AS Core Studies and Psychological Investigations

PSYCHOLOGY

OCR

Third Edition

Philip Banyard and
Cara Flanagan

Ψ **Psychology Press**
Taylor & Francis Group

LONDON AND NEW YORK

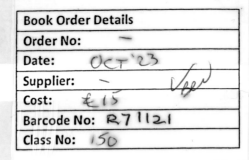

Third edition published 2013 by Psychology Press
27 Church Road, Hove, East Sussex, BN3 2FA

Simultaneously published in the USA and Canada
by Psychology Press
711 Third Avenue, New York, NY 10017

www.psypress.com

*Psychology Press is part of the Taylor & Francis Group,
an Informa business*

First edition published by Psychology Press 2006
Second edition published by Psychology Press 2008

British Library Cataloguing in Publication Data
A catalogue record for this book is available from the British Library

ISBN: 978-1-84872-116-6 (pbk)

ISBN: 978-0-203-50582-3 (ebk)

Typeset in Franklin Gothic and project managed by
GreenGate Publishing Services, Tonbridge, Kent
www.ggate.co.uk

Printed and bound in Great Britain by
Bell & Bain Ltd., Glasgow

MIX
Paper from
responsible sources
FSC® C007785

Contents

Introduction

Welcome to psychology   viii

The AS examination   x

The AS examination: mark schemes   xii

What is a core study?   xiv

Chapter 1

Psychological investigations   1

Research methods

Chapter 1 is concerned with the research methods that psychologists use to investigate human (and animal) behaviour.

This topic is assessed in **Unit G541**.

Throughout the chapter there are **questions and activities** to enhance your understanding. The chapter ends with some **exam-style questions with student answers and teacher's comments**.

Chapter 2

Cognitive psychology   37

Chapter 3

Developmental psychology   73

Chapter 4

Physiological psychology   109

Chapter 5

Social psychology   145

Chapter 6

Individual differences   181

The core studies

Each of these five chapters is concerned with the core studies examined in **Unit G542**.

In total there are 15 core studies, three in each of the chapter areas.

Each chapter starts with a two-page **introduction** to the area of psychology (cognitive, developmental, etc.).

There are then three core studies, each presented following the same format:

- **Starters**: background material.
- **Core study in a nutshell**: a simplified version of the study giving you information about what you must know about the context, aims, method and results of the study, plus a discussion.
- **Core study in detail**: a detailed description of the core study. There are also questions to answer, activities and biographical notes.
- **Evaluation**: some themes to consider.
- **Afters**: research that came afterwards plus links to other studies.
- **Questions for you**: multiple choice questions and exam-style questions to assess your knowledge and understanding.

Each chapter ends with a set of **exam-style questions with student answers and teacher's comments**.

Chapter 7

Approaches, perspectives, issues and methods   217

The **G542 exam** requires that you know the core study but also requires you to answer questions relating the core study to various approaches, perspectives, issues and methods. In this chapter we provide material to help you with this.

The chapter ends with some **exam-style questions with student answers and teacher's comments**.

Throughout this book there are questions for you to answer to help your understanding. You can find suggested answers to all the questions in this book – as well as lots of other useful materials at www.psypress.com/cw/banyard

Answers to multiple choice questions   247

References   248

Glossary with index   255

Acknowledgements

The authors would like to acknowledge the contribution of the following to the development of the first two editions of this book: Patrick Hylton, Mark Griffiths, Alex Haslam, Beth Black, James Stiller, Mark Holah, Kathy Bach and Mike Cardwell.

In preparing this third edition we are very grateful for the considerable help given by Caroline Farnsworth as well as invaluable feedback from Jamie Davies, Mark Holah, Jenny Baines and Caroline Parsons.

We would also like to thank Psychology Press for their confidence in this project and their relentless good nature in dealing with us, especially Lucy Kennedy, Rebekah Edmondson and Mandy Collison (we mean that most sincerely!). Thanks also to Carrie Baker and the team at GreenGate for the design of the text and their willingness to accommodate the demands of the authors.

Phil Banyard would like to acknowledge the encouragement and support he received from the teachers and examiners of the OCR specification. Their contributions and enthusiasm were the major drivers in the development of the course. He would also like to acknowledge the patience of his co-author, the hope that swirls around the City Ground, Nottingham, the diverting and always interesting company of Christian Adey, and the unforgettable piano playing of Mrs Mills.

The authors

Phil Banyard

Phil Banyard is Reader in Psychology at Nottingham Trent University. He has been involved in GCSE and A Level Psychology for more years than he can count and has marked more exam papers than he has brain cells left. He wrote the original OCR specification and was Chief Examiner for 14 years. It is testament to medical science that he still teaches, writes texts and ties his own shoes. His continued support of Nottingham Forest shows extreme loyalty or lack of imagination, depending on your point of view.

Cara Flanagan

Cara Flanagan is an experienced teacher and senior A Level examiner. She has written a wide range of articles and textbooks for A Level Psychology students, as well as editing the *Foundations of Psychology* Series (Routledge) with Phil Banyard. Aside from her writing, Cara regularly speaks at student conferences and teacher CPD courses. Her home is in the Scottish Highlands where she writes while enjoying the glorious landscape.

Illustration credits

Introduction

Chapter 1

Chapter 2

Welcome to psychology

What is psychology?

I know we pretend to be interested in everybody and everything but when it comes down to it, the most interesting thing in life is ME. This is partly a selfish thing because we clearly care more about what happens to ourselves than what happens to anyone else (oh don't pretend it's anything else), but it is also a logical thing. Let's face it, I am the person that I know most about. For everyone else I have to guess what is going on and rely on them to tell me about it.

When you think about yourself then you are confronted by some BIG QUESTIONS. These questions are so big that they are bigger than anything you can possibly imagine and then some. They are so big that it is not possible to get a full answer. Not now, nor in the future. We can only ponder and speculate on these things. The biggest question is 'Who am I?' and following on from this are three questions that form the core of any psychology course:

- Why do I think like this?
- Why do I feel like this?
- Why do I behave like this?

Thinking, feeling and doing

It is helpful to break down our experience of the world into these different spheres of thinking, feeling and doing. As a first thought you'd probably think that they are all connected and our feelings match up with our thoughts and the things we do are driven by these thoughts and feelings. Nothing could be further from the truth and that is one of the first puzzles of psychology and one of the things that makes people so interesting.

Take one of the author's (Phil's) response to global warming for example. He THINKS that global warming is real and that we should all try to reduce our carbon footprint. On the other hand although he FEELS sad when he sees films of penguins falling off an ice floe, the depth of his feeling does not match his belief that the world will suffer big consequences if we don't act soon. In fact he FEELS sadder when Nottingham Forest lose than when he watches films about the environment. And what does he DO about it? Well he doesn't consume that much but he still goes on holiday abroad when he can, he keeps his house warm and he has never been to a bottle bank (unless you include Threshers that is). This is not a unique state of affairs and it highlights how our feelings do not necessarily match with our thoughts or our behaviour.

Psychology doesn't have the answers to why we think, feel and behave in the ways that we do, but it does give us some evidence that helps us understand these processes a little better. In the introduction to Chapter 1 we develop this idea a bit further and look at how we can measure what we think, what we feel and what we do.

What is psychology about?

Psychology is mainly interested in individuals. What makes them tick, how they make decisions and how they interact. This distinguishes it from sociology which is mainly interested in groups of people and how they develop and react. At this time, psychology is very popular in Western countries because we are looking for individual solutions to personal problems and it seems as if psychology might provide some of the answers. Psychology is about how we make sense of the world and how we behave in it. It's about how we see, hear and touch, how we think, remember and concentrate, how we develop and maintain our identities and how we interact with others.

If you watch daytime television you might well think that psychology is mainly about relationships, body language and the lives of celebrities, but you would be wrong. If you study the subject at college or university, then you will probably not deal with any of these issues. What happens on the daytime television sofa is that self-appointed experts tell you things you probably already know. Listen closely, they won't tell you anything new, they are just filling time with harmless nonsense. We think that the psychology you will study on your course is much more interesting.

Defining psychology

In 1890 the US psychologist William James defined psychology as *'the science of mental life'*. Today it is commonly defined as *'the science of mind and behaviour'*. The key word for us is 'science' because it emphasises that the study of psychology is one that looks at evidence rather than opinion, and is prepared to put that evidence up for public scrutiny.

A common expectation of psychology is that it is about therapy and long conversations with bearded strangers about your mother. Nothing could be further from the truth.

Try this

Talk the talk

Any subject has its own language. If you take your car to the garage then the mechanic will use words that you have never heard before in explaining why your expensive motor is actually a heap of junk. And if you go to buy a computer, then the talk of Ram, Rom, Rum and Rim leaves you baffled and confused. To start with you might find some of the language of psychology quite confusing but don't be put off. Learn the terms and the ideas will become much more clear. Try and use a new psychological word every day. Start with **cognitive**. Use that word in a sentence with your friends/ mum/cat in the next hour.

Other words to try:

Defence mechanism

Validity

Hippocampus

Depersonalisation

You are already a psychologist

It's true. You already use psychology in your daily life. If you didn't, you would find life very difficult indeed. For example, when you walk down a shopping street how often do you physically bump into someone? Very rarely I would guess. The trick with not bumping into someone is to estimate how fast they are travelling and what direction they are going in. That way you can compute whether your paths are likely to collide. This is quite clever but it is also something a fairly basic computer can do. What is more remarkable is that you can read the intentions of the other person and guess which way they are going to go. We all change direction several times as we dodge down a busy street but we are able to judge where the other people are going to go and therefore avoid bumping into them. In effect you have to read their minds to see where they are planning to go and this is something that even the most sophisticated computer cannot do.

Not only are you a mind reader, you are also an emotion reader. You are a pretty good judge of a person's emotional state and you are able to judge when someone is angry or happy or sad. This is a very handy skill and can get you out of some tricky situations. We are not perfect at this skill but by and large we get these judgements right more often than we get them wrong.

So, in summary, you already use psychology to judge speed and distance in the world, you also use it to read people's minds and you can also read their emotions. These are all very remarkable skills and they are only the start of the many amazing things that you can do and which you commonly take for granted. In this text we want to build on the psychology you already know and use and show you some of the other things we know about how people tick.

To walk down a street without bumping into people you have to be a mind reader.

Core studies in psychology

Some subjects are based mainly around theories. Psychology is not one of these. The core of psychology is made up of evidence gained from research studies. Psychology is a patchwork of scientific studies that, at their best, give us some new insights into what it means to be a human being. These studies give us our next level of questions as we try and get some insights into the BIG QUESTIONS mentioned on the left. For example, in this text we will be looking at the following questions:

- If you split someone's brain in half will they become two people?
- Can you teach language to a chimpanzee?
- How easy is it to tell the difference between the sane and the insane?
- Do London taxi drivers have bigger brains than the average?
- If someone asked you to kill another human being would you do it?
- Does watching violence make children more likely to be violent?
- What is it that makes some people gamble?
- Can two personalities exist in the same body?
- How reliable is **eyewitness testimony**?

You've got to admit that there are some pretty good questions here. And each one of these questions is at the heart of one of the core studies in this text. It would be untrue to say that the studies give clear answers to the questions but they give us some clues and many of them will make you think differently about yourself and other people.

All the studies can be seen as a story, and this is probably a good way to study them. They all have a back-story, the things that happened before this story commences. This back-story is often the reason for the study being carried out. For example, the study by **Milgram** was an attempt to explore the behaviour that was observed during the Second World War. The studies also have some afters to them (a sequel if you like) where the ideas have been developed after the original study. With the Milgram study, for example, it is still referred to even though it is more than 50 years since it was carried out. We put each of the core studies in context by showing the ideas that stimulated the study and some of the work that has been carried out since.

How do they know that?

One of the very big advantages of looking at a small number of key studies in psychology is that you get a feel for how psychology is carried out. And if you get a feel for how psychologists get their evidence then you can make up your own mind about quite how good that evidence is. A question to ask anyone who is telling you some FACTS is 'how do you know that?'

The more we know about how evidence is collected and how people come up with their conclusions then the less we are going to be taken in by dodgy science and dodgy newscasts.

Wonder and scepticism

We think the best way to approach psychology is with a twin sense of WONDER and SCEPTICISM. The sense of wonder is necessary because the more you think about human behaviour the more wonderful it becomes. For example, how did you manage to learn language without ever having a lesson? And how are some people able to create fantastic pieces of music or original art that can inspire a generation?

On the other hand we need to keep a sceptical eye on the information that is fed to us. What is their evidence? And how did they get it? In the USA it is estimated that around five million people believe that they have been abducted by aliens. Despite the number of people reporting this experience it still seems very unlikely to the authors that this has in fact happened to anyone.

We hope that this text helps you develop your sense of wonder about people and how they think, feel and behave while at the same time developing a healthy scepticism about the conclusions that are sometimes drawn from the flimsiest of evidence.

Final thought

In this text we have tried to follow the suggestion of the great twentieth century scientist Albert Einstein who is credited with saying, *'Everything should be made as simple as possible, but not simpler.'*

The AS examination

There are two exams, which are outlined on this spread.

Unit G541 Psychological investigations

1 hour

Total 60 marks

30% of total AS mark

All questions are compulsory

See question examples on pages 34–35

The paper is divided into three sections: Sections A, B and C. Each section is worth 20 marks.

The questions will refer to the following four techniques for collecting/analysing data: self-report study, experiment, observation or correlation.

In each section of the exam there will be a piece of source material:

A brief outline of a piece of research

Candidates could be asked to:

* Identify strengths and weaknesses of the research method in general.
* Identify strengths and weaknesses of the specific research described in the source material.
* Suggest improvements to the research and their likely effects.
* Consider issues such as reliability and validity of measurements.
* Consider ethical issues raised by the source material.

The data produced by a piece of a research

Candidates could be asked to:

* Suggest appropriate descriptive statistics/graphical representations of data. (Note: no **inferential statistics** are required for this unit.)
* Draw conclusions from data/graphs.
* Sketch summary tables/graphs.

An outline of a proposed piece of research

Candidates could be asked to:

* Suggest appropriate hypotheses (null/alternate, one-tailed/two-tailed).
* Suggest how variables might be operationalised/measured.
* Suggest appropriate samples/sampling methods.
* Outline possible procedures.
* Evaluate the suggestions they have made.

How to get an A Grade on G541

It's all about interpreting source material and *applying* your knowledge, called **contextualisation**.

For example:

Describe **one** strength of using an opportunity sample in this study.

Answer: One strength of an opportunity sample is that it is easy to do because you just use those people most available such as people in your class.

This answer would not receive full marks because it is a general answer that could be used in relation to any study. For top marks there must be a specific reference to the source material.

There is further exam advice for G541 in Chapter 1.

Unit G542 The core studies

2 hours

Total 120 marks

70% of total AS mark

In Section A all questions are compulsory

In Section B there is one question but a choice between three core studies

In Section C you have a choice between two questions

The paper is divided into three sections: Sections A, B and C

Section A Core studies
Total 60 marks

For each core study there will be one question worth four marks (a total of 15 questions). This question may be parted. The questions will ask about specific aspects of the core studies.

Section B Core studies, methods and issues
Total 36 marks

Questions will cover aims, procedures and results of core studies as well as research methods used and issues named in the specification. For example:

*Choose **one** of the following core studies [three studies named] and answer parts (a)–(f) on this study.*

(a) Outline the aim of this study. [2]

(b) Describe the sample used in this study and suggest one advantage of using this sample. [6]

(c) Outline the procedure of this study. [6]

(d) Outline the findings of this study. [6]

(e) Discuss the reliability of the findings of this study. [6]

(f) Describe and evaluate changes that could be made to the way this study was conducted. [10]

Section C Approaches and perspectives
Total 24 marks

Questions take the following form:

*(a) Outline **one** assumption of the XXX approach. [2]*

(b) With reference to the named core study, describe how the XXX approach could explain the topic studied. [4]

*(c) Describe **one** similarity and **one** difference between any core studies that take the XXX approach. [6]*

(d) Discuss strengths and weaknesses of the XXX approach using examples from any core studies that take this approach. [12]

www You can read the specification yourself – download it from the OCR website (www.psypress.com/cw/banyard).

You can also look at examples of past examination papers.

Detail

When answering exam questions the number of marks available gives you some guidance about how much you should write – a 2 mark question requires less than a 3 mark question. However, it isn't just about the number of words because one student may write a lot but gain fewer marks than another student because their answer lacks **detail**. Consider the two examples below:

Student A: *In the study by Baron-Cohen, there were three groups of participants in the sample. The three groups were the children with a kind of autism, There were 16 people in this group. The second group with normal adults, There were 50 in this group. Finally there was a group of 10 people with Tourette syndrome. (55 words)*

Student B: *In the study by Baron-Cohen there were 16 individuals with autism (14 had Asperger), sex ratio was 13 males: 3 females. All had normal IQ. There was a second control group of normal age-matched adults (equal males to females). The third group of 10 had Tourette syndrome, again age-matched. Sex ratio 8 males: 2 females. (55 words)*

Bearing in mind that detail is important, a rough guide to length would be:

- 2 mark answers should be about 50 words.
- 8 mark answers should be about 200 words.
- 10 mark answers should be about 250 words.

How to get an A Grade on Section A
Thorough knowledge of the core studies is essential. You need to know the specific **details**.

How to get an A Grade on Section B

1 **Detail**
   The mark schemes on the next spread show that detail is used to assess your answer. Include numbers!

2 **Focus**
   Many students make the mistake of including irrelevant information. For example, when asked about the procedures of a study they include information about the sample or the findings. Irrelevant information gains no marks (but also read 'if in doubt, stick it in', see below).

3 **Contextualisation**
   Your answer must refer to the core study.

4 **Elaboration**
   You must state your answer and then explain it.

Contextualisation – the drop-in

Contextualisation is described at the bottom of the facing page. It applies to many of your examination questions. One way to test whether or not you have contextualised your answer is to imagine taking your answer to one question and dropping it into another question – would it read OK? In which case it has not been contextualised. For example:

*Outline **one** weakness of using independent measures in this study. [2]*

Answer: One weakness of using independent groups design is that you cannot control participant variables so that the participants in one group may be different in some way to the participants in the other group. If the participants in one group were more able that would explain why they did better rather than because of the independent variable.

The problem is that there is nothing in that answer that relates to a study. There is no **CONTEXT**. The same answer could be **dropped in** to any question and would not score full marks.

How to get an A Grade on Section C

Detail, focus, contextualisation and elaboration are all important.

Question (a) The word 'behaviour' must appear in your answer.

Question (b) Must refer back to the assumption in part (a).

Question (c) Use specific examples. You can use one core study for the similarity and a second one for the difference.

Question (d) 'Discuss' means that you first of all must *describe* the strength/ weakness and then must *evaluate it*, e.g. consider why it is a strength/weakness.

Elaboration – the **three-point rule**

S **State** your point.

C **Context** provide evidence to support your point.

C **Comment** on the significance of your point, or add an explanation, or any further comment.

For example:

S *One criticism of the study is that it lacks ecological validity.*

C *The study tested memory using a film of a car accident which doesn't reflect how eyewitnesses would actually experience an accident.*

C *Lack of ecological validity means you can't generalise the findings to everyday life.*

S *One strength of the physiological approach is that it has practical applications.*

C *For example, you can use evidence from Maguire's study to help people with brain damage.*

C *The evidence in the study suggests the brain can develop in response to demand so patients could be encouraged to exercise their brain to make it regrow.*

If in doubt, stick it in
In some questions you may not be sure what is required. For example, in one question candidates were asked to describe how data were gathered in a named study – however, they did not gain full marks if they just described how; they also had to include a statement of what data were gathered. The moral of the story is – if in doubt, stick any details in.

The AS examination: mark schemes

If your really want to do well in the AS examination, then you need to understand how examination answers are marked. Examination mark schemes are published on the OCR website. On this spread we give a general picture of these mark schemes.

The common marking criteria for description are:
- Accuracy
- Detail
- Elaboration
- Evidence of understanding
- Expression
- Use of psychological terminology

How mark schemes are used

At the end of each chapter in this book there are student answers that have been marked by a teacher.

The examiner decides on the appropriate mark using mark schemes similar to those on this spread. The mark band that best describes the answer is selected to determine the mark to award.

The mark schemes shown on this spread are not the only ones used, but they show the essence of what is likely to be there.

INTRODUCTION

2 mark question
For example:
Outline the aim of your chosen study. [2]

0 marks	No or irrelevant answer.
1 mark	Partial or vague answer, i.e. the aim has **no elaboration** or is **not fully contextualised**.
2 marks	Outline is clear and **fully contextualised**.

3 mark question
For example:
*Give **one** strength of using observation in your chosen study. [3]*

0 marks	No or irrelevant answer.
1 mark	Peripherally relevant strength identified, not linked to chosen study (**no contextualisation**) and with little or **no elaboration**.
2 marks	Appropriate strength identified but is basic and **lacks detail**. A vague/weak link is made to the study (**weak contextualisation**) showing **some understanding**.
3 marks	An appropriate strength is **accurately** explained and **elaborated**. There is a clear, developed link to the study (**contextualisation**) showing **good understanding**.

6 mark question
For example:
Outline the findings of your chosen study. [6]

0 marks	No or irrelevant answer.
1–2 marks	Outline is very basic and lacks in **detail** (e.g. one or two general statements are identified). Some **understanding** may be evident. **Expression** is poor with few, if any, **psychological terms**. The answer is not linked to the chosen study (**contextualisation**).
3–4 marks	Outline is mainly **accurate** with **some details** missing. Fine details may occasionally be present and **understanding** is evident. **Expression** and use of **psychological terminology** is reasonable. The answer is clearly linked to the study (**clear contextualisation**).
5–6 marks	Outline has **increasing accuracy** and **detail** with several fine details included. Detail is appropriate to level and time allowed. **Understanding**, **expression** and use of **psychological terminology** is good. There are clear and appropriate links to the study (**clear contextualisation**).

A general summary of 2, 3 and 6 mark questions

Mark		Relevance	Detail	Context	Elaboration	Understanding	Expression	Psychological terminology
1	1–2	Peripheral	Basic, lacking detail	None	Little or none	Some	Generally poor	Few
2	3–4	Appropriate, generally accurate	Lacks detail (may be some fine details included)	For questions out of 3, a vague/weak link. For questions out of 6, a clear link is required.	Some	Some	Reasonable	Reasonable
3	5–6	Appropriate and accurate	Detailed	Clear, developed link	Elaborated	Good	Good	Good

10 mark question

For example:

Describe and evaluate changes that could be made to the way your chosen study was conducted. [10]

0 marks	No or irrelevant answer.
1–2 marks	Description of change(s) are **peripheral** to the study. Description is basic and **lacks detail**. **Limited understanding**. Not linked to the chosen study (**no contextualisation**). Evaluation may be just discernible. The answer is unstructured, muddled, probably list–like.
3–4 marks	Description of change(s) is **appropriate** to the study. Description is basic and **lacks details** with **some understanding**, though **expression** may be limited. **Some evaluation** may be evident.
5–6 marks	Description of change(s) is **appropriate** to the study. Description is reasonable with **some understanding** though **expression** may be limited. Some evaluation is evident. There may be an **imbalance** between description and evaluation.
7–8 marks	Description of **two or more changes** is appropriate to the study. Description is **detailed** with understanding and **clear expression**. **Evaluation is reasonably effective** and informed. There may be a **balance** between description and evaluation. The answer has **some structure** and organisation.
9–10 marks	Description of **two or more changes** is appropriate to the study. Description is **detailed** with **good understanding** and **clear expression**. **Evaluation is effective** and well informed. There is a **good balance** between description and evaluation. The answer is competently structured and organised. Answer is mostly grammatically correct with occasional spelling errors.

12 mark question

For example:

Discuss the strengths and limitations of the social approach using examples from any core studies that take this approach. [12]

0 marks	No or irrelevant answer.
1–3 marks	There may be **some** strengths or weaknesses which are appropriate or **peripheral** to the question, or there may be an **imbalance** between the two. **Discussion** is poor with limited or **no understanding**. **Expression** is poor. **Analysis is sparse** and argument may be just discernible. Sparse or no use of **supporting examples**.
4–6 marks	There may be **some** strengths and weaknesses which are **appropriate** to the question, or there may be an **imbalance** between the two. **Discussion** is reasonable with **some understanding** though **expression** may be limited. **Analysis is effective** sometimes and **argument limited**. Sparse use of **supporting examples**.
7–9 marks	There may be a **range** of strengths and weaknesses which are **appropriate** to the question, or there may be an **imbalance** between the two. **Discussion** is good with **some understanding** and **good expression**. **Analysis** is reasonably effective and **argument is informed**. Some use of **supporting examples**.
10–12 marks	There is a **good range** of strengths (2 or more) and weaknesses (2 or more) which are appropriate to the question. There is a **good balance** between the two. **Discussion** is detailed with **good understanding** and clear **expression**. **Analysis** is effective and **argument well informed**. Appropriate use of **supporting examples**. The answer is competently **structured and organised**. Answer is mostly grammatically correct with occasional spelling errors.

Longer questions involve evaluation and include some other marking criteria:

- **Evaluation** entails looking at strengths and weaknesses.
- **Structure and organisation** involves the use of paragraphs.
- **Argument**, putting material together in a logical order (telling a story).
- **Balance** between elements in the answer, such as strengths and weaknesses or description and evaluation.
- **Analysis**, being able to break the question/answer into smaller components.

Evaluation

'Evaluation' literally means to 'establish the value of something'. There are many ways to do this, such as using the key issues.

An important part of knowing about a core study is being able to evaluate it. Evaluation is a personal business. We can tell you the facts of the study but deciding whether the study is good or bad is up to you.

Throughout the book we have provided you with the tools to evaluate studies rather than the answers. After each study there is a page with some suggested considerations to help you think about the issues. There are suggested answers to these questions at www.psypress. com/cw/banyard.

What is a core study?

The OCR AS specification is based around 15 psychological studies. The studies have been selected either because they are classic studies in psychology or because they illustrate important issues in psychology.

What is a 'psychological study'? When psychologists (and other scientists) conduct research they write a report, published in a magazine or 'journal'. One report might contain details of several investigations. Each core study is one of these reports (also called an article).

*The core studies are presented in the order they appear in the specification but there is no law that says you have to study them in this order. We have endeavoured to write the book so it can be read in any order. You can do all cognitive core studies first or just one cognitive core study and then a social one. We have tried to make each core study 'stand alone', but inevitably this is not exactly possible. There are some concepts that occur all over the place, such as ethics or **ecological validity** or **experiments**. You may need to skip around to other sections of the book – it won't be a bad thing to read some of the key issues several times, in the context of different core studies.*

Journal articles are usually divided up as follows:

Abstract
A summary of the study.

Introduction/aim
What a researcher intends to investigate. This often includes a review of previous research – theories and studies – which leads up to the aims for this particular study. The researcher(s) may state their research prediction(s) and/or a **hypothesis/es**.

Method
A detailed description of what the researcher(s) did, a bit like writing the recipe for making a cake. The main point is to give enough detail for someone else to replicate (repeat) the study. **Replication** is important to be able to check the results – if someone repeated the same procedure, they should get the same results and this shows that the results weren't just a fluke.

The method includes describing the participants (the **sample**), the testing environment, the procedures used to collect data, and any instructions given to participants before (the **brief**) and afterwards (the **debrief**).

Results
This section contains what the researcher(s) found, often called statistical data, which includes **descriptive statistics** (tables, averages and graphs) and **inferential statistics** (the use of statistical tests to determine how **significant** the results are).

Conclusions
The researcher(s) attempt to indicate what the results mean, for example making generalisations about people based on how the participants behaved in the study and with reference to other research studies.

Discussion
Finally, researchers discuss the results of the study. They might propose one or more explanations of the behaviours that they observed. The researchers might also consider the implications of the results and make suggestions for future research.

Read the originals

*The page below is from the actual article by **Loftus and Palmer** (Core Study 1) reporting their research. In this book we have provided fairly detailed accounts of each core study but it is a good idea to look at the original articles yourself. In many cases these can be found on the web and we have given the links at the end of each core study.*

JOURNAL OF VERBAL LEARNING AND VERBAL BEHAVIOR 13, 585–589 (1974)

Reconstruction of Automobile Destruction: An Example of the Interaction Between Language and Memory[1]

ELIZABETH F. LOFTUS AND JOHN C. PALMER

University of Washington

Two experiments are reported in which subjects viewed films of automobile accidents and then answered questions about events occurring in the films. The question, "About how fast were the cars going when they smashed into each other?" elicited higher estimates of speed than questions which used the verbs *collided, bumped, contacted,* or *hit* in place of *smashed.* On a retest one week later, those subjects who received the verb *smashed* were more likely to say "yes" to the question, "Did you see any broken glass?", even though broken glass was not present in the film. These results are consistent with the view that the questions asked subsequent to an event can cause a reconstruction in one's memory of that event.

How accurately do we remember the details of a complex event, like a traffic accident, that has happened in our presence? More specifically, how well do we do when asked to estimate some numerical quantity such as how long the accident took, how fast the cars were traveling, or how much time elapsed between the sounding of a horn and the moment of collision?

It is well documented that most people are markedly inaccurate in reporting such numerical details as time, speed, and distance (Bird, 1927; Whipple, 1909). For example, most people have difficulty estimating the duration of an event, with some research indicating that the tendency is to overestimate the duration of events which are complex (Block, 1974; Marshall, 1969; Ornstein, 1969). The judgment of speed is especially difficult, and practically every automobile accident results in huge variations from one witness to another

[1] This research was supported by the Urban Mass Transportation Administration, Department of Transportation, Grant No. WA-11-0004. Thanks go to Geoffrey Loftus, Edward E. Smith, and Stephen Woods for many important and helpful comments, Reprint requests should be sent to Elizabeth F. Loftus, Department of Psychology, University of Washington, Seattle, Washington 98195.

as to how fast a vehicle was actually traveling (Gardner, 1933). In one test administered to Air Force personnel who knew in advance that they would be questioned about the speed of a moving automobile, estimates ranged from 10 to 50 mph. The car they watched was actually going only 12 mph (Marshall, 1969, p. 23).

Given the inaccuracies in estimates of speed, it seems likely that there are variables which are potentially powerful in terms of influencing these estimates. The present research was conducted to investigate one such variable, namely, the phrasing of the question used to elicit the speed judgment. Some questions are clearly more suggestive than others. This fact of life has resulted in the legal concept of a leading question and in legal rules indicating when leading questions are allowed *(Supreme Court Reporter, 1973).* A leading question is simply one that, either by its form or content, suggests to the witness what answer is desired or leads him to the desired answer.

In the present study, subjects were shown films of traffic accidents and then they answered questions about the accident. The subjects were interrogated about the speed of

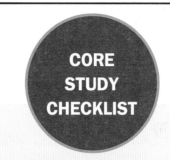

Core study checklist

Copy this checklist for each core study and place a tick in the final column when you can produce an appropriate answer from memory!

What you need to know about each core study		How much to write (NB detail)	Tick
Section A and B questions			
Context/previous research		2 marks	
Aims		2 marks	
Sample	Describe the sample.	3 marks	
	One strength and **one** weakness of the sample.	3 marks each	
	Explain how the sample was obtained.	3 marks	
Research methods/techniques	Describe research methods/techniques used (use of a laboratory, use of observation, conducting an experiment).	6 marks	
	One strength and **one** weakness of each method/technique.	3 marks each	
Procedures	How the data was collected.	8 marks	
Data collected	What quantitative and/or qualitative data collected.	4 marks	
	One strength and **one** weakness of the data collected.	3 marks each	
Ethical issues	Describe two.	6 marks	
The results (findings)		8 marks	
Improvements	Changes that could be made.	8 marks	
	Implications of the changes.	8 marks	
Evaluate the approach	**One** strength and **one** weakness of the approach using examples from the core study.	4 marks	

What you need to know about each core study		How much to write (NB detail)	Tick
Section C questions			
Use approach	to explain the topic studied.	4 marks	
Comparison	to one other core study from the same approach.	6 marks	
Evaluate the approach	One strength and one weakness of the approach using examples from the core study.	4 marks	

Subjects or participants?

In most of the core studies in this book the people in the studies were called 'subjects'. We have changed this in most cases to the more modern 'participants'.

During the 1990s there was a move to use the term 'participant' instead of 'subject' in order to reflect the recognition that participants are not passive but are actively involved. They search for cues about how to behave and this may mean that they behave as researchers expect rather than as they would in everyday life. The use of the term 'participants' acknowledges this participant reactivity.

The term 'subjects' also reflected a power relationship in research studies. Typically the researcher holds the power in the research setting because he/she knows what the experiment is about and knows the procedures to be followed. This often leaves the 'subject' powerless. It is to be hoped that the change of the term from 'subject' to 'participant' is more than just a cosmetic one and that, in more recent studies, the participant isn't quite as powerless. It may not be a good idea to rewrite the old studies and start calling the subjects 'participants', because they weren't. They were treated as passive respondents to the experimental situations set up by psychologists and they were rarely dealt with as colleagues. However, we have generally adopted the term 'participants' in this book to encourage its use and the meanings that go with it.

Specification for Psychological Investigations (G541)

Candidates should be able to:		Tick here when you can do it!
Describe the four techniques	For self-report this should include a knowledge and understanding of rating scales and open and closed questions and the strengths and weaknesses of each.	
	For experiment this should include a knowledge and understanding of experimental design (independent measures and repeated measures) and the strengths and weaknesses of each.	
	For observation this should include a knowledge and understanding of participant and structured observation, time sampling and event sampling and the strengths and weaknesses of each.	
	For correlation this should include a knowledge and understanding of positive and negative correlations and the interpretation of scattergraphs.	
Identify strengths and weaknesses of the four techniques, both in general terms and in relation to source material.		
Frame hypotheses (null and alternate, one- and two-tailed).		
Identify variables (for experiment – identify and explain the difference between independent and dependent variables).		
Suggest how variables might be operationalised/measured.		
Suggest (in relation to source material) strengths and weaknesses of measurement and alternative forms of measurement.		
Comment on the reliability and validity of measurement.		
Describe opportunity sampling, random sampling and self-selected sampling techniques.		
Identify strengths and weaknesses of opportunity, random and self-selected sampling techniques.		
Identify strengths and weaknesses of sampling techniques described in source material.		
Suggest appropriate samples/sampling techniques in relation to source material.		
Suggest appropriate procedures in relation to source material.		
Identify and describe the differences between qualitative and quantitative data.		
Identify strengths and weaknesses of qualitative and quantitative data.		
Suggest appropriate descriptive statistics for data in source material (mean, median, mode).		
Sketch appropriate summary tables/graphs from data in source material (bar charts, scattergraphs).		
Draw conclusions from data/graphs.		
Describe ethical issues relating to psychological research with human participants.		
Identify ethical issues in source material and suggest ways of dealing with ethical issues.		

Specification for Core Studies (G542)

Candidates should be able to:	Tick here when you can do it!
Candidates need to know specific aspects of the 15 core studies:	
• The background to the studies (the context). • Theories on which studies are based. • Psychological perspectives applicable to the studies. • Other research pertinent to the studies. • The information in the studies. • The methods used in the studies. • The way the results are analysed and presented. • The conclusions that can be drawn from the studies. • Strengths and limitations of the studies. • The general psychological issues illustrated by the studies. Evaluations of all of the above.	
Loftus and Palmer (eyewitness testimony)	
Baron-Cohen, Joliffe, Mortimore and Robertson (autism)	
Savage-Rumbaugh et al. (animal language)	
Samuel and Bryant (conservation)	
Bandura, Ross and Ross (aggression)	
Freud (Little Hans)	
Maguire et al. (taxi drivers)	
Dement and Kleitman (sleep and dreaming)	
Sperry (split brain)	
Milgram (obedience)	
Reicher and Haslam (BBC prison study)	
Piliavin, Rodin and Piliavin (subway Samaritan)	
Rosenhan (sane in insane places)	
Thigpen and Cleckley (multiple personality disorder)	
Griffiths (gambling)	
In addition, candidates need to be aware of the approaches/perspectives, issues and methods arising from the core studies: • Approaches: cognitive, developmental, physiological, social, individual differences. • Perspectives: behaviourist, psychodynamic. • Methods: experimental (laboratory and field), case study, self-report, observation, methodological issues such as reliability and validity. • Issues: ethics, ecological validity, longitudinal and snapshot, qualitative and quantitative data.	

This chapter looks at how psychologists conduct research. Like all scientists, psychologists use systematic techniques for collecting and analysing data in order to produce objective and verifiable data.

Psychological investigations

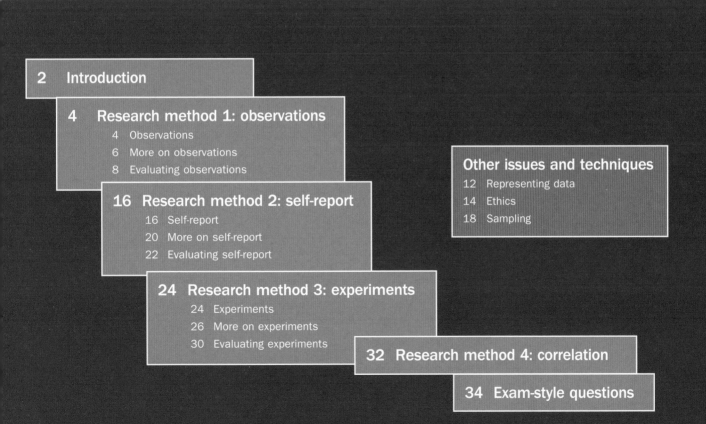

2 Introduction

4 Research method 1: observations
   4 Observations
   6 More on observations
   8 Evaluating observations

16 Research method 2: self-report
   16 Self-report
   20 More on self-report
   22 Evaluating self-report

24 Research method 3: experiments
   24 Experiments
   26 More on experiments
   30 Evaluating experiments

32 Research method 4: correlation

34 Exam-style questions

Other issues and techniques
   12 Representing data
   14 Ethics
   18 Sampling

Introduction

We use research methods to *find out information* about the world. We try to collect information that will help us understand our world a bit better. The alternative is to *make up information* – just guess why things happen; this is less likely to help our understanding.

The first way to find out things is to look at what is happening around you and record it. To start with we tell a story about what we see and then we try to put it in categories. This is the process of **observation**; we all use it in everyday life to make sense of our world. This intuitive method of 'research' has been developed by psychologists to increase our knowledge of the world. Sometimes they record things that are usual in everyday life, such as people's behaviour in a library, and sometimes they record rather unusual things that are rarely experienced, such as response to emergencies.

The main subject for psychological research is the behaviour and experience of people, and if you want to know what someone thinks, feels or does the first thing to do is to ask them. This gives us first-hand accounts called **self-reports**. These are excellent sources of data but not necessarily accurate. We are not always the best witnesses of ourselves because we forget what we did, or we want to put over a good impression of ourselves, or because sometimes we just don't know why we do things.

As we build up our evidence (from observations and self-reports) we start to develop theories which we want to test to see if they are right or not. For example, observations of children with **autism** led to the theory that children with this condition had a specific deficit in their way of interpreting the world. The study by **Baron-Cohen et al.** tested this theory using the *Eyes Task* that examines how accurate we are at reading emotion in another person. They compared the judgements of people with autism against the judgements of other people. Psychologists use **experiments** to see if one factor (in this case autism) causes a difference in behaviour (in this case difficulty interpreting emotion). These results can then be used to challenge or support their theories.

Some issues can be explored by looking at differences between groups while others are better explored by looking for associations between scores. For example, we might measure a person's level of stress and also their sense of control over their behaviour (locus of control). Our hypothesis might be that the more control we feel we have over our lives the less stress we will experience. We can examine this **hypothesis** using a test of **correlation**.

In this chapter we look at these four ways of collecting data and comment on the relative strengths and weaknesses of them.

Basics of scientific research

Scientific research starts with theories which explain things in the world about us. However, for a theory to be any good it must stand up to being tested. For example, the science of **phrenology** was based on the idea that the shape of the brain determined personality. However, this has not been supported by any evidence and so cannot be held to explain any facts.

Testable

If a result is sound it ought to be possible to repeat it. If it is not possible to get the same result again it raises a question about the original study. Sometimes studies are not repeated because of **ethical issues**, for example **Milgram**'s study of obedience but the question still remains.

Replicable

Objective

If we are objective then we try to remove as much bias as possible from our study (the opposite is to be subjective and personal). We can do this by using controls and by, for example, recording exactly what we observe rather than our interpretations. **Freud**'s study is a very subjective account of **Little Hans**' fears.

Valuable

Psychological research doesn't have to have direct benefit to the general public but many people think it should make a contribution to our understanding of ourselves and others. In other words it should be useful. Whatever criticisms are made of **Milgram**'s study, it has provided a valuable insight into human behaviour.

Try this 1.1

Play with psychological methods

Why not use your phone or iPod to carry out some research? If you haven't got an iPod then just make one out of pink cardboard and white string; nobody will notice. You can *observe* people's behaviour with an iPod: do they make less eye contact in the street? Do they hum out loud, or move in rhythm? You can *experiment* whether people do better at simple tests when listening to the iPod than when not listening. Or you can compare the effects of different types of music on performance. You can make a *questionnaire* about iPod playlists or colours, or attitudes to people who have iPods. And you might *correlate* the amount of time people use shuffle (compared to listening to whole albums) with some personality variable (such as extraversion – find a questionnaire on the web).

The mobile phone has pushed us to develop a whole new range of behaviours. Do people use hand gestures when they are on the mobile phone? Why? You could compare the gestures and facial expressions of mobile phone users with the gestures and expressions of face-to-face conversation. And what about asking people about how and when they use it, how many texts they send, and whether they save any texts, if so from whom? You could send the same message to males and females and look at the different answers. People love to talk about their phones so a questionnaire should be easy enough.

Measurement in psychology – some things to think about

What to measure

A key element of any psychological enquiry is the collection of data. This commonly, but not always, involves measuring the variable we are interested in. We don't just want to say what something is, we want to compare it to other similar things. How many, how big, how often, how strong, how unusual, are all questions we might ask. But what do we want to ask about in psychology and what do we want to measure? The big questions in psychology are: Why do I think like this? Why do I feel like this? Why do I behave like this? We usually phrase the question to focus on other people rather than ourselves (e.g. 'why do people think like this?') but the same principles apply. We look at these three areas of human life below and consider how we might get data and measure them.

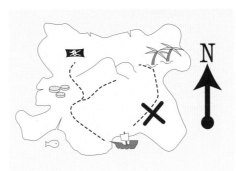

Mental treasure map

Measuring mental events can sometimes provide surprising insights. Kosslyn (1975) asked people to draw a map of a treasure island with some key features such as the beach, a hut, a coconut tree and buried treasure. When the drawing was finished Kosslyn asked the participant to close their eyes and imagine exploring the island. Kosslyn would choose a route, for example start at the beach and go to the hut. When they had reached the end they were asked to press a button which recorded how long they had been on the mental journey. Remarkably, the time taken to complete the mental journey was longer for items that were further apart. The mental world seems to have the same characteristics as the physical world and we move about it in the same way.

THINK

How can we measure what people are thinking? We can't see thinking, although we sometimes believe that we can. 'I know what you're thinking' we sometimes say to someone, but what gives us that belief? It comes from our observation of their behaviour. The changes in their facial expression or the pose they have adopted. We can't read or hear their thoughts but we can make an intelligent guess about what is going on inside their head.

We can measure thinking by asking people about their thoughts. Sometimes psychologists ask people to try and say out loud what they are thinking as they think it. If you try to do this you'll realise how difficult it is. **Griffiths** used this technique in his gambling study. We can also measure thoughts by giving people puzzles to solve and seeing how they solve them and how successful they are. The autism study by **Baron-Cohen et al.** uses these sort of techniques.

A modern technique for measuring *cognitive* processes is an eyetracker which follows the movement of your eyes and records where you fixate on a scene or a page when you are looking at it. This technique has been especially useful in research on reading.

FEEL

Measuring feelings is no easier than measuring thoughts. We can see some of the physical changes that emotions bring about but as adults we are very skilled at hiding our emotions so people don't know what we are really feeling. If you know someone quite well then you can often tell their mood by observing them. You are able to compare how they look with how they usually look so you can spot whether their eyes look more steely than usual or their jaw is set tighter than usual.

When you observe these changes you are making a basic form of measurement by noting whether someone, for example, looks MORE or LESS tense than usual. Behavioural observations like these are one way to measure emotions. Another way is to take the obvious route and ask someone how they feel. We might get measures here by asking them to rate themselves on some emotion scales or to respond to a standard list of questions.

Emotions often bring about bodily changes and we can measure these changes. We might measure the galvanic skin response (GSR) which records the level of sweat and is commonly used as part of a lie detector test. We might also measure changes in hormones associated with stress and **Reicher and Haslam** used this technique in the prison study.

BEHAVE

This ought to be the easy one to measure. We can observe what people do and what people say and what people produce, and we can record this behaviour. With thinking and feeling we have to use other measures to try and estimate the variables we are interested in, but with behaviour we can measure the thing we are studying. But life is never quite that easy because just recording behaviour is sometimes not quite enough.

In the **Bobo doll** study (**Bandura et al.**) the behaviour of the children was observed and recorded. But there is more to aggression than behaviour alone. We often give people a thump in a friendly way but if we did the same thing in anger we might not hit them any harder but the experience would be very different. Also, some people refer to passive aggression (a Freudian term) to describe awkward and obstructive behaviour that is used instead of confrontation.

Another issue for behavioural measures is that some behaviour is hidden from view. For example, we behave differently when we are being watched to when we are alone and by definition it is impossible to observe someone who is alone (unless we don't tell them). There are also some social behaviours that are kept very private.

Try this   1.2

Use your common sense to suggest how you can investigate the following questions. When you've done that, try to connect your suggestions to the psychological methods you know about.

- What makes people happy?
- How do parents in Nottingham bring up their children?
- How does someone react to another person when they have a romantic interest in them?
- Do people get better after a series of therapy sessions?
- At what age do babies recognise a human face?

...Connections...

To understand any evidence you have to understand how the data was collected. You might ask the question 'How do you know that?' and throughout this text we have tried to answer that question. The 15 core studies illustrate a wide range of data collection techniques in psychology. We have our own views on which evidence is the strongest and which should be taken with a pinch of salt. We hope that by studying how the evidence was collected you can make up your own mind about which you think is most valuable.

4 Research method 1: observations

The starting point for scientific enquiry is **observation**. We observe what is going on and then try and make sense of it. For example, people started to observe their surroundings thousands of years ago. They observed that the sun rose on one side of the landscape and set on the other and that this happened at regular and predictable intervals. They observed and recorded and then made the best sense of this, which was to believe that there was a bloke in a fiery chariot driving across the sky every day. Of course the conclusions were nonsense but the observations were sound.

The same principles and problems are there in psychological observations. We observe behaviour, record it, look for patterns in the behaviour and then try and make sense of it. The first task is to make good observations and to devise ways of categorising it and recording it. The tricky bit is to make sense of it and say what it means. What we are looking for is an explanation that tells us something we didn't already know about behaviour and does not involve flying blokes in flaming vehicles.

Ethics

Whenever conducting research you must treat your participants with respect. On pages 232–233 we consider ethics in detail but, for now, you need to have some awareness of **ethical issues** if you are going to conduct your own research. Ethics relates to the rightness or wrongness of our conduct. An ethical issue arises because there are conflicts between what a researcher would like to do and being respectful of participants.

You might like to just observe anyone – but the person you are observing may not want you to be watching and listening. The issue is one of **privacy**. A general rule (as we will see later) is that people should not be observed in a study unless it is in a public place, in other words one where they might be expect to be observed by others.

Consider the following studies:

One researcher sat in a café and recorded the conversations that people around him were having.

How would you feel if you found out that a psychologist had been listening to you talking with your mates and recorded what you were saying? Would you feel that this was an invasion of your privacy? It was a public place afterall ...

Another researcher recorded the behaviour of men in public toilets (public places). Humphreys (1970) sought to demonstrate that certain common prejudices about homosexuals were mistaken. To do this he pretended to be a 'watchqueen' in a 'tearoom'. A 'tearoom' is a public toilet where men meet for sex with other men. A 'watchqueen' is someone who is allowed to watch the sexual activity and, in exchange, acts as a lookout.

Do you think this is acceptable? Does the purpose of the research justify the methods?

You can see why psychologists have to spend time thinking about what is or is not acceptable.

The second ethical issue that causes problems when conducting observations is **informed consent**. Participants should be informed about their participation in a psychological study and given the option of taking part or not. However, in observational research, people may change their behaviour if they know they are being watched.

One way to deal with this is to **debrief** the participants afterwards, explaining the aims of the study and asking permission to use their data. Another way to deal with this is to use videotapes of people after they have given informed consent.

1.3

Try this

In class, work with a partner and take turns observing each other. Perhaps observe one partner working on a difficult task while the other person just reads a magazine. The person doing the observing should note down any aspect of their partner's behaviour.

OR ... you know you want to do this one (you probably do it anyway for fun). Take a seat in a public space such as a shopping centre and watch people go by. Try to describe what they are doing. Maybe choose to look at the bus queues. Devise some categories to capture most of their behaviour. Use the categories to see if there are differences in behaviour between different groups of people such as young and old.

- Can you draw any conclusions from your observations?
- Was it easy or difficult to record all behaviours?

Making observations

You might think that making observations is easy but if you tried the activity above, you should now realise it is difficult.

1. It is difficult to work out what to record and what not to record.
2. It is difficult to record everything that is happening. For example, in the activity above, you might have missed some behaviours while you were busy writing.

Observational research, like all research, aims to be objective and rigorous. For this reason it is necessary to use **observational techniques**.

Psychologists have methods to deal with the two points above, as we consider on the facing page.

Qs 1.1

1. On the left (in the light grey box) two studies are described that involved making observations. For each study explain how it might be conducted in a way that both respected the participants and satisfied the researcher's needs.

2. In each of the following observations state which sampling procedure (time or event sampling) would be most appropriate and explain how you would do it:
   a. Observing the different activities young children engage in at a nursery school.
   b. Observing what dog owners do when they are walking their dogs in a park.
   c. Observing the products bought by shoppers in a supermarket.

3. A university department undertakes an observational study of the behaviour of football fans at a live game.
   a. List **three** specific behavioural categories you might use.
   b. Identify a suitable sampling procedure and explain how you would do it.
   c. How could you observe target individuals so that they were not aware that they were being observed?
   d. Explain how videotaping could be used to deal with possible ethical issues.

4. A school decides to collect data about student behaviour in the cafeteria throughout the day. Answer questions a–d above.

1.4

Try this

Aim: To consider individual differences in anxiety when speaking in public. (You could compare males and females.)

1 **Pilot study**: Begin by conducting an **unstructured observation**. Ask several volunteers (males and females) to stand up in front of your class and deliver a one-minute talk on any topic. The rest of the class should make a note of any non-verbal behaviours, for example: scratching nose, licking lips, waving hands, saying 'um'.

2 **Devise your behaviour checklist**: Use your unstructured observations to create a *behaviour checklist* (explained below). It might be best to work in small groups to do this (a possible example is shown on the right). Each group can report back to the whole class with their ideas and the class can produce a final version.

3 **Use your behaviour checklist to record** structured observations of people speaking. Make a record for each speaker.

4 **Results**: Summarise your findings in a table showing totals for each behavioural category for each speaker. You can also illustrate the behavioural categories using a **bar chart**. Draw some conclusions from your data.

Behaviour checklist

	Person 1	Person 2	Etc.
Extraneous vocalisation e.g. 'um'			
Hand touches face			
Etc.			

Which would be best to use – time or event sampling?

---

1 Deciding what to record and what not to record
One of the hardest aspects of using the observational method is deciding what you are going to record and how the different behaviours should be categorised. This is because our perception of behaviour is often seamless; when we watch somebody perform a particular action we see a continuous stream of action rather than a series of separate behavioural components.

In order to conduct systematic observations we need to break up this stream of behaviour into different categories, called **behavioural categories**. In order to do this a researcher has to break the behaviour being studied into a set of components. For example, when observing infant behaviour, having a list such as smiling, crying, etc.

This list of behavioural categories (called a **behaviour checklist**) may be adopted from a previous research study (see an example on the right) or may be developed after first making preliminary observations. It should:

- Be objective. The observer should not have to make inferences about the behaviour. For example, a category such as 'Target person looks happy' means the observer has to think about whether the target person looks happy. The categories must relate to explicit actions such as smiling or laughing.

- Cover all possible component behaviours and avoid a 'waste basket' category (i.e. a category where you can include anything that isn't already covered).

- Have no overlapping categories. If categories are not mutually exclusive then observers may feel unsure which category to tick. The end result is that two different observers wouldn't produce the same record of behaviour.

2 Recording only some of the things that are happening
An observer needs to decide when and how often to make observations. This may be continuous, where the observer records every instance of behaviour in as much detail as possible. This is useful if the behaviours of interest do not occur very often.

However, usually continuous observation is not possible because there would be too much to record. Therefore observers use a systematic method. For example:

Event sampling Counting the number of times a specific behaviour (event) occurs in target individuals each and every time it occurs throughout the whole duration of the observation period. For example, counting how many times a person smiles in a one hour period.

Time sampling The observer decides on a time interval, such as once a minute or once every 30 seconds. Throughout the observation period the observer notes what behaviours are being shown at that time, i.e. every minute or every 30 seconds.

Time sampling also describes taking a sample at different times of day (or month, etc.) and possibly comparing different samples.

Try this

1.5

Observing bears in a zoo
Robert Jordan and Gordon Burghardt (1986) devised a behaviour checklist and used it to record bears' behaviour in two different zoos – one zoo where a lot of people were around and one zoo where the bears were less observed by people. Jordan and Burghardt found that the bears were much more active when there were more people about.

You could conduct your own observational study at a zoo. The researchers spent one hour each day making recordings over a two-and-a-half year period. Observations were recorded every 30 seconds (time sampling) using a behaviour checklist similar to the one below.

Behaviour checklist with codes (called a coding system) for recording postures and locations of captive black bears

Activity level 1: Reclining postures
Lying on back (P6)
Lying on front (P7)
Lying on side (P8)
Lying/sitting in a tree (P28)

Activity level 2: Sitting or standing
Standing on all fours (P3)
Standing on two feet (P29)
Sitting erect or semi-erect (P4)

Activity level 3: Bipedal standing and slow locomotion
Standing on two feet while touching an object (P1)
Walking on all fours (P11)
Rolling over (P18)

Activity level 4: Vigorous activity
Running (P19)
Ascending (e.g. trees) (P24)
Descending (e.g. trees) (P27)
Running a short distance and then walking (P32)
Jumping (all legs off ground) (P35)

What you have learned on this spread

- How to make observations.
- How to design an observational study.
- Ethics and ethical issues related to observations.
- Behavioural categories and behaviour checklists.
- Time and event sampling.

More on observations

On this spread we continue to explain how observational methods are used in research.

Thus far you have discovered why it helps to use structured observational techniques such as behavioural categories and methods of sampling (time and event sampling). You might even have tried some out for yourself.

Qs 1.2

1 Explain the difference between:

> On every spread of this chapter you will find QUESTIONS. Use these to help you read through and understand the contents of the spread.

    a Unstructured and structured observational techniques.

    b Naturalistic observation and controlled observation.

    c Participant and non-participant observation.

    d Disclosed and undisclosed observation.

2 A group of students decided to study student behaviour in the school library.

    a How could you conduct this as a naturalistic observation using unstructured techniques?

    b How could you conduct this as a controlled observation using unstructured techniques?

    c Identify **at least three** suitable behavioural categories that you could use in this study.

    d How could you observe the students so that they were not aware that they were being observed (undisclosed observation)?

    e Discuss **one** ethical issue that might arise in this research.

Observational TECHNIQUES
i.e. the system used to record observations.

Unstructured observations
In **unstructured observations** the researcher records all relevant behaviour but has no system.

Structured observations
In a **structured observation** the researcher uses various 'systems' to organise observations, such as **behavioural categories** and **time** or **event sampling**.

Observational METHODS
i.e. the environment in which an observation is conducted.

Naturalistic observations
In a **naturalistic observation** everything is left as it normally is. The environment is unstructured, i.e. uncontrolled. For example:

- Watching animals in their 'normal' or natural environment. This might be a zoo if that's where they usually live.
- Listening to children talking in their classroom or at home.

Controlled observations
In **controlled observations** some variables are controlled by the researcher (i.e. structured) to some extent. The study might be conducted in a **laboratory** in order to control variables in the environment. For example:

- Watching gorillas in a zoo where they have been provided with specific play items.
- Listening to children who have been asked to talk about their families.

An example of a naturalistic observation

Do little boys criticise each other if they behave like girls? Do little boys 'reward' each other for sex-appropriate play? Is the same true for little girls?

One study observed boys and girls aged 3–5 years during their free-play periods at nursery school. The researchers classified activities as male, female or neutral and recorded how playmates responded. Praise and imitation constituted some of the positive responses. Criticism and stopping play were some of the negative responses. The researchers found that children generally reinforced peers for sex-appropriate play and were quick to criticise sex-inappropriate play (Lamb and Roopnarine, 1979).

An example of a controlled observation

The same research as described on the left could be conducted by controlling some of the variables.

*For example, the researchers might have set up a special playroom in their laboratory with certain types of toys available (male, female and neutral). They could have observed the children through a **one-way mirror** so the children would be unaware of being observed.*

More techniques

Participant and non-participant observation
In many cases the observer is merely watching the behaviour of others and acts as a non-participant. However, in some studies observers also participate, which may affect their objectivity (see example on the right). This is not so much an either/or as a sliding scale of participation.

Disclosed and undisclosed observation
One-way mirrors can be used to prevent participants being aware that they are being observed. This is called undisclosed (**covert**) observation. This method was used in the core study on aggression by Bandura et al. (see page 88). Knowing that your behaviour is being observed is likely to alter your behaviour.

An example of a participant observation

In the 1950s the social psychologist Leon Festinger read a newspaper report about a religious cult that claimed to be receiving messages from outer space predicting that the end of the world would take place on a certain date in the form of a great flood. The cult members were going to be rescued by a flying saucer so they all gathered with their leader, Mrs Keech. Festinger was intrigued to know how the cult members would respond when they found their beliefs were unfounded. In order to observe this at first hand Festinger and some colleagues posed as cult followers and were present on the expected eve of destruction. When it was apparent that there 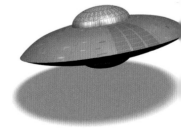 *would be no flood, the group initially became disheartened but Mrs Keech announced that she had received a new message from the aliens saying that the group's efforts had saved the day. Although some cult members soon left the cult, others took this as proof of the cult's beliefs and became even more enthusiastic supporters. The question of just how involved the psychologists were, and how much they contributed towards the false beliefs, remains uncertain (Festinger et al., 1956).*

Exam focus ... on BIG MARK QUESTIONS

The exam on Psychological Investigations (G541) consists of 'source material' describing a study and the questions that follow relate to this. Occasionally there are BIG MARK QUESTIONS, such as question number 1 on the right. You need these marks because they are critical in determining whether you get a high or low grade. The difference between each grade (e.g. a Grade A and B, B and C, etc.) is usually about 4 marks. If you do badly on a big mark question that alone may cost you two grades.

How do you answer these questions? Let's start with the 'describe' part. To describe an appropriate procedure you must provide enough detail for **replication**, *i.e. enough information for someone else to be able to repeat your procedure.* <u>*This means you need to be very specific in what you write.*</u> *Gaining a good mark is not about writing lots, examiners say that simple answers are often best as long as the specific details are included.*

When describing an observational study you should provide details of:

- ● *What?* *What are the aims of your study?*
- ● *Who?* *Who are the target individuals you are going to observe? How many? What are their characteristics?*
- ● *Where?* *The geographical location of the observations, and also the position of where the observer would be placed.*
- ● *Materials?* *The behaviour checklist and the behavioural categories.*
- ● *How?* *Should include whether using* **time** *or* **event sampling**.

The evaluate part is discussed on page 8.

> Researchers want to conduct an observation investigating the differences in the way young boys and girls play.
>
> 1 Describe and evaluate an appropriate procedure that could be used in this study. **[10]**
>
> 2 Outline **one** strength and **one** weakness of using time sampling in this study. **[6]**

Try this   **1.6**

Here are some more observational studies to try. You will need to make decisions about who, what, when, where and how.

At the end of any study you should present your results in a graph and draw conclusions.

Observe students in a common room or cafeteria

In this observation you can decide to be a participant or non-participant observer. You can also decide whether to use undisclosed or disclosed methods.

You can use the behaviour checklist below, adapted from one used by Fick (1993) in a study looking at the effects of a dog on the nature and frequency of social interactions in nursing home residents.

> ❑ *Non-attentive behaviour:* participant is not engaged in group activity.
>
> ❑ *Attentive listening:* participant maintains eye contact with other group members.
>
> ❑ *Verbal interaction with another person:* participant initiates or responds verbally to another person.
>
> ❑ *Non-verbal interaction with another person:* participant touches, gestures, smiles, nods, etc. to another person.

Decide on your research aims, for example you could compare social interactions in the morning and afternoon, or differences between boys and girls, or between different environments (such as in class and in the cafeteria).

For homework: observe your pet

If you are a pet lover (and have a pet) sit down and watch your pet, noting down any behaviours. Use this unstructured observation to produce a behaviour checklist and then observe the animal at different times. Is his or her behaviour different when there are lots of people in the room? Or at different times of day? Or different room temperatures?

Qs 1.3

1 In the box above there is advice about how you should describe an appropriate procedure for a study. Your answer should include details of what, who, where, materials and how.

  In the examples below, describe an appropriate procedure that could be used in each study. *The amount of detail you provide should be sufficient for replication.*

  a Researchers wish to record the social behaviour of monkeys in a zoo.

  b A study was made of the differences in the kinds of things young boys and girls play with.

  c What do drivers do when they stop at traffic lights? A group of psychology students conducted an observational study.

  d Observe students in a common room or cafeteria (see left).

  e Observe your pet study (see left).

2 With reference to the 'observe students' study on the left, discuss the following issues:

  a Explain whether you think it would be better to do this as a non-participant or a participant observation. Explain your reasons.

  b Explain whether you think disclosed or undisclosed observations would be most suitable. Explain your answer with reference to both ethical and practical issues.

What you have learned on this spread

- ● Observational techniques: structured or unstructured, participant or non-participant, disclosed or undisclosed.
- ● Observational methods: naturalistic or controlled.

To summarise		Techniques	
		Structure	No structure
Method (environment)	Structure	Controlled observation with structured observational techniques	Controlled observation with unstructured observational techniques
	No structure	Naturalistic observation with structured observational techniques	Naturalistic observation with unstructured observational techniques

- ● How to describe the procedures of an observational study (what, who, where, materials and how).
- ● The importance of replication in exam answers.

Evaluating observations

The next step on our journey is to consider the relative strengths and weaknesses of **observational studies**, i.e. to consider their value.

We will look at two important means of evaluation: reliability and validity.

Qs 1.4

1 Explain why reliability and validity are important.

2 A psychologist decided to conduct a naturalistic observation of the behaviour of people shopping in a supermarket.

 a Draw a suitable table for recording observations, showing some of the possible behavioural categories that might be used.

 b Identify **two** ways you could evaluate the reliability of the observations to be made. (In other words, consider issues that might affect whether this study is reliable as well as methods used to assess reliability).

 c Describe **two** features of the study that might reduce the validity of this study.

 d Explain how you could deal with these two features that might reduce validity.

 e Describe **one** way of ensuring that this study would be carried out in an ethically acceptable manner.

 f Evaluate your method of dealing with ethics (i.e. did it actually deal with the ethical issues).

3 You are asked to see if it is possible to use facial expressions to tell whether someone is lying or not.

 a Describe an appropriate procedure for such a study. Your answer should include details of what, who, where, materials and how.

 b Would you describe your study a naturalistic or a controlled observation?

 c Evaluate the reliability and validity of carrying out the study in the way described in part (a).

4 Below there are two graphs showing the observations of two children made by three observers. Do you think that the graphs indicate an acceptable level of inter-observer reliability? Explain your answer.

Exam focus ... on BIG MARK QUESTIONS

Big mark questions are also about reliability and validity, for example 'Evaluate the reliability and validity of this research. [10]

One way to approach such questions is to write 'One reason the reliability in this study is good is because ...'

Reliability

The term **reliability** refers to consistency.

If you use a ruler to measure the height of a chair and the following day you find that the measurement is different, you would probably think the chair must have changed magically overnight. You would expect the ruler to be reliable (consistent) so any change must be because the chair changed. If, in fact, the fluctuation was due to some change in the ruler it would be pretty useless as a measuring instrument – it wouldn't be dependable, consistent or reliable.

Evaluating the reliability of observations

When making observations of a person (or animal or event) we require the observations to be something we can depend on. If they are reliable we would expect to end up with the same data if the observations were made a second time.

For example, you could compare the observations made by two people of the same event. Both sets of observations should be the same, in the same way as using two tape measures to measure a table should produce the same result if they are reliable. This is called **inter-rater reliability**. Just doing this doesn't make the observations reliable but calculating inter-rater reliability enables us to evaluate how reliable the observations are.

Another way to evaluate reliability would be to consider how good a **behaviour checklist** is. If the categories are clear then all observers will be looking for the same things and are likely to be reliable.

Dealing with low reliability

Reliability can be improved by making sure that observers are trained in the use of the behavioural checklist.

It might also be necessary to review the behaviour checklist and see if some categories are unclear or need sub-dividing to make for more accurate recording.

Note that simply having more observers does *not* increase reliability.

Calculating inter-rater reliability

*In order to calculate inter-rater reliability a count can be kept of the number of times the observers agree with each other. Consider the table below which shows the observations from two observers recording the behaviour of a student in a mock interview. Data was recorded using **event sampling**. The data doesn't look like it would have high inter-rater reliability. A **correlation coefficient** can be calculated between the observers' records (see page 32). A general rule is that if the correlation between observers is greater than 80% this represents high inter-rater reliability.*

	Observer 1	Observer 2
Behaviour 1 (saying 'um')	10	3
Behaviour 2 (scratching face)	3	5
Behaviour 3 (nervous giggle)	1	2
Etc.		

	No social participation
1	Occupied alone participation
2	Hanging around alone
3	Alone – onlooker
4	Alone – unclear
	Social participation
5	Parallel behaviour 1
6	Parallel behaviour 2
7	Loosely associated but interactive
8	Role play – identifiable
9	Social participation unclear
	Not identifiable
10	Child not in view, generally unclear

An example of evaluating reliability

*The Behavioural Observation unit (BEO) at the University of Bern trains people in the use of observational techniques (BEO, 2004). They have a nursery school at the unit where children can be observed through a **one-way mirror**, using a **coding system** called KaSo 12 (see below).*

The graphs on the right show observations made of two children. Each time three observers were used (blue, red and yellow line). The figures represent the relative duration of a specific behaviour category expressed as a percentage of the total time.

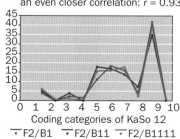

Child 2: Showing a markedly different distribution of behaviour patterns but an even closer correlation: r = 0.93

Coding categories of KaSo 12
F2/B1   F2/B11   F2/B1111

Child 1: **Mean** correlation of the 3 profiles: r = 0.86

Coding categories of KaSo 12
F2/B1   F2/B11   F2/B1111

*To achieve high marks you should clearly separate material on reliability and validity, and should aim to write about **four** issues (two on reliability and two on validity).*

Do not include procedural details in such a question – a mistake students often make.

Reliability and validity are discussed again throughout this chapter and also on pages 234, 235 and 242–243. They are both key concepts for psychological researchers because a study that lacks reliability and/or validity is simply meaningless.

Validity

The term **validity** refers to the extent to which a research study has measured what it intended to measure.

It is also concerned with the extent to which we have measured what is really 'out there' – reality – which is what the researcher did intend to measure.

Evaluating the validity of observations

Behavioural categories
Observations will not be valid if the behaviour checklist is flawed. For example, some observations may belong in more than one category, or some behaviours may not fit in any category. The result is that the data collected does not truly represent what was observed (the researcher has not measured what he/she intended to measure).

Observer bias
When an observer records what they see or hear their observations are inevitably influenced by their expectations. For example, if you believe that boys are more aggressive in their play than girls then you are likely to interpret their behaviour differently. If a little boy puts his hand on a friend the observer may say he was 'hitting' his friend whereas the same action may be interpreted differently when a little girl does it. **Observer bias** reduces the objectivity and validity of observations.

Other issues
There are other issues that affect validity, such as who is observed or where the observations are made. **Ecological validity** may be a problem if, for example, you only observe middle-class children who live in a city. Then the results of the study may only apply to middle-class, urban children and we say the study lacks ecological validity because the results cannot be applied to all children.

Dealing with low validity
Behavioural categories can be tested by using a **pilot study** (described on page 21). They can then be refined so they better fit the behaviour-to-be-observed.

Using more than one observer can reduce observer bias by averaging data across observers (balances out any biases).

Conducting observations in varied settings with varied participants improves ecological validity.

The psychomeasure of intelligence

It has been suggested that the circumference of a person's head could be used as a measure of intelligence. This is likely to be a fairly RELIABLE measure of intelligence because adult head size is consistent from one year to the next.

You may even feel this is a VALID measure of intelligence. Afterall, if you have a bigger brain then you might have more intelligence. However research doesn't bear this out. Intelligence is not related to brain or head size. This means this measure of intelligence lacks VALIDITY.

Try this   1.7

Children's books and gender stereotypes
In this example you could try reviewing the validity and reliability of your observations.
Peter Crabb and Dawn Bielawski (1994) examined American books for pre-school children and found that female characters were more likely to be pictured using household objects whereas males were more likely to be using production objects (e.g. things related to agriculture, construction, transportation – i.e. work outside the home).

*   Develop your own behaviour checklist to record the way males and females are represented in children's books (or you could look at TV ads). Start by looking at some children's books and the activities that men and women, boys and girls are engaged in. You may just use two categories (household objects and production objects), or you might want to add further categories.

*   Once you have developed a behaviour checklist, compare the observations made by yourself and some of your classmates. How reliable are your observations? Was there any evidence of observer bias? How valid were your observations? Were some of the behavioural categories ambiguous?

Reliable, but not valid

Not reliable, not valid

Reliable and valid

Being reliable is being consistent (far left and far right); being valid is being on target, in relation to what you are aiming to do (far right).

What you have learned on this spread
*   Reliability and inter-rater reliability.
*   Validity and observer bias, ecological validity.
*   How to evaluate the reliability and validity of an observational study.

Evaluating observations

One way to evaluate observational techniques and methods is to consider **reliability** and **validity**, as we did on the previous spread. However, there are other issues to consider. The table below covers the main strengths and weaknesses of observational methods and techniques, including issues related to reliability and validity.

When answering the questions on the facing page, you should draw on the information in the table below, but be aware of two things:

1 Always contextualise your answers.

2 Answers are likely to combine several categories, e.g. a study might be a naturalistic observation that uses a behaviour checklist and disclosed observations – so you can use the strengths/weakness for all of these techniques. Be inventive with your answers, combining more than one category.

Football fans are very aggressive. If you believe that they are aggressive you would probably produce biased observations of the behaviour of football fans – an example of observer bias.

	Strengths	Weaknesses
Observational techniques/methods	What people say they do is often different from what they actually do, so observations give a different take on behaviour than other research methods. Able to capture spontaneous and unexpected behaviour.	Observers may 'see' what they expect to see (**observer bias**). Observations cannot provide information about what people think or feel. Key behaviours may be missed due to people obscuring the view.
Unstructured observation	A means of conducting preliminary investigations in a new area of research, to produce ideas for future investigations. This technique may be used because the behaviour to be studied is largely unpredictable.	The behaviours recorded will often be those which are most visible or eye-catching to the observer but these may not necessarily be the most important or relevant behaviours.
Behaviour checklist (structured observations)	Enables systematic observations to be made so important information is not overlooked. Without such structure an observer may be overwhelmed by a stream of information and be unable to record everything.	Categories may not cover all possibilities and so some behaviours go unrecorded. This results in low **validity** because not measuring what was intended to be measured. A poorly designed behaviour checklist also reduces reliability (low **inter-rater reliability**).
Naturalistic observation	Gives a realistic picture of natural, spontaneous behaviour, therefore high **ecological validity**. (Although participants may know they are being observed.)	There is little control of all the other things that are happening, which may mean that something unknown to the observer may account for the behaviour observed.
Controlled observation	Can control the environment so observations can focus on particular aspects of behaviour, such as providing a certain selection of toys to observe the differences in what boys and girls play with.	The environment may feel unnatural and then participants' behaviour is unnatural (observations lack validity).
Participant observation	Likely to provide special insights into behaviour, from the 'inside', that may not otherwise be gained. Able to monitor and record behaviour in closer detail.	Objectivity may be reduced (observer bias). More difficult to record and monitor behaviour unobtrusively if the observer is part of the group being observed.
Disclosed observations	Avoids **ethical issues** because participants can decide whether to participate or not (**informed consent**).	If participants know they are being observed they are likely to alter their behaviour.
Undisclosed observations	Participants behave more naturally because they are not aware of being observed.	Raises ethical concerns about observing people without their knowledge (**deception** and **invasion of privacy**).
Time sampling	Makes the task of observing behaviour more manageable rather than being overwhelmed by every single behaviour that happens.	Observations may not be representative. May decrease **reliability** as it is more difficult to be consistent if recording behaviour during many different time intervals.
Event sampling	Useful when behaviour to be recorded only happens occasionally and might be missed if time sampling is used. Missing events would reduce validity.	Observer may miss some observations if too many things happen at once.

Exam focus on CONTEXTUALISED QUESTIONS

We looked at the exam question on the right earlier in this chapter. Both of the questions in this example require evaluation.

- *Question 1 requires you to describe and evaluate the procedure you devise. 'Evaluation' means providing strengths and weaknesses. As part of a 10 mark question your evaluation should include two or more* **APPROPRIATE** *evaluation issues in* **CONTEXT**.

- *Question 2 requires strengths and weaknesses again, one of each for a total of 6 marks. If you just describe* **one** *strength and* **one** *weakness you would receive low marks. If you include the* **CONTEXT** *you should receive top marks. The difference between getting low marks and top marks can be as much as one grade.*

So you can see that the **CONTEXT** *part of evaluation is critical in your quest for a good exam grade. 'Context' means relating your answer to the particular study described in the source material. For example, one strength of time sampling is that:*

> *Low mark answer: ... you don't have to note down every single behaviour that happens.*

> *Middle mark answer: ... you don't have to note down every single behaviour that happens. For example you would just look at one boy every 30 seconds.*

> *Top mark answer: ... you don't have to note down every single behaviour that happens. For example you would just look at one boy every 30 seconds and note down what he is doing then, rather than watching the boy while he is playing and recording every target behaviour you see.*

> *To receive top marks there is both CONTEXT and DETAIL.*

Researchers want to conduct an observation investigating the differences in the way young boys and girls play.

1. Describe and evaluate an appropriate procedure that could be used in this study. **[10]**

2. Outline **one** strength and **one** weakness of using time sampling in this study. **[6]**

> *In order to receive better than basic marks, some CONTEXT related to the source material must be included.*
>
> *OR you could add extra DETAIL, for example '... you don't have to note down every single behaviour that happens so you will not have to concentrate so hard as you would with event sampling.'*

Qs 1.5

At the bottom of this column there are descriptions of three observational studies. For each study answer the following questions:

1. Outline **one** strength and **one** weakness of conducting an unstructured observation in this study.

2. Identify **three or more** possible behavioural categories that could be used.

3. Outline **one** strength and **one** weakness of conducting a participant observation in this study.

4. Outline **one** strength and **one** weakness of conducting an undisclosed observation in this study.

5. Outline **one** strength and **one** weakness of using time sampling in this study.

6. Outline **one** strength and **one** weakness of using event sampling in this study.

7. Describe and evaluate an appropriate procedure that could be used in this study. For the 'describe' part, remember what, who, where, materials and how, and remember REPLICATION. For the evaluate part include two or more evaluation issues in your answer and make sure they are CONTEXTUALISED.

Study A A primary school is concerned about the way children cross the road after school. There is a road safety warden outside the school gates but some students cross further up the road where it is less safe. To check students' behaviour the school organises an observational study over a one week period.

Study B The department of medicine at Nottingham University is conducting research about what makes a good GP. As part of this they wish to observe the behaviour of GPs when they are consulting with their patients.

Study C The captain of the school football team analyses the playing styles of his team members by observing their behaviour during one match.

Try this   1.8

Self-presentation on Facebook
A rich source of data can be found on the phenomenon that is Facebook.

One line of investigation might concern the way people present themselves in their photograph – some people have a face only portrait, others are pictured with friends or put in some other image.

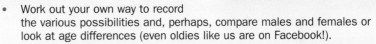

- Work out your own way to record the various possibilities and, perhaps, compare males and females or look at age differences (even oldies like us are on Facebook!).

- Consider ethical issues. People have decided to place their personal information in the public domain, so is it acceptable to make observations of what they have done? Should you inform your friends about what you are doing?

- Consider how to present your findings to others.

...Links to core studies...

In this text the **Rosenhan** study gathers the bulk of its data from observational techniques and so is commonly referred to as an observational study. The study by **Bandura et al.** also uses observational techniques but the main question of the study is answered using an experimental hypothesis and so this study is commonly referred to as an experiment. In the study by **Milgram** the behaviour of participants was observed and recorded, and aspects of the environment were controlled. It isn't usually called a controlled observation but it could be. **Savage-Rumbaugh** also controlled the apes' environment and observed their behaviour.

It is may be best to think of observation as a technique for gathering data rather than as a research method.

What you have learned on this spread

- How to contextualise your evaluations.
- Strengths and weaknesses of observational techniques and methods.
- How to evaluate an observational study.

Representing data

Researchers collect data. For example in the observational studies you have studied so far, the end result was often numbers – counting how many times a person scratched their nose or how many times a bear rolled over. This is numerical or **quantitative data**. On this spread we will explore both quantitative and **qualitative data**.

Quantitative data can be represented using **descriptive statistics**, which you will be familiar with from your study of mathematics – averages and bar charts. You need to use such **descriptive statistics** to represent findings from research and draw conclusions.

Painting in the style of The Kiss *by Gustav Klimt. You can describe this qualitatively or quantitatively.*

Quantitative data	Qualitative data
Quantity	Quality
Deals with numbers	Deals with descriptions
Data that can be measured	Data that are not measured
Psychologists develop measures of psychological variables	Observing people through the messages they produce and the way they act
Looking at averages and differences between groups	
	Concerned with attitudes, beliefs, fears, emotions

The Kiss **by Gustav Klimt**	
Painted between 1907 and 1908, when the artist was 45 years old	Representative of a style of art called *Art Nouveau*
Painting measures 180 × 180 cm	Shows a couple locked in a kiss
Bought for 25,000 crowns when it was first painted	Shows how bright, beautiful and golden everything is when you first kiss someone
33% of surface covered in gold leaf	
Listed as no. 12 on list of most popular paintings	Painted in oil and gold leaf on canvas
	Probably Klimt's most famous work

A psychology class	
24 students	Very enthusiastic about psychology
18 girls, 6 boys	Mixture of boys and girls
72% gained Grade A on mock exam	Hardworking students
10 plan to go on to study psychology at university	School located in an inner-city area
80% psychology teachers are female	Teacher's name is Mrs Jones

	Strengths	Weaknesses
Quantitative data	Easier to analyse because data are in numbers which can be summarised using descriptive statistics (averages as well as simple graphs). This generally makes it easier to draw conclusions because, for example, you can see at a glance that men did better on a particular maths test than women, or that the average rating for a particular film was 7 out of 10.	Oversimplifies reality and human experience because it suggests that there are simple answers (statistically **significant** but humanly insignificant).
Qualitative data	Represents the true complexities of human behaviour because access is gained to thoughts and feelings that may not be assessed using quantitative methods. Provides rich details of how people behave because they are given a free range to express themselves.	More difficult to detect patterns and draw conclusions because of the large variety of information collected, and because words cannot be reduced to a few simple points.

Qs 1.6

1   On the left of this page are descriptions of Klimt's painting *The Kiss* and of a hypothetical psychology class. Qualitative and quantitative descriptions are given of both. Try to do the same activity for the following:
    a   A television series.
    b   The town or city you live in.
    c   A major world event such as the London Olympics or the 9/11 bombing in New York.

2   Based on your answers to question 1, consider what kind of data is 'better':
    a   Outline the strengths and weaknesses of using quantitative data in the examples above.
    b   Outline the strengths and weaknesses of using qualitative data in the examples above.

3   Two psychology students observe each other and write down everything the other person does.
    a   Give **two** examples of the data collected in this study.
    b   Have they collected quantitative or qualitative data? Explain your answer.
    c   Outline **one** strength and **one** weakness of the kind of data collected in this study.

4   A group of psychology students visit a zoo and use a set of behavioural categories to make observations. They each select a target animal and count each time the animal performs one of the behaviours.
    a   Would they be using event or time sampling? Explain your answer.
    b   Give **one** strength and **one** weakness of the sampling technique used in this study.
    c   Have they collected quantitative or qualitative data? Explain your answer.
    d   Outline **one** strength and **one** weakness of the kind of data collected in this study.

Descriptive statistics

Descriptive statistics are used to describe and summarise data. Psychologists also use **inferential statistics** to check whether their results are significant, i.e. have not occurred by chance – however you only have to use such tests as part of the A2 course, you'll be glad to know!

Averages

There are three different ways to express the average or typical value of a set of data:

1 The **mean** is calculated by adding up all the numbers and dividing by the number of numbers. Not appropriate for data in categories.
2 The **median** is the *middle* value in an *ordered* list. Not appropriate for data in categories.
3 The **mode** is the value that is *most* common. When using frequency data the **modal group** is the group that has the highest value.

Graphs

A picture is worth a thousand words! Graphs provide a means of 'eyeballing' your data and seeing the results at a glance.

- **Bar chart**: the height of the bar represents frequency. Suitable for words and numbers.
- **Line graph**: illustrating frequency of continuous data.
- **Scattergraph**: suitable for **correlational** data (see page 32).

	Strengths	Weaknesses
Mean	It makes use of the *values* of all the data. Note the use of the word 'values'. All measures of central tendency use all the data and use the data values. But the mean is the only one that uses *all* the values when making the final calculation.	It can be unrepresentative of the numbers if there are extreme values. For example 2, 4, 5, 6, 9, 10, 12 mean = 6.86 2, 4, 5, 6, 9, 10, 29 mean = 9.42
Median	Not affected by extreme scores. For example in the data sets above right, the median in both cases would be 6.	Not as 'sensitive' as the mean because not all values are reflected in the median.
Mode	Useful when the data are in categories. For example, asking people to name their favourite colour. The mode would be the colour that received the most votes.	Not a useful way of describing data when there are several modes. For example if 12 people choose yellow and 12 people choose red and 10 people chose purple. The modal groups are yellow and purple but this isn't very informative.

1 For each of the following sets of data (a) calculate the mean, (b) calculate the median, (c) calculate the mode, (d) state which of the three measures would be most suitable to use and why.

i	2, 3, 5, 6, 6, 8, 9, 12, 15, 21, 22
ii	2, 3, 8, 10, 11, 13, 13, 14, 14, 29
iii	2, 2, 4, 5, 5, 5, 7, 7, 8, 8, 8, 10
iv	cat, cat, dog, budgie, snake, gerbil

2 The following data was collected in an observational study of how people present themselves on facebook:

	Males	Females
Face only	4	3
Face and body	8	12
With one friend	4	5
With several friends	1	9
With another item	3	0
Something else	9	8

a Explain why this is quantitative data.
b Outline **one** strength of using quantitative data in this study.
c How could you collect qualitative data in this study?
d Identify the mode for the male scores and the female scores.
e How would the mean score be calculated for the scores?
f When would the descriptive statistic called the 'median' be more appropriate and why?
g Sketch an appropriate bar chart for this data.
h Outline **two** findings from the data displayed in this graph.

Don't draw meaningless graphs

*Imagine that you did a study where there were two groups of 10 participants. One group were given a list of words organised into categories (items of food, precious metals, etc.), the other group were given the same list of words in **random** order. The recall scores are shown in the graphs below.*

The top graph on the right is a participant-by-participant graph – it is meaningless, yet many students do this kind of graph. The bar chart below may look too simple but it is all you need to present a clear summary of your results.

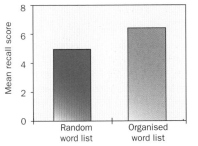

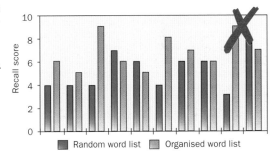

What conclusion(s) can you draw from the graphs above?

Ethics

The topic of ethics concerns standards of behaviour that distinguish between right and wrong, good and bad, and justice and injustice. Some ethical standards are highly general and apply to all situations, such as being honest or being helpful to others. Other standards apply to specific situations such as medical ethics or ethics when conducting research.

An **ethical issue** is a conflict between what the researcher wants and the rights of participants. These conflicts are discussed on this spread.

Psychologists have developed ways to deal with ethical issues, guided by their professional organisation. In the UK this is the British Psychological Society (BPS). The BPS publishes a code of practice.

Informed consent

What is it? Participants must be given comprehensive information concerning the nature and purpose of a study and their role in it.

Participant's view: Participants wish to know what they are letting themselves in for. This is necessary in order to be able to make an informed decision about whether to participate in a study.

Researcher's view: Providing comprehensive information may reduce the meaningfulness of the research because such information will reveal the study's aims and this could affect participants' subsequent behaviour.

For example, a researcher may want to see how obedient people are when given an order by someone in authority. If the researcher tells participants this at the outset of the study, participants might deliberately act more obediently.

Dealing with the issue: The issue is lack of informed consent. If informed consent is not possible then participants should be fully **debriefed** after the study. Debriefing gives the researcher an opportunity to assess the effects of the research procedures and offer some form of counselling if necessary. If deception has been involved in the study, the researcher will explain the true aims of the study and offer participants the right to withhold their data.

However, you can't turn back the clock. If a participant was distressed by taking part in a research study this is difficult to undo. Participants may say they didn't mind and say they enjoyed the experience as a form of self-reassurance.

Another way to deal with not being able to gain informed consent is called **presumptive consent**. There are situations where it is not possible to obtain informed consent (such as when you are observing people in a supermarket). An alternative is to gain informed consent from others. This can be done, for example, by giving the full research details to a group and asking if they would be willing to take part. We then *presume* that the participants themselves would have felt the same, if they had been given the opportunity to say so.

The problem with presumptive consent is that what people say they would or wouldn't mind is different from actually experiencing it.

Deception

What is it? This occurs when a participant is not told the true aims of a study, or is deliberately misled. If a researcher simply omits certain information to avoid alerting the participant to the aims of the study, this is not deception   however, the researcher will have failed in their duty to offer informed consent.

Participant's view: This is an issue because it prevents participants being able to give truly informed consent as they don't have all the necessary information to make that decision.

Researcher's view: Some deception is relatively harmless and/or can be compensated for by adequate debriefing. For example, in a memory study a participant might not be told that, at the end of the study, they will be tested for recall. Such a deception would not cause significant embarrassment or harm to the participants.

Dealing with the issue: Participants should be fully debriefed at the end and all deception explained to them. They should be offered the right to withhold their data.

Right to withdraw

What is it? Participants have the right to know that they can freely decide not to continue participation in a study at any time. This ensures that they feel comfortable at all times.

Participants should also have the right to withdraw their data at the end of a study if they were unhappy about their participation in the study.

Participant's view: A participant may have agreed to take part but, once the study is underway, may change their mind when they actually realise what is involved.

Researcher's view: The loss of participants may bias the study's findings because the participants who leave might be the more confident ones or the more intelligent ones.

Dealing with the issue: It must be made clear that participants can withdraw at any time. Participants may feel pressured to remain in a study. For example, they may think it will spoil the study if they leave or they may have been paid and feel it is wrong to leave.

Protection from harm

What is it? Harm includes any negative physical effects, such as physical injury or asking someone to smoke or drink alcohol, or any negative psychological effects, such as embarrassment or creating self-doubt.

Participant's view: Participants have no desire to be harmed! They would expect to be in the same state at the end of the study as they were at the beginning.

Researcher's view: It may not be possible to estimate all possible negative effects before conducting a study.

Dealing with the issue: Participants should not be exposed to risks greater than or additional to those encountered in their normal lifestyles.

Harm should be avoided by using other methods, such as **role play** (though this also may create **psychological harm**).

The BPS Code of Human Research Ethics (2010)

The information on this spread is based on the British Psychological Society (BPS) Code of Human Research Ethics. A few other points have been included below.

Scientific value

Research should be designed, reviewed and conducted in a way that ensures its quality, integrity and contribution to the development of knowledge and understanding. Research that is judged within a research community to be poorly designed ... can have the potential to cause harm.

On informing participants

*It is recommended that at least one **pilot study** of the processes for informing and debriefing participants be carried out with a naïve person having a literacy level at the lower end of the range expected in the planned research **sample**.*

Who can give consent

The consent of participants in research, whatever their age or competence, should always be sought, by means appropriate to their age and competence level. For children under 16 years of age and for other persons where capacity to consent may be impaired the additional consent of parents or those with legal responsibility for the individual should normally also be sought.

Privacy

What is it? Privacy refers to a person's right to control information about themselves.

There is a subtle distinction between privacy and **confidentiality** – we have a right of privacy, if this is invaded confidentiality or anonymity should be respected.

Participant's view: People have an expectation of privacy. Each person has the right to decide who knows and who doesn't know personal information about them, such as what they are talking about or what they are doing.

Researcher's view: Protecting privacy might be difficult, for example when conducting an **observational study**. Often observers do not wish to alert participants to the fact that they are being studied because that is likely to affect the participant's behaviour.

Dealing with the issue: Do not observe anyone without their informed consent unless it is in a public place.

However, there isn't universal agreement on what constitutes a public place, for example a couple kissing on a park bench may not feel that it is acceptable to be observed for a psychological study despite being in a public place.

Ask participants to give their retrospective consent and offer them the right to withhold their data.

Anonymity and confidentiality

What is it? Concerns the communication of personal information from one person to another, and the trust that this information will be protected either through keeping participants anonymous or keeping their information safe (confidential).

Participant's view: The Data Protection Act gives participants the legal right to have their personal information protected. No one should be able to make a connection between what the participant does in the study and his or her name or personal details.

Researcher's view: It may not be possible to keep information anonymous or confidential because details of a study may lead to an individual's identification. For example, individuals in a **case study** may be recognisable by unique features of the case.

Dealing with the issue: Researchers should not record the names of any participants. They should use numbers instead or use false names.

If anonymity or confidentiality cannot be guaranteed, participants should be informed in advance.

Qs 1.8

In each of the studies described below, describe **one** ethical issue that the researchers need to consider when conducting this study and suggest how this could be dealt with. **Make sure your answers are clearly contextualised**.

Study A: A researcher intends to observe children playing in the playground.

Study B: Psychology students plan to observe teachers' behaviour as they park their cars in the morning.

Study C: A teacher aims to investigate the behaviour of students in the library. She tells the students she is observing them to see how much time they spend working. In fact she is making notes on the conversations they have.

Try this   1.9

Ethics committee

All institutions where research takes place have an ethics committee (sometimes called an institutional review board) and the committee must approve any study before it begins. The committee looks at all possible ethical issues and at how the researchers plan to deal with these, weighing up the value of the research against the possible costs in ethical terms.

Try this for yourself. Divide your class into groups. Each group should devise a study that raises one of the ethical issues listed on this spread – but not a wild idea! Something that might be just acceptable. Look through your psychology textbook for ideas.

Write a research proposal that identifies the ethical issues and how you intend to deal with them. You should also be clear about the aim of the research and why it is important.

Then present your proposal to an ethics committee consisting of some of your class members. An ethics committee should be composed of people who represent the different interests: university, psychology department, participants – so each class member on the committee should take one of these roles.

What you have learned on this spread

- Ethical issues (informed consent, deception, right to withdraw, protection from harm, privacy, anonymity and confidentiality).
- How to deal with these ethical issues.

Research method 2: self-report

Observational studies provide insights into behaviour but they can't tell us what people are thinking or feeling. The most obvious way to find out what a person feels, thinks or does is to ask them.

The term **self-report** refers to any data collection method that involves asking people to report on their thoughts, feelings or behaviour. This data can be collected by asking people to write about themselves (a **questionnaire**) or talk about themselves (an **interview**). Questionnaires/ interviews can be structured which means that there are a set of pre-determined questions. Or they can be unstructured which means that questions are developed as the interview goes along. We will concentrate on structured techniques, and in particular on questionnaires. Commonly, questionnaires require short responses and allow us to easily compare the results between one person and another, and also to calculate average responses.

These are all self-report techniques:

Questionnaires: *Respondents record their own answers. The questions are predetermined.*

Structured interview: *Pre-determined questions, i.e. a questionnaire that is delivered in real-time (e.g. over the telephone or face-to-face).*

Semi-structured interview: *New questions are developed as you go along, similar to the way your GP might interview you. He or she starts with some pre-determined questions but further questions are developed as a response to your answers. For this reason this semi-structured approach is sometimes called the* ***clinical interview***.

Unstructured interview: *No questions are decided in advance.*

Try this   1.10

Investigating dreams

Aim

To find out about people's dreams. Research questions: What do people dream about? Do people dream in colour? How often do people have nightmares?

Method

You can use the questionnaire below or extend it with some of your own questions. Brief all participants about the purpose of the questionnaire and what will be involved; gain **informed consent**; hand out the questionnaire (or record the answers for interviewee); then debrief all participants.

QUESTIONNAIRE

What are your dreams like?

Think of a recent dream and answer the following questions related to your dream (you may tick more than one answer to each question):

1   What characters were in the dream?
   ☐ Known (e.g. family, friends)
   ☐ Generic (e.g. a policeman or a teacher but not a specific teacher)
   ☐ Animals
   ☐ Fantasy figure (e.g. angel, dragon)
   ☐ Other (please specify) _____

2   What kind of dream was it?
   ☐ Positive   ☐ Negative

3   How meaningful was your dream?
   Can you remember a lot of details?   YES/NO
   Was the dream just fragments?   YES/NO
   Was it related to specific day-time events?   YES/NO

Drawing conclusions

You can use various **descriptive statistics** (see page 13), such as stating the **modal** answer for each question and showing the answers to each question in a bar chart.

You could compare the content of male and female dreams, or dreams of teenagers and older people.

Writing good questions

There are three issues to consider when writing questions:

1 Clarity

Questions must be written clearly so that the respondent can understand what is being asked. If a respondent doesn't understand the question he or she will give a meaningless answer, which reduces the **validity** of the data collected.

There should be no ambiguity.

What does ambiguity mean? Something that is ambiguous has at least two possible meanings. For example, 'Did you see the girl with the telescope?' could mean 'Did you see the girl when you were using the telescope' or it could mean 'Did you see the girl who was using a telescope'.

2 Bias

The way a question is phrased may lead respondents to give particular answers. For example, some questions contain a hint about the desired answer – 'Was that film interesting?' is likely to produce a different answer to 'Was that film boring?' These are called **leading questions** – in the core study by Loftus and Palmer (**eyewitness testimony**) the leading question is asking 'How fast were the cars travelling when they smashed into each other?' The word 'smashed' suggests the drivers were travelling fast. If the word 'contacted' is used instead, it suggests the drivers were travelling at a slower speed.

An even greater problem is **social desirability bias** – people often prefer to answer questions in a way that makes them look better. For example, if you are asked 'Are you generally honest?', you might say 'yes' rather than 'no' because 'no' makes you look like a liar.

Sometimes questionnaires include a *lie scale* to test how honest people are being – the questionnaire includes questions such as 'Do you always think of other people's feelings?' If a person agrees with such questions then it suggests that they are trying to show themselves in a good light rather than being honest.

Ethical issues

It is expected that any self-report study will obtain **informed consent** from all participants unless **deception** is necessary.

• Where deception is necessary all respondents should be **debriefed** and offered the **right to withdraw** their data.

Qs 1.9

1   Explain what is meant by an 'open question' and a 'closed question'.

2   Explain what is meant by a rating scale.

3   A group of students decide to conduct research on the relationships adolescents have with family and friends.

   a   One of the questions on the questionnaire is 'Who do you love most?' Give **one** strength and **one** weakness of this question as a means of finding out about relationships.

   b   Explain why the question in (a) is an open-ended question.

   c   Write **one** closed question that the students could include in their questionnaire.

   d   Outline **one** strength and **one** weakness of using this closed question.

   e   The students' teacher suggests they could use a rating scale to gather information about the adolescents' different relationships. Suggest a suitable question.

   f   Outline **one** strength of using a question involving a rating scale in this study.

   g   Suggest **one** ethical issue that might arise when conducting this study and explain why it would be a problem.

   h   Explain how the students might deal with the ethical issue.

   i   Describe an alternative method of collecting data about adolescents' relationships rather than using a questionnaire.

   j   Explain what effect this change might have on the results.

3 Kind of question: open or closed

Examples of open and closed questions are shown on the right.

- **Open questions** invite respondents to provide their own answers.
- **Closed questions** have limited choices.

Open questions tend to produce **qualitative data**, i.e. data which can't be immediately counted.

Closed questions provide **quantitative data**, i.e. answers that can be counted. For example, in question 3 on the right you can count how many people ticked each of the answers provided.

Question 4 is an example of a question using a **rating scale** where respondents are asked to give a rating for their answers.

	Strengths	Weaknesses
Open question	Provides rich details of how people behave because they are given a free range to express themselves. They can express what they actually think rather than being restricted by preconceived categories.	More difficult to detect patterns and draw conclusions because respondents' answers are likely to be different. Therefore a researcher may look for trends rather than using **descriptive statistics**.
Closed question	Easier to analyse because data are in numbers which can be summarised using averages as well as simple graphs. This generally makes it easier to draw conclusions	May not permit people to express their precise feelings and tend not to uncover new insights. Oversimplifies reality and human experience because it suggests that there are simple answers.
Rating scale	A reasonably objective way to represent feelings and attitudes about something, producing quantitative data.	Respondents may avoid ends of scales and go for 'middle of the road', thus answers do not represent true feelings.

Examples of open questions

1   What factors contribute to making work stressful?

2   How does it feel when you are in love?

Examples of closed questions

3   Do you find work stressful? Yes/no/not sure

4   Which of the following factors at work makes you feel stressed? (You may tick as many answers as you like)

   ❒ Noise at work   ❒ Lack of control

   ❒ Too much to do   ❒ Bored

   ❒ Workmates   ❒ No job satisfaction

5   How many hours a week do you work?

   ❒ 0 hours

   ❒ Less than 10 hours

   ❒ Over 10 hours but less than 20 hours

   ❒ More than 20 hours

6   How much stress do you feel? (Circle the number that best describes how you feel.)

At work

   A lot of stress   5 4 3 2 1   No stress at all

At home

   A lot of stress   5 4 3 2 1   No stress at all

Travelling to work

   A lot of stress   5 4 3 2 1   No stress at all

Questions should not cause **psychological harm** (e.g. cause unnecessary embarrassment or loss of **self-esteem**), they should avoid where possible invasion of **privacy** (e.g. asking personal questions) and must respect **anonymity** and **confidentiality**.

- Participants' names should not be recorded and their answers can only be stored if they have given their permission.

What you have learned on this spread

- Self-report methods of investigating human behaviour.
- Writing questions for a questionnaire or interview.
- Leading questions and social desirability bias.
- Open and closed questions, rating scales and their strengths and weaknesses.

Sampling

Before continuing with the story of **self-report** methods we pause for a moment to consider **sampling**. In order to conduct any study (such as a **questionnaire** or **interview** or **observation**) the researcher has to decide who they will talk to or watch and listen to. This is called the 'sample' – a small group of people.

One way to do this is simply to use those who happen to be around, but there are other methods too.

Participants are drawn from a **target population** (the group of people that the researcher is interested in).

Target population

This is a sample of the target population

Try this   1.11

Testing different sampling techniques
Measure the height of 30 people in your school or college (alternatively make up 30 heights if you can't find a tape measure). Work out the average height by adding them together and dividing by 20. You now know the mean height of your target population.

This activity gives you a chance to try out the different sampling methods.

1 *Random sample:* Put all 20 names in a hat. Pick out 10 of the names and work out their mean (add them up and divide by 10). How close is it to the actual **mean**? A good sample should represent the target population. Repeat this two or three times.

2 *Opportunity sample:* Look at the heights of the first 10 people to be measured. Is this method more or less representative?

3 *Self-selected sample:* Ask your original 30 participants if they would volunteer for another study. Take the first 10 volunteers and calculate their mean height from the data you already have.

Look at the mean scores for each sample and compare them to the true mean (the one you originally calculated).

Think about how you might display your results. Which was the best way to select a sample?

Selecting a sample

When studying any behaviour, researchers can't test everyone in the world or even everyone in their own town. Therefore, when conducting research, psychologists select a **sample** from a **target population** (the group of people they are interested in – such as adolescents in the UK).

Once the research is conducted the researcher hopes to be able to *generalise* from the study to the target population. In other words, if the study looks at the dreams experienced by a sample of UK adolescents, then the results will be used to make statements about all UK adolescents.

Generalisability
This principle of GENERALISABILITY is very important for research. Researchers want to be able to draw conclusions about PEOPLE from the research they conduct with a small sample.

The problem is that it is only acceptable to make generalisations about 'people' (i.e. the target population) based on what the sample says or does if the sample is REPRESENTATIVE of the target population. The aim of all sampling methods is to produce a **representative sample**.

Some sampling techniques

Opportunity sample
Selecting people who are most easily available at the time of the study.

How? Select those most easily available, for example, ask people walking by you in the street or people sitting in school library, i.e. the first people you come across.

Self-selected sample (volunteer sample)
Produced by asking for volunteers. The participants select themselves.

How? For example, advertise in a newspaper or on a noticeboard.

Random sample
Every member of the target population has an equal chance of being selected.

How? Using a **random** technique, such as placing all names in a hat and drawing out the required number of names. You can also number each participant and use random number tables.

> Many students mistake a **systematic sample** for a random sample. Don't make that mistake! In a systematic sample you select every nth person from a list.

You may be wondering about time sampling **and** event sampling ...

Earlier in this chapter we explained how **observational studies** *can be* **structured** *so that observations are made in an organised way. For example, a researcher might observe the behaviour of people at a football match using event sampling. The researcher would watch a group of people and note down every time any of the people performed a specific action such as shouting.*

In this case the term 'sampling' refers to how the observations are sampled. The researcher in this football study would also need to select who to study. The target individuals observed would form the sample and another sampling technique would be used to select these target individuals. For example, the researcher might use opportunity sampling.

So you have both event sampling and opportunity sampling. Two forms of sampling in one study. Confusing, we know.

You're very special

Your mother has probably told you at some time or other that you are very special. And it's true, you are. In fact you are unique. There is no one quite like you (even if you are an identical twin).

However, when psychologists investigate human behaviour they end up making generalisations about people because they want to know about general trends. We have to be careful about making generalisations because, although we share common features with other people, we are all unique and quite unlike anyone else.

	Strengths	Weaknesses
Opportunity sample	Easiest method because you just use the first participants you can find, which means it is quicker than other methods.	Inevitably biased because the sample is drawn from a part of the target population rather than being drawn from the whole target population. For example, asking people in the street on a Monday morning which is likely to exclude professional people (because they are at work) or people from rural areas. You might think the target population is all UK adults but you have only selected people from a small part of this target population.
Self-selected sample	Access to a variety of participants (e.g. all the people who read a newspaper). This may make the sample more representative. A convenient way to find willing participants. If the research task is quite time-consuming then opportunity sampling may not work very well. You need participants who are committed.	The sample is biased because participants are likely to be more highly motivated and/or with extra time on their hands. Therefore they might be more helpful than most people or might be more inquisitive. This results in a **volunteer bias**.
Random sample	Potentially unbiased because all members of the target population have an equal chance of selection. Although you may end up with a biased sample because not all of the participants who are identified will agree to participate.	This form of sampling takes more time and effort than other methods because you need to obtain a list of all the members of your target population, then identify the sample and then contact the people identified and ask if they will take part. This process is even more difficult with a very large target population.

How many participants should be in a sample?

The number of participants or respondents in any study varies enormously. When using questionnaires it is relatively easy to distribute them to hundreds if not thousands of people (your sample).

*When conducting an **experiment** numbers are usually much smaller, as few as 25 is acceptable (Coolican, 1996). Small samples can still be representative and may have advantages over using samples that are too big. For example, large samples can obscure important individual differences – consider a study looking at the effect of noise on memory, it might be that noise has no effect on most people's memory but does affect people with sensitive hearing; if you have a very large sample it may include enough people with sensitive hearing to affect the results so that it appears that all people's memory is affected by noise.*

1 Explain **one** strength and **one** weakness of using an opportunity sample rather than a self-selected sample.

2 A group of students decide to find out what people think and feel about soap operas on TV.
   a Write **one** closed question they might use in this study.
   b Would your question produce quantitative or qualitative data? Explain your answer.
   c Suggest a suitable sampling technique for this study.
   d Describe how you would use this method to obtain your sample.
   e Outline **one** strength and **one** weakness of using this method to obtain a sample in this study.
   f Suggest which sampling technique might be used to overcome the weakness identified in (c) and explain why.

3 The college principal asks a group of psychology students to produce information about A Level courses in the college. The principal wants to know which A Levels are most interesting and rewarding, and which are most difficult.
   a Write **one** question for this interview using a rating scale.
   b Give **one** strength and **one** weakness of using a rating scale in this study.
   c Suggest a suitable sampling technique for this study and explain how you would use this in this study.
   d Outline **one** strength and **one** weakness of using this method to obtain a sample in this study.
   e Describe how you would use an alternative sampling technique and explain why this might be better.

4 An observational study is conducted to look at the different things men and women buy in a supermarket. Researchers examine the contents of their shopping trolleys at the checkout.
   a Identify a suitable technique for sampling behaviours in this study.
   b Identify a suitable technique for selecting participants in this study.

What you have learned on this spread

- Sampling and sampling techniques.
- The strengths and weaknesses of opportunity, self-selected and random sampling techniques.

More on self-report

So far you have learned about how to write good questions for a **self-report** study. Such questions are combined into a **questionnaire** or **interview** to use in finding out what people think and feel. On this spread we look at the design of self-report techniques, looking at questionnaires in particular (interviews are similar though some of the questions may not be decided in advance).

From the point of view of the exam it is important to grasp the essentials of self-report design because you may be asked to describe an appropriate procedure for a self-report study.

Try this   1.12

What are you afraid of?
Find out what things people are most frightened of – is it snakes, or spiders, or roller coasters? (The core study on **Little Hans** is about **phobias**.)

Design
Prepare a questionnaire to ask people what they are most scared of. You might use a combination of **closed questions**, **open questions** and **rating scales**.

One study investigated people's fears by giving participants a list of 29 animals and asking participants to rate each animal on a 3-point rating scale for ugliness and sliminess as well as fearfulness (Bennett-Levy and Marteau, 1984). For example:

1 = not afraid, 2 = quite afraid, 3 = very afraid
1 = not ugly, 2 = quite ugly, 3 = very ugly

Conduct a pilot study
Test your questionnaire out with a small group of people and make adjustments to the design. It might work better (in terms of later analysis) to use a 7-point scale.

Drawing conclusions
You could present the results for different questions in a table or **bar chart**, showing the **modal groups**.

For each animal you could provide a **mean** score for fearfulness, ugliness and sliminess.

It may be possible to produce a **scattergraph** of your results (see page 32), correlating fearfulness and sliminess (however this may only work if you have used a 7-point scale).

Designing a self-report study

When designing a questionnaire there are further issues beyond writing good questions (covered on pages 16–17).

Decide on the aims of the investigation
The aims shouldn't be too broad, such as 'to study dreams' or 'to study smoking'. It is better to narrow down to a more specific focus, such as investigating the content of dreams or attitudes about the risks of smoking.

Design the questionnaire
You need a range of questions related to the topic you intend to investigate. These should obviously be 'good' questions as described earlier, and may include a mixture of both **open** and **closed questions**.

Then you need to decide on a sequence for the questions. It is best to start with easy ones, saving difficult questions or questions that might make someone feel anxious until the respondent has relaxed.

It is also a good idea to include some 'filler questions'. These are irrelevant questions to mislead the respondent from the main purpose of the survey. If participants guess the aims of the questionnaire this may affect the answers they provide. For example, if they realise that the questionnaire is about the risks of smoking they may provide 'politically correct' answers rather than telling you what they really think about the risks of smoking. This tendency for participants to seek and respond to cues about a study's aims is called **demand characteristics**.

Examples of self-reports

HEALTH WARNING: *It is easy and fun to devise your own **psychological tests** (which are essentially questionnaires) and try them out on yourself and others.*

You can also use an established test from one of the sites below, but don't take any of them too seriously. They won't tell you anything about yourself that you don't already know. If you reflect on your own personality you'll be able to say much more about it than any test can hope to do. Also remember, if you do a test on someone else, you should be sensitive about how they may feel about the results.

You can find lots of questionnaires and psychological tests to try out on the internet:

http://www.queendom.com claims to be the world's largest testing centre, tests and questionnaires on everything.

http://www.yorku.ca/rokada/psyctest provides access to copyrighted psychological tests that can be downloaded and used by student researchers including dieting beliefs scale and self-esteem scales.

*http://ipip.ori.org/ipip/index.htm The International Personality Item Pool allows you to put together your own test using the subscales from many established **psychometric tests**.*

*A **pilot study** is a small-scale trial run of a research design conducted before doing the real thing. It is carried out in order to see if certain things don't work. For example, participants may not understand the instructions or may find that some questions are ambiguous. They may get very bored answering the questions because there are too many and the end result is they don't answer honestly. So perhaps fewer questions might be better.*

A pilot study is conducted with a small group of participants from the intended target population. The pilot study sample should represent the participants to be tested in the real study. For example, if the real study intends to use adults and children then both should be represented in the pilot study.

The researcher uses feedback from the pilot study to improve the research design. Then the 'real' study can be conducted.

Conduct a pilot study

It is a good idea to conduct a pilot study to test out the clarity of the questions and any other difficulties that might be encountered for respondents when answering the questionnaire. The questionnaire can then be amended accordingly.

Decide on sampling technique and sample size

One of the methods on the previous spread can be used, or a common method used in self-report studies is **quota sampling**. Subgroups within a population are identified (e.g. boys and girls or age groups: 10–12, 13–14, etc.). Then a quota is taken from each subgroup. For example, you give your questionnaire to 10 boys and 10 girls, or to 10 people aged 10–12, 10 people aged 13–14 and so on. The sample within each subgroup is selected using an **opportunity sample**. This method is more **representative** than other methods because there is equal representation of the subgroups that a researcher is interested in.

In a **stratified sample** the sample from each subgroup is obtained using a **random** method.

Exam focus ... on BIG MARK QUESTIONS

On page 7 we discussed exam questions that say 'Describe and evaluate an appropriate procedure for such a study'. These questions may make a big difference to the grade you receive.

*To describe an appropriate procedure for a self-report study you must provide enough detail for **replication**, i.e. enough details for someone else to be able to repeat the procedure. This means you must provide details of:*

- ***What?** The research aims.*
- ***Who?** The people you would use in your **sample** (i.e. the **target population**).*
- ***Where?** The physical environment where respondents answer the questions.*
- ***Materials?** A selection of the questions you would use. This can include information about the structure of the questionnaire.*
- ***How?** The **sampling technique** you would use.*

Remember – marks are not awarded for writing more, nor are they awarded for complex designs. Keep the design simple and make sure you include specific details so that replication would be possible.

Qs 1.11

1   A health psychologist plans to investigate children's attitudes about dieting and what they eat. He plans to use a self-report method to question children aged between 8 and 12.

  a   Suggest a suitable sampling technique for this study.

  b   Describe how you would use this method to obtain your sample.

  c   Outline **one** strength and **one** weakness of using this method to obtain a sample in this study.

  d   Suggest which sampling technique might be used to overcome the weakness identified in (c), and explain why.

  e   Suggest **two** examples of qualitative data that could have been collected in this study.

  f   Describe **one** ethical issue that the researchers need to consider when conducting this observation and suggest how this could be dealt with.

2   A class of psychology students decide to investigate people's belief in horoscopes. They intend to use a self-report method.

  a   Describe an appropriate procedure for such a study.

  b   Describe **two** ways of ensuring that this study would be carried out in an ethically acceptable manner.

3   We described a study about relationships on page 17 – a group of students decide to conduct research on the relationships adolescents have with family and friends. In their questionnaire the students asked their respondents to identify the person they felt closest to: 34% said their boyfriend/girlfriend, 28% said their best friend, 15% said their mother, 2% named their father, and 11% said their brother/sister.

  a   Is this an open or closed question?

  b   Place this information in a summary table.

  c   Sketch a bar chart to display the results.

  d   What conclusion(s) can you draw from your bar chart?

  e   Describe an alternative method of collecting data about adolescents' relationships rather than using a questionnaire.

What you have learned on this spread

- Designing questionnaires.
- How to describe the procedures of a self-report study (what, who, where, materials and how).

Evaluating self-report

We have already considered some of the problems related to **self-report** methods, such as leading questions and social desirability bias (on page 16) and demand characteristics (on page 20). Such problems threaten the validity of a self-report study. On this spread we will consider these issues in the context of reliability and validity.

Reliability and validity

Students find it difficult to distinguish these two concepts. But it is important because exam questions often ask about reliability AND validity and it is good to be able to write separately about each.

Reliability = consistency

Validity = whether you measured what you intended to measure, and also whether you actually found out what the person really thinks/feels.

Reliability

The concept of **reliability** was introduced on page 8. If the same **questionnaire** or **interview** is repeated with the same person it should produce the same outcome. This is called **test–retest**.

Evaluating the reliability of self-report

The consistency of a person's answers may be affected by a number of things. For example:

- The time of day – a person may be less willing to answer fully if questioned later in the day when they are tired.
- Presence of other people – a person may be less willing to answer truthfully if surrounded by other people who may hear their answers.
- Ambiguous questions – participants interpret these differently each time they are asked.

The test–retest method

The interval between test and retest must be long enough so that the participant can't remember their previous answers but not too long because then their thoughts or feelings may have changed and we would expect their score to be different, and then we're not checking reliability any more.

Dealing with low reliability

Problems with ambiguous questions can be discovered by looking at respondents' answers and rewriting those that produce the most inconsistent answers.

Reliability can be improved in the case of interviews, by training interviewers so they ask questions more consistently and avoid giving extra information that may affect respondents' answers.

Validity

The concept of **validity** was also introduced on page 9. The validity of a questionnaire or interview concerns whether it really measures what the researcher intended to measure.

Validity also concerns whether a respondent tells you their true thoughts. If a respondent does not provide an honest answer, then the researcher is not measuring what they intended to measure. For example, if you ask respondents 'How many pieces of fruit do you eat a day?' they may inflate their answer because they want to appear healthy! So they say 'five pieces' because they know they ought to be eating lots of fruit. The end result is the answers collected are meaningless.

Evaluating the validity of self-report

The truthfulness of a person's answers may be affected by:

- **Social desirability bias** – participants give answers that make them appear to be a 'good' person.
- **Leading questions** – participants give the answer desired by the researcher because of the form of the question (the form of the question 'suggests' what answer is desired).
- **Demand characteristics** – participants respond to other cues from the researcher, trying to help the researcher fulfil the research aims. For example, if the participant thinks the point of the questionnaire is to show that adolescents do have a healthy lifestyle then the participant will shape his/her answers in that way.

Concurrent validity

Another way to assess validity is called **concurrent validity**. This is established by comparing the current questionnaire/interview with a previously established one on the same topic. Participants take both tests and then their scores on both are compared using **correlation**.

Dealing with low validity

If validity is poor then the self-report measure should be revised by changing some of the questions. Researchers can identify which questions are suspect by removing some questions to see if this improves the correlation with an existing measure. Then they can assume that these questions are not relevant.

But what can you do if respondents are not giving honest answers? The researcher might change the **standardised instructions** so the importance of the questionnaire/interview is emphasised.

Qs 1.12

1 A researcher wishes to investigate internet use in 16–18 years olds.
   a Why might it be preferable to use a questionnaire rather than an interview for this study?
   b Why might it be better to use an interview instead of a questionnaire for this study?
   c The researcher decides to use a questionnaire. How could the reliability of this questionnaire be evaluated?
   d How could the validity of this questionnaire be evaluated?
   e The researcher writes one question using a rating scale. Suggest a possible question using a rating scale.
   f Evaluate the reliability and validity of using a rating scale in this study. (Make sure you separate your answer into reliability and validity.)

2 Explain why low reliability is a problem in a study using self-report.
3 Explain why validity is a problem in a study using self-report.
4 In the following studies describe and evaluate an appropriate procedure that could be used.
   a Researchers seek to find out about people's attitudes about politics using self-report.
   b A psychological study intends to look at the experience of going to university. First year students are asked to complete a self-report measure.

Exam advice

*Don't forget that exam questions are likely to ask you to describe strengths and weaknesses in relation to the source material, i.e. 'Describe **one** strength and **one** weakness of using self-report techniques in this study'.*

This means that you have to make sure you select an appropriate strength and weakness for the study described in the question and make sure you relate your answer to the particular study.

YOU NEED TO BE READY TO THINK ON YOUR FEET.

Strengths		Weaknesses
Self-report methods	Permits a researcher to find out what people think and feel. In an **observational study** we observe behaviour and may then infer what is going on inside someone's head. With self-report we ask them directly.	Answers may not be truthful, for example because of leading questions and social desirability bias.
Questionnaire	Can be easily repeated so that data can be collected from large numbers of people relatively cheaply and quickly (once the questionnaire has been designed). Respondents may feel more willing to reveal personal/confidential information in a questionnaire than in an interview. If **closed questions** are used, the findings can be easily analysed and displayed in bar charts.	The **sample** may be biased because only certain kinds of people fill in questionnaires – literate individuals who are willing to spend time filling them in.
Structured interview	Can be easily repeated. Easier to analyse than unstructured interviews because answers are more predictable.	The interviewer's expectations may influence the answers the interviewee gives (this is called **interviewer bias**).
Semi-structured or unstructured interview	Generally more detailed information can be obtained from each respondent than in a structured interview because the questions are specially shaped to the participant. Can access information that may not be revealed by predetermined questions.	More affected by interviewer bias than structured interviews because the interviewer is developing questions on the spot – they may inadvertently ask leading questions. Requires well-trained interviewers, which makes it more expensive to produce reliable interviews.

Try this   1.13

How extravert are you?

Answer yes or no to the questions below

1 Do you prefer to make instant decisions rather than reflecting for a while on what to do?
2 Would you prefer to take up a course in sketching rather than karate?
3 At parties do you prefer to listen to people rather than do the talking yourself?
4 Do you work best in a quiet atmosphere?
5 Have you got a wide circle of friends?
6 Have you done something stupid just for a dare?
7 Is it quite hard to know you?
8 Do you avoid spending too much time on your own?

9 Do you make new friends easily?
10 Are you the life and soul of a party?
11 Do you feel it is important to say what you think rather than keeping some opinions to yourself?
12 Do you prefer staying in rather than going out?
13 Do you ever dream of flying?
14 Do you prefer to work independently?
15 Are you too shy to tell people what you really think of them?
16 Do you discuss your decisions with other people?

Score 2 if you answered yes to questions 1, 5, 6, 8, 9, 10, 11, 13, 16
Score 2 if you answered no to questions 2, 3, 4, 7, 12, 14, 15

A score above 20 Little Miss (or Mr) Extravert – you are one outgoing cool cookie, living life to the hilt and having fun. You are full of energy and everyone loves being around you – just make sure you don't burn yourself out, or turn out to be just too much for your friends.

Scores between 10 and 20 Little Miss (or Mr) Balance – you love people but you also don't mind your own company. You love a bit of daring and adventure but you're also happy curled up at home with a good book. Good on ya!

A score below 10 Little Miss (or Mr) Shy – you're an introvert, independent and cautious. Excitement is too much for you to cope with, scary rollercoaster rides freak you out. It pays to be careful but perhaps once in a while you should venture outside your shell. Remember all work and no play makes for a dull dude.

- Evaluate the reliability of this questionnaire. What factors might affect the consistency of a person's responses?
- Evaluate the validity of this questionnaire. What factors might affect the truthfulness of a person's responses?
- Check concurrent validity by comparing the results with another measure of extraversion (search the internet).

...Link to the core studies...

Many of the core studies use self report as at least one of their measures. The study of **Thigpen and Cleckley**, for example, uses a range of psychological tests (which are a form of questionnaire) as well as the clinical interviews. These tests included personality tests, IQ tests and projective tests (see page 199). The prison study by **Reicher and Haslam** uses a number of tests to assess the thoughts and feelings of the participants. It is the sheer amount of data in this study that adds weight to their conclusions. The case studies of **Freud** and **Sperry** also use self reports as an essential part of their data. You might also argue that the chimp studies (**Savage-Rumbaugh et al.**) also use self-report but that is, of course, open to debate.

What you have learned on this spread

- Reliability and validity of self-report.
- How to evaluate the reliability and validity of a self-report study.
- Strengths and weaknesses of self-report methods.
- How to evaluate the procedures of a self-report study.

Research method 3: experiments

When psychologists want to investigate causal relationships they use the **experimental** method. For example, if we want to know whether listening to music helps students study, we would have some students listen to music and some not (these are the two conditions or 'levels') and then give them a memory test (to assess quality of studying) to see who does better. It is logical and simple.

In this case we would be seeking to demonstrate that music is the cause of better (or worse) memory performance.

- The experimenter manipulates one variable – in this case music or not, which is called the **independent variable** (IV).
- The experimenter measures the effect on behaviour – in this case memory performance, which is called the **dependent variable** (DV).

There are two basic **experimental designs**:

- **Repeated measures**: you test each individual in both conditions comparing their performance in both parts of the experiment.
- **Independent measures**: you test one group of people in the first condition and a different group of people in the second condition, and then compare the two sets of scores.

Many people use the word 'experiment' quite loosely, *as if an experiment was just another word for an investigation. It isn't. In an experiment, the experimenter:*

- *Alters the levels of one variable (the IV).*
- *Observes the effects of the IV on the DV.*

Only by doing this can we discover a causal relationship because the experimenter can claim that any change in the DV must be due to the changes made to the IV – except if there are **extraneous variables** *(to be explained on page 28).*

RESEARCH METHOD 3: EXPERIMENTS

Try this   1.14

Here are some ideas of possible topics to study:

- Music and studying (Do people work as effectively if they work while music is playing? Do people who listen to quiet music study better than those listening to loud rock music?)
- Weather and mood (Are people in a better mood on a sunny day?)
- Audience effects (Do people get a better score at a computer game if they are being cheered on (or jeered) by an audience rather than when they play the game by themselves?)

STEP 1 Work with a small group of other students and discuss how you might investigate one of the topics using the experimental method.

1 What will you need to measure?
2 Will you have two different conditions? What will you change across the two conditions?
3 Will everyone do both conditions? Or will you have two groups of participants, one doing each condition?
4 What will you expect to find out?
5 What will the participants do?
6 What do you need to control?
7 How many participants will you need and how will you get them?

STEP 2 When you have worked out what you will do, join with another group and explain your ideas to each other. The other group may ask useful questions which will help you refine your ideas.

STEP 3 Conduct your study. You may be able to do this in class or each member of your group could go away and collect some data.

STEP 4 Pool the data collected by your group and prepare a poster to present your results and conclusions.

How to design an experiment

The activity on the left essentially takes you through the key steps in designing an **experiment**. The technical terms for each step are:

1 Identify and *operationalise* the DV (see below).
2 Identify and *operationalise* the IV.
3 Select the **experimental design** (repeated measures or independent groups).
4 Write the *hypothesis*.
5 Decide on the *procedures*.
6 Decide on *controls* (discussed on next spread).
7 Choose the **sampling technique** (see page 18).

Operationalisation

The term **operationalise** means to specify a set of operations or behaviours that can be measured. For example, in the introduction box for this spread we suggested an experiment to see whether music helps students study. The IV is music and the DV is studying.

We operationalised 'studying' by saying we would give the students something to learn and test their memory of it. In other words, we have specified how we will measure their ability to have studied well.

- How else could you operationalise or measure the ability of participants to have studied well? What task could you give them to do and how might you assess their performance?
- The IV is music. How could you operationalise this? You need to specify what music you would use and for how long.

Behavioural categories are a form of operationalisation.

Ethical issues

Some experiments involve **deception** because, if you tell participants the true aims of the experiment beforehand, this may affect how they behave in the experiment. This means that experimenters have to give false information (such as in the core study by **Loftus and Palmer**).

- Experimenters can still obtain a form of **informed consent** because they can tell the participants as far as possible what they will be doing in order to help participants decide whether they are willing to take part.

Experimenters must avoid **psychological harm** – which includes embarrassment and loss of **self-esteem**, and also changing a person.

- The BPS code of ethics states that participants should experience no risks greater than encountered in their everyday lives.

In an **observational study** *you might observe what people do when sitting in their car at traffic lights. In order to do this you create a set of behavioural categories. In a sense you are operationalising the behaviour – because you are breaking 'sitting in a car' down into measurable units.*

You actually conduct experiments without thinking. For example, when you start a class with a new teacher you might make a joke or hand in your homework on time (both IVs) to see if the teacher responds well (the DV). You are experimenting with cause and effect.

Many people also have the wrong image of an experiment. On the right is a chemistry experiment. Psychology experiments aren't like this. For a start people rather than test tubes are involved. Experiments may be conducted in a **laboratory** setting – but can be conducted outside a laboratory too.

Hypotheses

At the outset of an experiment an experimenter will state what they expect to discover. This is done in the form of a statement of what the experimenter believes to be true. In the case of our experiment:

People who listen to music while studying perform less well on a memory test than people who work in silence.

There are several things to notice about this **hypothesis**:

- The IV is stated, including both levels of it (music and no music).
- The DV is also stated (performance on a memory test).

This hypothesis identifies the expected direction of the results, i.e. we expect people who listen to music to perform *less* well. This is called a **one-tailed hypothesis**. The other possibility would be a **two-tailed hypothesis**, where the direction is not predicted:

People who listen to music while studying perform <u>differently</u> on a memory test than people who work in silence.

The alternate hypothesis and the null hypothesis

The hypothesis described above (which states what the experimenter believes to be true) is called the **alternate hypothesis** (H_1) because it is an *alternative* to the **null hypothesis** (H_0). The null hypothesis is a statement of no difference or no relationship:

There is <u>no difference</u> between the memory test scores of people who listen to music or don't listen to music when studying.

Note that the null hypothesis is not the opposite of the alternate hypothesis – it is null, i.e. a statement of nothingness! This seems very odd but is used for statistical reasons that needn't worry you!

When you look at a one-tailed cat you know which way it is going. A two-tailed cat could be going either way.

Qs 1.13

1 The aims of a research study are different to the hypothesis for the research study. Aims begin 'To see whether …' A hypothesis must identify the IV and the levels of the IV, and identify the DV. Rewrite the following statements so they would count as hypotheses (in some cases you will need to add a second level of the IV):

   a To see if blondes have more fun than brunettes.

   b Arts students are less clever.

   c Whether alcohol causes goldfish to have poor memories.

   d Positive expectations lead to differences in performance.

2 A good hypothesis should also state the operationalised variables. In the statement 'Blondes have more fun than brunettes' the DV 'have more fun' is not operationalised.

   a Suggest how you could measure (operationalise) having more fun (you might use a rating scale or an observational technique). Explain your answer fully, using examples.

   b Outline **one** strength and **one** weakness of the way you have operationalised fun.

3 For each of the following, decide whether it is a one-tailed or two-tailed hypothesis.

   a Boys score differently on aggressiveness tests than girls.

   b Students who have a computer at home do better in exams than those who don't.

   c Participants remember the words that are early in a list better than the words that appear later.

   d Participants given a list of emotionally charged words recall fewer words than participants given a list of emotionally neutral words.

   e Hamsters are better pets than budgies.

   f Words presented in a written form are recalled differently to those presented in pictorial form.

4 The following questions relate to the studies proposed in 'Try this 1.13' on the facing page. Even if you haven't conducted one of these studies, answer the following questions for all three suggestions:

   a Identify and operationalise the IV and DV in the study.

   b State a one-tailed alternate hypothesis for the study.

   c State a null hypothesis for the study.

   d What experimental design would you use? Describe how you would use this design.

   e Describe how you could conduct this study using a different experimental design.

   f What sampling technique would you select? Explain the reason for your choice.

   g How could you have investigated the same topic using a different research technique (i.e. not an experiment)?

What you have learned on this spread

- Independent and dependent variables.
- Operationalisation of variables.
- Experimental designs: repeated measures and independent measures.
- One-tailed and two-tailed hypotheses.
- Alternate and null hypotheses.

More on experiments

On the previous page we looked at how to design an **experiment**, including decisions about **experimental design**. You may feel confused by 'designing an experiment' and 'experimental design', which are two different things. Some of the terms are confusing.

- 'Experimental design' refers very specifically to the decision about whether to use **repeated** or **independent measures**.
- 'Designing an experiment' refers to any decisions a researcher has to make when planning an experimental study. These decisions are outlined on the right.

On this spread we look at the strengths and weaknesses of experimental designs.

Exam focus

*To describe an appropriate procedure for an experiment you must provide enough detail for **replication**, i.e. enough information for someone else to be able to repeat the procedure. This means you must focus on specific details of:*

- **What?** *Operationalise the independent and dependent variable, and write a suitable **hypothesis**.*
- **Who?** *The people you would use in your **sample** (i.e. the **target population**).*
- **Where?** *The physical environment where participants are tested.*
- **Materials?** *What you will use in the experiment, such as a **questionnaire** to assess the DV.*
- **How?** *The **sampling technique** you would use.*

Qs 1.14

1 What is 'experimental design'?

2 Explain the difference between independent measures and repeated measures.

3 For each of the following experiments state whether it is repeated or independent measures. When trying to decide it might help you if you ask yourself 'Would the findings be analysed by comparing the scores from the same person or by comparing the scores of two (or more) groups of people?'

  a Boys and girls are compared on their IQ test scores.

  b Hamsters are tested to see if one genetic strain is better at finding food in a maze compared to another group.

  c Reaction time is tested before and after a reaction time training activity to see if test scores improve after training.

  d Participants are asked to give ratings for attractive and unattractive photographs.

4 Suggest at least **two** ways that you could operationalise the following variables:

  a Being drunk or not drunk.

  b A young child or an older child.

  c Being hungry or not hungry.

5 A researcher conducts a study to see whether people are happier if they are married or unmarried. The questions below overlap in terms of what you should put in the answers, i.e. you may find yourself saying the same thing twice. Write enough for 10 marks.

  a Describe and evaluate **one** way of measuring participants' happiness in this study.

  b Evaluate the reliability and validity of the way the dependent variable (DV) has been measured in this study.

  c Describe and evaluate an appropriate procedure that could be used in this study.

Repeated measures

All participants receive the same IV. For example: A study to test the effect of music on ability to study. Noise is the **Independent variable** (IV) and ability to study is tested using a memory test (the **dependent variable**, DV).

- *Condition A:* each participant does the memory test with music (the IV).
- *Condition B:* then each participant later does the test with no music (no IV).

To assess whether music does have an effect on studying, we consider the difference between each participant's score in condition A and condition B.

Weaknesses	Dealing with the weaknesses
In a repeated measures design one condition differs from the second condition because of the two different levels of the IV. However, the conditions may differ in other ways. In the case of the study above the researcher might use two different tests of memory – test 1 in condition A and test 2 in condition B. (You need to use two different tests because otherwise a participant may do better on the second test because they have done it once before.) It might be that participants do better in condition 2 because the test was easier rather than because the music was less loud. In this case changes in the DV (performance on the memory test) would be due to what is called an **extraneous variable** (e.g. an easier test) rather than the IV.	You can make sure the tests are equivalent by testing another group of participants beforehand and seeing whether they do equally well on both tests. Or half the participants in condition A do test 1 and half do test 2. And do the same for condition B. This counterbalances any differences in the tests because both conditions are affected equally.
When participants do the second memory test they might guess the purpose of the experiment, which could affect their behaviour. For example, some participants may purposely do worse on the second test because they want it to appear as if they work less well in the afternoon.	You can use a cover story about the purpose of the test to try to prevent participants guessing what the study is about (called **single blind** because one person – the participant – cannot 'see' the research aims).
When using repeated measures, if you do Condition A first it might affect your score in Condition B. With staggering originality (but also clarity) this is called an **order effect**. Participants may do better on the second condition because of a **practice effect** (even when the two tests are different) or because they are less anxious. Or participants may do worse on the second test because of being bored with doing the same test again (**boredom** or **fatigue effect**).	One way to control order effects is to use **counterbalancing** which ensures that each condition is tested first or second in equal amounts. For example: • Group 1: participants study with music, do a memory test, study with no music, do a second memory test. • Group 2: participants study with no music first, do a memory test, study with music, do a second memory test. Even though there are two groups this is still a repeated measures design because, at the end, we compare the two scores for each participant.

An example of an experiment using observational techniques

One of the core studies provides an example of how different methods and techniques are combined. In the 'Bobo doll study' (Bandura et al., 1961) children either watch an adult behaving aggressively or watch an adult who is not aggressive. This is the independent variable. Later they are observed playing with toys and a score is calculated for how aggressive they are. This is the dependent variable. But how is the dependent variable measured (operationalised)? A behaviour checklist was used (see page 5).

Independent measures

The participants are placed in two separate groups.

- *Group A* does the memory test with music (one level of the IV).
- *Group B* does the memory test with no music (the other level of the IV).

To assess whether music does have an effect on studying, we consider the difference between the scores of group A and group B.

Weaknesses	Dealing with the weaknesses
In an independent measures design there is no control of **participant variables** (i.e. the different abilities or characteristics of each participant). For example, participants in group A might happen to be better at concentrating than those in group B.	**Randomly allocate** participants to conditions which (theoretically) distributes participant variables evenly. This can be done by placing all participant names in a hat. The first name selected goes in group A, the second name goes in group B and so on. Alternatively use **systematic allocation** such as person number 1 is placed in group A, person number 2 in group B, etc. This should also distribute participant variables evenly.
You need twice as many participants to get the same number of results.	Be prepared to spend more time and money!

Where are the strengths for experimental designs?

You can work out the strengths of each design. This can be done by looking at the weaknesses of the other measure.

For example, one weakness of repeated measures is that participants may do better on the second test because they have had some practice after doing the first test. This is a strength of independent measures because participants just do one test.

In an exam? Can't remember what 'experimental design' means?

If you know this happens to you, then do something about it. Find a way to remember the link between experimental design and repeated and independent measures.

*Many students also draw a blank when they see a question with the phrase **descriptive statistics** in it. They lose marks because they can't answer the question. Don't let that happen to you.*

Try this   1.15

The effects of organisation on recall

Aim: to investigate the effects of organisation on the recall
Generate a master list of 50 words in categories. For example, select food as one category and then think of four food items in that category (gives you five words: category name plus four category words).

Method 1: repeated measures
Using your master list create two lists of 25 words each.

List A – 25 words organised in categories.

List B – 25 different words in random order.

Participants should have five minutes to study list A + list B (total = 50 words). Then they should have five minutes to recall as many words as possible.

Counterbalance the conditions so that half the participants get list A first and then list B, and the other participants get list B first and then list A.

Method 2: independent measures
Use the same master list and a different set of participants. This time:

Group A – given all 50 words organised in categories.

Group B – given the same 50 words in random order.

Randomly allocate participants to the two groups. Allow them five minutes to study the words and then test their recall.

Results for both methods
Display your results from methods 1 and 2 in a table.

Use descriptive statistics to summarise your results. Calculate the **mean** number of words remembered in the organised condition and the random condition, and display this in a **bar chart**.

What you have learned on this spread

- How to describe the procedures of an experiment (what, who, where, materials and how).
- Experimental designs (repeated measures and independent measures).
- Strengths and weaknesses of experimental designs.

More on experiments

The key feature of an **experiment** is that it can demonstrate a causal relationship – it can show that the **independent variable** (IV) *caused* a change in the **dependent variable** (DV) because the experimenter deliberately *controlled* the independent variable. Therefore any change in the dependent variable must be due to this cause.

There is another way that control is important in experiments – this is the control the experimenter has over other variables: **extraneous variables**. Uncontrolled extraneous variables will spoil an experiment as shown on the right because you cannot conclude that the IV caused a changed in the DV.

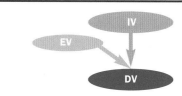

Changes in the dependent variable (DV) may be due to an extraneous variable (EV) rather than being due to the independent variable (IV). Therefore you cannot conclude that the IV affected the DV.

Extraneous variables

Extraneous variables may be classed as **participant variables** or **situational variables**.

Participant variables

Characteristics of individual participants may influence the outcome of a study.

Age, intelligence, motivation, experience
Any personal variables might act as an extraneous variable – but only if **independent measures** are used because then people in one group may be more intelligent, more highly motivated, etc. than the people in the other group. When **repeated measures** are used participant variables are controlled.

One example of a possible extraneous variable in the experiment on music and studying might be music experience – participants who never listened to music might be more affected by the music than participants who listened regularly.

Gender
Women and men differ on some behaviours. For example, research has shown that women are more compliant than men possibly because they are more oriented to interpersonal goals (Eagly, 1978). This means that if there are more women than men in one condition of an experiment this might mask the effects of the IV. However, it is important to realise that gender doesn't always matter so there is no need to control gender unless there is a reason to suspect a gender difference in the behaviour being studied.

Situational variables

Any feature of a research situation which influences a participant's behaviour acts as a situational extraneous variable.

Order effects
In an experiment using repeated measures design **order effects** (see previous spread) act as an extraneous variable – **practice**, **boredom** and **fatigue effects**.

Time of day, temperature, noise
Many environmental variables may act as extraneous variables but only under the following conditions:

- The variable does affect the behaviour tested, e.g. time of day is known to affect **cognitive** performance (people who are tested in the morning do better than those tested in the afternoon because people are more alert in the morning).
- The variable does vary systematically with the IV, e.g. participants in group 1 are all tested in the morning and those in group 2 are all tested in the afternoon. If all participants are tested in the morning it wouldn't matter.

Investigator or experimenter bias
Investigator bias is the term used to describe the effects of an investigator's expectations on a participant's behaviour. (The term **experimenter bias** applies just to experiments.)

Any cues (other than the IV) from an investigator that encourage certain behaviours in the participant leading to a fulfilment of the investigator's expectations will act as an extraneous variable.

For example, an experimenter might unconsciously be more encouraging to participants in group A than group B so this would explain why participants in group A do better on that task, rather than the IV being responsible. Or an experimenter might be more encouraging to some participants – one study found that male experimenters are more pleasant, friendly and encouraging to female participants than male participants (Rosenthal, 1966).

Demand characteristics
Demand characteristics are cues in an experimental situation that communicate to participants what is expected of them and may unconsciously affect a participant's behaviour. People always seek cues about how to behave, particularly in a new environment, and particularly if a person knows they are in an experiment. The result is that participants may not behave as they usually would.

Controlling participant variables
Participant variables can be controlled by using repeated measures design – each participant acts as his/her own control.

Alternatively, when using independent measures, experimenters can **randomly** or **systematically allocate** participants to groups and it is presumed that participant variables will be evenly distributed.

Controlling situational variables
Order effects can be controlled by using an independent measures design. Environmental factors such as time of day and temperature, etc. are controlled by keeping them constant – for example, always conducting a study in the morning or making sure that all participants do the study in the same kind of room conditions.

Controlling investigator effects and demand characteristics is less easy.

- **Single blind** Participants are not told the true aims of a study. This discourages them from seeking certain cues and altering their behaviour accordingly.
- **Standardised instructions** are a way of controlling investigator effects because they ensure that all participants have the same instructions and reduces the hints that can be given.

Qs 1.15

1 Orne's panic button study (see below) is an example of demand characteristics. Outline the demand characteristics in this study.

2 Explain the difference between investigator bias and experimenter bias.

3 Explain the difference between experimenter bias and demand characteristics.

4 Participants' memory was tested in the morning and in the afternoon, to see if there was any difference in their ability to recall numbers.

   a Give an example of **one** possible participant effect in this study.

   b Describe how you might deal with this participant effect.

   c Give an example of **one** possible investigator effect in this study.

   d Describe how you might deal with this investigator effect.

   e Give an example of **one** possible demand characteristic in this study.

   f Describe how you might deal with this problem.

5 An experiment is conducted to investigate whether only children do better at school than children who have one or more siblings.

   a Identify the IV and the DV in this experiment, and state how each could be operationalised.

   b Suggest a suitable two-tailed hypothesis for this study.

   c What kind of experimental design would be used in this study?

   d Suggest **two** extraneous variables that you would need to control.

   e Describe an appropriate procedure that could be used in this study. (Remember what, who, where, materials and how.)

6 Another psychological study looks at the effect of eating chocolate on moods.

   a Describe how you could investigate this by doing an experiment with a repeated measures design.

   b How might experimenter bias affect the results of this study?

   c Describe how demand characteristics might affect the results of this study.

   d Describe how you could study this topic using a method other than an experiment.

Try this   1.16

Are you only as good as your last CD?

There are two schools of thought as far as impression formation goes. One view is that people make up their minds about you as soon as they meet you and such impressions are quite enduring (a *primacy effect*). The other view is that what counts most is whatever you did more recently (people say 'he is only as good as his last CD' – a *recency effect*).

A classic study by Solomon Asch (1946) looked at the primacy and recency effects in an experiment. Some participants were given a list of adjectives that described a target person:

intelligent, industrious, impulsive, critical, stubborn, envious.

Other participants were given the same list but in reverse order. All participants were asked to fill in a rating sheet to evaluate the target person – for example, they were asked to rate how happy, sociable, etc. the person was. The first group gave higher ratings presumably because their list started with positive descriptions, thus supporting a primacy effect.

Other studies have found recency effects, for example Luchins (1957).

Design your own study to test the primacy and recency effects.

Smiling makes you happy

You might think that you smile because you are feeling happy but psychological research shows it works the other way round too. If you ask someone to tighten certain facial muscles (essentially making them smile) people say they feel happier and also rate cartoons as more funny, as shown in a study by Laird (1974), who told participants he was measuring facial muscular activity, attaching surface electrodes to participants' faces between their eyebrows, at the corners of their mouths and on their jaws. Then participants were asked to contract their muscles at these points. By using this procedure, Laird was able, without ever mentioning an emotion or an emotional expression, to induce participants to either smile or frown.

You can conduct a similar experiment by asking some participants to hold a pencil in their mouth while rating cartoons (holding a pencil between your teeth widthways simulates smiling). Compare ratings made by the smilers and nonsmilers.

Right brain left brain

If you perform two tasks that occupy your left **hemisphere** you should be slower than when doing two tasks that involve separate hemispheres.

Participants should tap their right finger while reading a page from a book (both involve left hemisphere) and repeat the same task without reading. Count the number of taps in 30 seconds. You should counterbalance conditions.

Demand characteristics

Martin T. Orne invented the term demand characteristics.

'The totality of cues that convey the experimental hypothesis to the [participant] become determinants of the [participant's] behaviour' (Orne, 1962).

In one of Orne's studies participants had to sit in a room on their own for four hours. One group of participants were asked at the beginning of the study to sign a form releasing the experimenter from responsibility if anything happened to them during the experiment. They were also given a panic button to push if they felt overly stressed. The other group were given no information to arouse their expectations. The first group showed extreme signs of distress during isolation and this can only be explained in terms of the demand characteristics created (Orne and Scheibe, 1964).

What you have learned on this spread

- Extraneous variables.
- Participant and situational variables.
- Experimenter and investigator bias.
- Demand characteristics.

Evaluating experiments

Extraneous variables reduce the validity of any experiment because the changes to the dependent variable (DV) were not caused by the independent variable (IV). This means that any causal conclusions are wrong. On this spread we will consider some further issues related to the validity of experimental research, as well as the issue of reliability. In addition we consider the different shapes and sizes that experiments come in.

Reliability

Experiments involve measurement of some kind. For example, in the experiment on music and studying, we decided to measure 'studying' by testing memory. In this case we would be concerned about the reliability of the memory test and the same considerations would apply as for any self-report measure. We could evaluate the reliability using the test–retest method (see page 22).

Alternatively, in the same experiment, we might have measured the dependent variable (studying) by observing participants' behaviour when studying to see if it differed when studying with or without music. The independent variable would remain the same but in this case the DV might be a count of how often each participant looked away from their books. Reliability would be concerned with the consistency of the observations and, as in the any observational study we could assess this using inter-rater reliability (see page 8).

Validity

The validity of measurements concerns whether an experimenter was testing what he/she intended to test. For example, you might decide to measure helping behaviour by dropping your scarf and seeing how long it took for people to pick it up in two different situations. Would this really test helping behaviour? If your answer is no, then the measurement lacks validity.

Participant's awareness
In some experiments (and other studies) participants do not realise they are being studied. In such situations participants will behave more naturally than they would when they know their behaviour is being recorded. For example, demand characteristics are only a problem if a person knows they are in an experiment.

Control
Another aspect of 'testing what an experimenter intended to test' concerns control. If an experimenter fails to control extraneous variables then changes in the DV may not be due to changes in the IV. This means that the findings would lack validity – the experimenter might claim a causal link was demonstrated between IV and DV but this would not be true.

Realism
The problem with high levels of control in an experiment, is that the situation begins to be very artificial. The experiment may lack realism which means that we can't generalise the findings to everyday life. This issue of generalisability is called ecological validity, the extent to which the findings of a study can be generalised to everyday life. Ecological validity is discussed further on pages 234–235. It is a complex topic but one that is important when understanding how meaningful psychological research is.

Replication
One of the strengths of the experimental method is that experiments can be repeated because the procedures are well controlled. This is a way of demonstrating validity. If an experiment is conducted again and produces the same result this suggests the original result was 'true' (i.e. did demonstrate a truth about human behaviour).

Qs 1.16

1 A psychologist conducted a field experiment to investigate the power of touch. The experimenter stood in a shopping centre and stopped passers-by to ask them if they would complete a questionnaire. There were two conditions in this experiment. In one condition the experimenter touched some participants lightly on the forearm as he made his request. In the other condition there was no touching. He recorded which participants were willing to stop and answer the questionnaire. The results are shown below.

- 10 participants who were touched on the arm said 'yes', whereas 5 said 'no'.
- 8 participants who were not touched on the arm said 'yes', whereas 12 said 'no'.

a Explain why this would be classed as a field experiment.

b Give one strength and one weakness of this experiment.

c Identify the IV and DV in this experiment and explain how they have been operationalised.

d Identify the experimental design that was used and give one strength and one weakness of this experimental design in this study.

e Explain how the psychologist might deal with the weakness you have identified in (d).

f Outline one ethical issue that the experimenter should consider and suggest how he might deal with it.

g Put the results in a table.

h Sketch an appropriately labelled bar chart to illustrate the results.

2 A group of psychology students decided they would like to assess the benefits of different revision techniques. They selected two methods that students commonly use to see which was more effective.

a How could this study be conducted as a repeated measures experiment?

b Give one strength and one weakness of using this experimental design in this study.

c Explain how you would measure the dependent variable.

d Describe one weakness with the method of measuring the DV described in (c).

e Evaluate the reliability and validity of the study you would conduct.

3 A news article claims that children who have music lessons do better at school. In order to test this a psychologist advertises for GCSE students who either take piano lessons outside school or who have never studied a musical instrument.

a Name and briefly describe the sampling technique used in this study.

b Evaluate the sampling technique that was used.

c Describe how you could investigate this by doing an experiment with an independent measures design.

d Evaluate the reliability and validity of carrying out the study in this way.

e Describe and evaluate one other way to measure the DV in this study.

EVALUATING EXPERIMENTS

Different kinds of experiment

	Strengths	Weaknesses
Laboratory experiment A **laboratory** is a special environment where causal relationships can be investigated under controlled conditions. Note that some **observational** studies are also conducted in laboratories.	Well controlled. Extraneous variables are minimised (increasing validity). Can be easily replicated because most aspects of the experimental environment have been controlled (enhances validity).	Artificial, a contrived situation where participants may not behave naturally (as they would in day-to-day life). Demand characteristics and experimenter bias may reduce validity.
Field experiment An experiment conducted in more everyday surroundings than a laboratory. Note that a **field study** is a study conducted in a natural environment where no IV has been manipulated.	Less artificial, and usually higher ecological validity. Avoids demand characteristics and **experimenter bias** when participants are not aware of being studied, and this may increase validity. (In some field experiments participants are aware of being studied.)	Less control of extraneous variables (reduces validity). More time consuming and thus more expensive.
Quasi-experiment The experimenter does not manipulate the IV but uses an IV that would vary even if the experimenter wasn't around. Strictly speaking an experiment involves the deliberate manipulation of an IV by an experimenter, therefore quasi-experiments are not 'true experiments' because no one has deliberately changed the IV in order to observe the effect on the DV.	Allows research where an IV can't be manipulated for ethical or practical reasons. Enables psychologists to study 'real' problems, such as the effects of a disaster on health (increases ecological validity).	Cannot demonstrate causal relationships because IV is not directly manipulated. Less control of extraneous variables (reduces validity). Can only be used where conditions vary naturally. Participants may be aware of being studied (reduces validity).

Try this   1.17

Date of birth*
Various studies have shown that in any year group the students who are older tend to do better at school. You can test this within your class. Divide the class into those born in the first six months of the school year (Sept, Oct, Nov, Dec, Jan, Feb) and those born in the last six months. For each group of students calculate a numerical score based on their GCSE results.

Is there a difference between the two groups?

Boys and girls*
Obviously boys are different from girls in many ways but there are some differences that are rather surprising. For example, boys tend to have higher digit ratio than girls. The reason is to do with hormones because the male hormone testosterone affects finger length.

Digit ratio is calculated by dividing the length of the index finger by the length of the ring finger. Calculate digit ration for all members of your class (measure both hands and work out the **mean**) for each participant.

Is there a difference between boys and girls?

*You might think these are quasi-experiments because the IV has not been deliberately changed. However, just to be picky, in a quasi-experiment the IV has to be changed by someone – and in these cases no one caused it to vary so they are just 'difference studies'.

...Links to core studies...
Experiments are still the most common method used by psychologists so it is no surprise that many of the core studies use this method. Interestingly the **Milgram** study is commonly referred to as an experiment but is really a demonstration of obedience because it doesn't manipulate any independent variable.

Laboratory experiments: **Loftus and Palmer** (eyewitness testimony), **Baron-Cohen et al.** (autism) and **Samuel and Bryant** (conservation), all use the experimental method. However, even though Baron-Cohen's study was conducted in a laboratory it is more a quasi-experiment because the independent variable was autism, which can't be manipulated directly. And although the Bobo study (**Bandura et al.**) is often described as an observation it tests some tightly controlled experimental hypotheses.

Field experiments: The study by **Piliavin et al.** (subway Samaritan) is an example of a field experiment.

Quasi-experiments: The study by **Sperry** (split brain) is an example of a quasi-experiment because you obviously can't allocate people randomly to the split-brain/whole-brain conditions. No really, you can't. The study by **Maguire et al.** compares the brains of taxi drivers with other drivers.

What you have learned on this spread
- Reliability and validity in experiments.
- How to evaluate the reliability and validity of an experiment.
- Ecological validity.
- Different kinds of experiment (laboratory, field and quasi) and their strengths and weaknesses.
- How to evaluate an experiment.

Research method 4: correlation

A **correlation** is a way of measuring the relationship between two variables – instead of looking at the difference (which is what we do in an **experiment**).

- Age and beauty co-vary. As people get older they become more beautiful. This is a **positive correlation** because the two variables increase together.
- You may disagree and think that as people get older they become less attractive. You think age and beauty are correlated but it is a **negative correlation**. As one variable increases the other one decreases.
- Or you may simply feel that there is no relationship between age and beauty (a **zero correlation**).

*You can collect both **quantitative** and **qualitative data** using **observation** or **self-report** techniques. In an experiment or correlation the data is strictly quantitative – though you can also collect qualitative data and convert this to a numerical score.*

Try this

1.18

Assertiveness and watching TV

Aim
To see whether watching TV is related to assertiveness (because many programmes encourage such behaviour).

Method
You need to obtain two pieces of data from everyone in your class:

The number of hours they watched TV in the last 48 hours (presuming that the more TV watched, the more 'assertive' programmes were watched).

An 'assertiveness' score – each person should rate themselves (or be rated by someone else) on a scale of 1 to 10 where 10 is very assertive. Alternatively look for an assertiveness questionnaire on the internet.

Results
Plot the scores for each person on a scattergraph.

Calculate a correlation coefficient to assess the strength of the correlation (use the Excel method below right).

Intelligence tests
There are many IQ tests on the internet (see, for example, http://www.queendom.com).

Correlate IQ scores with a memory test (give participants a word list to learn and test their recall the next day), or with reaction time, or anything else you can think of.

You can test reaction time using a metre ruler – one person stands on a chair holding the ruler in the air while the second person loosely holds the lower end. When person 1 drops the ruler and says 'Grab', person 2 has to grab it. The point at which the ruler is clasped equals reaction time. Alternatively search the internet for reaction time tests.

*In an experiment the variables are **independent** and **dependent** variables. In a correlation they are co-variables. NEVER refer to an IV and DV when discussing correlational research.*

Correlation and scattergraphs

A **scattergraph** is a graph that shows the correlation between two **co-variables** by plotting dots to represent each pair of scores. For each individual we obtain a score for each co-variable, in our case the co-variables are age and beauty.

The top graph on the right illustrates a positive correlation. The middle graph shows a negative correlation. The bottom graph is an example of very little correlation.

The extent of a correlation is described using a **correlation coefficient**. This is a number between +1 and –1, +1 is a perfect positive correlation and –1 is a perfect negative correlation.

The correlation coefficients for the graphs on the facing page are +.76, –.76 and +.002

The plus or minus sign shows whether it is a positive or negative correlation. The coefficient (number) tells us how closely the co-variables are related. –.76 is just as closely correlated as +.76. It's just that –.76 means that as one variable increases the other decreases (negative correlation) and +.76 means that both variables increase together (positive correlation).

Strong or weak?

The benefit of using graphs to represent data is that you can 'eyeball' the results – you can see at a glance whether there is a strong or a weak correlation between co-variables. You may be asked, in the exam, to comment on the kind of relationship shown in a scattergraph and can use the table on the right to help you.

In order to get a 'feel' for scattergraphs and correlation coefficients you might have a go at constructing scattergraphs and seeing what correlation coefficients are produced. Try the Excel method below.

The closer a correlation is to 1 the stronger it is (remember the sign doesn't matter, +1 is as strong as –1)

Correlation coefficient	Type of correlation
1.0	Perfect
.80	strong
.50	moderate
.30	weak
.10	very weak

Playing with correlation coefficients: the Excel method

Using Microsoft Excel you can enter and alter pairs of numbers to see how this affects a scattergraph and correlation coefficient.

- *On an Excel sheet enter your data in two columns.*
- *To see a scattergraph click and drag your cursor from the top left to the bottom right of the two columns. From the toolbar menu select 'chart' and select 'XY scatter'.*
- *To obtain the correlation coefficient, place the cursor in an empty box and type '=correl('. Then select with your cursor one column of your data and type a comma in the box and then select your other column of data and finish with a closing bracket. The formula should look something like: =correl(a6:a13,b6:b13). When you press return the correlation coefficient should appear in this box.*

(If you are confused look on YouTube where there are a number of guides for using Excel to plot a scattergraph.)

Try this ...

- *Alter one of the values and see how this affects the scattergraph and correlation coefficient.*
- *Produce a scattergraph with the following correlation coefficients: –.10, +.10, –.90, +.90.*
- *There are also a number of websites where you can enter data and a scattergraph will be produced with the correlation coefficient for you – try http://www.alcula.com/calculators/statistics/scatter-plot*

When considering a correlation study on age and beauty ...

A **one-tailed alternate hypothesis** would be 'There is a positive relationship between age and beauty'.

A **two-tailed alternate hypothesis** would be 'There is a relationship between age and beauty'.

The **null hypothesis** would be 'There is no relationship between age and beauty'.

The top graph illustrates a positive correlation. The middle graph shows a negative correlation. The bottom graph is an example of very little correlation.

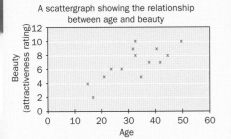

A scattergraph showing the relationship between age and beauty

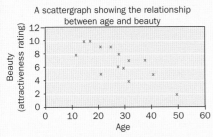

A scattergraph showing the relationship between age and beauty

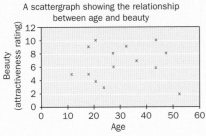

A scattergraph showing the relationship between age and beauty

Strengths	Weaknesses
Can be used when it would be unethical or impractical to conduct an experiment.	Cannot show a cause-and-effect relationship.
If the correlation is not strong then you can rule out a causal relationship. You can't demonstrate a causal relationship but if there is no correlation between co-variables then there can't be a causal relationship.	People often misinterpret correlations and assume that a cause and effect have been found whereas this is not possible.
If the correlation is strong then further investigation is justified because there may be a causal link.	There may be **intervening variables** that can explain why the co-variables being studied are linked. For example, research studies have shown a positive correlation between amount of TV watched and aggressiveness. However, it is wrong to conclude that watching TV is directly related to aggressiveness because it could be that a low boredom threshold was the cause of both of them, an intervening factor.
	The method used to measure either co-variable may lack **reliability** or **validity**.

...Links to core studies...

Correlational analyses are commonly used in applied research. This is because it is often not possible to carry out controlled experiments in applied settings. For example, studies on health can't put people in health damaging situations but they can look at whether where someone lives can predict their long term health (it does) or whether smoking 20 cigarettes a day is associated with shorter life span and more amputations (it is). Applied research is more the focus in A2 on this course and on the AS the chosen studies don't use correlation extensively.

One example is **Dement and Kleitman** who correlated the length of REM episode with the number of words a person used to describe the dream experienced in that REM episode. The correlations were all positive and ranged between .40 and .71 for each participant.

Qs 1.17

1   A psychological study investigates whether there is a relationship between how well students do in exams and how highly motivated the students are, in order to see if motivation and performance are linked. Motivation is measured by assessing how much the students participate in class (for example, counting how often they answer a question in class or how much of class time is spent working).

   a   Suggest **one** problem that might arise with the way class participation has been assessed.

   b   Describe how you could use time sampling to assess class participation, and give **one** strength of using this instead of event sampling.

   c   Describe and evaluate a different way to assess motivation.

   d   At the end the researchers plot a scattergraph of average exam scores and level of motivation. Their graph looks like the third graph above. What would you conclude from this?

2   A class of psychology students want to investigate whether there is any relationship between how hungry you feel and how good the food you are about to eat looks!

   a   In order to assess hunger the students devise a rating scale. Give an example of what this rating scale might look like.

   b   Describe **one** problem with measuring hunger in this way.

   c   Write a suitable operationalised one-tailed hypothesis and two-tailed hypothesis for this study.

   d   The students find a strong positive correlation between the co-variables. Sketch a graph to show what this should look like.

   e   One of the students concludes that hunger must have caused the food to look better. What is wrong with this conclusion?

   f   Describe **one** ethical issue that might arise in conducting this study and say how it could be dealt with.

What you have learned on this spread

- Correlation, strengths and weaknesses.
- Positive, negative and zero correlation.
- Scattergraphs.
- How to describe the procedures of an observational study (what, who, where, materials and how).
- How to evaluate the reliability and validity of a correlation.
- How to evaluate a correlation.

Exam-style questions

The example exam-style questions here are set out like the exam but there aren't as many. In the exam the total number of marks will be 60.

Section A

An experiment is designed to find out whether people like a product name because it is familiar. Participants were given a list of invented product names to read out loud. Some of the names appeared 10 times in the list whereas others only appeared once. After reading the list participants were asked to rate how much they liked each of the words on a rating scale from 1 to 10 where 10 represents 'like it a lot' and 1 is 'don't like it at all'. This was a repeated measures design.

The results are shown in the graph on the right.

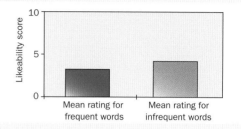

Bar chart showing mean ratings for likeability

1   Identify the independent variable and the dependent variable in this study. [2]

Stig's answer

The IV is the words and the DV is rating.

Chardonnay's answer

The independent variable is whether the words were familiar or not, and the DV was the ratings for likeability given to the words.

Teacher's comments

Stig, you are a man of few words. Given that the question is only worth 2 marks your answers are not sufficient for any marks. You need to at least say 'frequency of words' to get 1 mark for the IV and some extra detail of the rating (e.g. 'rating of likeability' to get 1 mark for the DV). Chardonnay has given an operationalised description of each of the variables. Take care Stig, brevity is a dangerous course of action.

Stig (0 out of 2 marks) Chardonnay (2 out of 2 marks)

2   Outline **two** conclusions that could be drawn from the graph. [4]

Stig's answer

One conclusion is that people didn't seem to like the words much at all. A second conclusion is that they liked the frequent words more.

Chardonnay's answer

1   You could conclude from the graph that in fact people actually like the infrequent words, on average, more than the frequent ones.
2   You could also conclude that this shows that people don't necessarily like things because they are familiar.

Teacher's comments

The question requires two conclusions which both students have provided. There are no marks for 'elegance' although Chardonnay's presentation makes for easier reading.

Stig, here each conclusion is worth two marks so brevity will be penalised. Neither of your conclusions will be worth 2 marks because they are each lacking detail. Your first answer is an unusual conclusion but actually a fair conclusion – the mean ratings for both groups of words were low. You would need to spell this out for full marks,

Chardonnay, you are again scooping up the marks with a thorough and clearly expressed answer.

Stig (2 out of 4 marks) Chardonnay (4 out of 4 marks)

3   The sampling technique used was a self-selected sample. Suggest **one** strength and **one** weakness of the sampling technique used in this study. [6]

Stig's answer

The strength of a self-selected sample is that it is easy to obtain because people volunteer. The weakness is that you may get a biased sample because you only ask certain kinds of people (those who volunteer).

Chardonnay's answer

The strength of choosing this method was to get those people who would really want to take part so hopefully they would really think about the task. This is quite important when asking participants to rate something like likeability because they could just write anything. The weakness of choosing this method is that volunteers are not typical of all other people, they are possibly more highly motivated and more willing to please so the students who volunteered in this study might have tried to guess what the researcher wanted and realised it was to do with familiarity.

Teacher's comments

Stig, this is quite a short answer. You have essentially identified one strength and one weakness but you have not elaborated or explained further. Most importantly neither strength or weakness has been related to the study, as required by the question.

Chardonnay, for each strength and weakness you have identified it, you have explained it a little bit further and also, crucially, related it to the study. Generally speaking, if the question mentions 'in the study', you do have to ensure the answer is framed within the context of the study and not just any study!

Stig (1+1 out of 6 marks) Chardonnay (3+3 out of 6 marks)

Section B

An observational study was conducted of the behaviour of children in a school playground. Two researchers kept a record of acts of aggression by boys and girls using time sampling. They recorded a total of 43 acts by boys and 23 by girls.

1   Produce an appropriate summary table for this data. [2]

Stig's answer

Aggressive acts	Boys	Girls
	43	23

Chardonnay's answer

Table showing aggressive acts observed in a school playground

	Boys	Girls
Number of aggressive acts	43	23

Teacher's comments

You have drawn a table, Stig, and put the data in correctly but some important details are missing, as you can see if you look at Chardonnay's table. Maybe you thought the question just meant 'fill the data in a table', but the titles are an integral part of any table.

Stig (1 out of 2 mark) Chardonnay (2 out of 2 marks)

2   Suggest **one** problem with using time sampling in this study. [3]

Stig's answer

It is difficult to do because there is so much you have to look at and you might not get it right.

Chardonnay's answer

The difficulty with time sampling is that at each observational moment you have to make a note of what all the children are doing and if there was a lot of children in the playground you could easily miss out some of the children which means that your observations wouldn't be very accurate.

Teacher's comments

Stig, it's good to be to the point and long answers are not always the best ones – but a bit too brief again here! Your answer suggests a good understanding but you need to explain yourself more clearly so the examiner can see that you do understand. For example, 'there is so much you have to look at' – what is the 'so much' you have to look at? And what do you mean by 'get it right'? Presumably you are talking about making an accurate record. Just a little more care would have meant a lot more marks.

Chardonnay, being the thorough student that you are, you have provided loads of detail and wisely used an example to aid your explanation.

Stig (1 out of 3 marks) Chardonnay (3 out of 3 marks)

3   How could the researcher check the reliability of the observations in this study? [3]

Stig's answer

One way to check the observations would be to use inter-rater reliability which means that you correlate each set of observations from each of the observers and the agreement should be better than 80%.

Chardonnay's answer

Reliability means how consistent you are. Reliability can be checked by looking at the observations made by both of the observers and seeing how much they agree with each other. They should agree with each other most of the time to show consistency in the aggressive behaviours of the children they are observing.

Teacher's comments

Stig, you have given an excellent definition of inter-rater reliability. Unfortunately you have forgotten to add the context of the observation so although your description is really better than Chardonnay's she has contextualised her answer.

Chardonnay, this is not a great description but you have added some context and it is good enough for full marks.

Stig (2 out of 3 marks) Charonnay (3 out of 3 marks)

Section C

You have been asked to produce a questionnaire investigating the correlation between stress and health.

1   Suggest a fully operationalised null hypothesis for this study. [4]

Stig's answer

There will be no relationship between stress (1 to 5 scale, where 1 is high) and health (1 to 5, where 5 is good health).

Chardonnay's answer

There will be no difference between stress rating (1 to 10, where 1 is low stress and 10 is very stressed) and self rating of health (1 to 10, where 1 is poor health and 10 is excellent).

Teacher's comments

At first it looks like Chardonnay has the better answer as she has operationalised her variables more clearly. However, appearances can be deceptive!

Stig this is a good null hypothesis where your operationalisation is good enough for full marks.

Chardonnay you have stated no difference (not no relationship or no correlation). A difference implies two groups of participants, so unfortunately this gets no credit whatsoever.

Stig (4 out of 4 marks) Chardonnay (0 out of 4 marks)

2   Outline and evaluate the procedure you could use for collecting data. [10]

Stig's answer

I could use a questionnaire from the internet on stress and then ask people how many times they were off school to measure their health. I would print 20 copies of this questionnaire and add some instructions for the participants about what to do, asking for their consent.

I would then give the questionnaires out to a range of people I know so that I got a good range of ages and both males and females. I would thank them for taking part at the end and ask if they had any further questions.

Chardonnay's answer

For this study I would create a structured questionnaire containing 20 questions, some open and some closed. The questions would be about how much stress people felt they were experiencing and also about their health (or illness). I would conduct a small pilot study to check that the questions were clear and make any changes necessary and then give the questionnaires out to a lot of different people. I would approach people and ask them if they could spare 10 minutes for my psychology project. I would then further explain the aim of the project to respondents so they could give their informed consent.

Teacher's comments

Stig, you have covered the basics of your procedure, but there are some details which would prevent me from replicating your study. Incidentally, a good way of checking your procedure is to get a friend to read it and see if they feel they could conduct a perfect replication of your study. If not, there is something missing and you will not get full marks. Here, I do not know where your respondents filled in the questionnaire, whether they were on their own or in groups, whether you gave them a time limit or not. As I do not have access to the questionnaire, it also might be useful if you gave a quick summary of the instructions!

Chardonnay, this is a good answer, covering all the main details to allow replication. You have included information given to the participants, location, time taken as well as the step-by-step information.

Stig (2 out of 10 marks) Chardonnay (4 out of 10 marks)

3   Describe what psychologists mean by the term validity in this study. [3]

Stig's answer

It means that the psychologist found out what he was hoping to find out. The results were what he had predicted.

Chardonnay's answer

Validity means how true the results are. Are they really what happens in everyday life or did some aspect of the study mean that the results are meaningless. Validity is about whether you are testing what you meant to test.

Teacher's comments

Stig, this is not the right answer at all!

Chardonnay, you have got round to the right answer in the end (validity refers to whether you are measuring what you claim to be). Also, you have referred to a form of validity (ecological validity), by way of expansion. So you have done (just) enough for two marks. Unfortunately you have not included any context. Remember when you see this phrase 'in this study' you must include something about what the study is about in your answer.

Stig (0 out of 3 marks) Chardonnay (2 out of 3 marks)

CHAPTER 2

This chapter looks at three core studies in cognitive psychology:

- *Loftus and Palmer's work on memory for events.*

- *Baron-Cohen, Joliffe, Mortimer and Robertson's study of the thought processes of autistic adults.*

- *Savage-Rumbaugh, McDonal, Sevcik, Hopkins and Rubert's observations of chimpanzees experience of acquiring human language.*

Cognitive psychology

38 Introduction to cognitive psychology

Core study 1
40 Loftus and Palmer (eyewitness testimony)

40 Starters: research into memory
42 The study in a nutshell
43 The study in detail
47 Evaluation
48 Afters: memory research after the car crash studies
49 Multiple choice questions
49 Exam-style questions

Core study 2
50 Baron-Cohen *et al.* (autism)

50 Starters: the history of autism
52 The study in a nutshell
54 The study in detail
57 Evaluation
58 Afters: more studies on autism
59 Multiple choice questions
59 Exam-style questions

Core study 3
60 Savage-Rumbaugh *et al.* (animal language)

60 Starters: animal language
62 The study in a nutshell
63 The study in detail
67 Evaluation
68 Afters: just monkeying around
69 Multiple choice questions
69 Exam-style questions

70 Exam-style questions

What is cognitive psychology?

Cognitive psychology is the study of all mental processes:

- How do we see the world?
- How do we store and recall information?
- How do we communicate?
- How do we think?

Cognitive psychology takes a mechanistic approach, which means that it largely looks at people as if they are machines. Modern research looks at human cognitive processes and compares them to those of a computer. Computers can do several of the things that people can do, and they can do some of them better. They can respond to the environment, store information, calculate and much more. There are, however, many cognitive tasks that we do far better than even the best computer.

Try this 2.1

How do we see?

Think about these puzzles:

- Your eyes are moving all the time (stare into a friend's eyes to check this out) but your view of the world is stable.
- The screen at the back of your eye (the retina) is flat, but you see the world in 3D.
- The image on the retina is upside down and back to front, but you see things the right way round.
- Light never reaches the brain. It hits the back of the eye (the retina) and is transferred to your brain as electro-chemical messages.

Is the eye like a camera?

Yes and no. A diagram of the eye shows that it looks like a camera. It has a lens and a screen to collect the light, but if you could capture the images that appear on the retina they would not look like anything you would recognise. The eye is the first line of our battle to make sense of the world. It does not just record the information that comes in, it starts to interpret it. You might think of it as a bit of brain on a stick rather than a camera.

The puzzles of cognitive psychology

Making sense of the world is something we take for granted. Most of us are able to see, hear, think, taste, talk and listen (though many of us struggle a bit with the listening). But how do we do this? And what do we mean by seeing and hearing and thinking? In the items on these pages we are not trying to give you all the answers to these questions but merely trying to show you what the puzzle is. The more you think about it the more puzzling it becomes.

Take sound for example. What is it? If you did school physics then you'll know that our ears respond to changes in air pressure. These changes in air pressure are experienced by us as sound. You might well have come across the riddle 'If a tree falls in a forest and no one is there to hear it, does it make a sound?' Certainly it creates some changes in air pressure but the experience of sound is your response to these changes so we would argue that the answer is no. Sound is in your head and is created by you. It's remarkable and almost unbelievable.

Sensation and perception

What is the difference between the physical stimuli that hit us (like light and sound) and the images that appear in our minds? The physical stimuli create *sensations* in our sense organs but we then use these sensations to create our *perceptions* of the world. If we think about the example of sound given above then the changes in air pressure are the sensation we receive and our perception of it is sound. We say that 'seeing is believing' but is what we see sometimes the invention of our minds? And are some of our memories also part invention?

Look at the two rows of characters. If you read the top row they are clearly all letters, and if you read the bottom row then it is a sequence of numbers. Look again and you will see that the middle figure in both rows is exactly the same. So what is it? The letter 'B' or the number '13'? In fact, it is neither and it is both. You understand the character not just by the shape that you sense but also the meaning you perceive it to have. Your perception of the object is affected by the sensation the shape makes on your eye but this sensation is added to and interpreted by you to give it meaning.

The figure and ground phenomenon

We perceive one part of an event as the *figure* (the object) and the other as the *ground* (the background). **Edgar Rubin** demonstrated the phenomenon by creating his classic example of an ambiguous figure–ground situation. In Rubin's figure, there is no *true* figure and ground. We can either see the light area as background in which case we see two faces, or we can see it as an object in which case we see a vase. We can't see both at the same time. Our perception makes sense of this figure and of the world by deciding what is figure and what is background.

This is the feature of perception that is played with when people want to camouflage an object or themselves. If you can blur the boundaries between an object and its background you make it less visible.

Visual illusions

Visual illusions show how our minds can be confused by sensations to create a false perception. Look at the images on any illusions website. You may well have seen some of them before but think how they are playing tricks on your mind. For a more dramatic demonstration go to **Richard Gregory**'s website (www.richardgregory.org) and look at the Charlie Chaplin mask. The remarkable thing here is that you know what is really there but you cannot see it. Your mind insists on seeing something that is clearly not there.

The Necker cube

This is one of the simplest illusions to create and one of the most puzzling. This figure is a flat drawing of two squares joined at the corners but it looks like a cube. And not just any cube. The orientation of the cube appears to change as you look at it. Sometimes it seems to point upwards and sometimes it seems to point downwards. You are seeing something that you know is not really there (a cube) and because it is not really there your mind's eye cannot decide which way round it is, so it tries out the different orientations and inverts it. Try keeping the cube in one position and you'll find it can't be done. You can't stop seeing 3D even though it is on a flat page.

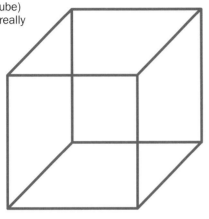

The Necker cube

The eyes of a child

What does a newborn baby see when it opens its eyes? We can never know this because they can't, or won't, talk to us. And when they can talk, they can't remember what it was like in the delivery room or the back of the car on the way home.

One of the most quoted views on this comes from the great US psychologist **William James** who wrote, *'The baby, assailed by eyes, ears, nose, skin, and entrails at once, feels it all as one great blooming, buzzing confusion'* (James, 1890, page 488). In other words babies don't see shapes or patterns, just a moving array of colours. Over time they start to see patterns in the confusions and eventually learn to build up the three-dimensional picture that greets most of us when we open our eyes.

We can't know what a baby sees but what if you find someone who has been blind all their life and then is given their sight as an adult? What will they see?

There are a few recorded cases of this including SB who was studied by Richard Gregory (you can read the story of SB at www.richardgregory.org). Until the age of 52 SB lived a successful and active life as a blind man until advances in surgery meant that his sight could be restored. When the bandages were first removed, and SB could see, he heard the voice of the surgeon. He turned towards the voice but could only see a blur. Although he realised this must be a face he could not 'see it'. After a few days he was able to make sense of the visual information. He was best at recognising things he had been able to touch when he was blind. Some things surprised him, for example he had believed that a quarter moon would be like a quarter of a circle rather than a crescent.

People who recover their sight after blindness often experience depression. This was the case with SB and he found his new visual world brought him more sadness than happiness. He soon chose to spend a lot of his time in darkness.

Cognitive puzzles in everyday life

1 Why do my photos look so rubbish?

You were on the beach and saw a giant lizard. It was massive and you were really brave to get that close to take a picture, but when you looked at the image you could barely see the lizard at all. And that giant ship on the horizon has become a dot. Is the camera rubbish? Probably not. Your mind's eye adjusts the size of objects so you perceive them to be bigger. The camera records what is really there, but your mind's eye distorts it to help you concentrate on the important objects.

Maybe your mind is monitoring all sorts of information below the level of your awareness and selects the important bits for you to attend to. But what is doing this monitoring and how does it decide what is important?

2 How do children learn language?

I was trying to make excuses for my lack of a foreign language by explaining to a Spanish friend that their language was difficult for English people to learn. My friend commented that this was remarkable because in his country there were many five year olds fluent in it. Children do not need instruction to learn language, and in fact it is almost impossible to stop them developing language. Language is a complex set of sounds and rules that almost defy description yet we have no difficulty in developing them and being understood. And what is even more remarkable is that they do not copy all the features of what they hear but develop their own pattern of speaking.

3 How do we tune in to conversations?

You are in a large group of people talking to a friend. You don't know what everyone else in the room is talking about but all of a sudden you hear your name from the other side of the room. Someone is talking about you. You immediately tune out of the conversation with your friend and listen to what is being said about you.

This is remarkable in itself. You don't have movable ears so the tuning in has taken place inside your head rather than outside. Even more remarkable is how you heard your name. If you weren't listening to that conversation how did you hear your name?

...Connections...

Cognitive psychology is about understanding how we make sense of our world and communicate within it. It has links to all the other areas of psychology in this text. In **Individual differences** we look at the cognitive skill of intelligence; in **Developmental psychology** we look at how children think; in **Social psychology** we look at how people make social judgements, and in **Physiological psychology** we look at how the brain carries out cognitive tasks. One of the fastest growing areas in psychology is cognitive neuroscience which focuses on the connections between brain structures and cognitive abilities.

Research into memory

Everybody has a tale about memory: how they forgot an important appointment, or the fact that their granny can remember everyone's name in the family over the last 200 years. Sometimes we surprise ourselves by what we can recall when we go back somewhere we haven't been for many years, or at an important moment in a quiz. 'How did I know that?' you ask yourself. Mind you, when you are in the exam room trying to answer the questions you are more likely to ask yourself why you can't remember things.

Making adverts work

Advertisers use retrieval cues to help us remember their product. One way of using retrieval cues is to place pictures from television adverts on the packaging of the product. The Campbell Soup Company, for example, reported that sales increased by 15% when their point-of-sales materials (items in the shops) were directly related to their television advertising (Keller, 1987).

Two traditions

There are two routes to studying memory:

- The experimental study of mental mechanisms (see right).
- The study of everyday experience (see below).

The most commonly researched of these in psychology is the **experimental** study of mental mechanisms. This might seem a little disappointing because the interesting bits are the phenomena of everyday life. In fact, the **cognitive** psychologist **Ulrich Neisser** (1982) suggested that a basic principle of memory research was:

'If X is an interesting or socially significant aspect of memory, then psychologists have hardly ever studied X.' (page 4)

Neisser goes on to make a more remarkable claim:

'I think that "memory" in general does not exist.' (page 12)

This sounds ridiculous because it is obvious that we remember objects and events, but is there really a thing we can call a memory? There does not seem to be any one part of the brain that controls memories, so thinking of memory as a mechanism, like a DVD recorder, is probably not helpful. In fact it would be very misleading because, as we will see later, we do not store and recall exact records of events. Far from it: we recreate our memories and in so doing we distort them.

The experimental study of mental mechanisms

The earliest systematic work on the psychology of memory was carried out by **Hermann Ebbinghaus** at the end of the nineteenth century. He carried out a range of highly controlled experiments most commonly using himself as the sole participant. He measured his ability to remember nonsense syllables. These are three letter syllables that sound like words but mean nothing, for example 'wib', 'fut', 'wol', etc. He used nonsense syllables so that any past knowledge would not affect the results. The studies were methodical, and provided a wide range of findings which had a big influence on how memory research was conducted, and on theories of memory.

Bartlett (see below) criticised Ebbinghaus' work by noting that the use of nonsense syllables created a very artificial situation, and therefore lacked **ecological validity**. He also suggested that Ebbinghaus concentrated too closely on the material that was being remembered, and ignored other important features like the attitudes of the subject and their prior experience. There is also an issue about whether anything is completely nonsense. If you look at the three examples of nonsense syllables above then maybe one of them has some meaning for you. 'Fut' reminds me of football and 'wol' is the sign above Owl's house in Winnie the Pooh.

Later work developed a two-stage model of memory (long-term memory and short-term memory) which became a multi-store model as more boxes were added to the model. Although this research did not use nonsense syllables it commonly used word lists or other tasks that did not have much connection to everyday memory.

Try this 2.2

Try the method of repeated reproduction (see right) to see how much a message or a picture changes as it passes from one person to another.

Start off with a simple image and ask someone you know to look at it and then draw it. Then take their drawing and show it to someone else and then ask them to look at this image and then draw it, and so on. After 10 drawings compare the 10th drawing with the first one. Are the differences the same as Bartlett found?

The study of everyday experience

In contrast to Ebbinghaus, Bartlett carried out a series of studies into the memory of meaningful material like stories and pictures. One of Bartlett's methods was to ask someone to look at some material and then recall it. This recalled material was then shown to someone else who had to recall what they had seen, and so on. This is called the method of serial reproduction.

Bartlett used another method (the method of repeated reproduction), where the same person is asked to keep remembering the same material over a period of time. An example of how the recall of an image changed over successive reproductions is shown on the right. The drawing is a representation of the Egyptian 'mulak', a conventionalised reproduction of an owl, which may have been used as the model for our letter 'M'. With each recall of the image the drawing changed and by the tenth version the person believed they had initially seen a black cat.

In his studies Bartlett (1932) found that memories change in a number of ways:

- *They become more conventional:* Drawings became more like common objects such as a cat in the example shown. Also when people were asked to recall stories these memories were also modified to be more conventional.

Flashbulb memory

Some events have a big effect on us and we are able to say where we were and what we were doing when we heard about the event or when we witnessed it. It is almost as if a flashbulb has gone off in our minds to highlight the scene and fix the image. Flashbulb memories are typically remarkably vivid and seem to be permanent. These memories are usually of very emotional and personal events in your life. Flashbulb memories can also be related to events that are public but affected you emotionally, such as the death of a famous person (like Princess Diana) or a dramatic news event (like the destruction of the World Trade Center on 9/11).

Maybe there is a flashbulb mechanism that is responsible for capturing these events and storing them in memory for an indefinite period of time. Maybe these memories are not encoded any differently from others but we remember them because we rehearse them by retelling them often.

A problem with much of the work on flashbulb memories is that data are not checked. If I say I remember I was in the bath when I heard the news that a famous person had died, how would you know this was correct? In fact, how would I know?

A flashbulb memory is a memory about what you were doing when you heard about something significant. It is not the memory for the event itself.

Neisser doubts whether these memories are any more accurate than our other memories and he carried out a number of studies including one on memories of the Challenger space disaster.

In 1986 the Challenger space shuttle exploded on take-off killing the entire crew. It was seen live on television and shown repeatedly on newscasts. The next day Neisser and Harsch (1992) asked students to give their recollections of the time when they first heard of the disaster. They went back to the same students two-and-a-half years later and asked them the same question. They discovered that at least 25% of them were wrong about every major detail. Only 10% gave all the same details. He also discovered that the students' confidence in the memories had no **correlation** with their accuracy. Students who had inaccurate recall were just as likely to be confident in their memories as students whose memories were unchanged. These studies were repeated after the World Trade Center was destroyed in 2001. The results were very similar and if you are interested just search online 'flashbulb memory and world trade center' to read about it.

9/11 World Trade Center

- *They are simplified:* Stories and pictures become simpler when they are recalled.
- *Labels or names affect recall:* For example, in the images shown once a label 'cat' has been used, the recalls become more and more like a common view of a cat rather than the original image.
- *Elaboration takes place:* Some items are introduced into the story or the picture by the person remembering it. In the example shown a tail develops from one of the lines of the mulak but by the last drawing it has no connection to the original.
- *Emotional distortion takes place:* The way someone was feeling during the tests tended to affect the memory of the stories they were told.

Bartlett found that our memories are not exact recordings of events and images. This is obviously important when we look at evidence in court but it was more than 40 years before this idea was looked at again by Elizabeth Loftus (see next page).

Recall cues

We often have the experience of knowing something but not quite being able to recall it. This commonly happens in quizzes, examinations and when you forget to take your shopping list to the Co-op. What we need is a memory cue and then it all comes back to us. This is why advertisers use visual displays in shops that remind people of the TV adverts (see facing page).

One of the cues that helps us is the context in which we first came across the information. If we heard about something when we were on the bus then we might well remember it again when we next get on the bus.

The simple message here is that you should do your examination revision in a situation that is as close as possible to the exam room. So set yourself up with a wobbly desk and an uncomfortable chair and get your mum to walk up and down and keep staring at you.

...Link to the core study...

We are very confident about our own memories: 'I was there, I saw it, I know what happened.' Psychology tells us, however, that this is not the case and memory is far from an accurate record of events. Does this matter? Well, not if you are telling the story of a good night out, but yes if you are giving evidence in a court of law. Perhaps our memories are susceptible to suggestion and if so, the leading questions of barristers and police might have an effect on evidence given to them about a crime.

Loftus and Palmer: the core study

Elizabeth Loftus and John C. Palmer (1974) Reconstruction of automobile destruction. *Journal of Verbal Learning and Verbal Behavior, 13,* pages 585–589.

See the CORE STUDY CHECKLIST on page xv for details of what you need to know for the exam.

In a nutshell

Context
Past research has shown that memory can be very inaccurate, for example when estimating the speed a car is travelling at. Such inaccuracy may be influenced by **leading questions**.

The study consists of two **experiments**:

Experiment 1

Aim
The aim of the first experiment was to investigate the accuracy of memory and, in particular, the effect of leading questions on what people remember.

Participants
45 students (divided into 5 groups).

Procedure
This was a **laboratory experiment**, using an **independent measures design**.

1   Shown film clips of car accidents.
2   Asked questions about the film clips including a critical question 'How fast were the cars going when they hit each other?'

Participants were in one of five different conditions:

Group 1: Asked 'How fast were the cars going when they hit each other?'

Group 2: Asked 'How fast were the cars going when they contacted each other?'

Group 3: Asked 'How fast were the cars going when they smashed into each other?'

Group 4: Asked 'How fast were the cars going when they bumped each other?'

Group 5: Asked 'How fast were the cars going when they collided into each other?'

Results
The **mean** speed estimates differed for each group:

• The verb 'smashed' gave the highest estimate.
• The verb 'contacted' gave the lowest estimate.

Conclusions
This suggested that estimates of speed are affected by leading questions.

Key term: leading questions
A **leading question** suggests what answer is desired or leads a person to give a desired answer.

For example, 'Was the person in the street a young man?' The question suggests what you saw.

Such questions are especially problematic in **eyewitness testimony**, *when a witness to a crime is asked to provide details. Policeman and lawyers may unconsciously ask leading questions and this affects the answers they get. It also may affect what an eyewitness subsequently remembers.*

Experiment 2

Aim
Does the critical word (e.g. 'smashed' or 'hit') change a person's subsequent memory of the event they witnessed?

Participants
150 students (divided into 3 groups).

Procedure
1   Shown a film of a car accident.
2   Asked questions about the film clips.

Group 1 was asked 'How fast were the cars going when they smashed into each other?'

Group 2 was asked 'How fast were the cars going when they hit each other?'

Group 3 were not asked about the speed of the cars. This is a **control group**.

3   The participants were asked to return the laboratory a week later. They were asked some more questions about the film clips they saw a week earlier. One of the questions was 'Did you see any broken glass?' (There was no broken glass in any of the film clips.)

Results
Participants in the 'smashed' condition (who tended to think the car was travelling faster) were more likely to say there was more glass.

Discussion
This suggests that the original leading questions had actually affected what they remembered (as opposed to biasing their recall).

Qs 2.1

Experiment 1
1   What was the critical question?
2   Identify the five verbs used in this experiment.
3   Explain in what way this is an independent measures design.
4   Identify the independent and dependent variables in this experiment.
5   How was the independent variable manipulated in this experiment?

Experiment 2
6   Explain why this study is described as a laboratory experiment.
7   There is a control group in this experiment. How was the control group different?
8   Explain why a control group is necessary.
9   Why did the participants have to return to the laboratory one week later instead of answering the question about the broken glass immediately?

The detailed version: Experiment 1

Context and aim

How accurate is your memory? More specifically, how well can you estimate details of a car accident such as how long did it take from beginning to end or how fast were the cars travelling?

Psychological research has found that people are very inaccurate. For example, Marshall (1969) found that when Air Force personnel, who knew in advance that they would be asked to estimate the speed of a vehicle, observed a car travelling at 12 mph, their estimates ranged from 10 to 50 mph.

This suggests that it might be quite easy to influence the answers that people give to such numerical questions. One way to influence answers is by phrasing a question in such a way that it leads a person to give a particular answer. Some questions are more 'suggestive' than others; in legal terms such questions are called *leading questions* – a question that '*either by its form or content, suggests to the witness what answer is desired or leads him to the desired answer*' (Loftus and Palmer, 1974, page 585).

Aim

The aim of the first experiment was to see if the estimates given by participants about the speed of vehicles in a traffic accident would be influenced by the wording of the question asked. For example, participants asked about how fast the cars were travelling when they *hit* each other would give different speed estimates and have different expectations than participants asked the same question with the word 'smashed' instead.

Method

Participants
The participants in this study were 45 American students.

Procedure
The participants were shown seven film clips of different traffic accidents. The clips were originally made as part of a driver safety film.

After each clip the participants were given a **questionnaire** which asked them to describe the accident and then answer a series of specific questions about the accident.

There was one critical question: 'About how fast were the cars going when they hit each other?' One group of participants was given this question. The other four groups were given the verbs 'smashed', 'collided', 'bumped' or 'contacted' in place of the word 'hit'. Thus there were five **experimental groups** in this laboratory experiment.

Results

The mean speed estimate was calculated for each experimental group, as shown in the graph below. The group given the word 'smashed' estimated a higher speed than the other groups (40.8 mph). The group given the word 'contacted' estimated the lowest speed (31.8 mph).

Speed estimates for verbs used in Experiment 1

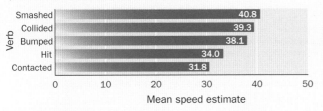

Try this   2.4

Do you get headaches frequently?

According to Loftus' research this is a leading question. People asked this question reported an average of 2.2 headaches per week whereas those who were asked 'Do you get headaches occasionally, and if so, how often?' reported an average of 0.7 headaches! The way the question was asked had a significant effect on the answer given.

Try it out yourself. Consider how you will design this study:

- *How will you select participants?*
- *How will you decide which question to ask each participant?*
- *How will you analyse the data you collect?*

Qs 2.2

1 Write a suitable alternate hypothesis for this experiment. Make sure it is clearly operationalised (good practice for the Psychological Investigations paper).

2 Identify the experimental design used in this study and give **one** strength of using this design.

3 List the experimental groups in this study.

4 Why was it a good idea to ask 10 questions rather than just asking the critical question alone?

5 Each group of participants was shown the films in a different order. Why do you think this was done?

6 The participants all knew they were taking part in a psychology experiment. How do you think this might have affected their behaviour?

7 How do you think this also may have affected the results from the study?

8 Can you think of a way that this problem might have been overcome?

9 Describe a possible sampling technique that might have been used in this study.

10 Give **one** strength and **one** weakness of this sampling technique.

11 Outline **one** finding from Experiment 1.

12 State **one** conclusion that can be drawn from this finding.

Experiment 1 continued

Discussion

The results show that the form of a question can have a significant effect on a witness' answer to the question. In other words, **leading questions** can affect the accuracy of memory.

The issue is – how does this happen?

Loftus and Palmer proposed two explanations for this result:

1. Response-bias factors

The different speed estimates occur because the critical word (e.g. 'smashed' or 'hit') influences or biases a person's response. In other words, hearing the verb 'smashed' leads you to think of a noisy high impact accident and therefore leads you to estimate a higher speed than for the verb 'hit'.

2. The memory representation is altered

The critical verb changes a person's perception of the accident – some critical words would lead someone to have a perception of the accident being more serious. This perception is then stored in the person's memory of the event.

If the second conclusion is true, we would expect participants to 'remember' other details that are not true. Loftus and Palmer tested this in their second **experiment**.

Try this   2.5

Try repeating one of the experiments from the study by Loftus and Palmer, using a photograph of an automobile accident and devising a set of questions, one of which will be the critical question.

Each person in your class should give the questionnaire to two people: one has the 'smashed' version, one has the 'hit' version. Make sure they don't know that there are two different versions.

Put all the results together, and calculate the mean speed estimate for all those questionnaires that used the word 'smashed' and the mean speed estimate for all those questionnaires that used the word 'hit'.

Draw a bar chart to illustrate your class results.

Biographical notes

'Just because someone thinks they remember something in detail, with confidence and with emotion, does not mean that it actually happened ... False memories have these characteristics too.'

Elizabeth Loftus *is Distinguished Professor at the University of California, Irvine. She was born in Los Angeles, California in 1944 and planned to be a maths teacher but discovered psychology at university. She received her PhD from Stanford University in 1970.*

She began her research with investigations of how the mind classifies and remembers information. In the 1970s, she began to re-evaluate the direction of her research. In 'Diva of disclosure' (Neimark, 1996) published in Psychology Today*, she stated 'I wanted my work to make a difference in people's lives'. She began her research on traumatically repressed memories and eyewitness accounts and suddenly found herself in the midst of sexual abuse stories and defending accused offenders. Loftus has been an expert witness consultant in hundreds of cases on the unreliability of eyewitness testimonies based on false memories, which she believes to be triggered, suggested, implanted or created in the mind.*

Loftus has received numerous awards for her work from psychology and from other disciplines. She has received four honourary doctorates including one from the UK. She received the William James Fellow Award from the American Psychological Society, 2001 for 'ingeniously and rigorously designed research studies ... that yielded clear objective evidence on difficult and controversial questions'. She remains a respected figure in psychology and in a review of twentieth-century psychologists published by the Review of General Psychology *she was the top-ranked woman on the list.*

'I study human memory. My experiments reveal how memories can be changed by things that we are told. Facts, ideas, suggestions and other forms of post-event information can modify our memories. The legal field, so reliant on memories, has been a significant application of the memory research. My interest in psychology and law, more generally, has grown from this application.'

 Elizabeth Loftus' home page www.seweb.uci.edu/cls/faculty/loftus.uci

The detailed version: Experiment 2

Aim

Loftus and Palmer conducted a second experiment to further investigate the effects of leading questions on memory.

This time going one step further to see if the leading question altered subsequent expectations about the likely consequences. In particular they wanted to see if such questions simply create a response-bias (explanation 1) or if they actually alter a person's memory representation (explanation 2).

'The difference between false memories and true ones is the same as for jewels: it is always the false ones that look the most real, the most brilliant.'

(Spanish artist Salvador Dali)

Qs 2.3

1 What did Loftus and Palmer decide to investigate in their second experiment?
2 What is an 'experimental group'?
3 Outline **one** difference between the responses given by the two experimental groups.
4 A possible hypothesis for Experiment 2 would be 'Participants are more likely to report seeing broken glass when they are given the word "smashed" in a previous question than when they have the word "hit"'. Is this a one-tailed or two-tailed hypothesis?
5 State a suitable null hypothesis for experiment 2.
6 Outline **two** findings from Experiment 2.
7 What conclusions can you draw from the probability table on the right?
8 How do the aims for Experiments 1 and 2 differ?
9 The mean speed estimates for Experiments 1 and 2 were quite different. How might that be explained?
10 Describe **two** quantitative measurements recorded in this study (Experiments 1 and 2).

Try this   2.6

Draw a bar chart of the table probability below. This may help you understand the results of the study and what to conclude.

Method

Participants
The participants in this study were again American students but a new group of 150 students.

Participants
Part 1
Participants were shown a one-minute film which contained a four-second multiple car accident. The participants were asked a set of questions including the critical question about speed. There were three groups:

- Group 1 was asked: 'How fast were the cars going when they smashed each other?'
- Group 2 was asked: 'How fast were the cars going when they hit into each other?'
- Group 3 was asked no question about the speed of the vehicles. This was a **control group**.

Part 2
One week later the participants were asked to return to the psychology **laboratory**. They were asked some further questions including 'Did you see any broken glass?' There was no broken glass in the film but, presumably, those who thought the car was travelling faster might expect that there would be broken glass.

Results

Part 1
The results from Part 1 are shown in the graph on the right. Participants gave a **significantly** higher speed estimate in the 'smashed' condition, as before.

Part 2
In Part 2 (a week later) they found that participants in the 'smashed condition' were also more likely to think they saw broken glass (see graph below).

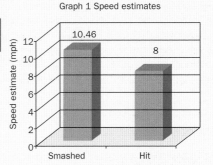

Graph 1 Speed estimates

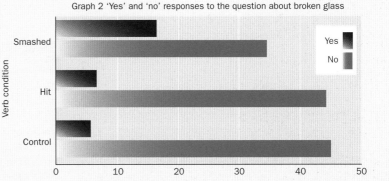

Graph 2 'Yes' and 'no' responses to the question about broken glass

Verb condition	Speed estimate (mph)			
	1–5	6–10	11–15	16–20
Smashed	0.09	0.27	0.41	0.62
Hit	0.05	0.09	0.25	0.50

The table above shows the probability of saying 'Yes' to the question 'Did you see any broken glass?' in relation to the original question asked about speed estimates.

Experiment 2 continued

Discussion

The results from Part 1 of Experiment 2 again show that the way a question is asked can influence the answer given, and confirm that the word smashed creates a perception that the car is travelling faster.

The results from Part 2 of Experiment 2 suggest that this effect is not just due to a response-bias because **leading questions** actually altered the memory a participant had for the event.

Loftus and Palmer propose that memory is determined by two sources:

1   One's own perception gleaned at the time of the original event.

2   External information supplied after the fact (such as leading questions).

Over time information from these two sources is integrated in such a way that we are unable to tell which source any particular piece of information came from. All we have is one 'memory'.

In the second **experiment** the two pieces of information combine to form a memory of an accident that appears quite severe and therefore generates certain expectations, for example that there is likely to be broken glass.

Links to other research

This research can be linked to earlier studies of the way a verbal label given to an object alters the to-be-remembered form, such as in the study by Carmichael *et al.*, 1932 (see right).

Another study by Daniel (1972) found that participants' recognition of objects was similarly affected, and thus concluded that verbal labels cause a shift in the way information is represented in memory in the direction of being more similar to the suggestion given by the verbal label.

The two studies mentioned in this discussion (Carmichael et al. and Daniel) are both quite old, so you might wonder why we have included them.

They were cited by Loftus and Palmer in their discussion, which is why we have included them here – your task is to know the core study paper inside out.

Research suggests that if you were shown this picture but told it was a beehive – then that's what you might well remember it as.

Carmichael et al. gave participants a set of drawings (central column) and then provided a verbal description (to left or right). When participants were later asked to redraw the image, the resulting object was typically affected by the verbal label.

Sample reproduced figures	Description presented	Figures presented	Description presented	Sample reproduced figures
	← Curtains in a window		Diamond in a rectangle →	
	← Bottle		Stirrup →	
	← Cresent moon		Letter 'C' →	
	← Beehive		Hat →	
	← Eyeglasses		Dumbell →	
	← Seven		Four →	
	← Ship's wheel		Sun →	
	← Hourglass		Table →	
	← Kidney bean		Canoe →	

Things you could do ...

Read the original article by Loftus and Palmer. See if you can find it online, or obtain a copy from your local library (they will order a copy if you provide a full reference).

Read other accounts of the research:

Two classic books by Elizabeth Loftus *Eyewitness Testimony* (new edition 1996, Harvard University Press) and *The Myth of Repressed Memory* (1996, St. Martin's Press), as well as *Witness for the Defense* written with Katherine Ketcham (St Martin's, 1992).

Research by Elizabeth Loftus is discussed in a chapter of *Skinner's Box* by Lauren Slater, a book which contains the background to a number of key studies in psychology though this has received some serious criticism (search online).

Watch a video on YouTube about the accuracy of memory 'False memory and eyewitness testimony' (http://tinyurl.com/bv9pv24).

...Links to core studies...

The issue of leading questions comes up elsewhere in this text.

* The study by **Samuel and Bryant** looks at the effect of questions on the responses of children to a simple cognitive task.
* The case study by **Freud** on Little Hans contains evidence from the child's father who put some very leading questions to Hans.
* Most controversial is the connection to **Thigpen and Cleckley's** study on multiple personality. Are the memories and the multiples created by the therapy?

Evaluating the study by Loftus and Palmer

The research method
This study was a laboratory experiment.

What are the strengths and weaknesses of this research method in the context of this study?

The experiment used an independent measures design.

What are the strengths and weaknesses of this experimental design in the context of this study?

The sample
American students were used in this study. In what way is this group of participants unique?

How would the unique characteristics of the sample in this study effect the conclusions drawn?

You might consider that America is an **individualist** culture, i.e. a society where its citizens are more concerned with individual gains than the 'common good'. This may affect their willingness to be influenced by leading questions.

You might also consider the unique characteristics of students – they are more intelligent and tend to have good memories, and thus might be less likely to be affected by leading questions.

Ethics
*What **ethical issues** should have concerned the researchers in this study, and how might they have dealt with these?*

Reliability
Reliability concerns measurement.

What aspects of human behaviour were measured in this study? How could the reliability of these measurements be assessed?

Ecological validity
Real-life eyewitnesses may be feeling scared or anxious.

How do you think this might affect their memory?

In this study eyewitness testimony was tested by showing participants video clips. The contrived nature of the task might affect the generalisability of this study.

In what way is this different to a real life accident? In what way do you think the tasks in this experiment were contrived or artificial?

To what extent do you think we can generalise the findings from this study to other situations, such as everyday life?

Snapshot or longitudinal?
Experiment 1 is a snapshot study. Experiment 2 is a (very short) longitudinal study because it takes place over the period of one week.

Consider the strengths and weaknesses of each design in the context of this study.

Qualitative or quantitative?
The data collected in this study was quantitative.

Explain in what way it is quantitative and explain the strengths and weaknesses of producing this kind of data in the context of this study.

Applications/usefulness
How might the findings from the two experiments be used in real life?

How valuable was this study?

What next?
*Describe **one** improvement to this study, and say how you think this might affect the outcome.*

There are no simple answers.

Evaluating a study requires you to think.

*We have provided some pointers here, linked to the **RESEARCH METHODS** and **KEY ISSUES** covered in Chapter 1 (Psychological investigations) and Chapter 7 (Key issues).*

You can read suggested answers on our website www.psypress.com/cw/ banyard.

Producing effective evaluation
When you produce your own answers to the issues on the left there are two things to ensure:

1 Contextualisation
2 Elaboration

The key to **CONTEXTUALISATION** is to ensure that your answer includes some information about this particular study. For example:

> *Question:*
> Outline **one** strength of the sample used in this study. **[2]**

2 mark question

> *Answer:*
> **STATE**: The strength of this kind of sample is that it is easy to get hold of the participants.
> **CONTEXT**: In the Loftus and Palmer study this would have been true because the study was conducted in a university so it would have been easy to just get some students to come in and participate.

The key to **ELABORATION** is the three-point rule (see page xii). For example:

> *Question:*
> With reference to the study by Loftus and Palmer, suggest **one** strength of conducting snapshot studies. **[2]**

3 mark question

> *Answer:*
> **STATE**: Snapshot studies allow the researcher to compare individuals or groups at one period in time to see how they may be similar or different.
> **CONTEXT**: Loftus and Palmer compared, in one snapshot, the effects of different leading questions on the memory of groups of American students.
> **COMMENT**: The alternative would have been to study the effect of each question on participants over a longer period of time, which would take a lot longer.

The cognitive approach

On pages 38–39 and 218–219 we have discussed the **cognitive approach**.

The study by Loftus and Palmer concerns human memory.

- In what way is this an example of the cognitive approach?
- Discuss the strengths and weaknesses of the cognitive approach using examples from the Loftus and Palmer study.

Loftus and Palmer: afters

Memory research after the car crash studies

At first glance the topic of memory seems to be free from much controversy. Nothing could be further from the truth and this topic has become a hot issue. Seeing glass that wasn't there (in Loftus' second **experiment**) suggests that we invent memories or to put it another way we have some false memories. Now read on.

Mis-identification

Experimental research have found that people can make errors when asked to identify someone who might have taken part in a crime. People were shown a grainy surveillance video of a man and told them that he had shot a security guard. Then they were presented with five mug shots and asked which one was the perpetrator. It was an impossible task, because none of the five mug shots really matched the man in the video. Nevertheless, every one of the 352 subjects identified one of the mug shots as the man they had seen (Wells and Bradfield, 1998). It seems that people are good at picking a criminal out of a line-up if he or she is there, but they are not good at being able to spot that he or she is not actually in the line-up.

False and recovered memories

Elizabeth Loftus is most famous today for her work on false memory. During the 1980s a number of therapists, mainly in the USA, reported that their adult clients had been recalling traumatic memories of childhood abuse that they had previously been unaware of. Many people were accused of child abuse as a result of these recovered memories and a number ended up in prison. Very few of the recovered memories were backed up with other evidence. Loftus, among others, became concerned about the type of therapy being offered and the quality of the memories. She came to believe that *some* of these memories were being created in the therapist's consulting room. It will not be a shock to the reader to say that this work is very controversial.

It is a sad fact of modern life that some children suffer abuse. They commonly find it difficult to talk about this and often only deal with it as adults, if at all. What Loftus is challenging is the memories that suddenly appear when the person is an adult and only in the therapist's chair. As she comments, people who suffer traumatic events have problems forgetting not remembering. If you want to find out more then search the internet for 'lost in mall loftus' and you'll find loads of articles and even some YouTube clips of Loftus talking about the research.

Lost in the mall

Can false memories be planted in people? Elizabeth Loftus believes so and conducted a study with her associate, Jacqueline E. Pickrell (1995) to see if they could demonstrate that memories can be planted. For ethical reasons they could not try to plant memories of childhood sexual abuse. They wanted to plant a memory that would have been distressing but had a happy ending. They decided to use a 'lost in the mall' story. They created a book for each participant that had stories from their childhood. Included in this was one made-up story about being lost in a shopping centre (mall) that was supposed to have been added by a close relative. It was, in fact, false. A quarter of their participants came to believe that this event had happened to them and they could recount features of the incident that were not part of the original planted story. In other words they had started to embellish the story and make it their own. The story was well and truly planted and started to take on a life of its own.

Loftus (1997) provides other evidence of false memories, from one of many cases from the US courts. Nadean Cool was a nursing assistant when in 1986 she received therapy to help her deal with a traumatic event that had happened to her daughter. The therapist used hypnosis among other techniques to dig out any hidden memories. The digging produced a remarkable haul of horrible memories. Cool came to believe that she had been in a satanic cult, that she had eaten babies and had sex with animals. She also came to believe that she had more than 120 personalities including children, angels and a duck. Some years later she realised that none of these events had happened and she sued the psychiatrist for malpractice. She was awarded $2.4 million in an out-of-court settlement.

Weapon focus

Johnson and Scott (1976) identified the 'weapon focus effect'. There were two conditions in her experiment. In both conditions participants heard a discussion in an adjoining room. In condition 1 a man emerged holding a pen and with grease on his hands. In condition 2 the discussion was rather more heated and a man emerged holding a paper-knife covered in blood. When asked to identify the man from 50 photos, participants in condition 1 were 49% accurate compared with 33% accuracy in condition 2. This suggests that the weapon may have distracted attention from the man and might explain why eyewitnesses sometimes have poor recall for certain details of a crime.

It might be that the witness focuses his or her attention on the weapon, so not attending to other features of the scene. This might be because of heightened arousal or because it is an unusual event (Wells and Olsen, 2003).

When people witness an event with a gun involved then they are less likely to be able to describe the characters than if there is no gun. You might well remember this page as the one with the gun.

Multiple choice questions

1 Which of the following was not a cue word in the experiment by Loftus and Palmer?
a Smashed.   b Contacted.
c Knocked.   d Hit.

2 The DV in the first experiment was:
a Estimate of speed.
b The verb 'smashed'.
c The question about broken glass.
d The film.

3 In experiment 1, how many experimental conditions were there?
a 1   b 3
c 5   d 7

4 In experiment 2, how many experimental groups were there?
a 1   b 2
c 3   d 4

5 In Experiment 2, participants were tested immediately and then asked to return for some more questions. How long afterwards was this?
a 1 day.   b 3 days.
c 1 week.   d 2 weeks.

6 In experiment 2, which group saw the most broken glass?
a The 'smashed' group.
b The 'collided' group.
c The 'hit' group.
d The control group.

7 Which of the following is true?
a Experiment 1 and 2 were both repeated measures.
b Experiment 1 and 2 were both independent groups.
c Only Experiment 1 was repeated measures.
d Only Experiment 1 was independent groups.

8 The conclusion drawn from Experiment 2 was that:
a The leading question creates a response-bias.
b The leading question alters memory.
c a and b.
d Memory is not affected by leading questions.

9 The participants in this study were:
a Children.   b Students.
c Teachers.   d Adults.

10 A demand characteristic may act as an:
a IV.
b DV.
c Extraneous variable.
d All of the above.

Answers are on page 247.

Exam-style questions

There are three kinds of question that can be asked about the Loftus and Palmer study, as represented here by sections A, B, and C.

See page x for further notes on the exam paper and styles of question.

Section A questions

1 The study by Loftus and Palmer used film clips of car accidents. Outline **two** ways that this might affect the ecological validity of the study. [4]

2 Loftus and Palmer concluded, at the end of the first experiment, that there were **two** possible explanations for why leading questions affect the accuracy of memory. Outline these two explanations. [4]

3 Identify **two** conclusions that can be drawn about memory from the study by Loftus and Palmer. [4]

4 (a) Loftus and Palmer asked participants to estimate the speed of two cars in a traffic accident. They used different verbs in the questions they asked. Name **two** of the verbs. [2]
(b) What was the effect of using the different verbs you identified in (a)? [2]

5 Loftus and Palmer used the same set of standardised procedures with each participant. Describe **two** of these procedures. [4]

6 (a) Explain the difference between the two experiments in the study by Loftus and Palmer. [2]
(b) Explain the reason why a control group was used in this study. [2]

7 Loftus and Palmer concluded that leading questions do affect memory. Describe **two** findings that support this conclusion. [4]

8 Loftus and Palmer used the experimental method in their study. Outline **one** strength and **one** weakness of using this method in this study. [4]

9 The study by Loftus and Palmer used an independent measures design. Explain **one** strength and **one** weakness of using this design in this study. [4]

10 (a) Describe the two samples used in the study by Loftus and Palmer. [2]
(b) Outline **one** weakness of the sample. [2]

Section B question

Answer the following questions with reference to the Loftus and Palmer study:

(a) State **one** of the hypotheses investigated in this study. [2]

(b) Describe the sample used in this study and give **one** weakness of using this sample. [6]

(c) Outline the procedure of this study. [6]

(d) Outline the findings of this study. [6]

(e) Discuss the reliability of the findings of this study. [6]

(f) Describe and evaluate changes that could be made to the way this study was conducted. [10]

Section C question

(a) Outline **one** assumption of the cognitive approach. [2]

(b) Describe how the cognitive approach could explain the inaccuracy of eyewitness testimony. [4]

(c) Describe **one** similarity and **one** difference between the Loftus and Palmer study and any other core studies that take the cognitive approach. [6]

(d) Discuss strengths and weaknesses of the cognitive approach using examples from any core studies that take this approach. [12]

The history of autism

Leo Kanner

In the 1940s **Leo Kanner**, a psychiatrist at Johns Hopkins University in the USA, recognised that a number of children sent to his clinic displayed similar characteristics which he named 'early infantile autism'. The word autism comes from the Greek for 'self'. Kanner was able to describe the following features that were common to all of the autistic children:

- A lack of emotional contact with other people.
- Intense insistence on sameness in their routines.
- Muteness or unusual speech.
- Fascination with manipulating objects.
- Major learning difficulties but high levels of visuo-spatial skills or rote memory.
- An attractive, alert, intelligent appearance.

Kanner's pioneering work was slow to catch on but is now the focus of much international research.

Hans Asperger

Hans Asperger was working at the same time as Leo Kanner and published a paper which described a pattern of behaviours in several young boys who had normal intelligence and language development, but who also exhibited autistic-like behaviours and marked deficiencies in social and communication skills. The condition, **Asperger syndrome** (AS), was named after Hans Asperger. Children with AS are deficient in social skills but, unlike other autistics, have a normal IQ and many individuals (although not all) exhibit exceptional skill or talent in a specific area.

Transporters

The Transporters are a series of stories for children that introduce them to emotions in faces and encourage them to pay more attention to human faces. The characters are based on transport which fascinates many children especially those with autism.

Theory of Mind

Theory of Mind (ToM) is the ability to infer, in other people, a range of mental states, such as beliefs, desires, intentions, imaginations and emotions.

Simon Baron-Cohen argues that having some difficulty in understanding other people's points of view is not the only psychological feature of the **autistic spectrum**, but it is the core feature and appears universal among individuals with autism. At one extreme, there may be a total lack of any Theory of Mind, a form of 'mind-blindness'. More frequently, autistics may have some basic understanding, but not at the level that one would expect from observed abilities in other areas.

Animal cognition

The psychologists who first coined the term 'Theory of Mind' (Premack and Woodruff 1978), were interested in animal cognition and believed that primates could read others' intentions. Subsequent research has shown that primates are quite sophisticated in their relationships: they can deceive, form alliances and bear grudges for days. Chimpanzees can even tell what another chimpanzee can and cannot see. But after decades of studies, no one has found indisputable signs that chimps or other non-human primates have a Theory of Mind. It seems to be a unique human quality.

'Reality to an autistic person is a confusing, interacting mass of events, people, places, sounds and sights. There seems to be no clear boundaries, order or meaning to anything. A large part of my life is spent just trying to work out the pattern behind everything.'

A person with autism (www.nas.org.uk)

What are the characteristics of autism?

People with autism generally experience three main areas of difficulty; these are known as the triad of impairments:

- *Social interaction:* difficulty with social relationships, for example appearing aloof and indifferent to other people.
- *Social communication:* difficulty with verbal and non-verbal communication, for example not fully understanding the meaning of common gestures, facial expressions or tone of voice.
- *Imagination:* difficulty in the development of interpersonal play and imagination, for example having a limited range of imaginative activities, possibly copied and pursued rigidly and repetitively.

Other features commonly associated with autism are:

- learning difficulties
- obsessive interests
- resistance to change in routine
- odd mannerisms
- repetitive behaviour patterns.

Causes of autism

There is evidence that some people have a genetic predisposition towards autism. The condition appears to have family links but it isn't purely genetic. It is likely that autism develops as a response to environmental hazards though it is not clear at the moment what these hazards are. Currently a lot of research is looking at what happens during pregnancy and just after birth. The likely culprits are diet, hormones or vaccines (other than MMR – see below).

Rising rate of autistic spectrum disorders in the UK

For decades after Kanner's original paper on autism was published in 1943, the condition was considered to be rare with an incidence of around 2 per 10,000 children. Studies carried out over the last 100 years have shown an annual increase in incidence of autism in pre-school children. The data below show how dramatic this increase has been:

1966: 1 in 2,222
1979: 1 in 492
1993: 1 in 141
2004: 1 in 110
2012: 1 in 110

(Source: National Autistic Society)

No one doubts that the diagnosis of autism is rising dramatically but there is some debate about why. Is this due to more cases and if so what is causing this? Or is it due to changing patterns of diagnosis so people are now receiving the label of autism who would not have done so in the past? There was a scare during the 1990s that the rise might be due to childhood immunisation (the MMR vaccine for measles, mumps and rubella) but there is no evidence to support this and a lot to challenge it (see the evidence at www.bmj.org).

What is it like to be autistic?

There is a surprising lack of first-hand accounts of autism especially as there are so many people with the condition. Frith and Happé (1999) have collected some accounts from autistic people of what it is like to be autistic:

'When I was very young I can remember that speech seemed to be of no more significance than any other sound ... I began to understand a few single words by their appearance on paper.'

'It was ages before I realised that people speaking might be demanding my attention. But I sometimes got annoyed once I realised that I was expected to attend to what other people were saying because my quietness was being disturbed.'

'There are two ways to be a nobody nowhere. One is to be frozen and unable to do anything spontaneously for yourself. The other is to be able to do anything based on mirrored repertoires without any personal self-awareness yet being otherwise virtually unable to do anything complex with awareness.'

Einstein, Newton and Asperger syndrome

It is a tradition of psychology to try to diagnose historical figures and explain modern conditions in terms of these people. Baron-Cohen and James (see Muir, 2003) believe **Albert Einstein** and **Isaac Newton** may have had Asperger syndrome.

Newton seems like a classic case. He hardly spoke, was so engrossed in his work that he often forgot to eat, and was lukewarm or bad-tempered with the few friends he had. If no one turned up to his lectures, he gave them anyway, talking to an empty room.

As a child, Einstein was also a loner, and repeated sentences obsessively until he was seven years old. He became a notoriously confusing lecturer. And despite the fact that he made intimate friends, had numerous affairs and was outspoken on political issues, Baron-Cohen and James suspect that he too showed signs of Asperger syndrome.

It's fair to say that not everyone is impressed with these diagnoses and suggest that Baron-Cohen and James are being selective with the biographical information they are using. They also wonder about the value of this type of speculation about historical figures.

Autistic savants

Daniel Tammet is an autistic savant. He can carry out mind-boggling mathematical calculations at fantastic speeds. Unusually for a savant, Tammet can describe how he does it. He speaks seven languages and is even devising his own language.

An estimated 10% of the autistic population (and 1% of the non-autistic population) have savant abilities, but no one knows exactly why. Autistic savants have displayed a wide range of talents, for example the blind American savant Leslie Lemke played Tchaikovsky's Piano Concerto No. 1 after he heard it for the first time and he had never had so much as a piano lesson. And the British savant Stephen Wiltshire was able to draw a highly accurate map of London from memory after a single helicopter trip over the city. Wiltshire's pictures are world famous and he has had a number of successful art gallery shows.

A few years ago Tammet broke the European record for recalling pi, the mathematical constant, to the furthest decimal point. He found it easy, he says, because he didn't even have to 'think'. To him, pi isn't an abstract set of digits; it's a visual story, a film projected in front of his eyes. He learnt the number forwards and backwards and, last year, spent five hours recalling it in front of an adjudicator. He wanted to prove a point. *'I memorised pi to 22,514 decimal places, and I am technically disabled. I just wanted to show people that disability needn't get in the way.'*

David Tammet created *Optimnem* which is a website company providing language instruction. His book *Born on a Blue Day* that describes his life as a savant has sold over half a million copies worldwide and has been translated into 18 languages.

www   Tammet's website can be found at http://www.danieltammet.net. Search online for 'David Tammet' and you'll find YouTube clips and articles about him.

Daniel Tammet

...Link to the core study...

The characteristics of people who receive a diagnosis of autism are varied and puzzling. Does this behaviour all derive from just one cognitive deficit? **Baron-Cohen et al.** used a task that would give an insight into the thought processes of young children and establish whether they have a Theory of Mind. The beauty of this study is that it provides a simple and obvious test of an interesting hypothesis.

Victor: the wild boy of Aveyron

In 1799, a boy was found naked in the Caune Woods in France looking for roots and acorns. He was taken by three sportsmen to a neighbouring town, where he lived with a widow, escaping after a week, but returning back to civilisation of his own accord. He was eventually taken to Paris, where he was cared for by **Jean-Marc Gaspard Itard** who set about trying to socialise the wild child. Itard was interested to see what were the basic characteristics of human beings and whether he could teach a child to overcome the deprivations of early life. The child, who was given the name Victor, was mute and had probably been isolated from human contact from an early age. Despite a lot of work by Itard, Victor only developed some very basic social skills.

The reason that Victor comes into this text is that modern commentators suggest he displayed a number of characteristics of autistic children. In particular, Victor:

• never learned to speak,
• had a 'decided taste for order',
• pulled people towards objects that he wanted to use,
• would not play with toys in a constructive manner.

Itard also noted that whilst he could instruct Victor into how to behave in a social context, when that context was repeated in a different location he would revert to his previous behaviour.

French film director Francois Truffaut was inspired by the story to make a film of the case in 1970 called *L'Enfant Sauvage*. You should find a clip on YouTube if you search online.

Baron-Cohen *et al.*: the core study

Simon Baron-Cohen, Therese Joliffe, Catherine Mortimore and Mary Robertson (1997) Another advanced test of Theory of Mind: evidence from very high functioning adults with autism or Asperger Syndrome. *Journal of Child Psychology and Psychiatry, 38,* pages 813–822.

See the
CORE STUDY
CHECKLIST
on page xv for
details of what you
need to know for
the exam.

In a nutshell

Context
It has been suggested that autism and Asperger syndrome are caused by the inability to develop a **Theory of Mind (ToM)**.

However, this is not supported by all research. It appears that adults with **autistic spectrum disorder (ASD)** do possess ToM. This is based on studies that show adults are able to pass second order ToM tests (see facing page). It is possible that they are able to pass these tests because the tests were designed for six year olds. They are not complex tests and therefore are much easier for an adult whose abilities have developed through experience.

Aim
In order to assess whether high functioning ASD adults do really have ToM a new test was devised, the *Eyes Task*.

Participants
Three groups of participants were tested:
- Group 1: Participants with autism/AS, normal intelligence, 13 males and 3 females.
- Group 2: 50 normal adults, age **matched** with individuals in Group 1.
- Group 3: Participants with Tourette syndrome (TS), age matched, 8 males and 2 females.
- Groups 2 and 3 served as controls to see if 'normal' adults could cope with the test, and also to see if individuals with other developmental disorders (such as TS) could cope.

Procedure
This was a **quasi-experiment** as the **independent variable** (autism/no autism) varied naturally.

Participants were given the following tasks:
- Task A: *Eyes Task*, 25 forced choice questions about emotion expressed in a person's eyes. This tested both basic and more complex emotions.
- Task B: Strange *Stories Task*, this was used to confirm (validate) the results from the *Eyes Task*.
- Task C: *Gender Recognition of eyes*, a control task involving face perception but not mindreading.
- Task D: *Basic Emotion Recognition Task*, a control task, participants had to identify basic emotions in whole faces to demonstrate they could recognise emotional states in a simple test.

Tasks C and D were control tasks only given to group 1. Group 2 only did task A. Group 3 did tasks A and B.

Key term: autistic spectrum disorder
Autistic spectrum disorder (ASD) includes *autism* at one end of the spectrum and *Asperger Syndrome (AS)* at the other end. All individuals share certain characteristics (such as lack of emotional and social skills, desire for sameness) but at the AS end the individuals have normal intelligence and language development whereas autism is associated with learning difficulties.

Key term: Tourette syndrome
Tourette syndrome is a neurological disorder which is characterised by tics – sudden involuntary movements or vocalisations (such as swear words) that are repeated. These tics occur in spasms and may appear many times a day or only occasionally throughout a year. An individual may have long spells without any tics. Individuals have some control over the tics but usually feel a compulsion to produce them. If the person tries to hold back the tics, this eventually leads to a strong outburst.

There are similarities between Tourette and autism:
- Individuals generally have intelligence in the normal range.
- Individuals suffer from the disorder from childhood.
- The disorder disrupts normal schooling and peer relations.
- Both conditions have been related to abnormalities in the **frontal lobe** of the brain.
- A genetic basis has been suggested for both.
- Both disorders affect males more than females.

Results
Mean scores for the *Eyes Task*:
- 16.3 (out of 25) for individuals with autism/AS.
- 20.3 for the normal adults, males did less well than females.
- 20.4 for the participants with TS.

Strange Stories Task
Group 1 (individuals with autism/AS) had more difficulty with this task, supporting the **validity** of the *Eyes Task* as a test for autism.

Control tasks
There were no differences between groups 1 and 3.

Discussion
Contrary to previous studies of adults with autism/AS, the results of this study provide evidence of a lack of Theory of Mind even in high functioning individuals with autism/AS.

BARON-COHEN *ET AL.*: THE CORE STUDY

Qs 2.4

1 If a person lacks a Theory of Mind, what does that mean?
2 There were three groups of participants in this study. Identify the experimental design that was used.
3 Give **one** strength and **one** weakness of this design in the context of this study.
4 Identify the independent and dependent variables in this experiment.
5 Identify the **two** control groups used in this study.

6 Identify the **two** control tasks used in this study.
7 In the *Eyes Task* (see facing page) the pictures were standardised. Why was this necessary?
8 In the *Eyes Task*, what were the 'foils'?
9 What does this study tell us about Theory of Mind?
10 The conclusion refers to 'high-functioning individuals with autism/ AS'. Explain what this means.

Testing for Theory of Mind

First order Theory of Mind test

There are a number of different tests used to assess whether someone has a Theory of Mind (ToM). One of the classic tests used is called the *Sally Anne Test*. In this test a person is introduced to two dolls – Sally and Anne – and a sequence of events is described (pictures 1 and 2 below). In the third picture the first order question is asked 'Where will she look for her ball?' A person with ToM would say that Sally will look in the basket despite the fact that they know the ball is in the box. They are able to separate what is in their mind from what is in the other person's mind.

A person lacking ToM would say that the ball is in the box. ToM enables us to recognise that others have beliefs about the world that are wrong (false beliefs).

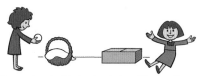

Sally puts her ball in her basket and leaves the room.

Anne moves the ball to her box.

Sally returns – where will she look for the ball?

Second order ToM test

There is a second question that can be asked, which is called 'second order' because it involves not just reading someone else's mind but interpreting what another person thinks about another person's thoughts.

Where does Anne think that Sally will look for the ball?

The *Eyes Task*

The *Eyes Task* consists of photographs of the eye region of 25 different faces (male and female).

The photos were taken from magazines and were **standardised**: same size (15 × 10 cm), all black and white and all of the same region (from midway along the nose to just above the eyebrow).

Each picture was shown for three seconds and participants were given a forced choice question – they had to select between two mental state terms printed under each picture.

These mental state terms were either 'basic' mental states (such as sad or afraid) or more 'complex' (such as reflective, arrogant, scheming, etc). The two terms for each photo were one mental state term and its 'foil', i.e. a term with the opposite meaning – for example 'concerned' and 'unconcerned' or 'friendly' and 'hostile'. The full list is given on the right.

The decision about what would count as the 'correct' answer was made by a panel of four judges (male and female) and confirmed by a further panel of eight raters working independently.

The target mental state terms that were used, and their foils.

No.	Target term	Foil
1	Concerned	Unconcerned
2	Noticing you	Ignoring you
3	Attraction	Repulsion
4	Relaxed	Worried
5	Serious message	Playful message
6	Interested	Disinterested
7	Friendly	Hostile
8	Sad reflection	Happy reflection
9	Sad thought	Happy thought
10	Certain	Uncertain
11	Far away focus	Near focus
12	Reflective	Unreflective
13	Reflective	Unreflective
14	Cautious about something over there	Relaxed about something over there
15	Noticing someone else	Noticing you
16	Calm	Anxious
17	Dominant	Submissive
18	Fantasising	Noticing
19	Observing	Daydreaming
20	Desire for you	Desire for someone else
21	Ignoring you	Noticing you
22	Nervous about you	Interested in you
23	Flirtatious	Disinterested
24	Sympathetic	Unsympathetic
25	Decisive	Indecisive

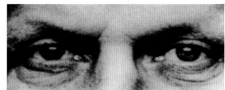

Examples from the Eyes Task. Right picture is serious vs playful, left picture is reflective vs unreflective.

Perceptual versus conceptual perspective-taking

There is a link between the Sally Anne test and the core study on Piaget's research (see page 76). The Sally Anne task involves conceptual perspective-taking, whereas Piaget tested perceptual perspective-taking using the three mountains task. Children were shown a model of three mountains and a set of pictures, and asked to choose which picture showed a doll's perspective. Three- and four-year-old children tended to choose their own perspective, rather than the perspective of the doll. These children are bound by the egocentric illusion, that is they fail to understand that what they see is relative to their own position, and instead take it to represent the world as it really is.

Such perceptual tasks depend solely on visuo-spatial skills and do not involve imputing beliefs to others. A study by Hobson (1984) has shown that autistic children cope with this task in line with their mental age.

This shows that the failure to cope with the Sally Anne task is due to the conceptual skills required.

A child (on the far right) is shown a model of three mountains and asked to identify the view that the doll (on the near right) would see. Young children cannot take the perspective of another. This is perceptual perspective-taking.

The detailed version

Context and aim

One explanation for **autism** is that the disorder is caused by a core **cognitive** deficit – an impaired **Theory of Mind (ToM)**. Such a deficit would explain the social, communicative and imaginative abnormalities that are characteristic of autism (see page 50).

However, some research (for example Bowler, 1992) has contradicted this, finding that adults with **Asperger syndrome** (AS) or with high-functioning autism can pass *second-order* Theory of Mind tests (described on previous page). This suggests that people with autism/AS may have ToM.

However, it may be that the tests used in these studies are not sufficiently complex tests of ToM. The tests were designed for six year olds and can only demonstrate that the adults tested have ToM skills equivalent to those of a six year old. This does not mean the adults tested necessarily have an intact ToM. In essence such tests produce a **ceiling effect** – whereby data cannot take on a value higher than some 'ceiling' and thus the task is not assessing abilities above the ceiling. It's similar to the effect that would be produced if you used a metre rule to measure everyone's height in your class – everyone would be recorded as one metre tall, an artificial ceiling because your measuring tool does not go high enough.

In the case of existing ToM tests the task is challenging for six year olds but too easy for adults, so they all pass even though they may not actually have a fully functioning ToM.

Happé (1994) developed a more advanced ToM test, the *Strange Stories Task*, pitched at the level of a normal 8–9 year old. In this task participants had to judge the mental state (**experimental condition**) or physical state (**control condition**). On this task both adults with autism or AS had more difficulty with the experimental task than 'normal' control participants.

Aims

Baron-Cohen *et al.* developed a new test – the *Reading the Mind in the Eyes Task* (*Eyes Task* for short). This test aims to assess mind-reading but Baron-Cohen *et al.* argue that this is essentially the same as ToM.

Interestingly, previous research has found that parents of children with AS do worse on this task than matched controls, suggesting that ToM deficits are inherited and predispose individuals to develop autism/AS.

The text of the study uses the phrase 'individuals with autism' rather than autistics because the latter term implies that autism affects the whole personality; a person with autism becomes nothing but their condition. A person who has measles is not a measlic, they remain a person with measles. The current trend is to avoid using labels such as 'autistics' or 'diabetics'.

Method

Participants

Three groups of participants were tested:

Group 1 16 people with high functioning autism (HFA) or with Asperger syndrome (AS). They were all of normal intelligence, which is relatively rare with autism (but Asperger syndrome is not associated with mental handicap). There were 13 men and 3 women. The participants were recruited using an advertisement in the *National Autistic Society* magazine as well as being recruited through doctors.

Group 2 50 age-**matched** controls (25 men and 25 women) with no history of psychiatric disorder and presumed to be of normal intelligence.

Group 3 10 adult patients with **Tourette syndrome** (TS), also age matched with Groups 1 and 2. There were 8 men and 2 women, mirroring the sex ratio of Group 1, all of normal intelligence. The reason for using people with TS was because of the similarities between autism, AS and TS, for example they all suffered a developmental disorder since childhood, these disorders disrupted normal schooling and normal peer relations, they all have a significant genetic basis (i.e. are likely to be inherited) and all have been associated with abnormalities in the **frontal lobe** of the brain.

The fact that participants in each group were matched means that this is a **matched participants design**.

First and second-order false belief tasks

All participants in GroupS 1 and 3 were able to pass the first- and second-order false belief (ToM) tasks. This meant that any failure on the *Eyes Task* could be attributed to problems with mind-reading problems beyond that of a six year old.

It was expected that only participants in Group 1 would be **significantly** impaired on the *Eyes Task*.

Procedure

There were four different tasks. Group 1 did all four tasks. Group 2 only did the *Eyes Task*. Group 3 did the *Eyes Task* and the *Strange Stories Task*.

1. The *Eyes Task*

See previous page for details. All participants did this test.

2. Strange Stories Task

Participants in Groups 1 and 3 were tested on Happé's *Strange Stories Task* in order to demonstrate the **validity** of the *Eyes Task* as a test of ToM. If it is a valid test then performance on the *Eyes Task* should **correlate** significantly (and positively) with performance on the *Strange Stories Task* (this is an example of **concurrent validity**).

3. Control Tasks

In order to check whether difficulties with the *Eyes Task* might be due to other factors participants in Group 1 were given two control tasks:

Gender Recognition Eyes Task identifying the gender of the eyes used for the *Eyes Task*. Such a judgement does not involve mind-reading but does involve face perception, perceptual discrimination and/or social perception. Therefore this controls for any difficulties in those areas.

Basic Emotion Recognition Task (Emotion Task), participants were asked to judge photos of whole faces which displayed the six basic emotions identified by Ekman (1992) (happy, sad, angry, afraid, disgust and surprise). This was done to check if difficulties on the *Eyes Task* were due to difficulties with basic emotional recognition. This task is not the same as the *Eyes Task* for two reasons – it involves whole faces and it tests only the basic six emotions rather than a fuller range of mental states. Such differences mean that it is easier to recognise emotional states on this basic task than on the *Eyes Task*.

Results

Eyes Task

The **mean** scores for each group of participants are shown in the table below (maximum score possible was 25).

	Mean score	Range
Autism/AS	16.3	13–23
Normal	20.3	16–25
TS	20.4	16–25

This shows that the normal and TS participants performed identically, whereas the autism/AS group were significantly less able to cope with the *Eyes Task*.

One thing to take into account is how many answers a participant could get right just by chance. If a participant had simply given **random** answers without even looking at the eyes Baron-Cohen *et al.* calculated (using Binomial theory) they should score 15 out of 25 by chance. On this basis it could be calculated that only 8 of the autism/AS group performed better than chance.

The range of scores for each group indicates that there was a ceiling effect for the normal and TS groups because some participants were able to gain full marks.

In the normal group the females performed significantly better than the males (mean 21.8 versus 18.8). The normal males were still significantly better than the autism/AS group.

Other Tasks

On the *Strange Stories Task* no participants with TS made any mistakes but the participants with autism/AS were significantly impaired. The results for this part of the study were reported elsewhere (Joliffe, 1997).

On the control tasks Group 1 performed normally.

Try this   2.7

- Try a version of the *Eyes Task* at http://glennrowe.net/BaronCohen/Faces/EyesTest.aspx or http://www.questionwriter.com/samples/eyesquiz
- You can try a different (and more difficult) *Eyes Task* as part of an assessment that looks at males versus female brains at http://www.bbc.co.uk/science/humanbody/sex/add_user.shtml
- Or construct your own test using magazine pictures.

Qs 2.5

1 Research has been conducted previously on adults with autism, finding that they had ToM. So why was the study reported here necessary?
2 Write a suitable alternate hypothesis and a null hypothesis for this study.
3 Explain a 'ceiling effect' in the context of this experiment.
4 In Group 1 there were 13 men and 3 women. In what way might this gender bias be important? (See the 'Key term' box for Tourette Syndrome on page 52).
5 The normal adult participants were 'age-matched'. What does this mean?
6 Explain why adults with Tourette Syndrome were selected as a control group.
7 Explain why it was desirable to use a control group in this study.
8 Explain why it was desirable to use control tasks in this study.
9 Explain what each of the control tasks were controlling.
10 Why did only Group 1 do the control tasks?
11 The tasks were presented in random order to participants. Why was this necessary? (Look up 'order effects' on page 26.)
12 Write a set of standardised instructions for the *Eyes Task*.
13 What did participants do on Happé's Strange Stories Task?
14 In what way is this study an experiment?
15 What kind of experiment is it?
16 Outline **three** conclusions you could draw from the results. (Do this by stating the result and then 'This suggests that …')

Biographical notes

Simon Baron-Cohen

His cousin Sacha Baron-Cohen as Borat

Simon Baron-Cohen *is co-director of the Autism Research Centre (ARC) in Cambridge where he is Professor of Developmental Psychopathology. His first cousin is the comedian Sacha Baron-Cohen, a.k.a. Ali G and Borat.*

Baron-Cohen is looking to identify the basic mental processes that are common to all cases of autism and that link autistic behaviour to its biological roots. In 1985 he made a breakthrough discovery of one such process. With his advisers Uta Frith and Alan Leslie, he used the Sally Anne test and demonstrated the unusual thought patterns of children with autism.

In an interview for Psychology Today *(Kunzig, 2004) he describes his motivation for studying people with mental disabilities. He grew up with an older sister who is severely disabled, both mentally and physically. Today she lives in an institution, is confined to a wheelchair and has a very low IQ.*

'Yet despite that,' says Baron-Cohen, 'as soon as you walk into the room, she makes eye contact, her face lights up. Even though she has no language, you feel like you're connecting to another person.'

Discussion

The results show that:

1 Adults with **autism** or **Asperger syndrome (AS)** were impaired on a **Theory of Mind (ToM)** test despite having normal intelligence.

2 Within the normal population, females do better on this test of ToM than males.

The autism/AS impairment is:

- Not due to low intelligence because performance on the *Eyes Task* was not correlated with IQ.

- Not the result of just any developmental 'neuropsychiatric'* disability since participants with TS were unimpaired on the test. (*neuropsychiatric refers to a mental disorder which has a neurological or 'brain' component).

- Not due to 'weak central coherence' (Frith, 1989) i.e. having difficulty interpreting context. Some psychologists have suggested that individuals with autism have difficulty dealing with some tasks because they cannot separate themselves from reality and answer questions out of context. In the case of the *Eyes Task* there was no context – it consisted of items that were relatively 'pure' ToM.

Additionally the results showed:

- No support for a link between ToM and **frontal lobe** processes. Previous research had suggested that the frontal part of the brain might be involved in ToM but the fact that TS participants had no greater difficulty than normal participants on the ToM task suggests otherwise. (Remember that TS has been associated with frontal abnormalities.)

Conclusion

The results of this study seem to provide evidence of ToM deficits in adults with autism or AS, contrary to previous research with adults. One criticism might be that the *Eyes Task* is not actually measuring ToM. However, this can be countered:

- The target words are mental state terms.

- The terms are not just referring to emotions but refer to mental states.

- The pattern of performance on the *Eyes Task* was mirrored in the pattern of performance on the Strange Stories Task, providing **concurrent validity**.

- The performance on the *Eyes Task* was *not* mirrored in the performance on the two control tasks, suggesting that poor performance was not due to using eyes as stimuli, or to difficulties extracting social information from minimal cues, or to subtle perceptual deficits, or to lack of basic emotion recognition.

Finally it should be noted that some of the autism/AS group hold university degrees which suggests that this aspect of social ability is independent of general intelligence.

Ecological validity

This 'very advanced test' of ToM is still much simpler than real life social situations. One important difference is that the *Eyes Task* is a static one whereas in real life social situations people are in motion. A more realistic task might involve making judgements of people in movies. Many of the participants with autism/AS reported that they found it very hard to comprehend what was going on in a movie – they couldn't work out who knows what and who doesn't, and why people laugh at particular points. The reason that movies were not used to test ToM is that comprehension of what goes on in movies involves more than *pure* ToM.

Mentalistic significance of the eyes

The *Eyes Task* involved interpreting the mentalistic significance of the eyes, which is similar to other problems exhibited by individuals with autism. For example, young children with autism have difficulty interpreting the direction of a person's gaze as a sign of what the person is thinking or intends to do.

Gender difference

The female strength on the *Eyes Task* may be due to genetic factors or may be due to the way girls are socialised differently to boys, encouraging them to pay more attention to what people are thinking. Either way previous research has not found a gender difference on mind-reading tests but this may be because previous tests showed a **ceiling effect**. Therefore the *Eyes Task* offers a new method of investigating this difference. (Baron-Cohen has increasingly become interested in such gender differences – see 'afters' on page 58.)

...Links to core studies...

The work on ToM is also relevant to the study on Kanzi by **Savage-Rumbaugh *et al.*** It is important for our understanding of the 'thought processes' of animals and machines. What do they understand? And what do they think we understand?

Related to **Piaget**'s views on cognitive development and the core study by **Samuel and Bryant**.

This study also illustrates the difficulties of studying children (see the studies in the **Developmental psychology** section).

Things you could do ...

Read the original article by Baron-Cohen, Joliffe, Mortimore and Robertson
http://docs.autismresearchcentre.com/papers/1997_BCetal_Anotheradvancedtest.pdf

Read:

About a high-functioning academic with autism – Temple Grandin http://www.guardian.co.uk/education/2005/oct/25/highereducationprofile.academicexperts

Books by Simon Baron-Cohen, such as 'Zero degrees of empathy'.

Autism is engagingly dealt with in the book *The Curious Incident of the Dog in the Night-time* by Mark Haddon.

Watch videos about Theory of Mind on YouTube, or watch the film *Rainman* with Tom Cruise and Dustin Hoffman, which explores the issue of people who think in unusual ways.

Evaluating the study by Baron-Cohen *et al.*

The research method
This study was a quasi-experiment because the IV (autism versus normal) was not something controlled by the experimenter.

What are the strengths and weaknesses of this research method in the context of this study?

The study used an independent measures design.

What are the strengths and weaknesses of this experimental design in the context of this study?

The sample
To what extent do you think the sample was representative of all people with autism/AS? Consider the sampling techniques used in this study.

How would this affect the conclusions that can be drawn?

Ethics
The participants in this study were all adults. However, there might be issues about whether people who lack a Theory of Mind are able to understand what is involved in the study.

What ethical issues should have concerned the researchers in this study, and how might they have dealt with these?

Reliability
Reliability concerns measurement.

What aspects of human behaviour were measured in this study? How could the reliability of these measurements be assessed?

Validity
The study uses concurrent validity as a means of establishing the validity of the *Eyes Task*.

Explain what this means and discuss how the control tasks were also used to establish validity.

Ecological validity
The task used to assess ToM was simpler than the real demands of a live social situation.

What are the strengths and weaknesses of investigating ToM in a way that is not representative of everyday situations?

To what extent can we generalise the findings from this study to other situations?

Quantitative and qualitative
The data collected in this study was mainly quantitative. *Explain in what way it is quantitative and explain the strengths and weaknesses of producing this kind of data in the context of this study?*

Some qualitative data was collected, related to the experience of the participants with autism/AS and watching movies. *Describe how this part of the study might be extended and explain the strengths and weaknesses of producing this kind of data in the context of this study?*

Applications/usefulness
The findings from this study might be used for theory or practice. *How do you think psychologists might apply the results from this investigation to developing new theories or to helping people in everyday life?*

What next?
*Describe **one** change to this study, and say how you think this might affect the outcome.*

> There are no simple answers.
>
> *Evaluating a study requires you to think.*
>
> *We have provided some pointers here, linked to the RESEARCH METHODS and KEY ISSUES covered in Chapter 1 (Psychological investigations) and Chapter 7 (Key issues).*
>
> *You can read suggested answers on our website www.psypress.com/cw/banyard.*

Producing effective evaluation
When you produce your own answers to the issues on the left there are two things to ensure:

1 Contextualisation
2 Elaboration

The key to **CONTEXTUALISATION** is to ensure that your answer includes some information about this particular study. For example:

Question:

With reference to the study by Baron-Cohen *et al.*, outline **one** strength of using quantitative data. **[2]**

Answer:

STATE: One strength of quantitative data is that it is easy to analyse and produce descriptive statistics such as the mean for different experimental groups.

CONTEXT: In the study by Baron-Cohen they compared the mean scores for each group on the *Eyes Task* which clearly showed that the participants with autism/AS performed less well than either of the other two groups.

The key to **ELABORATION** is the three-point rule (see page xii). For example:

Question:

With reference to the study by Baron-Cohen *et al.*, describe **one** similarity with any core studies that take the cognitive approach. **[3]**

Answer:

STATE: One similarity is that any research that takes the cognitive approach is related to mental processes.

CONTEXT: Baron-Cohen and his co-workers were interested in Theory of Mind, the mental process of understanding what other people are thinking.

COMMENT: Loftus and Palmer also takes the cognitive approach and considers memory, specifically how language can alter the way people remember things.

The cognitive approach
On pages 38–39 and 218–219 we have discussed the **cognitive approach**.

The study by Baron-Cohen *et al.* concerns autism.

- In what way is this an example of the cognitive approach?
- Discuss the strengths and weaknesses of the cognitive approach using examples from the Baron-Cohen *et al.* study.

Baron-Cohen *et al.*: afters

More studies on autism

The increase in the diagnosis of autism in this country has been matched by the expansion in research programmes in universities. Foremost among these is the Autism Research Centre (www.autismresearchcentre.com).

The Lovaas programme

During the 1970s **Ivar Lovaas** developed an intensive **behaviour therapy** for children with autism and other related disorders. The treatment is widely used but remains controversial not least because of its expense but also because of questions about its effectiveness.

What does the programme involve?
Lovaas recommends that treatment should begin as early as possible, and ideally before the child reaches three and a half years. This is believed to be necessary in order to teach basic social, educational and daily life skills. It can also reduce disruptive behaviours before they become established.

The treatment takes place in the home and consists of 40 hours therapy a week. This therapy is on a one-to-one basis, six hours a day, five days a week, for two years or more. Because the therapy is so intense a team of therapists needs to be trained for each child. You can see why it is so expensive.

The intervention programme progresses very slowly from teaching basic self-help and language skills to teaching non-verbal and verbal imitation skills. The treatment then moves on to encourage the basics of playing with toys. When the child can do these tasks they learn the basics of expressing themselves and how to interact and play with other children.

As with many therapies much of the research on the Lovaas treatment is carried out by therapists using the treatment. A review of the research (Bassett *et al.*, 2000) came to the conclusion that intensive behaviour therapy with children with autism had some benefits but the claims that they developed normal functioning could not be supported. This treatment is an example of the **behaviourist perspective** which is described on page 228.

Male brains?

Autism affects far more boys than girls. At the **Asperger** end of the **autistic spectrum**, the ratio is about 10 : 1. The sex difference, says Baron-Cohen, is *'one puzzle that has been completely ignored for 50 years. I think it's a very big clue. It's got to be sex-linked'* (quoted in Kunzig, 2004).

Baron-Cohen suggests that men and women think in different ways due to physical features in the brain. In particular there are two key abilities, empathy and systemising.

- *Empathising ability:* reading the emotional and mental states of other people and responding to them.
- *Systemising ability:* making sense of the world through categorising things, though this can take the form of seemingly purposeless obsessions such as plane spotting, or memorising train timetables.

In brief, Baron-Cohen's most recent theory is that autism is characterised by low empathising ability and high systemising ability. Baron-Cohen's theory goes beyond people diagnosed with autism and includes all of us. The essential difference between men and women, according to Baron-Cohen, is that women are better at empathising and men are better at systemising. These are average differences and there are plenty of male brains in female bodies, and female brains in male bodies. There are even female autistics, but there are many more male ones: in Baron-Cohen's theory, autism is a case of the 'extreme male brain'.

Baron-Cohen developed a *Systemising Quotient questionnaire*. Here is an example item:

When I read the newspaper, I am drawn to tables of information, such as football scores or stock market indices.
Strongly agree? Slightly agree? Slightly disagree? Strongly disagree?

Facilitated communication

Which hand is doing the pointing?

There are many possible reasons why an individual doesn't communicate very well. It might be that they don't want to, or don't understand or they don't have the abilities to produce communications. The carers of people who are not communicating often hope that communication is in fact possible if only a way can be found to do it.

Facilitated communication (FC) is a technique which is used to allow communication by those previously unable to communicate by speech or signs due to autism, mental retardation, brain damage or such diseases as cerebral palsy. It involves a facilitator who helps a patient use a keyboard by lightly balancing their hand above the letters; patients who have previously not communicated are able to recite poems, carry on high-level intellectual conversations, or simply chat.

Parents are grateful to be told that their child does not have severe learning difficulties but is either normal or above normal in intelligence. FC allows their children to demonstrate their intelligence by giving them a new technique to express themselves with. But is it really their child who is communicating? Sometimes people using FC make quite startling claims about messages from God or, more worryingly, childhood abuse (see page 48 on false memories). Most scientific observers are sceptical about FC but carers are more willing to believe.

Another study by Baron-Cohen

In order to be able to arrange pictures into simple stories a child has to imagine what the story character is thinking. Baron-Cohen *et al.* (1986) tested three groups of children (autistic, Down's and 'normal') on three types of stories; autistic children found most difficulty with the belief story but did better than 'normal' children on the mechanical story.

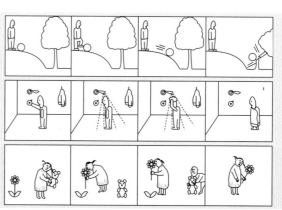

Mechanical story

Behavioural story

Belief story

Multiple choice questions

1 Earlier research showed that:
   a Adults with autism can pass second-order ToM tests.
   b Childen with autism can pass second-order ToM tests.
   c Adults with autism did not pass second-order ToM tests.
   d No participants with autism pass second-order ToM tests.

2 Which of the following tasks test ToM?
   a *Eyes Task*.
   b Strange Stories Task.
   c Basic Emotion Recognition Task.
   d Both a and b.

3 Which of the following is not true of individuals with TS?
   a Have normal intelligence.
   b Have suffered from a developmental disorder since childhood.
   c Have experienced disruptions to their schooling.
   d Are more likely to be male than female.

4 The control group in this study was:
   a Adults with AS.
   b Normal adults.
   c Adults with TS.
   d Both b and c.

5 The participants were matched in terms of:
   a Age.   b School experience.
   c Gender.   d All of the above.

6 The *Eyes Task* uses a form of questioning called:
   a Multiple choice questions.
   b Open questions.
   c Difficult questions.
   d Forced choice questions.

7 Which of the following is a 'foil' word for 'friendly'?
   a Repulsion.   b Hostile.
   c Happy reflection.   d Disinterested.

8 The validity of the *Eyes Task* was confirmed using the:
   a Strange Stories Task.
   b Gender Recognition Task.
   c Basic Emotion Recognition Task.
   d Both a and b.

9 The mean scores on the *Eyes Task* was:
   a The same for all three groups.
   b Groups 1 and 2 were similar.
   c Groups 2 and 3 were similar.
   d Groups 1 and 3 were similar.

10 A more realistic test of Theory of Mind than the *Eyes Task* might be:
   a The Strange Stories Task.
   b Talking about your own feelings.
   c Explaining what people were thinking in a movie.
   d Both a and b.

Answers are on page 247.

There are three kinds of question that can be asked about the Baron-Cohen et al. study, as represented here by sections A, B, and C.

See page x for further notes on the exam paper and styles of question.

Exam-style questions

Section A questions

1 (a) In the study by Baron-Cohen *et al.* why did they need to devise a new test of Theory of Mind? [2]
   (b) Explain what is meant by the term 'Theory of Mind'. [2]

2 In what way are individuals with autism the same as those with Asperger syndrome, and in what way are they different? [4]

3 (a) From the study by Baron-Cohen *et al.*, describe **one** of the control tasks that was used. [2]
   (b) Outline the findings from this task. [2]

4 Identify **one** similarity and **one** difference between the participants in the autism/Asperger group and the normal adults tested. [4]

5 (a) In the study by Baron-Cohen *et al.* Theory of Mind was tested using the *Eyes Task*. Describe this task. [2]
   (b) Describe a different way to test Theory of Mind. [2]

6 (a) Baron-Cohen *et al.* say that earlier tests of Theory of Mind produced ceiling effects if used with participants aged over six years. Explain the term 'ceiling effects'. [2]
   (b) Explain how such effects were avoided by the newer *Eyes Task*. [2]

7 (a) Explain what is meant by the term 'ecological validity'. [2]
   (b) Explain in what way the study by Baron-Cohen *et al.* may be described as lacking ecological validity. [2]

8 (a) Give **one** example of a word pair in the *Eyes Task*. [2]
   (b) Outline **one** finding from the *Eyes Task*. [2]

9 (a) Identify **two** ways that quantitative data was collected in this study. [2]
   (b) Give **two** examples of quantitative data collected in this study. [2]

10 What evidence from this study suggests that adults with autism do not have a Theory of Mind? [4]

Section B questions

Answer the following questions with reference to the Baron-Cohen *et al.* study:

(a) Outline the aim of this study. [2]

(b) Describe **two** examples of quantitative data recorded in this study. [4]

(c) With reference to this study, suggest **one** strength and **one** weakness of quantitative data. [6]

(d) Describe the procedures of this study. [8]

(e) Suggest how this study could be improved. [8]

(f) Outline the implications of the improvements you have suggested for this study. [8]

Section C questions

(a) Outline **one** assumption of the cognitive approach. [2]

(b) Describe how the cognitive approach could explain autism. [4]

(c) Describe **one** similarity and **one** difference between the Baron-Cohen *et al.* study and any other core studies that take the cognitive approach. [6]

(d) Discuss strengths and weaknesses of the cognitive approach using examples from any core studies that take this approach. [12]

Savage-Rumbaugh *et al.*: starters

Animal language

Communication is inevitable. We can't stop sending messages to other people and interpreting their actions. Humans also have a remarkable way of communicating using symbols which we call language. But what is language and can other animals use it? It is clear that we can communicate with animals because they will respond to us and we will respond to them. There is no dispute about this, but what do animals understand during this communication, and what messages are they able to communicate back to us? In language we talk about things that aren't there, events that are not happening now and not in a place near here. For example, we might say 'I went to the 2012 Olympics in London and dropped my choc ice on the Jubilee line'. Can animals use this sophisticated communication we call language or do they just communicate immediate events and wants such as 'give me biscuit now!'?

Kanzi (left) and his mother, Matata, two of the chimpanzees in this core study.

Early attempts to teach language to chimps

Vicki

Catherine and Keith Hayes (1952) tried to train a chimpanzee, Vicki, to talk. Their intensive training sessions used rewards to encourage her to make sounds and imitate the lip movements of the trainers. The chimp learned a lot of skills but sadly not the skill of using language. She did learn four sounds, 'Mama', 'Papa', 'cup' and 'up', but her use of them was not very language-like and the sounds were not very convincing either (Hayes and Nissen, 1971). The clear finding is that chimps do not have the vocal apparatus to talk to us.

Gua

A different approach to language training was used by the Kelloggs (*they sound like a pair of flakes – ed.*) who brought up a chimpanzee called Gua with their son Donald. As far as possible they treated the two alike. Gua seemed to treat the Kelloggs as his parents and showed a trait common in chimpanzees and children – disrupting their parents' love life. This meant that Gua was banned from the Kelloggs' bedroom though why he was ever let in is another matter. Sadly, Gua did not learn to talk. We have no information about Donald's tree climbing behaviour or liking for bananas (Kellogg and Kellogg 1933).

If you scout around on YouTube you can find clips of both Vicki and Gua.

Sarah

Premack and Premack (1983) raised a chimpanzee, Sarah, and taught her to use different coloured and shaped discs to represent words. She placed these on a board to make sentences. First she learned the symbol for an object or concept (for example, apple), then she put symbols together to form sentences (first 'Mary + apple', next 'Mary + to give + apple', and finally 'Sarah + to give + apple + Mary'). At the end she had acquired 130 symbols and could make sentences up to eight units long. However, Sarah did not spontaneously use language to ask questions although she would practise sentences on her own.

Washoe

The breakthrough study in the field of animal language was of Washoe (Gardner and Gardner, 1969). Washoe was born in Africa, around September 1965. She was taken to the US where Drs Allen and Beatrix Gardner adopted her for their research, naming her after Washoe County, Nevada where they lived. She was between 8 and 14 months old at the start of the project. Much later she moved with Roger and Deborah Fouts to Central Washington University where a special facility was set up for her and other chimpanzees involved in their language programme (see www.friendsofwashoe.org).

Washoe has been claimed to be the first animal to acquire human language. She was taught American Sign Language and it has been reported that Washoe could **reliably** use about 250 signs. 'Reliable use' was established when a sign was seen by three different observers in three separate spontaneous instances in the correct context and used appropriately, and then seen 15 days in a row.

Chimpanzees are remarkable imitators, and in the early interactions, Washoe was encouraged to imitate the gestures of the humans. She would be rewarded for her efforts with tickles! Later in the programme, when Washoe made an incorrect sign or a badly formed sign, then she would be encouraged to imitate the correct one. However, if she was pressed too hard for the right sign, Washoe sometimes became diverted from the original task, or ran away, or went into a tantrum, or even bit the tutor.

The jury is still out on whether Washoe developed language or not. The Gardners pointed to the range of signs and the situations she used them in, but others noted that she never developed a regular word order which is a basic feature of any language. The controversy did not affect her celebrity status, however, and her progress was avidly followed by millions of people around the world.

Washoe died in October 2007, aged 42. It is reported on her website that she died at home surrounded by her family and friends. She was probably the best known and best loved primate ever – truly she was the people's chimpanzee (© T. Blair).

Language and communication

Language: A small number of signals (sounds, letters, gestures) that, by themselves are meaningless, can be put together according to certain rules to make an infinite number of messages.

Communication: The way in which one animal or person transmits information to another and influences them.

Everyone agrees that animals can communicate with each other. The disagreement is over whether they can use something similar to human language to do this.

Aitchison (1983) suggests there are 10 criteria that distinguish communication from language including:

- arbitrariness of the symbols (the symbol is not like the object or the action it is describing);
- semanticity (the use of symbols to mean objects or actions);
- displacement (refers to things that are distant in time and space);
- it being used spontaneously;
- it involving turn-taking;
- it being structure dependent (the symbols are combined according to the rules of grammar).

ELIZA

Although Washoe and Kanzi respond to language it does not mean they understand it. For 30 years computers have been able to simulate conversation. For example, in the 1960s Weizenbaum created a programme called ELIZA that was able to respond to a user's input as if it were a non-directive psychotherapist. Expert judges were not always able to tell the difference between ELIZA's responses and those of a real therapist (see Boden, 1977). If you want some therapy from ELIZA, then just do a search for her on the internet and start the consultation.

Noam Chomsky, the respected American linguist, on animal language.

'It is about as likely that an ape will prove to have language ability as that there is an island somewhere with a species of flightless birds waiting for human beings to teach them how to fly.' (cited in Terrace, 1979)

Samuel Pepys (1633–1702), probably the first diarist

'I do believe it already understands much English: and I am of the mind it might be taught to speak or make signs.' (Diary, 24th August 1661)

Animals and humans

What is the difference between animals and humans? Are humans just another animal that is a bit more intelligent or is there a qualitative difference between us and them? This is a question that challenges scientific and religious beliefs.

One of the crucial differences between humans and animals is that we have language, and it is argued that this shows our uniqueness. The work on Kanzi and the other chimpanzees is important because, if Sue Savage-Rumbaugh and her team can show that the chimpanzees have language, then it breaks down one of the last big divides between the species.

The chimpanzees, like many other animals, can communicate and respond to messages but is this the same as language? Linguists argue that a true language is one that can generate novel messages. To do this you need to have a set of rules (a *grammar* or *syntax*) to combine symbols. One example of a rule is the use of word order to change the meaning of messages. For example, 'the beer is on the table' has a different meaning to 'the table is on the beer'. If Kanzi can put words in order she is showing the rules of grammar. And if she makes spontaneous communications then that would be a further marker of language. And if she can go into a pub and ask for a pint of beer, that will nail it.

Monkey suit

When we look at an ape are we misinterpreting what we see? Do we see an animal or do we treat them as if they are a human in a hairy suit?

Anthropomorphism is the attribution of human characteristics to inanimate objects, animals, forces of nature and others.

When we say dogs are loyal or foxes are cunning we are treating the animals as if they think and behave like humans. We often take this a step further and attribute human qualities to machines, for example talking to your computer as if it is deliberately messing you about.

When we are anthropomorphic we are assuming that the animals or machines have a **Theory of Mind**, that they know what they are doing and they are also responding to us (see the study on autism on page 52).

Thomas the Tank Engine is another example of anthropomorphism. We hope we're not spoiling anything if we tell you that tank engines aren't really alive.

Clever Hans

It is a common human error to overestimate the abilities of animals. Many dog owners will say things like 'he understands every word' about their pets. Unfortunately they are completely deluded as dogs do not understand language even though they learn to respond to 'walkies' and 'biscuit'.

There is a long history of making this mistake. In 1904 a scientific commission, including a psychologist, assembled to examine the intelligent horse known as Clever Hans. Russian aristocrat Wilhelm Von-Osten claimed to have taught Clever Hans basic arithmetic over a period of two years using skittles, an abacus and a blackboard with carrots for a reward. Hans gave the answers to problems by tapping his hoof on the ground. The commission were convinced by the demonstration.

Oskar Pfungst, however, carried out more tests on the horse and discovered that his skills were indeed clever, but not arithmetical. He found that Hans only got the questions right when Von-Osten knew the answer, and could be seen by the horse. Pfungst's studies showed that when Hans was counting with his hoof Von-Osten inclined his head downwards to see the hoof. When the correct answer was reached he would either straighten up slightly or raise an eyebrow or even slightly flare his nostrils. Pfungst himself was able to get the same level of performance out of Hans using these tricks himself. Von-Osten died a disillusioned man in 1909. It is not recorded what happened to Hans, though rumour has it he ended up in a frozen lasagne.

Clever Hans and his trainer Wilhelm Von-Osten enjoy some after-dinner chit chat about the runners in the 3.30 at Kempton Park.

...Link to the core study...

If only we could speak to the animals, what would they say? If **Savage-Rumbaugh et al.** can show that chimpanzees have the capacity for language they will have smashed the last great divide between people and other animals. Mind you, if they are successful it begs the question of why chimps don't use language on a daily basis. But then perhaps they do.

Savage-Rumbaugh *et al.*: the core study

Sue Savage-Rumbaugh, Kelly McDonald, Rose A. Sevcik, William D. Hopkins and Elizabeth Rupert (1986) Spontaneous symbol acquisition and communicative use by Pygmy Chimpanzees (*Pan paniscus*). *Journal of Experimental Psychology, 115(3)*, pages 211–235.

See the
CORE STUDY
CHECKLIST
on page xv for
details of what you
need to know for
the exam.

In a nutshell

Context
Past research has shown that **apes** can acquire language, but there are two key issues:

1. Whether chimpanzees can acquire language without any specific training, in the same way that human infants acquire language.
2. Whether animals can understand words. For example, a dog can respond to the command 'sit', but true understanding involves more than this.

Aim
The aim of this research was to investigate the human language capabilities of pygmy chimpanzees.

Subjects
The report concerns four chimpanzees:

- Kanzi and his sister Mulika were studied most intensively. They were both pygmy chimpanzees (also called Bonobos). Kanzi was 30 months old at the start of the study and Mulika was 11 months.
- Austin and Sherman belonged to the order 'common chimpanzees'. They had been previously trained and studied by Savage-Rumbaugh. This report uses the two common chimpanzees as a point of comparison.

Procedure
This study is a **longitudinal case study**, spanning 17 months. Kanzi and Mulika learned to use lexigrams by:

- watching others using the lexigrams
- through natural communication with the researchers, rather than being specifically trained.

Recording language acquisition:

1. *Record kept* of Kanzi and Mulika's vocabulary use during the period of this report indicating (1) correctness and (2) whether it was spontaneous, imitated or structured.
2. *Behavioural verification* was used to demonstrate that the chimpanzees did understand the symbols used, i.e. the chimpanzee responded to a symbol in an appropriate way. The **reliability** of **observations** was checked.
3. *Formal testing* at the end of the study to assess the chimpanzees' vocabulary. This was carefully controlled to rule out the effect of cueing.

*The **lexigrams** were displayed on a computer or, when outdoors, the chimpanzees had a board with the lexigrams on it. Each symbol brightened when touched. A speech synthesiser was added when it became apparent that Kanzi could comprehend words, so the appropriate words were spoken when a symbol is touched.*

Results
- Kanzi and Mulika used explicit gestures more than Sherman and Austin.
- Kanzi started using lexigrams when his mother went away (age 17 months). Mulika started using the lexigrams earlier (at 12 months).
- Both chimpanzees used a new term in an associative context first, similar to children.
- In total, during the period covered by this report, Kanzi acquired 46 words and Mulika 37.
- Kanzi also produced an impressive total of non-imitative combinations (about 2,500).
- All the four chimpanzees could match photographs to lexigrams but only Kanzi and Mulika could select the appropriate lexigram or photograph when prompted with the spoken word. Kanzi was the only one tested with the synthesised voice and did less well than with the spoken voice.
- Kanzi was also able to lead a visitor who knew nothing of the forest at the Language Learning Centre to the various sites on request.

Discussion
This report demonstrates a number of key differences between pygmy and common chimpanzees in (1) the ease of language acquisition, (2) the ability to comprehend spoken English, (3) the specificity with which the lexigrams were used and (4) use of syntactical structure.

Overall the results suggest that it is possible for a chimpanzee to spontaneously acquire human language.

Try this 2.8

Try learning to use lexigrams yourself. Some people should be researchers and others chimpanzees. The researchers should create a list of made up words such as 'TARK' and 'BLOP' and draw a symbol for each new word. They should also decide on the meaning for the word.

Now try to teach your chimpanzees to use this vocabulary.

Qs 2.6

1. Describe the two main subjects of this study.
2. Two common chimpanzees were also subjects in this study. What was their involvement?
3. How did Kanzi and Mulika acquire language?
4. Explain what 'behavioural verification' means.
5. Identify the **two** other methods used to judge language acquisition.
6. Explain why it is important to check the reliability of the observations.
7. Outline **three** results from this study.
8. Give **one** piece of evidence that supports the conclusion that a chimpanzee can acquire human language.

The detailed version

Context and aim

A number of research projects have focused on the ability of apes to acquire language (as discussed on the previous spread). Savage-Rumbaugh conducted her own research with two common chimpanzees (*Pan troglodytes*) called Sherman and Austin. This research led her to identify three steps in language development.

1 Associative symbol use: This is the ability to associate or link a symbol with an object. For example Sarah linked the coloured disc representing apple to that object and Washoe, using American Sign Language, was able to link the sign for tickle with that activity.

2 Referential symbol use involves directing attention to an object, i.e. referring to it. So there is a distinction between using a symbol to name (or label) an object (e.g. use the symbol for apple to identify that object) and using a symbol to refer to (or request) an object. Savage–Rumbaugh *et al.* use the following example:

'A child requests a teddy bear, but instead his mother holds up a duck and asks "Can you tell me what this is?" – the child is able to set aside her own interest in obtaining a teddy bear long enough to respond appropriately to the question, and as she does so, she does not become confused about which sounds are associated with the object she desires and which are associated with the object she is asked to name.'

So in this example there is a request (referring to the teddy bear) and a naming (being asked to name the duck). The point is that children can switch from requests to naming naturally, whereas apes cannot.

Savage-Rumbaugh found that Sherman and Austin could not differentiate between requesting (referencing) and naming. She found that they could name some things but not refer to them, and with other things they could refer to them but not name them. However, after special training, they were able to develop this skill and once they mastered referential naming, the next stage of representational usage followed naturally.

3 Representational symbol use is the ability to use language to stand for objects that are not present. For example, being able to respond to the request 'get your ball' is an example of association when the ball is in the room, however being able to respond to this request when the ball is in another room requires representation. Once Sherman and Austin did acquire referential usage, they then followed the same developmental path as children, i.e. representational usage appeared. For example, Austin:

- Initiated word games.
- Extended his symbol usage beyond the original context. He learned the word *scare* in the context of a game where an individual put on a mask and tried to scare someone else, and then used the word to refer to another chimpanzee who was screaming loudly outside the building.
- Began to acquire new symbols without specific training.

Aim of this study: understanding spoken words

One of the barriers in training apes to use human language is their difficulty in producing speech because they lack the necessary vocal apparatus. However, they may still be able to comprehend it. True comprehension is more than just responding to words (association), for example a dog can respond to the command 'sit'. Furthermore, children acquire true comprehension without any training, unlike dogs.

Additionally most animals cannot provide a differential response on cue. Dogs can produce a different motor response in relation to verbal cues (e.g. 'fetch' or 'sit') but have more difficulty producing a different selection in response to a verbal cue (e.g. select a ball from a group of objects when requested).

Thus it should be possible to demonstrate human language capabilities in apes by (a) needing no training and (b) being able to provide differential responses on cue. This report aims to demonstrate these abilities in pygmy chimpanzees (*Pan paniscus*), contrasting them with the abilities of common chimpanzees.

Method

Subjects

The principal subject was a pygmy chimpanzee (Latin name *Pan paniscus* and also commonly called Bonobo chimpanzees). Kanzi was aged between 30 and 47 months during the time of this report. This particular species of great ape is rare both in captivity and in the wild. Observational studies of *Pan paniscus* suggest they are a more social species than other apes and display more highly developed social skills such as food sharing. Other research has also found indications that they might be a brighter species. This would suggest they might be better able to acquire language.

A second pygmy chimpanzee was studied, Kanzi's younger sister, Mulika, aged between 11 and 21 months during the period of this report. Both spent several hours a day with their mother and were attached to her, but they appeared to prefer human company.

Two other chimpanzees (common chimpanzees – *Pan troglodytes*) are included in this study as comparisons – Austin and Sherman. They were part of earlier training programmes.

The small number of subjects is inevitable because of the time required in conducting an in-depth longitudinal study.

Biographical notes

Kanzi (on the left in the picture above) using a lexigram panel to communicate with Sue Savage-Rumbaugh at the Language Research Centre at Georgia State University, USA. The Centre is a 55 acre forest where Kanzi and a number of other chimpanzees live, including Kanzi's mother Matata. Kanzi was aged four at the end of this core study. Now he is in his 30s (typical life span is 40) and the alpha male of the community of **Bonobos**, described as an old patriarch 'balding and paunchy with serious, deep-set eyes' (Raffaele, 2006).

There is an interesting link with the core study on **autism**. In 2010 Kanzi fathered a son, Teco, who has been displaying autistic-like behaviours such as repetitious behaviours and avoiding eye contact (English, 2011). This claim leads to a further question as to whether humans are unique in experiencing mental disorders or whether such behaviour is something else, like language, which we share with our close primate relatives.

Sue Savage-Rumbaugh's work with Kanzi, the first ape to learn language in the same manner as children, was selected by the Millennium Project as one of the top 100 most influential works in cognitive science in the twentieth century by the University of Minnesota Center for Cognitive Sciences in 1991.

Method continued

Procedure

Creating the learning environment

Communication system – Kanzi and Mulika used a visual symbol system consisting of geometric symbols (**lexigrams**) which brightened when touched. These symbols were on an electronic keyboard, or on a pointing board for use outside. A speech synthesiser was added when it became apparent that Kanzi could comprehend words, so the appropriate words were spoken when a symbol is touched.

Rearing and exposure to lexigrams – Kanzi was exposed to the use of symbols, gestures and human speech from the age of six months as he watched the interactions between his mother (Matata) and her keepers. Kanzi was separated from Matata at two and a half years so she could take part in a breeding program. When she returned four months later Kanzi had developed a preference for human company.

Kanzi's sister Mulika was born nine months later and Kanzi enjoyed spending time with his sister. Mulika did not observe Mutata learning to use the lexigrams but she did observe Kanzi using them.

In contrast with Sherman and Austin, Kanzi and Mulika were not trained to use lexigrams. People around them **modelled** symbol use in the course of communicating with each other and the chimpanzees. The researchers emphasised their activities vocally and visually by pointing to appropriate lexigrams. For example, if they were engaged in a tickling bout the teacher would say '[teacher's name] tickle Kanzi' via the keyboard and also vocally.

Naturalistic outdoor environment – During the warmer months of the year food was placed at 17 named locations within the 55 acre forest used by the Language Research Centre (see map on facing page). The name of each site matched the food that was placed there (e.g. 'Raisins' and 'Hotdog'). To get food the chimpanzees had to go to these places.

At first Kanzi was shown photos of various food items and asked to indicate which he wanted to eat, and then taken to the right location. Within four months Kanzi could select a photo and guide others to the right place, sometimes carrying Mulika on the way. Later he could use the symbols alone and Mulika too began to use the symbols to initiate travel.

Indoor environment – Kanzi and Mulika helped in a variety of activities such as changing bed sheets, doing the laundry and preparing food. They played with dolls and watched videotapes of people they knew. All of these activities were similar to those enjoyed by Sherman and Austin.

Procedures for recording language acquisition

Data recording – When the chimpanzees used a lexigram indoors on the computer this could be automatically recorded.

Outdoors the record was made by hand and entered into the computer at the end of each day. This meant there was a complete record of Kanzi's utterances from 30–47 months of age and for Mulika from 11–21 months.

Each utterance was classified as:

- Accuracy – correct or incorrect.
- Spontaneous (no prior prompting).
- Imitated (if it included any part of a companion's previous utterance).
- Structured (initiated by a question, request or object). Structured questions were used to determine whether the chimpanzees could give a specific answer.

Vocabulary acquisition criterion – In order to count a word as being 'acquired' it was not sufficient that the chimpanzees produced context-appropriate words since this can happen without comprehension.

What was required was a spontaneous utterance which could be verified by observing what the chimpanzee actually did. This was called 'behavioural verification' and had to be confirmed in 9 out of 10 cases. For example, Kanzi might indicate he wanted to go to the tree house and this would be verified if he then took the researcher to this location, producing a positive concordance score.

In order to establish the **reliability** of the **observations** the researchers used one four and a half hour block of observations. They compared the observations recorded at the time ('real time') with a set of observations made from a video recording of the same four and a half hours. They found 100% agreement with regards to the lexigrams used and their correctness but one disagreement about whether it was spontaneous or not. In addition the videotape observer recorded an extra nine utterances.

Formal tests of productive and receptive capacities – At the end of the period covered by this report, Kanzi and Mulika were formally tested on all the words in their vocabulary. This was done formally to ensure that their performance was not due to contextual cues or inadvertent glances. They were tested by:

(a) Being shown photographs and then asked to select the right lexigram.

(b) Listening to a word and then asked to select the right photograph.

(c) Listening to a word and then asked to select the right lexigram.

(d) Listening to a synthesised version of the word and then asked to select the right lexigram (only Kanzi was tested).

Controls – A number of controls were used in the testing to avoid cueing. For example:

- The order of presentation was varied to ensure that the researcher didn't know what item was being tested.
- The alternatives were **randomly** selected on each trial.
- Synthesised version was used to avoid the effect of intonation when the word was spoken.

Qs 2.7

1 Explain the three key 'stages' of language acquisition (see previous page).

2 Explain the differences between the four chimpanzees in this report.

3 What symbol system did the chimpanzees use and how did they indicate their choice of symbol to the researchers?

4 How did the researchers communicate with the chimpanzees?

5 'People around them modelled symbol use.' What does this mean?

6 Explain what was meant by 'structured questions'.

7 The article says that context-appropriate words can be produced without comprehension. Think of your own example.

8 Give your own example of behaviour verification.

9 Why was it necessary to use formal tests?

10 Describe **one** of the controls used to avoid cueing.

11 Explain the importance of producing non-imitative combinations.

Results

Untutored gestures

Kanzi and Mulika naturally used gestures to communicate. Their gestures were often more explicit than those used by Sherman and Austin, for example, when Mulika wanted a balloon blown up she placed it in a person's hand and then pointed to the person's mouth and even pushed the balloon towards their mouth.

First use of lexigrams

Kanzi first started to actually use the lexigrams when his mother went away (age two and a half years). He immediately had a fair vocabulary which suggested that he had already learned the meaning of some of the lexigrams (by watching Matata using the symbols).

Mulika began using symbols at 12 months, much earlier than Kanzi. At first she used particular symbols (such as for milk) for a variety of all-purpose things such as asking to be picked up or requests for food or even for milk.

At about 14 months Mulika began using a number of lexigrams appropriately – her new words over the next few months were *milk, surprise, Matata, peanut, hotdog, cake, mushroom, melon, cherry, banana, jelly, go* and *blueberry*. Mulika occasionally reverted to using milk as an all-purpose communication.

Neither Kanzi or Mulika had difficulty identifying a lexigram when it was in a new position or on another keyboard.

Associative usage

It was observed that both chimpanzees started using a new term in an associative context first. For example, Kanzi first 'heard' the word *strawberry* when he was at the mushroom site. He and a researcher then went to the strawberries site where he tasted some. Initially Kanzi's spontaneous usage of *strawberries* was restricted to the mushroom site, i.e. where the word was first imitated. Eventually this extended beyond the 'initial acquisition routine' to context-free situations. It seems likely that children go through the same initial process of associative usage before being able to use symbols independent of context (i.e. representationally).

Progress

In total, during the period covered by this report, Kanzi acquired 46 words and Mulika 37. Mulika's initial rate of acquisition was slower than Kanzi's. This was probably because Kanzi had acquired some words in the period before his mother's departure but not produced them. Comprehension preceded production in the case of 63% of the words.

Combinations

One of the key characteristics of human language acquisition is the ability to combine words to produce novel meanings. Kanzi's multi-symbol expressions appeared quite early, within the first month of lexigram usage. Such combinations were far fewer than single symbol utterances. In total, over the 17 months, Kanzi produced 2,540 non-imitative combinations plus 265 which were prompted or partially imitated. All but 10 were judged to be appropriate and understandable; 764 were only produced once.

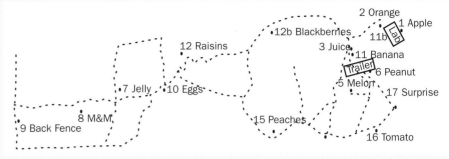

Map of the 55 acre forest at the Language Research Centre, showing Kanzi's food sites.

Kanzi's rate of non-imitative combinations was a lot less than Nim (another chimpanzee trained to use human language – see page 68) who produced 19,000 combinations during a similar period of time. Kanzi's three-word utterances never referred to himself whereas all of Nim's did (e.g. 'more eat Nim'). Nim's most frequent combinations related to food whereas Kanzi's were more likely to relate to games (e.g. 'chase bit person').

Imitation

Like human children Kanzi and Mulika imitated most often when they were learning new words. The proportion of imitated to spontaneous utterances was similar to children's – about 15% of utterances were imitation and 80% were spontaneous. Imitation seems to be a strategy used by language learners when they don't know what to say.

Formal tests

All four chimpanzees could correctly match photographs when prompted with the lexigram. However, only Kanzi and Mulika showed an understanding of spoken English. Kanzi was the only one tested with the synthesiser and performed less well with this, although even the researchers found it hard to identify the synthesised words.

Bar chart showing percentage success on formal tests

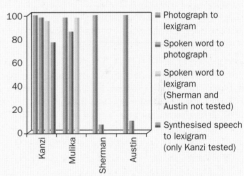

Travel plans

When Kanzi was about three years old a **blind** test was arranged with someone who had never been in the wooded area and therefore could offer no cues. Kanzi was able to select a symbol or photograph from a selection and then go to the correct place.

When he was showing the 'blind' visitor around he directed him to the back of the 55 acres, an area where he was not usually allowed to go, possibly because he just wanted to explore this area of dense bush. He then directed the visitor back to the trail. There were two locations not selected by Kanzi; the visitor used spoken English to ask Kanzi to lead him to these places as well, which Kanzi was able to do.

This test was not given to Mulika because, at the time, she did not like to travel without Kanzi.

General observations regarding symbol usage

Both Kanzi and Mulika made generalisations beyond the particular meaning of a word. For example, they used *tomato* to refer to different round red fruits.

Kanzi also used words in different ways. For example, if he said *juice* and then went to that location in the forest he didn't then look for the juice – indicating that he meant *juice* as the location and not the drink.

Sometimes Kanzi took the lexigram keyboard and went off by himself to use it, as if he wanted just to practise. Kanzi had also used the keyboard to indicate when he wants 'no play'.

Savage-Rumbaugh *et al.*: the core study *continued*

Discussion

This report is the first time the entire body of symbol usage and comprehension has been recorded for apes. Previous studies have been criticised because they included anecdotal records. For example, an **ape** might sign *coffee* when someone walks past with coffee (an appropriate usage) but might also sign the same word on occasions when it is inappropriate. Therefore it is not clear whether the ape has a true comprehension of the word. In this study the formal tests demonstrated usage and accuracy.

The number of apes studied means that it may be unreasonable to make generalisations. However, some preliminary comparisons can be made between species.

Difference 1 regards the ease of language acquisition. Kanzi and Mulika acquired language with greater ease than Sherman and Austin, who required extensive training. It took three years for a clear concordance to develop between what they said and what they did, something that was spontaneously grasped by Kanzi and Mulika. Like normal children, Kanzi and Mulika usually used words appropriately from the start.

Matata did not acquire symbols spontaneously and required even more training than Sherman and Austin. This suggests that there may be a critical age for the development of language in chimpanzees. In addition Sherman and Austin's difficulties might be due to their different learning environment (as compared to Kanzi and Mulika's learning environment).

Difference 2 is the ability to comprehend spoken English words. Kanzi and Mulika are the only chimpanzees recorded who have been able to respond to spoken language without any contextual cues. It is important to note that no one ever tried to specifically teach them to respond to English commands. They were spoken to normally at all times. This understanding of spoken English gave them an advantage with the keyboard because they understood the words first and then they just had to link the word to the **lexigram** in order to use the lexigram. This suggests that the way the pygmy chimpanzees acquired understanding of the graphic symbols (lexigrams) is fundamentally different from the way the common chimpanzees learnt to use symbols.

Difference 3 is in the specificity with which the lexigrams were used. Sherman and Austin were inclined to acquire broad differentiations, such as between drink and eat, whereas Kanzi and Mulika spontaneously learned to differentiate between specific words (e.g. between juice and coke). Even after Sherman and Austin were taught to differentiate, they often 'drifted' back into more general usage so that terms such as juice and coke were used interchangeably.

Difference 4 was that Kanzi could direct someone other than himself to do something (to request A to act on B where he was neither A or B). This is regarded as the beginnings of a use of syntax – the rules that govern the structure of sentences. These rules enable us to understand the difference between 'the beer is in his hand' and 'his hand is in the beer' (the different structures tell a different story).

Conclusion

Given that this study involved a very small sample, it is not possible to make any sweeping generalisations. However, the results suggest that at least pygmy chimpanzees have a greater capacity for human language than other species.

The fact that the capacity to use speech appears to be there, untapped, suggests that exposure to the appropriate culture might be all that is required. It might be that just one ape, who developed an innovative way to use sounds, might push the behaviour of a group of wild apes towards the development of language.

Participants and subjects

In this study we have described the apes as 'subjects' rather than participants. Psychologists used to describe all of the people they studied as 'subjects'. However, in the last decade opinions have changed. The term 'subject' suggests that the researcher holds the power in the research setting because he/she knows what the study is about and knows the procedures to be followed. This power relationship is reflected in the use of the term 'subject' for the research participants other than the researcher. The concept of a 'subject' may encourage researchers to be less sensitive to the needs and rights of individuals involved in research. In the 1990s there was a move to use the term 'participant' instead of 'subject' in order to reflect the much more active involvement of participants and to emphasise their important rights.

Qs 2.8

1   Four differences between the abilities of common and pygmy chimpanzees are described on the left. Select the one that you think is most important and explain why you think it is important.

2   How could one ape 'push the behaviour of a group of wild apes towards the development of language'?

3   What conclusion do you think is appropriate about whether this study shows that animals can use language? Provide evidence to support your view.

...Links to core studies...

This study has clear links to the autism work of **Baron-Cohen *et al.*** because the aim of both strands of research is to unlock our understanding of an individual by developing ways for them to communicate.

Central to the work on animal language is the concept of Theory of Mind. Do animals have a sense of their own existence and can they create a mental model of an another individual in their minds?

This study also uses the techniques of **behaviourism** (see page 228) outlined in the study by **Bandura *et al.***

Things you could do ...

Read the original article by Savage-Rumbaugh *et al*. See if you can find it online, or obtain a copy from your local library (they will order a photocopy if you provide the full reference).

Read:

Sue Savage-Rumbaugh's account of Kanzi: Savage-Rumbaugh, S. and Lewin, R. (1996) *Kanzi: The ape at the brink of the humand mind*. John Wiley & Sons.

About the Great Ape Trust, where Kanzi and his family live: http://kanzi-superstar.blogspot.co.uk

Watch videos about Kanzi (and other apes) on YouTube. Videos show the use of lexigrams and also Kanzi being tested with novel sentences. There is also a recent film about Nim, called *Project Nim* (played by himself).

Evaluating the study by Savage-Rumbaugh *et al.*

The research method

This research could be described as a longitudinal case study.

What are the strengths and weaknesses of this research method in the context of this study?

It was also an observational study.

What are the strengths and weaknesses of this research method in the context of this study?

It could also be argued that this study is a quasi-experiment. The IV is type of chimpanzee and the DV is success on formal testing.

What are the strengths and weaknesses of this research method in the context of this study?

The sample

Various chimpanzees were used in this study, belonging to different species. It was recognised as a small sample.

How would the size of the sample affect the conclusions that can be drawn from this study?

Ethics

Part of the process of teaching language to an animal is to enculturate them into the human world.

Is it ethical to teach human language to animals? (You might consider the costs and benefits.)

If pygmy chimpanzees share human characteristics (such as language), what are the implications for using them as research subjects?

Reliability

Reliability concerns measurement.

What aspects of behaviour were measured in this study? How was the reliability of these measurements assessed?

Ecological validity

Each chimpanzee may not have been representative of his/her own species, and may have had certain unique characteristics. For example, Nim seemed more interested in food than Kanzi, who talked about games.

How might such individual differences affect the representativeness and ecological validity of the observations in this study?

Snapshot or longitudinal?

This was a longitudinal study as it took place over a period of 17 months.

Consider the strengths and weaknesses of this design in the context of this study.

Qualitative or quantitative?

Both qualitative and quantitative data were collected in this study.

Give examples of both kinds of data and the strengths of each kind in the context of this study.

Applications/usefulness

If animals can learn to use human language, then what can we conclude about the uniqueness of human beings?

What next?

*Describe **one** change to this study, and say how you think this might affect the outcome.*

There are no simple answers.

Evaluating a study requires you to think.

*We have provided some pointers here, linked to the **RESEARCH METHODS** and **KEY ISSUES** covered in Chapter 1 (Psychological investigations) and Chapter 7 (Key issues).*

You can read suggested answers on our website www.psypress.com/cw/banyard.

Producing effective evaluation

When you produce your own answers to the issues on the left there are two things to ensure:

1 Contextualisation
2 Elaboration

The key to **CONTEXTUALISATION** is to ensure that your answer includes some information about this particular study. For example:

> *Question:*
>
> Outline **one** strength of the use of qualitative data in this study. **[2]**
>
> *Answer:*
>
> **STATE:** One strength of qualitative data is that it represents the richness of experience.
>
> **CONTEXT:** In the study by Savage-Rumbaugh the acquisition of language was demonstrated not just by counting the words and phrases (quantitative data) but also by giving examples of the kinds of things the chimpanzees could say (qualitative data). For example, Kanzi's spontaneous usage of *strawberries* was restricted to the mushroom site.

 2 mark question

The key to **ELABORATION** is the three-point rule (see page xii). For example:

> *Question:*
>
> With reference to the study by Savage-Rumbaugh, describe **one** weakness of using the case study method. **[3]**
>
> *Answer:*
>
> **STATE:** One weakness of the case study method is that it is difficult to make generalisations from individual cases as each one has unique characteristics.
>
> **CONTEXT:** The two chimpanzees in this study were different to 'normal' chimpanzees because they had been reared in a language environment whereas other members of their species are reared in their natural (wild) environment.
>
> **COMMENT:** This means that we cannot generalise from this study to how all pygmy chimpanzees in the wild would behave.

3 mark question

The cognitive approach

On pages 38–39 and 218–219 we have discussed the **cognitive approach**.

The study by Savage-Rumbaugh *et al.* concerns language.

- In what way is this an example of the cognitive approach?
- Discuss the strengths and weaknesses of the cognitive approach using examples from the Savage-Rumbaugh *et al.* study.

Just monkeying around

The jury is still out on animal language. There are strong supporters of the view that the chimps are using language and equally strong critics of this view. Maybe we want to believe in it too much (a good scientist is also sceptical).

Nim Chimpsky

Nim is another famous chimpanzee (mentioned in the core study). He was studied by **Herbert Terrace** (1979). Nim Chimpsky (named after the linguistics expert, **Noam Chomsky**) learnt 125 different signs and put them together in combinations. However, when Terrace examined the tapes of all of Nim's communications he was disappointed to find a marked difference between Nim's communication and child language.

1 There was no increase in the length of Nim's communications (children show a steady increase).

2 Only 12% of Nim's communications were spontaneous (children initiate more communications than they respond to).

3 Imitation increased (it declines in children) as language developed.

4 Nim made frequent interruptions and did not learn to take turns (very young children learn to take turns).

Although Terrace set out to **replicate** the Washoe study (see page 60) he was not able to find any evidence that Nim was using anything like human language. Nim could communicate to get things he wanted, but not to communicate ideas or thoughts or meanings. A pigeon could be taught the same skill using the techniques of **operant conditioning** (see page 229).

A good illustration of the limitations of Nim's communication can be seen in his longest recorded sentence, *'Give orange me give eat orange me eat orange give me eat orange give me you.'* It's not just that it doesn't resemble a Shakespearean sonnet, but it doesn't resemble the language of a toddler.

Terrace concludes his paper by writing:

'Sequences of signs, produced by Nim and by other apes, may resemble the first multiword sequences produced by children. But unless alternative explanations of an ape's combination of signs are eliminated, in particular the habit of partially imitating teachers' recent utterances, there is no reason to regard an ape's utterance as a sentence' (Terrace et al., 1979).

The question of animal language remains controversial because **replication** studies are difficult to carry out. The key theoretical issue concerns whether the animals are learning the rules of a language or just learning to imitate for rewards.

> *'That which distinguishes man from the lower animals is not the understanding of articulate sounds, for as everyone knows, dogs understand many words and sentences'* Charles Darwin *'Descent of Man'* (1871).

Kanzi or can't he?

Remarkable animals have always been able to capture the public imagination. The example of Clever Hans (see page 61) shows how easy it is to overestimate what they can do. At the Kanzi website (www. greatapetrust.org/bonobo/meet/kanzi.php) it is possible to see another example of this. They claim that *'his vocabulary includes more than 500 words! His comprehension of spoken language is at least equivalent to that of a two-and-a-half-year-old child.'*

The most famous feature of bonobos is that they are very sexually active. Sex plays a big part in bonobo daily life and is used as a greeting, a way of resolving conflicts, a way of making up with another individual after a conflict and a form of bartering for food and treats.

Kanzi's social behaviour does not appear to be recorded on the website so we have no idea if he has used his communication skills to help make friends. We are told, however, that Kanzi's achievements are not limited to language, but include tool use and tool manufacturing. According to the great ape trust website, *'Kanzi has shown skills as a stone tool maker and he is very proud of his ability to flake Oldowan style cutting knives. Kanzi's stone knives are very sharp and he's able to cut hide and thick ropes with them.'*

The website goes on to say that Kanzi has also demonstrated his unspecified and musical skills, having played with Sir Paul McCartney and Peter Gabriel. It is not recorded what songs they played together nor whether he engaged with traditional bonobo behaviour with them afterwards.

Kanzi is supported by the Great Ape Trust and at www.greatapetrust.org you will find a load of information, including images and videos of Kanzi and Savage-Rumbaugh. There is also a Great Ape Trust channel on YouTube.

Talking to pets

Millions of pet owners will tell you their animal 'understands every word I say'. Check this out with the dog translation device. It is called the *Bowlingual* and it claims to be able to interpret about 200 phrases or words – grouped in six different emotional categories: fun, frustration, menace, sorrow, demand and self-expression.

The inventors of the Bowlingual were awarded the 2002 IgNoble Peace Prize (like a Nobel Prize, but not quite) for promoting peace and harmony between species (see www.improb.com).

So can other animals really acquire human language skills?

Despite the obvious fun of the Bowlingual the simple fact is that your pets can not communicate with you. They have no problems hearing words that we use and recognising them but they do not understand them. What they do is to learn an association (see the key issue on **behaviourism**) between specific words and specific activities (like going for a walk) or other rewards (like food).

This repertoire of words can become quite extensive, maybe even as much as 20–30 words or more but this is not language comprehension. For example, if you say: 'Fang lets go out and have a nice walk in the park and chase rabbits', then what Fang hears is most likely 'FANG blah blah blah WALK blah blah blah' and this is enough to get Fang jumping around the kitchen with excitement. And the fact that you picked up the lead and ball is also a big clue to the mutt.

Fang can also probably respond to the non-verbal emotional tones you use when you say the words and is able to make different responses to your different emotional states. It is a big jump to think that the animal understands your emotional state but it is clear that it can recognise the change and respond to it.

Our willingness to believe in the intelligence of our pets is another example of animism or anthropomorphism (see page 61).

Multiple choice questions

1 Kanzi belonged to which species:
 a Old world chimpanzees.
 b Pygmy chimpanzees.
 c Forest chimpanzees.
 d Common chimpanzees.

2 Kanzi's mother was called:
 a Mulika.   b Austin.
 c Matata.   c Mamosa.

3 The symbol system that was used with the chimpanzees was:
 a Flexiforms.   b Lexiforms.
 c Flexigrams.   d Lexigrams.

4 Which of the following is not a name of one of the sites in the forest?
 a apple.   b campfire.
 c peaches.   d raisins.

5 In total how many words did Kanzi learn during the period of this report?
 a 41   b 43
 c 46   d 53

6 Which chimpanzee had the fastest initial rate of acquisition of language?
 a Kanzi.   b Mulika.
 c Matata.   c Austin.

7 Which of the following is true for both the pygmy chimpanzees and children?
 a They imitated more words than they produced spontaneously.
 b A new term was used in an associative context first.
 c They preferred to use words related to games rather than food.
 d All of the above.

8 How many months old was Mulika at the end of the study?
 a 21   b 25
 c 30   d 47

9 One of the formal tests of comprehension required the chimpanzees to:
 a Select the right lexigram for a photograph.
 b Combine lexigrams.
 c Lead a researcher around the forest.
 d Speak English.

10 Which of the following is not a difference between the pygmy and common chimpanzees?
 a The ease of language acquisition.
 b The ability to use lexigrams in a specific context.
 c The ability to understand spoken English words.
 d The ability to use lexigrams to communicate.

Answers are on page 247.

> There are three kinds of question that can be asked about the Savage-Rumbaugh *et al.* study, as represented here by sections A, B, and C.
>
> See page x for further notes on the exam paper and styles of question.

Exam-style questions

Section A questions

1 From the study by Savage-Rumbaugh *et al.* outline **two** methods that were used to record the lexigrams used by the chimpanzees. [4]

2 Describe **two** differences between the language acquisition of pygmy chimpanzees and common chimpanzees. [4]

3 Savage-Rumbaugh *et al.* claim that Kanzi and Mulika were exposed to language in a different way to Sherman and Austin.
 (a) Explain in what way this was different. [2]
 (b) How might this difference have affected their development of language? [2]

4 (a) Savage-Rumbaugh *et al.* conclude that Kanzi's use of language might be 'a precursor of syntactical structure'. Explain what is meant by 'syntactical'. [2]
 (b) Describe **one** other conclusion from the study by Savage-Rumbaugh *et al.* [2]

5 Identify **two** similarities between Kanzi's acquisition of language and the way children acquire language. [4]

6 (a) Savage-Rumbaugh *et al.* used formal tests with the chimpanzees. Why were such tests necessary? [2]
 (b) Describe **one** of the formal tests that was used to test Kanzi. [2]

7 In the study by Savage-Rumbaugh *et al.* explain the criterion used to decide whether a chimpanzee had acquired true comprehension of a word. [4]

8 In the Savage-Rumbaugh study quantitative data was gathered.
 (a) Identify **two** methods used to collect this quantitative data. [2]
 (b) Give **two** examples of the quantitative data that was collected in this study. [2]

9 The study by Savage-Rumbaugh involved two subjects who were studied over a long period of time.
 (a) Describe the subjects studied by Savage-Rumbaugh. [2]
 (b) Explain why these subjects may not have been representative of their own species. [2]

10 In the study by Savage-Rumbaugh qualitative data was recorded.
 (a) Describe **one** example of qualitative data that was recorded. [2]
 (b) Give **one** advantage of using qualitative data. [2]

Section B questions

Answer the following questions with reference to the Savage-Rumbaugh *et al.* study:

(a) Briefly outline the previous research or event which was the stimulus for this study. [2]

(b) Describe **two** ethical issues raised by this study. [6]

(c) Give **two** strengths of the case study method as used in this study. [6]

(d) Give **two** weaknesses of the case study method as used in this study. [6]

(e) Outline the results of this study. [8]

(f) Suggest how this study could be improved. Give reasons for your answer. [8]

Section C questions

(a) Outline **one** assumption of the cognitive approach. [2]

(b) Describe how the cognitive approach could explain language acquisition in apes. [4]

(c) Describe **one** similarity and **one** difference between the Savage-Rumbaugh *et al.* study and any other core studies that take the cognitive approach. [6]

(d) Discuss strengths and weaknesses of the cognitive approach using examples from any core studies that take this approach. [12]

Exam-style questions

The example exam-style questions here are set out like the exam but in Section A of the exam there will be only one question on each of the three cognitive core studies, i.e. three cognitive questions, each worth 4 marks in total.

Section A

1 In the study by Loftus and Palmer, the participants were shown film clips of car accidents.

(a) Describe **two** differences between witnessing these film clips and witnessing a real accident. [2]
(b) For each difference, say how this might affect the results of the study. [2]

Stig's answer

(a) One difference is that the film clips weren't real. Another difference is that people are scared in real life but wouldn't be scared in a lab.
(b) The fact that they weren't real means that people don't react like they would in real life. Being less scared might mean their memories could be better.

Chardonnay's answer

(a) The first difference is that which means that people don't behave like they do in real life.
(b) This means that the results can't be generalised to help us understand eyewitness testimony.

Teacher's comments

Don't just repeat the question, Stig. Of course the clips weren't real. Your suggestion about the absence of fear in the laboratory is a good point, so one mark for part (a). In part (b) of your answer only the second sentence is creditworthy – the first sentence doesn't say how the results would be affected.

Chardonnay, your answer for part (a) is OK but only just. You really should have referred to something in the study such as films clips or accidents whereas your answer could apply to any study. In parts (a) and (b) you have lost marks because there is no second difference. Other factors which would be important would include the effect of emotional arousal or being distracted by other events. Both of these might reduce the accuracy of recall – though some research suggests that emotion enhances memory (e.g. flashbulb memories).

Stig (1 + 1 out of 4 marks) Chardonnay (1 + 1 out of 4 marks)

2 In the study by Savage-Rumbaugh *et al*.

(a) Outline **one** similarity between the way that Kanzi acquired language and the way a child would acquire language. [2]
(b) Outline **one** difference between the way that Kanzi acquired language and the way a child would acquire language. [2]

Stig's answer

(a) It was similar because Kanzi first of all used words in an associative context which is like what young children do.
(b) It was different because she didn't learn that much in 17 months. Human children learn language very quickly and this is quite slow.

Chardonnay's answer

(a) One similarity was that Kanzi learned the lexigrams spontaneously without any specific training. He learned it just be watching his mother and also communicating with the researchers.
(b) One difference was that Kanzi didn't speak the words.

Teacher's comments

Both Stig and Chardonnay have provided clear similarities and would receive the full 2 marks. There are a large range of other similarities to choose from including the use of imitation and combination of words to form novel utterances.

In terms of the differences, Stig has provided an adequate answer (though he has made one of the most common (though trivial) mistakes in referring to Kanzi as a 'she' (Kanzi is male). Chardonnay has slipped up. It is true that Kanzi didn't speak the words and children do – but the question focuses on a difference in the way language is acquired, not just a difference. With some elaboration this could have been turned into a fully creditworthy answer, for example 'One difference was that Kanzi had to be taught using symbols rather than listening to and producing spoken words'.

Stig (2 + 2 out of 4 marks) Chardonnay (2 + 0 out of 4 marks)

3 Loftus and Palmer reported their results for the second experiment in a table similar to the one below. Describe **two** conclusions that could be drawn from this data. [4]

Table 1. Response to the question 'Did you see any broken glass?'

Response	Verb condition		
	Smashed	Hit	Control
Yes	16	7	6
No	34	43	44

Stig's answer

More people were affected by the word smashed and less people were affected by the word hit.

Chardonnay's answer

Conclusion 1: Leading questions alter what we remember.

Conclusion 2: Even people who are not asked a leading question make mistakes in what they remember.

Teacher's comments

This is not two points, Stig. It is the same point said backwards. You could also be more specific than just saying they were 'affected'. Just look at Chardonnay's answer, she's got the right idea. She makes two good points, especially the second one which is commonly missed when people describe this study.

Stig (1 + 0 out of 4 marks) Chardonnay (1 + 2 out of 4 marks)

4   In the study by Baron-Cohen *et al.*, the autism/Asperger syndrome group was compared with two other groups of adults.

  (a) Describe the other two groups of adults. [2]
  (b) Explain why it was necessary to have these comparison groups. [2]

Stig's answer

(a) The groups were autistic, normal and Tourette sydrome. In the first group there were 16 high functioning adults with autism or Asperger. In the normal group there were 50 adults who were age-matched and the gender split was even. In the TS group there were 10 adults with more males to mirror the gender split in group 1. All participants had normal IQ.

(b) It meant you had a way of comparing the performance of the autistic/AS group on the Eyes Task.

Chardonnay's answer

(a) Normal adults and adults with Tourette syndrome.

(b) You needed to have other groups so you could see if the autistic spectrum participants were different in terms of Theory of Mind. The groups were all similar in age and intelligence so that couldn't be the explanation for any difference. The TS participants had a developmental disorder so that couldn't be an explanation. The only difference between the groups was the lack of social competence in the autism/Aspergers group.

Teacher's comments

Part (a) You're really doing well now, Stig. Unfortunately you only need to write a couple of phrases to get all the marks and you didn't need to include a description of the autism/Asperger group. Chardonnay has saved precious time by answering the question simply but sufficiently for full marks.

Part (b) This isn't an easy question to answer – you may well understand but find it hard to put your thoughts into words (which is why practice is so important). Stig hasn't quite managed to explain himself clearly but there is certainly enough for one mark. Chardonnay has expressed herself well for the full two marks. Comparison groups are used to control for extraneous variables that might act as an alternative independent variable, for example inability to score well on the *Eyes Task* might be due to general developmental delay, therefore we need to control for this by having some participants (those with Tourette syndrome) with the same problem. It also might be that all adults find this task difficult therefore we need to control for this by having a group of normal adults as a comparison.

Stig (2 + 2 out of 4 marks) Chardonnay (2 + 2 out of 4 marks)

5   In the study by Baron-Cohen *et al.* the *Eyes Task* tested Theory of Mind.

  (a) Explain what is meant by Theory of Mind. [2]
  (b) Describe **one** difficulty that might be experienced by someone in everyday life who does not have a Theory of Mind. [2]

Stig's answer

(a) 'Theory of Mind' is having a theory about what is in someone else's mind, knowing what they are thinking.

(b) If you haven't got a Theory of Mind you don't know what other people are thinking.

Chardonnay's answer

(a) 'Theory of Mind' refers to the ability to represent the mental states of another person and understand what they are likely to be thinking.

(b) One difficulty that might arise would be having problems understanding what is going on in a movie, like understanding why someone has got annoyed with someone else.

Teacher's comments

Part (a) asks for a simple definition of 'Theory of Mind'. We can't know what someone else is thinking but we can build up a model in our heads so we can guess what people will think and say. Chardonnay's answer is clear and precise and worth all the marks. Stig has had a good go but maybe will only get 1 mark for part (a).

There are a number of everyday difficulties that arise if you do not have a Theory of Mind, for example social interactions with others or understanding a book or a movie. Stig has not given any example of everyday life – he really has just repeated his answer to part (a). Chardonnay's answer is correct and contains sufficient detail for two marks.

Stig (1 + 0 out of 4 marks) Chardonnay (2 + 2 out of 4 marks)

6   In the study by Savage-Rumbaugh *et al.* the chimpanzees communicated with the researchers using lexigrams.

  (a) Why did the chimpanzees use lexigrams rather than spoken language? [2]
  (b) Explain **one** method used by Savage-Rumbaugh *et al.* to test the chimpanzees' ability to comprehend lexigrams. [2]

Stig's answer

(a) They used lexigrams because chimps aren't very good vocally whereas they are very good with their hands so they should find it easy to point at the lexigrams.

(b) One way this was tested was to show the chimpanzees a range of photographs and lexigrams and they had to match them up.

Chardonnay's answer

(a) Because it is easy to learn to use the lexigrams and the chimps don't actually have to speak.

(b) Comprehension was tested in lots of ways, for example the chimps were shown a photograph and asked to select the correct lexigram, or they heard a word in spoken English and had to select the right photograph or lexigram.

Teacher's comments

Stig's answer is fine for part (a) but Chardonnay's doesn't explain why lexigrams might be easier than spoken language. Early studies found that chimps can't vocalise very well. They don't have the biology for it. They are, however, good with their hands.

In part (b) Chardonnay has given a lengthy answer covering more than the 'one method' required by the question. Stig's answer is along the right tracks but is not precisely right because at any time there was always just one item that had to be matched with a selection of lexigrams or photos.

Stig (2 + 1 out of 4 marks) Chardonnay (0 + 2 out of 4 marks)

Exam-style questions

Section C

7 (a) Outline **one** assumption of the cognitive approach in psychology. [2]

(b) Describe how the cognitive approach could explain autism. [4]

(c) Describe **one** similarity and **one** difference between any **two** core studies that take the cognitive approach. [6]

(d) Discuss the strengths and limitations of the cognitive approach using examples from any of the core studies that take the cognitive approach. [12]

Total [24]

Chardonnay's answer

(a) One assumption of the cognitive approach is that humans behave rather like computers. In particular, the way the mind works is like a computer in that it has information inputted (stimuli), it does some processing (e.g. storing information) and it gives some output (e.g. recalling information).

(b) The cognitive approach would explain autism along the lines of a cognitive deficit. So, it wouldn't explain it in terms of genes, or biology or neurotransmitters, or brain areas, but in terms of some faulty information processing. For autism, a popular cognitive explanation is lack of Theory of Mind (ToM) as suggested by Baron-Cohen. This means that an autistic person is not able to infer in other people mental states such as beliefs and emotions. So, an autistic child might think that someone else is also thinking and feeling the same way as they do, and knows the same things.

(c) One similarity between Baron-Cohen et al. and Loftus and Palmer is that they both use a kind of experimental approach and this is a popular methodology for cognitive studies. In Baron-Cohen, the IV is whether the participant is autistic, Tourettes or normal. The DV is measured through a task (the Eyes Task). In Loftus and Palmer, the IV is the word given to the participants and again, the DV is measured through a task (recall of speed of the car in the video). One difference between Baron-Cohen and Savage-Rumbaugh is that Baron-Cohen uses a large sample whereas Savage-Rumbaugh uses a small sample and is therefore really more like a case study and not so generalisable.

(d) One strength of the cognitive approach is that it focuses upon what people think and this is really important to the study of psychology! For example, in Baron-Cohen's study, he has demonstrated how autistic people are not able to conceive of what other people are feeling as easily as non-autistic people, i.e. not capable of 'mind reading'. This is shown because the autistic/AS participants scored less well on the Eyes Task than the non-autistic sample. This is useful research because it can help people know how best to communicate with and treat autistic children.

Another strength of the cognitive approach is that it is quite scientific. For example, in Baron-Cohen it is scientific because it uses the experimental method and there are many controls (e.g. matched ages, two control groups, standardised tasks, etc.). This means we can be more sure that the findings are valid.

One weakness of the cognitive approach is that it ignores emotion. We do not know from this study how it feels to be an autistic child or person and what their experience is. This means that the cognitive approach is reductionist.

Another weakness of the cognitive approach is that really it is only guessing about how people think as you cannot directly observe thinking in the way that you can observe behaviour. So, in the Eyes Task, we do not know why the autistic people did less well – it might not be because of poor Theory of Mind or it might have been for some other reason, e.g. they didn't understand the adjectives, or they didn't concentrate, etc. Really, we are only guessing because thought processes cannot be directly observed.

Teacher's comments (see mark schemes on pages xii–xiii)

Overall, Chardonnay, your answer is about the right length and you have devoted proportionate time to each of the four question parts.

(a) You have accurately <u>and</u> clearly described one assumption of the cognitive approach. You have remembered to include reference to 'behaviour' for full marks.

(b) It is helpful to say how the cognitive explanation contrasts with alternative (e.g. physiological) explanations and this shows that you clearly understand the focus of this cognitive explanation of autism. However, you could have provided more elaboration or detail. This could be achieved in many ways, such as providing an example of how lack of Theory of Mind might manifest itself in real life; or perhaps distinguishing between first and second order tasks.

(c) For the similarity, the description is good, accurate and you have elaborated your point by detailing the IVs and DVs. Of course, some might argue whether Baron-Cohen is a 'true' experiment. It is really a natural experiment (or quasi-experiment); but essentially, you have made a valid point here and it is good enough for 3 marks.

For the difference, your description is just a little above basic (as well as being quite a superficial difference). You manage to push it out of the one mark category by referring (albeit briefly) to the fact that Savage-Rumbaugh's research is a case study and thus has doubtful generalisability – just enough for 2 marks.

Your answer for the similarity is better so you will get that mark only.

(d) I like the way you have structured this part to make it organised and clear. You have identified and explained two valid strengths and two weaknesses and your answer is reasonably balanced. This automatically puts you into one of the top two bands (7–9 marks and 10–12 marks). The rest hinges upon the detail of your discussion, the effectiveness of your analysis, use of supporting examples, and finally, the quality of your language. Thus, it is worth noting that your answer to part (d) is marked as a whole and not for each particular strength or weakness.

Certainly, your use of examples is, on all occasions, appropriate and there is evidence of analysis (e.g. in offering alternate interpretations of the Baron-Cohen results in your second weakness); but there is not much in the way of discussion ... how much of a weakness/strength is this? Is there a counter-argument? You could discuss whether it is necessarily always a bad thing to ignore emotion; or whether controls necessarily have a negative impact upon ecological validity and so on.

Thus, while your use of examples is good, the lack of discussion prevents you from getting into the top band, and the fact that you have only illustrated with the use of the Baron-Cohen study is a weakness. Thus a mark of 8 for this section.

Chardonnay (2 + 3 + 3 + 8 marks = 16/24 marks)

CHAPTER 3

This chapter looks at three core studies in developmental psychology:

- *Samuel and Bryant's study of children's ability to conserve quantities.*

- *Bandura, Ross and Ross' demonstration of how aggression is learned through imitation.*

- *Freud's classic study of Little Hans and the Oedipus complex.*

Developmental psychology

74 Introduction to developmental psychology

Core study 4
76 Samuel and Bryant (conservation)
76   Starters: how do children think?
78   The study in a nutshell
79   The study in detail
83   Evaluation
84   Afters: Piaget revisited
85   Multiple choice questions
85   Exam-style questions

Core study 5
86 Bandura, Ross and Ross (aggression)
86   Starters: learning
88   The study in a nutshell
89   The study in detail
93   Evaluation
94   Afters: still kicking ass
95   Multiple choice questions
95   Exam-style questions

Core study 6
96 Freud (Little Hans)
96   Starters: psychoanalysis
98   The study in a nutshell
99   The study in detail
103   Evaluation
104   Afters: the legacy
105   Multiple choice questions
105   Exam-style questions

106   Exam-style questions

Introduction

What is developmental psychology?

Developmental psychology is sometimes understandably but misleadingly thought of as child psychology: understandably because the major part of the literature in developmental psychology is about children; misleadingly because it gives the impression that psychological development stops as the child enters adulthood. A truly comprehensive developmental psychology should concern itself with the whole lifespan of human development. Having said this, the studies in this chapter reflect the traditional preoccupation with children.

Try this 3.1

Make friends with your elderly relatives and ask them what they did when they were children. Try and sort out what was the same as your childhood and what was very different. How did they play? Who were their friends? What was school like?

Culture corner

Development is something that interests many people other than psychologists. They have observed how we go through different stages in our lives and they have recorded these changes in plays and pictures and novels. The speech from Shakespeare's As You Like It suggests men go through seven stages in their progress from the cradle to the grave, and the picture by Hans Baldung Grien (The seven ages of women, above) shows a similar progression for women, though why they have to have their clothes off all their life is anyone's guess.

Early work in developmental psychology

There are three main themes in the study of child development: cognition, emotion and behaviour.

Cognitive development

In Europe one of the pioneers of **cognitive development** was Jean Piaget (see the study by **Samuel and Bryant**, page 78) who provided an account of how children pass through various stages of thinking as they progress towards adult thought. More recently psychologists in this tradition have looked at children who show unusual patterns of thought. One such pattern is labelled as **autism** and many psychologists including **Simon Baron-Cohen** (see page 52) have carried out studies to investigate the nature and causes of this.

Emotional development

A different tradition in developmental psychology has focused on emotional development rather than cognitive development. The most cited figure in this tradition is **Sigmund Freud** (see page 96). This concern with the emotional life of the child can be seen in the work of **John Bowlby** and **Mary Ainsworth** on attachment (see below).

Behavioural development

A third tradition in developmental psychology comes from the **behaviourists** (see pages 228–229). The underlying principle here is of the effect of rewards and punishments on behaviour. If a child responds to these (and they do) then it is important that we reward the behaviour we want the child to develop and punish or ignore the behaviour we don't want to see again. You can watch this being played out on the many child behaviour shows on television. In the behaviourist tradition the most famous and enduring study is **Bandura's** Bobo doll experiment (see page 88).

Attachment

One important research area in developmental psychology concerns the study of the strong emotional bond between two people, commonly referred to as *attachment*. This term is often taken to mean the emotional tie between a child and its adult caregiver. It is a popular belief in Western culture that the emotional experiences we have in our early years will have a critical effect on our adult behaviour and experience. This belief has been supported by Freud and also by John Bowlby.

John Bowlby

The social disruption caused by the Second World War (1939–45) created thousands of orphans across the world and prompted concern about the effects of bringing children up in institutions. Also, many thousands of children in this country were separated from their parents to keep them safe from the bombing that was happening in the cities. Parents were encouraged to send their children into the country. In 1951, Bowlby produced a report for the World Health Organisation (WHO) in which he suggested that *'mother love in infancy and childhood is as important for mental health as are vitamins and proteins for physical health'* (see Bowlby, 1965, page 240). In the WHO report Bowlby put forward the concept of 'maternal deprivation' which is what happens when a child does not receive a *'warm, intimate and continuous relationship with his mother'*.

Although many children might experience mild deprivation, Bowlby was most concerned with those who experience severe deprivation. This was said to occur when a child under the age of two and a half was deprived of its mother for a period of more than three months. Bowlby argued that research from orphanages and hospitals showed that such deprivation will have a dramatic and lifelong effect on the child's emotional health and ability to form relationships.

Effects of this research

The clear implication of Bowlby's account is that mothers are a crucial part of a child's development and that many of the problems of later life can be traced back to inadequate mothering. In the 50 years since Bowlby's report, research has confirmed the importance of a warm and stable emotional environment for a child; it has not supported the notion that this environment must be created by the biological mother. In fact Bowlby never suggested that mothering can only be done by a child's biological mother but his use of the terms 'mother' and 'maternal' led to this common misinterpretation. A *mother* is a woman who gives birth to a child, whereas *mothering* is a collection of activities that can be carried out by anyone, though most commonly this person is the child's mother.

Although Bowlby's work has been challenged over the years there is an acknowledgement that it led to a change in the way that children are cared for in institutions and helped to raise the standards of child care in this country (Tizard, 1986).

Different images of childhood

Babies in Zambia and the USA

Do babies from different cultures behave differently? **T. Berry Brazelton** *et al.* (1976) studied the behavioural differences between a group of urban Zambian newborns, and urban American newborns. They made extensive **structured observations** of 10 newborn babies from each culture. The babies were measured in a variety of ways on the first, fifth and tenth days of their lives. The most important measure was the *Neonatal Behavioral Assessment Scale* (Brazelton, 1973). This scale measures infants on more than 24 dimensions to do with interactive, perceptual and motor abilities. Examples of these dimensions are: social interest in researcher, motor activity, hand-to-mouth activity, alertness and following with eyes.

On day one the Zambian infants scored lower on a number of measures, mostly to do with alertness and activity. The researchers put this down to the relatively stressed intra-uterine environment of the Zambian babies, resulting in early dehydration and an overall lack of energy. By the tenth day, however, the Zambian group had started to score more highly than the US group on measurements of social interaction (for example, social interest and alertness).

The reason for this turnaround might be to do with the differences between the environments of the two groups of children. Due to the good health and diet of their mothers the US infants had a good physiological environment in the womb but after birth they had a *'relatively nonstimulating environment'* (page 106). The US babies were less likely to be handled than the Zambian infants and their mothers followed the *'cultural emphasis in the United States on quieting the infant and protecting him from external stimulation'* (page 106). By contrast, the Zambian infants improved as they began to be rehydrated and to receive nutrition by feeding from their mother. The increased social responsiveness of the Zambian babies may have been influenced by the more active, contact oriented, stimulating child-rearing practices of the Zambian women.

Not all childhoods are the same

It is estimated that there are 300,000 child soldiers worldwide (UNICEF website) in at least 18 countries. Although the term 'child soldier' commonly brings up a picture of gun-waving teenage boys, the reality is a little different. A number of child soldiers are girls, maybe as many as 40% in some countries and many of the soldiers are as young as seven or eight. Not all of these children carry weapons but their roles as support to weapons units puts their lives in danger.

Some children take up arms to deal with poverty, abuse or discrimination. Some are seeking revenge for violence against themselves or their families. Sometimes they are abducted and forced to join armed groups, and sometimes they become separated from their families and the armies are the only source of food and shelter.

The effect of being a child soldier
However they came to be soldiers, children suffer from their involvement in military activity. It is an abuse of their right to be protected from the effects of conflict. Not only is their childhood destroyed, but they are also separated from their homes, communities and families. Children's

education is brought to a brutal end and military activity damages them physically and mentally as many of them have witnessed or taken part in terrifying acts of violence – even against their own families and communities.

Child labour then and now

The exploitation of children was outlawed in the UK by a series of laws including the 1819 Cotton Mills and Factories Act which prohibited children under the age of nine years from working in cotton mills, and restricted those over the age of nine to a 12-hour day. The special status for young people in these laws reflected a changing view of childhood. If only all international clothing companies could follow suit today.

Romanian orphanages

It is now more than 20 years since the world found out about the thousands of children locked away in Romania's state institutions. When British teacher Monica McDaid first came across the orphanage in Siret she was horrified. *'One thing I particularly remember was the basement. There were kids there who hadn't seen natural light for years. I remember when they were brought out for the first time. Most of them were clinging to the wall, putting their hands up to shield their eyes from the light'* (BBC website, 2005). Many children were adopted by families across Europe and the USA, but did they manage to adapt and recover? A group of these children, adopted by UK parents, has been studied by **Michael Rutter** from the Institute of Psychiatry in London. When they arrived in the country as babies, more than half the 165 children he studied showed severe delays in development compared with British children. Later he found that, even at the age of 11, many of these children had not caught up. *'Contrary to popular opinion at the time, we found there were definite long-term effects from being in an institution'* (Rutter, 2005) and the effects were more damaging the longer the child had spent in institutionalised care.

'A child's mind is a blank book. During the first years of his life, much will be written on the pages. The quality of that writing will affect his life profoundly.' Walt Disney (Pinker, 2002).

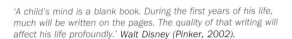
...Connections...

The studies that are included in this chapter are not the only ones in this book that relate to developmental psychology. In a very real sense all psychology is developmental since it is the study of things (people and processes) which change and develop over time. For too long psychology as a whole has tended to study static snapshots of people, frozen in time and space, and thereby has risked missing some things which lie at the very core of human existence. Elsewhere in the book we look at the development of thought (**Baron-Cohen** *et al.*), the development of language (**Savage-Rumbaugh** *et al.*) and the development of mental distress (**Thigpen and Cleckley**).

Samuel and Bryant: starters

How do children think?

Do children think in the same way as adults or do they have their own distinctive ways of seeing and thinking about the world? **Jean Piaget** started his academic career working on the early IQ tests in Binet's **laboratory** (see page 227). Piaget found the task of devising the test items very dull and he never finished the work. However, during his work he noticed that children of the same age appeared to make the same types of mistake. Piaget wondered whether the IQ testers were asking the wrong kind of questions in their attempts to understand the development of intelligence. Instead of looking at what children get wrong, Piaget asked how they get it wrong.

Piaget spent a lot of time watching and listening to children. He would play games with them to find out how they created rules for their play. He found that children don't think like adults. Piaget came to the conclusion that their amusing and apparently illogical thought and talk actually had a logic all of its own. Albert Einstein called it a discovery 'so simple that only a genius could have thought of it'. To Piaget, children are not just little adults but they are **cognitive** aliens: they appear to think like us but in fact there is something very different going on in their minds.

Stages of development

According to Piaget (1954) children develop their ability to think through a series of stages that occur as we mature (age). Children move from one stage to the next when they are 'ready' – which partly results from experiences in the world but is mainly driven by maturation.

- **Sensory motor stage** (birth to around 18 months), during which the child is learning to match their senses (what they see and hear, etc.) to what they can do.
- **Pre-operational stage** (18 months to about seven years), during which the child is learning to use symbolism (and language in particular), and is developing some general rules about mental operations.
- **Concrete operational stage** (seven to around 12 years), during which the child is able to use some sophisticated mental operations but is still limited in a number of ways; for example, the concrete operational child tends to think about the world in terms of how it is, and finds it hard to speculate on how it might be.
- **Formal operational stage** (12 years and above), which is the most sophisticated stage of thinking and is mainly governed by formal logic.

Piaget said that it is possible to observe these different thought patterns through the errors of reasoning that children make. He devised some ingenious tests to illustrate this different style of thinking. The most famous of these tests relate to the pre-operational stage. In this stage Piaget said that children's thought has the following features:

- They are unable to conserve (see right). For example, they do not appreciate that if you change the shape of an object it keeps the same mass.
- They are unable to reverse mental operations. If they have seen some action take place they can not mentally 'rewind the tape'.
- They rely on their intuitions about what they can see rather than what they can reason.
- They are perceptually egocentric, finding it difficult to imagine a viewpoint different to their own.

Try this   3.2

What is the difference between children and adults?

Make a list of as many differences between children and adults as you can think of. The answers don't have to be psychological. You might try using the following three headings for your list: what they think, what they feel, what they do. This will give you a clue as to why it is so difficult to carry out studies on children.

Animism

Young children readily see psychological characteristics such as consciousness, feelings and motives in physical objects and events. In other words they animate everything, and so we call this process 'animism'. Piaget said that to start with a child will believe that almost anything can be alive whether it moves or not. Later, the child comes to believe that only things that move are alive, but this includes things like trains and clocks. The next step is to see life only in those objects that can move on their own, but this still includes objects such as the sun and the moon. Finally, the child comes to believe that only animals and maybe plants are alive.

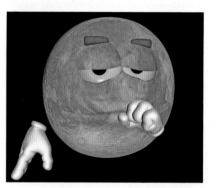

The Man in the Moon – sorry to spoil it for you but it really is just a lump of rock.

Conservation studies

An example of one of Piaget's **conservation tasks** is carried out with some counters. The child is shown two equal rows of counters.

The adult asks, 'Which one has more counters?' and the child replies 'They're both the same'.

Then, in full view of the child, the adult spreads out one row of counters.

The adult now asks the same question; many pre-operational children point to the bottom row and say, 'This row has more'. Piaget believes that the child does not realise that quantity stays constant (is conserved) even though it may appear to have changed. If children at this developmental stage were able to 'rewind the tape' of the adult spreading out the counters, reversing the adult's actions in their minds, they would realise that the number of counters had not changed.

Up to the age of about seven children find it difficult to conserve or to reverse the tape in their minds. They therefore use their intuition to answer the question about which line has more counters. This is a reasonable strategy to use and one that adults also use when they do not have enough information. In using their intuition to examine what it looks like, the question then becomes 'which line looks as if it has more?'. The logical answer is then to say the spread out one has more because that is what it looks like.

Magic

Magic is the label we give to events we can't explain. To a child, an adult is a magician because they can do all manner of things a child can't.

Because Phil knows the local traffic system quite well, he can say 'abracadabra' just before the lights turn to green and a child will believe that Phil has changed the lights by magic (he knows it's sad but it amuses him). This is the basis of most magic tricks. The magician has more knowledge than you but you don't know how much more so you can't estimate the extent of his powers.

Adults encourage children's belief in magic by telling them about mystical creatures that don't really exist like Father Christmas (sorry if you hadn't heard already) and the Tooth Fairy (ditto). Even as adults we believe in magical things such as special medicines or love potions. The practice of homeopathy has no scientific support yet a large number of people continue to purchase homeopathic remedies that have no demonstrably active ingredients.

Maybe in Piaget's studies when the children see an adult spread out the counters or pour the liquid from one beaker to another they think the adult is doing some magic. In which case it is plausible to believe that the taller beaker has more fluid in it because it was put there by magic.

Biographical notes on Jean Piaget

Piaget grew up near Lake Neuchatel in a quiet region of French-speaking Switzerland. His father was a professor of medieval studies and his mother a strict Calvinist. He was a child prodigy who soon became interested in the scientific study of nature. When he was 11 he wrote a short scientific paper on an albino sparrow. This paper is considered as the starting point of his long and brilliant academic career.

In 1923 he married Valentine Chatenay and had three children, Jacqueline, Lucienne and Laurant. Like many developmental psychologists, Piaget studied his own children and reported on their intellectual and language development.

The main theme in Piaget's work is how knowledge develops. How do we come to know what we know and think what we think? His answer was that knowledge develops through our interactions in the world, and we develop through predictable stages.

In the past 20 years Piaget's work has been challenged in a number of ways. For example, research has demonstrated that new-born infants already have some of the knowledge that Piaget believed children had to develop for themselves.

There are also many studies that challenge Piaget's description of child thought processes. These new studies challenge the detail of Piaget's theories but not the central theme that children have qualitatively different thought

Jean Piaget (1896–1980)

processes to adults – before Piaget's time psychologists thought that children just knew less; Piaget helped us to realise that they don't simply know less, they think differently.

The appearance–reality distinction

This is another characteristic of pre-operational thought, which is related to difficulties with conservation. Pre-operational children are 'overwhelmed' by what they see – how things appear – and let that dominate their thinking. Three year olds (pre-operational) were shown Maynard the cat and then watched while the cat went behind a screen and a mask was placed over his head. When they saw the post-transformation 'dog' the children said it was a dog even though they had watched the whole transformation (DeVries, 1969).

What makes the wind?

In one of his most famous experiments, Piaget asked children, 'What makes the wind?' A typical conversation went like this:

Piaget: What makes the wind?

Julia: The trees.

Piaget: How do you know?

Julia: I saw them waving their arms.

Piaget: How does that make the wind?

Julia: [Waving her hand in front of his face] Like this. Only they are bigger. And there are lots of trees.

Piaget: What makes the wind on the ocean?

Julia: It blows there from the land. No. It's the waves...

This is the sort of conversation that delights parents, who then bore you to death telling you about it. Julia is wrong but her answer makes sense. Classifying the answers as 'true' or 'false' misses the point. Piaget was looking for a theory that would show how children come up with answers like this. (Conversation reported in Papert, 1999)

...Link to the core study...

The core study by **Samuel and Bryant** directly challenges Piaget's explanation of why children make mistakes in the conservation tasks. It looks at three of those tasks and compares children across different ages. It is asking whether there is something in the design of Piaget's tasks that creates a problem for the children.

Samuel and Bryant: the core study

Judith Samuel and Peter Bryant (1983) Asking only one question in the conservation experiment. *Journal of Child Psychology, 22* (2), 315–318.

See the CORE STUDY CHECKLIST on page xv for details of what you need to know for the exam.

In a nutshell

Context

Piaget developed a theory of how children's thinking changes as they get older (as described on the previous spread). One of his key methods of research was the **conservation task**. This task was used to assess whether a child had reached the concrete operational stage of thinking, i.e. was able to think in a systematically logical way.

Piaget found that children under the age of seven or eight years could not think in this way. However, Piaget's methods were criticised because of the way he asked the questions. It was argued that the use of two questions might confuse children (he asked the same question twice: 'Are they the same?'). Children might think they had to give a different answer the second time.

Key term: Conservation task

In the standard **conservation task** a child is first shown two equal quantities and asked 'Are they the same'?

Then the display is transformed in front of the child by pouring the liquid from one glass into a taller, thinner one. Then children in all conditions are asked 'Are they the same quantity?' Pre-operational children are likely to say yes.

Pre-operational children base their decisions on current appearance and on their intuition because they cannot 'rewind the tape' to remind themselves what actually happened. They do not use consistent logic – the logic that says quantities can't change.

Aim

Rose and Blank (1974) tried asking just one question and found that children coped better, i.e. they were more likely to show conservation. The aim of Samuel and Bryant's study was to extend Rose and Blank's research.

Participants

The children in the study came from Devon, England.

Four age groups were tested: 5, 6, 7 and 8 years old. There were 63 children in each age group (total = 252 children).

Procedure

This was a **laboratory experiment**, using both **repeated measures** and **independent measures**.

Each child was tested four times on each of the three materials (= 12 tests):

- *Mass:* children were shown a Plasticine cylinder, which was then transformed by being made flatter (and thus *looked as if* there was more).
- *Number:* a row of counters which was then transformed by being spread out so the row was longer.
- *Volume:* a glass filled with water, which was then transformed by being poured into a taller thinner beaker so the water level was higher.

Each age group was subdivided into three task groups:

- *Standard condition,* as used by Piaget, where the key question ('Are they the same?') was asked twice.
- *One question condition,* as used by Rose and Blank, where the key question was only asked after the transformation of the display.
- *Fixed array* was a **control condition** where the key question was asked once and there was no transformation.

Results

Samuel and Bryant found:

- *Age difference:* Older children performed consistently better than younger children.
- *Materials difference:* All children made fewer errors on the number task (an error is when a child fails to conserve).
- *Condition difference:* All children made fewer errors when asked one question post transformation.

Discussion

The results of this study show that Piaget's methods were flawed.

Asking two questions on the conservation task may have confused the younger children and therefore they did not truly demonstrate their abilities.

It might be possible that the children in the one question condition simply ignored the information in the pre-transformation display and that's why they did better – however, this cannot be the case because otherwise the children in the fixed array control would also have done well, and they didn't. The results nevertheless do also support Piaget because there was still an association between age and ability to conserve.

SAMUEL AND BRYANT: THE CORE STUDY

Qs 3.1

1 Identify the dependent variable in this experiment.
2 Three independent variables are identified above. Name each of them and explain how they were manipulated in this experiment.
3 What is the 'transformation'?
4 How is the ability to conserve measured in this study?
5 Explain why this study would be described as having a longitudinal, independent measures design.
6 Describe the sample used in this study.
7 Describe **one** conclusion that can be drawn from this study.

Try this · 3.3

You will increase your memory for the steps involved in this experiment if you do it yourself. Here are some suggestions:

1 Role play the 12 separate trials.
2 If you know someone with a child aged between four and eight, try doing one of the conservation tasks with them – either the standard or one question condition. Compare your results with your classmates.

Please note that special care must be taken when using young children as research participants. Make sure you have full parental consent and brief/debrief both child and parents.

The pre-operational child

The detailed version

Context and aim

Piaget's theory of cognitive development

Jean Piaget developed a theory to explain how children develop their abilities to think – we described this theory on the previous spread. One of the key transitions in Piaget's theory is moving from the stage when a child cannot think in a logical way to the stage when they can think logically. This is the transition from the pre-operational stage to the concrete operational stage, a transition that happens around the age of seven. In fact children do think logically during their early years but this logic has no internal consistency. For example, a child of five might argue that the amount of coins in a row is greater because it looks greater. This is a kind of logic but it will let you down if you are trying to design a rocket to go to the moon.

Piaget illustrated these two stages of development using the concept of conservation, which is explained on the previous spread and on the facing page. According to Piaget we can see the point at which a child moves from being pre-operational (i.e. not logical) to being operational in their ability to conserve. The ability to conserve illustrates the beginning of the operational stage of thinking.

The conservation task is flawed

Margaret Donaldson (1982) pointed out that Piaget's demonstration of this transition using the conservation task was flawed. The experimenter may be unwittingly forcing children to produce wrong answers because of the way the questions are asked. In Piaget's conservation experiments, children were asked whether the two displays were the same. This question was asked both before the transformation and again afterwards.

Based on Donaldson's criticisms, Rose and Blank (1974) conducted a variation of Piaget's conservation experiment. They conducted the number experiment (with counters) and asked only one question instead of two. They only asked whether the rows were the same *after* the transformation. This alteration had a **significant** effect – children who failed the traditional test often succeeded when only one question was asked. This finding suggests that the reason children fail is not because they cannot conserve quantity but because they have been confused by the questions.

Rose and Blank only looked at the number tasks and only tested six-year-old children, therefore Samuel and Bryant's study aimed to find out if the same results would occur with other conservation tasks and a wider age range of participants.

Aim

The intention of this study was to investigate the question of whether children under the age of seven or eight years are able to understand the principle of invariance of quantity, i.e. conservation. It is claimed that they can't but that may be due to the use of flawed research methods.

Method

Participants

252 boys and girls aged between five and eight and a half years from Crediton in Devon, England. The children were divided into four age groups, whose **mean** ages were:

- five years, three months
- six years, three months
- seven years, three months
- eight years, three months.

What this means is that, for example, the children with a mean age of six years, three months may actually have ranged in age from about five years, six months to six years, six months. Their mean age was six years, three months.

Based on your knowledge of conservation, would a preschool child rather be given a pound coin or a 50 pence piece?

Qs 3.2

1 Explain the concept of conservation.
2 Briefly explain the aim of this study.
3 Outline Donaldson's criticism of Piaget's research.
4 How was Samuel and Bryant's study different to the study by Rose and Blank?
5 A longitudinal study tests the same children repeatedly, as they get older, to monitor developmental change. An alternative method is to use a snapshot design where development is seen by comparing the behaviour of children of different ages. Which design was used here?
6 What might be the strength(s) of using this design in this study?
7 What might be the weakness(es)?
8 Identify **two or more** features of the sample that was used.
9 Identify and explain **two** strengths of this sample and **two** weaknesses.
10 Identify the sampling technique that was used.

Method continued

Procedure

Conditions

Condition 1: Standard condition
Children in this condition were given the traditional **conservation task** where they were asked two questions. One question was asked after the first display ('Are they the same?') and the same question was asked again after the transformation.

Condition 2: One question condition
Children in this condition were asked the question only once, after the display was changed (i.e. post-transformation).

Condition 3: Fixed array control
Children in this condition only saw one display, the post-transformation one, i.e. they were just shown the last column in the table (see bottom of page) and asked whether the two were the same mass/number/volume.

This was a **control condition** to check whether children took the transformation into consideration. This is important because children being tested with the one question procedure could focus solely on the perceptual configuration of two displays. In this case, children's performance would not be a sign of conservation thinking.

Experimental control

*In Chapter 1 we discussed experimental control. One way that the experimenter controls an experiment is to control the **independent variable** (IV).*

*Control is also used to reduce the effect of **extraneous variables** (variables other than the IV which may affect the **dependent variable** – see page 28).*

One potential extraneous variable is that participants in one subgroup might be older (and therefore more likely to be able to conserve). To make sure that the three subgroups were equivalent in terms of age the experimenters matched the ages of children in each subgroup.

Control was also used to ensure that the researchers were testing what they intended to test. It is possible that participants in the one question task were not using information from the pre-transformation display. They may have just based their answer on the post-transformation display and therefore weren't conserving anything. To control for this Samuel and Bryant used the fixed-array condition – if the pre-transformation display is critical to success on the post-transformation task then the fixed array control participants should do worse. This is what happened.

Age
Each age group was subdivided into the three conditions.

Mean age in years	Number of children		
	Condition 1	Condition 2	Condition 3
5¼ years	21	21	21
6¼ years	21	21	21
7¼ years	21	21	21
8¼ years	21	21	21

Within each group the children were closely **matched** for age. In order to do such matching it means putting children together in groups of three that are the same age, such as three children all age five years one month. Then one of these children is placed in condition 1, one is placed in condition 2 and one is placed in condition 3.

Materials
Each child had four trials with each of the three kinds of material (i.e. 12 trials in total). The materials used were:

1 Plasticine cylinder to assess conservation of mass.
2 Counters to assess conservation of number.
3 Glasses with water to assess conservation of volume.

Trials (equal and unequal quantities)
For each of the four trials with each material:

- **Equal trials** – trials 1 and 2: the quantities before and after transformation were the same, so the correct answer to the final question 'Are they the same' is yes.
- **Unequal trials** – trials 3 and 4: the quantities before and after transformation were different, so the correct answer to the final question 'Are they the same' is no.

Qs 3.3

1 Identify **three** factors that might affect a child's ability to conserve.

2 There were three conditions, three kinds of material and two kinds of trials. Draw a table to represent this.

3 The order of the tasks was varied so that each child got them in a different order. Why is it a good idea to do this?

4 Explain the purpose of the one judgement condition.

5 Explain the purpose of the fixed array control.

6 Why were the children matched for age?

7 How do you think the children's behaviour might be affected by being questioned by a 'strange' adult?

8 Why do you think Samuel and Bryant included both equal and unequal trials in the pre-transformation display?

9 How could demand characteristics affect the behaviour of the participants in the two-question condition?

	Pre-transformation		Post-transformation
	Equal quantities trials	**Unequal quantities trials**	
Mass	Two equal Plasticine cylinders.	Two unequal Plasticine cylinders, one longer than the other.	One cylinder is squashed so it looks like a sausage or a pancake.
Number	Two rows of 6 counters, each arranged identically.	One row of 6 counters and one of 5 arranged to be equal in length.	One row was either spread out or bunched up so the two rows were not of equal length.
Volume	Two identical glasses, with the same amounts of liquid.	Two identical glasses, with different amounts of liquid.	The liquid from one glass is poured into a narrower or wider one.

Results

Conditions

Children made fewest errors when asked only one question. An error is a failure to conserve.

Mean number of errors for each child (rounded to the nearest whole number)	Standard	One question	Control
	5	4	6

Children did worse on the fixed array control condition. This shows that children who conserved must have been using information from the pre-transformation display in order to answer the final question correctly (because the fixed array group did not have this information).

Age

Older children made fewer errors.

Mean age in years	Mean errors per child (out of 12). Mean errors (out of 12). The errors have been rounded to one decimal place
5¼ years	8.1
6¼ years	5.5
7¼ years	3.6
8¼ years	2.1

Materials

Children made fewer errors on the number task and most on the volume task.

Material	Mean errors (out of 12). The errors have been rounded to one decimal place
mass	4.4
number	4.0
volume	5.9

Trials

There were no differences found in the equal and unequal trials and therefore the results for these two conditions were combined in the analyses for materials.

Age and conditions

This is the result we are most interested in because it shows:

- For every condition the youngest children made most errors and errors decreased with age. This means that age has an important effect on ability to conserve.

- For all age groups (except the seven year olds) the children performed better on the one question condition than the standard, two question condition. This shows that the form of questioning has an important effect on ability to conserve.

Altogether this means that both age and form of questioning affect the ability to conserve.

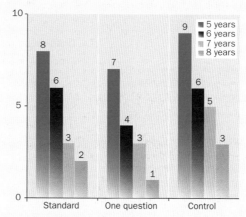

Graph showing mean number of errors (out of 12) for each child

Biographical notes

Peter Bryant was Watts Professor of Psychology at the University of Oxford from 1980 to 2004. He is currently involved in a variety of different research projects on how children learn to read and to do mathematics.

Bryant worked with Piaget and his team of researchers in the 1960s and observed their research first hand. In his view Piaget completely transformed the subject of child psychology and was an astonishingly gifted experimenter.

'No one in the history of psychology, apart perhaps from Pavlov, has contributed as much as Piaget did to the creation of new, ingenious and highly successful ways of investigating people's behaviour. However ... the actual experimental designs that he and his colleagues adopted were often flawed.'

The flaw was that they failed to have control conditions that would exclude other possible explanations for a child's abilities, such as failure at the conservation task. Other researchers, such as Samuel and Bryant, have been left to do this.

'Our point was that one of the factors that determines the children's success in the conservation task is the context in which the problem is given to them' (personal communication).

Judith Samuel is Head of Psychology Services (Learning Disability Division) for Southern Health NHS Foundation Trust. Her main area of research and service development is with people with profound intellectual disabilities (in particular Intensive Interaction). She links this work to her early research:

'I have built on my initial interest in the social context of cognitive development and learning' (personal communication).

Discussion

The results indicate that failure on the traditional two-question conservation task may be at least partly due to being asked two questions rather than because young children are unable to conserve. Presumably, the experimenter's repetition of the same question makes children think they must change their answer the second time. This is shown by the fact that:

- The children must have been using their knowledge of conservation when they solved the one-question task.
- The children must have used their knowledge of the pre-transformation display to do this because they all did much better than the fixed-array **control group**.

This means that the repetitive questioning used in the traditional conservation **experiment** actively misleads the child.

The important lesson is that children may possess certain **cognitive** abilities (such as conservation) but may not display these when tested if the method used is flawed.

*Participants are required to give **informed consent** in any experiment – however, in the case of a child participant, parents are asked to provide consent. The child should be asked as well, especially in situations that might cause confusion or distress.*

Qs 3.5

1   What did Samuel and Bryant conclude about the techniques used by Piaget to investigate conservation?

2   What piece of evidence did they use to support this conclusion?

3   Samuel and Bryant did not draw any conclusions about Piaget's theory. It could be argued that the findings continue to support Piaget's theory. Explain how this could be true.

Children as participants

Practical issues

One issue that concerns researchers when studying children is that children are more 'suggestible' than adults. They are more likely to respond to researcher's cues because they are more uncertain of themselves. Therefore they may unwittingly fulfil the researcher's expectations, leading to findings which are not valid.

*The two main types of 'cues' are **demand characteristics** and **investigator bias** (see page 28). **Leading questions** may also affect performance.*

Ethical issues

*A second issue that concerns researchers working with children is ethics. The same **ethical issues** are important with child participants as with adults (see pages 14–15 and 232–233).*

1   ***Informed consent:** Researchers cannot obtain the informed consent of children and must seek that of a parent or guardian. They should also ask the child for his/her own consent.*

2   ***Psychological harm:** Researchers would be even less willing to distress or **deceive** a child than any other participant. The long-term effects of research on impressionable children should be considered.*

...Links to core studies...

The work of Piaget along with Samuel and Bryant has connections to the work on autism by **Baron-Cohen et al.** They both use imaginative techniques to explore child thought and they both develop theories about the development of cognitive processes.

In the 1920s Piaget became interested in psychoanalysis and moved to Zurich, where he attended Carl Jung's lectures. This gives us a link to **Freud**'s work.

Piaget's work also gives us an explanation for how children learn right from wrong and that also connects to Freud's and **Bandura et al.**'s studies.

Things you could do ...

Read the original article by Samuel and Bryant on PsychExchange (http://www.psychexchange.co.uk/file124.html)

Read: some interesting background reading relating to Piaget is in the classic book *Children's Minds* by Margaret Donaldson (1978).

An article by Baucal and Stepanovic´ (2006) includes a thorough review of studies that have looked at the validity of the conservation task as well as studies of the 'repeated question hypothesis', concluding with their own experiment. See http://www.doiserbia.nb.rs/img/doi/0048-5705/2006/0048-57050603257B.pdf

Watch videos about conservation – type 'Piaget conservation' into the search box on YouTube.

Listen to the *Mind Changers* on Piaget, an excellent BBC radio series on key psychological studies. You can find copy of programme at http://www.bbc.co.uk/radio4/science/mindchangers2.shtml

Evaluating the study by Samuel and Bryant

The research method
This study is a laboratory experiment.

What are the strengths and weaknesses of this research method in the context of this study?

In some ways this study is also a quasi-experiment (because the IV age isn't 'manipulated', it just exists).

What are the strengths and weaknesses of this research method in the context of this study?

The sample
The participants in this study were all children aged five to eight and a half years.

In what way do children make good or bad participants?

Ethics
Ethical issues are important in all studies but there are special issues to consider with children (see feature on the facing page).

What ethical issues should have concerned the researchers in this study, and how might they have dealt with these issues?

Reliability
Reliability concerns measurement.

What aspects of behaviour were measured in this study? How was the reliability of these measurements assessed?

Validity
The study used a number of methods to control extraneous variables and therefore improve validity.

Discuss how the control tasks were used to improve validity.

Ecological validity
The study was a laboratory experiment, however the tasks were nevertheless quite similar to real life activities.

To what extent is this study representative of real life? To what extent would the children behave as they would in everyday life?

Snapshot or longitudinal?
This was a snapshot study as each child was only studied briefly.

Consider the strengths and weaknesses of this design in the context of this study.

What would be the relative advantages of conducting a longitudinal study?

Qualitative or quantitative?
What kind of data were collected in this study? Use examples to illustrate your answer.

What are the strengths and weaknesses of producing this kind of data in the context of this study?

Suggest how a different kind of data might have been collected in this study.

Applications/usefulness
Piaget's theory has been used in education, for example, the theory suggests that children should only do certain activities when they are 'ready' for that kind of thinking.

How might you use the findings from this experiment?

What next?
*Describe **one** change to this study, and say how you think this might affect the outcome.*

There are no simple answers.

Evaluating a study requires you to think.

*We have provided some pointers here, linked to the **RESEARCH METHODS** and **KEY ISSUES** covered in Chapter 1 (Psychological investigations) and Chapter 7 (Key issues).*

You can read suggested answers on our website www.psypress.com/cw/banyard.

Producing effective evaluation
When you produce your own answers to the issues on the left there are two things to ensure:
1 Contextualisation
2 Elaboration

The key to **CONTEXTUALISATION** is to ensure that your answer includes some information about this particular study – but if you have already done this in your first sentence you must add a comment to gain the full 2 marks. For example:

2 mark question

> *Question:*
> Outline **one** weakness of the way in which data was gathered in this study. **[2]**
>
> *Answer:*
> **STATE**: One weakness of the way data was collected is that Samuel and Bryant just conducted their study with one group of students from Devon.
>
> **COMMENT**: These students may have unique characteristics. Devon is a rural county and may be more middle-class than elsewhere in the UK. These children may have more highly developed cognitive skills and therefore we can't generalise the findings to all UK children.

The key to **ELABORATION** is the three-point rule (see page xii). For example:

3 mark question

> *Question:*
> With reference to the study by Samuel and Bryant suggest **one** strength of laboratory experiments. **[3]**
>
> *Answer:*
> **STATE**: One strength of laboratory experiments is that the experimenter can control extraneous variables more easily than in a field experiment.
>
> **CONTEXT**: Samuel and Bryant controlled a number of important extraneous variables such as some groups containing slightly older children.
>
> **COMMENT**: To make sure that the three subgroups were the same in terms of age the experimenters matched the ages of children in each subgroup.

The developmental approach

On pages 74–75 and 220–221 we have discussed the **developmental approach**.

The study by Samuel and Bryant concerns thinking.

- In what way is this an example of the developmental approach?
- Discuss the strengths and weaknesses of the developmental approach using examples from the Samuel and Bryant study.

Samuel and Bryant: afters

Piaget revisited

Piaget's work has had a major effect on schooling in the UK and forms part of many teacher training courses. One consequence of this has been an army of student teachers heading off to primary schools equipped with beakers and plasticine.

Naughty Teddy

Another study that revisited Piaget's conservation tests was devised by McGarrigle and Donaldson (1974). In Piaget's test of conservation of number, he showed children two rows with an equal number of counters and then spread the counters in one of the rows so the row looked longer. Children in the pre-operational stage tended to say there were more counters in the row that looked longer. There are a number of explanations for this including Piaget's (the child cannot conserve) and Samuel and Bryant's (the second question requires a different answer to the first).

Another possible reason might be in the task itself. Is it the way the counters are moved or even who does the moving that leads the children to make the mistake? To a child an adult has magic powers. Who knows where those powers end? Perhaps the child thinks that the adult can actually change the number of counters?

McGarrigle and Donaldson used a 'naughty teddy' puppet to mess up the counters rather than get an adult to do this. When Naughty Teddy did the messing up of the counters most of the four to six year olds (70%) made the correct judgement about the rows (the quantities in each row are the same).

Very Naughty Teddy

It is not clear why they are more likely to make the correct judgement when the puppet is involved and Moore and Frye (1986) suggested the improvement was because the children were distracted by the naughty teddy antics. Perhaps they were so distracted that they didn't notice the change.

Moore and Frye demonstrated this by getting Naughty Teddy to actually take away a counter as well as messing up the row. The children still said the quantities were the same even though now they weren't.

This all goes to show that it is very difficult to investigate children's thinking, and it also confirms Piaget's basic idea that children appear to have different thought processes to adults.

Cognitive development and culture

Does Piaget's theory describe how all children develop or just those in Western societies? To answer this we have to break down the question and look at three smaller questions:

Q: *Do Piaget's stages occur in the same order in different cultures?*

A: *Probably yes.*

A cross-cultural study of children in the UK, Australia, Greece and Pakistan found that children developed an ability to complete the conservation tasks in the same order (Shayer et al., 1988).

Q: *Do children from different cultures go through the stages at the same age?*

A: *Probably no.*

Various studies have found differences of up to six years in the age that children reach the third and fourth of Piaget's stages (Matsumoto, 1994). However, there is always an issue about whether the children were just doing badly on the task even though they actually had the ability to make the correct judgement.

Q: *Do all cultures see scientific reasoning as the highest form of thought?*

A: *Clearly no.*

Different societies place different values on styles of behaviour and thought. In the West we appear to think that abstract and hypothetical thought processes are the highest form of intelligence. Many other cultures, however, value thought processes that are more social and take other people into account (Matsumoto, 1994).

Children's drawings

Another illustration of the different way that children see the world to adults is in their drawings of people. The drawings follow a predictable developmental pattern that is nothing like the way adults draw people. Most remarkably, they start off by leaving out the body and draw the arms and legs coming out of a big head. This is like the famous Mr Men, but it is the Mr Men that copy children rather than children copying the Mr Men.

Another test of conservation

Miller (1982) designed a conservation **experiment** where no experimenter was involved in the transformation. It involved insects in one condition and boats in another. As the children watched, the insects/boats just drifted apart, so there was no experimenter doing anything. Despite the fact that the children were not distracted by an experimenter, they still failed the conservation task.

Multiple choice questions

1 This study was a replication of a study by:
   a Piaget.
   b Samuel and Bryant.
   c Rose and Blank.
   d Both a and c.

2 What was the age range of participants in this experiment?
   a 4½ to 8½ years.
   b 5 to 8 years.
   c 5½ to 8 years.
   d 5 to 8½ years.

3 Which of the following were used to control for extraneous variables?
   a Different age groups.
   b Matching participants.
   c Fixed array task.
   d Both b and c.

4 Which of the following is true?
   a This was a repeated measures design.
   b This was an independent groups design.
   c This was a mixed groups design.
   d Both a and b.

5 What were the three kinds of material that were used in the experiment?
   a Height, number, volume.
   b Height, quantity, volume.
   c Mass, quantity, speed.
   d Mass, number, volume.

6 Which is the post-transformation question?
   a The question asked before the change was made.
   b The question asked while the change was made.
   c The question asked after the change was made.
   d All of the above.

7 Which of the following were IVs in this experiment?
   a Children's age.
   b Ability to conserve.
   c The three conditions (one question, two questions, control).
   d Both a and c.

8 Which of the kinds of material did the children find easiest to conserve?
   a Height.   b Number.
   c Volume.   d Mass.

9 Which group of children made most errors on the conservation tasks?
   a Five year olds.   b Six year olds.
   c Seven year olds.   d Eight year olds.

10 The results showed that:
   a More children can conserve when only asked the post-transformation question.
   b Fewer five year olds can conserve than eight year olds.
   c Piaget underestimated what children can do in terms of conservation.
   d All of the above.

Answers are on page 247.

Exam-style questions

There are three kinds of question that can be asked about the Samuel and Bryant study, as represented here by sections A, B and C.

See page x for further notes on the exam paper and styles of question.

Section A questions

1 From the study by Samuel and Bryant on conservation, identify **two** factors that affect a child's ability to conserve. For each factor explain why it increases the chances of a child giving a correct answer. [4]

2 Samuel and Bryant's study on conservation had three conditions. Briefly describe **two** of these conditions. [4]

3 The study by Samuel and Bryant involved conducting interviews with children.
   (a) Describe **one** problem that psychologists have to consider when they interview children. [2]
   (b) Suggest how psychologists might deal with this problem. [2]

4 Outline **two** conclusions that can be drawn from Samuel and Bryant's study into conservation. [4]

5 Samuel and Bryant's study considered the validity of Piaget's methods of assessing conservation.
   (a) Explain what 'validity' means. [2]
   (b) Outline **one** difference between the method used by Piaget and the method used by Samuel and Bryant. [2]

6 From Samuel and Bryant's study on conservation, give **one** piece of evidence that supports Piaget's claims and **one** piece of evidence that challenges Piaget's claims about children's ability to conserve. [4]

7 The study by Samuel and Bryant is a laboratory experiment.
   (a) Identify **two** independent variables in this study. [2]
   (b) Explain the findings for one of these variables. [2]

8 (a) Outline **one** way the results from the study by Samuel and Bryant show that cognitive development has taken place. [2]
   (b) Explain how the results of this study show that the form of questioning is important. [2]

9 Outline **two** ethical issues raised in the study by Samuel and Bryant. [4]

10 (a) Identify **two** features of the sample used in the study by Samuel and Bryant. [2]
   (b) Outline **one** weakness of the sample used in this study. [2]

Section B questions

Answer the following questions with reference to the Samuel and Bryant study:

(a) Identify an independent variable and dependent variable from the study by Samuel and Bryant. [2]

(b) Describe the sample used in the study by Samuel and Bryant, and give **one** weakness of the sample. [6]

(c) Describe ethical issues that might arise in this study and explain why they are problematic. [6]

(d) Explain how the validity of these measurements could be assessed. [6]

(e) Outline the results of the study by Samuel and Bryant. [8]

(f) Suggest **two** changes to the study by Samuel and Bryant and outline how these changes might affect the results. [8]

Section C questions

(a) Outline **one** assumption of the developmental approach in psychology. [2]

(b) Describe how the developmental approach could explain conservation. [4]

(c) Describe **one** similarity and **one** difference between the study by Samuel and Bryant and any other core studies that take the developmental approach. [6]

(d) Discuss strengths and weaknesses of the developmental approach, using examples from any core studies that take this approach. [12]

Learning

How do we learn? Some of our behaviour is moulded by **reinforcement**. We do things that bring about pleasant consequences (rewards), such as warmth or praise or money, and we do things to avoid unpleasant consequences, such as cold or disapproval. Some of our learning comes through trial and error, but we also appear to learn by watching other people. It is, after all, safer to let others make the mistakes. When any behaviour appears to have positive consequences, we store it away for an appropriate occasion and then try it for ourselves.

When we are successful at something we become more confident of being able to do that task again. We develop a sense of **self-efficacy** which is a belief about our ability to succeed. As we interact with our environment, it becomes a two-way process: as we change the environment, the environment changes us (reciprocal determinism). Learning is therefore a combination of watching, thinking and trying. We learn most from people with whom we identify. When we are very young this is our parents; later it is peers, and later still it is attractive and famous people as well as people in authority.

History

Learning has been one of the key topics in psychology for over one hundred years. It can be defined as:

a relatively permanent change in behaviour (or potential behaviour) as the result of experience.

John B. Watson (1878–1958) was the first to study how the process of learning affects our behaviour, and he formed the school of thought known as **behaviourism**. Behaviourists are basically interested in explaining behaviour simply in terms of the stimuli in the environment. Although it can explain some examples of human learning there is a lot of behaviour it cannot explain.

Social learning theory

The behaviourism of Watson took on a more human dimension with the publication of the book *Social Learning* and *Imitation* (Miller and Dollard, 1941). This approach added imitation to the known principles of learning. The book was written to explain how animals and humans imitate observed behaviours (a process called **modelling**); in other words you don't just learn because you have been rewarded but because you see someone else rewarded and store this memory for future reference. You then may imitate or model the behaviour given appropriate circumstances and will only continue to repeat it if directly reinforced. **Social learning theory** explains human behaviour in terms of a continuous interaction between **cognitive**, behavioural and environmental influences. It is now most closely associated with **Albert Bandura**.

Why are people aggressive?

Aggression has a lot of forms. It can be giving someone a funny look, or it can be shouting at them or it can involve physical violence. Sometimes we think aggression is a good thing, such as in sport where we want sports people to show controlled aggression. Some people believe it is important to fight and even kill people for your beliefs. Mostly, however, we judge aggression to be a bad thing, though strangely we appear to enjoy watching violence and murder for entertainment.

Is aggression learnt?
Perhaps we are born with the potential to be peaceful and calm but learn how to be aggressive as we grow up. This is where the work of Bandura comes in.

Why road rage?

Is aggression an instinct?
A lot is made of research into animal aggression and one influential book was On Aggression *by Konrad Lorenz (1966). He defined aggression as 'the fighting instinct in beast and man which is directed against members of the same species' (page IX).*

Is aggression cathartic?
Catharsis is the cleansing effect of releasing intense, stored emotion. The term was used by Freud to describe the effect of releasing painful memories during therapy. It is suggested that being aggressive will release the tension and make someone less likely to engage in further violence.

Role models

The idea of role **models** is one of the most overused concepts in popular psychology. It is often used to criticise people who are in the public eye. For example, the wife of the former British Prime Minister, Cherie Blair, was blamed by psychologist Sandi Mann for being too successful and so causing stress to ordinary mothers who tried to copy her. *'Whilst Mrs Blair is a very impressive lady,'* said Dr Mann, *'she may not necessarily be the best role model for women if the perception is that she rarely gets time to take any time out for herself'* (BBC, 2000). England footballer Wayne Rooney was banned from coaching kids at a schools match because he was not considered a 'good role model' by the English Schools Football Association (Manchester Evening News, 2005).

These two examples illustrate the power of the role model and how the idea is used to attack the behaviour of people in the news. It is a common feature to put pressure on women to be less successful in their careers, and on young working-class men not to get above their presumed station in life.

What is aggression?
This is harder to define than you would think. Not least because what one person sees as being aggressive another person might see as a bit of a laugh. One definition is:

'any behaviour directed toward another individual that is carried out with the proximate (immediate) intent to cause harm. In addition, the perpetrator must believe that the behaviour will harm the target and that the target is motivated to avoid the behaviour.' (Bushman and Anderson, 2001, page 274)

The important issue is intention. If you injure someone accidentally by tripping on the carpet and throwing a cup of coffee on them this would not be seen as aggressive. But if you stood in the middle of the room and deliberately threw it at them, this would be an aggressive act. The action is the same, the injury is the same but the intention is different.

Is aggression a response to frustration?
Dollard, for example, made the assertion that 'the occurrence of aggressive behaviour always presupposes the existence of frustration' and that the 'existence of frustration always leads to some form of aggression' (Dollard et al., 1939, page 8).

Superman: a role model to copy or to be put off by?

Biographical notes on Albert Bandura
Albert Bandura was born on December 4, 1925 in the province of Alberta, Canada. He studied at the University of British Columbia and of Iowa. In 1953 Bandura accepted a teaching position at Stanford University, USA where he continues to teach today.

He is most associated with the development of 'social learning theory' which he has recently renamed 'social cognitive theory' to take in further developments of the theory. In 1986 Bandura wrote *Social Foundations of Thought and Action* which outlines his social cognitive theory. Bandura has made a large contribution to the field of psychology, as seen in the many honours and awards he has received including several honorary degrees from universities all over the world.

Albert Bandura (1925–)

To introductory psychology students, however, he is still best known for the Bobo studies. Recently he wrote of this,

'In my earlier life, I conducted research on the power of social modeling. … The studies of aggressive modeling were conducted over 40 years ago. But the Bobo doll continues to follow me wherever I go. The photographs are published in every introductory psychology text and virtually every undergraduate enrols in introductory psychology. I recently checked into a Washington hotel only to have the clerk at the registration desk asked, "Did you do the Bobo doll experiment?" I explained that "I am afraid that will be my legacy." He replied, "Hell, that deserves an upgrade. I will put you in a suite in the quiet part of the hotel." So there are some benefits to the wide exposure.' (Bandura, 2004, page 626)

How do people learn to be non-aggressive?
One example can be found in the behaviour of the !Kung people of the Kalahari Desert described by Draper (1978). The parents were observed to have some distinctive ways of dealing with conflict between children:

1 *'When two small children argue or begin to fight, adults don't punish or lecture them; they separate them and physically carry each child off in an opposite direction. The adult tries to soothe and distract the child and to get him interested in other things.'* (page 36)

2 *'[P]arents do not use physical punishment, and … aggressive postures are avoided by adults and devalued by the society at large.'* (page 37)

3 *'Adults consistently ignore a child's angry outburst when it does not inflict harm. A child's frustration at such times is acute, but he learns that anger does not cause an adult to change his treatment of the child, and the display of anger does not get the adult's attention or sympathy.'* (pages 37–8)

So does this have an effect on adult behaviour? According to Draper, the !Kung were very successful in discouraging harmful and malicious behaviour in young people. During the 12 months she lived with the !Kung she saw no conflicts between adults, which resulted in serious injuries.

Oh Superman...
In the popular imagination, role models inspire us to do more and achieve more, but is this always the case? What if you think you can't match up to the role model? It seems that Superman is too good a role model. Fans of the man from Krypton seem to compare themselves to the superhero, and realise they can't measure up. And as a result, they are less likely to help other people (Nelson and Norton, 2005).

In a study on decision making, students were asked to list the characteristics of Superman, or alternatively superheroes in general, as part of a larger **questionnaire**. Later on the students were given the opportunity to volunteer for a fictitious community programme. Students who had been prompted to think about Superman volunteered less often than those who had thought about other superheroes. One explanation for this is that thinking about someone exceptional makes you think about your own shortcomings and think about what you can't do rather than what you can.

...Link to the core study...
This study looks at how aggressive behaviour develops in children. It is now over 50 years old but it still attracts a lot of attention and is still quoted in many texts. The study addresses two key questions, first, 'is aggression an innate feature of our behaviour or do we learn it?' Our answer to this question affects how we develop social policies to deal with aggressive behaviour. The second question, which follows on from the first, is 'if aggression is learnt then how is it learnt?'

Bandura *et al.*: the core study *continued*

Albert Bandura, Dorothea Ross and Sheila A. Ross (1961) Transmission of aggression through imitation of aggressive models. *Journal of Abnormal and Social Psychology, 63(3),* 575–582.

In a nutshell

See the CORE STUDY CHECKLIST on page xv for details of what you need to know for the exam.

Context
Research has shown that children imitate what other people do. At least they imitate a behaviour in the immediate environment where they see it happening. For example, if a child sees someone being aggressive to a particular toy then the child will also behave aggressively towards that doll.

Aim
Bandura *et al.* aimed to see if children would generalise this learning to other situations and perform the same actions even when the **model** is not present (the model is the person being imitated). This is the essence of imitative learning or **social learning**.

Participants
A group of 72 children participated in this study (36 boys and 36 girls). The children were aged three to five years old and all attended a university nursery school.

Two **confederates** were also involved, a male and a female who acted as the 'models' for aggressive or non-aggressive behaviour. In this context a 'model' is someone who is imitated – a 'role model'.

Procedure
A **laboratory experiment** was conducted.

Phase 1: modelling
The children played in an experimental room, watching a model playing with toys. The effects of three **independent variables** were studied:

1 Exposure to an aggressive or non-aggressive model. The children were placed in one of three **experimental groups**:
   - *Group 1:* observed an aggressive model.
   - *Group 2:* observed a non-aggressive model.
   - ***Control group:*** no model was present while the children were playing.

   The aggressiveness of each child is a potential **extraneous variable**. Therefore it was important that the children in each group were similar in terms of aggressiveness. All the children were rated for aggression and then distributed evenly between the three groups. This is called **matched participants design**.

2 The effects of model's gender. Some children watched a male model and others watched a female model.

3 The effects of child's gender. Half the participants were boys and half were girls.

Phase 2: aggression arousal
The children were taken to another room where they were then allowed to play with some attractive toys. This play was abruptly stopped in order to make the children feel frustrated.

Phased 3: test for delayed imitation
The children were taken to another room where they were observed playing with toys, including the Bobo doll.

Key term: social learning
In this article Bandura et al. *refer to 'imitative learning', i.e. learning to perform a new behaviour as a consequence of imitating a model's behaviour. This later became known as* **social learning** *because learning takes place in a social context – it is 'social' because it involves watching other people.*

Results
The children who observed the aggressive model were more likely to exhibit the same specific acts of violence shown by the model than the other two groups, for example they said 'pow' and hit the doll with a mallet.

The children who observed the aggressive model were later generally more aggressive, although the difference between groups was very small.

The boys were more affected by same-sex models than the girls were. Both boys and girls were more affected by the male models in terms of physical (but not verbal) aggressiveness.

Discussion
The results showed that children do imitate behaviour of models beyond the specific situation where the behaviour was viewed.

The aggressive models affected behaviour in two ways: they provided information about specific behaviours and also generally increased levels of aggression.

Male models appear to have a stronger influence possibly because aggression is a masculine-type behaviour and therefore boys and girls attend more readily to male models.

A Bobo doll is an inflatable doll about five-foot tall. There is a weight in the bottom that makes it bob back up when you knock it down.

Qs 3.6

1 Bandura *et al.* were aiming to see if children would 'generalise their learning'. Explain what this means.
2 Identify **three** characteristics of the sample that was used.
3 What kind of experimental design is used in this study (independent or repeated measures)?
4 Identify the **three** independent variables (IVs) in this study.
5 What is the dependent variable (DV)?
6 In what way could aggressiveness be an extraneous variable in this study?
7 Explain why the children were 'matched'.
8 What aspects of this experiment might be harmful to a child?
9 Why was it important that the children were taken to a very different setting for the 'aggression arousal'?
10 Describe **two** findings from this study.

The detailed version

Context and aims

Previous studies have shown that children will imitate what someone else (called 'the model') is doing when they remain in the same immediate setting. However, a more crucial test of imitative learning is to see whether a child will generalise the imitative response patterns to new settings when the model is absent. In other words, whether they will still display the newly learned behaviour in a new setting when the model is no longer present. This is a more crucial test of the principles of imitative learning (or **social learning theory**).

Aims

The research predictions are:

1 Observing an aggressive model will lead a subject (participant) to reproduce aggressive acts similar to their models, whereas this will not be true of participants who observed non-aggressive models or who observed no model.

2 Observing an aggressive model will lead a participant to behave in a generally more aggressive manner, whereas those who observed a non-aggressive model would be inhibited from behaving aggressively.

3 Participants will imitate the behaviour of a same-sex model to a greater degree than a model of the opposite sex. This is based on previous research that has shown that parents reward imitation of sex-appropriate behaviour and discourage or punish sex-inappropriate imitation. For example, boys are unlikely to be encouraged to engage in female appropriate activities such as cooking or looking after a baby, whereas such behaviours would be welcomed in a girl.

4 Boys will be more likely than girls to imitate aggressive behaviour because it is a highly masculine activity.

Qs 3.7

1 Briefly summarise the four research predictions.

2 The researchers predicted that the child participants in this study would be more likely to imitate the behaviour of a same-sex model because children are generally encouraged to behave in sex-appropriate ways. Give an example of how children are encouraged to behave in a sex-appropriate way. Do you think children today are also encouraged to behave in sex appropriate ways? Explain your answer.

3 Another research prediction is that boys are more disposed to aggressive behaviour. Do you agree with this prediction? Explain your answer.

4 What kind of sampling procedure was probably used In this study?

5 Why is it necessary to have a control condition?

6 Aggressiveness was also controlled. How was this done?

7 Besides the Bobo doll and the mallet, name a few other toys in the room. Why were these other toys selected?

8 Why was it important that the toys were in the same position for every child?

Method

Participants

The participants were American children from a university nursery school (Stanford in California, the University where this study was conducted). There were 36 boys and 36 girls in the **sample,** aged between 37 and 69 months (approximately three to five years). The **mean** age was 52 months (about four and a half years).

There were two adult 'models', a male and a female, plus a female experimenter.

Procedure

In order to assess the effect of the model's behaviour, there were three conditions:

• *Group 1*: observed an aggressive model.

• *Group 2*: observed a non-aggressive (and subdued) model.

• *Control group*: were not exposed to any model.

In addition the effects of gender were assessed (the interaction between the model's gender and the child's gender). In order to do this each of the experimental groups was subdivided into four groups: boys watching same-sex model, boys watching opposite sex model, and the same for the two girl groups (making a total of eight experimental groups each with six participants). The control group were not exposed to a model.

	Boy participant		Girl participant	
	Male model	Female model	Male model	Female model
Group 1	6	6	6	6
Group 2	6	6	6	6
Control group	12		12	

Controlling aggressiveness

In order to ensure that each group contained equally aggressive children (and thus control this potential extraneous variable), aggressiveness ratings of the children were taken beforehand by one of the children's teachers, an experimenter who knew the children well.

On the basis of these ratings the participants were arranged in threes and assigned at **random** to one of the three groups. Thus the children were matched across conditions.

Phase 1: modelling

Each child was taken individually by the experimenter to an experimental room in the main nursery building and the 'model' was invited to join them. The experimenter seated the child at a small table in one corner of the room and encouraged the child to design a picture using stickers and potato prints. Once the child was settled, the experimenter escorted the model to the opposite corner which contained a small table, chair, tinker toy set, a mallet and a five-foot Bobo doll. The experimenter then left the room.

A tinker toy set, one of the neutral toys available for the children to play with.

(The procedural details continue on next page.)

Method *continued*

Phase 1 *continued*

The experimental and **control conditions** were **operationalised** as follows:

Aggressive condition The **model** spent the first minute playing quietly but then turned to the Bobo doll and spent the rest of the time being aggressive towards it. This included specific acts which might later be imitated, namely laying the doll on its side, sitting on it and repeatedly punching it on the nose. Then picking the doll up and striking it on the head with the mallet, throwing the doll in the air and kicking it about the room. This was done three times accompanied by various **standardised** comments such as 'Hit him down', 'Pow' and 'He keeps coming back for more'.

Non-aggressive condition The model assembled the tinker toys in a subdued manner and ignored the Bobo doll.

Control The report does not say what treatment these children received.

The experimenter re-entered the room after 10 minutes and informed the child that it was time to go to another game room.

Phase 2: aggression arousal

Before testing the children's imitation of the models it was necessary to mildly provoke them. This was done partly because observing aggressive behaviour may reduce the probability of behaving aggressively, making it less likely that those observing the aggressive model would behave aggressively.

It was also done because the children who watched the non-aggressive model might be inhibited from behaving aggressively because of what they observed.

The children were taken to a room in another building that contained some attractive toys (e.g. fire engine, jet fighter plane, colourful spinning top, complete doll set with a wardrobe and a baby crib). The child was allowed to play with the toys but, after about two minutes, the experimenter said that she had decided to reserve the toys for the other children. The experimenter and child then moved to the adjoining experimental room. It was presumed that this intervention made the children frustrated which would lead to a greater likelihood of becoming aggressive.

Phase 3: test for delayed imitation

This third room contained a variety of toys:

- 'Aggressive' toys, that could be used to express aggression, including a mallet, dart gun, tether ball with a face painted on it hung from the ceiling and a three-foot Bobo doll.
- Non-aggressive toys including a tea set, crayons and paper, a ball, dolls, cars and plastic animals.

The toys were arranged in a fixed order for each session. The experimenter sat quietly in the corner working while the child played for 2 minutes.

The child was observed through a **one-way mirror** by the male model. A second observer was present for half of the subjects and recorded his **observations** independently. This enabled **inter-rater reliability** to be calculated.

The observers did not know which condition the child had participated in (except if the child had been in one of the sessions with the male model).

The observers recorded what the child was doing every five seconds (providing 240 observations). Responses were recorded in the following categories and provided an 'aggression score' for each child:

1 Imitative aggression responses
- *Physical:* any specific acts which were imitated.
- *Verbal aggression:* any phrases that were imitated, such as 'Pow'.
- *Non-aggressive verbal responses:* such as saying 'He keeps coming back for more'.

2 Partially imitative responses
- *Mallet aggression:* uses mallet on toys other than Bobo.
- *Sits on Bobo doll* but doesn't behave aggressively.

3 Non-imitative aggressive responses
- *Punches Bobo doll:* strikes, slaps, pushes the doll.
- *Non-imitative physical and verbal aggression:* aggressive acts directed at toys other than Bobo, saying hostile things not said by the model.
- *Aggressive gun play.*

Qs 3.8

1. Explain why it was necessary to have a control condition?
2. Explain why Phase 2 of this experiment was necessary.
3. How was the DV operationalised in this study?
4. Describe the behaviour checklist used in this study.
5. Is this study an experiment or an observation? Explain your answer.
6. Why was a one-way mirror used to observe the children?
7. Explain 'inter-rater reliability' and why it was desirable to calculate this.
8. In phase 3 identify **two or more** controls that were used.
9. Identify the three rooms that were used in this study.
10. Describe **two** ethical problems that might arise in this study and explain how the experimenters are likely to have dealt with them.
11. It would have been necessary to gain informed consent from the children's parents. What information would you give them if you were seeking their informed consent?

A female model kicking Bobo around the room. When Bandura et al. *refer to a 'model' they don't mean a fashion model – the term 'model' is used in **social learning theory** to refer to anyone who is imitated. And when someone is 'modelling' a behaviour, it means they are 'imitating' it.*

Results

Imitation of aggression

The children imitated the models both in terms of specific acts and in general levels of their behaviour.

- **Complete imitation** Children in the aggressive condition imitated many of the models' physical and verbal behaviours, both aggressive and non-aggressive behaviours. In fact about one-third of their imitations were of non-aggressive verbal behaviour. By contrast, children in the non-aggressive and control conditions displayed very few aggressive behaviours (in fact 70% of them had zero scores).

- **Partial imitation** There were differences for partial imitation in the same direction as those found for complete imitation.

- **Non-imitative aggression** The aggressive group displayed more non-imitative aggression than the non-aggressive group, but the difference was small and not **significant**.

- **Non-aggressive behaviour** Children in the non-aggression condition spent more time playing non-aggressively with dolls than children in the other groups.

Gender effects

- **Same-sex imitation** There was some evidence of a 'same-sex' effect' for boys but not for girls.

- **Gender of model** The male models had a greater influence in general than the female models.

- **Gender of child** Boys imitated more physical aggression than girls but the groups didn't differ in terms of verbal aggression.

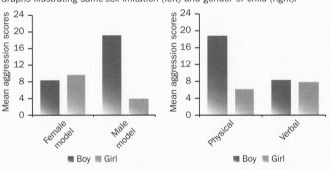

Graphs illustrating same-sex imitation (left) and gender of child (right).

*In the aggressive condition, one of the things that the model did was to kick the Bobo doll. Later the children were watched as they played with toys, including the Bobo doll. Was the little girl imitating the model's act of kicking the doll? Or was this behaviour due to **demand characteristics** – an inflatable doll kind of 'invites' being kicked or punched?*

The graph shows that in all conditions children behaved aggressively but children only displayed imitative aggression (physical and verbal) when the model was aggressive.

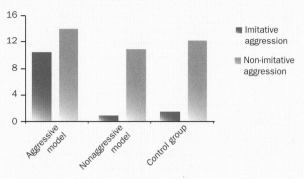

Qs 3.9

1. What conclusion(s) can you draw from the graph above?
2. Refer back to the four original research predictions. For each of one state the finding associated with this prediction.
3. The difference between the two experimental groups in terms of non-imitative aggression was not significant. What conclusion can we draw from this?

Try this   3.5

The actual data produced in the report of this study are shown in the table below. It is interesting to examine these data for yourself and decide on what conclusions *you* would draw.

For example, the children with the aggressive model were sometimes *less aggressive* than the children with the non-aggressive model. How would you explain that?

There were also occasions when boys were *more* aggressive with a female model rather than the male model. How would you explain this?

*Raw data from study by Bandura et al., **mean** aggression scores (page 578).*

Response category	Experimental groups				Control groups
	Aggressive		Non-aggressive		
	F model	M model	F model	M model	
Imitative physical aggression					
Female subjects (F)	5.5	7.2	2.5	0.0	1.2
Male subjects (M)	12.4	25.8	0.2	1.5	2.0
Imitative verbal aggression					
F	13.7	2.0	0.3	0.0	0.7
M	4.3	12.7	1.1	0.0	1.7
Partially imitative: mallet aggression					
F	17.2	18.7	0.5	0.5	13.1
M	15.5	28.8	18.7	6.7	13.5
Partially imitative: punches Bobo doll					
F	6.3	16.5	5.8	4.3	11.7
M	18.9	11.9	15.6	14.8	15.7
Non-imitative aggression					
F	21.3	8.4	7.2	1.4	6.1
M	16.2	36.7	26.1	22.3	24.6
Non-imitative: aggressive gun play					
F	1.8	4.5	2.6	2.5	3.7
M	7.3	15.9	8.9	16.7	14.3

Discussion

This study shows that people will produce new behaviours that they have observed and generalise these behaviours to other situations. This extends the scope of the principle of **operant conditioning**. According to this principle we learn through reward and punishment – for example, if you act aggressively and are rewarded for this behaviour then you are likely to repeat the behaviour. If you are punished for the behaviour, then you will be less likely to reproduce the behaviour in the future.

However, operant conditioning will only work if a person produces a particular behaviour. The results of this study show that the observation of someone else's behaviour may also lead to learning new behaviours.

Greater influence of male models

The greater influence of the male **models** might be explained in terms of the fact that males in general have a higher reward value. Research by Rosenblith (1959) found that male experimenters were more effective than females in influencing children's behaviour, and suggested that the fact that males are less commonly found in school settings might enhance their status and thus 'reward value'.

A second explanation for the greater influence of male models is that physical aggression is a male-type behaviour. Both girls and boys were not surprised by the male model's behaviour, in fact they were quite impressed (saying things like 'Al's a good socker, he beat up Bobo'). Whereas they were surprised by the female models ('That's not the way for a lady to behave'). Thus they may have been more ready to imitate the appropriate behaviour of the male model and more prone to ignore the inappropriate behaviour of the female model.

Imitations were of physical rather than verbal behaviour because that is highly masculine-type behaviour.

Explaining imitative learning

It might be argued that the reason why participants behaved more aggressively after watching an aggressive model is it weakened their usual reluctance to be aggressive. However, the fact that children imitated specific acts shows that the new behaviour was due to learning rather than an altered level of what is acceptable.

It is possible to explain imitative learning in terms of Freud's 'Identification with aggressor' (Freud, 1946). According to this, one deals with aggressive behaviour by adopting the attributes of the threatening person to allay anxiety. This is the process of identification. However, this study suggests that identification may not be necessary for imitative (social) learning to take place because the children imitated the models regardless of the quality of the relationship.

That's no way for a lady to behave

Bandura et al. *suggest that the children may have been more likely to imitate the behaviour of male models because it is more acceptable for males to behave that way. It may be that the women who behave aggressively were not imitated because it was seen as inappropriate behaviour.*

Qs 3.10

1 Identify **three** conclusions that can be drawn from the results.
2 How does this study extend the principle of operant conditioning?
3 What suggestions do Bandura *et al.* offer as to why boys and girls are more likely to imitate the male model in terms of physical aggression?
4 Bandura *et al.* suggest that the model's aggressive behaviour may weaken a child's reluctance to be aggressive. What evidence is there to suggest this is not the explanation for the increased levels of aggression?
5 How can identification be used to explain social learning?
6 What evidence is there to suggest that identification is not the explanation for social learning?
7 This research was conducted a long time ago. Do you think children would behave the same today? Why or why not?

Things you could do ...

Read the original article by Bandura, Ross and Ross at http://psychclassics.yorku.ca/Bandura/bobo.htm

Read: This research suggests that aggression is caused by experience. However, there is plenty of evidence that aggression may also be inherited. Read about the other side of the evidence. A good starting place is the 'Genetics of aggression' on Wikipedia, or look up 'Aggression, nature or nurture' on the internet.

Watch videos, for example:

A video put together by some students, providing description and evaluation http://www.youtube.com/watch?v=Mljor9txWJw&feature=related

Bandura's description of his research with clips from this study (http://www.youtube.com/watch?v=hHHdovKHDNU).

A lecture by Albert Bandura (but skip the first nine minutes!), which includes how his theory has been usefully applied to universal global problems (http://www.youtube.com/watch?v=xjIbKaSXM3A).

...Links to core studies...

This study links to **Freud**'s theory because the concept of identification is used to explain social learning.

This study gives an explanation of how our social behaviour develops and so links to social psychology studies such as **Reicher and Haslam** and **Piliavin *et al.***

The study extends the theory of **behaviourism** and so links to that key issue.

The sophisticated method used has a tight experimental method and uses observational techniques to collect the data. Observation is also used in **Rosenhan**'s study.

Evaluating the study by Bandura *et al.*

The research method
This study was a laboratory experiment.

What are the strengths and weaknesses of this research method in the context of this study?

Data collection
Observational techniques were also used in this study (to measure the dependent variable).

What are the strengths and weaknesses of this research method in the context of this study?

The sample
The participants were young children from one middle-class US nursery school.

What impact would such characteristics (age, class and culture) have on the results? How much can you generalise the results of this study to people in general?

Ethics
There are a number of important issues to consider: the fact that the participants were children, that they were asked to witness aggressive behaviour, that the expected outcome was that they would acquire some aggressive behaviours, that they were mildly provoked to feel aggressive and finally, that they were observed covertly.

Which aspects of the study were ethically acceptable and which aspects weren't?

Reliability
Reliability concerns measurement.

What aspects of human behaviour were measured in this study? How could the reliability of these measurements be assessed?

Validity
The techniques used to measure the dependent variable (aggression) may be affected by observer bias.

To what extent might this reduce the validity of this study?

Ecological validity
This study involved aggressive behaviour towards an inflatable doll.

To what extent is this study representative of everyday life?

This study looked at short-term effects.

To what extent can we generalise the findings from this study to other situations?

Qualitative or quantitative?
What kind of data were collected in this study? Use examples to illustrate your answer.

What are the strengths and weaknesses of producing this kind of data in the context of this study?

Suggest how a different kind of data might have been collected in this study.

Applications/usefulness
How might you use the findings from this study, for example in understanding the effects of media violence on children and adults?

What next?
*Describe **one** change to this study, and say how you think this might affect the outcome.*

> *There are no simple answers.*
>
> *Evaluating a study requires you to think.*
>
> *We have provided some pointers here, linked to the* **RESEARCH METHODS** *and* **KEY ISSUES** *covered in Chapter 1 (Psychological investigations) and Chapter 7 (Key issues).*
>
> *You can read suggested answers on our website www.psypress.com/cw/banyard.*

Producing effective evaluation
When you produce your own answers to the issues on the left there are two things to ensure:
1 Contextualisation
2 Elaboration

The key to **CONTEXTUALISATION** is to ensure that your answer includes some information about this particular study. For example:

> *Question:*
> With reference to the study by Bandura *et al.*, describe **one** similarity with any core studies that take the developmental approach. **[3]**
>
> *Answer:*
> **STATE:** One similarity is that any research that takes the developmental approach is related to how people's behaviour changes (develops) over time and the factors that create this change.
> **CONTEXT:** Bandura *et al.*'s study looked at how children's aggressive behaviour might develop because of what they see other people doing.
> **COMMENT:** This is similar to the study by Samuel and Bryant which looked at a different aspect of development – how children's ability to conserve quantity changes as they get older.

The key to **ELABORATION** is the three-point rule (see page xii), but you don't need three points when there are only 2 marks! For example:

> *Question:*
> In the study by Bandura *et al.*, the children were taken into a second room to create mild frustration. Explain why this was necessary. **[2]**
>
> *Answer:*
> **STATE:** It was necessary because the children might otherwise have reacted to the model by being less likely to behave aggressively.
> **COMMENT:** Without some kind of provocation they had no reason to be feeling aggressive themselves.

The developmental approach

On pages 74–75 and 220–221 we have discussed the **developmental approach**.

The study by Bandura, Ross and Ross concerns aggressive behaviour.

- In what way is this study an example of the developmental approach?
- Discuss the strengths and weaknesses of the developmental approach using examples from the Bandura, Ross and Ross study.

Bandura *et al.*: afters

Still kicking ass

It is remarkable that more than 50 years after this study was conducted it is still commonly used as evidence in our understanding of children's development. The simple message from the study would seem to be that children copy what they see, but maybe we are not ready to deal with that yet because this would mean switching off our televisions.

Video games

Does watching and taking part in video games make children more aggressive? The video game industry would have you believe that there is no link between video violence and real-life violence. For example, Sacher (1993) reviewed research in this area and found that seven studies did link video games to aggressive behaviour but 19 studies found no link.

A different argument is put forward by ex-US army officer and psychologist David Grossman (1995). He suggests that playing violent video games will desensitise people and make them emotionally disengaged from violence. Grossman points out how difficult it is to get soldiers to fire guns. The history of warfare shows that fewer than one-fifth of soldiers fire their guns at another human being. To counteract this and improve their 'kill rate' the US army used psychological techniques to train the shooting response in their soldiers. Part of the training uses video combat simulations.

Today the US army has made its own video game, 'America's Army', that you can download for free. In the game, you get to kill people with cool weapons that look and respond like the real things. You get to ambush terrorists and, when caught in a firefight, you can hear bullets whistle past your ears. The game has been downloaded many millions of times since the original version was launched in 2002 and appears in the 2008 *Guinness Book of Records* as the most downloaded war game.

For a different point of view there is 'Special Force' produced by the Islamic group Hezbollah in which you can be a Palestinian fighter attacking Israeli soldiers and settlers (Ryan, 2004).

The uncomfortable truth is that the best evidence shows that exposure to violent video games is a risk factor for increases in aggressive behaviour and decreases in empathy and pro-social behaviour (Anderson *et al.*, 2010). In other words, Bandura's findings still stand today.

Violence on terrestrial television

An analysis of two weeks' prime-time viewing on UK terrestrial television looked at the levels of violence in a range of programmes (BSC, 2002). It found an increasing trend towards violence in programmes compared with previous years.

The study found that on average there were 5.2 acts of violence per hour in 2001, whereas in 1997 the figure was 4.1 acts per hour. The programmes containing the most violence were films (8.4 scenes per hour), the news (8.3 scenes per hour) and drama (6.6 scenes per hour). There is a common belief that programmes before the watershed (9pm) are less violent than those after it. Although this used to be the case it is no longer true and in 2001 there were more scenes of violence before the watershed than after it.

The jury is out on whether television and video game violence comes out of the screen and affects the players in their everyday lives, but to be fair the jury is getting its sponsorship from the video game industry.

The most common context for violent scenes was crime and police action which accounted for 31% of all violent scenes. And the most common reason for violence was shown as anger or frustration (16% of scenes). Although 83% of the programmes were made in the UK, the programmes from the USA accounted for 35% of the violent scenes. The analysis also found that there is a growing trend to show violence in a realistic way. In the two weeks of prime-time programmes there were 335 deaths of which 35% were shown as murders. Over half of the deaths occurred as the result of gunshots.

In brief, the average viewer in the UK watches a regular diet of violence and murder. Two questions come from this: first, does this violent wallpaper have an effect on levels of violence in our communities, and second, why is watching violence an essential part of our daily entertainment?

Observing violence at home

All children with a TV observe aggressive behaviour every day on the screen. Most, however, do not see real-life aggression. One exception to this is children who witness, or are victims of, domestic violence.

In the UK it is estimated that 13% of women and 9% of men experience domestic violence (abuse, threats or force) in the course of any one year (Hall and Smith, 2011). Of the people who experience domestic violence women are much more likely to receive a serious injury than men (6% women, 1% men) and experience far more incidents on average than men (women 20, men 7). No other crime has such a high repeat victimisation rate.

Violence is a family affair. For every parent experiencing domestic violence there will often be children who are also suffering. It is estimated that in 90% of incidents involving domestic violence, the children are in the same or the next room (Hughes, 1992). During violent assaults on a parent children might well intervene to protect the parent or their brothers and sisters.

Effect on children

The jury is out on the effect on children of observing domestic violence. Some children show a range of responses such as poor school performance, aggression to peers and rebelling against adults. Some children don't show any negative effects at all and may even show signs of improvement such as better school work. There is no clear pattern of response to observing domestic violence (Women's Aid, 2012). For more information see the Women's Aid website at www.womensaid.org.uk.

Multiple choice questions

1 What age children were used in this experiment?
   a Nursery school.
   b Primary school.
   c Secondary school.
   d A mixture of all three.

2 Which of the following was not one of the research predictions?
   a Children will imitate specific acts performed by an aggressive model.
   b Children who observe an aggressive model will become generally more aggressive.
   c Boys will be more aggressive than girls.
   d Boys will be more likely to imitate a same-sex role model than girls.

3 The IV in this experiment was:
   a Sex of the child.
   b Aggressiveness of the model.
   c Sex of the model.
   d All of the above.

4 Which experimental design was used in this study?
   a Single participant.
   b Independent measures.
   c Repeat measures.
   d Matched participants.

5 Which of the following was an ethical issue in this study?
   a Deception.
   b Right to withdraw.
   c Psychological harm.
   d All of the above.

6 In phase 2 of the study the children were:
   a Not allowed to play with the toys.
   b Allowed to play with the toys but stopped after two minutes.
   c Watched while they played with the toys as long as they liked.
   d Shown a film.

7 The non-aggressive model was:
   a Happy.   b Joking.
   c Silent.   d Subdued.

8 Observations were made every:
   a 5 seconds.   b 5 minutes.
   c 10 seconds.   d 10 minutes.

9 One of the behaviours that was observed was 'sits on Bobo doll'. Which category did this come in?
   a Imitative aggressive responses.
   b Partially imitative responses.
   c Non-imitative aggressive responses.
   d Non-imitative responses.

10 Which of the following is true?
   a Boys imitated less physical aggression than girls.
   b Boys imitated more verbal aggression than girls.
   c Boys behaved less aggressively than girls.
   d Boys were more likely to imitate male models than female models.

Answers are on page 247.

Exam-style questions

There are three kinds of question that can be asked about the Bandura, Ross and Ross study, as represented here by sections A, B and C.

See page x for further notes on the exam paper and styles of question.

Section A questions

1 In the study by Bandura *et al.* the observers classified the children's aggressive behaviour as imitative or non-imitative.
   (a) Give **one** example of imitative aggression and **one** example of non-imitative aggression in the study. [2]
   (b) Why did they look at both types of aggression? [2]

2 The study by Bandura *et al.* was a well-controlled experiment.
   (a) Identify **two** variables that were controlled. [2]
   (b) Explain how each of these variables was controlled by the researchers. [2]

3 In the study by Bandura *et al.* the children were mildly provoked to arouse aggression.
   (a) Outline how the children were subjected to mild arousal of aggression. [2]
   (b) Why was this necessary? [2]

4 Bandura *et al.* concluded that aggression may be learned through imitations. Give **two** differences between the way the children witnessed the violence in the experiment and the way children witness violence in everyday life. [4]

5 (a) Describe **one** of the predictions made at the beginning of the study by Bandura *et al.* [2]
   (b) To what extent do the results support this conclusion? [2]

6 The children in the study were matched in terms of aggressiveness.
   (a) Describe how this was done. [2]
   (b) Explain why it was necessary to match the children on aggressiveness. [2]

7 Outline **two** findings from the study by Bandura *et al.* [4]

8 Bandura *et al.* studied children.
   (a) Outline **one** practical difficulty with studying children. [2]
   (b) Outline **one** ethical difficulty with studying children. [2]

9 In the study by Bandura *et al.*
   (a) Outline **two** of the independent variables. [2]
   (b) Explain how the behaviour of the model was manipulated. [2]

10 In the study by Bandura *et al.*, explain what happened during the final stage when the children were observed playing with toys. [4]

Section B questions

Answer the following questions with reference to the Bandura *et al.* study:

(a) Describe the aims of the study by Bandura *et al.* [2]

(b) Describe the data collected in the study by Bandura *et al.* and **one** strength of collecting this kind of data. [6]

(c) Describe how the children's behaviour was observed in the study by Bandura *et al.* [8]

(d) Explain how the reliability of these measurements could be assessed. [6]

(e) Outline the conclusions of the study by Bandura *et al.* [6]

(f) Suggest **two** changes to the study by Bandura *et al.* and outline how these changes might affect the results. [8]

Section C questions

(a) Outline **one** assumption of the developmental approach in psychology. [2]

(b) Describe how the developmental approach could explain aggression. [4]

(c) Describe **one** similarity and **one** difference between the study by Bandura *et al.* and any other core studies that takes the developmental approach. [6]

(d) Discuss strengths and weaknesses of the developmental approach, using examples from any core studies that take this approach. [12]

FREUD: STARTERS

Psychoanalysis

You can't get more interesting or more controversial than this. Basically it's about sex and death, two topics that we obsess about but find it difficult to discuss in a sensible way. The name of Sigmund Freud will always get a reaction. Many people seek to dismiss his work and many others will argue that he was the greatest thinker of the last century. Love him or hate him, you can't ignore him.

It is over 70 years since Sigmund Freud died in London but he is still one of the most influential thinkers in the Western world. Type his name into Google and you'll get more than two million hits. Site after site gives summaries of his work, interprets it, applies it to life, the universe and everything, and carries on arguments with other sites about what the theory means. In this text it is only possible to hint at the importance of the theory, so if you are interested then check out the many websites.

The unconscious mind

Perhaps Freud's most important contribution to the way we think about ourselves has been the unconscious mind. He didn't invent the concept but developed the idea and applied it to a wide range of events. Freud proposed that our awareness is in layers and there are thoughts occurring below the surface. He suggested that the power of the unconscious can be seen in dreams which he called the 'royal road to the unconscious'. According to Freud, dreams may appear to be nonsense but they are meaningful and reveal your hidden thoughts, feelings and desires. We hide the true meaning of the dream in symbols. The trick is to interpret the symbols and find the cause of the dream.

Psychic structure

Freud developed the idea of the unconscious by proposing a 'psychic structure'. This structure is divided into the id, ego and superego.

You are born with a mass of pleasure-seeking desires (I want it, and I want it now!). This is the id. As you become socialised your ego develops and controls the desires of the id. Finally you take on the ethics of other people and these appear in your mind as the superego. One way to think of the superego is as your conscience or maybe as the voice of your mother, which you can hear even when she isn't there. The task of the ego is to maintain a balance between the id and the superego. Too much id and you get in all sorts of trouble, too much superego and you get consumed by guilt. Much of the id is in the unconscious because if you had half an idea of what your desires are telling you to do you'd die of shock.

The talking cure

Freud believed that the answer to a number of psychological and physical problems lay deep in the unconscious mind. The task of the therapist was to help the patient get access to these unconscious thoughts and feelings. After he studied with **Jean-Martin Charcot** in Paris, Freud briefly used hypnosis to achieve this. He later moved on and developed the method of free association, which is one of the techniques used in **psychoanalysis** – commonly called 'the talking cure' – to get people to say whatever is going through their minds. He believed that if he could guide his patients to a relaxed mental state their thoughts would automatically drift towards any areas of conflict and pain.

The couch

When Freud carried out psychoanalysis on his patients he got them to lie on a couch. In fact, Freud's original couch can be seen at the Freud Museum in London. Many psychoanalysts still use a couch with their patients. They believe it is useful because when lying down the patient will focus less on objects in the environment and more on images and feelings that come from their own minds. Also they are unable to see the reaction of the analyst which prevents them playing the game of trying to guess what the analyst is thinking or feeling. Maybe the lack of eye contact also helps the patient to relax and be less concerned by the reaction to what they are saying (Ross, 1999).

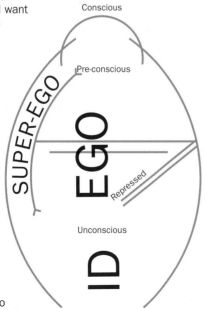

Freud sketched out a diagram of his conception of psychic structures as shown here.

Ego defence mechanisms

We can protect ourselves from a full awareness of unpleasant thoughts, feelings and desires with **defence mechanisms**. They are ego defences because the ego (our rational, conscious mind) uses them to protect itself from anxiety. For example:

Denial is the refusal to accept reality and to act as if a painful event, thought or feeling did not exist.

Displacement is the redirecting of thoughts feelings and impulses from an object that gives rise to anxiety to a safer, more acceptable one. For example, being angry at the boss and kicking the dog.

Projection means placing your undesired impulses onto someone else. For example, an angry spouse accuses their partner of hostility.

Repression is the blocking of unacceptable feelings or memories from consciousness. However, things which are placed in the unconscious mind are expressed through, for example, dreams or mental disorders such as **phobias**. This is a key theme in the study of Little Hans – he repressed his anxieties about his mother, father and sister; this anxiety was then attached to something else (horses) which made him fearful of horses.

Isolation is sometimes called *intellectualisation* and means that in certain situations or when recalling particular memories, a person will show no emotion or feeling. They may recall painful events without recalling the emotion that they felt at the time. An example may be that the person recalls how they were abused as a child, but acts as if it meant nothing to them.

Regression is where a person behaves in a way that in the past may have brought about relief from the anxiety-provoking situation. An example may be of an older child reverting to sucking their thumb when another child is born into the family. Or an adult may throw a tantrum if things aren't going the way they want them to.

Biographical notes on Sigmund Freud (1856–1939)

Sigismund Schlomo Freud (later shortened to Sigmund by himself) was born to a middle-class Jewish family in Freiberg in central Europe. When he was four years old the family moved to Vienna where he stayed until 1938 when he was forced to leave the city to escape the Nazi regime. The anti-Semitism that he had lived with all his life finally drove him out of Vienna. Four of his sisters were subsequently unable to get out and died in the death camps.

During his childhood Freud had some hostility towards his father but was very close to his mother. This family dynamic is thought by some to have influenced his later theories of, for example, the **Oedipus complex**.

He studied medicine and became a respected neuropathologist. One condition that interested him was hysteria, where patients would exhibit extreme physical symptoms such as paralysis without an obvious physical cause. A visit to the French neurologist Jean-Martin Charcot convinced him that hysteria was caused by mental events rather than physical ones. He started to explore the mental reasons for hysteria and developed his techniques of free association. With Joseph Breuer he published *Studies in Hysteria* in 1895.

Freud continued to develop and publish his theories for the next 40 years. *The Interpretation of Dreams* (1900) and *Three Essays on the Theory of Sexuality* (1905) made Freud famous. They also made him very controversial especially because of his views on infantile sexuality. He developed his theories from his **clinical** work and some of his case studies are published, including the story of Little Hans. He also engaged in a lot of self-reflection and analysis.

Freud tackled the big questions about life and came up with many uncomfortable answers. He attracted devoted followers though there were many splits in the community of psychoanalysis. Wider society recognised the extraordinary contribution Freud made to our understanding of the human mind and in 1935 he was appointed Honorary Member of the Royal Society of Medicine.

Sigmund Freud (1856–1939)

The Oedipus complex

Freud believed that children are born with powerful emotions and drives. As a child develops, the drives focus on different parts of their body. After birth, the focus is on the mouth and children explore the physical and emotional world through it (this is called the oral stage). As children start to gain control of their bodily functions they move into the **anal stage** where they get pleasure from retaining or expelling faeces. Then comes the phallic stage where the focus is on their genitals. Between the ages of 7 and 11 Freud suggested children go through a latency period where sexual feelings are repressed before moving into the adult genital stage at puberty.

The part of this theory most relevant to the study of Little Hans is the phallic stage and, in particular, the Oedipus complex: *'I want a girl, just the girl that married dear old dad.'*

Part of the Greek myth of Oedipus refers to a child who is brought up not knowing who his parents are. As a man he goes to the city of Thebes where he kills the tyrant king and marries the queen. Unfortunately for Oedipus he then discovers that the king was his father and the queen, now his wife, is also his mother. Well it would upset anyone.

Freud saw the story as describing a childhood drama for all little boys. Their mother is their first source of affection and is the focus of their erotic feelings. During the phallic stage of development the boy wants to possess his mother and recognises a competition with his father. He fears he will be punished for such wishes by castration but resolves the conflict by 'identifying the aggressor' and taking on the values and behaviour of his rival.

Freudian slips

Freud became interested in the trivial errors of everyday life such as forgotten appointments or saying the wrong thing. Freud believed that these events were not due to chance but were the result of unconscious attitudes, for example he quoted Charles Darwin who always made a written note of research findings that disagreed with his own ideas because he found that these facts and ideas were more likely to slip the memory than those that agreed with him. Today we use the term *Freudian Slip* to describe those occasions when we say something we didn't mean to but what we say actually reflects what we really believe or are thinking about. Commonly they involve saying a sexual word by mistake. Search online 'freudian slips' and check out the YouTube clips for some good examples.

Book burning

It's difficult to imagine in the UK today that a government would organise events to burn the books of people they believed had degenerate views. This is what happened to Freud among others during the 1930s in Germany.

Freud (1933) commented: 'What progress we are making. In the Middle Ages they would have burned me. Now they are content with burning my books.'

Anti-Semitism

'My language is German. My culture, my attainments are German. I considered myself German intellectually, until I noticed the growth of anti-Semitic prejudice in Germany and German Austria. Since that time, I prefer to call myself a Jew.' (Freud, 1925)

...Link to the core study...

Freud used case studies as evidence for his theories. Much of his theory on children was based on the recollections of adults which are, of course, coloured by their subsequent experiences. Little Hans is one of the few children that Freud had direct experience of, and even then most of the contact was made indirectly through interviews with Hans' father. The full study is the length of a short novel which might be a bit off-putting to you. However, if you enjoy a good read then we recommend that you look it out.

Freud: the core study

Sigmund Freud (1909) Analysis of a phobia in a five-year-old boy. In J. Strachey (ed. and trans.) *The Standard Edition of the Complete Psychological Works: Two Case Histories* (vol. X), pages 5–147. London: The Hogarth Press.

This case study is over 100 pages long, containing lots of detail of what Hans said and did. What we have presented here is very much a selection!

See the
CORE STUDY CHECKLIST
on page xv for details of what you need to know for the exam.

In a nutshell

Context and aims
Freud used the study of Little Hans to support his ideas about child development and the treatment of mental disorder:

- Freud proposed that adult personality is shaped by childhood events. In this study he sought evidence of infantile sexuality and the **Oedipus complex**.
- Freud proposed that mental disorder can be explained in terms of **ego defence mechanisms**. In this **case study** he consider what caused Hans' **phobia** about horses.
- Freud developed a therapy to treat mental disorder, **psychoanalysis**, and used this case study to demonstrate the value of this method.

Method
This case study concerns one boy, 'Little Hans', during the time he was aged between three and five years old. The data was collected by Hans' father, a man who was interested in Freud's work. Both Freud and Hans' father analysed the events that unfolded.

Results
Freud divided the results of the study into three parts.

Key term: psychoanalysis

*The term **psychoanalysis** is used to refer to Freud's theory of personality development and also a form of therapy – his 'talking cure' (see page 96). As a form of therapy psychoanalysis aims to help patients become consciously aware of their unconscious, repressed feelings. By consciously acknowledging these feelings the patient can accept them and recover.*

Key term: the Oedipus complex

*Freud explained how boys go through a stage in their development where they desire their mothers and regard their fathers as a rival, wishing them dead. This death wish creates anxiety. The **Oedipus complex** is eventually resolved when a boy comes to identify with his father.*

FREUD: THE CORE STUDY

Part I: introduction
The background to the case study begins when Hans is three. There are three sources of his anxiety:

- *His mother* with whom he would like to have a sexual relationship. She has rejected his advances and he fears castration.
- *His father* who is a rival for Hans' mother. At the same time Hans loves his father.
- *His sister Hanna* who is also a rival. He wishes his mother would drown her, but then fears his mother might harm him too.

Part II: case study and analysis
Hans' father and Freud considered things that Hans said and did, and provided explanations for Hans' phobias. For example:

- *Phobia of being bitten by white horses*: Hans reported that (1) a real event where a little girl was told that she might be bitten if she touched a particular white horse and (2) asking his mother to touch his penis and being told that wasn't proper. The anxiety caused by the latter became attached to the former, created a phobia of white horses.
- *Phobia of horses and their black nosebands*: Hans wished to become a man (and gain his mother's love). He also wished his father was dead, a wish that created anxiety. The black nosebands represented manhood and his father. His anxiety became attached to the horse and its nosebands.
- *Generalised anxiety (a form of phobia)*: Hans was afraid of leaving the house probably because he became afraid of horses with laden carts. Laden carts represented pregnancy, which was related to his anxieties about his sister.

Hans' phobias were resolved when he was able to express his true feelings to his father through his fantasies and eventually to identify with his father.

Part III: discussion
This case study might be criticised for lacking objectivity. For example Hans' father used **leading questions**.

This case study does show that young children are interested in their sexuality, as Freud predicted, and illustrates the Oedipus complex.

This case study also shows how phobias are an expression of unconscious anxieties.

The patient may overcome such a phobia by gaining a conscious understanding of their **repressed** fears.

Qs 3.11

1. This was a case study. Outline **one** strength and **one** weakness of a case study with reference to this study.
2. Describe how the data was collected in this study.
3. Explain why the data collected might not be valid.
4. Explain why his mother was a source of anxiety for Hans.
5. Explain why his father was a source of anxiety for Hans.
6. Explain why his sister was a source of anxiety for Hans.
7. Identify **two** of Hans' phobias.
8. Select **one** of Hans' phobias and outline Freud's explanation of why this phobia developed.
9. How did Hans resolve his phobia(s)?
10. Describe one of Hans' fantasies (see page 101).
11. In what way is this resolution an example of psychoanalysis?
12. Describe **one** ethical issue related to this study.
13. In what way is Hans a 'little Oedipus' (see previous page for a description of the Oedipus complex)?

The detailed version

Context and aims

Freud developed a theory of child development – how a person's experiences during childhood shape their adult personality. Freud based this theory on the recollections of his adult patients about their childhood. In his work, Freud listened to many patients describing the events of their childhood and he proposed that these events explained the mental disorders and difficulties they experienced as adults.

Aims

The opportunity to study young Hans meant he could see if his theory about personality development would be supported. In particular the case of Little Hans related to the development of infantile sexuality and the Oedipus complex.

There was a second aim for this study. During the period when Hans' father was recording **observations**, Hans developed an intense phobia of horses. This provided Freud with an opportunity to also test his explanation of how phobias develop. Additionally it meant he could use his method of treatment (psychoanalysis) and demonstrate its usefulness.

Qs 3.12

1 Briefly explain why Freud was interested in this case study.
2 Describe the sample in this case study.
3 Explain why Hans' father decided to undertake this case study.
4 Explain why Hans developed a castration anxiety.
5 Explain the concept of repression.
6 Explain why Hans came to fear having baths.
7 How did the holiday at Gmunden affect his relationships with his father and mother.
8 Why did Hans resent his baby sister?

Method

Participant

The participant in this case study is a boy called Little Hans who was aged between three and five during the period of this case study. The other main people involved were his father, mother and sister. They lived in Vienna, Austria at the beginning of the twentieth century (Hans was born in 1904).

Procedure

Hans' father was one of Freud's closest 'followers', a member of Freud's Wednesday night study group. He was keen to put Freud's ideas of psychoanalysis into practice. Psychoanalysis involves the interpretation of a patient's thoughts and fantasies so that the patient can come to understand them himself.

Hans' father recorded events and conversations with Hans and sent these regularly to Freud. Both Freud and the father offered interpretations of Hans' behaviour. On one occasion during the case study Hans was taken to meet Freud.

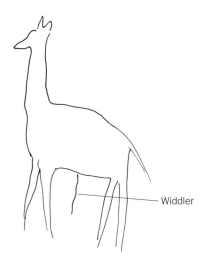

A drawing Hans made of a giraffe. He asked his father to add the widdler but his father said 'Draw it yourself'.

— Widdler

Results: Hans' early life

Little Hans and his 'widdler'

Just before he was three, Hans started to show a lively interest in his 'widdler'. Hans observed that animals had big ones, especially an animal like a horse. He assumed that both his parents must have big ones because they were fully grown.

He got pleasure from touching his widdler and also from excretion. Later, when he imagined having his own children, he supposed he would help them widdle and wipe their bottoms – performing those things which had given him much pleasure. He kicked about when urinating/ defecating showing the pleasure associated with such activity.

His mother found him playing with his penis: *'If you do that, I shall send for Doctor A. to cut off your widdler'* (page 8).

This led Hans to develop a **castration anxiety** (fear of having his penis removed), which meant he had to repress his feelings of pleasure to prevent the accompanying sense of anxiety.

Hans also felt sexual desire for his mother, which was repressed and expressed as an interest in other girls and wanting to kiss them.

Death wish towards his father

During his summer holiday at Gmunden, Hans spent much time alone with his mother while his father returned to work in Vienna. When they returned home, Hans had to share his mother once again with his father and wished his father to be permanently away.

Hans expressed his conflicting aggression and love towards his father by hitting him and then kissing the spot where he had hit his father.

Baby sister

When Hans was three and a half his baby sister Hanna was born (October 1906), further separating him from his mother. Having a baby sister also reminded him of the attentions he used to receive from his mother when he was a baby.

Hans admitted that he had watched his sister having a bath and wished his mother would let her go. This unconscious desire to see his sister drown became translated into a fear that his mother might equally let Hans go in the bath.

Baths were womb-like and so also related to the process of being born.

Sources of his anxieties

In summary, Hans felt anxious about his:

• *Mother* – he had sexual fantasies about her but these resulted in anxieties. For example she had threatened that his penis would be cut off and that led to castration anxiety.

• *Father* – Hans saw his father as a rival for his mother, and wished him dead. But at the same time he loved his father and this created conflict and feelings of anxiety.

• *Sister* – he wished Hanna would drown, which led to anxiety and a fear that his mother would drop him.

An example of a conversation between Hans and his father

*This extract was recorded by Hans' father which shows how his father often used **leading questions** (questions which may 'suggest' a certain answer from the respondent – see study by **Loftus and Palmer** for more on leading questions).*

I: *Did you often get into bed with Mummy at Gmunden?*

Hans: *Yes.*

I: *And you used to think to yourself you were the Daddy?*

Hans: *Yes.*

I: *And then you felt afraid of Daddy? Can you remember the funeral at Gmunden? You thought then that if only Daddy were to die you'd be Daddy.*

Hans: *Yes.*

(From Freud, 1909, page 90)

Timeline

Year	Hans' age	Event
1903		Hans born.
1906	3–3¾	First reports.
	3¼–3½	Summer holidays, first visit to Gmunden.
	3½	Castration threat.
	3½	Hanna born.
1907	3¾	First dream.
	4	Removal to new flat.
	4¼–4½	Second visit to Gmunden, episode of biting horse.
1908	4¾	Episode of falling horse, start of phobia.
	5	Recovery, end of analysis.

Exam advice

In this description of Freud's case study we have tried to be true to the original document. However, the structure of the case study doesn't match exactly to the exam requirements.

In an exam, you may be asked to describe the results of this study. You should focus on the evidence rather than the analysis – but, arguably, the analysis is also part of the results.

(From Freud, 1909, page 49)

Results: case study and analysis

The phobia starts (January 1908)

When Hans was four and a half, he developed a fear that a white horse would bite him – Hans referred to his fear as *'my nonsense'*.

Freud felt that Hans' real fear was that he would lose his mother. His anxieties had been **repressed** into his unconscious mind and eventually expressed as a **phobia**. Freud explained the links between Hans' anxieties and horses in the following way:

1 It was partly based on a real event. Hans heard a father warn his daughter that a white horse might bite her if she touched it.

2 This was linked to Hans' mother telling him that it would not be proper if she touched his penis – Hans had asked her to touch his 'widdler' once when she was drying him after a bath. The link was: if you put your finger on a white horse it will bite you, if someone puts their finger on your widdler this was not proper.

3 Hans feared that his mother might leave him because she disapproved of his request. Hans' desire for his mother was a consequence of his sexual **libido** (his sexual drive). This sexual desire was now linked to a sense of anxiety.

4 In order to cope with this Hans unconsciously transferred the anxiety (attached to his libido) to white horses and therefore he became afraid of a white horse biting something that touched it.

5 His anxiety was exacerbated because his father told him that women don't have widdlers. Freud suggested that Hans would think 'My mother had a widdler before and now she hasn't. It must have been cut off. She said mine might be cut off if I touched it. She obviously wasn't joking because it happened to her'.

   This would lead to **castration anxiety**.

6 Horses also represented his father (see Hans' visit to see Freud, below) and the anxiety associated with his father.

Further horse anxieties

A new fear developed of horses pulling heavily laden carts or a bus. This created a **generalised anxiety disorder** where Hans became afraid of leaving his home.

This again was related to an actual event: Hans recalled an occasion when he was walking with his mother and they saw a horse pulling a bus. The horse fell down and kicked its legs about. This terrified Hans because he thought the horse was dead, creating anxiety.

The horse kicking also represented many repressed anxieties:

- Hans secretly wished his father would fall down dead. Seeing the horse fall over increased his anxiety about this death wish.

- Hans had become preoccupied with bowel movements ('lumf'). A laden cart was like a body full of faeces. Lumf falling in the toilet made a noise similar to the noise of a horse falling.

- A heavily laden cart was also like a pregnant woman and babies are also lumf-like. Therefore laden vehicles represented pregnancy. When a heavily laden cart tips over it represents giving birth (see passage below).

- The anxieties about pregnancy were linked to Hans' repressed feelings about his sister.

- Hans was particularly concerned about the horse 'kicking about' when it fell over which was linked to his own behaviour when defecating.

The phobia also served a real purpose of keeping him at home with his mother.

> *Hans played with dolls and had one that he named 'Lodi', the word for 'sausage'. His father pointed out that a sausage is like a lumf. 'When you sat on the chamber and a lumf came, did you think yourself you were having a baby?' Hans said yes. 'You know when the bus-horses fell down? The bus looked like a baby-box, and when the black horse fell down it was just like ...' Hans finished the sentence '... like having a baby'. And the noise of the horses' hooves was like Hans' noise he made with his feet when on the chamber.*

Hans visits Freud (March 1908)

Freud proposed that a horse might be symbolic of Hans' father because the black around the horses' mouths and the blinkers in front of their eyes might be symbols of his father's moustaches and glasses – symbols of manhood (i.e. things that Hans might envy because he wanted to be grown up and able to have his mother's love).

*Freud told Hans that he was afraid of his father because he was so fond of his mother. Freud's revelation appeared to release Hans and enable him to deal more directly with his phobia. He started to be able to go out into the street again and to the park. This is an example of **psychoanalysis** (the talking cure), where a psychological problem may be cured by making unconscious thoughts conscious.*

Fantasies

Hans reported many fantasies or 'dreams' which each expressed different aspects of his anxieties.

The dream about giraffes

A week or so before they visited Freud, Hans told his father the following 'dream' of two giraffes, *'In the night there was a big giraffe in the room and a crumpled one; and the big one called out because I took the crumpled one away from it. Then it stopped calling out; and then I sat down on top of the crumpled one'* (page 37).

Hans' father perceived that the big giraffe was him (the father) or his penis, and the crumpled one was his wife's genital organ.

The scene is a replay of what usually happened in the mornings – Hans came into their bed, welcomed by his mother but his father warned her not to do this (this is the big giraffe calling out). Hans stayed a little while (sits on the crumpled one).

Criminal fantasies

Hans dreamt about doing forbidden things with his father. He dreamt, for example, that he went *'with [my father] in the train, and we smashed a window and the policeman took us off with him'* (page 41), This represented wishing to do something forbidden to his mother which his father was also doing.

The resolution

Hans had several fantasies which enabled him to express his repressed feelings and finally fully recover from his phobias.

Fantasy 1: the plumber

Hans related the following to his father *'I was in the bath, and then the plumber came and unscrewed it. Then he took a big borer and stuck it in my stomach'* (page 65).

Hans' father interpreted this to mean: *'I was in bed with Mummy. Then Daddy came and sent me away. He pushed me away with his big penis'* (page 65).

Hans also had another fantasy: *'The plumber came and first he took away my behind with a pair of pincers, and then he gave me another, and then the same with my widdler'* (page 98). Presumably both the new behind and widdler were bigger, like Daddy's.

These fantasies showed that Hans was now identifying with his father by (apparently) wanting a behind and a widdler as well as a moustache like his father's. Thus Hans was becoming more conscious of his feelings about his father and resolving those feelings.

Fantasy 2: where babies came from

Hans' continued fear of baths represented an unconscious understanding of where babies come from. His interest in laden carts revealed his own attempt at providing an answer – he called laden carts 'stork-box carts' because his parents told him a stork brought the baby, and the box that brings the baby is the mother's womb. So stork + box = stork-box cart which is where babies come from.

Hans' parents finally explained where babies really came from – from inside 'Mummy'. This meant Hans no longer had a need for the cart analogy. After this he played outside, not fearing the carts.

Fantasy 3: becoming the daddy

Hans had always had an ongoing fantasy about his own children and how he was going to look after them. One day he was playing a game with these imaginary children and his father asked *'Are your children still alive?'* (page 96).

Hans replied that boys couldn't have children, he had been their mummy but now he was their daddy. And Hans' father was the Grandaddy.

So Hans had worked out a solution where his father was still part of the family and both of them were married to Hans' mother.

This led Freud to conclude that Hans had at last overcome his **Oedipus complex** because he was able to identify with his father.

And after this Hans managed to go all the way to the park!

Many students are somewhat dismissive of Freudian psychology. Try a bit of psychoanalysis yourself.

Write a short story about yourself. The story should show you in the past, the present and the future. Include:

- a scene from your early childhood
- a scene about a conflict in your current life
- a scene from your imagined future in which the conflict is resolved and elements of the first two scenes are also present.

You may present the scenes in the story in any order you choose. You might then share your story with other students and consider what you learned from the exercise.

Did you make unconscious thoughts and feelings conscious? Do you think this may be helpful? If so, in what way? Has the task changed what you think about psychoanalysis?

1 Give an example of a 'leading question' from the conversation between Hans and his father.

2 Give **two** reasons why Hans developed a fear of white horses.

3 Suggest **one** reason why Hans might have been afraid of a horse pulling a laden cart.

4 Freud explained Hans' behaviour in terms of 'deep meanings'. What alternative explanation (without deep meanings) might account for Hans' wish to stay at home?

5 Give an example of Freud's search for 'deep meanings' (i.e. hidden meanings).

6 Hans regarded his father as a rival for his mother. Explain how the giraffe fantasy represents this.

7 Explain why the plumber fantasy helped Hans to recover.

8 What is the link between anxiety and phobia?

9 In what way were Hans' fantasies important?

10 What might have led both Freud and Hans' father to draw biased conclusions?

11 List at least **two** different methods that were used to collect data in this case study.

12 Freud says that children do not respond to the therapist's 'suggestion'. What does this mean?

Freud: the core study *continued*

Postscript

Hans was interviewed much later when he was 19. At that time he appeared entirely normal and had experienced no difficulties during adolescence. He had no recollection of the events of his childhood.

More recently Hans' true identity was revealed – Herbert Graf (on the right below). He became an opera producer in America and died in 1973.

Qs 3.14

1   Freud suggests **two** possible criticisms of this case study. What were they?

2   How did Freud respond to the **two** criticisms of the study?

3   How does this study support Freud's theory of sexuality?

4   How does Freud explain Hans' recovery from his phobias?

5   Do you think Little Hans would have recovered without Freud's help? Why or why not?

Discussion

Support for Freud's theory of sexuality

Freud suggests that there are two possible criticisms that could be made about this case study:

1   If Hans was 'abnormal' we can't draw conclusions about normal development.

2   The analysis was conducted by his father and lacked objective worth.

Freud's response was:

1   That such **neuroses** in early childhood are relatively normal. This means it is reasonable to use this case to increase our understanding of normal development.

2   That, even if a response is triggered by suggestion, it is not arbitrary. In other words there is some meaningfulness to Hans' dialogue even if his father led him to give some of these answers. Freud argued that, in fact, Hans did sometimes disagree with his father's suggestions, so it was not always a case of being lead to give certain responses. In addition there were benefits from the close, subjective relationship between father and son. For example, more intimate details are likely to be revealed than when talking to a stranger.

Freud concluded that the **case study** of Hans does support his ideas about infant sexuality. For example, Hans' interest in his 'widdler' showed that he was focused on his sexuality in line with Freud's predictions about children's interest in their sexuality.

Hans was also a perfect example of a 'little **Oedipus**'. He had a wish to be close to his mother and to engage in sexual relations with her. His father was his rival whom he wished dead, but also loved deeply.

Understanding phobias

Freud explained **phobias** as the conscious expression of **repressed** anxieties. Hans' case fitted this well. In order to help Hans, Freud's task was to throw out hints so that Hans could obtain a conscious grasp of his unconscious wishes.

Hans' phobias were triggered by real events but represented unconscious anxieties created by conflicts over his feelings towards his mother and father. Freud traced Hans' initial anxieties to his sexual feelings towards his mother and a jealousy of his father. Freud told Hans that his fear of horses biting him represented a fear of his father.

This enlightenment enabled Hans to delve deeper into his other fears – the fear of horses falling down and a new fascination with 'lumf' which was variously associated with pleasure in defecation, pregnancy, understanding where babies come from and laden carts. The final bath/plumber fantasy was again a composite one which *'exhausted the content of the unconscious complexes which had been stirred up by the sight of the falling horse'* (page 131).

Views on life and the upbringing of children

Hans' conflicts were relatively 'normal' and therefore the same could be said of the phobias. It might be generally useful to apply these same principles of **psychoanalysis** to all children to free them of repressed wishes that inevitably arise during childhood.

...Links to core studies...

Such is Freud's influence that there are links all through this text. The work of Elizabeth **Loftus** looks at repressed and false memories; the case study of **Thigpen and Cleckley** deals with the unconscious mind.

Freud contributes to our understanding of moral development in children and offers an opposing view to the social learning theory of **Bandura**.

Freud's **psychodynamic perspective** is one of the key issues.

Things you could do ...

Read: the original case study by Freud, which gives you the real flavour of psychoanalysis, *Complete Psychological Works Of Sigmund Freud, The Vol 10: Two Case Histories* ('Little Hans' and 'The Rat Man'), published by Vintage Classics.

Watch videos on YouTube, for example a great animated conversation between Freud and Hans' father (Freud's Little Hans Case Study) and a documentary about Freud in 3 parts.

Listen to the *Mind Changers* on Little Hans, an excellent BBC radio series on key psychological studies. You can find a copy of the programme at http://www.bbc.co.uk/programmes/b00bg335.

Evaluating the study by Freud

The research method
This study was a case study.

What are the strengths and weaknesses of this research method in the context of this study?

Data collection
Hans' father collected data about Hans by observing what Hans did and said.

What are the strengths and weaknesses of observation in the context of this study?

Hans' father also questioned Hans (interviewed him).

What are the strengths and weaknesses of interviewing in the context of this study?

The sample
Hans and his family were the participants in this study. Hans was a European boy from an intelligent middle-class family and from a specific period of time (circa 1900).

In what way might these characteristics affect the results and conclusions drawn from the study?

Ethics
What ethical issues should have concerned the researchers in this study, and how might they have dealt with these issues?

Reliability
Reliability concerns measurement.

What aspects of behaviour were measured in this study? How was the reliability of these measurements assessed?

Validity
Hans' father may have influenced the information Hans provided by using leading questions.

Explain how this might affect the validity of this study.

Hans' father and Freud explained Hans' behaviour.

In what way were these explanations biased and thus might lack validity?

Snapshot or longitudinal?
This was a longitudinal study as it took place over a period of years.

Consider the strengths and weaknesses of this design in the context of this study.

Qualitative or quantitative?
What kind of data were collected in this study?

What are the strengths and weaknesses of producing this kind of data in the context of this study?

Applications/usefulness
Freud used the results from this study to support his theory of personality and also to enhance our understanding of the development of mental disorder (phobias).

How valuable do you think this study was?

What next?
*Describe **one** change to this study, and say how you think this might affect the outcome.*

> There are no simple answers.
>
> *Evaluating a study requires you to think.*
>
> *We have provided some pointers here, linked to the **RESEARCH METHODS** and **KEY ISSUES** covered in Chapter 1 (Psychological investigations) and Chapter 7 (Key issues).*
>
> *You can read suggested answers on our website www.psypress.com/cw/ banyard.*

Producing effective evaluation
When you produce your own answers to the issues on the left there are two things to ensure:

1 Contextualisation
2 Elaboration

The key to **CONTEXTUALISATION** is to ensure that your answer includes some information about this particular study. For example:

The key to **ELABORATION** is the three-point rule (see page xii). For example:

Question:
From Freud's study of Little Hans, suggest **one** strength of using the case study method. **[3]**

3 mark question

Answer:
STATE: Case studies provide rich, in-depth information giving us an opportunity to understand the complexities of human behaviour.

CONTEXT: In Freud's case study a great deal of information is presented about the things that Hans said and did, as well as the interpretations given by Freud.

COMMENT: This information gives the reader an opportunity to have greater insights into the causes of behaviour than you would get from an experiment.

The issues of **CONTEXT** and **ELABORATION** apply to all exam questions. For example:

Question:
From Freud's study on Little Hans, outline **one** piece of evidence that shows he was a 'little Oedipus'. **[2]**

2 mark question

Answer:
STATE: A little Oedipus is a child who desires his mother and therefore is jealous of his father, and wishes him dead. This creates anxiety.

CONTEXT: In Hans' case this anxiety was expressed as a fear of horses because they represented his father.

The developmental approach

On pages 74–75 and 220–221 we have discussed the **developmental approach**.

The study by Freud concerns the development of personality and mental disorder.

- In what way is this study an example of the developmental approach?
- Discuss the strengths and weaknesses of the developmental approach using examples from the Freud study.

Note: this study is also an example of the psychodynamic perspective – so you should try answering these questions for that perspective.

The legacy

It is hard to think of many people who have had such a deep and enduring effect on the Western world as Sigmund Freud. It is also difficult to think of people who have inspired such strong feelings both for and against their work. The theories and practice of **psychoanalysis** are still fiercely debated. What is undeniable is that Freud has affected the ideas we hold about identity, memory, sexuality and childhood. A brief search of the internet will find a wealth of resources on the man and his work. Like him or loathe him, you can't really ignore him.

Freud merchandise

Can't afford a therapist but want someone to talk to? You can get the Sigmund Freud Beanbag Doll ('Soft, squeezable, and oh so smart! Great gift for anyone in the mental health field'), or maybe the Freud and Couch finger puppet, or the ever-popular movable Freud action figure ('captures Freud in a pensive pose, holding a distinctly phallic cigar. Put him on your desk or nightstand to inspire you to explore the depths of your unconscious and embrace the symbolism of your dreams'). You can even buy Freudian Slippers.

These items and others available from The Unemployed Philosopher's Guild (www.philosophersguild.com).

The legacy

Since Freud first published his theories whole forests have been destroyed printing what people have to say about them. Bookshop shelves still groan with texts about Freud and by people following his ideas. In mainstream psychology, however, Freud does not feature very highly in UK university courses and many psychologists would not cite Freud as an important influence on the modern subject. Having said that, he still has the greatest recognition of any psychologist and when students are asked to identify the most important psychologist they give Freud twice as many votes as his nearest rival.

Freud's influence is massive both in psychology and beyond. Most obvious is the effect on therapy. Although traditional psychoanalysis is relatively rare in this country, the ideas about the importance of the first five years, the role of the unconscious and the power of defence mechanisms influence many therapists. Freud is commonly cited in texts on critical theory and his influence is seen in literature and the arts.

Freud's family continue to be prominent in British life and the diversity of their work perhaps reflects the enduring influence of the man.

The Freud dynasty

The only one of Freud's children to continue his work as a therapist was **Anna Freud** who came to the UK with him in 1938. Famous in her own right, her legacy is the Anna Freud Centre in Hampstead, London dedicated to the well-being of children and their families.

Of Freud's grandchildren, Lucian Freud (1922–2011) was one of Britain's most famous (and expensive) artists. His daughter is the fashion designer Bella Freud.

Lucian's brother, Clement Freud, was a popular broadcaster for over 40 years and was a Liberal Party MP for the Isle of Ely between 1973 and 1987. His daughter Emma Freud is a British broadcaster and cultural commentator. She is married to the writer Richard Curtis which therefore gives us a link from Freud to *The Vicar of Dibley*. He'd be so pleased.

Emma's brother Matthew Freud is one of the most powerful PR men in London. He had close connections with the last Labour Government and his clients include companies such as Pepsi, BT and BskyB. He is married to Elizabeth Murdoch (Rupert's daughter) who is a media executive.

The careers of the family members reflect the areas of life that continue to be influenced by Freud: therapy, broadcasting, the arts, advertising and public relations.

Anna Freud with her father.

Farting as a defence against unspeakable dread

Psychoanalyst **Mara Sidoli** was famous for her willingness to deal with difficult cases. She took on a severely disturbed 'latency boy' (named from Freud's latency period between the ages of 7 and 11 years) called Peter who frankly didn't smell too good.

According to Sidoli (1996) *'Peter held loud conversations with imaginary beings and made loud anal farts as well as farting noises with his mouth whenever he became anxious or angry.'* He also tended to soil himself when anxious. Sidoli describes this behaviour in terms of Freud's **defence mechanisms** and suggested he was testing his parents' commitment to him.

After a year of therapy that seemed to be having little effect Sidoli took the nuclear approach and started to make farting noises herself. This so surprised Peter that it finally broke through the defences and he was able to express his dread, affection and humour about his parents in a less noxious way.

For this report and for her courage and tenacity Mara Sidoli was awarded the 1998 igNoble Prize (like the Nobel Prize but not really) for literature.

Behaviourist explanation of phobias

Freud's explanation of Little Hans' **phobia** is not the only possible explanation. The **behaviourist Hobart Mowrer** (1947) analysed the same situation using the learning theory concepts of association and **reinforcement**. According to this behaviourist view a fear is learned when something that was previously neutral (such as a horse) is paired with something that provokes fear (the experience of watching the horse fall down dead). Once this association has been learned other things reinforce it. In this case the fact that Hans' phobia meant staying away from horses and thus spending more time at home with his mother was reinforcing.

Multiple choice questions

1 How old was Hans when his father started recording the case study?
   a Two years old.   b Three years old.
   c Four years old.   d Five years old.

2 When Hans was three and a half what important event occurred?
   a He developed a phobia.
   b His sister Hanna was born.
   c He worked with a plumber.
   d All of the above.

3 In the dream of the giraffes, Hans dreamed that the big giraffe called out because:
   a He sat on the big one.
   b He sat on the crumpled one.
   c He took the crumpled one away.
   d He hit the big one.

4 What animal represented his father?
   a Horse.   b Giraffe.
   c Lion.   d Both a and b.

5 What is 'castration anxiety'?
   a Fear of becoming a man.
   b Fear of having one's penis removed.
   c Fear of sexual rejection.
   d All of the above.

6 What kind of horse was Hans afraid of?
   a Large horse.   b White horse.
   c Spotted horse.   d Police horse.

7 Hans used his own word for his phobia, which was his:
   a Troubles.   b Illness.
   c Babble.   d Nonsense.

8 What did a laden cart represent?
   a His father.
   b A full stomach.
   c A pregnant woman.
   d All of the above.

9 The term 'lumf' referred to:
   a Faeces.   b Horses.
   c Mountains.   d A penis.

10 The final fantasy Hans had was about:
   a Giraffes.
   b Breaking into a train.
   c A plumber.
   d His pretend children.

Answers are on page 247.

Exam-style questions

> There are three kinds of question that can be asked about the Freud study, as represented here by sections A, B and C.
>
> See page x for further notes on the exam paper and styles of question.

Section A questions

1 Freud suggested that Hans' fear of horses symbolised his fear of his father. Outline **two** pieces of evidence that support this suggestion. [4]

2 In Freud's study of Hans, several dreams or fantasies are described. Outline **two** of these. [4]

3 Freud describes Hans as a 'little Oedipus'.
   (a) Explain briefly what the Oedipus complex is. [2]
   (b) Give **one** example from the study by Freud of how Hans was a little Oedipus. [2]

4 In the study of Little Hans by Freud.
   (a) Briefly outline **one** of Hans' anxieties. [2]
   (b) Outline Freud's explanation of this anxiety. [2]

5 The study by Freud of Little Hans provided an explanation of how a phobia develops.
   (a) Outline Freud's explanation of the development of Hans' phobia of horses. [2]
   (b) Give **one** piece of evidence that he used to support this explanation. [2]

6 The study by Freud contains the following extract of a conversation between Hans and his father:
   Father: When the horse fell down did you think of your daddy?
   Hans: Perhaps. Yes it's possible.
   (a) Explain why Hans might think of his father when the horse fell down. [2]
   (b) Give **one** problem with this type of questioning. [2]

7 From Freud's study of Little Hans:
   (a) Outline **two** items of data that were collected. [2]
   (b) Give **one** weakness of the way in which this data was collected. [2]

8 Freud's study of Little Hans was a longitudinal case study.
   (a) Outline **one** strength of this research method in Freud's study. [2]
   (b) Outline **one** weakness of this research method in Freud's study. [2]

9 In the study of Little Hans by Freud explain how horses symbolised Hans' fear of his father. [4]

10 From Freud's study of Little Hans:
   (a) Describe the main individual who was studied. [2]
   (b) Outline **one** conclusion from this study. [2]

Section B questions

Answer the following questions with reference to the Freud study:

(a) Describe the aim of the study by Freud. [2]

(b) Describe how data was collected in the study by Freud. [6]

(c) Give **one** strength and **one** weakness of the method used to collect data in the study by Freud. [6]

(d) Describe **two** ethical issues that are important in the study by Freud. [6]

(e) Outline the conclusions of the study by Freud. [8]

(f) Suggest **two** changes to the study by Freud and outline how these changes might affect the results. [8]

Section C questions

(a) Outline **one** assumption of the developmental approach. [2]

(b) Describe how the developmental approach could explain the development of phobias. [4]

(c) Describe **one** similarity and **one** difference between the study by Freud and any other core studies that take the developmental approach. [6]

(d) Discuss strengths and weaknesses of the developmental approach, using examples from any core studies that take this approach. [12]

Exam-style questions

The example exam-style questions here are set out like the exam but in Section A of the exam there will be only one question on each of the three developmental core studies, i.e. three developmental questions, each worth 4 marks in total.

Section A type questions

1 The study by Samuel and Bryant showed that younger children were less able to conserve than older children.

    (a) Explain what the ability to 'conserve' is. [2]

    (b) Describe **one** of the methods used by Samuel and Bryant to test whether the children could conserve or not. [2]

Stig's answer

(a) They mean that children are able to work out that something stays the same even if it looks like it is different.

(b) You can test for conservation using mass, volume or number – counters in a row. You show a child two identical rows of counters and then space the counters out in one row so it looks longer and see if the child says they are the same or different.

Chardonnay's answer

(a) The same quantity of water may look more or less in a shorter or taller glass but it doesn't actually change.

(b) One way to test for conservation is using volume – a liquid in two beakers.

Teacher's comments

Stig, you are showing off now. These are two sound answers. Although part (a) could be more tightly phrased, it is accurate. Part (b) is very clear.

Chardonnay, you talk about conservation of water … which is actually conservation of volume. You're a bit confused. You're not wrong, but you're not totally right either. In part (b) for full marks you need to describe and not just identify; you have just said that there was a liquid in two beakers but not actually said what is done to test conservation (the liquid from one beaker is poured into a taller and thinner one and the child asked whether they are the same).

Stig (2+2 marks out of 4) Chardonnay (1+1 out of 4 marks)

2 Samuel and Bryant's study on conservation compared Piaget's original method of testing conservation (two-question condition) with a 'one-question' condition.

    (a) Outline **one** key difference between these two conditions in terms of the results. [2]

    (b) Explain why Samuel and Bryant thought the children would do better in the one-question condition. [2]

Stig's answer

(a) In Samuel and Bryant's study young children did less well when they were asked only one question than when they were asked two questions.

(b) One reason is that they might have been confused. Being asked two questions could be confusing.

Chardonnay's answer

(a) In Piaget's original experiment (with two questions) he found that younger children did less well than those over the age of seven. In the one-question experiment more of the younger children got the question right but there were still differences.

(b) The reason why more younger children did better with only one question might be due to demand characteristics. They might have thought that when they were asked a second question they were supposed to give a new answer.

Teacher's comments

Stig you have got it the wrong way round. Children did better in the one-question condition, making fewer errors on the conservation task. Despite getting part (a) wrong, you strangely are on the right lines for part (b). You would need further explanation for the full 2 marks, for example, why does asking two identical questions cause confusion?

Chardonnay's turn to show off now. Part (a) is a very full answer and you also talk about one-question/two-questions in terms of another IV – age. This is almost surplus to the requirements for 2 marks for this question. Part (b) is also very strong! You have identified 'demand characteristics' as one reason for doing better and then explained this concept in the context of the question asked for the full 2 marks.

Stig (0+1 out of 4 marks) Chardonnay (2+2 out of 4 marks)

3 When studies are conducted with children, researchers need to consider ethical issues especially carefully. Outline **two** ethical issues that were important in the study by Bandura *et al.* on the imitation of aggressive behaviour. [4]

Stig's answer

The children should not have experienced harm and there were two ways they could have been psychologically harmed. First the children who watched the aggressive model might have been stressed and they also learned to be violent. They also were made to feel aggressive because the toys they were playing with were taken away.

Chardonnay's answer

One issue is of informed consent. The younger children couldn't give their own informed consent. Their parents must have been asked and they might not have wanted to take part. A second issue is that they might have felt distressed because of the frustration of having the toys taken away from them.

Teacher's comments

This is all true, Stig, but you have sadly not identified two separate ethical issues as both stress and mild aggression arousal relate to the same issue – protection from harm.

Chardonnay has outlined two different ethical issues. However, informed consent is not strictly speaking, according to the ethical guidelines, a problem here. As the parents and carers gave consent, the guidelines indicate this is acceptable. The second issue is sufficient for 2 marks – identified and outlined.

Stig (2+0 out of 4 marks) Chardonnay (1+2 out of 4 marks)

4   (a) Explain how **one** of the controls was used in the study by Bandura *et al*. [2]
     (b) Give **one** reason why it is difficult to generalise from the findings of this study to aggression outside the laboratory. [2]

Stig's answer

(a) One control that was used in Bandura's study was that the children were matched for their aggressiveness.

(b) It's difficult to generalise from Bandura's findings because the study was done in a lab.

Chardonnay's answer

(a) Bandura had a control group who did not observe any aggression. This controlled for the fact that the children may have behaved aggressively even if they didn't see any aggression.

(b) One reason why it might be difficult to generalise from this study is because the children were American children and they might be more aggressive than children from other countries in the world.

Teacher's comments

Stig, you have identified a control used in the study, and this automatically gets you one mark. However, the question asks you to 'explain how', so you are required to give a brief (one or two sentences) description of how they were matched. In part (b) you haven't provided enough for two marks as you have only identified the reason. For 2 marks you could have added 'and children might not behave in the same way in everyday life'.

Chardonnay, in part (a) you have identified a control and explained how it was used. So, 2 marks. In part (b) you have identified that they were American, so limiting generalisability to other cultures. Another point you could have made is that the nursery was for the children of university staff, who were probably middle-class, thus limiting generalisability to other groups. Anyway, you have written enough for 2 marks.

Stig (1+0 out of 4 marks) Chardonnay (2+2 out of 4 marks)

5   In Freud's study of Little Hans, one of the main events was the birth of his sister.

     (a) Describe what Hans felt about his sister. [2]
     (b) What explanation did Freud give linking Hans' sister and Hans' fear of death? [2]

Stig's answer

(a) Hans did not like his little sister. He wished she hadn't been born and was dead.

(b) The connection was that his wish that his sister was dead made him fear that he might die too.

Chardonnay's answer

(a) Hans had mixed feelings about his sister. He loved her but also wished her dead because she was a rival for his mother's affections.

(b) I think it might be due to the bath and Hans' worries that his mother would let him go and he would drown. This was because he wished that she would let his sister go.

Teacher's comments

A bit too simple, Stig. Hans did appear to have a bit of a death wish thing going on with his little sister, but it wasn't necessarily a conscious wish. We do not know if Hans liked his little sister or not. Chardonnay has provided a fuller picture and brought in the important theme of jealousy and rivalry for his mother's affections.

Part (b) for both Stig and Chardonnay is good enough to attract full credit.

Stig (1+2 out of 4 marks) Chardonnay (2+2 out of 4 marks)

6   From Freud's study of Little Hans, Hans' father recorded what Hans said and did, sometimes asking Hans questions about his behaviour. Outline **one** strength and **one** weakness of the way in which the data was gathered. [4]

Stig's answer

One strength is that this was a study about a normal child rather than Freud's usual work with patients who were mentally ill.

One weakness is that there were lots of different ways the data could be interpreted. Freud's way is only one possibility, not necessarily the right one.

Chardonnay's answer

One strength about the way the data was collected is that Hans knew his father well and therefore felt freer to tell him everything.

On the downside his father talked to him a lot and often gave 'leading questions' about the meaning of what Hans did or said, and this might have led him to give answers that were what his father expected.

Teacher's comments

Stig, I don't really think that you were concentrating on the question. The key phrase here is 'the way in which data was gathered' and this is different from the sample or the interpretation. The question is asking about how the data was collected from Hans. Your first answer is not appropriate to the question (it is related to the aims of the study rather than to *how* the data was collected). Your second answer is about how the data was *interpreted*, so again it is not appropriate.

Chardonnay's answer is along the right lines and contains sufficient elaboration for the full marks. A key issue in this study (although Freud was in denial about this!) was that the person collecting the data (Hans' dad) was biased, being instilled with Freudian ideas, and this is apparent in his use of leading questions.

Stig (0+0 out of 4 marks) Chardonnay (2+2 out of 4 marks)

Exam-style questions

The example exam-style question here is set out as in Section C of the exam. However, there is no guarantee, in Section C, of a question related to the developmental approach.

Section C type questions

7 (a) Outline **one** assumption of the developmental approach in psychology. [2]
   (b) Describe how the developmental approach could explain conservation. [4]
   (c) Describe **one** similarity and **one** difference between any core studies taking the developmental approach. [6]
   (d) Discuss strengths and limitations of the developmental approach, using examples from any core studies that take this approach. [12]

Total [24]

Chardonnay's answer

(a) One assumption of the developmental approach is that as we get older, we change and develop.

(b) The developmental approach would say that conservation is something which changes according to age – so that while some children under, say, age seven cannot conserve, in general, those aged more than seven will be able to conserve. Developmental theories often use stages and the ability to conserve is something which indicates whether a child has reached the concrete operational stage or not. Ability to conserve is, according to Piaget, whether a child has the logical operations to understand that just because, e.g. something looks longer or taller, it doesn't necessarily mean it is bigger – in other words being logical and not just going on the appearance of things.

(c) One similarity between the studies by Bandura and Samuel and Bryant is the method used. Both were lab experiments. In Bandura one of the IVs was the type of model (aggressive or passive), in Samuel and Bryant one of the IVs was age of child.
One difference between Freud and Samuel and Bryant is the size of the sample. Freud used a study of one child, a four year old boy. Samuel and Bryant used 72 children from Stanford University nursery.

(d) One strength of the developmental approach is that it is a particularly useful branch of psychology. If we can better understand how children learn and develop, these can become strategies and policies in nurseries and schools in order to improve people's lives and help education. For example, in the Samuel and Bryant study, we know that by asking children the same question twice (as in the standard judgement condition), this encourages them to give the wrong answer. This means that teachers should avoid doing this in class and people who set Key Stage 1 tests should avoid this sort of thing. However, some might say that this is all obvious and most of developmental psychology is common sense.

One weakness of the developmental approach is that it focuses too much on children. The developmental approach should really be a lifespan approach, from the cradle to the grave, and while a lot of developmental psychologists do believe this, most of the research has been done on childhood development. For example, in the case of cognitive development (e.g. Samuel and Bryant) most of the theories and studies are about changes in childhood. This ignores any changes in patterns of cognition in adulthood and assumes that it all remains the same after 18.

Another weakness of the developmental approach is that it ignores individual differences between children and looks instead at overall patterns. For example, in Samuel and Bryant, even though it wasn't true that all seven year olds could conserve all of the time, the study isn't interested in why some children can and some children cannot – is it personality, education, nature or intelligence which explains this? Therefore, developmental psychology overgeneralises.

Teacher's comments (see mark schemes on page xii–xiii)

(a) Chardonnay, your answer is to the point, brief and true. However, it is lacking in detail of the fine points that are necessary for full marks. You could have mentioned different aspects of development, for example emotional, cognitive, attachment or learning factors. You have also omitted to mention the key term 'behaviour' which is essential when writing about an assumption. Just 1 mark.

(b) You clearly understand conservation itself and how it fits into Piaget's theory of cognitive development. Certainly, it was perceived as a key test of whether a child had reached the concrete operational stage or not. You use terminology appropriately and there is a good level of detail. On the downside, however, your answer is not linked to your assumption. The answer really needed to emphasise the 'change and develop' aspect to your answer to part (a), so not quite enough for full marks.

(c) Your similarity is correct and well illustrated for both studies. The difference you have selected is also very good. However, you are incorrect in the number of participants in the study by Samuel and Bryant – it was 252 children. 3 + 2 marks here, for a total of 5 marks.

(d) Chardonnay, you have one strength and two weaknesses. In fact, you need at least two of each to be able to get more than 6 of the 12 available marks here and the mark scheme is very specific about this requirement. This is a real shame, because the quality of your answer otherwise is very good – relevant examples, detailed discussion, clear expression and effective analysis, as well as being well-structured and organised. All your points are coherent and show excellent understanding, although it would be better if you used more than one of the developmental studies to illustrate your points rather than sticking to Samuel and Bryant each time. As I said, a real shame … had you supplied a second strength of the same calibre, this would have certainly been a top band response. But as it is, it can only get the maximum of 6.

Chardonnay (1 + 3 + 5 + 6 marks = 15/24 marks)

CHAPTER 4

This chapter looks at three core studies in physiological psychology:

- Maguire et al.'s study of the role of specific brain structures in memory for places.

- Dement and Kleitman's research into the link between REM sleep and dreaming.

- Sperry's investigation of what happens when you deconnect the two hemispheres of the brain.

Physiological psychology

110 Introduction to physiological psychology

Core study 7
112 Maguire, Gadian, Johnsrude, Good, Ashburner, Frackowiak and Frith (brain scans)
112   Starters: brain scanning: a new technology
114   The study in a nutshell
115   The study in detail
119   Evaluation
120   Afters: scan on
121   Multiple choice questions
121   Exam-style questions

Core study 8
122 Dement and Kleitman (sleep and dreaming)
122   Starters: sleep and dreams
124   The study in a nutshell
125   The study in detail
129   Evaluation
130   Afters: dream on
131   Multiple choice questions
131   Exam-style questions

Core study 9
132 Sperry (split-brain)
132   Starters: one brain or two?
134   The study in a nutshell
135   The study in detail
139   Evaluation
140   Afters: more brains
141   Multiple choice questions
141   Exam-style questions

142 Exam-style questions

What is physiological psychology?

Physiological psychology explores human behaviour and experience by looking at people as if they are physiological machines. This idea has some value because it is clear that our biology affects our behaviour and experience. On a simple level we know that certain foodstuffs, such as coffee or alcoholic drinks, will affect the way we see the world and the way we behave. Also, it has been observed for a long time that damage to the brain and nervous system can have an effect on behaviour and experience. So the action of chemicals and the structure of the nervous system are the two main themes of physiological psychology. However, the question that arises is how much does our biology affect us and what other factors intervene to affect the response.

The selection of studies in this chapter look at the structure and function of the brain. They also look at how we can map physiological processes onto physiological changes. The goal of the physiological psychologist is to map all behaviour onto chemical and neurological changes.

Golgi stains

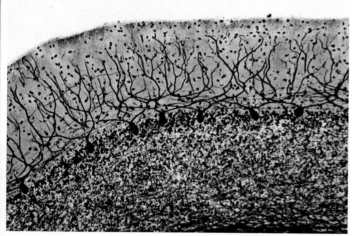

Our knowledge of the brain has advanced as scientists have found new techniques for viewing and recording its structure and functions. Camillo Golgi discovered a technique to stain nerve tissue so that the structure of nerve cells could be seen and investigated. This enabled scientists to map the paths of nerve cells in the brain for the first time. The Golgi stain, as it is now called, highlights a few cells in their entirety and creates striking images such as the one shown above. It is not fully understood even today how this process works.

Mapping the brain

*It is a relatively recent discovery that the brain is the powerhouse of our behaviour and experience. It had been known for some time that the brain had something to do with controlling physical things like movement but in 1861 a French physician, **Paul Broca**, came across a young man who was fit and healthy in every way except he could not say any more than one word. That word was 'tan' and he became known by that name. Broca wondered whether the reason for the language problem was due to a problem in the brain. This turned out to be the case and the affected area is now known as Broca's area (though really it ought to be called 'Tan's area' because it was his brain). Most importantly Broca had demonstrated that the brain has an effect on mental events (such as how we think) as well as physical events (such as how we move).*

Brain and behaviour

We now know that what goes on in our brains will affect what we think, what we feel and what we do (our cognitions, our emotions and our behaviour). The relationship between the brain and our behaviour is still only partly understood but the research gives us some fascinating questions that make us think about who we are and what makes us tick.

Brains and personality

The case of Phineas Gage is often cited as an example of the effects of the brain on personality. Gage was a US railway worker in the nineteenth century who had an industrial accident in which a large bolt was blasted through his skull and blew a hole in his brain. The bolt was 1 m in length, over 3 cm in diameter and weighed over 6 kg. It blasted through Gage's left cheek bone and came out of the top of his head. It is reported that Gage regained consciousness after just a few minutes.

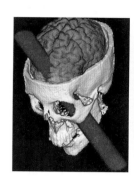

An artist's impression of Phineas Gage's skull with the metal rod that was fired through his head.

The story of Phineas Gage appears in many psychology texts because of the changes that were then observed in the man. His behaviour changed dramatically after the event and he stopped being a conscientious worker. The railway company who had been employing him would not give him his job back when he regained his health because of these behavioural changes. The changes are described below in an account written at the time of the incident by a doctor.

'Gage was fitful, irreverent, indulging at times in the grossest profanity (which was not previously his custom), manifesting but little deference for his fellows, impatient of restraint or advice when it conflicts with his desires, at times pertinaciously obstinate, yet capricious and vacillating, devising many plans of future operations, which are no sooner arranged than they are abandoned in turn for others appearing more feasible. A child in his intellectual capacity and manifestations, he has the animal passions of a strong man. Previous to his injury, although untrained in the schools, he possessed a well-balanced mind, and was looked upon by those who knew him as a shrewd, smart businessman, very energetic and persistent in executing all his plans of operation. In this regard his mind was radically changed, so decidedly that his friends and acquaintances said he was "no longer Gage".' (Harlow, 1868)

Some of the details of the case are disputed but the incident highlights the question of how much our behaviour is affected by our brains. Was Gage a different man because some of his brain had gone or had the shock of being injured and then rejected by his employer changed his world view? Whatever the explanation the case shows how the brain can continue to function even when some parts are damaged.

This is a story that never goes away. For example, recent research has discovered that Gage actually had an impressive recovery and worked as a stagecoach driver along a 100 mile route in Chile. That is a job that would require a lot of physical and social skill.

Gage's skull has recently been scanned and compared with the scans of a hundred men of the same age to estimate exactly which bits of his brain were damaged (Van Horn et al., 2012).

INTRODUCTION

Localisation and the brain

The studies on Phineas Gage and by Broca (see facing page) point to the idea that different parts of the brain (localities) do different things. This idea is called **localisation**. The studies in this chapter by **Sperry** and by **Maguire et al.** both tell us something about localisation. These studies and the ones that follow in this section give us a lot of information but also give us some new puzzles to think about.

The man with no brain

It's a great headline and even though it is not quite true it does describe one of the remarkable findings of the brain scan revolution. **John Lorber** was a neurosurgeon in Sheffield who was interested in people who had survived *hydrocephalus* as a child. This condition (hydro = water, cephalus = head) can be fatal if not treated as the ventricles (spaces) in the brain fill up with cerebrospinal fluid.

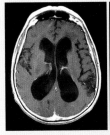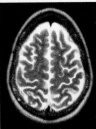

CAT scan of a hydrocephalus patient (left) and a normal brain (right). The dark areas are fluid and the grey areas are the brain.

A young man in perfect health was referred to Lorber because he had a slightly larger than average head which can be a sign of hydrocephalus. When Lorber looked at the **CAT scans** he found that the man's brain was a thin smear around the skull and the bulk of his head contained spinal fluid. According to all theories of brain structure the man should not have been alive, but not only was he alive but he had a degree in maths and economics. Lorber went on to scan more than 600 people with hydrocephalus and found numerous cases where the ventricles were filling more than 50% of the head with fluid (Lewin, 1980).

Lorber liked to give dramatic talks and entitled his paper on this topic 'Is your brain really necessary?' Partly because of his style of presentation and partly because the results are difficult to explain, the work does not appear in many textbooks.

Murderers

What if our behaviour can be changed by small changes in our brains? Would we become a different person and do different things? One curious case which raises these questions is the story of Charles Whitman. On 1 August 1966, Charles Whitman murdered his mother, drove home and murdered his wife then climbed the tower at the University of Texas with a high velocity rifle. For several hours he shot at everything he saw, killing 14 people and wounding 31 before he was gunned down by police. After the tragedy it was found that Whitman had sought psychiatric help for bad headaches and violent feelings. In a diary he requested an autopsy to be carried out after his death. This autopsy discovered a tumour the size of a walnut pressing on his *amygdala* which is a small area of the brain associated with aggressive behaviour.

The case illustrates the question of making connections between physiological changes and behavioural changes. The more you read about the Whitman case the more confusing it gets (if you are interested just Google his name). Whitman had been experiencing a depressed mood over a long period of time and had even told his therapist of his dreams of shooting people from the tower. On the day of the murders he was observed to be very calm and left long diary entries describing the reasons for his actions.

One explanation of his behaviour focuses on the brain tumour and therefore sees the man having only limited control of his actions. Another explanation, however, focuses on his history of poor behaviour in the army and at college including firearms offences. So was it the tumour? Or something else? Although we always want to know the reason why someone does something, the truth generally turns out to be more complicated than one simple explanation.

Emotion and the brain

There are a range of brain structures that are associated with emotions. Perhaps the most researched is the series of small structures hidden deep in the brain called the *limbic system*. It is this system that is the difference between mammals (us) and reptiles (e.g. crocodiles) – well, that and the teeth of course.

The discovery of the importance of these structures in emotion was made by Papez (1937) by looking at the brains of people and animals that had suffered emotional disorders.

Bulls

Two structures are particularly important; the *hypothalamus* which controls the bodily changes associated with emotion and the *amygdala* which has an effect on aggression. This has been demonstrated by a range of **experimental** and **case study** evidence. For example, the Spanish psychologist, **José Delgardo** is a pioneer in the implantation in the brain of radio activated electrodes. His ability to find an exact spot in the animal's brain is so precise that he has trusted his life to it in dramatic demonstrations. He implanted an electrode in the amygdala of a bull and then got into the bullring with it. When the bull started to charge, Delgardo activated the electrode and the bull halted its charge. After repeated experiences of this, the animal became permanently less aggressive. Not many people would put their science on the line in his way.

No need to fear a charging bull – if its amygdala is disabled.

...Connections...

Many psychologists will argue that all psychology will eventually be physiological psychology. They believe that concepts such as **free will** or consciousness will be found to be controlled by simple physiological processes when we have unlocked more secrets of the brain. Other psychologists are more sceptical about what we are able to discover about the brain. Elsewhere in this text **Piaget** and **Freud** both look to biological explanations of behaviour and **Milgram** argued that being **obedient** is our destiny because it is part of our nature. The biological approach also gives us explanations for unusual behaviours such as **autism** (**Baron-Cohen et al.**) and **mental disorder** (**Rosenhan**) and for other individual differences such as intelligence or personality. There is no doubt that biological explanations have contributed to our understanding of a range of conditions but if we follow the argument too far we arrive at biological solutions for all our social problems.

Brain scanning: a new technology

In the final quarter of the twentieth century, scanning technology stimulated a dramatic breakthrough in brain research. Before scans there were **EEGs** but these only provided general information about electrical activity in the whole brain. And before EEGs, the only way to investigate brains was to deal with the real thing. This meant operations where the brain was altered in some way by the use of surgery or chemicals or electrical stimulation. . The work of **Sperry** and **Penfield** (see page 133) was also part of this. There were also studies that were carried out on people with brain injuries though, in such cases, the final analysis often had to wait until the person died and their brain could be fully examined. Phineas Gage (see page 110) and the Texas tower murderer (see page 111) are examples of this evidence. This type of early research on brain function is clearly limited because it can't really see the brain at work.

Scanning allows scientists to view the brain while it is working. The advent of such techniques meant that scientists could now study the brain without cutting it open. A whole new world appeared to be available to them. But things are never so simple and the issue is to be able to interpret what the scans tells us and recognise what they can't tell us.

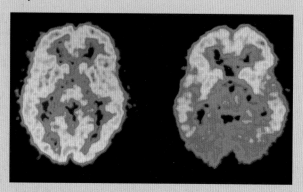

The images above show two PET scans. The normal brain on the left shows a lot of activity throughout the scanned area; the one on the right is the scan of a person with Alzheimer's Disease, showing far less activity.

Different kinds of scanning technique

Types of scan include:

CAT (computerised axial tomography)
CAT scans are built up from taking a series of x-rays 180° around the head. The images show areas of damage and will highlight, for example, the area where a person has experienced a cerebral haemorrhage (a type of stroke).

MRI (magnetic resonance imaging)
People are slid into a machine looking like a giant pencil sharpener and subjected to a strong magnetic field which is turned on and off rapidly in the presence of a radio wave. The atoms of the brain change their alignment (spin) because of the magnetic field when it is on and produce characteristic radio signals when it is turned off. A detector reads those signals and, using a computer, can map the structure of the tissue. There are no radioactive materials used in an MRI scan.

fMRI (functional magnetic resonance imaging)
fMRI scans are the most recently developed forms of brain imaging and the scan of choice for psychologists. The scans use MRI technology to measure the changes in the blood oxygen levels that are connected to neural activity in the brain or spinal cord.

PET (positron emission tomography)
Patients are injected with slightly radioactive glucose (sugar). The most active brain tissue uses the glucose and so attracts the radioactive substance. Radiation sensors detect where the radiation is greatest and so build up a picture of activity in the brain. The scans take between 10 and 40 minutes to complete and are painless. Mind you, there is the slight issue of radioactive substances in your brain.

The data from the scan is usually presented as a coloured picture where the 'hot' colours such as orange and red are used to represent the areas where there is greatest activity and the 'cold' colours such as green and blue represent the areas with least activity. The scans tell us which bits are busy but not what they are doing.

The new phrenology?

It was not until the end of the eighteenth century that Western science realised that the brain was the control centre for the body. **Franz Josef Gall** was the man who came up with the revolutionary idea and he also proposed that different parts of the brain control different aspects of behaviour and experience. He reasoned that everyone's brain will be different in shape and that this shape will have an effect on their character. He further reasoned that as the skull fits around the brain then the shape of the skull will reflect the shape of the brain. Therefore if we examine the skull we are also examining the brain. This is the **pseudoscience** of **phrenology**. We call it a 'pseudoscience' because sadly there is no evidence to support it which is a shame because it would be fun to feel the bumps on someone's head and 'read' their personality.

It sounded such a good idea that Gall was able to make a good living doing skull readings. He is sadly remembered for this rather than his revolutionary ideas about the brain.

Moving on from the phrenology of Gall, the pictures of the brain we get from modern scanning techniques are very pretty but what do they really tell us? Have we been taken in and just replaced bumps on the head with coloured pictures? Are the images we get from scans an example of a new phrenology (Uttal, 2003)? There are many reasons to be excited about the information we get from neuroscience but it is important to stay critical of the evidence we are given and not be over-impressed by pretty pictures and machines that go 'ping'.

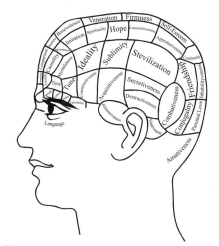

Phrenology is the attempt to identify personal characteristics by 'reading' the bumps of the skull. It is based on the idea that certain functions are located in certain parts of the brain and that these will be visible in the shape of the skull.

You will often find a modern phrenology head on the desks of psychology lecturers. Nobody knows why this is.

The Knowledge

Some of the participants in this core study were London taxi drivers. To obtain an 'All London' taxi licence you need to acquire *The Knowledge*. This means you must have a thorough knowledge of London, including the location of streets, squares, clubs, hospitals, hotels, theatres, government and public buildings, railway stations, police stations, courts, diplomatic buildings, important places of worship, cemeteries, crematoria, parks and open spaces, sports and leisure centres, places of learning, restaurants and historic buildings; in fact everything you need to know to be able to take passengers to their destinations by the most direct routes.

'I had a brain surgeon in the back of my taxi the other day ...'

The 'All London' licence requires you to have a detailed knowledge of the 25,000 streets within a six-mile radius of Charing Cross with a more general knowledge of the major arterial routes throughout the rest of London. The difficulty here is that the centre of London is still based on a medieval road map and there are numerous small paths and tortuous routes. It is very easy to get lost and lose your sense of direction. *The Knowledge* is a unique skill that requires learning a very detailed mental map of the area.

Drivers are assessed by means of an initial written test which determines whether they have reached the required standard to start 'appearances'. These are a series of one-to-one oral examinations conducted by a qualified Knowledge of London Examiner. The examiner grades each applicant according to his or her performance. The higher the grade on each appearance, the quicker the applicant can expect to receive a licence. Some applicants pass *The Knowledge* with as few as 10 or 12 appearances while others take longer. The whole process usually takes between two and four years. And you thought A Levels were tough! (See www.taxiknowledge.co.uk.)

Alzheimer's disease and memory

The hippocampus is believed to be one of the areas that is damaged in Alzheimer's disease, leading to severe loss of memory. The Spanish film director Luis Bunuel watched his mother develop the disease and wrote:

'You have to begin to lose your memory, if only in bits and pieces, to realise that memory is what makes our lives ... Our memory is our coherence, our reason, our feeling, even our action. Without it we are nothing ... we can only wait for the final amnesia, the one that can erase an entire life, as it did my mother's.'

The case of HM's hippocampus

Henry Molaison is very famous in psychology: *'...he has probably had more words written about him than any other case in neurological or psychological history'* (Ogden and Corkin, 1991, page 195). In texts, he is usually referred to by the initials HM to protect his identity, although that might seem ironic after you read about what the psychologists did to him. It is doubly ironic because his name is now well know so we will refer to him by name. Henry Molaison was born in 1926 and had a head injury at the age of seven that started a lifetime of epileptic seizures. These seizures got worse over the years and in his mid-20s he was having uncontrolled grand mal attacks (health-threatening seizures). It was proposed to attempt a brain operation to cure the epilepsy. At that time there were some surgeons who were very enthusiastic about brain surgery and William Scoville was one of these, having carried out hundreds of **frontal lobotomies** (an operation to sever connections to the brain's **frontal lobe**). These operations, based on minimal theory and with limited or no success, were used to change the behaviour of people thought to be aggressive or psychologically disturbed.

Experimental brain surgery

Scoville carried out an **experimental** piece of surgery on Molaison to reduce his epilepsy. Among the brain tissue he removed were parts of a small structure named the **hippocampus**. On the good side, Molaison survived the operation and his epilepsy was now less damaging, but on the very big down side he had profound retrograde and anterograde amnesia. More precisely, he had lost much of his memory for the 10 years prior to the operation (anterograde amnesia), and even more damagingly, he had lost the ability to store new information (retrograde amnesia). He had a memory span of just a few minutes, so he was effectively waking up every few minutes not knowing where he was or who he was talking to.

This was clearly a disaster for Molaison but he probably never understood that because he could never remember what happened to him, or if he did he would forget it within a couple of minutes. This tragedy for Molaison was a great opportunity for psychologists who became aware of the case. They queued up for the next 40 years to study his memory, assessing it with all kinds of tests and checking out a wide range of **hypotheses** concerning the theoretical distinctions between long-term and short-term memory, and between explicit and implicit memory. They used all sorts of stimuli including electric shocks and white noise (for a review see Corkin, 1984, or Parkin, 1996). Henry Molaison died in 2008 aged 82 and his brain is preserved at the University of California.

HM and ethics

The story of Henry Molaison is commonly presented without comment in psychology books, but ask yourself this, how did he give **informed consent** for the 40 years of constant experimentation? He did not know what was being done to him or even who was doing it. And who gave permission for his brain to be removed and preserved? Is this ground-breaking science or cruel exploitation of a man whose life has been ruined by experimental brain surgery?

...Link to the core study...

The core study by Eleanor **Maguire**'s team at University College London is an excellent example of the remarkable discoveries that we can find from modern scanning technology. They help us to map the brain and find out more about the way that activities are distributed around the brain. Some studies, such as this one, take pictures of the structure of the brain (the bits) while others take pictures of the functions (the brain in action). This type of research is fascinating and frustrating in equal measure because it raises as many questions as it answers.

Maguire *et al.*: the core study

Eleanor A. Maguire, David G. Gadian, Ingrid S. Johnsrude, Catriona D. Good, John Ashburner, Richard S.J. Frackowiak and Christopher D. Frith (2000) Navigation-related structural changes in the hippocampi of taxi drivers. *Proceedings of the National Academy of Science*, USA, 97, 4398–4403.

See the CORE STUDY CHECKLIST on page xv for details of what you need to know for the exam.

In a nutshell

Context

Many birds and small animals have a need for spatial memory, for example they need it to find food they have hidden – they have to remember where they put it and find their way there again.

Research has shown one area of the brain in particular to be involved – the **hippocampus** (or 'hippocampi' since all animals have two hippocampi, one in each **hemisphere** of the brain).

In species that have a need for spatial memory the hippocampi are larger than in other species when overall brain and body size are taken into account.

In some animals the size of the hippocampi (*hippocampal volume*) increases during seasons when they use their spatial memory most.

Aim

This study aims to see if the human brain responds in the same way – whether the form and shape of the hippocampi change in response to behaviour requiring a spatial memory.

Participants

London taxi drivers were used because their work involves spatial memory and navigation.

The **experimental group** consisted of 16 right-handed male taxi drivers. Their **mean** age was 44 and mean experience of taxi driving 14.3 years.

This group was matched (age, gender and handedness) with a **control group**. This is a **matched participants design**.

Procedures

MRI scanning was used to collect data about the participants' hippocampi. This data was analysed using two techniques:

* *VBM* (voxel based) is a technique that measures the volume of specific brain areas by comparing each brain area to a template. MRI scans were made of 50 healthy male brains to produce the template.

* *Pixel counting* – MRI scans of slices through the hippocampus produce a two dimensional picture. Pixels can be counted to produce a measure of hippocampal volume. A pixel is a single point in a picture.

Key term: MRI scanning

*Magnetic resonance imaging (**MRI**) is just one of the methods used to study the brain. This, and other methods of brain scanning, are described on the previous spread. The particular strength of MRI scanning is that it produces a more detailed picture of soft tissue than **CAT scans** do. MRI scanning is used to scan other parts of the body as well the brain. **fMRI scanning** is even better because it shows changing activity levels in the brain – but this kind of scanning was not required in the taxi driver study because they only needed to measure the volume of the hippocampus.*

Results

There are three significant regions of the hippocampus: the anterior hippocampus, the body of the hippocampus and the posterior hippocampus. There are two hippocampi: right and left (RH and LH).

1   *Results from VBM*

    There was more **grey matter** in both left and right hippocampi of taxi drivers compared with controls. This difference was restricted to the *posterior* region of RH and LH. By contrast, the controls had relatively more grey matter in the *anterior* region of the RH and LH.

2   *Results from pixel counting*

    In the control group two areas of the hippocampus were larger (i.e. had more volume): the *anterior* RH and the *body* of the RH.

    In the taxi drivers both the *posterior* RH and LH had greater volume than in the controls.

3   Overall there was no difference in total volume of the hippocampi in the controls and taxi drivers.

4   There was a **positive correlation** between time spent taxi-driving and volume of the *posterior* RH and a **negative correlation** between time and the volume of the *anterior* RH and LH.

Discussion

The results suggest that a 'mental map' is stored in the right posterior hippocampus. This fits with data from previous studies.

This shows functional differentiation within the hippocampus, i.e. some regions are concerned with spatial memory whereas other regions of the hippocampus have other functions.

This study shows how experience affects the organisation of the brain and has implications for the rehabilitation of patients with brain damage.

Qs 4.1

1 Why did Maguire *et al.* use taxi drivers in this study?

2 Why was it necessary to just use male drivers who were all right-handed?

3 Explain the reason for having a control group.

4 'This group was age and gender matched with a control group.' What does this mean?

5 In what way is this study a quasi-experiment?

6 Identify the independent and dependent variables in this experiment.

7 Two measures were made of each participant's brain. Briefly describe these measures.

8 In essence what was the purpose of both of these measures?

9 Describe the findings that relate to the anterior hippocampus.

10 Describe the findings that relate to the right hippocampus.

11 Which region(s) of the hippocampus are associated with spatial memory? Provide evidence to support your answer.

12 Explain the idea of a 'mental map'.

The detailed version

Context and aims

Past research has indicated that the hippocampus plays a role in spatial memory, i.e. the ability of animals and humans to remember locations in space and navigate between them.

For example, research studies have found that:

- Small mammals and birds who engage in exceptional behaviours requiring spatial memories (such as storing food and locating it again) have increased hippocampal volume (relative to their brain and body size) when compared to animals who do not use spatial memories.
- Hippocampal volume increases in some species during seasons where demand for spatial ability is greatest.
- There are structural brain differences in the hippocampi of healthy human brains, such as differences between males and females, and musicians and non-musicians.

Research questions to answer
There are several questions that have not been answered by past research:

1   Are brain differences predetermined or is the brain capable of changing in response to environmental stimulation – i.e. is it **nature or nurture**?

2   What is the precise role of the hippocampus? Studies that have involved lesioning (severing links in parts of the brain) and brain scanning (neuroimaging) have shown that the hippocampus plays a role in spatial memory and navigation but such studies have not demonstrated its precise role.

3   Does the human brain respond to experiences requiring spatial memory in the same way as the brains of lower mammals and birds? Previous research found structural changes in the brain of these animals in response to behaviour requiring spatial memory, which leads us to expect structural changes in the human brain.

Aim
The present study will look at morphological change in the healthy human brain associated with spatial memory and navigation. (Morphology is the study of the form and shape of things.) The prediction is that the hippocampus is the most likely region to show morphological changes.

Qs 4.2

1   Why is the term 'hippocampal volume' used instead of just talking about the size of the hippocampus?

2   The text states 'Birds have larger hippocampal volume relative to brain and body size'. Why is it important to relate hippocampal volume to body size?

3   What explanation is offered for this increased hippocampal volume?

4   Give **one** reason why Maguire et al. predicted that the hippocampus was the region most likely to show changes related to spatial memory.

5   Write a suitable hypothesis for this study.

6   Describe the taxi drivers' experience and explain why the range in experience might have an impact on the results of the study.

7   Why did they exclude people with health problems and those over the age of 62?

8   Explain exactly how the researchers would have matched the experimental and control participants.

The hippocampus

The Latin name for 'seahorse' is 'hippocampus' (hippo = horse). The structure in the brain was called hippocampus because it was thought to look like a seahorse.

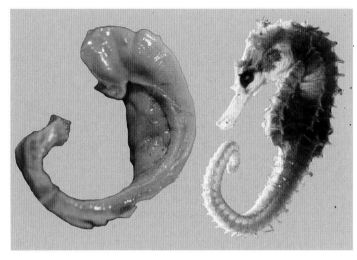

The hippocampus is located in the temporal lobe deep inside the brain as shown in the diagram below. There is one hippocampus on each side of the brain (i.e. one in each hemisphere).

The brain has been cut in half so we are viewing it from the middle.

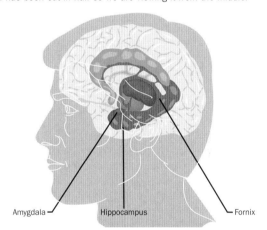

Amygdala — Hippocampus — Fornix

Method

Participants

An ideal group to use in studying spatial memory and navigation are London taxi drivers. They have to undergo extensive training to acquire *The Knowledge* – learning to navigate between thousands of places in London. Learning *The Knowledge* takes an average of two years, culminating in a very stringent set of police examinations (see previous spread).

All 16 participants were right-handed, male London taxi drivers, mean age 44 (range 32–62). There was an even spread of participants in each age group (e.g. 31–40, 41–50, 51–60) and all had been licensed drivers for more than 1.5 years (mean 14.3 years, range 1.5–42 years).

All of the taxi drivers had healthy medical, neurological and psychiatric profiles. Participants were excluded if they were younger than 32 or over 62, and also if they were female, left-handed, or had any health problems.

There was a control group of 16 men, none of whom were taxi drivers. The mean age and the age range were the same for the control group as for the experimental group of taxi drivers.

Maguire *et al.*: the core study *continued*

Method continued

Procedure

Data was collected using **MRI scans** and then these scans were analysed using two techniques.

Image analysis method 1: VBM

VBM stands for *'voxel-based morphometry'*. This technique was a very new method for measuring the volume of areas of the brain. 'Morphometry' is the measurement of the size and shape of an object, i.e. the form.

Traditionally, morphometry is achieved by using images from brain scans and calculating the volume from the size and shape of the image. However, it is difficult to do this with small regions such as the **hippocampus**.

VBM is performed by comparing every brain to a template brain in order to identify overall differences in brain size between the brain-being-studied and the template brain.

In this study the template was generated from MRI scans of the brains of 50 healthy males. The brains of all experimental and **control group** participants were then compared to this template to calculate the volume of different regions of the brain.

In particular VBM identifies differences in the density of **grey matter** in different parts of the brain. In the brain there is **white matter** and grey matter. Grey matter lies on the surface of the brain and also deep inside, in structures such as the **hypothalamus** and hippocampus. It is the part of the brain that is most dense in neural connections (which makes it look grey) and associated with higher order thinking.

Image analysis method 2: pixel counting

Hippocampal volume was calculated using a well-established pixel counting technique. The pixels were counted in the images produced by the **MRI scans**. Each scan was of a slice made through the hippocampal region of participants' brains (see diagram on the right). There were at least 26 contiguous slices (i.e. slices lying next to each other). Each slice was 1.5 mm thick, therefore covering a total length of approximately 4 cm (1.5 mm thick × 26 slices = 3.9 cm).

The images were analysed by one person experienced in the technique who counted the pixels in each slice. This person was **blind** to whether a participant was a taxi driver or control, and also 'blind' to the VBM findings.

In the final analysis only 24 slices were used. Total hippocampal volume was calculated by adding up the pixels from each slice and multiplying this by the distance between adjacent slices (i.e. 1.5 mm). Finally a correction was made in relation to the total *intracranial volume* (ICV). This is the area within the cranium (skull). This was done to account for the fact that some people have larger brains than others and therefore we would expect their hippocampi to be correspondingly bigger.

Pixels and voxels

A pixel is a single point on a graphic image ('pixel' stands for pix + element).

A 'voxel' is a volumetric pixel i.e. a pixel with 3 dimensions (height, width and depth).

Brain slices used for pixel counting

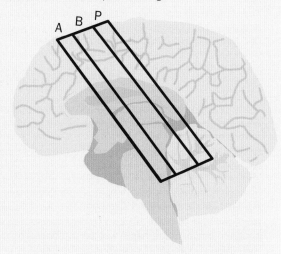

The diagram above shows where the photographic slices were taken through the brain. The slices cut through the length of the hippocampus covering three regions:

A – anterior hippocampus (6 slices)

B – body hippocampus (12 slices)

P – posterior hippocampus (6 slices)

Qs 4.3

1. Two measures were made of each participant's brain. In essence what was the purpose of each measure?
2. The VBM was described as 'unbiased'. What does this mean?
3. The person doing the pixel counting was 'blind' as to whether a participant was a taxi driver or control, and also blind to the VBM findings. What does this mean and why is it necessary?
4. Explain what the term 'intercranial volume' means.
5. Why was a correction made to the ICV?
6. Identify the **three** regions of the hippocampus that were studied.
7. Why do you think there were 12 slices through the body but fewer through the other two regions?

Try this 4.1

Get to know your brain

Use a cauliflower to label the key areas of the brain (see page 132) just to get a 'feel' for it!

Later you can attach new labels showing what the study found for each of these key areas.

Finally, you can add a few onions and make a stir fry – education and nutrition!

Results

VBM analysis

There were only two brain regions with **significantly** increased grey matter in the taxi drivers (as compared with the **control group**) – the right and left hippocampi (RH and LH). No differences were observed anywhere else in the brain.

In the taxi drivers the increase was limited to the posterior hippocampus in both **hemispheres** of the brain.

In the controls there was relatively more grey matter in the anterior hippocampus in both hemispheres of the brain than there was in the brains of the taxi drivers.

Results from the VBM

The brain scans above show the additional grey matter (coloured in yellow) in the posterior left hippocampus (LH) and posterior right hippocampus (RH) in taxi drivers as compared to the control group.

This illustrates how VBM works – it highlights the differences in grey matter.

Pixel counting

There was no significant difference between the taxi drivers and the control group in terms of (1) intercranial volume and (2) total hippocampal volume.

However, there were differences in specific regions of the hippocampus:

Control group

- **Anterior RH** was larger (i.e. had a greater volume) than the anterior LH in the controls than in taxi drivers.
- **Body of the RH** was again larger on the right than the left in the controls.

Taxi drivers

- **Posterior LH and RH** were larger in taxi drivers than in the controls.

Results from pixel counting

*Graphs showing the **mean** of the cross-sectional area measurements for the three regions of the hippocampi.*

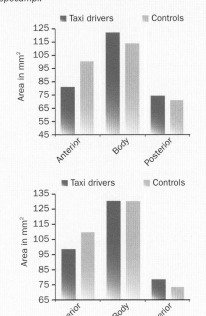

	Left hippocampus	Right hippocampus
Anterior		CONTROL
Body		CONTROL
Posterior	TAXI DRIVERS	TAXI DRIVERS

Results from pixel counting

The table shows the regions of the brain that have the largest volume for both groups of participants based on pixel counting, e.g. control participants had the largest volume in the anterior right hippocampus (RH).

Changes with navigation experience

Correlations were examined between the amount of time spent as a taxi driver (including both training to be a taxi driver and time spent as a qualified driver) and the volume of specific brain regions.

Time spent as a taxi driver was:

- **Positively correlated** with the volume of the posterior RH.
- **Negatively correlated** with the volume of the anterior RH and LH.

Biographical notes

Eleanor Maguire *and her team won the 2003 IgNobel medicine prize 'for presenting evidence that the brains of London taxi drivers are more highly developed than those of their fellow citizens' (http://www.improbable.com/ig/ig-pastwinners.html#ig2003). In fact the research didn't show that the taxi drivers' brains are more developed – but this seems to be a typical media exaggeration of the research findings.*

Dr Maguire has won other awards, including the Royal Society Rosalind Franklin Award – made for outstanding contributions to science.

Dr Maguire works in London as the Professor of Cognitive Neuroscience at the Wellcome Trust Centre for Neuroimaging, University College London, UK. She first became interested in the neural basis of memory while working with patients with brain damage.

Qs 4.4

1. Outline **one** conclusion that can be drawn from the VBM analysis.
2. Write at least **two** conclusions that can be drawn from the graphs above, based on the pixel counting.
3. Explain why there was no difference in the total hippocampal volume in taxi drivers and controls.
4. Correlations were calculated between time spent as a taxi driver and the volume of the posterior right hippocampus. What can you conclude from this correlation?
5. A correlation was also examined between experience as a taxi driver and the anterior hippocampi. What can you conclude from this correlation?
6. Based on the results of this study, what area of the brain would you identify as being important in spatial memory? Explain the basis of your answer.

Discussion

The results from both methods of data analysis indicate a difference between taxi drivers and **control group** – in the taxi drivers there was **significantly** greater volume in the posterior **hippocampus** whereas in the control group there was significantly greater volume in the anterior hippocampus. This suggests a relationship between navigational skills and the relative distribution of **grey matter** in the hippocampus.

Nature or nurture
The question is whether this distribution is an *effect* of spending time navigating (**nurture**) or whether this particular arrangement of hippocampal grey matter is present in some individuals and *predisposes* them to take up a job that requires navigational skills (**nature**).

This possibility was tested by looking at the **correlation** between hippocampal volume and time spent as a taxi driver. The fact that right hippocampal volume was significantly correlated with driving experience suggests that such changes are acquired. There was an increase in posterior hippocampus (**positive correlation**) and a decrease in anterior hippocampus (**negative correlation**). This implies there is *local plasticity in the structure of the healthy adult human brain as a function of exposure to environmental stimuli'* (page 4402).

Previous research and current conclusions
These findings are supported by other research:

- Rodent and monkey studies have found the *posterior* hippocampus is involved in spatial navigation.

- In rats the *posterior* hippocampus is richer in *place cells* than other areas of the hippocampus – these are cells related to spatial perception.

- Studies in humans using functional neuroimaging (**fMRI**) show that the *posterior* hippocampus is active when recalling or using previously learned navigational information.

- Patients with damage to the hippocampus that has spared the *posterior* region can still recall routes learned before damage occurred.

The *posterior* hippocampus seems to be related to *previously learned* spatial information. The *anterior* hippocampus may be more involved in encoding *new* information (which would also involve the *posterior* region). This demonstrates *functional* (morphological) differentiation within the hippocampus.

The results of this study suggest that taxi drivers store a mental map of London permitting increased understanding of how routes and places relate to each other. The consequence of this is an increase in tissue volume.

These findings challenge the traditional view that the hippocampus has only a transient role in memory. The hippocampus is an 'old' part of the brain, i.e. if we look back through evolution this was a part of the brain that was present in very primitive animals. The need to navigate would be an important behaviour for all animals and therefore it is not surprising that it is a function within the old part of the brain. Undoubtedly in humans the hippocampus has evolved to take on other functions, such as **episodic memory** (this refers to memory for events, places, associated emotions, and other conception-based knowledge in relation to an experience; as distinct from, for example, *procedural memory* which is memory for how to do things).

Right and left hippocampus
The study found differences between the right and left hippocampus (RH and LH). LH volume did not correlate with taxi-driving experience. This suggests that the LH has a different role in spatial memory and navigation than the RH. It is possible that the role of the LH is to store memories of people and events (episodic memories) associated with the context of taxi driving. This would complement the role of the RH which integrates information into an existing map.

The data in this study are not at a microscopic level but one might speculate about how the observed changes take place. The simplest explanation is that the cells of the hippocampus are re-organised in response to the increased demand to store navigational information. The increase in grey matter in the *posterior* region would 'borrow' material from *anterior* region to cope with the demand.

The demonstration that normal activities can bring about changes in the relative volume of grey matter has important implications for rehabilitating people who have suffered brain damage – by making demands on the brain it may respond by enlisting the use of grey matter from other regions.

However, this study only demonstrates such plasticity in the hippocampus and it remains to be seen whether other regions of the brain respond to experience in a similar way.

 Qs 4.5

1 What evidence was used to argue that the observed differences between taxi drivers and controls were due to experience (nurture) rather than predisposition (nature)?

2 The discussion includes a quote from the article about plasticity (see left). Explain this quote.

3 Describe **one** finding from previous research that supports the results of this study.

4 One of the conclusions is that the results demonstrate functional differentiation within the hippocampus. Explain this conclusion.

Things you could do ...

Read the original article by Maguire *et al.* (and other related articles) at http://www.fil.ion.ucl.ac.uk/Maguire/a_level.html

Read:

The biography of HM, a young man who lost his memory when his hippocampi were removed, *Memory's Ghost* by Philip J. Hilts. Raises some interesting ethical questions.

Cabbies' brain power. Some interesting anecdotes http://news.bbc.co.uk/1/hi/677048.stm

Watch Eleanor Maguire talking about her research (it's in English despite the fact that the title is in Spanish!) and about how her research can be used http://www.youtube.com/watch?v=0GvYHtx3Xfo

...Links to core studies...

This study maps some cognitive processes to specific areas of the brain. The attempt to map psychological changes to physical areas in the brain is creeping into all aspects of psychology. Any identifiable group of people, for example gamblers (see the core study by **Griffths**) can be examined to see if their brains show any measurable differences from non-gamblers. Likewise people with autism (**Baron-Cohen *et al.***) and people with mental health issues (**Rosenhan**) have been studied in this way. This particular brain scanning study tells us something very specific about memory and so links to the study by **Loftus and Palmer**.

Evaluating the study by Maguire *et al.*

The research method
This study was a quasi-experiment because the independent variable was whether a participant was a taxi driver or not. Participants were not assigned to these groups by the experimenter.

What are the strengths and weaknesses of this research method in the context of this study?

Research technique
The technique used to measure the independent variable was based on MRI scanning.

What are the strengths and weaknesses of this research technique in the context of this study?

The sample
The participants were all men aged between 32 and 62.

How would the unique characteristics of the sample in this study affect the conclusions drawn?

Reliability
Reliability concerns measurement.

What aspects of human behaviour were measured in this study?

How could the reliability of these measurements be assessed?

Validity
Taxi-driving may represent a very specific form of navigational ability.

How do you think this would affect the validity of the results?

Snapshot or longitudinal?
This was a snapshot study as each participants' brain was studied at one moment in time.

Consider the strengths and weaknesses of this design in the context of this study.

The alternative would be to conduct the study as a longitudinal design.

Explain how this could be done.

Consider the strengths and weaknesses of this design in the context of this study.

Qualitative or quantitative?
What kind of data were collected in this study?

What are the strengths and weaknesses of producing this kind of data in the context of this study?

Applications/usefulness
Maguire *et al.* suggest how the results from this study could be used.

Describe this application and say how valuable you think this study was.

What next?
*Describe **one** change to this study, and say how you think this might affect the outcome.*

There are no simple answers.

Evaluating a study requires you to think.

*We have provided some pointers here, linked to the **RESEARCH METHODS** and **KEY ISSUES** covered in Chapter 1 (Psychological investigations) and Chapter 7 (Key issues).*

You can read suggested answers on our website www.psypress.com/cw/banyard.

Producing effective evaluation
When you produce your own answers to the issues on the left there are two things to ensure:

1   Contextualisation
2   Elaboration

The key to **CONTEXTUALISATION** is to ensure that your answer includes some information about this particular study. For example:

Question:

Outline **one** weakness of the sample in the study by Maguire *et al.* **[2]**

Answer:

STATE: The sample in this study was all men, so the findings can't apply to all people.

CONTEXT: It might be that female brains are different and spatial memories are stored in a different way in female brains.

The key to **ELABORATION** is the three-point rule (see page xii).

Question:

With reference to the study by Maguire *et al.* suggest **one** weakness of conducting a snapshot study. **[3]**

Answer:

STATE: One weakness is that you have to assume that any differences between the groups are due to the independent variable (IV) whereas that may not be the case.

CONTEXT: In the Maguire study the IV was being a taxi driver or not, but there might have been other differences between the two groups.

COMMENT: It would be better to observe how taxi driver's brains change with experience by measuring the hippocampal volume over time.

The physiological approach

On pages 110–111 and 222–223 we have discussed the **physiological approach**.

The study by Maguire *et al.* concerns how memories are stored in the brain.

- In what way is this an example of the physiological approach?
- Discuss the strengths and weaknesses of the physiological approach using examples from the Maguire *et al.* study.

Scan on

The future is clearly in brain scanning as psychology departments fall over themselves to buy scanners and take ever more pictures of people's brains. The jury is still out, however, on how much value we will get from all these pictures.

Scanning race

Scanning techniques are now being used to investigate social issues and social judgement. Which parts of our brain are being used when we laugh or when we are attracted to someone or when we meet someone different to us? **Jennifer Eberhardt** is a prominent researcher in racial stereotyping, prejudice and stigma. Recently she has been examining brain scans to see what they tell us about racism and racial differences (Eberhardt, 2005).

Jennifer L. Eberhardt

Working in the USA, Eberhardt's research team have used **fMRI** to study the face recognition of people of the same and different race to the viewer. Previous studies have shown that people find it easier to recognise faces from the same race as themselves and that this effect is stronger for European American than African American participants. The researchers were able to identify differences in brain activity that correlated with the race of the face they were identifying (Golby *et al.*, 2001).

Other work (Richeson *et al.*, 2003) found a relationship between **frontal lobe** activity and racial prejudice, and that the greater the brain differences in the face recognition task the greater the level of prejudice.

This work sounds very interesting, if difficult to interpret, but there are dangerous issues that can be raised by scanning studies on race. For example, what if you looked for differences in the average scans of different racial groups? There is little doubt that any scientific argument would soon be drowned under the weight of social prejudice. The history of brain science is littered with attempts to prove one group superior to another.

Adrian Raine

Adrian Raine and the search for the murderer's brain

One line of investigation with brain scans has been to look for differences in the brains of people with mental health issues or a history of criminality. An influential figure in this research is the British psychologist **Adrian Raine** (www-rcf.usc.edu/~raine). Raine is confident that he has discovered that the brains of murderers are different to those of non-murderers (hopefully most of the population). He writes:

'There are now 71 brain imaging studies showing that murderers, psychopaths, and individuals with aggressive, anti-social personalities have poorer functioning in the prefrontal cortex – that part of the brain involved in regulating and controlling emotion and behaviour.

More dramatically, we now know that the brains of criminals are physically different from non-criminals, showing an 11% reduction in the volume of grey matter (neurons) in the prefrontal cortex.

Violent offenders just do not have the emergency brakes to stop their runaway aggressive behaviour. Literally speaking, bad brains lead to bad behaviour ... One of the reasons why we have repeatedly failed to stop crime is because we have systematically ignored the biological and genetic contributions to crime causation.' (Raine, 2004)

You will not be surprised to know that a lot of people do not agree with Raine and think he is greatly overstating the case. For example, Steven Rose puts forward an alternative view (see http://news.bbc.co.uk/1/hi/programmes/if/4106217.stm).

The main concern with brain scanning work like this is that it seems to propose some very simple solutions to very complex problems. The bottom line is that we know very little about why people choose to be violent or passive, or whether they choose to murder someone or count to 10 and have a cup of tea instead. The recent history of psychosurgery (brain surgery to change behaviour) has not been a positive one and that is why many people urge caution with this research.

The brain on trial

Should brain scans be allowed in court as evidence? It's a tricky question. Clearly a picture of our brain says something about us, but what exactly? In 1992 in the USA Herbert Weinstein was charged with strangling his wife and then, in an attempt to make the death look like suicide, throwing the body out of their 12th floor apartment window. His legal team argued that he should not be held responsible for his actions because he had an abnormal cyst resting on his brain. Before it came to court the prosecution agreed to allow Weinstein to plea guilty in return for a reduced charge of manslaughter. They felt the evidence might sway the jury to find him not guilty of murder.

In the USA it is now common for defence lawyers in murder cases to use brain scans and then argue that a brain impediment has affected their client and made them not responsible for their actions (Rosen, 2007). Among the many problems with this is that people are often very impressed by scientific evidence but might not understand how it was collected and what alternative explanations there might be.

Lie detecting

Another use of brain scans in court has been the development of fMRI lie detectors. The company *'No Lie MRI'* (look it up online) claims that by asking people questions while they are being scanned their technique bypasses conscious **cognitive** processing and that they can get better readings than traditional lie detector tests. If this technique was **reliable** then it would be a very useful tool but like all lie-detector tests it is not foolproof and there is evidence that people can bluff the test (Ganis *et al.*, 2011).

Despite the problems with the technology people are likely to be more impressed with lie-detector evidence from brain scanning than other technologies (McCabe *et al.*, 2011).

Check out the BPS Research Digest blog (http://bps-research-digest.blogspot.co.uk) for more information on this.

Multiple choice questions

1 The method of brain scanning used in this study was:
a CAT scan.   b PET scan.
c MRI.   d VBM.

2 The control group was matched with the taxi drivers on the basis of:
a Age.   b Gender.
c Experience.   d Both a and b.

3 The method of VBM was used to calculate:
a The amount of grey matter.
b The density of grey matter.
c The volume of the hippocampus.
d Both b and c.

4 The method of pixel counting was used to calculate:
a The amount of grey matter.
b The density of grey matter.
c The volume of the hippocampus.
d Both b and c.

5 The thickness of each cross-sectional scan was:
a 1.5 mm   b 2.5 mm
c 1.5 cm   d 2.5 cm

6 When co-variables are negatively correlated:
a They both increase together.
b They both decrease together.
c As one increases the other decreases.
d There is no relationship.

7 Which of the following is not true?
a The hippocampus is a newer part of the brain.
b There are two hippocampi in a person's brain.
c The hippocampus is named after a sea horse.
d The hippocampus is divided into three regions.

8 The hippocampal volume in the control participants was:
a The same as the taxi drivers.
b Greater in the anterior hippocampus than taxi drivers.
c Greater in the posterior hippocampus than taxi drivers.
d Both a and b.

9 Which side of the hippocampus correlated with taxi driving?
a Right.
b Left.
c Right and Left.
d We don't know.

10 Maguire et al. concluded that:
a Taxi drivers are born with an enlarged hippocampus.
b Observed differences in the hippocampus are due to experience.
c All parts of the brain have the same plasticity as found in the hippocampus.
d Both b and c.

Answers are on page 247.

Exam-style questions

> There are three kinds of question that can be asked about the Maguire et al. study, as represented here by sections A, B and C.
>
> See page x for further notes on the exam paper and styles of question.

Section A questions

1 (a) Explain why Maguire et al. used taxi drivers in their study. [2]
(b) Identify **two** criteria used to select the taxi-drivers as participants in this study. [2]

2 (a) Describe **one** finding from this study. [2]
(b) Suggest how the findings from this study might be used. [2]

3 Outline **two** major ideas of the physiological approach to psychology that are in the study by Maguire et al. [4]

4 (a) Outline **one** control that was used in the study on brain scanning by Maguire et al. [2]
(b) Explain why it was important to use this control. [2]

5 In the study by Maguire et al.:
(a) Describe **one** method used to analyse the brain scans. [2]
(b) Describe **one** result obtained using this method. [2]

6 Maguire et al. found a positive correlation in their study of taxi drivers' brains.
(a) Explain the term 'positive correlation', using examples from this study. [2]
(b) State **one** conclusion that can be drawn from this result. [2]

7 In the study by Maguire et al., the taxi drivers and control participants were matched.
(a) Explain how the participants were matched. [2]
(b) Explain why it was important to match the two groups of participants. [2]

8 In the study by Maguire et al.:
(a) Identify **one** independent variable (IV) and **one** dependent variable (DV). [2]
(b) Describe the effect of **one** of the IVs on the DV. [2]

9 In the study by Maguire et al. describe the participants involved in the study. [4]

10 In the study by Maguire et al.:
(a) Identify **two** techniques used to analyse the size of the participants' hippocampus. [2]
(b) Outline **one** difference that was found between the taxi drivers and control participants. [2]

Section B questions

Answer the following questions with reference to the Maguire et al. study:

(a) Outline the aim of this study. [2]

(b) Explain why this study can be considered a snapshot study. [4]

(c) Suggest **one** strength and **one** weakness of conducting snapshot studies. [6]

(d) Describe the procedure followed in this study. [8]

(e) Suggest how the procedure followed in this study could be improved. [8]

(f) Outline the implications of the procedural changes you have suggested for this study. [8]

Section C questions

(a) Outline **one** assumption of the physiological approach. [2]

(b) Describe how the physiological approach could explain memory. [4]

(c) Describe **one** similarity and **one** difference between the Maguire et al. study and any other core studies that take the physiological approach. [6]

(d) Discuss strengths and weaknesses of the physiological approach using examples from any core studies that take this approach. [12]

Sleep and dreams

Sleep does not mean switching off and closing down the body's activity. Far from it. Sleep is a very active state, both physically and mentally. Our bodies move frequently and, more interestingly for psychologists, our brain activity is even more varied during sleep than it is during the normal waking state.

Measuring sleep

Sleep researchers commonly look to three measures to describe the stages of sleep. First, gross brain wave activity, as measured by an electroencephalogram (**EEG**). This machine provides the summary of electrical activity from one area of the brain. Second, the electrical activity of a muscle is measured with an electromyogram (EMG). Third, eye movement is recorded via an electro-oculogram (**EOG**).

Stages of sleep

Awake
In an awake state the pattern of our **brain waves** (measured by EEG) are typically beta waves. However, when you become relaxed, your brain waves become slower and more regular and have a greater amplitude (the height of the wave). This pattern is called an *alpha wave* which can be observed during meditation.

Asleep: stages 1 and 2
As you go to sleep, your brain waves slow down further (greater wave frequency – the distance from the crest of one wave to the next) and the amplitude also becomes greater. This wave form is called a *theta wave*. The transition from relaxation to stage 1 and then stage 2 sleep is quite gradual. This is very light sleep and a sleeper, awoken at this time, will often say that they weren't actually asleep. The brain waves in stages 1 and 2 are also characterised by **sleep-spindles** and K complexes which are sudden increases in wave frequency and wave amplitude respectively.

Asleep: stages 3 and 4
Deeper sleep is characterised by the *delta waves* of stages 3 and 4. These waves are the slowest and have the highest amplitude. It is very difficult to wake someone up from deep sleep and if you do rouse them, they will be quite confused and disoriented. However, the brain is not dead to the world and will respond to significant noises such as if a mother hears her baby crying this will wake her. Delta sleep is also when sleepwalking and sleep talking are most likely to occur.

REM sleep
There is another form of sleep, **REM** or **rapid eye movement** sleep, named after the darting eye movements that occur during this stage (measured by the EOG). This sleep stage is associated with the experience of dreaming. It is also characterised by a lack of muscle tone (measured by the EMG) which results in temporary paralysis (which explains why you sometimes can't move in a dream). This stage is also associated with a unique brain wave pattern – fast, desynchronised EEG activity resembling the awake state.

Normal night
At the start of a night a sleeper progresses through the four sleep stages ending up in deep sleep. This is followed by a return back through the stages from 4 to 3 to 2 but then, instead of stage 1, REM sleep occurs. This cycle is repeated through the night taking approximately 90 minutes. During the course of the night the length of REM episodes increases and the length of delta sleep decreases in each cycle. By the end of the night there is no delta activity at all.

The puzzle of dreams

Dreams have puzzled people for centuries. Why do we dream, and what do they mean? Some people believe that dreams can prophesy the future, some think they tell us about our emotions and some think they are just **random** firing of the brain that mean nothing.

Dream worlds and real worlds
When I am dreaming then I feel as if I am there. I get scared or I get happy depending on what is happening in my dream world. But it is not real and when I wake up I know that. But do I really know that? Maybe this is all a dream and one day I will wake up from this. What is the difference between the awake world and the dream world? When I'm awake I use the sensations I get and my experience of the past events to create a perception of the world. This 'real' world is as much in my head as my dream world. So how do I tell the difference?

Shakespeare had a lot to say about dreams in his plays and he ponders on this idea in *The Tempest* (IV, i) when Prospero says:

We are such stuff
As dreams are made on, and our little life
Is rounded with a sleep.

'Do androids dream of electric sheep?'
If dreams are just the random thoughts of a mind that is switched off then do computers dream? The little red light is on and it sometimes whirrs and gurgles. Is it dreaming and if so what is it dreaming of? Possibly the best ever title for a science fiction book asks the question, *Do Androids Dream of Electric Sheep?* The book, written by Philip K. Dick, was adapted to make the cult film *Blade Runner*.

The sidewinder sleeps tonight

The band R.E.M., formed in 1980, got their name when Michael Stipe picked it out of a dictionary while searching for something that the band members would all accept. 'How about REM?' he said. 'What does it mean?' they asked. 'Rapid eye movements,' Stipe was said to have replied.

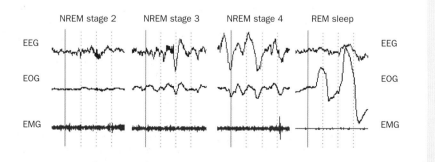

NREM stage 2	NREM stage 3	NREM stage 4	REM sleep

EEG   EOG   EMG   EEG   EOG   EMG

*Brain, eye and muscle activity associated with each sleep stage. **NREM** is non-REM sleep.*

Famous dreams: the discovery of the benzene ring

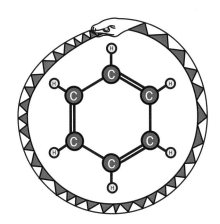

The form of the benzene ring first appeared to Friedrich Kekulé in a dream as a serpent seizing its own tail.

One of the most famous dreams in science was reported by the German chemist **Friedrich August Kekulé von Stradonitz**. He was puzzling over the properties of benzene which did not fit into the theories of chemical structure that existed at the time. He describes what happened next:

'... I turned my chair toward the fire place and sank into a doze. Again the atoms were flitting before my eyes. Smaller groups now kept modestly in the background. My mind's eye sharpened by repeated visions of a similar sort, now distinguished larger structures of varying forms. Long rows frequently rose together, all in movement, winding and turning like serpents; and see! What was that? One of the serpents seized its own tail and the form whirled mockingly before my eyes. I came awake like a flash of lightning. This time also I spent the remainder of the night working out the consequences of the hypothesis.'

Perchance to dream

In perhaps the most famous speech from a Shakespeare play, Hamlet considers whether he should take his own life or not. To be or not to be is a question about whether to go on or not. But as he muses about this he starts to consider what death is like. Is it an extension of sleep? It is common to see this idea represented on grave stones and in newspaper memorial notices, for example 'Although we sit at home and weep, we surely know that you just sleep.' But what if our nightmares persist in this endless sleep?

To die, to sleep;
To sleep: perchance to dream: ay, there's the rub;
For in that sleep of death what dreams may come
When we have shuffled off this mortal coil,
Must give us pause: there's the respect
That makes calamity of so long life;
Hamlet (III, i)

There are numerous other examples of how dreams have inspired people. For example, the most famous horror story of all time, Frankenstein, was dreamt by Mary Wollstonecraft Shelley in 1816. Musicians have also found inspiration and success with their dreams. Paul McCartney composed his hit song 'Yesterday' following a dream in 1965.

Sleep and the brain

We don't just fall asleep. Our brains make us go to sleep. Sleep is a specialised state which has evolved in all animals to serve particular functions. If sleep serves vital functions then it is important for survival for the brain to 'make' us sleep.

Brain research has identified some of the key areas. The *hypothalamus* appears to be an important region for controlling non-REM sleep and may well keep track of how long we have been awake and how large our sleep debt is. There is a special group of cells in the hypothalamus called the *suprachiasmatic nucleus* (SCN) which receives information about light from the eyes and 'tells' the brain when it is safe to sleep. Cells in the hypothalamus are also sensitive to rises in body temperature and send a message to sleep-related cells. This explains why having a warm bath makes you feel sleepy.

The area of the brainstem known as the *pons* is important in REM sleep. During REM sleep, the pons sends signals to the visual system of the *thalamus* and to the *cerebral cortex*. The pons also sends signals to the *spinal cord*, causing the temporary paralysis that is part of REM sleep. Other brain sites are also important in the sleep process. For example, the thalamus generates many of the brain rhythms in non-REM sleep that we see as EEG patterns.

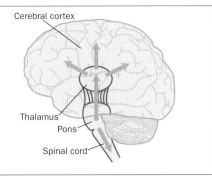

Cerebral cortex

Thalamus

Pons

Spinal cord

Slow wave sleep disorders

Sleepwalking
Some of the most puzzling sleep disorders are associated with **slow wave sleep** (also known as deep sleep, stages 3 and 4), the most notable being sleepwalking and night terrors (which are different from the nightmares of REM sleep). They mainly occur in childhood and tend to have some hereditary basis. Sleepwalking peaks in adolescence, but declines rapidly by the late teens. Episodes are often triggered by anxiety; in susceptible children, the worry can be trivial – the loss of a favourite toy, or just a frustrating day.

Sleep talking
Some people talk in their sleep. Fortunately for many of them they only talk nonsense. Sleep talking, like sleepwalking, can't normally occur in REM sleep because of the general paralysis at this time. Sleep talking is common in adults and even more so in children. In fact, almost all children will do this if they are talked to during light sleep. Then there is some sort of confused reply that has little relevance to what was originally said. If two or more children share a bedroom, and one starts sleep talking, then the other might well join in and create a bizarre meaningless conversations like those that we have come to know and love from the Big Brother house.

...Link to the core study...

Remarkably, when **Dement and Kleitman** carried out this study, they were testing for the first time the idea that the observed physical response of rapid eye movement during sleep was connected to the almost mystical state of dreaming. The physiology of sleep was only just beginning to be unravelled and suddenly the world of dreams seemed to be coming into the domain of science.

Dement and Kleitman: the core study

William Dement and Nathaniel Kleitman (1957) The relation of eye movements during sleep to dream activity: An objective method for the study of dreaming. *Journal of Experimental Psychology, 53 (5)*, 339–346.

See the
CORE STUDY CHECKLIST
on page xv for details of what you need to know for the exam.

In a nutshell

Context
Research has found that people in **rapid eye movement (REM) sleep** are likely to be dreaming, so this might provide a very useful way of knowing when someone is dreaming and would permit the study of dreams.

Aim
To conduct a rigorous assessment of the relationship between REM sleep and dreams:

1 Do dreams occur just in REM sleep or also during quiet sleep (**NREM sleep**)?

2 Is there a **positive correlation** between the length of an REM episode and how long a person thought they were dreaming?

3 Does the pattern of eye movements during REM relate to the visual experience of a dream?

Participants
Nine adults were studied, five were studied more extensively.

Procedure
Participants slept and were observed in a sleep **laboratory**. Their eye movements and **brain waves** were recorded through the night using **EOG** and **EEG** (see previous spread for information).

They were awoken by a bell at various intervals, either in REM or NREM sleep, and asked to speak into a recording machine to prevent any cueing from the researcher. They were asked to report:

a Whether they had been dreaming, and if so ...

b The content of the dream.

c Whether they were dreaming for 5 or 15 minutes.

They were also awoken during episodes of vertical or horizontal eye movement and asked to describe their dream.

Key tems: REM and NREM sleep
REM sleep is characterised by the rapid movement of the closed eyes while a person is sleeping. This has sometimes been called 'paradoxical sleep' because the eyes and brain are active but the body is paralysed except for the eyes.

NREM sleep refers to sleep when there is no rapid eye movement – non-rapid eye movement.

Results
*   *Occurrence of REM activity*
    On average REM activity lasted 20 minutes and occurred every 92 minutes. The frequency was characteristic for each individual. Episodes tended to be longer later on in the night. REM activity was accompanied by a relatively fast EEG pattern.

*   *REM versus NREM activity*
    Participants frequently reported having a dream when woken during REM sleep (65–90% of the time) but were less likely to report a dream in NREM sleep (3–12.5%). Most of recall in NREM periods was within eight minutes of the end of an REM episode.

*   *Length of REM periods and dream duration estimates*
    Participants were 83% correct in estimating whether REM activity lasted for 5 or 15 minutes. There was also a **significant** positive correlation between the duration of REM activity and the number of words used to describe a dream.

*   *Eye movement patterns and visual imagery of dream*
    These were linked, for example horizontal eye movements during REM sleep were linked in one participant to a dream about two people throwing tomatoes.

*   *Effects of practice*
    Participants didn't report more dreams in the second half of the series of tests.

Discussion
There appears to be a clear and (almost) exclusive relationship between dream states and REM activity, providing an objective means of studying dream states.

Qs 4.6

1 Name **two** characteristics of REM sleep.

2 Explain the main aim of this study.

3 With respect to this aim, what is the independent variable (the variable which varied) and the dependent variable (the variable that was measured) in this experiment?

4 Describe the sample in this study.

5 Describe **one** weakness with this sample.

6 What recording machines were used and why?

7 The sleep patterns in this study of the participants may have differed from their normal sleep habits. Why would this be important?

8 Identify **two** controls used in this study and explain why they were necessary.

9 There were **three** research aims. Explain how each of these was measured.

10 For each research aim, state **one** piece of evidence that was found.

11 Outline **two** other findings and explain why these were important.

12 The participants didn't report more dreams in the second half of the series. Why was it important to check this?

The detailed version

Context and aims

In order to be able to study dream activity it is necessary to have an objective means of knowing when someone is dreaming. This is possible if a link can be established between dreaming and some specific physiological activity. Aserinsky and Kleitman (1955) observed that periods of rapid eye movements during sleep were associated with a high incidence of dream sleep.

This study further investigated the relationship between eye movements and dreaming to demonstrate that dream experiences and REM activity are two facets of the same thing.

Aims
Research has investigated a possible link between REM sleep and dreams. This study aimed to conduct a more rigorous test of the association between REM sleep and dreams, using three approaches:

1. Comparing what dreams people recall when awoken in either REM sleep or quiet periods of sleep (NREM sleep). There should be no contact between the researcher and participant to eliminate any possible cueing effect.

2. Looking at the relationship between subjective reports of dream duration and the length of eye movements before awakening. If REM sleep is the physical manifestation of dreaming then there should be a **positive correlation**.

3. Observing the patterns of eye movements during REM sleep to see if they represented the visual experience of the dream or were simply **random** motor discharge.

Qs 4.7

1. Would it matter if participants knew the purpose of the study? Why or why not?
2. Does the size of the sample matter? Explain your answer.
3. Identify **one** other potential weakness of the sample, other than size.
4. Why were participants told to abstain from caffeine and alcohol?
5. Explain **one** problem with the instruction to abstain from alcohol and caffeine.
6. What happened after the participants were woken?
7. Why was it important that the participants didn't know if they had just been having REM activity when they were awoken by the bell?
8. It is difficult to believe that the participants had a normal night's sleep. How might this affect REM and NREM activity?

Method

Participants

There were nine American adults, seven adult males and two females. Each was referred to by their initials.

Five of them were studied intensively. The other four were only studied to confirm the results from the first five.

Procedure

Sleep laboratory
The research sessions were repeated many times. Typically the participant reported to the sleep laboratory just before their usual bedtime. They had been told to eat normally but abstain on the day of the study from alcohol or drinks containing caffeine.

Recording eye and brain
Electrodes were attached around the participant's eyes to measure electrical activity and hence eye movement (using EOG), and attached to the participant's scalp to record brain waves (using EEG) as a measure of depth of sleep. The recordings were made continuously through the night. The participant then went to sleep in a quiet darkened room.

At various times during the night participants were woken by a bell, placed by their bed. The awakenings were done either during an REM period or at varying time periods after REM activity had stopped (i.e. during NREM sleep). On average the participants were awoken 5.7 times a night and slept for six hours.

Waking participants
The investigators used various different patterns for awakening the five most intensively studied participants. This variety was necessary to avoid any unintentional pattern. For example, with two participants they used a table of random numbers, and another participant was told he would only be awoken during REM sleep but in fact was awoken randomly during REM and NREM sleep.

None of the participants were told whether they had just been displaying REM activity when they were awoken.

Participants were also awoken if they displayed patterns of mainly vertical or mainly horizontal eye movements, or a mixture of both, for more than one minute. They were then asked to describe the content of their dream.

Data collection
The participant was instructed to speak into a recording machine near their bed, (a) stating whether they had been dreaming, (b) describing, if they could, the content of the dream and (c) saying, if they had been dreaming, whether they had been dreaming for 5 or 15 minutes. Recording their answers was done in this way because direct contact might mean that the investigator would 'cue' certain responses from the participant.

An investigator was listening outside the room and occasionally entered the room to further question the participant on some particular point of the dream. The participants usually fell back to sleep within five minutes.

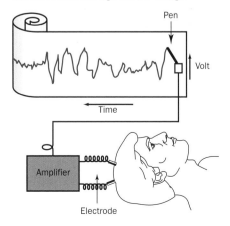

In a sleep study electrodes are placed around a participant's eyes and on his scalp and connected to an EEG monitor which records electrical activity from networks of neurons in the brain.

The illustration below shows how an EEG recording in made. The electrical activity recorded by the electrodes is translated into a series of wavy lines representing the amount of volts being produced in the brain at any time. A 'brain wave' is the rapid alternation between high and low voltage.

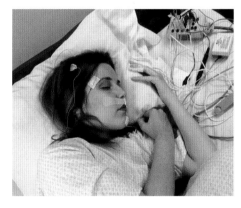

Dement and Kleitman: the core study *continued*

Results

The occurrence of REM activity

There are some general observations about **REM** activity:

- All participants had REM activity every night.
- REM activity was accompanied by a relatively fast **EEG** pattern.
- When REM activity was absent there were periods of deeper sleep, indicated by either **slow wave sleep** or **sleep-spindles**.
- No REM activity occurred during the initial onset of sleep.
- REM periods lasted between 3 and 50 minutes, with a **mean** of about 20 minutes. The REM period tended to get longer the later in the night it occurred. The eyes were not constantly in motion during REM activity, instead there were bursts of between 2 and 100 movements.
- REM periods occurred at fairly regular intervals. The frequency was characteristic for each individual. The participant WD averaged one REM period every 70 minutes, for KC it was once every 104 minutes. The average was one REM episode every 92 minutes.
- Despite the disturbance of being regularly awakened, the REM periods were as frequent as those recorded in a previous study of uninterrupted sleep.
- REM periods during the final hours of sleep tended to be quite long. If a participant was awakened during one of these long periods, they often went back into REM sleep as if the heightened brain activity had not run its course.

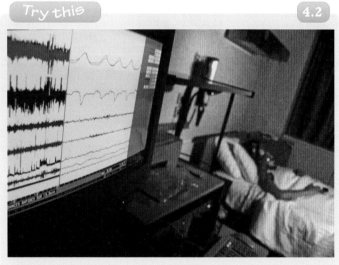

Try this 4.2

A modern-day sleep lab.

Role play

Set up your 'pseudo sleep lab' in your classroom. You need a bed, an 'EEG machine' near the head of the bed, and a 'recording device' nearby. Students can take turns being sleep researchers, equipment monitors and sleep volunteers.

- The sleep researchers should brief the volunteer.
- Then the equipment monitor should attach some 'bluetack' electrodes to the scalp and eyes of the volunteer, with strings to the EEG machine.
- Follow the procedures on the previous spread.

When these procedures are completed, discuss ways in which the methodology of this study may have affected the outcome.

You can also discuss how dream descriptions could have been subject to misinterpretation.

Three approaches

Three different approaches were used to establish the link between REM and dreams.

1 REM versus NREM recall

Participants were considered to be dreaming only if they could provide a coherent, fairly detailed description of dream content.

The table below shows how many dreams were recalled after being awoken in REM or **NREM sleep** in the five most intensively studied participants.

Participant	REM sleep		NREM sleep	
DN	17/26	65%	3/24	12.5%
IR	26/34	76%	2/31	6%
KC	36/40	90%	3/34	9%
WD	37/42	88%	1/35	3%
PM	24/30	80%	2/25	8%

- For all participants there was a high incidence of recall of dreaming during REM periods, and a low incidence of recall during NREM periods (see pie charts below), regardless of the patterns used to determine awakenings.
- However, there were times when REM activity was not associated with a coherent dream and times when NREM sleep did produce coherent dream recall.

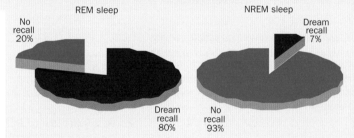

Graphs showing mean percentage of dreams recalled in REM and NREM sleep.

- There were individual differences – some participants were better able to recall their dreams.
- When participants were awoken in NREM sleep (characterised by high voltage, slow waves), the likelihood of having a dream was related to the recency of an REM episode. If participants were awoken more than eight minutes after the end of an REM period, very few dreams were recalled (6 dreams in 132 awakenings) whereas if participants were awoken *within* eight minutes of an REM period the proportion recalled rose (5 dreams in 17 awakenings).
- When participants were awoken during deep NREM sleep they sometimes were rather bewildered and reported that they must have been dreaming but couldn't remember the dream. They recalled a mood, such as anxiety or pleasantness, but no specific content.
- Most of the instances when dreams could not be recalled during REM sleep occurred during the early part of the night (there were only 39 reports of having no dreams during REM awakenings and 19 of these were during the first two hours of the night).

2 Length of REM and dream duration estimates

A further way to establish the link between REM sleep and dreaming is to show that the length of REM activity was related to the estimated duration of a dream. This was done by awakening participants either 5 or 15 minutes after the onset of REM activity and asking them to decide which was the correct duration.

You can see in the table below that some but not all of the participants were very accurate in their estimations. On average they were 83% correct (92 times correct out of 111).

| | 5 minutes | | 15 minutes | |
	Right	Wrong	Right	Wrong
DN	8	2	5	5
IR	11	1	7	3
KC	7	0	12	1
WD	13	1	15	1
PM	6	2	8	3
Total	45	6	47	13

A different way of assessing duration of REM activity in relation to length of dream was to calculate a **correlation** between how long the REM episode lasted and the number of words the participant used to describe the dream. The results showed a **positive correlation** and were **significant** for each participant, ranging between .40 and .71.

3 Eye movement patterns and visual imagery of the dream

There was great variation in eye movements during REM periods. It was proposed that the movements might correspond to where and at what the dreamer was looking in his/her dream. To investigate this the participants were woken when their eye movements were mainly vertical or horizontal or both or neither, as shown in the table below:

Type of eye movement	Content of dream reported by participants
Mainly vertical There were 3 such dreams reported	Standing at bottom of cliff and looking at climbers at different levels.
	Climbing ladders and looking up and down.
	Shooting at a basketball net and looking down to pick up the next ball.
Mainly horizontal 1 dream	Two people throwing tomatoes at each other.
Both vertical and horizontal 10 dreams	Looking at things close to them, e.g. talking to a group of people, fighting with someone.
Very little or no movement 21 dreams	Watching something in the distance or just staring fixedly at some object.

Effects of practice

The table below compares performance in the first half of the tests with the last half, showing that participants didn't recall more dreams as they got more practised.

| | First half | | Second half | |
	Dream recall	No recall	Dream recall	No recall
DN	12	1	5	8
IR	12	5	14	3
KC	18	2	18	2
WD	19	2	18	3
PM	12	3	12	3
Total	73	13	67	19

There did appear to be a link between eye movement and the content of a dream. When one participant was dreaming about climbing a series of ladders, looking up and down as he climbed, his eyes moved vertically.

When another participant had a dream about throwing tomatoes, this was accompanied by horizontal eye movement.

Qs 4.8

1 When were participants most likely to report that they had been dreaming?

2 How was dreaming operationalised?

3 What evidence was there that the participants' sleep was following a fairly normal pattern, not affected by being in a laboratory?

4 There were individual differences. Participants showed a different ratio of recall/no recall in REM sleep. Give an example of this individual difference.

5 How might this be important when interpreting the results?

6 Another difference was that some participants were better able to recall their dreams than others. In what way is this important?

7 Outline **three** pieces of evidence that support the view that dreaming is linked to REM sleep.

8 Describe **one** piece of evidence that challenges this conclusion.

9 Give **one** example of a piece of qualitative data and **one** example of a piece of quantitative data recorded in this study.

10 How could you explain why dreams were not always reported in REM sleep?

Discussion

This study showed that dreaming is accompanied by **REM activity**. It cannot be stated with complete certainly that dreaming doesn't occur at other times. The few instances of NREM dreaming can be best explained by assuming that the memory for a dream persisted for some time and thus appeared to occur during NREM sleep.

Past research
Wada (1922) suggested that dreaming was connected to gastric contractions and McGlade (1942) identified a link with foot twitching. The associated research showed weak support for these claims and the studies lacked **reliability**.

Other research has investigated the REM-dreaming link, providing support for the results of this study. For example, Ramsey (1953) found that most dreams were recalled during the later hours of sleep.

Why don't all people have REM sleep?
Previous research by Aserinsky and Kleitman (1955) found that some people don't have REM sleep. This may be due to **sampling** behaviour during sleep rather than making continuous **observations**. It could be that REM periods occurred between when the samples were taken, thus escaping observation. Alternatively it might be that REM activity in some people involved very little movement and it was not detected by the **EOG**.

Conclusion
It seems reasonable to conclude that an objective measurement of dreaming may be accomplished by recording REMs during sleep.

Qs 4.9

1 What explanation is offered for why dreams may seem to occur in NREM sleep?
2 What evidence supports this claim? (See previous spread.)
3 Previous research has found that not everyone appears to have REM sleep. What explanation(s) do Dement and Kleitman offer for this?
4 How could the researchers have used a continuous method of observation?
5 When people are deprived of REM sleep they suffer 'REM rebound' – they need more REM sleep. How do you think this may have affected the results in this study?
6 Why do you think it is important to have a means of objectively being able to measure when dreaming is occurring?

Try this 4.3

What are dreams like?
People have very different, and quite characteristic, dreams. Work out a system to record the kind of dreams experienced by members of your class. There is a 'Dream questionnaire' on page 16 which you might use. Or look for something on the internet.

Brain waves
There are a number of apps available which will measure your brain wave patterns during sleep. Try, for example, *Sleep cycle alarm clock* or even *Dream On* which aims to influence the content of your dreams.

Links to core studies

This core study makes an interesting link to **Freud's** approach to dreaming. In the **Little Hans** study he makes use of some dreams that Hans has to interpret the boy's feelings for his parents. This core study also links to the work of **Rosenhan** because of the well-established connection between sleep deprivation and symptoms of mental disorder. This core study has a methodological simplicity used to look at the seemingly very complex phenomenon of dreaming. This same methodological simplicity can be seen in the study comparing taxi drivers' brains with those of non-taxi drivers (**Maguire *et al.***) and also the experiment on eyewitness testimony by **Loftus and Palmer**.

Biographical notes

William Dement's career started in the 1950s as a medical student in Kleitman's lab. Today he is a Professor at Stanford University where he also runs a sleep disorders clinic. He has researched sleep disorders, circadian rhythms, sudden infant death syndrome, jet lag, sleep loss and sleep hygiene. He has been feted with a long list of awards including 'Profound Thinkers of the Bay Area Award' and 'Man of the Year of the Société de Distinction Internationale'.

William Dement

Nathaniel Kleitman died in 1999 at the age of 104, so he was in his 60s at the time this research was conducted. He was born in Russia and immigrated to the US at the age of 20. He has been described as 'the father of modern sleep research'. Before him, few scientists had systematically investigated the intricacies of sleep, dismissing it as a state where very little happens. Kleitman's discovery, with Eugene Aserinsky, of REM sleep was the beginning of a whole new area of study. The subjects for this first study were their own children. He was no stranger to the role of subject himself. Kleitman and an associate spent more than a month 150 feet underground in Mammoth Cave, Kentucky to investigate the 'free-running' sleep–wake cycle.

Nathaniel Kleitman (left)

Things you could do ...

Read the original article by obtaining a photocopy from your local library – give them the full reference and order a photocopy.

Read:

Jacob Empson and Michael Wang's book *Sleep and Dreaming*.

A BBC feature on sleep http://www.bbc.co.uk/science/humanbody/sleep

Watch YouTube series 'How the body works', includes programme on EEG http://www.youtube.com/watch?v=M9XVm-ks1ME&mode=related&search=Brain%20waves

Evaluating the study by Dement and Kleitman

The research method
This study could be considered a controlled observation – because the experimenter controlled when the participants woke up.

What are the strengths and weaknesses of this method in the context of this study?

It could also be considered to be a quasi-experiment because the IV (REM/NREM sleep) wasn't controlled by the experimenter.

What are the strengths and weaknesses of this method in the context of this study?

The research techniques
One of the techniques used in this study was self-report.

What are the strengths and weaknesses of this research technique in the context of this study?

The sample
The participants were nine adults. *In what way are the participants in this sample unique?*

To what extent were the participants different from each other in terms of their recall in REM sleep? How does this affect the conclusions drawn from the study?

Sampling was also used to record behaviour associated with REM activity. This was used instead of making continuous observations.

What are the strengths and weaknesses of these methods in the context of this study?

Ethics
What ethical issues should have concerned the researchers in this study, and how might they have dealt with these?

Reliability
Reliability concerns measurement.

What aspects of human behaviour were measured in this study? How could the reliability of these measurements be assessed?

Ecological validity
Participants slept in a lab with electrodes on their head and were awakened throughout the night.

To what extent does the behaviour in this study reflect 'normal' sleep and dreaming?

In what way could this study be described as 'low in ecological validity'?

How might this affect the conclusions drawn from the study?

Qualitative and quantitative
Both quantitative and qualitative data were collected in this study.

Give examples of each. What are the strengths and weaknesses of producing each kind of data in the context of this study?

Applications/usefulness
How valuable is this study? Find out more about sleep research in general and consider all the benefits (or not) of this landmark study.

What next?
*Describe **one** change to this study, and say how you think this might affect the outcome.*

There are no simple answers.

Evaluating a study requires you to think.

*We have provided some pointers here, linked to the **RESEARCH METHODS** and **KEY ISSUES** covered in Chapter 1 (Psychological investigations) and Chapter 7 (Key issues).*

You can read suggested answers on our website www.psypress.com/cw/banyard.

Producing effective evaluation
When you produce your own answers to the issues on the left there are two things to ensure:
1   Contextualisation
2   Elaboration

The key to **CONTEXTUALISATION** is to ensure that your answer includes some information about this particular study. For example:

> *Question:*
> With reference to the study by Dement and Kleitman, explain why this study might be considered a quasi-experiment. **[2]**
>
>
>
> *Answer:*
> **STATE**: A quasi-experiment is a study with an independent variable and dependent variable, as in any experiment. However, in an experiment the experimenter causes the independent variable to change. In a quasi-experiment the experimenter uses an independent variable that was varying naturally.
> **CONTEXT**: In the study by Dement and Kleitman the independent variable was having REM sleep and NREM sleep, a sleep state that varied naturally and was not controlled by the experimenter.

The key to **ELABORATION** is the three-point rule (see page xii), but you don't need three points when there are only 2 marks! For example:

> *Question:*
> Discuss **one** strength of the physiological approach, using examples from any study that takes this approach. **[3]**
>
>
>
> *Answer:*
> **STATE**: One strength of the physiological approach is that physical behaviours lend themselves to being measured precisely and objecively.
> **CONTEXT**: In the study by Dement and Kleitman the aim was to be able to measure dreaming objectively.
> **COMMENT**: For example they found that the number of words to describe a dream was related significantly to the duration of the dream.

The physiological approach

On pages 110–111 and 222–223 we have discussed the **physiological approach**.

The study by Dement and Kleitman concerns the brain activity that is associated with dreaming.

• In what way is this an example of the physiological approach?

• Discuss the strengths and weaknesses of the physiological approach using examples from the Dement and Kleitman study.

Dement and Kleitman: afters

Dream on

The work of Dement and Kleitman was the spark for an avalanche of research into sleep and its effects. Much of this work has been used to good effect but as you can see on this page, this is not always the case. This research has only answered some of the many questions about sleep. If we know a lot more about sleep because of psychological research it is also fair to say that we know only a little more about dreaming. What are dreams and nightmares? When we dream at night we have fragmentary experiences over which we have very little control. People appear and disappear, change into giant frogs and then start eating your left leg. Before you know what has happened you're buried up to your waist on Skegness beach and you've just married Jeremy Kyle. At which point, of course, you wake up screaming. These dream events are strangely powerful and can stay with us for years. The great Italian artist **Leonardo Da Vinci** mused *'Why does the eye see a thing more clearly in dreams than the imagination when awake?'*

World record

So how long do you think you can stay awake? The world record was set in 1964 by Randy Gardner in San Diego, USA. He wanted to enter a science fair and decided to make a project of a world record attempt at sleep deprivation. His attempt attracted a lot of attention and after a week **William Dement** (yes the very same) got in touch.

'I immediately called Randy's home, explained to him and his parents who I was, and asked if I could observe him attempt to break the record.' (Dement, 2001).

Gardner had to be watched all the time to make sure he did not fall asleep and Dement took his turn in keeping him awake.

'If [Gardner] began to fall asleep, I would hustle him outside to the small basketball court in his backyard or drive him around the deserted San Diego streets in a convertible with the top down and the radio playing loudly.'

Dement spent the tenth day of the attempt walking around the town with Gardner and records how the teenager was able to beat him on arcade games and also at basketball. On the eleventh day Gardner hosted a press conference where he spoke without slurring or stumbling over his words and appeared to be in excellent health. At 6:04am he finally fell asleep having set a world record for sleeplessness that has never been broken.

The remarkable aspect of this achievement is Gardner's apparent good health throughout the time without sleep. This has not been observed on other attempts where people quickly show severe psychological effects including hallucinations. One possible explanation is that he was able to indulge in 'microsleep' – small periods of sleep during the day which allow some physiological recovery to take place.

Sleep debt

Surveys in the UK find that young adults report sleeping about 7–7.5 hours each night. A hundred years ago the average person slept nine hours each night. This means that today's population sleeps one to two hours less than people used to sleep (Webb and Agnew, 1975).

The key change is probably artificial light which triggers wakefulness. People probably sleep 500 hours less each year than they used to and this might well be less sleep than evolution intended. When people go out of their daily routine, for example on holiday, they tend to sleep longer. In fact, in less industrialised societies, the total daily sleep time tends to still be around nine to 10 hours (Coren, 1996).

A group of researchers spent a summer above the Arctic Circle where there is continuous light 24 hours a day (Palinkas *et al.*, 1995). All their watches, clocks and other timekeeping devices were taken away, and they chose when to sleep or wake according to their 'body time'. At the end of the study, the participants' overall average daily sleep time was 10.3 hours. Every member of the team showed an increase in sleep time, with the shortest logging in at 8.8 hours a day, and the longest at almost 12 hours a day.

People who are living with a sleep debt are less efficient and the common effects of a large sleep debt are lapses in attention, reduced short-term memory capacity, impaired judgement and having 'microsleeps' which the sleeper is commonly unaware of – obviously not good if you're driving. It is estimated that 20% of UK motorway accidents are caused by sleepiness (Horne and Reyner, 1995) and over 300 people are killed each year by drivers falling asleep at the wheel (THINK, 2004).

There is now evidence that many major disasters have been due to sleep-debt effects. The evidence shows that these include the oil spill of the Exxon Valdez, the nuclear accidents at Chernobyl and Three Mile Island, and the loss of the space shuttle Challenger (Coren, 1996).

Sleep and torture

Barney the purple dinosaur sings 'I Love You'. But how would you feel if you had to listen to it for 24 hours non-stop?

Sleep deprivation has been used by many countries as an interrogation technique. For example, during the occupation by US and UK forces at the start of this century, some prisoners in Iraq were deprived of sleep by playing them loud heavy metal music for long periods of time. The US Psychological Operations Company (PsyOps) reports that their aim was to break a prisoner's resistance through sleep deprivation and playing music that was culturally offensive to them (BBC, 2003).

To say this is controversial is to understate the issue. Amnesty International, for example, says these techniques may well be psychological torture and therefore breach the Geneva Convention.

Sergeant Mark Hadsell, of PsyOps, comments *'These people haven't heard heavy metal. They can't take it. If you play it for 24 hours, your brain and body functions start to slide, your train of thought slows down and your will is broken. That's when we come in and talk to them.'*

Sergeant Hadsell's favourites are said to be 'Bodies' from the *XXX* film soundtrack and Metallica's 'Enter Sandman'. The theme tune from the US children's programme *Sesame Street* and songs from the purple singing dinosaur Barney are also on his hit list.

One US serviceman said *'In training, they forced me to listen to the Barney "I Love You" song for 45 minutes. I never want to go through that again'* (BBC, 2003).

To be fair, it is argued by members of PsyOps that these tactics only have temporary effects on the prisoners. For example, Rick Hoffman in an interview with the BBC said *'There have been other kinds of non-lethal, non-harmful techniques, such as sleep deprivation... which leave no long-lasting effects but do have the end result of breaking down the individual's will to resist questioning.'* It is a fine line between using pressure on people and straying into torture (BBC, 2003).

Multiple choice questions

1 REM stands for:
   a Random eye movements.
   b Random eye motion.
   c Rapid eye motion.
   d Rapid eye movements.

2 How many participants were studied intensively?
   a 3   b 5
   c 7   d 9

3 Which of the following are characteristics of REM activity?
   a No EEG activity.
   b Different kinds of EEG activity.
   c Relatively fast EEG activity.
   d Relatively slow EEG activity.

4 In this study, the recall of dreams was:
   a The DV.
   b The IV.
   c An extraneous variable.
   d A confounding variable.

5 Which of the following procedures acted as a 'control' in this study?
   a Participants reported their dreams without direct contact with the experimenter.
   b Participants were not told if they had been woken from REM activity or not.
   c The study was conducted in a laboratory.
   d All of the above.

6 Almost all of the dreams reported in NREM sleep were reported within how many minutes of REM activity?
   a 2   b 4
   c 6   d 8

7 At what time of the night were REM episodes absent?
   a At the beginning.
   b In the middle.
   c Towards the morning.
   d REM episodes were always present.

8 At what time of the night were REM episodes longest?
   a At the beginning.
   b In the middle.
   c Towards the morning.
   d The duration of REM did not differ during the night.

9 On average REM episodes lasted:
   a 10 minutes
   b 20 minutes
   c 30 minutes
   d 40 minutes

10 When eye movement patterns were observed during REM periods, the least common form of eye movement was:
   a Mainly vertical movement.
   b Mainly horizontal movement.
   c A mixture of horizontal and vertical.
   d Little or no movement.

Answers are on page 247.

Exam-style questions

There are three kinds of question that can be asked about the Dement and Kleitman study, as represented here by sections A, B and C.

See page x for further notes on the exam paper and styles of question.

Section A questions

1 Dement and Kleitman's study on sleep linked REM activity to dreaming. Describe **two** pieces of evidence that supported this link. [4]

2 In the study of sleep by Dement and Kleitman there was some evidence that dreams also occurred in NREM sleep.
   (a) Explain how they collected this evidence. [2]
   (b) How did they explain the dreams being reported in NREM sleep? [2]

3 Dement and Kleitman used an electroencephalogram (EEG) to record sleep activity.
   (a) Explain what the EEG shows. [2]
   (b) Describe **one** limitation of using an EEG to investigate dreaming. [2]

4 (a) Identify **two** of the controls used by Dement and Kleitman in their study of sleep and dreaming. [2]
   (b) Outline why controls are used in psychological research. [2]

5 In the study of sleep by Dement and Kleitman, participants were told to abstain from two substances on the day of the experiment.
   (a) Identify these **two** substances. [2]
   (b) Outline **one** problem with this instruction. [2]

6 (a) Identify **one** of the hypotheses of Dement and Kleitman's study on sleep and dreaming. [2]
   (b) Outline the results of the study in relation to this aim. [2]

7 Outline **two** ways that the study by Dement and Kleitman can be said to be low in ecological validity. [4]

8 With reference to the study by Dement and Kleitman,
   (a) Outline **one** piece of evidence that shows that REM sleep is linked to dreaming. [2]
   (b) Outline **one** piece of evidence that challenges this relationship. [2]

9 Dement and Kleitman investigated aspects of dreaming.
   (a) Explain **one** method they used to measure the duration of a person's dream. [2]
   (b) Explain how the reliability of this method could be determined. [2]

10 In the study by Dement and Kleitman, describe the methods that were used to control extraneous variables. [4]

Section B questions

Answer the following questions with reference to the Dement and Kleitman study:

(a) Briefly outline the research method used in this study. [2]

(b) Describe **two** examples of quantitative data recorded in this study. [4]

(c) With reference to this study, suggest **one** strength and **one** weakness of quantitative data. [6]

(d) Describe the procedures of this study. [8]

(e) Suggest how this study could be improved. [8]

(f) Outline the implications of the improvements you have suggested for this study. [8]

Section C questions

(a) Outline **one** assumption of the physiological approach. [2]

(b) Describe how the physiological approach could explain dreaming. [4]

(c) Describe **one** similarity and **one** difference between the Dement and Kleitman study and any other core studies that take the physiological approach. [6]

(d) Discuss strengths and weaknesses of the physiological approach using examples from any core studies that take this approach. [12]

Sperry: starters

One brain or two?

The brain is a truly remarkable organ. Think about it. The brain creates our world for us every time we wake up. **Roger Sperry** said, *'Before brains there was no color or sound in the universe, nor was there any flavor or aroma and probably little sense and no feeling or emotion'* (Sperry, 1964). All these qualities only exist in our brains. I know you think a tree is green and the sky is blue and Rudolf's nose is red but it isn't so. The world is full of radiation of different wavelengths and it is our brain that senses that radiation and creates the colours we use to interpret our surroundings. It's almost too amazing to think about.

During his career Sperry made some startling discoveries about the brain, none more so than the ones described in this core study. I think this study challenges what we know about ourselves and what we can become.

A lot was already known about the brain before Sperry's study and some of that is summarised on this spread. Every year sees our knowledge of the brain growing with the promise of finding out more about why we do the things we do. Brain scientist Wilder Penfield (see facing page) believed that the brain represented the most important unexplored field in the whole of science and it is hard to argue with him. We have only scratched the surface in our understanding of the brain.

What the brain does

The brain has two relatively symmetrical halves (left and right). The illustration shows a brain that has been cut down the middle. You can see that the top third of the brain (i.e. the cerebral cortex) is not joined to its other half: the only part that has been cut through is where the two halves are joined – at the commissural fibres, which include the corpus callosum.

Cerebral cortex

This is the clever bit of the human brain and the largest part. The cerebral cortex actually covers the brain like a tea cosy and is highly wrinkled which increases the surface area and probably increases its power. Structures that are 'sub-cortical' lie under the tea cosy. Such sub-cortical structures are concerned with more basic processes like emotion and are present in all animals, whereas the cortex is specific to higher animals such as mammals.

The cortex is divided into four lobes which are believed to control different functions:

- **Frontal lobe** (front of the brain, above the eyes): reasoning, planning, parts of speech, movement, emotions and problem solving.
- **Parietal lobe** (top, towards the back): movement, orientation, recognition, perception of stimuli.
- **Occipital lobe** (back): visual processing.
- **Temporal lobe** (sides): perception of auditory stimuli, memory and speech.

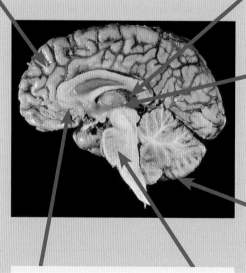

Corpus callosum

The corpus callosum connects the left and right cerebral hemispheres and carries most of the communication between the two halves of the brain. A number of claims have been made about sex and racial differences in the corpus callosum. The idea is that the greater the traffic across the two halves the greater the person's intelligence (favouring women and white people). Such claims are made in popular magazines but they have little scientific support (Bishop and Wahlsten, 1997).

Thalamus

The simple story is that the thalamus (a sub-cortical structure) is a 'relay station' for signals from the senses (skin, stomach, eyes, ears but not the nose) to the cerebral cortex. The real story is more complicated, because the thalamus does more than just send the signals on – it also does some initial analysis of the signals.

Hypothalamus

This is located below the thalamus (hence hypo-thalamus). It is the size of half a baked bean but plays a very important role as the major control centre for a range of essential functions. For example, it controls body temperature, hunger and thirst. It also appears to be involved in emotional and sexual activity. A lot of work for half a baked bean.

Cerebellum

The cerebellum, or 'little brain', is similar to the cerebral cortex in that it has two **hemispheres** and has a highly folded surface or cortex. This structure is associated with regulation and coordination of movement, posture and balance.

Brain stem

The brain stem is the stalk of the brain below the cerebral hemispheres. It is the major route for communication between the forebrain and the spinal cord and peripheral nerves. It also controls various functions including respiration and regulation of heart rhythms.

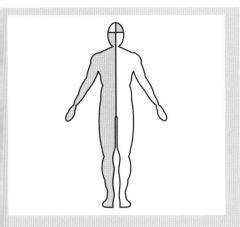

Cross-wired

The left side of the body and the left visual field are controlled by the right hemisphere, and the right side of the body and the right visual field by the left hemisphere.

Control of the auditory fields is more complex, while our sense of smell, the most neurologically ancient of the senses, is not crossed over at all, each nostril being 'wired' to the hemisphere on the same side of the body.

Wilder Penfield (1891–1976)

Penfield was a Canadian surgeon and researcher who was interested in finding cures for epilepsy and other brain disorders. With his colleagues, Penfield developed a new surgical approach in which he was able to examine the exposed brain of a conscious patient using just a local anaesthetic. As the patient described what they were feeling, Penfield pushed a probe into sections of the brain and located the damaged tissue that was the source of the epileptic seizures. The damaged tissue was removed and many patients then had relief from their seizures.

Of course, once you have an open brain in front of you, it is only natural to poke about a bit to see what is going on. This is exactly what Penfield did and he made some astounding discoveries. For example, he found that careful administration of a mild electric shock to one of the temporal lobes could make some patients recall precise personal experiences that had long been forgotten.

This brain technique also allowed him to create maps of the sensory and motor areas of the brain. These maps are commonly represented as distorted models of a person that show how much of the brain area is associated with each part of the body (if you find it difficult to visualise this then Google 'Penfield homunculus'). He first published this work in 1951 and it is still being used today. Penfield's research also gave us a lot of information about how different areas of the brain have different effects on our behaviour and experience (lateralisation of function).

Penfield's research into the structure and function of the brain was prompted by his desire to discover a physical basis for the belief in the human soul, an idea that was followed up some years later by V.S. Ramachandran (see his website).

Penfield's work has captured the imagination of many people and he gets a mention in a number of works of fiction. For example, in the science fiction classic Do Androids Dream of Electric Sheep? *by Philip K. Dick (also filmed as Blade Runner) characters use a household device called a Penfield Mood Organ to dial up emotions on demand.*

Sperry's animal experiments

It is an uncomfortable part of medical science that many advances come from research on animals. Pictures of animals in painful apparatus illustrate one side of the story and life-saving medicines illustrate the other.

It can be no surprise that Sperry carried out a lot of research on animal brains before he operated on people. Those of a nervous disposition should stop reading now.

Sperry was able to show that a number of functions are 'hard-wired' into the nervous system and cannot be learned. For example, he swapped wiring round on a rat's foot so that when it tried to move its left foot the right foot moved instead. The rat was not able to adapt to this new arrangement. He also cut the optic nerves of salamanders and then rotated them before allowing the nerves to regenerate and reconnect to the eye. The salamander then saw the world upside down and it was not able to adapt to this. And of course, the split-brain technique of severing the corpus callosum was tried out on cats and monkeys before being used on people.

The full gory details of the animal work does not make good reading and many readers might object to the zoo full of animals who had their brains rearranged by Sperry. On the other hand, the patients with epilepsy who had the split-brain operation were better able to live an ordinary life and so might disagree. It's a moral maze.

Epilepsy

Epilepsy is the term given to a collection of disorders that are associated with uncontrolled seizures. The severity of the seizures can differ from person to person. Some people will just experience a trance-like state for a few seconds, or minutes, whereas others will lose consciousness and have convulsions (uncontrollable shaking of the body). Epilepsy is a relatively widespread condition affecting around 456,000 people in the UK. The condition usually begins during childhood but it can start at any age. Around 1 in every 280 children is affected by epilepsy. Modern medications can usually control epilepsy but not cure it and surgery is still sometimes used in difficult cases.

It is not clear what causes epilepsy, although one of the main risk factors (common to many other disorders) is being poor. Parts of the world that are less developed than the West have up to twice the incidence of epilepsy.

A common myth about epilepsy is that it is brought on by flashing lights, but around only 10% of people with epilepsy are sensitive to lights in this way.

St. Valentine, patron saint of lovers and people with epilepsy.

Epilepsy in history

The split-brain operation used in this study was performed as a means of treating severe epilepsy. Epilepsy has been recognised as a condition for many centuries and people have tried to explain it in a number of ways. In the fourteenth and fifteenth centuries seizures were commonly seen as being a curse or the work of demonic forces. People with seizures made pilgrimages to the Priory of St Valentine, a monastery on the border between France and Germany, for spiritual healing. They went there because, as well as being the patron saint of lovers, Valentine moonlights as the patron saint of people with epilepsy.

In the Middle Ages epileptics were pointed in the direction of medical 'cures' ranging from blood-letting to burning.

Treatments and attitudes are much better today but it is fair to say that people with epilepsy still experience discrimination and negative responses in the UK.

www   If you are interested to find out more about the brain then you might start your exploration at the whole brain atlas (www.med.harvard.edu/AANLIB/home.html).

...Link to the core study...

The idea of splitting a person's brain in half is shocking and fascinating. You just have to know what happens. If your personality is merely something in your brain, rather than in a mystical idea like a soul, then maybe cutting the brain in half will create two personalities. Of course you can't do this to people just for the sake of investigating this question but sometimes extreme surgery is the only option. In this study the split-brain operation was done to relieve epilepsy, but also afforded scientists the ideal opportunity to assess the psychological effects of splitting the brain.

Sperry: the core study

Roger Wolcott Sperry (1968) Hemispheric disconnection and unity in conscious awareness. *American Psychologist, 23*, 723–733.

See the
CORE STUDY CHECKLIST
on page xv for details of what you need to know for the exam.

In a nutshell

Context
Previous research suggests that functional removal of areas of the brain, such as the **frontal lobe**, results in major behavioural changes. Whereas removal of the **corpus callosum** has a much less serious effect in both humans and monkeys.

Aim
Split-brain surgery was performed on severe epileptics to relieve their symptoms. The aim of this study was to record the associated behavioural changes.

Participants
Eleven epileptic patients who had undergone the split–brain operation took part in this study.

Note that the operation was not done for the purpose of this study, which would have been unethical.

Procedure
Participants were seated in front of a screen and focussed on a cross in the middle of the screen.

Images were shown on the left and right of the screen.

Images on the left are processed by the left visual field (LVF) of both eyes. The brain is cross-wired for vision so information from the LVF of both eyes goes to the right hemisphere.

Information from the right side of the screen is processed by the right visual field (RVF) of each eye and sent to the left hemisphere.

In split-brain patients some of this information won't 'get through', e.g. information from the RVF in the right eye won't get through to the left hemisphere (see diagram on page 137).

The images were displayed for very brief periods (0.01 seconds) so participants could not turn their head. There was a gap under the screen so that the participant could identify objects placed behind the screen, out of sight.

The brain is also cross-wired for touch, so the right hand is controlled by the LH (and vice versa).

In most people, language is controlled by the LH but hearing is processed on both sides of the brain.

Key terms: hemispheric deconnection, the split-brain operation and epilepsy

*The brain is divided into two halves called **hemispheres**. The two halves of the brain are connected by the corpus callosum as well as some smaller connections (the anterior commisure, **hippocampal** commisure and the massa intermedia). The importance of these connections is that they enable both hemispheres to communicate with each other. Without them you have, in essence, two brains.*

*__Hemispheric deconnection__ (also called the **'split-brain' operation**) involves cutting through the connections. The purpose of the operation was to separate the two hemispheres in order to alleviate the symptoms of severe epilepsy. Epilepsy is a condition where the brain experiences a severe electrical storm. The neurons of the brain generate electrical currents to transmit their messages. In epilepsy some neurons discharge electrical signals inappropriately creating a 'storm'. In cases of severe epilepsy this storm is not confined to one area of the brain but spreads from hemisphere to hemisphere, magnifying the storm. This can be alleviated by deconnecting the hemispheres.*

Results	Conclusion that can be drawn
Display to LVF and RVF	LVF linked to RH, RVF linked to LH.
$ sign to LVF and ? sign to RVF	Left hand linked to RH (and LVF).
Participant draws $ sign with left hand	Right hand linked to LH (and RVF).
Participant reports he saw the ? sign	Language centres are in LH.
	The function of corpus callosum is to enable communication between RH and LH.
Visual material to LVF Participant reports he saw nothing or a flash of light on his left side.	RH has language weaknesses.
Visual material to LVF Participant can select objects that are *similar* with left hand, e.g. selecting a wrist watch when seeing a wall clock.	RH is not completely 'word blind', shows some language comprehension.
Pin-up to LVF Participant displays appropriate emotional reaction (such as a giggle) but says he saw nothing.	RH is still 'human' because it demonstrates an appropriate emotional response.
Two objects placed simultaneously one in each hand and then hidden in a pile of objects. Participant's right hand can select object presented to it and same for left hand, but each hand ignores the other hand's objects.	We effectively have two minds. Split-brain patients are two rather than one individual.
Everyday life Participants continue to watch TV or read books with no complaints; intellect and personality are unchanged.	Split-brain patients cope relatively well with everyday life, developing some strategies to compensate.

Qs 4.10

1 Why might it be considered unethical to perform a split-brain operation just for the purpose of this study?

2 What ethical issues are raised in this study?

3 Describe the sample used in this study and explain why they were selected.

4 In what way is Sperry's study a quasi-experiment?

5 What was the main brain structure that was cut for the split-brain operation?

6 In a split-brain patient, if information is presented to the LVF only, why can't they report what they are seeing?

7 What would have happened if the patients could turn their heads in time to see both images?

8 Why can normal individuals say what they see in the left visual field?

9 Why couldn't participants recognise material presented to the LVF with their right hand?

10 Describe **three** findings from this study and for each state what this piece of evidence shows.

11 What overall conclusion can you draw about the way the two hemispheres of the brain function?

The detailed version

Context and aim

Some forms of brain surgery have been shown to result in major functional deficits, i.e. behaviour is changed dramatically. Examples include **frontal lobotomy** or unilateral lobotomies performed to treat epilepsy. A lobotomy is an operation where connections to specific areas of the brain are cut so that part of the brain is no longer functional. In a frontal lobotomy connections to the **frontal lobe** are severed.

Studies of split-brain surgery have produced contradictory results. Animal operations resulted in numerous behavioural effects (e.g. Myers, 1961). Whereas Akelatitis (1944) observed no important behavioural effects in humans. Sperry's own research with humans and monkeys found less damaging effects than for lobotomies.

The implication is that cutting the corpus callosum does not have the damaging effects that occur when functionally removing other parts of the brain. ('Functional removal' means that the part of the brain is not actually removed but connections are severed so it is as if the part has been removed.)

Aim

To study the psychological effects of hemispheric disconnection in split-brain patients with severe epilepsy, and to use the results to understand how the right and left hemispheres work in 'normal' individuals.

Method

Participants

The participants were a group of 11 American patients who suffered from severe epileptic seizures that could not be controlled by medication. The split-brain operation is a possible remedy; it involves cutting through the most or all of the **cerebral commisures** that connect the left and right hemispheres of the brain (e.g. corpus callosum and some of the other structures listed on the facing page). The result of this is that no communication is possible between the left and right hemispheres.

For most patients the operation reduced the frequency and severity of their seizures.

Procedure

The main setup for testing the behavioural effects of hemispheric deconnection is shown on the right. Information can be presented selectively to the left hemisphere (via the right visual field, RVF) or to the right hemisphere (via the left visual field, LVF).

Qs 4.11

1 Akelaitis conducted earlier studies of split-brain patients. What effect did he find the procedure had on the behaviour of patients?
2 Why do you think Sperry projected the slides so briefly?
3 Explain how the brain is cross-wired to visual fields (see previous spread for information on cross-wiring).
4 Why was it important that participants couldn't see their hands?
5 Explain why a participant can't say what they see in the left visual field.

Apparatus for studying split-brain patients

The participant has one eye covered and is asked to gaze at a fixed point in the centre of a projection screen. Visual stimuli are back-projected onto the screen, either to the right or left of the screen, at a very high speed – one picture every 0.01 second or less. This means that the eye only has time to process the image in the visual field where it was placed (i.e. if the image was shown to the left visual field there is not time for the participant to move their eye or head so that the right visual field might also receive the image). Below the screen there was a gap so that the participant could reach objects but not see his or her hands.

Biographical notes

Roger Sperry, who was one of the premier neurobiologists of his time, started out studying English at university and only later took an interest in psychology. Like many remarkable people he had a range of interests and talents: he was a star athlete in javelin and played basketball at University, an avid fisherman, and an exceptionally talented sculptor, painter and ceramicist. He also was a keen paleontologist who collected prehistoric molluscs from around the world and, according to one colleague, was known for hosting great parties where he served his special 'split-brain' punch.

Sperry had a profound effect on the progress of physiological psychology specifically and brain science generally. He revolutionised neuroscience. In later years he turned more and more to philosophy and formulating a non-reductionist view of consciousness. He proposed that consciousness emerges from the activity of cerebral networks as an independent entity.

Roger Sperry (1913–1994) received the Nobel Prize in Medicine in 1981. In his acceptance speech he said:

'The great pleasure and feeling in my right brain is more than my left brain can find the words to tell you.'

Try this   **4.5**

Right brain left brain

It is possible to demonstrate right and left field advantages in normal individuals (without split brains).

Present two words (one on the right and one on the left) on a computer screen for less than 100 milliseconds. You can do this using an automatic PowerPoint display. Participants should show a preference for reporting the word on the right.

If you present two pictures (one left and one right), there should be a preference to report the picture on the left because the right hemisphere is better at analysing pictures.

You can also have a go with the right versus left brain optical illusion at http://www.youtube.com/watch?v=9CEr2GfGilw

Results

Baseline results

- If a projected picture is shown and responded to in one visual field, it is only recognised again if it appears in that visual field (VF).

- If visual material appears in the right visual field (RVF, processed by left **hemisphere**), the participant could describe it in speech and writing as normal.

- If the same visual material is projected to the left visual field (LVF, processed by the right hemisphere) then the participant says he did not see anything or says there was just a flash of light on his left side. (Language centres are in the left hemisphere.)

- If you then ask the same participant to use his left hand (right hemisphere control) to point to a matching picture or object in a collection of pictures/objects, he points to the item he just insisted he couldn't see.

These results confirm that the right hemisphere cannot speak or write (called **aphasia** and **agraphia** respectively).

$ and ? signs

What do you see?

What do you see?

Partcipant draws a $ with left hand

I see a "?"

If a $ sign is flashed to the LVF and a ? sign flashed to RVF the participant will draw (using his left hand out of sight) the figure $ which was shown to LVF but will tell you that he saw the ?, the sign shown to RVF.

Sperry says *'the one hemisphere does not know what the other hemisphere has been doing'* (page 726).

Composite words

What do you see?

What do you see?

Participant selects a key with left hand

'The word is "case"'. Participant spells the word with right hand

When words are flashed partly to the LVF and partly to the RVF, the letters are responded to separately. For example if 'keycase' is projected ('key' to the LVF and 'case' to the RVF) then a participant would:

- Select a key from the collection of objects with his left hand (LVF goes to right hemisphere which controls the left hand).

- Spell out the word 'case' with his right hand (RVF goes to left hemisphere which controls the right hand).

- Say 'case' if asked what word was displayed (RVF goes to left hemisphere which controls speech).

EXAM TIP

When you get into the exam, write down the following to help you remember:

RVF ⟶ LH ⟶ right hand
LVF ⟶ RH ⟶ left hand

Left eye		Right eye	
LVF	RVF	LVF	RVF
	LH		RH
Left hand		Right hand	

 Try the split-brain game: http://nobelprize.org/medicine/educational/split-brain/index.html.

4.6

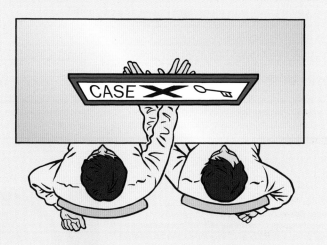

Role play

Two right-handed people should sit next to each other (on one chair if possible). They should be in front of a table with a screen on it, divided into left and right with an X in the middle. Person A (on the left) represents the left hemisphere and Person B (on the right) represents the right hemisphere.

The two volunteers should put their outer hands behind their backs. They should place their inner hands on the table and cross them over (ideally under the screen). The two hands represent the split-brain patient's left and right hands.

Members of the class should act as experimenters and conduct Sperry's mini-experiments on this spread. The volunteers should try to react as a split-brain patient.

(Adapted from http://www.rrcc-online.com/~psych/RLExpire.htm)

Using touch

What can you feel?

'This hand is numb.'

What can you feel?

'It's a hammer.'

Objects placed in the right hand (controlled by left hemisphere) can be named in speech and writing.

If an object is placed in the left hand participants can only make wild guesses and may seem unaware that they are holding anything.

However, if the same object is placed in a grab bag with other objects, the participant can find the original object with his left hand. They cannot retrieve the object with their right hand if it was first sensed with the left hand.

When asked to name objects held in their left hand participants frequently said something like 'This hand is numb' or 'I don't get messages from that hand'. If they successfully identified an object with their left hand they would comment 'Well, I was just guessing' or 'I must have done it unconsciously'. In other words, they had developed a way of explaining their rather strange behaviour to themselves.

Dual processing task

If two objects are placed simultaneously one in each hand and then hidden in a pile of objects, both hands can select their own object from the pile but will ignore the other hand's objects. Sperry said *'It is like two separate individuals working over a collection of test items with no cooperation between them'* (page 727).

Everyday effects

In everyday life split-brain patients don't usually notice that their mental functions are cut in half. They continue to watch TV and read books unaware of the separate visual input. This is because all the problems described in the study only arise when visual material is displayed very briefly. In everyday life deconnection can be overcome by moving the eyes or saying an answer out loud so information is shared between right and left hemisphere.

However, this doesn't mean split-brain patients are better off in their 'deconnected' state. It is true that their IQ scores and personality were little changed; however, in most complex activities people with cooperating hemispheres appear to do better, for example all the patients had some problems with short-term memory and had limited attention spans.

On the other hand, there are some tasks that are actually performed better by split-brain patients. They could carry out a double reaction-time task as fast as they could carry out a single task. In normal patients the introduction of a second task causes interference.

Qs 4.12

1. Describe the outcome of the mini-experiment using the $ and ? signs.
2. Explain why this occurs.
3. Describe the outcome of the mini-experiment using the composite words.
4. Explain why this occurs.
5. Describe the outcome of the mini-experiment using touch.
6. Explain why this occurs.
7. Describe the dual processing task.
8. What did the findings from the dual processing task demonstrate?
9. Explain in what way the two halves of the split-brain represent two minds.
10. Identify **three** things controlled by the left hemisphere.
11. Identify **three** things controlled by the right hemisphere.
12. The right hemisphere is sometimes referred to as the 'minor' hemisphere. Explain why.
13. What does 'functional lateralisation' mean?
14. Some patients had their surgery over four years ago whereas for others the surgery was very recent. What effect might this have on their performance?
15. Explain how the split-brain patients manage to watch the TV without noticing their abnormal visual input.
16. Describe what split-brain patients could do better than normal people?

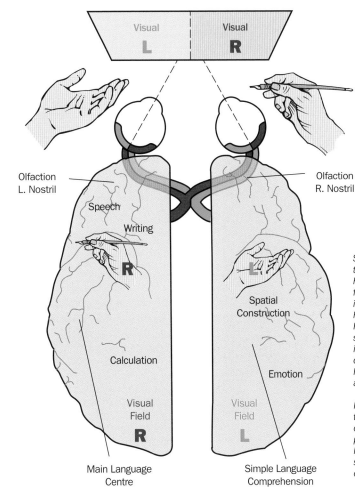

Sperry showed that the right and left hemispheres display functional lateralisation, in other words each side has different functions. For example, the left side (or hemisphere) is the main language centre and the right side has centres for spatial awareness and emotion.

In split-brain patients the signal from the LVF of the left eye will not pass through to the right hemisphere. And the same is true for the RVF of the right eye.

Sperry: the core study *continued*

Discussion

Abilities of the right hemisphere

Before Sperry conducted his split-brain research little was known about what the right, 'silent' **hemisphere** could do. Tests with the split-brain patients revealed a range of higher-order mental abilities, including some verbal comprehension. These capacities are described in the table on the right. In fact there are some abilities that are even dominant in the right hemisphere, such as spatial awareness and emotion.

Closing statements

Patients appear to have two independent streams of consciousness, each with its own separate memories, own perceptions, own impulses to act; in a sense two minds in one body.

Sperry ends the article by saying *'The more we see of these patients and the more of these patients we see, the more we become impressed by their individual differences'* (page 733).

Such differences might explain the contrasting results collected by different investigators. For example, some patients display some **ipsilateral** control (right hemisphere can communicate with right hand, i.e. same side of the body). Such patients would not display some of the behavioural effects described here.

This table shows some of the things the right (minor) hemisphere could do in the split-brain patients.

Human mental capacities	If a patient is holding an object in their left hand, they can then point to the name of the object displayed in their LVF. This demonstrates that the right brain has some distinctly human mental capacities since a monkey could not perform such tasks.
Understanding of general categories	Patients can select objects that are related to a pictured item presented to LVF, a task that requires mental processing. For example, if a picture of a wall clock was shown to the right hemisphere (LVF), the left hand will select a toy wrist watch. This shows that the right hemisphere has grasped the general category (timepiece) and is not just searching for a physical match.
Simple arithmetic problems	For example, if numbers are shown to the LVF, the left hand (held out of sight) can signal the correct answer. If two different pairs of numbers were shown to RVF and LVF separately, the right and left hands could signal two separate answers but the patient will only say the answer for the RVF.
Responding to spoken cues	If an object is named out loud, the left hand (right hemisphere) can locate the object because hearing is partially **bilateral** (about 10% goes to same side and 90% goes to opposite hemisphere).
Sorting	The left hand can sort objects into groups by touch on the basis of shape, size and texture.
Spatial awareness	On some tests the right hemisphere was found to be superior to the left (major) hemisphere – on tests that involve drawing spatial relationships and performing block design tests.
Emotion	If a pin-up picture is shown in a series of geometric figures to the LVF there is an emotional reaction (such as a giggle) but the patient usually says he saw nothing or just a flash of light. The patient who saw the picture with his LVF cannot explain why he giggled.
	Odours to right nostril (right hemisphere) can't be named but can be identified as pleasant or unpleasant – the patient might grunt or turn away. The patient can also identify the correct object with his left hand which shows that the right hemisphere can identify the smell-object.
	This emotional responsiveness is used to effect by some patients in ordinary testing – if the right hemisphere hears the left hemisphere stating an incorrect answer, the right hemisphere expresses annoyance.

Dr Strangelove's name was derived from the fact that he could not control his right hand, which had a mind of its own (strange glove).

There are real conditions that are similar – the 'alien hand syndrome' and 'anarchic hand'. Both are neurological disorders, i.e. caused by some malfunction of the brain. The conditions may also occur as a consequences of the split-brain operation.

Qs 4.13

1 Describe **one** function where the right hemisphere is dominant.
2 Describe **two** other functions of the right hemisphere.
3 Sperry pointed out the fact that there were important individual differences in the split-brain patients. What is the importance of this for interpreting the study's results?
4 State, in your own words, the overall conclusion you would draw from this study.

...Links to core studies...

The most striking connection is to the multiple personality study of **Thigpen and Cleckley**. Both studies look at split consciousness. In the case of Sperry, some of his patients appeared to have two consciousnesses that were not always aware of each other. In the case of Eve, there are more than two consciousnesses, but could this have a physiological cause like Sperry's patients? Both studies challenge us to consider what we understand about identity and personality.

Things you could do ...

Read the original article. See if you can find it online, or obtain a copy from your local library (they will order a photocopy if you provide the full reference).

Read:

One remarkable science fiction book that draws directly on the work of Roger Sperry is *A Scanner Darkly* by Philip K. Dick. The book and the subsequent film with Keanu Reaves explores the consequences of living with a split brain.

Watch YouTube videos of split-brain patients, e.g. http://www.youtube.com/watch?v=ZMLzP1VCANo

Evaluating the study by Sperry

The research method
This study can be described as a quasi-experiment because the independent variable (presence or absence of split-brain) varied naturally. The dependent variable is the participant's performance on a variety of tests.

However, as each of these people are described in detail it could also be argued that Sperry's work is a series of case studies.

What are the strengths and weaknesses of these research methods in the context of this study?

Research technique
Data was collected through self-report.

What are the strengths and weaknesses of this research technique in the context of this study?

The sample
We do not know to what extent the split-brain patients had brain damage caused by the severe epileptic fits (or the fits may have been caused by brain damage in the first place).

How does this affect the conclusions drawn from the study?

The sample contained patients who had recently had the operation.

To what extent might this affect the conclusions drawn?

Ethics
It is easy to be confused about ethical issues in this study – the split-brain procedure was not done for the purpose of the study and therefore is not an ethical issue. However, we might question the ethics of using patients for the purpose of scientific study and question their ability to give informed consent.

What ethical issues should have concerned the researchers in this study, and how might they have dealt with these issues?

Reliability
Reliability concerns measurement.

What aspects of human behaviour were measured in this study? How could the reliability of these measurements be assessed?

Ecological validity
To what extent can we generalise from this study to understanding the 'normal' brain?

Qualitative or quantitative?
What kind of data were collected in this study?

What are the strengths and weaknesses of producing this kind of data in the context of this study?

Applications/usefuless
How valuable was this study?

What next?
*Describe **one** change to this study, and say how you think this might affect the outcome.*

> *There are no simple answers.*
>
> *Evaluating a study requires you to think.*
>
> *We have provided some pointers here, linked to the **RESEARCH METHODS** and **KEY ISSUES** covered in Chapter 1 (Psychological investigations) and Chapter 7 (Key issues).*
>
> *You can read suggested answers on our website www.psypress.com/cw/banyard.*

Producing effective evaluation

When you produce your own answers to the issues on the left there are two things to ensure:

1 Contextualisation
2 Elaboration

The key to **CONTEXTUALISATION** is to ensure that your answer includes some information about this particular study. For example:

Question:
With reference to the study by Sperry, describe **one** strength of using self-report. **[2]**

Answer:
STATE: One strength of self-report is that people actually tell you what they are thinking or experiencing.

CONTEXT: In the case of Sperry's study it would have been much harder to discover the participants' experience of what they saw just by observing, for example, when they picked up the wrong object. It was easier to just ask them.

The key to **ELABORATION** is the three-point rule (see page xii), but sometimes it is a matter of providing two pieces of context to provide elaboration. For example:

Question:
With reference to the study by Sperry, describe **one** difference with any core studies that take the physiological approach. **[3]**

Answer:
STATE: One difference is the research methods used.

CONTEXT: In Sperry's study the capabilities of the participants was demonstrated by giving them certain tasks to do.

CONTEXT: In Maguire's study the participants' brains were simply measured for volume to see the effects of a naturally occurring independent variable. There was no need to test their capabilities.

The physiological approach

On pages 110–111 and 222–223 we have discussed the **physiological approach**.

The study by Sperry concerns the relationship between the brain and behaviour.

- In what way is this an example of the physiological approach?
- Discuss the strengths and weaknesses of the physiological approach using examples from the Sperry study.

Sperry: afters

More brains

The novel *A Scanner Darkly* by Philip K. Dick (and the film of the same name starring Keanu Reeves) turns around the idea of a split brain and actually quotes the work of Sperry as a central part of the plot. This film is described below along with some of the scientific legacy of Sperry's work.

Hemispherectomy

*Hemispherectomy involves the surgical removal or disconnection of one of the two halves of the brain. This **MRI** scan shows a brain after hemispherectomy. Most of the left hemisphere has been removed and the rest has been deconnected from the right hemisphere.*

If one part of the brain is damaged perhaps it would be best to remove it. One radical way to do this is the removal of one **hemisphere** of the brain (i.e. half the brain). Hemispherectomy was first attempted in 1928 by US neurosurgeon **Walter E. Dandy** as a treatment for brain cancer. In the 1950s the technique was first used for epilepsy and it continues to be used today.

It is most commonly used on children and only those with serious conditions that do not respond to other treatments. Sometimes the surgeons remove a large part of the hemisphere but more commonly they just disconnect the damaged part from the rest of the brain.

Children appear to have remarkable powers of recovery and hospital stays are commonly less than a week. The operation is very successful in that patients commonly stop having seizures yet are able to regain the ability to walk.

The modern use of the hemispherectomy was pioneered by **Benjamin Carson** who performed his first operation in 1985 in the USA. He specialises in child brain surgery. Talking about hemispherectomy he said: *'you can't get away with that in an adult, but a child has the ability to actually transfer functions to other parts of the brain. So you can take out half of the brain of a kid, and you'll see the kid walking around, you'll see him using the arm on the opposite side, and in many cases even engaging in sporting activities.*

The human brain is the thing that makes you who you are. I never get over my awe of the brain.' (Carson, 2002)

Hemispherectomy surgeon Benjamin Carson holding up a model of the skulls of conjoined twins.

More split brains

Split-brain research gave some major insights into how the functions of the brain are divided between the two hemispheres. It showed us, among other things, that people are capable of understanding language in the right hemisphere. **Michael Gazzaniga** worked with **Sperry** and is still working in the field today. An example of his work is a video shot in 1976 of a teenage boy being shown the word 'girlfriend' to his right hemisphere. The boy doesn't respond verbally and shrugs to indicate that he doesn't see any word. But then he giggles. This indicates a teenage embarrassment to the word 'girlfriend'. Then using his left hand the boy picks out three letters from an assortment in front of him and spells out L-I-Z. All this suggests he must have been able to understand it after all and so there must be some language ability in the right hemisphere.

Split-brain research is coming to an end now because the operations are carried out far less often due to advances in medical science. Also the original patients are getting quite old. The research focus is now on brain scans rather than the **cognitive** task given to patients with this extreme surgery. If you are interested in reading a bit more and seeing some videos of split-brain research just search online for 'split-brain studies'.

Right brain left brain

L R

Logic	Intuitive
Linear	Holistic
Symbolic	Concrete
Abstract	Analogic
Verbal	Non-verbal
Temporal	Non-temporal
Rational	Non-rational
Digital	Spatial
Analytic	Synthetic

One of the legacies of Sperry's research was to elevate the role of the right hemisphere from being the 'minor' hemisphere to one with special functions. This has led to the 'cult' of right versus left brained thinking. In 1972 Robert Ornstein suggested that society had placed too much emphasis on left-brained thinking and that we should liberate the creative powers of the right brain. Right-brain education programmes have been developed and tapes sold to develop 'whole-brain learning'. The right side was seen as the more intuitive, feminine side of human nature which was a feather in the cap of feminists. However, Corballis (1999) concludes that the differences between the hemispheres are minor and the right brain left brain movement should be regarded as little more than commercial exploitation.

Sperry at the movies

The novel A Scanner Darkly *by Philip K. Dick (released as a film in 2006) imagines a world where users of mind expanding drugs risk brain damage from taking large doses. The central character is a police agent whose own use of the drug severs the connection between the two hemispheres of his brain. The book quotes the work by Sperry and speculates on what happens when you have two disconnected brains in the same head. If one half of the brain doesn't know what the other is doing then maybe the police officer can become a secret agent without even knowing about it?*

Here's looking at you kid

'I used to think that the brain was the most interesting part of the body. Then I thought, "What part of my body is telling me that?"' (Emo Philips)

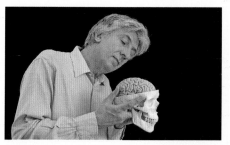

Think about this. When people carry out research into the brain what is doing the research? A brain looking at a brain?

SPERRY: AFTERS

Multiple choice questions

1 The split-brain operation was performed:
   a To conduct this experiment.
   b For patients with mild epilepsy.
   c For patients with severe epilepsy.
   d Both a and c.

2 Visual stimuli were flashed on the screen for:
   a 1 second.   b 0.1 seconds.
   c 0.01 seconds.   d 0.001 seconds.

3 The right hand and right nostril are connected to the:
   a Right hemisphere.
   b Left hemisphere.
   c Right and left hemisphere respectively.
   d Left and right hemisphere respectively.

4 When a $ sign was flashed to the left visual field, the patient could:
   a Draw the $ sign with his left hand.
   b Draw the $ sign with his right hand.
   c Tell you he saw a $ sign.
   d Both a and c.

5 When the word 'keycase' was flashed so that 'key' is presented in the LVF and 'case' in the RVF, the patient can:
   a Spell out the word 'case' with his right hand.
   b Spell out the word 'case' with his left hand.
   c Say the word 'key'.
   d None of the above.

6 When a patient held an object in their left hand, they could:
   a Say what it was.
   b Find a similar object with their right hand.
   c Find a similar object with their left hand.
   d Both a and b.

7 Split-brain patients had:
   a Personality changes.
   b Problems with short-term memory.
   c Short attention spans.
   d Both b and c.

8 The right hemisphere was found to be:
   a The main language centre.
   b Word blind.
   c Able to engage in some verbal functions.
   d Lower in IQ.

9 The patient gave an emotional response (a giggle) if a photograph of a pin-up was displayed to the:
   a Right visual field.
   b Left visual field.
   c Either field.
   d The patients never giggled.

10 Sperry ended his article by highlighting the fact that:
   a His patients were essentially abnormal.
   b The study was unethical.
   c There were important individual differences in what the split-brain patients could do.
   d All of the above.

Answers are on page 247.

Exam-style questions

> There are three kinds of question that can be asked about the Sperry study, as represented here by sections A, B and C.
> See page x for further notes on the exam paper and styles of question.

Section A questions

1 Sperry studied the abilities of split-brain patients.
   (a) Describe **one** difference between the ability of split-brain patients and 'normal' people to identify objects by touch alone. [2]
   (b) Give **one** explanation for this difference. [2]

2 (a) From the study by Sperry, explain why the split-brain operation was carried out on the patients in the study. [2]
   (b) Outline the major function of the corpus callosum. [2]

3 The results of Sperry's study of split-brain patients suggest that we effectively have two minds. Outline **two** pieces of evidence from the study that show this. [4]

4 (a) Describe the technique that Sperry used to present information to only one side of the brain? [2]
   (b) Explain why 'normal' people do not have any difficulty with the technique used to test the split-brain patients. [2]

5 From the paper by Sperry on split-brain patients, outline evidence which indicates that language is processed in the left hemisphere of the brain. [4]

6 (a) In Sperry's study, describe **one** problem with generalising from the sample. [2]
   (b) Explain what is meant by the term 'left visual field' as used in the paper by Sperry. [2]

7 In Sperry's study of split-brain patients,
   (a) Explain what is meant by 'hemispheric deconnection'. [2]
   (b) Outline **two** psychological effects of hemispheric deconnection. [2]

8 In Sperry's study, split-brain patients were found to have difficulties on some tasks.
   (a) Describe **one** conclusion that can be drawn from the observations of their behaviour. [2]
   (b) Explain why patients do not experience these difficulties in everyday life. [2]

9 With reference to Sperry's study, explain why split-brain patients:
   (a) Could not describe in speech material presented to their left visual field. [2]
   (b) Could describe an object that they held in their right hand. [2]

10 With reference to Sperry's study, outline tasks that are controlled by the right hemisphere. [4]

Section B questions

Answer the following questions with reference to the Sperry study:

(a) Briefly outline the previous research or event which was the stimulus for this study. [2]

(b) Describe the sample used in this study and suggest **one** strength of using this sample. [6]

(c) Give **two** strengths of the self-report method as used in this study. [6]

(d) Give **two** weaknesses of the self-report method as used in this study. [6]

(e) Outline the results of this study. [6]

(f) Describe and evaluate changes that could be made to the way this study was conducted. [10]

Section C questions

(a) Outline **one** assumption of the physiological approach. [2]

(b) Describe how the physiological approach could explain the way the brain controls behaviour. [4]

(c) Describe **one** similarity and **one** difference between the Sperry study and any core studies that take the physiological approach. [6]

(d) Discuss strengths and weaknesses of the physiological approach using examples from any core studies that take this approach. [12]

Exam-style questions

EXAM-STYLE QUESTIONS

Section A type questions

1 (a) Briefly describe the experimental group and the control group in the study on brain scanning by Maguire *et al*. [2]

   (b) Why do psychologists use control groups in experimental research? [2]

Stig's answer

(a) The experimental group was the taxi drivers. The control group was normal people.

(b) You have to use control groups to act as a comparison, to control for the results.

Chardonnay's answer

(a) The experimental group were 16 male taxi drivers who had a minimum of 1½ years experience. Their mean age was 44 (range 32–62). The control group were a group of normal adult males, age-matched with the taxi drivers.

(b) A control group means you have something to compare the experimental group to. If you found that one participant had a higher activity in the right hemisphere you don't know if this is abnormal or not unless you have something to compare this with.

Teacher's comments

Stig, your part (a) needs a bit more detail (look at Chardonnay's answer) to really show the examiner what you know. Part (b) is fine, but to ensure the full marks you need to communicate the idea of a control group acting as a benchmark or point of reference, i.e. 'comparing against the norm'.

Chardonnay, you are flaunting your knowledge in part (a) with bags of detail, more than sufficient for 2 marks.

Your part (b) communicates to the examiner a good understanding of the idea of the control group acting as a base line for comparing with normal brain activity.

Stig (1+1 out of 4 marks) Chardonnay (2+2 out of 4 marks)

2 (a) From the study by Maguire *et al*. outline **two** differences between the brain scans of the taxi drivers and the control group. [2]

   (b) Outline **one** conclusion that can be drawn from these differences. [2]

Stig's answer

(a) One difference is that the brains of the controls had a larger anterior hippocampus than in the brains of the taxi drivers whereas the posterior hippocampus was larger in the taxi drivers.

(b) These differences show that the brains of taxi drivers and normal people are different which must be due to the fact that taxi drivers use their spatial memory more than most people.

Chardonnay's answer

(a) In the taxi drivers there was a correlation between time spent driving taxis and the size of their hippocampus. There was a positive correlation for the posterior hippocampus and a negative correlation for the anterior hippocampus.

(b) We can conclude from this that the size of the hippocampus changes as a consequence of learning navigational skills, which suggests that the changes are not innate but due to experience.

Teacher's comments

Not the most elegant phrasing Stig but you have described the two key differences accurately. In part (b) you have failed to give a conclusion – you have just stated the finding (their brains are different) and then offered an explanation which is not the same as a conclusion. A conclusion is an interpretation of the results – what do they show us? It helps to start a conclusion with the phrase 'This suggests that …'.

Chardonnay has managed to provide a sound conclusion but her answer for part (a) falls short of the mark. In part (a) she has given a finding but not one which is a *difference* between the taxi drivers and controls. This means she fails to gain any marks for part (a) because it doesn't relate to differences, and therefore no marks for part (b).

Stig (2+0 out of 4 marks) Chardonnay (0+0 out of 4 marks)

3 Dement and Kleitman investigated the relationship between sleep and dreaming.

   (a) Outline **one** finding from this study about the relationship between sleep and dreaming. [2]

   (b) Give **one** reason why the conclusions of this study might not be valid. [2]

Stig's answer

(a) They found that dreaming occurred in one particular kind of sleep – REM sleep. Participants reported dreams almost every time they were woken from REM sleep but rarely at other times.

(b) One reason why this conclusion may not be valid is that the study only looked at adults and even then it was only a few adults so we can't be certain that this is representative.

Chardonnay's answer

(a) There was a correlation between the length of REM activity and the number of words a participant used to describe a dream.

(b) One problem with the study was that it lacked ecological validity.

Teacher's comments

Stig, a good answer and I am glad you conveyed the idea that whilst dreaming mostly occurred in REM sleep, it did also occur on a few occasions (11/160 wakings) in NREM.

In part (b) you give a thorough explanation of why the study might lack validity – because of certain unique characteristics of the sample but you have not linked this back to the study.

Chardonnay, spot on. You have reported a finding related to Dement and Kleitman's second hypothesis and this answers the question well.

Part (b) is too brief. Why is it lacking in ecological validity (it was conducted in a laboratory)? You also need to link to the study (mention a *sleep* laboratory for example).

Stig (2+1 out of 4 marks) Chardonnay (2+0 out of 4 marks)

4   Dement and Kleitman investigated the link between REM sleep and dreaming. Identify **four** characteristics of REM sleep. [4]

Stig's answer

They are rapid eye movements, faster brain activity, having dreams and can't remember another.

Chardonnay's answer

The four characteristics are that people have random eye movements. Fast EEG activity which shows that the brain is very active. The research by Dement and Kleitman showed that people very frequently have dreams in REM sleep and it is more likely to occur later in the night.

Teacher's comments

Tough question, but you've had a good stab at it Stig, identifying three characteristics.

Chardonnay, you are on sparkling form! You have correctly identified four characteristics of REM.

Stig (3 out of 4 marks) Chardonnay (4 out of 4 marks)

5   Sperry commented on his study of split-brain patients that: 'the second hemisphere does not know what the first hemisphere has been doing'.

  (a) Describe **one** piece of evidence from his study that supports this statement. [2]
  (b) Explain why split-brain patients do not experience problems as a result of this in their everyday lives. [2]

Stig's answer

(a) When Sperry showed a dollar sign to the right visual field and a question mark to the left visual field, the split-brain patient could recognise the dollar sign with his left hand but couldn't say what it was.

(b) In everyday life people don't see things for a split second so they have time for the thing to be seen by both hemispheres.

Chardonnay's answer

(a) Patients who were given two objects to hold in each hand then could recognise the objects but only using the hand that had originally held the object.

(b) This doesn't matter in everyday life because you usually can look at an object using both eyes rather than just touching it.

Teacher's comments

Stig, you have got a bit confused … easily done in this study. Remember, Left Visual Field is processed by the Right Hemisphere (no language) which, in turn, controls the left hand. It helps to find some way of remembering this, such as the diagram on page 136.

But Stig, you have got part (b) right …

… which is more than Chardonnay who has lost her fizz! Your part (a) is fine, but your part (b) is not clear. Be careful in this study not to confuse eyes with visual fields. They are not the same thing!

Stig (0+2 out of 4 marks) Chardonnay (2+0 out of 4 marks)

6   In Sperry's study of split-brain patients the capabilities of each brain hemisphere were studied.

  (a) Give **one** result from this study that demonstrates the language limitations of the right hemisphere of the brain. [2]
  (b) Give **one** result from this study that demonstrates that the right hemisphere is not completely unable to understand words. [2]

Stig's answer

(a) The right hemisphere doesn't have any language because if something is shown to the left visual field it can't be named.

(b) The right hemisphere is not totally word blind because, in some patients, they could identify an object with their left hand if the word was shown to their right hemisphere.

Chardonnay's answer

(a) In one of the studies that Sperry did, they showed the word 'keycase' to the patient. The patient only reported the word 'case' because this was in the right visual field (left hemisphere).

(b) The right hemisphere isn't completely word blind because it can sometimes respond to words.

Teacher's comments

Stig, you've got the visual field–hemisphere link right this time in part (a) and your part (b) is spot on too.

Chardonnay, your part (a) is on the right track, but really you should have explained why the patients could not report the word 'key', as this relates to the lack of language ability in the right hemisphere. This would have given your answer better focus. In part (b) you would get one mark for the word 'respond', but for the second mark you would need to say how, e.g. by pointing/picking up an object with the left hand.

Stig (2+2 out of 4 marks) Chardonnay (1+1 out of 4 marks)

Exam-style questions

Section C type questions

7   (a) Outline **one** assumption of the physiological approach in psychology. [2]
     (b) Describe how the physiological approach could explain navigation. [4]
     (c) Describe **one** similarity and **one** difference between core studies which take a physiological approach. [6]
     (d) Discuss strengths and limitations of the physiological approach, using examples from any core studies taking this approach. [12]

Total [24]

Chardonnay's answer

(a) One assumption of the physiological approach is that behaviour can be explained by biological or physiological occurrences or processes. Thus, genes, brain functioning, hormones are all very important for what we do and how we behave.

(b) The physiological approach could explain navigation in terms of a number of things. For example, as a species, we may all be somehow genetically predisposed to be able to find our way around and be able to find our way home as once upon a time our survival would have depended upon it. Also, the physiological approach would explain navigation in terms of which parts of the brain are specialised in storing mental maps. Maguire's study showed it is the hippocampus.

(c) Maguire is similar to Dement and Kleitman because they both are interested in the brain and use scanning technology. Maguire used MRI scanning and Dement and Kleitman used EEG.

Maguire is different from Dement and Kleitman because Maguire looks at a particular part of the brain – i.e. the hippocampus – and is interested in its size. Dement and Kleitman were not measuring any particular brain part, but overall brain activity as measured by the EEG. The EEG is used by attaching electrodes to the scalp and gives a live and continuous read out of changes in brain activity. MRI maps the structure of the brain tissue rather than activity. Also, it is a bit like a snapshot photo taken at one moment in time and does not show any changes as they are happening.

(d) One strength of the physiological approach is that it is very scientific. It uses scientific equipment and generally the experimental method. It always takes place in controlled conditions. Altogether this means that the results are usually valid and have high status. For example, in Maguire, they use some of the latest scanning technology and the study takes place in a laboratory. Using VBM and pixel counting to measure the volume of the hippocampus is very scientific. The downside to this is that this is quite a dehumanising way to study human beings – as if they were chemicals or lab rats.

Another strength of the physiological approach is that it can help develop treatments and therapies for certain illnesses or problems. For example, you can use drugs to treat insomnia or mental illnesses. In rarer cases, brain surgery may be a good treatment. However, all these treatments have side effects which are sometimes quite severe.

One weakness of the physiological approach is that it does not always show cause and effect. It might show that being a taxi driver is associated with a larger hippocampus (posterior region), but it doesn't show that this is *because* of being a taxi driver. It may be that the taxi drivers had this already and it helped them to pass The Test – i.e. that the larger hippocampus caused them to become taxi drivers. So, we do not always know the direction of cause and effect. However, Maguire might say that this is not true because she correlated the size of the hippocampus with number of years of taxi driving and found a positive correlation. This supports her idea that the brain has changed (morphed) because of the taxi driving.

Another weakness of the physiological approach is that it treats people like nothing more than complex machines or living organisms. This doesn't look at people as a whole. For example, the physiological approach ignores other important aspects of navigation such as the cognitive aspects.

Teacher's comments (see mark schemes on pages xii–xiii)

(a) Spot on Chardonnay – you have identified a range of physiological explanations for human behaviour. Full marks.

(b) This is excellent, Chardonnay. You show a good understanding of both the physiological approach as well as navigation. You use specialist terminology appropriately (genetically predisposed, hippocampus, mental maps, etc.) Full marks.

(c) You have provided one similarity and one difference, but these are not in equal depth. The similarity is a good valid point but you could have developed it a bit more.

The difference you identify is very good and shows a more than appropriate understanding in the differences between the two technologies and what they can measure in the brain. Therefore, 1+3 for a total of 4 marks for this question part.

(d) Some good material here, Chardonnay – your discussion of the scientific nature of the physiological approach is sufficiently detailed and well related to Maguire's study. You are able to pick out details of the procedure and make them relevant to your point. Your discussion of the issue of the *direction* of cause and effect is also presented in a well-balanced and even handed way, showing a good analysis of the results and alternative explanations.

However, there are also some little mistakes. One minor one is that the test taken by taxi drivers is called 'The Knowledge'. Perhaps more importantly is that, for your second strength (therapies), you did not manage to relate this to the study. Also, your second weakness could have done with further development – what do you mean by cognitive aspects (e.g. how we remember landmarks or find some road layouts more difficult to remember than others)? And could have done with some further discussion (are there any benefits to focusing upon a single feature such as the hippocampus for an experiment?).

All in all, your part (d) is still pretty good. There is a range of strengths and weaknesses, you have structured your answer coherently and you express yourself well. The quality of your evaluation is generally good. 9 out of 12 marks.

Chardonnay (2+4+4+9 marks = 19/24 marks)

CHAPTER 5

This chapter looks at three core studies in social psychology:

- Milgram's demonstration of obedience in situations requiring destructive behaviour.

- Reicher and Haslam's simulation of a prison environment to investigate the effects of group processes.

- Piliavin, Rodin and Piliavin's field experiment to study the factors that affect willingness to help in an emergency situation.

Social psychology

Introduction to social psychology   146

Core study 10
148 Milgram (obedience)
    148   Starters: do as you are told
    150   The study in a nutshell
    151   The study in detail
    155   Evaluation
    156   Afters: still following orders?
    157   Multiple choice questions
    157   Exam-style questions

Core study 11
158 Reicher and Haslam (BBC Prison study)
    158   Starters: tyranny and terror
    160   The study in a nutshell
    161   The study in detail
    165   Evaluation
    166   Afters: more tyranny
    167   Multiple choice questions
    167   Exam-style questions

Core study 12
168 Piliavin, Rodin and Piliavin (subway Samaritan)
    168   Starters: good, and not so good, Samaritans
    170   The study in a nutshell
    171   The study in detail
    175   Evaluation
    176   Afters: deciding to help
    177   Multiple choice questions
    177   Exam-style questions

178 Exam-style questions

Introduction

What is social psychology?

Social psychology is concerned with social interaction and the phenomena of social behaviour. It looks at the behaviour of the individual within a social context. One of the most influential US psychologists of the twentieth century was **Gordon W. Allport** who defined social psychology as:

'With few exceptions, social psychologists regard their discipline as an attempt to understand and explain how the thought, feeling and behaviour of individuals is influenced by the actual, imagined or implied presence of others. The term "implied presence" refers to the many activities the individual carries out because of his position (role) in a complex social structure and because of his membership in a cultural group' (1968, page 3).

This definition suggests that social psychology is mainly concerned with issues of social influence. Through the middle part of the twentieth century that was the case, but modern social psychology has wider interests.

Social psychology attracts a lot of attention because it is about the events and processes that make up our daily lives. It looks at our feelings, our thoughts and our behaviour, and tries to describe and explain aspects of the human condition such as love and hate, happiness and sadness, pride and prejudice, comedy and tragedy. It is the personal science and it is about me and you.

A big issue in social psychology that still has an impact today is the attempt to understand and reduce prejudice and discrimination. We look at that on the next page.

And what makes it even more compelling is that everyone is an amateur social psychologist and if we weren't we would not be able to function in everyday life. Just walking down the street I have to make judgements about other people. At the extreme end of the scale I might judge whether they are potentially dangerous and avoid them if I judge them to be a risk. If I couldn't judge when someone has finished talking I would always be interrupting them in conversation. I make judgements about whether people like me, or find me funny, and I also make judgements about whether someone needs some support or maybe whether they are telling lies. In daily life I am a relatively competent social psychologist. The task of academic social psychology is systematically to investigate these processes.

Investigating and making sense of our social behaviour is a complicated activity. If we try to carry out controlled studies then the situations we create are often very artificial and so we have to be very careful about the conclusions we draw. Concerns like this have led many social psychologists in the UK to use **qualitative approach** such as in-depth **interviews** or detailed analysis of text or images.

Key issues in social psychology

Early psychologists were most concerned with cognition and the measurement of personal characteristics. From the earliest days of psychology, however, there was also a lot of effort put into solving real life social problems in, for example, schools and business. Much of this work required the psychologists to come up with explanations of human behaviour and some suggestions of how to improve it – this was an early form of applied social psychology.

In your core studies you are focusing on three key issues, social influence, helping behaviour and resistance to **tyranny**.

Social influence
Social influence takes a lot of forms, such as the pressure from friends, the instructions from teachers and also the impact of role **models**. The London Olympics provided a new set of role models that will influence people to achieve even more in their lives. For example, Jonnie Peacock had his right leg amputated at age five after an illness. Now he is Paralympic champion at the 100-metre sprint.

Jonnie Peacock at London 2012

A Gamesmaker at London 2012.

Helping behaviour
Staying on the Olympics theme, one of the most spectacular features of London 2012 was the impact of the Gamesmakers. The 70,000 people who were selected from the quarter of a million applicants transformed London and impressed everyone who took part or spectated at the games. Their behaviour challenged our expectations about when and where people will help and what they expect in return.

Resistance to tyranny
Resistance comes in many forms and often involves joining with people, keeping your values and being prepared to accept some hardship for the things you believe in. Burmese politician Aung San Suu Kyi spent 15 years under house arrest because of her support for democracy. Although she was allowed to leave Burma she stayed in order to carry on with her campaign.

We often focus in psychology on the negative aspects of human behaviour but here we want to focus on the many positives illustrated by great role models, by the willingness to help others and by the courage to fight for what you believe in.

Burmese democracy campaigner Aung San Suu Kyi.

The social psychology of prejudice and discrimination

Psychology and prejudice

Psychology is the study of people carried out by people. Inevitably, the problems psychologists investigate also form part of their own experience. Psychologists study **prejudice** but they also have to struggle to deal with it. Early research in the first part of the twentieth century was based on US and European theories of racial superiority. As ever, the person who carries out the studies finds that the group they belong to is the best. For example, a review of 73 studies on race and intelligence in 1925 came to the conclusion that the *'studies taken all together seem to indicate the mental superiority of the white race'* (Garth, 1925, page 359). This work would not stand up to any scientific scrutiny today (or then to be fair) but it reflected the views of some psychologists at that time.

During the twentieth century psychology explored prejudice and if you are interested you can check out the famous work by **Richard LaPiere** (attitudes in hotels), by **Muzafer Sherif** (robbers cave) and **Henri Tajfel** (minimal group studies). At the same time as this work was gaining prominence black psychologists in the USA struggled to be recognised and accepted by their peers. For example, you could check out the excellent account of this by **Robert V. Guthrie** called *Even the Rat Was White*.

It is a struggle for every new generation to deal with issues of prejudice, to treat all people with respect and to read books rather than burn them. Psychologists are not immune to this struggle.

An American story

In the USA at the start of the twentieth century slavery was banned, but a new way to oppress people had been developed. Following a court ruling (referred to as Plessey vs. Ferguson, 1896) it became legal to create a segregated society under the principle of 'separate but equal'. Many states in the USA used this principle to have separate buses, drinking fountains and schools for white people and for black people.

The long legal battle against this law was led by the National Association for the Advancement of Coloured People (NAACP). One of the obvious challenges was that the principle of 'separate but equal' clearly did not apply because although black people had separate facilities they were clearly worse than those provided for white people. This was particularly true in basic schooling. In a number of test cases the lawyers used evidence from psychologists **Kenneth Clark** and **Mamie Phipps** on identity and **self-esteem** in black children. The Clarks devised the doll choice test and found that young black children in 1940's USA had a sense of racial inferiority. They repeated their tests in the states where the court cases were being brought. Clark and Clark were able to show scientifically something that is blindingly obvious today; that is, if you treat people like crap for long enough they end up feeling like crap.

The anti-segregation cases were eventually taken to the Supreme Court of the USA (the highest court in the country) and the Clarks prepared evidence on the effects of segregation. The Supreme Court acknowledged the work presented by Clark and Clark noting the following about the effects of segregation on black children:

'To separate them from others of similar age and qualifications solely because of their race generates a feeling of inferiority as to their status in the community that may affect their hearts and minds in a way unlikely ever to be undone ...' (Clark, 2001, page 271)

On 17 May 1954 (Brown vs Topeka Board of Education) the principle of 'separate but equal' was ruled illegal.

Mamie and Kenneth Clark

The pioneering work of Mamie and Kenneth Clark

Mamie Phipps (1917–1983) was born in Hot Springs, Arkansas, USA where, although she was from a middle-class family, she was not protected from the social policies of the time and attended a segregated school and used facilities that were reserved for 'Coloreds Only'. She began studying self-perception in black children as a graduate student at Howard University, where she met and married Kenneth Clark (1914–2005).

Between 1939 and 1940, the two published three major articles on this subject. Phipps Clark continued her work at Columbia University where, in 1943, she became the first African American woman and the second African American (after her husband) in the University's history to receive a psychology doctorate. Even after conducting, publishing and presenting significant research and earning her PhD, Mamie had difficulty finding work as a psychologist. She explained her frustration:

'Although my husband had earlier secured a teaching position at the City College of New York, following my graduation it soon became apparent to me that a black female with a PhD in psychology was an unwanted anomaly in New York City in the early 1940s' (Clark 2001, page 271).

Kenneth Clark (1914–2005) was the first African American to earn a doctorate in psychology at Columbia, to hold a permanent professorship at the City College of New York, to join the New York State Board of Regents and to serve as president of the American Psychological Association.

The work of the Clarks on black esteem and identity had a positive and enduring effect on their society. In fact it is difficult to think of any one piece of psychological research that has had such a major impact on the everyday life or millions of ordinary people.

...Connections...

If psychology is about human behaviour and experience then maybe all psychology is social psychology. Without other people we cannot survive our early years – it is very rare for an individual to survive and develop as an adult without social contact with other people. In this chapter we have included examples of research from mainstream social psychology, but elsewhere in the text there are many studies that have a social aspect to them. The cognitive study of **Loftus and Palmer** shows the influence of people on perceptual judgements, and the developmental studies of **Freud** and **Bandura et al.** are also about our social behaviour. In Chapter 6 on individual differences there are papers on identity (**Thigpen and Cleckley**) and our social judgements of abnormality (**Rosenhan**).

Do as you are told

The big moral question in the middle of the twentieth century was how the horrors of the Second World War (1939–45) could have happened and how they could be prevented in the future. During that war the Nazi government in Germany initiated a policy to exterminate 'worthless' ethnic groups. This led to the deaths of millions of people of Jewish descent, and the killing also extended to the mentally ill, homosexuals, gypsies and people of Slavic descent. It is not easy to kill this number of people and so death camps were set up to increase the killing efficiency. Auschwitz was the most efficient camp established by the Nazi regime, peaking at 12,000 deaths a day. Although the total number of Jewish dead in Auschwitz will never be known for certain, estimates vary between one and two-and-a-half million.

Who could do such a thing?

How could someone go to work each day to kill thousands of people and dispose of the bodies? The first response is to think of these people as monsters. They cannot be like us because we would not do these things. But can we be so sure of our humanity? Perhaps it was not monsters but ordinary people with ordinary lives who did these things. Social psychologists set out to investigate this and find out under what circumstances people will comply with authority.

Concentration camp victims

Milgram was of Jewish descent and the killings of the Second World War had an enduring effect on his life and his work.

'The impact of the Holocaust on my own psyche energised my interest in obedience and shaped the particular form in which it was examined.' *(Milgram, cited in Blass, 2004, page 62)*

Solomon Asch carried out some studies on conformity to group pressure (Asch, 1955). Subjects were recruited to take part in a test of perception. They were asked to say which line from a choice of three matched the target line. Unknown to one subject in each group the rest of the group members were **confederates** of the investigator and primed to give certain responses. For most of the trials they gave the obvious and correct answers, but on a few 'critical' trials they all gave the wrong answer. The subject was the last in the group to answer and had to listen to all the others giving their wrong answers. He then had to either give a different answer to the rest of the group or conform to the group pressure by giving a wrong answer. In around 40% of the trials, the subject conformed to the group.

Stanley Milgram worked with Asch while he was a postgraduate student and devised variations of Asch's study. In particular he carried out a cross-cultural version with data gathered in Norway, France and the USA (Milgram, 1960). He was interested in national character and devised an elaborate hoax to investigate it. As in the Asch study, subjects had to make a judgement in a group, but in this case they made the judgement in a single cubicle where they could not see the other subjects but only hear them. In fact there were no other group members and the subject just heard recorded voices. When he returned to the USA he devised plans for a new study. He wanted to make the Asch study more relevant to everyday behaviour. His moment of inspiration came when he stopped thinking about how to change the level of conformity and asked just how far a person would go under the investigator's orders. At that moment the obedience study was born.

Vietnamese civilians murdered by US troops during the My Lai massacre.

Atrocities

Atrocities happen in each generation. We commonly like to talk about them as being carried out by other people; people not like us and not part of our society but the truth is very different. In the history of Western Europe there are many atrocities big and small. One of the biggest was the slave trade that transported millions of Africans around the world with a callous disregard for life or welfare. There was also the incident, in 1937, when the Spanish dictator Franco invited the German airforce to bomb the market town of Gernika in the Basque region of Spain killing and injuring many people. The list is endless.

The Milgram study is commonly related to the Second World War but even as he conducted his studies a new horror was unravelling in South East Asia where the USA had started a major conflict with the people of Vietnam. It is often referred to as the Vietnam War, though not if you are Vietnamese. The USA was finally defeated by the peasant army of the Vietnamese in 1973 with a loss of 55,000 American lives. Less commonly reported are the 1.5 million Vietnamese lives lost, many of whom were civilian peasants.

My Lai

Milgram commented on one particular act of savagery by the US Army. On the morning of March 16, 1968 a company of soldiers moved into the peasant village of My Lai looking for armed fighters. They found only women, children and the elderly, but they treated them as insurgents and tortured, raped and finally murdered them. Somewhere between 350 and 500 villagers were slaughtered before the killing frenzy was stopped when a US Army helicopter crew famously landed between the American troops and the remaining Vietnamese hiding in a bunker. The 24-year-old pilot, Warrant Officer Hugh Thompson, Jr., confronted the leaders of the troops and told them he would open fire on them if they continued their attack on civilians. This helicopter crew are still hailed as heroes today in Vietnam (see www.cnn.com/WORLD/9803/16/my.lai) but were treated by many as traitors in the USA.

The massacre was covered up and denied for a year but eventually the information became public knowledge. Just one man (William Calley) was charged and eventually served three years under house arrest before being pardoned by President Nixon.

Milgram wanted to know how this event could happen. And there are many other issues to consider, for example:

- Some of the 120 soldiers on that patrol opted out of the killing. How did they manage to do that while the others felt they had to obey orders?
- What factors led the helicopter crew to decide to intervene against their own colleagues?

The remarkable work of Stanley Milgram

Milgram's obedience study had such an impact that the variety and originality of his other work is often missed. He was one of the most innovative psychologists of the last century. The items on this page are just a selection of his work. If you want to know more then try his book *The Individual in the Social World* (1992).

Six degrees of separation

'It's a small world, isn't it?' we say to each other when we discover a personal connection with someone who lives miles away from us. In one of his many innovative studies, Milgram set out to test this idea in 1967. He asked some people from Kansas (in the Midwest of the USA) to send packages to a stranger in Massachusetts, on the East Coast several thousand miles away. The senders were told the stranger's name, occupation, and roughly where they lived. They were told to send the package to someone they knew on a first-name basis who they thought was most likely, out of all their friends, to know the target personally. That person would do the same, and so on, until the package was personally delivered to its target.

Milgram reported the results enthusiastically but also selectively. One of the packages got through in four days but it was one of the few that did. Most didn't make it but the ones that did were able to get there in about six hops. This led to the famous phrase 'six degrees of separation' which commonly appears in writings on the experience of urban life. It suggests that any two people in the world can be connected by an average of six acquaintances. It is a delightful idea and may well be right but Milgram did not find the clear evidence to support this.

Modern communications allowed researchers to look at the small-world **hypothesis** again. A recent study of over 60,000 email users (Dodds *et al.*, 2003) attempted to reach one of 18 target people in 13 countries (including Estonia, India and Norway) by forwarding email messages to acquaintances. Most of the chain messages were not completed but there are many reasons for this, including apathy on the part of the people who were contacted and also email overload which is a new stress issue for many workers in the West. Using the chains that did reach their destinations the researchers calculated that social searches can reach their target in five to seven steps. So maybe Milgram was right after all.

Familiar strangers

Milgram noticed a strange phenomenon of city life: we regularly see people we recognise but never talk to or interact with. He called these people 'familiar strangers'. They might be the person who always gets on the same bus as you, or you see in the corner shop. Milgram got his students to carry out a novel study on these familiar strangers (Milgram, 1977). They chose a suburban railway platform and one morning photographed the commuters waiting for a train. The students numbered the people on the photograph and then a few weeks later gave out the pictures and a **questionnaire**. The students got on the train and by the time the train arrived in New York City 119 out of the 139 passengers had completed the survey.

On average the commuters reported seeing four familiar strangers in the picture but only having spoken to an average of 1.5. Other questions revealed that although 47% of the passengers had wondered about the familiar strangers, whereas less than one-third reported feeling even a slight inclination to start a conversation.

Other techniques

Milgram devised too many research techniques to even mention here. We have given two examples but there was also the *dropped letter technique* to measure prejudice and helping behaviour, where he would leave un-posted letters addressed to organisations lying around in public places to see which organisation would attract the most support and get their letter posted.

He also developed techniques to investigate *obedience requests* on the subway trains, the *cyranos* (people saying the words written by someone else) and the *mental maps* of cities (the mental images that people have of the streets in their town). Psychologists can usually retire if they develop one new method; Milgram developed many.

Biographical notes on Stanley Milgram

Stanley Milgram was born in New York City in 1933 to working class Jewish parents who had immigrated to the USA from Europe. Milgram excelled in all subjects at school where his classmate was Philip Zimbardo. His first degree was in political science but after a crash course in psychology he started a doctorate in psychology at Harvard University in 1954.

In 1960 he moved to Yale University and carried out the obedience studies for which he is most famous. The work was acknowledged by psychologists and the public but the controversy it caused affected his career. In 1967 he returned to New York to work at the City University where he stayed for the rest of his life. Milgram preferred to investigate topics that affected ordinary people in their everyday lives. For example, his mother-in-law is reported to have asked why people no longer give up their seats on subway trains so Milgram sent out teams of students to investigate this.

The Milgram family had a history of heart disease and Stanley survived four heart attacks before succumbing to the fifth in 1984. His work stills jumps off the pages of psychology books and magazine articles (see the excellent biography by Blass, 2004).

Stanley Milgram (1933–1984)

'The soldier does not wish to appear a coward, disloyal, or un-American. The situation has been so defined that he can see himself as patriotic, courageous, and manly only through compliance.' Stanley Milgram (www.stanleymilgram.com)

...Link to the core study...

Milgram's background as a political scientist and his concern to explain the Holocaust meant that he was drawn to the social psychology of conformity. His initial work looked at national differences in conformity to see whether it was the structure of a society that led people to carry out atrocities. He found that rates in different societies were fairly similar so Milgram came up with another approach. How far would you go in obeying unjust authority? Now read on.

Milgram: the core study

Stanley Milgram (1963) Behavioural study of obedience. *Journal of Abnormal and Social Psychology*, 67, 371–378.

See the
CORE STUDY CHECKLIST
on page xv for details of what you need to know for the exam.

MILGRAM: THE CORE STUDY

In a nutshell

Context

Obedience is important for social life but can be destructive, as was the case during the Second World War when German officers obeyed orders to kill innocent people.

Aim

The aim of this study was to demonstrate the power of a legitimate authority even when a command requires destructive behaviour.

Participants

The **sample** consisted of 40 male volunteers from various occupational backgrounds aged between 20 and 50 years.

There were two other participants: the experimenter (a part not played by Milgram) and the 'learner'.

Procedure

The study took place in a **laboratory** at Yale University. The true participant was always given the role of 'teacher'. He believed that both he and the 'learner' were **randomly allocated** to their roles and also believed the study was about learning (i.e. the true aim of the study was withheld).

Obedience to legitimate authority was tested by asking the 'teacher' to administer increasingly strong electric shocks to the 'learner' every time the learner made a mistake on a learning task.

The teacher (T) read questions out to the learner (L) who sat in a separate room in front of a four-way panel to select answers (see diagram on right). The learner was strapped into his chair and an electrode placed on his wrist. This was connected to the electric shock generator controlled by the teacher.

If the teacher expressed a desire to stop delivering shocks then the experimenter (E) had a set of statements ('prods') to deliver such as '*The experiment requires that you continue*'.

When the shock level reached 300 volts the learner had been instructed to bang on the wall. After that he stopped responding.

Participants were **debriefed** after the study.

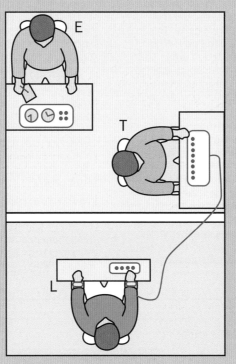

Try this   5.1

Before conducting this study, Milgram asked various people (psychiatrists, undergraduates and some ordinary people) to predict how the participants would behave in this study.

Try conducting a survey yourself – briefly outline the research procedure and ask people to predict how 100 hypothetical participants would behave.

Results

Prior to the study Milgram conducted a survey. Respondents predicted that less than 3% of participants would go to the maximum shock level.

In fact 65% of the participants continued to the maximum voltage.

Only five participants (12.5%) stopped at 300 volts.

Qualitative data was also collected in this study. For example **observations** of the participants showed that they experienced extreme anxiety.

Discussion

The extent of destructive obedience and the tension shown were unexpected.

Possible explanations for the high levels of obedience include:

- The prestige of the institution which made participants reluctant to disobey.
- The sense of obligation to continue with the study.
- The participants' lack of opportunity to think about or discuss what they were doing.

Qs 5.1

1 What did the participant believe was the aim of the study?

2 Outline the true aim of the study.

3 The sample was a volunteer sample. Give **one** weakness of this sample in this study.

4 Identify **three** other features of the sample used in this study.

5 Describe the other people involved in the study.

6 Why do people often think that Milgram was the 'experimenter'.

7 What was the role of the 'experimenter' in this study?

8 Explain why you think this study was conducted in a laboratory.

9 Participants were debriefed after this study. Why was that necessary?

10 What was the main finding from this study?

11 Both quantitative and qualitative data were collected in this study. Give **one** example of each kind of data from this study.

12 Explain why participants might have experienced extreme anxiety during the study.

13 Milgram provided a number of explanations for the high levels of obedience shown. Select **one** and explain this fully.

The detailed version

Context and aim

Obedience is an indispensable part of social life. In order to live in communities some system of authority is required. The issue of obedience was particularly relevant in the 1960s, when explanations were sought for the inhumane obedience of Germans who systematically slaughtered millions of innocent people during the Second World War.

Obedience may be deeply ingrained in the human character and may be thought to be destructive, but we should also remember that it serves productive functions as well, such as acts of charity and kindness.

Aim

The aim of this study was to investigate the process of obedience, to demonstrate the power of a legitimate authority even when the command requires destructive behaviour. The test has to involve destructive behaviour because, if participants were asked to obey a neutral or constructive order, then there would be little reason *not* to obey.

Specifically Milgram aimed to investigate whether participants would show obedience to an authority figure who told them to administer electric shocks to another person.

Method

Participants

Milgram worked in the psychology department at Yale University, which is in New Haven, Connecticut, USA. In order to recruit participants he placed an advertisement (see right) in a local paper and also sent out a mailshot in the post. As you can see in the advertisement he informed prospective participants that the scientific study was to be related to memory and that they would be paid $4.00 plus 50 cents car fare for an hour of their time (remember that $4.50 was a reasonable sum of money in those days).

Participants were to be American men between the ages of 20 and 50 and not high school or college students.

A final group of participants were selected from all those who volunteered, consisting of 40 men from various occupational and educational backgrounds (skilled and unskilled workers, salesmen and professionals). Participants were told that the money was theirs no matter what happened after they arrived.

The part of the experimenter was played by a biology teacher, dressed in a technician's coat. The learner (or victim) was played by a 47-year-old accountant, trained for the role. Both of these men were accomplices of Milgram (i.e. they were **confederates**).

The aim of Milgram's research

*The aim of this study is often described as the 'Germans are different hypothesis'. Milgram describes this in a film he made but this aim is not stated in the actual article published in 1963. He believed that the inhumane obedience of Nazi Germans could be explained by the fact that Germans are by disposition much more obedient than people from other cultures/ countries; it is in their national character. Milgram intended to conduct this study with Germans but first wanted to run a **pilot study**, to see if his procedure worked. He did not expect high levels of obedience from Americans. As you will see, in reading this article, he actually found that Americans were highly obedient, evidence that obedience is due to situational rather than dispositional (personality) factors.*

Note – you can obtain the film where Milgram describes his aims from Uniview, see http://www.uniview.co.uk/acatalog/psychology-resources.html.

Public Announcement

WE WILL PAY YOU $4.00 FOR ONE HOUR OF YOUR TIME

Persons Needed for a Study of Memory

*We will pay five hundred New Haven men to help us complete a scientific study of memory and learning. The study is being done at Yale University.

*Each person who participates will be paid $4.00 (plus 50c carfare) for approximately 1 hour's time. We need you for only one hour: there are no further obligations. You may choose the time you would like to come (evenings, weekdays, or weekends).

*No special training, education, or experience is needed. We want:

Factory workers	Businessmen	Construction workers
City employees	Clerks	Salespeople
Laborers	Professional people	White-collar workers
Barbers	Telephone workers	Others

All persons must be between the age of 20 and 50. High school and college students cannot be used.

*If you meet these qualifications, fill out the coupon below and mail it now to Professor Stanley Milgram, Department of Psychology, Yale University, New Haven. You will be notified later of the specific time and place of the study. We reserve the right to decline any application.

*You will be paid $4.00 (plus 50c carfare) as soon as you arrive at the laboratory.

TO:
PROF. STANLEY MILGRAM, DEPARTMENT OF PSYCHOLOGY, YALE UNIVERSITY, NEW HAVEN, CONN. I want to take part in this study of memory and learning. I am between the ages of 20 and 50. I will be paid $4.00 (plus 50c carfare) if I participate.

NAME (Please Print) ....
ADDRESS ....
TELEPHONE NO .... Best time to call you ....
AGE .... OCCUPATION .... SEX.....................
CAN YOU COME:
WEEKDAYS.......................................EVENINGS.............................WEEKENDS.............................

---

1 Milgram says that obedience is 'an indispensable feature of social life'. Do you agree? Why or why not?

2 How was obedience linked to the behaviour of Germans in the Second World War?

3 What is meant by 'destructive obedience'? Give an example.

4 Why were participants told that the study was about memory when the real aim was to study obedience?

5 Why do you think that Milgram did not want any students as participants?

6 Outline **one** strength of the sample used in this study.

7 Explain what the term 'confederate' means, using examples from this study.

8 Why was it necessary for the role of the learner to always be played by the same person?

The photograph shows the experimenter on the right in a lab coat. The learner is being strapped into an 'electric chair apparatus' and an electrode attached to his wrist so he can receive shocks if he makes a mistake on the learning task.

The generator (in photograph above) *had labels for every group of four switches, as shown below:*

Slight shock	15	30	45	60
Moderate shock	75	90	105	120
Strong shock	135	150	165	180
Very strong shock	195	210	225	240
Intense shock	255	270	285	300
Extreme intensity shock	315	330	345	360
Danger: Severe shock	375	390	405	420
XXX	435	450		

Standard prods were used by the 'experimenter' if the 'teacher' wished to stop.

Prod 1	*'Please continue, or 'Please go on'*
Prod 2	*'The experiment requires that you continue.'*
Prod 3	*'It is absolutely essential that you continue.'*
Prod 4	*'You have no other choice, you must go on.'*
Special prods	If the teacher asked whether the learner might suffer permanent physical injury, the experimenter said: *'Although the shocks may be painful, there is no permanent tissue damage, so please go on.'*
	If the teacher said that the learner clearly wanted to stop, the experimenter said: *'Whether the learner likes it or not, you must go on until he has learned all the word pairs correctly. So please go on'.*

Qs 5.3

1 Why was it necessary to conduct a 'preliminary run' for the teacher and learner?

2 Identify **five** aspects of the procedure that were designed to increase the concern felt by the participant.

3 Why do you think it was important to have a standardised set of responses for the experimenter?

4 Why do you think that it was important for the participants to be debriefed (dehoaxed) at the end of the study?

5 Informed consent is considered to be an issue in this study. What did the participants consent to?

6 Participants were told they would be paid just for turning up, i.e. they could leave any time they wished. Do you think this meant they understood that they had the right to withdraw? Explain your answer.

Method continued

Procedure
Each participant was told that the study aimed to see how punishment affected learning. The naïve volunteer participant was introduced to the other 'participant' (the accountant) and then lots were drawn for the parts of teacher and learner. The naïve 'true' participant always got the part of teacher.

Learner and teacher were taken to the **laboratory** where the learner was strapped into an 'electric chair apparatus' in order to prevent excessive movement when the electric shocks were delivered (see photograph on previous page). An electrode was attached to the learner's wrist and also attached to a shock generator in the next room. The experimenter advised them that, *'Although the shocks can be extremely painful, they cause no permanent tissue damage'* (page 373).

Learning task
The teacher was asked to read a series of word pairs to the learner, and then read the first word of the pair along with four terms. The learner had to indicate which of the four terms was originally paired with the first word.

Shock generator
This machine had 30 switches each labelled with a number of volts from 15 to 450, in increments of 15 (see left). There were also labels to describe the voltage intensity, for example 'strong shock'.

In order to convince the naïve participant that the shocks were genuine, they were given a sample shock of 45 volts, on their wrist.

The teacher was told to give a shock for a wrong response and, each time, to move one level higher on the shock generator. The teacher also had to announce the voltage each time, thus reminding him of the increasing intensity.

Preliminary and regular run
A **pilot study** showed that it takes some time before participants can get the procedure right so each participant was given 10 words to read to the learner. The teacher made seven errors on this practice run and so received seven shocks, reaching the moderate level of 105 volts.

Feedback from the victim
The learner had a predetermined set of responses, giving approximately three wrong answers to every correct answer. The learner made no sign of protest or any other comment until a shock level of 300 volts was reached. At this point he pounded on the wall but thereafter ceased to provide any further response to questions; the participant usually turned to the experimenter for advice and was told to wait 5–10 seconds before treating the lack of response as a wrong answer. He was to continue increasing the shock levels with each wrong answer. After the 315 volt shock the learner pounded on the wall again but after that there was no further response from the learner.

Experimenter feedback
If the participant turned to the experimenter for advice about whether to continue giving shocks, the experimenter was trained to give a series of standard 'prods' (see left) which were always made in sequence, i.e. prod 2 was only used if prod 1 was unsuccessful. If the participant refused to obey prod 4 then the study was terminated. The sequence was begun anew on each hesitation.

Further records
Most sessions were tape-recorded and some photographs taken through **one-way mirrors**. Notes were kept on any unusual behaviour and observers wrote descriptions of participants' behaviour.

Interview and dehoax
All participants were interviewed (**debriefed**) after the study and were asked various **open questions**. They were also given some **psychological tests**. After this, procedures were undertaken to ensure that the participant would leave the laboratory in a state of well-being. A friendly reconciliation with the learner was arranged.

Results

Preliminary predictions

Milgram described the research situation to 14 psychology undergraduates and asked them to predict how 100 hypothetical participants would behave. Their answers were in close agreement, expecting that no more than 3% of participants would continue to 450 volts.

Research results

Participants accept situation

With few exceptions the participants were convinced of the reality of the research situation. In the debriefing they were asked to indicate how painful the shocks had been. The **modal** response was 'extremely painful'.

Distribution of scores

The two key findings were:

- Five participants (12.5%) stopped at 300 volts, labelled as 'intense shock'. This was just after the participant had made his first pounding on the wall.
- Over half of the participants (26/40 or 65%) went all the way with the electric shocks, delivering the full 450 volts. This of course means that 35% were not fully obedient. At some point after 300 volts they had refused to continue.

The graph below shows the breakoff points – when participants refused to go further. Five stopped at 300 volts, eight stopped in the group labelled 'extreme intensity shock' (315–360 volts), one quit at 375 volts – 'danger severe shock', the rest continued to the end.

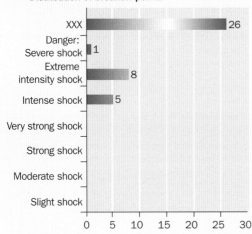

Distribution of breakoff points

Number of participants who stopped at this point

Experiment or investigation?

*There is some debate about whether or not this study is an **experiment**. We can be certain that it was conducted in a laboratory (a place specially designed for conducting research, a controlled environment). This leads many people to assume it was an experiment. However, in order for a study to be classed as an experiment there must be an **independent** and **dependent variable** (IV and DV).*

It could be argued that the shock levels were the IV and the DV was willingness to obey. Milgram himself described it as an experiment.

*However, others argue that the shock levels were just a means of assessing how obedient a person was. The shock levels did not cause obedience, which is what an IV does. An IV causes a behaviour and the DV measures its effect. In this case the study is simply an investigation or perhaps a **controlled observation**.*

Qualitative data

Signs of extreme tension

Many participants showed nervousness and a large number showed extreme tension, participants *'were observed to sweat, tremble, stutter, bite their lips, groan and dig their finger-nails into their flesh'.*

Fourteen displayed nervous laughter which seemed bizarre, and three had *'full-blown uncontrollable seizures'.*

Comments from participants

Milgram recorded two of the participants' comments:

'I think he's trying to communicate, he's knocking ... Well it's not fair to shock the guy ... these are terrific volts. I don't think this is very humane ... Oh, I can't go on with this.' (pages 375–376)

'He's banging in there. I'm gonna chicken out. I'd like to continue, but I can't do that to a man ... I'm sorry I can't do that to a man. I'll hurt his heart. You take your [money].' (page 376)

Some participants simply got up and left, without saying anything.

Those who continued to the end often heaved a sigh of relief and mopped their brows. Some shook their heads apparently in regret, some remained calm throughout.

Try this   5.2

It's a good idea to **role play** this study to get a clear idea of what happens between the teacher, learner and experimenter.

Qs 5.4

1. Give **one** example of some quantitative data collected in this study and **one** example of qualitative data collected in this study.
2. Why might the findings have surprised Milgram?
3. What conclusions can you draw from the graph?
4. Five participants stopped at 300 volts and a further four stopped at 315 volts. Why was this the critical breakoff point?
5. Milgram included comments from two of the participants (see above). What do these comments tell us?
6. Identify at least **three** features of this study that made it more likely that participants would behave more obediently than they would normally? (Note: in a sense these features are demand characteristics.)
7. Orne and Holland (1968) argued that the participants didn't really believe the shocks were real because such things don't happen in a psychology study. What evidence is there that the participants did believe the shocks were real?
8. Explain why the main part of the study might be considered to be a controlled observation.
9. Some of the data were collected using interviews and also using observation. Identify the data that was collected using these techniques.

Milgram: the core study *continued*

Discussion

Milgram suggests that two findings emerged which were surprising:

Finding 1
The sheer strength of the obedient tendencies that were displayed, despite the fact that:

- People are taught from childhood that it is wrong to hurt another person.
- The experimenter had no special powers to enforce his commands.
- Disobedience would bring no material loss to the participant.

This behaviour was not expected by the students in the pre-research survey, nor by the persons who observed the study through **one-way mirrors** who expressed complete disbelief at the participants' behaviour.

Finding 2
The extraordinary tension generated by the procedures. One observed related:

'I observed a mature and initially poised businessman enter the laboratory smiling and confident. Within 20 minutes he was reduced to a twitching, stuttering wreck, who was rapidly approaching a point of nervous collapse. He constantly pulled on his earlobe, and twisted his hands. At one point he pushed his fist into his forehead and muttered "Oh God, let's stop it." And yet he continued to respond to every word of the experimenter, and obeyed to the end.' (page 377)

Why did they obey?
Milgram put forward the following reasons to explain the high levels of obedience in this study:

1 The location of the study at a prestigious university provided authority.
2 Participants assume that the experimenter knows what he is doing and has a worthy purpose, so should be followed.
3 Participants assume that the learner has voluntarily consented to take part.
4 The participant doesn't wish to disrupt the experiment because he feels under obligation to the experimenter due to his voluntary consent to take part.
5 This sense of obligation is reinforced because the participant has been paid (although he was told he could leave).
6 Participants believe that the role of learner was determined by chance; therefore the learner can't really complain.
7 It is a novel situation for the participant who therefore doesn't know how to behave. If it was possible to discuss the situation with others the participant might have behaved differently.
8 The participant assumes that the discomfort caused is minimal and temporary, and that the scientific gains are important.
9 Since the learner has 'played the game' up to shock level 20 (300 volts) the participant assumes the learner is willing to continue with the experiment.
10 The participant is torn between meeting the demands of the victim and those of the experimenter.
11 The two demands are not equally pressing and legitimate.
12 The participant has very little time to resolve this conflict and he doesn't know that the victim will remain silent for the rest of the experiment.
13 The conflict is between two deeply ingrained tendencies: not to harm someone and to obey those whom we perceive to be legitimate authorities.

Qs 5.5

1 Milgram listed 13 explanations for the high levels of obedience that he observed. Select **three** of these explanations – the ones you feel are the 'best'.

2 There have been many ethical criticisms of this study. On balance do you think that Milgram was justified in conducting this study?

Further details of the study were provided by Milgram in his book Obedience to Authority *(1974). These may be useful when considering your evaluations.*

- *The participants were sent a follow-up **questionnaire**, which showed that 84% felt glad to have participated, and 74% felt they had learned something of personal importance.*
- *Milgram did think about abandoning the study when it became clear that some participants were quite stressed. However, he decided that 'momentary excitement is not the same as harm' (1974, page 212).*
- *Milgram questioned whether the reason so many people were shocked by the study might be more to do with the unanticipated findings rather than the methods used.*

Things you could do ...

Read the original article by Milgram. See if you can find it online, or obtain a copy from your local library (they will order a photocopy if you provide the full reference).

Read other accounts of the research:

Milgram's book *Obedience to Authority,* which includes interviews with participants and details of further studies.

Research by Milgram is discussed in a chapter of *Skinner's Box* by Lauren Slater, which also includes an interview with a participant.

Watch a video, there are many on YouTube, for example:

Derren Brown's fascinating recreation of the Milgram experiment ('The Heist').

The BBC's replication of the Milgram experiment in 2009.

The French TV show 'Game of Death', a replication of Milgram's study.

...Links to core studies...

Milgram's conclusion is that we are made by the situations we are in. The issue of situations and opportunity is also dealt with in the studies by **Griffiths** and also **Piliavin *et al.*** Both these studies share another characteristic with Milgram in that they attempted to explore human behaviour in real-life settings.

MIGRAM: THE CORE STUDY

Evaluating the study by Milgram

The research method

This study was conducted in a controlled laboratory environment.

What are the strengths and weaknesses of using a controlled environment in the context of this study?

Both observation and self-report were also used in this study.

What are the strengths and weaknesses of using these research methods in the context of this study?

The sample

The participants were US males and volunteers. *In what way are the participants in this sample unique?*

How might this affect the conclusions drawn from the study?

Ethics

What ethical issues should have concerned Milgram in this study?

To what extent do you think he dealt with these ethical issues successfully? What else might he have done?

Reliability

Reliability concerns measurement.

What aspects of human behaviour were measured in this study? How could the reliability of these measurements be assessed?

Ecological validity

Psychological research aims to find out about how real people behave in the real world.

To what extent do you think the participants in this study behaved as they would have done in everyday life when faced with a command from an authority figure?

Snapshot or longitudinal?

This is a snapshot study.

How could this study be conducted as a longitudinal study?

Consider the strengths and weaknesses of each design in the context of this study.

Quantitative and qualitative data

Some of the results can be described as quantitative data and other findings are qualitative. Give examples of both kinds of data in this study.

What are the strengths of quantitative data in the context of this study? What are the weaknesses?

What are the strengths of qualitative data in the context of this study? What are the weaknesses?

Applications/usefulness

Psychologists aim to conduct research that will help make people's lives better.

From your point of view, how valuable was this study?

What next?

*Describe **one** change to this study, and say how you think this might affect the outcome.*

> *There are no simple answers.*
>
> *Evaluating a study requires you to think.*
>
> *We have provided some pointers here, linked to the **RESEARCH METHODS** and **KEY ISSUES** covered in Chapter 1 (Psychological investigations) and Chapter 7 (Key issues).*
>
> *You can read suggested answers on our website www.psypress.com/cw/ banyard.*

Producing effective evaluation

When you produce your own answers to the issues on the left there are two things to ensure:

1. Contextualisation
2. Elaboration

The key to **CONTEXTUALISATION** is to ensure that your answer includes some information about this particular study. For example:

Question:
Describe **one** ethical issue raised in Milgram's study. **[2]**

Answer:
STATE: One ethical issue is informed consent.

CONTEXT: In Milgram's study the participants did consent to taking part in a study about memory but they weren't fully informed about the actual study and therefore were deprived of the right to give informed consent.

The key to **ELABORATION** is the three-point rule (see page xii). For example:

Question:
With reference to Milgram's study, outline **one** weakness of using qualitative data. **[3]**

Answer:
STATE: One weakness of qualitative data is that it is more difficult to detect patterns and draw conclusions because of the large variety of information collected.

CONTEXT: In the Milgram study this would have been true because the quotes from participants such as 'He's banging in there. I'm going to chicken out' couldn't be displayed in a graph.

COMMENT: However, in this particular case the quotes from participants did paint a similar picture so it was possible to detect patterns about the stress that participants experienced.

The social approach

On pages 146–147 and 224–225 we have discussed the **social approach**.

The study by Milgram concerns obedience.

- In what way is this an example of the social approach?
- Discuss the strengths and weaknesses of the social approach using examples from the Milgram study.

Milgram: afters

Still following orders?

The Milgram study is probably the most well known and most powerful piece of social psychology. It was a mixed blessing for Milgram's career, however, because its controversial nature meant that the most prestigious universities were not keen to employ him. The ethical issues mean that it has been difficult to **replicate** the study until now when the development of technology allows us to carry out the study in a virtual world (see Slater *et al.*, 2006).

Is evil banal?

One of the conclusions that is commonly drawn from Milgram's study is that evil acts can be done by ordinary people. But is this the best explanation?

At the time of Milgram's studies a trial was taking place in Jerusalem of one of the Nazi leaders involved in *Endlosung der Judenfrage* (the final solution to the Jewish question). Adolf Eichmann had been part of this project from the beginning and in 1942 he was given the job of Transportation Administrator which put him in charge of all the trains that carried Jews to the death camps in Poland. In 1960, some time after the war, he was captured and put on trial.

The question that Milgram was asking, and that also became the centre of Eichmann's trial, concerned what sort of person could carry out such evil actions. Eichmann's defence was that he was just following orders, but this was not accepted by the court which heard evidence of how he had gone beyond his orders to devise more efficient ways of working and to continue the slaughter even after he was ordered to stop. He was found guilty and hanged.

The analysis of the trial that interested Milgram was in a book by **Hannah Arendt** (*Eichmann in Jerusalem*, 1963) where she describes how ordinary Eichmann appeared to be. This observation led her to refer to the '*banality of evil*' suggesting that evil acts are carried out unthinkingly by people who are not aware of the consequences and not committed to what is going on. Milgram saw this as an explanation of his own work.

Recent reviews of the evidence, however, tell a very different story (see Haslam and Reicher, 2008). For a start, Arendt only attended the start of the trial when Eichmann was trying to portray himself as someone who was blindly following orders. Later in the trial he was to show how closely he identified with the Nazi ideology and how aware and proud he was of his role in the mass murder of the Jews.

Milgram's view that it is ordinary people who do these things does not square with the evidence. As Haslam and Reicher (2008) point out, '*people do great wrong, not because they are unaware of what they are doing but because they consider it to be right.*' Haslam and Reicher offer an alternative explanation in terms of **social identity theory** (see page 158).

Did they obey?

It seems strange to ask the question '*Did they obey?*' given everything that has been written about this study. The Milgram Obedience Study is probably the most talked about work in social psychology, ever. Nobody takes a course in psychology without coming across it. So why ask this question when the answer seems obvious?

Nobody doubts the data and the brilliance of the design but was Milgram on the right lines when he came to analyse it and have we failed to look at the details in the subsequent years?

There are several reasons to think that obedience is not the best explanation of the data (see Haslam and Reicher, 2012) but we will look at just one. Look again at the four prompts that encourage the teacher to continue,

Prod 1 '*Please continue*', or '*Please go on*'.

Prod 2 '*The experiment requires that you continue*'.

Prod 3 '*It is absolutely essential that you continue*'.

Prod 4 '*You have no other choice, you must go on*'. (Milgram, 1963, p.374)

The first three don't demand obedience but justify to the teacher why they should carry on. They are appeals to help with the 'science'. Only the fourth one demands their obedience.

And here is the punchline: a recent review of Milgram's original data showed that every time the fourth prompt was used the teacher stopped (see Haslam and Reicher, 2012). This is not just for the 40 participants in the baseline study but for the full 800 people tested by Milgram in the many variations of the original design and also the participants in the recent clever replication of the study by Burger (2009). In Milgram's book he describes one participant's reaction to being given the final prompt. The man says he won't do it and goes on '*If this were Russia, maybe, but not in America*' (Milgram, 1974, page 65).

If you look at the fourth prompt then perhaps this is the point where the study stops being something that the 'teacher' is doing with the 'experimenter'. It stops being a joint activity to do something scientific. The study stops being on the side of the 'teachers' and at that point the 'teacher' says '*No more!*' The Milgram studies seem to be less about people obeying orders and more about getting people to believe in what they are doing.

Milgram and ethics

Many text books use the obedience study as an example of lack of ethical sensitivity. We would argue that they are wrong to do so. It is true that after the study was carried out there was an ethical storm about it. For example, **Diana Baumrind** (1964) wrote a damning critique, arguing that just because someone volunteers for a study this does not take away the researcher's responsibilities towards them. She used direct quotes from Milgram's study to illustrate the lack of regard she believed was given to the subjects. For example:

'*In a large number of cases the degree of tension [in the subjects] reached extremes that are rarely seen in sociopsychological laboratory studies. Subjects were observed to sweat, tremble, stutter, bite their lips, groan, and dig their fingernails into their flesh. These were characteristic rather than exceptional responses to the experiment.*' (page 375)

Baumrind accepted that some harm to subjects is a necessary part of research, for example testing out new medical procedures, because the results could not be achieved in any other way. Social psychology, however, is not in the same game as medicine and is unlikely to produce life-saving results, thus does not justify harming subjects.

The case for the prosecution was very powerful. Milgram's application to join the American Psychological Association (APA) was put on hold while they investigated the study, and he was not given the post he hoped for at Yale.

The case for the defence, however, is overwhelming. At the time of study psychologists were less sensitive about **ethical issues** than today, however there were ethical guidelines in place. In fact Milgram took more care than his colleagues about such issues. His obedience study contains the first reference to **debriefing** in a psychological report and he kept in contact with his subjects after the study to check their progress.

His work was eventually endorsed by the APA and he was awarded the Prize for Behavioral Science Research of the American Association for the Advancement of Science in 1964.

Finally, the obedience study has created a mirror for the world to see itself in. We can't look on at atrocity and comfort ourselves that we would never do it. We have to confront the fact that ordinary people can do despicable things. The Milgram study still dominates social psychology as arguably its greatest piece of work.

Multiple choice questions

1   Identify the sampling technique used:
   a Self-selected sample.
   b Opportunity sample.
   c Random sample.
   d Male sample.

2   Which ethical issue was not really a problem in this study?
   a Right to withdraw.
   b Deception.
   c Debriefing.
   d Psychological harm.

3   At what shock level did the learner start banging on the wall?
   a 200 volts.   b 250 volts.
   c 300 volts.   d 350 volts.

4   How many prods did the experimenter use?
   a 2   b 4
   c 6   d 8

5   After the study, the subject was:
   a Introduced to the learner.
   b Dehoaxed.
   c Given psychological tests.
   d All of the above.

6   Students predicted that:
   a 1% would obey fully.
   b 3% would obey fully.
   c 5% would obey fully.
   d 10% would obey fully.

7   What percentage of participants stopped at 300 volts?
   a 12.5%   b 17.5%
   c 22.5%   d 27.5%

8   What percentage of participants stopped at 450 volts?
   a 50%   b 55%
   c 60%   d 65%

9   Milgram offered explanations for why the subjects obeyed. Which of the following was <u>not</u> one of his reasons?
   a Sense of obligation.
   b The setting was prestigious.
   c They were paid.
   d They didn't take the task seriously.

10 Does Milgram suggest that obedience is:
   a A bad thing?
   b A good thing?
   c Both bad and good.
   d Unusual.

Answers are on page 247.

Exam-style questions

There are three kinds of question that can be asked about the Milgram study, as represented here by sections A, B and C.

See page x for further notes on the exam paper and styles of question.

Section A questions

1   Milgram's study has been criticised for being low in ecological validity.
   (a)   Outline **one** argument demonstrating that it was low in ecological validity. [2]
   (b)   Outline **one** argument demonstrating that it was high in ecological validity. [2]

2   Identify **four** aspects of Milgram's study that encouraged the participants to behave in a highly obedient way. [4]

3   (a)   Describe **one** ethical issue raised in Milgram's study. [2]
   (b)   Describe what steps Milgram took to deal with this ethical issue. [2]

4   In Milgram's study the participants showed signs of stress.
   (a)   Give **one** example of the stress shown by participants. [2]
   (b)   Explain why the participants may have been stressed. [2]

5   (a)   Describe how Milgram measured obedience. [2]
   (b)   Suggest **two** factors that would explain why participants were so obedient in Milgram's study. [2]

6   Outline **two** pieces of evidence from Milgram's study that showed that the participants believed the shocks were real. [4]

7   Some people regard Milgram's study as being controversial.
   (a)   Give **one** reason why the results of Milgram's study might be judged to be controversial. [2]
   (b)   Outline Milgram's reason for doing this research. [2]

8   From Milgram's study of obedience:
   (a)   Describe the sample that was used. [2]
   (b)   Outline **one** strength of this sample. [2]

9   In Milgram's study of obedience, male volunteers were recruited. There were two other additional participants. Describe the role of the **two** additional participants. [4]

10 From Milgram's study of obedience:
   (a)   Outline **one** quantitative finding from this study. [2]
   (b)   Give **one** weakness of this data in this study. [2]

Section B questions

Answer the following questions with reference to the Milgram study:

(a)   Outline the aim of this study. [2]

(b)   Describe why the sample was selected for this study and suggest **one** limitation of this sample. [6]

(c)   Outline the procedure of this study. [6]

(d)   Outline the findings of this study. [6]

(e)   Discuss the ecological validity of this study. [6]

(f)   Describe and evaluate changes that could be made to the way this study was conducted. [10]

Section C questions

(a)   Outline **one** assumption of the social approach. [2]

(b)   Describe how the social approach could explain obedience. [4]

(c)   Describe **one** similarity and **one** difference between the Milgram study and any other core studies that take the social approach. [6]

(d)   Discuss strengths and limitations of the social approach using examples from any core studies that take this approach. [12]

Tyranny and terror

The big question of the Milgram study concerned the development of **tyranny** and our response to it. The social psychologists of the time focused their explanations on the events of the Second World War. This war is still used as a cultural reference point and it is common to hear politicians and commentators referring to Nazi Germany or to Hitler. These references are usually very simplistic and tap into a basic understanding that something very wrong happened there and it shouldn't be allowed to happen again. The problem with these references are that the world is a different place in the twenty-first century and looking back 50 years will not necessarily help us to understand the present and deal with our modern crises.

In today's world we want to understand about how terror and tyranny develop and we need to go beyond seeing it as being divided into the good guys (obviously us) and the bad guys (anyone who gets in our way or challenges us). The work of European social psychologists such as Steve Reicher and Alex Haslam is important in exploring the natures of tyranny and terror so that we can improve our understanding and respond in positive ways.

Social identity

Social identity theory (SIT) was developed by **Henri Tajfel**. It states that the social groups and categories to which we belong are an important part of our self-concept, and therefore a person will sometimes interact with other people, not as a single individual, but as a representative of a whole group or category of people. A simple example of this is the common experience of doing something to make your family proud of you and you feel as if you are representing your family and don't want to let them down. Sometimes you act as an individual and sometimes as a group member and during one conversation you might change between these two identities. In business meetings people sometimes suggest that they are wearing 'a different hat' to convey the idea that they are adopting a social identity.

There are three basic psychological processes underlying social identification. The first of these is *categorisation* which is a basic tendency to classify things into groups. This commonly leads to an exaggeration of the similarities of those items in the same group, and an exaggeration of the differences between those in different groups. This means that when we categorise people, we accentuate the similarities to ourselves of people in the same group, and exaggerate the differences from ourselves of people in other groups.

The second psychological process is that of *social comparison*. Social groups do not exist in isolation, but in a social context in which some groups have more prestige, power or status than others. Once a social categorisation has been made, the process of social comparison means that the group is compared with other social groups, and its relative status is determined. This comparison has an inbuilt bias in favour of groups like ourselves because we know more about them.

The third psychological mechanism underlying social identity concerns the way that *membership* of a social group affects our self-concept. According to Tajfel and Turner (1979), people want to belong to groups which will reflect positively on their **self-esteem**. If the group does not compare favourably with others, and membership of it brings about lowered self-esteem, people will try to leave the group, or to distance themselves from it. If leaving the group is impossible, then they may look for ways that group membership may provide a positive source of self-esteem.

Prisons

This core study is about prisoners and prisons. If putting people into prisons makes their behaviour worse and the behaviour of their guards brutal then we need to look again at our criminal justice policy. Over nine million people are held in prisons worldwide (Home Office, 2003) with about half of them being detained in just three countries (USA, Russia, China). In England and Wales in January 2008, 79,724 people were being held in prison (75,383 men and 4,321 women) (NOMS, 2008). The table on the right shows rates of people being imprisoned in selected countries. You might wonder why some countries lock up many more people than others.

Country	Prisoners per 100,000 population
Nigeria	32
Japan	53
France	93
Germany	98
China	117
England and Wales	141
South Africa	402
Thailand	404
USA	701

From International Centre for Prison Studies (2008)

Terrorists or freedom fighters? Some people see the Palestinian group Hamas as terrorists but others see them as fighters for the legitimate rights of the Palestinian people.

War on Terror

Terrorism was not invented on 11 September 2001 though the destruction of the World Trade Centre in New York on that day changed the way the West viewed the world. The attack on the twin towers was the first attack by an outside force on the USA, and suddenly people in the US didn't feel safe. It is perhaps worth noting 'the other September 11th' when, on 11 September 1973 a USA-backed military coup in Chile overthrew the democratic government of Salvador Allende. In the aftermath of the coup the loss of life was similar to that at the World Trade Centre. Terrorism has a complex history.

After the World Trade Center attacks, then-President of the USA George W. Bush used the phrase 'War on Terror' to describe the USA's response to this act. Some would argue, however, (Merrin, 2005) that the war was already over and the USA had lost. In one day the terrorists had destroyed the World Trade Centre, created a global media explosion that still reverberates today and destroyed the sense of safety held by citizens of the USA. Terror was created on a huge scale on one day and nothing that has happened since has reduced that. In modern history it is hard to think of an event that has created such a sense of shock and awe. It was The One Day War.

The most visible consequences of the War on Terror have been the invasions of Iraq and Afghanistan. One of the confusing things about these missions is the idea that you can fight a perception (a sense of terror) by sending in a terrifying army. It is not clear whether a sense of terror has been reduced by any of these actions.

The Stanford Prison simulation – a mock prison

The Stanford Prison Experiment (SPE) is one of the most famous of all psychology experiments. At the height of the American War in Vietnam, when opposition to the war was very strong on university campuses and students were involved in violent protests, the US Navy funded a study to investigate the effects of prison life on guards and prisoners. Philip Zimbardo was the lead psychologist in the team that created a mock prison in the basement of the Stanford University psychology department. Their work was dramatic and surprising, and the results are still commonly cited today.

The study

In brief, 24 subjects were selected from an initial pool of 75 respondents to a newspaper advertisement which had asked for male volunteers to participate in a psychological study of prison life. The volunteers were interviewed and completed a **questionnaire** designed to screen subjects, and the selected people were described as 'normal', healthy, male college students who were predominantly middle class and white.

Zimbardo took the role of Warden and his other researchers took on roles of day-to-day management of the prison. He also recruited an ex-convict for advice about the prison and also to intimidate the prisoners when they asked to leave. The subjects were **randomly allocated** their roles of either 'prisoner' or 'guard', and signed contracts on that basis. The contract offered $15 a day and guaranteed basic living needs, though it was made explicit to the prisoners that some basic civil rights (for example, **privacy**) would be suspended. The prisoners were given no information about what to expect and no instructions on how to behave. The guards were told to maintain a reasonable degree of order within the prison necessary for its effective functioning, though they were explicitly prohibited from using physical aggression.

Both sets of subjects were given uniforms to promote feelings of anonymity. The guards' uniform (plain khaki shirt and trousers, whistle, baton, and reflecting sunglasses) was intended to convey a military attitude and impression of power. The prisoners' uniform (loose-fitting smock, number on front and back, no underwear, light chain and lock around ankle, rubber sandals and a cap made from nylon stocking) was intended to be uncomfortable, humiliating and to create a sense of subservience and dependence.

Results

The **role play** soon took an ugly turn and following an attempted revolt by the prisoners, the guards became more and more extreme in their behaviour. Things that were originally rights for the prisoners soon became privileges. The prisoners were subjected to sustained intimidation and humiliation by the guards as the psychologists looked on.

Things deteriorated very quickly with some of the prisoners showing severe signs of distress. Eventually a combination of a lawyer appearing from one of the families of the prisoners and a confrontation between Zimbardo and his then girlfriend (and later wife) persuaded Zimbardo to bring the study to an end after six days instead of the planned 14 days.

Afters

Zimbardo has never published an account of the study in a refereed journal (i.e. where academic peers review the research before publication) and he has still not released all of the data. This control of the data means that Zimbardo has also been able to control the story that is told about the events. The main lesson that Zimbardo draws from the study is that the roles we are asked to play will structure our behaviour. The guards became brutal and cruel because they had been assigned to the role of guard. There are other explanations for what happened here,

In the mock prison the guards humiliate the prisoners in a line-up.

however, but the restriction on access to the data and the lack of scrutiny by other scientists limits the confidence we can have in the conclusions that Zimbardo makes.

Biographical notes on Philip Zimbardo

Philip George Zimbardo was born into poverty in New York City, the grandchild of Sicilian immigrants. The family were constantly on the move (31 times to be exact) because they couldn't pay the rent. Zimbardo was often ill as a child, including one spell of spending six months in a hospital aged five, which he describes as a formative experience in his development, leading him to recognise the importance of making and sustaining human relationships.

Zimbardo went to secondary school in the Bronx with Stanley Milgram. When asked if it was a coincidence that both of them developed an interest in social influence his response was *'We were both interested in situational influences because growing up poor, one sees failure and evil in your midst and you don't want to believe it is the dispositions of your family and friends, but rather in situational forces imposed on them.'* (Zimbardo, personal communication).

Professor Zimbardo has conducted research in many other areas of psychology, such as shyness, persuasion, hypnosis and most recently terrorism. He helped to create the US Public TV programme *Discovering Psychology* and acts as series host. Zimbardo has received numerous awards for his distinguished teaching, creative research, dedicated social action, and career-long contributions to psychology. He was recently president of the American Psychological Association.

www You can read about the SPE at http://www.prisonexp.org.

...Link to the core study...

Reicher and Haslam's study stands alone as an observation on the way that terror and tyranny develop but it also acts as a re-evaluation of the social psychology of the last century. In particular it gives us a new understanding of the issues raised by Milgram (see pages 154) and Zimbardo's SPE (see above).

In one sense the study is about prisons but in another it is a more general investigation of how groups of people negotiate power and responsibility.

Reicher and Haslam: the core study

See the
CORE STUDY
CHECKLIST
on page xv for
details of what you
need to know for
the exam.

Stephen Reicher and S. Alexander Haslam (2006) Rethinking the psychology of tyranny: The BBC prison study. *British Journal of Social Psychology*, 45, 1–40.

In a nutshell

Key term: tyranny

Tyranny *is defined by Reicher and Haslam as* 'an unequal social system involving the arbitrary or oppressive use of power by one group or its agents over another' *(page 2).*

Context

One explanation offered for the anti-social behaviour of groups is **deindividuation** – a loss of one's sense of personal identity. The consequence is that group members behave in ways they wouldn't as individuals. This was demonstrated in the Stanford Prison Experiment (SPE) described on the previous page.

Reicher and Haslam offer a different explanation for anti-social group behaviour. **Social identity theory** suggests that individuals behave in an anti-social manner because they identify with a group that has anti-social norms.

This study focuses in particular on **tyranny** (the anti-social behaviour of some groups). Tyranny exists because there are group inequalities – some groups are dominant whereas others are subordinate. People prefer to belong to dominate groups because such groups have power and group membership enhances their own identity. Members of subordinate groups feel powerless and unable to challenge dominant groups.

Aims

The aims of this study are to:

1 Study the interactions between dominant and subordinate groups.

2 Understand the conditions under which subordinate groups will challenge the inequalities between dominant and subordinate groups, and thus overthrow tyranny. The prediction is that:

- Members of dominant groups will identify with their group, they seek no change.
- Members of subordinate groups will identify with their group (and challenge inequality) when they are motivated by a lack of **permeability** and a lack of fairness (group divisions are not legitimate).

Participants

Male volunteers were sought and then selected through screening (e.g. assessment by **clinical psychologists**). The final 15 came from diverse social and ethnic backgrounds. They were divided into groups of three where all the members of each group were matched (**matched participants design**) in terms of, for example, racism, **authoritarianism** and social dominance. One member of each group was **randomly** selected to be a guard (N=5) and the rest were prisoners (N=10).

Procedure

A mock prison was created and filmed by the BBC. This was an **experimental case study**. It was a case study because one group were observed. It was experimental because of the planned interventions (**independent variables**):

- *Permeability* – prisoners were told they might be promoted to guards.
- *Legitimacy* – participants told on day 3 that roles had been **randomly allocated**, i.e. not legitimate, creating insecurity.
- *Cognitive alternatives* – prisoner 10 was introduced on day 4 to challenge inequality and creates insecurity.

Dependent variables were measured using **rating scales** related to social, organisational and clinical variables (e.g. social identification, **authoritarianism** and depression). **Observations** were recorded with video cameras.

Results

Phase 1: *Rejecting inequality* – social identification in prisoners started once the groups became impermeable. The guards showed little social identification which led to ineffective leadership. This in turn meant that the prisoners no longer perceived the inequalities as legitimate (the guards did not deserve their privileges) and this led to a collapse of the prisoner-guard system on day 6.

Phase 2: *Embracing inequality* – participants set up an egalitarian social system which soon failed. The suggested replacement was a tyrannical regime, reflected in a rise in right-wing authoritarianism. The new regime was judged unethical and therefore the study was stopped after 8 days.

Discussion

There are four possible critiques that can be made of this study: the role of television (were participants play-acting?), the role of personality (were there important individual differences?), the reality of the set up (were participants really engaged?), and the impact of interventions (did the IV cause the DV?).

The findings cannot be explained in terms of a 'natural' tendency to assume roles and assert power (as proposed by Zimbardo). Social identification provides a better account for both this study and the SPE.

More importantly, this study provides a new framework for understanding tyranny – the failure of groups renders members powerless and willing to accept alternatives that run against personal values and norms, thus making tyranny psychologically acceptable.

Qs 5.6

1 Two explanations are offered for the anti-social behaviour of groups. Outline each explanation.

2 Explain why subordinate groups find it difficult to challenge dominant groups.

3 Reicher and Haslam suggest conditions that would enable subordinate groups to challenge dominant groups. What are these conditions?

4 Identify **three** features of the sample.

5 Explain how the process of matching would have controlled individual differences.

6 In what way was this study an experimental case study?

7 Give examples of quantitative and qualitative data that were collected.

8 What was the effect on the prisoners of impermeability?

9 What was the effect on the prisoners of no legitimacy?

10 Give **one** criticism of this study.

The detailed version

Context and aim

The shadow of events of the Second World War continues to hang over academic psychology. The central question is 'how we come to condone the tyranny of others or else act tyrannically ourselves?'

At one time anti-social behaviours such as prejudice, discrimination and genocide were explained in terms of individual characteristics, i.e. such behaviours were due to the personality of the perpetrators. There has been a shift in psychology towards explanations that focus on group processes and explanations which suggest that when people get together in groups their behaviour becomes extremely anti-social.

This equating of anti-social behaviour (tyranny) with groups has a long history, for example Gustave LeBon (1895–1947) argued that individuals lose their sense of personal identity and responsibility when in a crowd and thus become capable of barbaric acts. Philip Zimbardo suggested that this process of deindividuation is an *ageless life force, the cycle of nature, the blood ties, the tribe'* (Zimbardo, 1969, page 249).

Zimbardo's research: Tyranny as role and power

Zimbardo's most famous research, the SPE, was important in shifting explanations for anti-social behaviour from an individual to a group focus. Zimbardo's study showed that immersion in a group undermines the constraints that normally prevent anti-social behaviour. In addition, when a group also has power this seems to encourage extreme anti-social behaviour.

The impact of the SPE was important ethically as well as theoretically, as the participants in the study experienced considerable stress. This meant that subsequent research was increasingly limited to **laboratory experiments** with minimal or no interaction between participants. The ultimate result has been that research on important social topics such as oppression and genocide has become remote from the social realities of such phenomena.

These **ethical issues** have also meant that the conclusions from the SPE have never been challenged because the study could not be **replicated**. Such a replication is long overdue for two reasons:

1   The conclusions that were drawn are questionable. Zimbardo and his team concluded that the behaviour of the SPE guards and prisoners was due to a natural acceptance of their roles. However, their behaviour may have been more to do with the instructions given to them by Zimbardo. When Zimbardo briefed the guards he told them to create fear and give the prisoners a sense of powerlessness.

2   These conclusions have been generalised to a wide range of real-life situations from prisons to terrorism, and thus the traditional analysis of the SPE has had profound social consequences. The implications from Zimbardo's study are that people have little choice in what they do – they simply behave according to assigned roles. This implies they have little responsibility for their actions and therefore tyrants cannot be held responsible for what they do. The conclusions also discourage the oppressed from challenging tyranny.

An alternative analysis: social identity

Social identity theory (SIT, described on page 158) proposes that people are only influenced by the norms and values of a group if they *identify* with the group. If the group norms are pro-social then the individuals who identify with the group will behave in a pro-social manner, such as being helpful. If the group norms are anti-social then group members will behave in an anti-social manner.

When there are two or more groups, inevitably one group is 'better' because it has more members, more money, higher status, etc. Other groups are inferior or subordinate to this dominant group. This creates group inequality and the dominant group has the power to oppress groups with a negative value (tyranny).

Members of subordinate groups may decide to take collective action against the dominant group but only under certain conditions:

*   *Permeability* – if group members believe that it is possible to move out of the group (i.e. permeability is high) they will not engage in collective action. *Impermeability* leads to stronger identity within the group and an increased likelihood of collective action against the dominant group.

*   *Security* consists of two strands: perceived fairness of intergroup inequalities (*legitimacy*) and the *stability* of these intergroup relations. If group members feel *insecure* they become aware of cognitive alternatives, and thus are more likely to take collective action to challenge inequalities.

Aims

1   One aim of this study was to create an institution that resembled 'typical' hierarchical institutions such as prisons, offices or schools.

    Specifically the aim was to create an environment where group inequalities could be manipulated in terms of power, status and resources. The main question is whether the concepts of social identity provide a more satisfactory account of group behaviour than Zimbardo's view of role acceptance.

2   A further aim was to investigate the conditions under which people identify with their groups. The predictions are that:

    *   dominant group members will identify with their group;

    *   subordinate group members will only identify with their group and challenge intergroup inequalities *if* relations between the groups are seen as *impermeable* and *insecure*.

3   Two further aims were to investigate the relationship between social, organisational and **clinical** factors in group behaviour, and to develop a practical and ethical framework to examine social psychological issues.

Qs 5.7

1   LeBon proposed that anti-social behaviour is linked to groups. What explanation did he provide for why this might happen?

2   Why has Zimbardo's research not been replicated?

3   Briefly describe social identity theory.

4   Explain, in your own words, what is meant by 'permeability'.

5   Explain, in your own words, what is meant by 'security'.

6   Under what conditions will subordinate group members seek 'cognitive alternatives'?

7   Outline one aim of this study.

8   Under what conditions will subordinate group members challenge tyranny?

Reicher and Haslam: the core study *continued*

Method

Participants

Male volunteers were sought through national newspapers and leaflets. An initial pool of 332 applicants was reduced to 27 through screening which involved assessment by **clinical psychologists**, and medical and character references. **Psychometric tests** were also used to assess, for example, **authoritarianism**, depression and **self-esteem**.

The final 15 participants were chosen to ensure a diversity of age, social class and ethnic background. These 15 were divided into five groups of three people matched as closely as possible on personality variables that might be **significant**, i.e. racism, authoritarianism and social dominance (**matched participants design**). From each group of three one person was **randomly** selected to be a guard and the other two were prisoners. One prisoner was not involved at the beginning of the filming.

Procedure

The study was conducted in December 2001 in conjunction with the BBC. The role of the BBC was to: (a) create the prison environment according to the researcher's design; (b) film the study over a period of up to 10 days at Elstree Studios in London; and (c) prepare the film for broadcast (four one-hour programmes screened in May 2002).

This programme is distinct from reality TV because reality TV programmes are designed for entertainment and academics are invited to comment afterwards as opposed to having an instrumental role in the design.

The method used was an **experimental case study**:

- It is experimental because interventions (**independent variables, IVs**) were introduced at specific points in the study to observe the effects on **dependent variables (DVs)**.
- It is a case study because the behaviour of only one group was observed.

Environment

Prisoners were allocated to lockable three-person cells off a central atrium. This was separated from the guards' quarters by a lockable steel mesh fence. There were facilities throughout for video and audio recording.

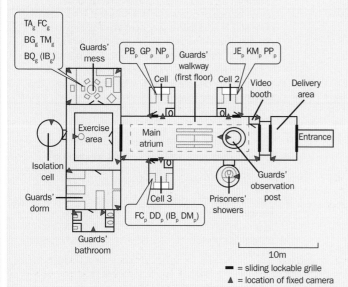

Plan of the prison showing where each prisoner (subscript P) or guard (subscript G) was located.'

Ethics

The study was considered by various **ethics committees** and was monitored throughout by independent psychologists and another ethics committee. Participants signed a comprehensive consent form which informed them of the potential psychological and physical risks (e.g. discomfort, confinement, constant surveillance and stress).

Guards

The guards were briefed the night before the study began. They were told that they were responsible for the smooth running of the institution and that they must respect the basic rights of the prisoners. The guards were allowed to lock prisoners up, see into prisoners' cells, and use rewards and punishments (such as a bread and water diet). The guards had far better accommodation and food than the prisoners. This created a sense of inequality.

Prisoners

The prisoners arrived one at a time. Their heads were shaved and they were given numbered orange uniforms. A set of rules and prisoners' rights were posted in their cells.

Independent variables

There were three planned interventions (IVs):

1 **Permeability** (the expectation of movement between groups). Participants were told that the guards were selected because of certain personality characteristics (e.g. reliability, initiative), and also told that if prisoners showed these traits they might be promoted to being guards. This created *permeability*.

On Day 3 one prisoner was promoted but after that participants were told no further promotions (or demotions) would be possible. This aimed to create *impermeability*.

2 **Legitimacy** (when decisions are based on real differences). On Day 6 participants were to be told there were actually no differences between guards and prisoners. This meant that the group division was, afterall, not legitimate. This aimed to create *insecurity* and trigger a search for *cognitive alternatives*.

3 **Cognitive alternatives** (being able to think about possible alternatives). After the legitimacy intervention a new prisoner was to be introduced. He was chosen because he was a trade union official and therefore would provide the skills to negotiate and organise collective action. This would provide *cognitive alternatives* and aimed to create *insecurity*.

Dependent variables

There were numerous DVs. Not all were measured every day because this would have overwhelmed the participants:

1 **Social variables** – social identification, awareness of cognitive alternatives, right-wing authoritarianism.

2 **Organisational variables** – compliance with rules, organisational citizenship. The 'organisation' refers to the interrelationships between all participants.

3 **Clinical variables** – depression and **self-efficacy**.

These were measured using:

- **Rating scales**, where participants were asked to rate statements (e.g. *'I think the relationship between prisoners and guards is likely to change'*).
- **Observations** of the interactions between prisoners and guards were audio- and video-recorded.
- Physiological measure – saliva swabs were taken daily to assess **cortisol** levels, a measure of stress.

Results

Phase 1: rejecting inequality

In the first phase of the study, the aim was to create group identification which should enable the subordinate group to challenge inter-group inequalities.

Social identification and permeability

As expected the prisoners showed little group identification until the group boundaries became *impermeable* (after the promotion on day 3). At this point they started to discuss how they could work together to improve conditions. Therefore impermeability enhanced *social identification* and *collective action.*

Contrary to expectations the guards did not identify with their group.

Graph showing changes in social identification

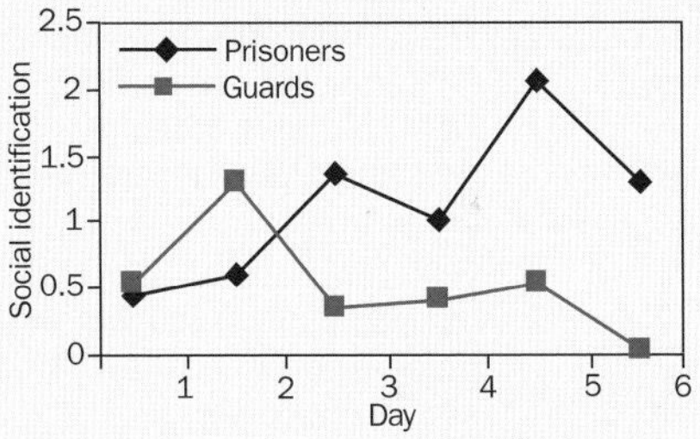

Legitimacy and security

Low group identity among guards led to ineffective leadership. This led the prisoners to have reduced regard for the guards' authority as legitimate, creating *insecurity* and ultimately enabling prisoners to feel able to challenge intergroup inequalities. For example, JE_p ($_p$ denotes prisoner) threw his plate on the floor, demanding better food from the guards.

This response meant there was no need for the legitimacy intervention which had been intended to create *insecurity*.

Cognitive alternatives

Prisoner 10 (DM_p) joined on day 5 (earlier than originally planned) and established a negotiating structure. Measurements using rating scales showed that participants did become increasingly aware of *cognitive alternatives*, as predicted.

Organisational and clinical measures

Measures of organisational variables dropped significantly on day 5 when the prisoners started to challenge the guards and no longer supported the organisation.

The unity of the prisoners led to increased self-efficacy scores and decreased depression scores, whereas the opposite was true for the guards who became more disorganised and mutually recriminatory.

Combined impact

On day 6 some prisoners broke out of their cells and occupied the guards' quarters, making the guards' regime unworkable.

Phase 2: embracing inequality

The participants met with the experimenters to draw up terms of a new commune. Within a day, however, this new social structure was in crisis because two ex-prisoners felt marginalised and violated communal rules.

A new group (one ex-guard and three ex-prisoners) formulated a plan for a new and harsher prisoner-guard hierarchy, for example PB_p said *'We want to be guards and f**king make them toe the line ... No f**king talking while you're eating'* (page 22).

Supporters of the commune were largely passive. Publicly they may not have wished to show support but privately, when later **debriefed**, some had warmed to the idea of a strong social order.

Biographical notes

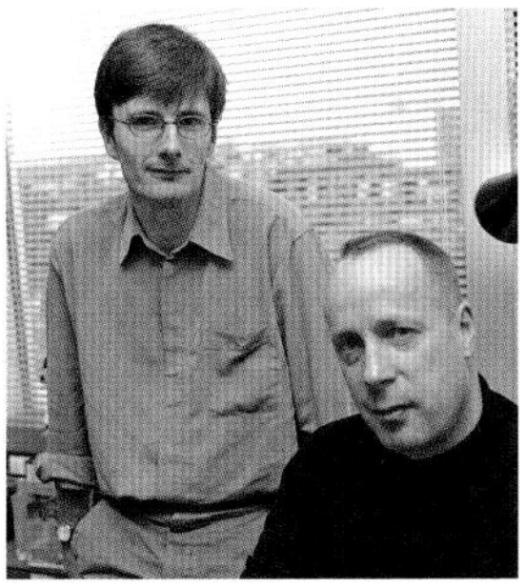

The picture shows Professors ***Steve Reicher*** *(on right) and* ***Alex Haslam*** *who head psychology departments at opposite ends of the world – St. Andrews in Scotland and the University of Queensland in Australia respectively.*

How did they come to work together? Alex explains, *'Steve and I have known each other (and been friends) for about 20 years. We have always worked on similar issues (leadership, group dynamics) and always from a similar perspective (the social identity perspective), due in large part to the fact that we had the same PhD supervisor, John Turner.'.*

Authoritarianism

This desire for a strong social order was reflected in an increase in right-wing authoritarianism.

However, a fascinating pattern emerged if the data were analysed as a function of the new guards/prisoners, as shown in the graph below. The new plan meant a re-assignment of participants to roles, those participants who sought to be guards actually showed a slight *decrease* in authoritarianism whereas this increased in participants who chose to be prisoners. At the end of the study the scores for guards and prisoners were nearly the same.

Graph showing changes in authoritarianism, which emerged when participants selected their own roles.

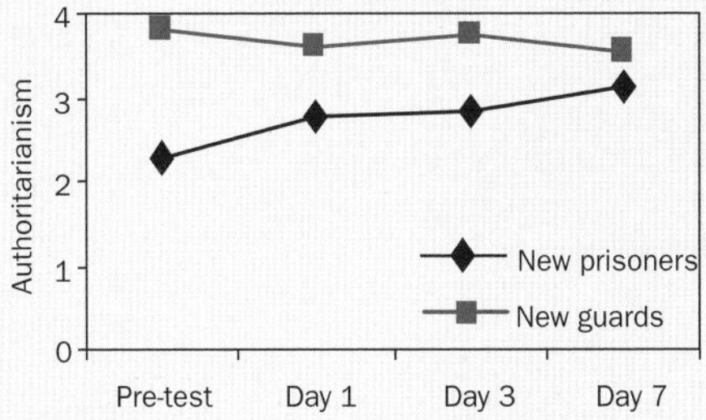

(Note that not all measures were taken on every day.)

Study ends prematurely

The new regime could not be imposed due to ethical constraints and the existing regime was not working so the study was stopped on day 8.

Qs 5.8

1. Why were the researchers so concerned about the ethics of this study?
2. What did they do to ensure the study was carried out ethically?
3. Explain how the procedures created a sense of (a) inequality, (b) impermeability and (c) insecurity.
4. Identify **two** of the dependent measures in this study and explain how they were measured.
5. Two graphs are shown on this page. State a conclusion that can be drawn from each of these.

Reicher and Haslam: the core study *continued*

Discussion

Four critiques of the study

1 The role of television
The participants may have been acting for the cameras. However, this would not explain why their behaviour changed at the times predicted, e.g. before and after **permeability**. In any case 'being watched' is not such an usual situation as we are all watched by surveillance cameras.

2 The role of personality
The 'prisoners' may have been especially strong characters. However, the fact that participants' 'character' on relevant dimensions (e.g. **authoritarianism**) changed over time suggests that personality cannot explain the course of events. In addition, dominance only occurred through shared identity rather than forcefulness of personality. For example FC$_p$ was a mild character who became a leading figure through shared identity.

3 The reality of inequality and power
It may be that the participants didn't become engaged with the **role play** and thus were not acting as they would if it was 'real'. However, the prisoners expressed a dislike of being locked up and being deprived of cigarettes; the guards' conversations reflected the seriousness they felt about the role. All of this points to engagement with the situation.

4 The impact of interventions and key variables
It could be argued that the **dependent variables** were affected by other, **extraneous variables**. For example, the introduction of DM$_p$ made prisoners feel uncertain about what would happen next. However, this is unlikely because there is no theoretical basis for this chain of events whereas there is theoretical justification for the suggested impact of the interventions.

Social identity account of tyranny

The conditions of social identification
This study shows that people do not automatically assume roles. Instead their behaviour relates to social identification which shifts with contextual factors such as permeability, security and legitimacy.

This study also demonstrates how extreme behaviours can be restrained by making actors visible and hence accountable. TQ$_g$ was a successful businessman which may explain his reluctance to play the part of a brutal guard. This shows that behaviour is not always dominated by the present context; past and future contexts matter.

The consequences of social identification
The study demonstrates the interrelationships between social, organisational and **clinical** variables. Shared social identity led to effective organisation (mutual support and trust) and positive mental states (lack of depression, anxiety and burnout).

Reactions to group failure
There were two instances of group failure: (1) failure of the guards to control the prisoners, (2) failure of the commune. In both instances group members were prepared to relinquish their existing norms and values and adopt new ones in order for a viable social order to be established.

Conclusions

1. The results support the SPE conclusions that collective conflict and **tyranny** cannot be understood by looking at individuals; any account must look at group processes.

2. The results contradict the traditional view that group processes are toxic, i.e. inevitably lead to uncontrolled, mindless and anti-social behaviour.

3. The results show that it is the breakdown of groups that creates the conditions under which tyranny can flourish.

4. This analysis can be applied to the SPE – tyranny flourished when the prisoners were told they could not leave and thus the group became disoriented and broke down.

5. This study shows it is possible to run ethical field studies into social processes rather than conducting sterile experiments.

Qs 5.9

1. Explain **two** of the criticisms that could be made of this study and, for each of them, outline Reicher and Haslam's defence.
2. In what way do Reicher and Haslam's findings support Zimbardo?
3. Refer back to the aims of this study on page 161. For each aim what can we conclude?
4. Explain what happened on the two occasions when the groups failed.
5. Explain how the breakdown of groups allows tyranny to flourish.

...Links to core studies...

This study is about real people in real situations. Although the prison is contrived it is clear the participants were not just acting out a part. This study falls in the tradition of social psychology studies such as **Milgram** and **Piliavin et al.** that observe the complexities of behaviour in real life settings. Having said that, the study has a wide range of controls that we associate with experiments (for example the **Loftus and Palmer** study).

Things you could do ...

Read the original article by Reicher and Haslam at http://www.bbcprisonstudy.org/pdfs/BJSP(2006)Tyrannny.pdf.

Read: Haslam and Reicher (2002). *A user's guide to 'The Experiment': Exploring the psychology of groups and power*. London: BBC Learning.

Watch a video and gets lots of other information at the official site for The Experiment, see http://www.bbcprisonstudy.org.

Evaluating the study by Reicher and Haslam

The research method
This study was conducted in a controlled laboratory environment.

What are the strengths and weaknesses of using a controlled environment in the context of this study?

The study was described as an experiment and a case study.

Describe the strengths and weaknesses of using these research method in the context of this study.

The sample
The participants were British males and volunteers.

In what way are the participants in this sample unique? How might this affect the conclusions drawn from the study?

Ethics
Do you think this study was ethically acceptable? Outline reasons for and against.

Reliability
Reliability concerns measurement.

What aspects of human behaviour were measured in this study? How could the reliability of these measurements be assessed?

Ecological validity
Haslam and Reicher suggest that the behaviour in this study had parallels with real life. For example, we are constantly filmed in our everyday lives. They also suggest that the participants took the task seriously.

To what extent do you think the participants in this study behaved as they would have done in everyday life? Is being filmed the same as everyday life? Did they take the task seriously? Are there other explanations for their behaviour?

Snapshot or longitudinal?
This is a longitudinal study because it takes place over the period of 8 days.

Consider the strengths and weaknesses of this design in the context of this study.

Quantitative and qualitative data
Some of the results can be described as quantitative data and other findings are qualitative.

Give examples of both kinds of data in this study.

What are the strengths of quantitative in the context of this study?

What are the strengths of qualitative in the context of this study?

Applications/usefulness
Psychologists aim to conduct research that will help make people's lives better.

From your point of view, how valuable was this study? Think of some real life instances of tyranny and how the findings from this study could be applied.

What next?
*Describe **one** change to this study, and say how you think this might affect the outcome.*

There are no simple answers.

Evaluating a study requires you to think.

We have provided some pointers here, linked to the RESEARCH METHODS and KEY ISSUES covered in Chapter 1 (Psychological investigations) and Chapter 7 (Key issues).

You can read suggested answers on our website www.psypress.com/cw/banyard.

Producing effective evaluation
When you produce your own answers to the issues on the left there are two things to ensure:

1 Contextualisation
2 Elaboration

The key to **CONTEXTUALISATION** is to ensure that your answer includes some information about this particular study. For example:

Question:

With reference to the study by Reicher and Haslam, suggest **one** strength of conducting a laboratory experiment. **[2]**

Answer:

STATE: One strength of a laboratory experiment is that causal relationships can be demonstrated because an independent variable is manipulated to observe its effect on a dependent variable, and extraneous variables can be minimised.

CONTEXT: In the Reicher and Haslam study there were several independent variables, such as high/low permeability. By changing this the researchers could demonstrate the effect this had on social identification.

The key to **ELABORATION** is the three-point rule (see page xii) but sometimes it is a matter of providing two pieces of context to provide elaboration. For example:

Question:

Describe **one** difference between the Reicher and Haslam study and any other study that uses the social approach. **[3]**

Answer:

STATE: One difference is in terms of the number and kind of participants that were studied.

CONTEXT: In the Reicher and Haslam study it was a relatively small group of 15 people and they were British.

CONTEXT: In Milgram's study the sample was larger (40 participants) and they were American.

The social approach

On pages 146–147 and 224–225 we have discussed the **social approach**.

The study by Reicher and Haslam concerns identity.

*   In what way is this an example of the social approach?
*   Discuss the strengths and weaknesses of the social approach using examples from the Reicher and Haslam study.

Reicher and Haslam: afters

More tyranny

Since the publication of Reicher and Haslam's work, Zimbardo has challenged the conclusions that have been drawn from their study and has launched a new account of his Stanford Prison Experiment in his book *The Lucifer Effect* (2007). This book contains many new details about the original study that had previously been unpublished. In this section we look at the two studies to see how they can used to explain more recent examples of **tyranny**.

Abu Ghraib

In 2004 accounts started appearing in the world media of abuse of Iraqi prisoners at the Abu Ghraib prison in Baghdad. These reports were accompanied by a number of photographs taken by the soldiers. These images were the driving force behind **Phillip Zimbardo** deciding to write his book *The Lucifer Effect*. In the book Zimbardo revisits the Stanford Prison Experiment and uses it to explain the behaviour of the guards at Abu Ghraib. The message that Zimbardo draws from the SPE is that there are no bad apples, only bad barrels. He argues that in the SPE ordinary members of the public found themselves in a far from ordinary situation and behaved in cruel and brutal ways to other people. It could have been you, says Zimbardo. The factors that facilitated this, according to Zimbardo, included the uniforms that the participants wore and the roles they were assigned.

Zimbardo suggests that when we look at Abu Ghraib we should see not the actions of the guards but the actions of the system that created them. He describes how in his role as expert witness for one of the guards, Staff Sergeant Ivan 'Chip' Frederick, he made this point to the military court, though with little success.

A different interpretation of Abu Ghraib, however, does not see the guards as

Iconic image of US troops abusing Iraqi prisoners at the Abu Ghraib prison.

victims of the US government but as the agents of their much closer Machiavellian masters. In this reading of events the uncomfortable truth for us is that the guards were responding to what they perceived to be the requests of PsyOps units (Psychological Operations). One of those charged, Private Lynndie England, who featured prominently in the first batch of photographs and was subsequently jailed, insisted she was acting on orders from *'persons in my chain of command'. 'I was instructed by persons in higher rank to "stand there, hold this leash, look at the camera", and they took pictures for PsyOps'* (see for example, Ronson, 2004).

Dying for the cause

On 7 July 2005, the day after London had been awarded the 2012 Olympics, four young British men got on public transport in London and detonated explosive devices, killing themselves and 52 other people. One of the four, Mohammed Sidique Khan, detonated his bomb on the Circle Line at Edgware Road killing six people and injuring a further 120. The picture shows him recording a message about his reasons for the attack.

How can we understand this behaviour? If we follow Zimbardo's approach then we need to look for the authority and the broken institutions that brought about these

London bomber, Mohammed Sidique Khan.

actions. However, if we look at the history of Sidique Khan then we see a story of a fairly ordinary young man working as a teaching assistant. He was well liked and well educated, and he had a young family. A picture does not emerge of a person driven by outside forces but of someone who made choices to become more involved in politics and religion and ultimately to die for a cause he believed in.

A way to start to understand this is to look at the social identities he took on and to try to see why he made the choices that he did. Read more at http://news.bbc.co.uk/1/hi/uk/4762209.stm.

The ethics of torture

If you can use psychological techniques to prevent acts of tyranny taking place what would you do? Is it OK to use psychological torture to interrogate suspected terrorists? The debate over this has split opinion in the American Psychological Association (APA). Most controversial is the role of psychologists at detention facilities such as Guantanamo Bay. Following growing concerns about this, the then APA President Ronald Levant visited Guantanamo Bay in 2005 saying *'I accepted this invitation to visit Guantanamo because I saw it as an important opportunity for the Association to provide input on the question of how psychologists can play an appropriate and ethical role in national security investigations.'* (Levant, 2007 page 2)

He was accompanied on the trip by Steven Sharfstein, President of the APA, who was so alarmed by what he encountered that he called for all psychiatrists to have nothing more to do with military interrogations. No such clear statement came out of the APA, and the involvement of psychologists continued at military interrogation facilities.

It should be remembered that Guantanamo is outside international law and even US law. The inmates have not been arrested and charged, they have been kidnapped and tortured. They are not prisoners of war according to the US, and so are not covered by the Geneva Conventions. They have no legal representation and no obvious chance of release.

Most revealing in Levant's description of what he encountered at Guantanamo is the following,

'We next visited the brand new psychiatric wing, which has both inpatient and outpatient services. I had a very unusual experience as we were standing at the nursing station, receiving a briefing from the psychiatrist. Behind me a voice asked "Dean Levant? Is that you?" That was the last thing I expected to hear at GTMO! I turned to see a former doctoral student in clinical psychology from Nova Southeastern University [NSU], who is now a military psychologist. I thought to myself, "NSU's graduates sure have done a good job of getting out into the world!"' (ibid, page 5)

Study psychology, see the world and use sensory deprivation techniques on kidnap victims. It could catch on.

In 2009 the psychologists finally made a clear ethical statement about involvement of psychologists with torture, but not before President Obama had been elected and passed legislation to close the camps. **Ethical issues** are difficult to resolve, though many would think that banning torture ought to be one of the easier ones.

Multiple choice questions

1 The study was:
a A case study. b An experiment.
c An observation. d All of the above.

2 At the start of filming there were:
a 5 prisoners. b 7 prisoners.
c 9 prisoners. d 10 prisoners.

3 The conclusion drawn from the SPE was that:
a Individual characteristics determine behaviour in groups.
b Groups are likely to behave pro-socially.
c Groups create social identification.
d The behaviour was due to role acceptance.

4 The study was planned to run for:
a 8 days. b 9 days.
c 10 days. d 14 days.

5 Which of the following was not a planned intervention in the study?
a Permeability. b Security.
c Legitimacy. d Cognitive alternatives.

6 How did Reicher and Haslam intend to trigger the search for cognitive alternatives?
a The introduction of prisoner 10.
b Telling prisoners there was no difference between prisoners and guards.
c Increasing sense of security.
d Removing permeability.

7 Which of the following was true?
a The prisoners showed a high level of identification when permeability was high.
b The prisoners showed a high level of identification when permeability was low.
c The guards showed a high level of group identification.
d Both b and c.

8 At the end of the study right-wing authoritarianism in the 'new' guards:
a Increased.
b Decreased.
c Was nearly the same as prisoners.
d Both b and c.

9 What evidence suggested that the participants were not play-acting?
a Their behaviour changed as predicted.
b They said they weren't play-acting.
c They appeared to be very distressed.
d None of them were actors.

10 The group failed when:
a The guards failed to control the prisoners.
b The commune collapsed.
c The 10th prisoner was introduced.
d Both a and b.

Answers are on page 247.

Exam-style questions

There are three kinds of question that can be asked about the Reicher and Haslam study, as represented here by sections A, B and C.

See page x for further notes on the exam paper and styles of question.

Section A questions

1 In Reicher and Haslam's study one of the interventions was intended to increase 'permeability'.
(a) Describe how 'permeability' was created. [2]
(b) Describe how the situation to create impermeability. [2]

2 In the Reicher and Haslam study one intervention did not have to be used.
(a) Describe this intervention. [2]
(b) Explain why it was not necessary to implement it. [2]

3 The BBC Prison study was an attempt to re-examine the conclusions of an earlier prison simulation – the Stanford Prison Experiment (SPE).
(a) State **one** conclusion that was the same in both studies. [2]
(b) State **one** conclusion that was different. [2]

4 From Reicher and Haslam's BBC prison study:
(a) Describe what is meant by the term 'tyranny'. [2]
(b) Describe **one** of the variables manipulated to create a situation in which tyranny could develop. [2]

5 Reicher and Haslam identified various potential criticisms of their prison study.
(a) Outline **one** of these criticisms. [2]
(b) Outline their answer to this criticism. [2]

6 From the prison study by Reicher and Haslam identify **four** self-rating scales that were used. [4]

7 From Reicher and Haslam's BBC prison study, outline **two** reasons why the prisoners were given uniforms. [4]

8 In the Reicher and Haslam study of a simulated prison:
(a) Describe **one** method used to ensure ethical acceptability. [2]
(b) Describe **one** reason in which the study had low ecological validity. [2]

9 Describe how the sample was recruited in Reicher and Haslam's study. [4]

10 Describe **one** quantitiative and **one** qualitative measure used in the Reicher and Haslam study. [4]

Section B questions

Answer the following questions with reference to the Reicher and Haslam study:

(a) State **one** of the hypotheses investigated in this study. [2]

(b) Describe how the sample in this study was selected and suggest **one** advantage of using this sample. [6]

(c) Explain why this study can be considered a laboratory experiment. [6]

(d) Outline the procedure used in this study. [8]

(e) Outline the findings of this study. [6]

(f) Suggest **one** change to the procedure of this study and explain how this might affect the results. [8]

Section C questions

(a) Outline **one** assumption of the social approach. [2]

(b) Describe how the social approach could explain identity. [4]

(c) Describe **one** similarity and **one** difference between the Reicher and Haslam study and any other core studies that take the social approach. [6]

(d) Discuss strengths and weaknesses of the social approach using examples from any core studies that take this approach. [12]

Piliavin *et al.*: starters

Good, and not so good, Samaritans

At first sight the city is a lonely and alien place. Buildings hover over the streets and cast long shadows over the faceless and nameless people who scurry beneath them. Many people only experience the city when they commute into work or to shop. To them it can be a dangerous and unfriendly place.

Every so often a news story captures the public imagination and turns into a modern parable of city life. The case of James Bulger in Liverpool is one of these stories (see page 176) and so was the case of Kitty Genovese (below), a young woman murdered in a New York street in 1964. This murder made the news because of the reported behaviour of the residents of the neighbourhood in which the attack took place.

Social psychologists including Stanley Milgram became interested in the newspaper accounts of the murder. **John Darley** and **Bibb Latané** devised a number of **laboratory** studies that demonstrated what became known as the 'bystander effect'.

Kitty Genovese

The assault

Kitty Genovese drove home from her bar job arriving at 3.15am. When she got out of the car she was approached by Winston Moseley who stabbed her. She screamed and her cries were heard by several neighbours but on a cold night with the windows closed only a few of them recognised the sound as a cry for help. When one of the neighbours shouted at the attacker, Moseley ran away, and Genovese made her way towards her own apartment around the end of the building. She was seriously injured but now out of view of those few who may have had reason to believe she was in need of help.

Other witnesses observed Moseley enter his car and drive away, only to return five minutes later. He searched the apartment complex, following the trail of blood to Genovese, who was lying in a hallway at the back of the building. Out of view of the street and of those who may have heard or seen any sign of the original attack, he proceeded to rape her, rob her and finally murder her. The time from the first assault until her death was about half an hour.

Later investigation revealed that at least 38 individuals nearby had heard or observed portions of the attack, but none could have seen or been aware of the entire incident.

Many were entirely unaware that an assault or homicide was in progress; some thought that what they saw or heard was a lovers' quarrel or a group of friends leaving the bar outside which Moseley first approached Genovese.

The *New York Times* ran the story under the headline *'Thirty-Eight Who Saw Murder Didn't Call the Police'* which was not exactly true. The article began, *'For more than half an hour thirty-eight respectable, law-abiding citizens in Queens watched a killer stalk and stab a woman in three separate attacks in Kew Gardens'*. It is from this semi-correct article that the murder became famous and the local residents were damned.

The Genovese family

It was a difficult call for us to know whether to describe the case of Kitty Genovese in this book. It appears in many psychology articles and most introductory texts and, remarkably, she is probably more famous with psychology students than most of the psychologists they study. She is famous, however, for the way she died and we doubt this is how she would have wanted to be remembered. She had family and friends and a full and interesting life. She was much more than a gruesome headline.

Doorway where Kitty Genovese died

Explanations of the bystand

The *bystander effect* (also known as bystander apathy) is a phenomenon where persons are less likely to intervene in an emergency situation when others are present than when they are alone.

There have been numerous attempts to explain this effect by psychologists and some of them are outlined here.

Pluralistic ignorance

Imagine this, you are walking down the street and you see some smoke coming out of a building. You are not sure it's smoke, it might be steam. It could be a fire but it might not be. How can you tell? The most obvious thing to do is to look at the reaction of other people. As you look around they seem to be relaxed about it and just walking on. It must be steam you think, so you walk on too. But maybe those other people were also unsure and they walked on because they saw you looking relaxed. Between all of you, and without saying a word, you have negotiated that the situation is not an emergency. This effect is called *pluralistic ignorance*.

In a laboratory study, participants were directed to a room to fill in **questionnaires**. They were either alone or with two other people. While they were in the room steam started to come through

Then there is her family. There can be no closure for the families of murder victims, especially for the Genovese family. The story still surfaces from time to time and still appears in psychology texts like this one. About 40 years after the murder yet another television programme was made. Kitty's brother Bill said *'I was consulted in a project for the History Channel not long ago. See, they're going to do the story anyway, so we may as well cooperate. At least we have some measure of control if we cooperate.'* (Gado, 2005)

Calling the police

Although the residents are always given the blame in the Kitty Genovese story, their perception of the local police contributed to the social climate. At the time of the attack one local resident commented, *'Shortly after moving in I heard screaming on the street several times, called the police and was politely told to mind my own business.'* (Rosenthal, 1964, page 46)

Another resident wrote to the *New York Times* saying, *'Have you ever reported anything to the police? If you did, you would know that you are subjected to insults and abuse from annoyed undutiful police such as "why don't you move out of the area" or "why bother us, this is a bad area" or "you will have a call answered 45 min".'* (Rosenthal, 1964, page 46)

effect

a vent in the wall. The question was how many people would report this. Seventy-five per cent of people left on their own reported the steam but only 38% of people in a group did so (Latané and Darley, 1968).

Diffusion of responsibility

It's such a relief when someone else sorts out an emergency. The more people there are in a group the less chance that it will be you, you hope. **Experimental** studies show that adding people to a group reduces the chance of an individual stepping up to help in an emergency (Darley and Latané, 1968).

In another experiment students were recruited to take part in some discussions via an intercom. Each student had to talk for two minutes, then comment on what the others said, though in fact there was only one real person taking part. The other 'students' were pre-recorded. As the student listened to one of the other voices the person appeared to have an epileptic seizure and started choking before lapsing into silence. If the student believed they were the only person to hear this emergency then 85% tried to help, but if they thought that the other people could also hear it the intervention rate dropped as low as 30% (Darley and Latané, 1968).

The tradition with firing squads is to load all of the guns with blanks except for one but not say which one has the bullet. This allows everyone in the firing squad to believe they did not shoot at the victim. This helps to diffuse their responsibility for the execution.

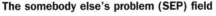

Try this   5.3

Write down some examples of when help is required, for example a beggar on the street, or an earthquake appeal or a fight in a bar. Think about occasions recently when you've thought about intervening. Try and get a long list.

Now put them in a line from those you would definitely intervene and help through to those that you would be unlikely to do anything about. What is the difference between the events at either end of the line? What are the things that would make you more likely to help in those situations that are nearer the 'no-help' end?

Parables

A parable is a story that is told to illustrate a religious, moral or philosophical idea. It is possible to see some psychology studies, such as the **Milgram** core study and the Stanford Prison Simulation, as parables.

The good Samaritan is a famous Christian parable (Luke: 10: 25–37), told by Jesus to illustrate the idea that it is important to show compassion for all people regardless of race. The parable tells of a man attacked, robbed and left for dead at the side of the road. He is ignored by two passers-by, both religious men. A third man, however, stops and helps. He is a Samaritan (i.e. from Samaria) and therefore of a different race from the man who was robbed. He would have less reason to stop than the first two men but his compassion was such that he could not pass by and do nothing. This story produces the term 'good Samaritan' to describe someone who helps a stranger. The charity group 'the Samaritans' in this country provides free support to people contemplating suicide.

The good Samaritan study

Students at a theological college were asked to present a sermon on helping; on their way to the sermon, they passed a man slumped and groaning in a doorway. If the students thought they were late 10% helped, compared with 63% who thought they were early. Some of those who didn't help said they didn't notice the victim (Darley and Batson, 1973).

Stimulus overload

People living in cities are bombarded every day with stimuli and with social interactions. Some days it is just too much. Strangers approach you with clipboards trying to sell you something. Traffic is continuous, noisy and unpredictable, and then there are the thousand text messages that demand your attention. Milgram (1970) suggested that people have stimulus overload and so restrict their attention to the events that they believe are most important. These are likely to be things that are personally relevant or connected to people they know. The lives of strangers will inevitably come way down the list.

The somebody else's problem (SEP) field

In an ironic take on the bystander effect The Hitchhiker's Guide to the Galaxy (by Douglas Adams) describes the somebody else's problem field (SEP field). This fictional technology is a cheaper and more practical alternative to an invisibility field. A SEP field can be created around a bizarre and unbelievable scene so that the unconscious mind of an observer defines it as 'somebody else's problem', and therefore doesn't see it at all.

An example of this was given in Adam's third book Life, the Universe and Everything, when a UFO landed in the middle of a cricket ground during a match, and the crowd didn't notice it. The SEP field requires much less energy than a normal invisibility field and a single flashlight battery can run it for over a hundred years.

The idea of the SEP field has some grounding in real life, in that people may not notice things that don't fit their view of the world: when people look at branded goods they see attractive design and not the sweat shop conditions in which many of them are made.

...Link to the core study...

The moral panic that arose in the 1960s about the alienation of people in cities stimulated a lot of laboratory experiments related to helping behaviour. There will always be questions over how far these studies can be applied to everyday life. A small number of brave researchers took their studies out into the city. The core study by **Piliavin et al.** is one example.

One of the issues to consider as you read the study is the view that is taken of people in the city. In particular they are seen as relatively passive with the most important variable being the number of other people near to them.

Piliavin *et al.*: the core study

Irving M. Piliavin, Judith Rodin and Jane Allyn Piliavin (1969) Good samaritanism: an underground phenomenon? *Journal of Personality and Social Psychology, 13 (4),* 289–299.

See the CORE STUDY CHECKLIST on page xv for details of what you need to know for the exam.

In a nutshell

Context
Following the murder of Kitty Genovese (see previous spread) psychologists have conducted numerous studies to investigate **bystander behaviour**. Past research has been mainly conducted in **laboratory experiments**.

Aims
To investigate, in a natural setting, factors that may influence bystander behaviour:

1 Type of victim (drunk or ill).
2 Race of victim (black or white).
3 Impact of **modelling**.
4 Group size.

Participants
A **field experiment** was staged on the New York subway during the middle of the day (11am to 3pm). The 4,450 participants were the passengers on the train. **Confederates** played the role of victim and **models** (a 'model' is a person's whose behaviour is imitated).

Procedure
There were four teams of students (aged 24–35), each team consisting of a male victim, male model and two female observers to record activity. In total there were 103 trials. A single trial was one ride on the express subway lasting 7½ minutes (from one stop to the next).

On each trial the team boarded a subway train. The observers sat outside the critical area, the victim stood in the critical area and the model varied his position. After 70 seconds the victim staged a collapse and remained on the floor until help was forthcoming or until the train stopped at the next station.

There were four **independent variables**:

1 Victim drunk or ill (carrying a cane).
2 Victim black or white.
3 Model intervened or not.
4 Group size.

The **dependent variables** were:

1 Time taken for first passenger to help.
2 Total number of passengers who helped.

Key term: bystander behaviour

Bystander behaviour refers to how bystanders behave in emergency situations, i.e. when someone else requires help because of an accident. Research (mainly conducted in laboratories) has indicated that people are actually less willing to help if there are other bystanders and more willing to help if they are the only bystander. This has led to the term 'bystander apathy', describing the reduced helpfulness of bystanders in large groups. Various explanations for this, including **diffusion of responsibility** *are outlined on the previous spread.*

Results
The frequency of helping was considerably higher than found in laboratory experiments. The main findings were:

- An apparently ill person is more likely to receive help than one who appears drunk (95% versus 50%), and help is forthcoming more quickly.
- The race of the victim has little effect except when the victim is drunk and then they are more likely to be helped by someone of the same race.
- The model intervening early (after 70 seconds) had slightly more effect than the late model (at 150 seconds). There was only a small amount of data on this as most victims were helped before a model could step in.
- The 'diffusion of responsibility' effect was not found in this situation. Helping was greater in seven-person groups than in three-person groups.
- The longer the emergency continued without help being forthcoming, the more likely that someone will leave the critical area.
- Participants' comments were recorded, for example *'I never saw this kind of thing before'.*

Discussion
The results can be explained in terms of a cost–reward model:

- (1) An emergency situation leads to (2) heightened arousal, (3) people wish to reduce this arousal, which can be achieved by helping or not helping.
- A person will decide to help if the rewards outweigh the costs of both helping and not helping.
- For example, the cost of helping may be time, the cost of not helping may be disapproval, the reward of helping may be a small amount of praise.
- This study indicated that bystander behaviour is a more complex process than suggested by the diffusion of responsibility model, which was based on only one factor.

Qs 5.10

1 Outline the real-life incident that formed the basis for this area of research.
2 State **two** alternate hypotheses for this study.
3 Describe the participants in this study.
4 Was the sample a random, self-selected or opportunity sample? Explain your answer.
5 Outline **one** weakness of the sample in the context of this study.
6 Why was a subway train a good place to conduct the experiment?
7 Which of the four independent variables varied naturally?

8 Identify **two** ethical issues raised in this study.
9 The victim in each of the four teams, was dressed identically. How did this control one extraneous variable?
10 Name **two** other controls that were used.
11 Outline the findings related to the hypotheses you wrote in question 2.
12 Both quantitative and qualitative data were collected. Give **one** example of each.
13 Outline **one** strength of qualitative data in this study.
14 State **one** conclusion that can be drawn from this study.

The detailed version

Context and aims

Psychologists have conducted many studies in order to find explanations for bystander behaviour. Recent findings by Darley and Latané (1968) suggest that the presence of more people by no means guarantees more help. They have explained this in terms of *diffusion of responsibility* (see previous spread).

Much of this previous research has been conducted in laboratories which is not a problem if some research is also conducted in the field to provide confirmation from a more natural setting.

Aims

The main aims of this study are outlined in points 1 and 2.

1   *To see if type of victim (drunk or ill) is* **significant**. People who are seen as partly responsible for their plight receive less help (Schopler and Matthews, 1965). In addition, bystanders might be reluctant to help a drunk because he/she may behave embarrassingly and/or become violent.

2   *To see if race of victim (black or white) is significant*. Research suggests that people would be more likely to help someone of their own race.

3   *To consider the impact of modelling*. Past research (Bryan and Test, 1967) shows that people are more likely to help in an emergency situation if they have seen someone else displaying the behaviour.

4   *To consider the effect of group size*. Darley and Latané (1968) found that increased group size led to decreases in frequency of responding and an increase in latency (how long it takes to offer help).

Qs 5.11

1   Outline Darley and Latané's research and the explanation they offered for bystander behaviour (i.e. diffusion of responsibility).

2   Describe the role of the victim and the role of the model in this study.

3   Outline how observation was used to collect data in this study.

4   Identify **two** difficulties that the observers may have encountered when recording data.

5   The observers also used self-report methods. Explain what they did.

6   Outline **one** weakness of using self-report techniques in this study.

Method

Participants

The participants were about 4,450 American people who were travelling on the 8th Avenue express subway train in New York City weekdays between 11am and 3pm over a two-month period in 1968. There were slightly more white people than blacks (55% versus 45%). On average there were 43 people in a compartment on any one trial and, on average, 8.5 people in the 'critical area' (see diagram below).

Procedure

On each trial, a team of four General Studies students boarded the train separately. There were four different teams and in each team there were four members. Two girls acted as observers and took seats outside the critical area. The male model and victim remained standing. After approximately 70 seconds the victim staggered forward and collapsed, and remained lying on his back staring at the ceiling until receiving help. The express train does not stop for 7½ minutes between 59th and 125th Street, the start and stopping points for this study. If no help was forthcoming when the train stopped the model helped the victim to his feet.

Victim

The four victims (one in each team) were aged 26–35; one was black. All were dressed identically. Each victim participated in both cane and drunk trials.

On 38 trials the victim was drunk and on 65 trials the victim was sober.

*   *'Drunk' condition*: victim smelled of alcohol and carried a bottle in a brown paper bag (as they do in New York).
*   *Cane condition*: victim appeared sober and had a black cane.

Model

Four white males aged between 24 and 29 played the models, to see if a 'model' (someone offering help) affected the behaviour of other passengers.

There were three possibilities:

*   *No model*: the model didn't help at all.
*   *Early model*: helped 70 seconds after the victim collapsed.
*   *Late model*: helped after 150 seconds.

On some trials the model was in the critical area and on some trials in the adjacent area.

Measures

On each trial one observer noted:

*   Race, sex and location of every person seated or standing in the critical area.
*   Total number of persons in the carriage.
*   Total number who helped the victim.
*   Race, sex and location of every helper.

The second observer noted:

*   Race, sex and location of every person in the adjacent area.
*   Time when help was first offered.

Both observers noted any comments made by nearby passengers and also tried to elicit comments from a passenger sitting next to them.

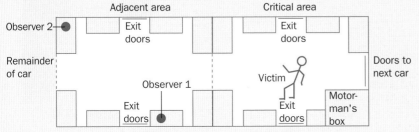

Above left, the layout of subway carriage showing the critical area and position of the victim. Above right, a New York subway train.

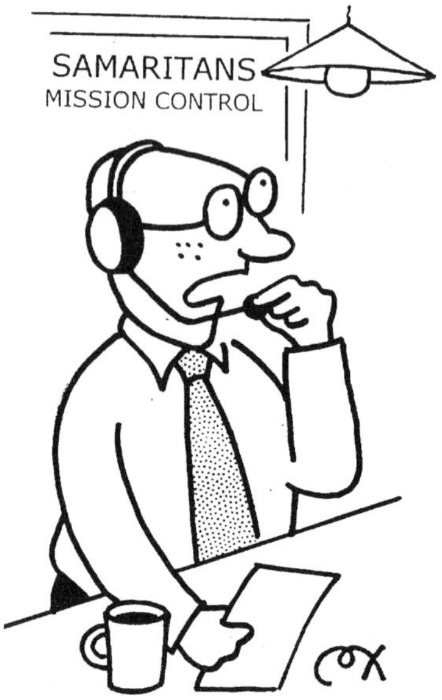

"Prepare to move! There's a man lying in the high street and one person's already passed by..."

www.CartoonStock.com

Results

Overall frequency of helping

Piliavin *et al.* first of all noted that the frequency of helping was impressive compared with previous **laboratory experiments**. On 81 of the 103 trials help was forthcoming within 70 seconds and therefore there was not time for the model to be involved on these trials.

Drunk versus cane condition

In total there were 103 trials – in 65 there was a cane victim and in 38 trials there was a drunk victim.

- The cane victim received spontaneous help 95% of the time (62/65 trials). In three trials the **model** stepped in after 70 seconds, Therefore help was no longer 'spontaneous'.
- The drunk victim was spontaneously helped 50% of the time (19/38 trials).

A further analysis was made of the time taken for help to be offered. The graph below shows that the speed of offering help was much slower in the drunk condition: 17% of victims in the drunk condition were helped within 70 seconds, 87% of the cane victims were helped within the same time frame.

The **median** latency (i.e. delay) for cane trials (no model condition only) was 5 seconds whereas it was 109 seconds for drunk trials.

Graph showing time taken for help to be offered

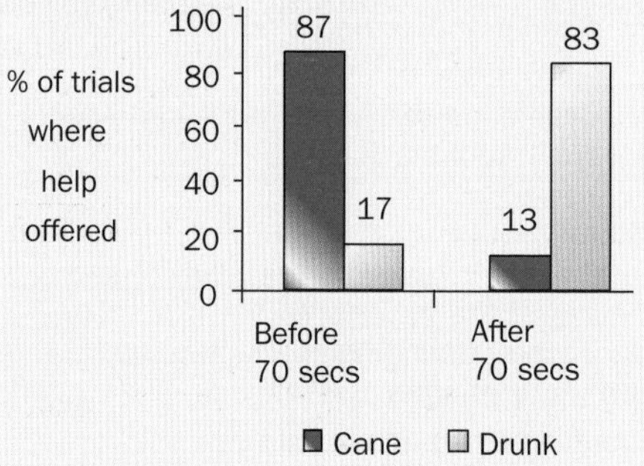

Race of victim

Considering the 81 spontaneous helpers it was found that certain trends emerged, though none of these trends were **significant**.

- White bystanders were slightly more helpful – 64% of the spontaneous helpers were white (in total 55% of the helpers were white so we would expect more white people to help).
- Black victims received help less quickly than white victims.
- In the drunk condition there was a slight '*same race effect*' – whites were slightly more likely to help whites than to help blacks. This may be because, in the drunk condition, people are generally less willing to help. However, Piliavin *et al.* suggest that when a white person is faced with a white drunk they may feel increased empathy and trust for their own race and therefore overcome their reluctance.

Modelling

The data on the impact of **modelling** was difficult to analyse because, in most cases, help was forthcoming within the first 70 seconds. Therefore the model had no time to act.

The model was involved in 19 trials in total, 16 of which were drunk trials (in all but three of the cane trials help was offered in under 70 seconds).

- In all early trials (model helps after 70 seconds), the model triggered help from a passenger.
- In four of the late trials (model helps after 150 seconds) no help was offered. Total number of late trials was seven.

A tentative conclusion could be drawn that, by the time 150 seconds has elapsed, anyone who was going to help would have helped!

Try this 5.4

Try **role-playing** this experiment. Arrange your classroom to look like the subway carriage. Make a list of all the different conditions and have a go trying them out while the observers keep a record of all data. You could even film it and place on YouTube.

Design a study to test the bystander effect – ethically!

One possibility is to replicate the 'smoke filled room' study by Latané and Darley (1968).

You can read about this study and watch a YouTube clip of a replication at http://www.weirduniverse.net/blog/permalink/the_smoke_filled_room

Biographical notes

***Irving and Jane Piliavin** started as teachers and studied to be social psychologists, both ending as professors of sociology at the University of Wisconsin at Madison. Jane tells the story of how the Samaritan study came about: '[Irv] was working with Bibb Latané on a post-doc designed to give people in other fields (his is social work) the opportunity to retrain. He was riding on the subway himself … when a drunk rolled off his seat and fell to the floor. Nobody did anything for a long time (until he did). By the time he got [home] a few hours later he had designed the study' (personal communication).*

Jane continues as an Emeritus professor. Irving died in 2009. He was an athlete all his life and was still taking tennis lessons up until a few weeks before he died aged 81, determined to improve.

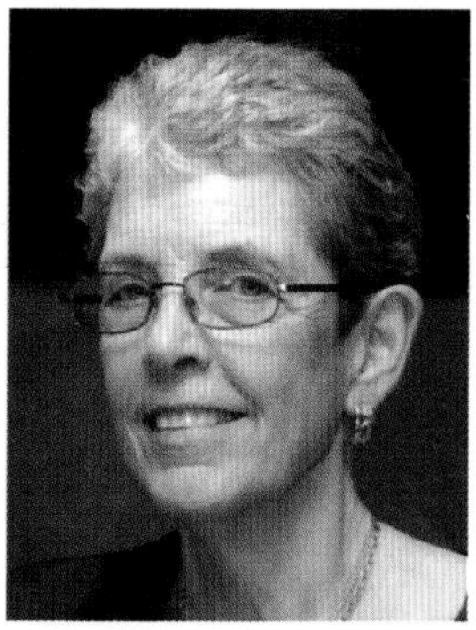

Jane Piliavin

Group size

Darley and Latané found that helpfulness decreased as group size increased, in a study where bystanders could not see each other nor could they see the 'victim'. In another study by Latané and Rodin (1969) the reduced helpfulness was found even when bystanders were face-to-face but the victim was heard but not seen. In the Piliavin *et al.* study bystanders were face-to-face with other bystanders and with the victim. Would reduced helpfulness still be found?

In order to analyse the relationship between helping and group size Piliavin *et al.* looked at only the no model conditions (N=81) and divided the trials into three groups according to the number of male bystanders in the critical area: (1) 1–3 males, (2) 4–6 males, (3) 7+ males.

For each group the **mean** response time for that group was calculated. This data showed that as group size increased, the response time also increased – which was the opposite of the earlier findings.

Further analysis

The problem is that these groups cannot really be compared because as group size increases it means that the *likelihood* of help also increases.

Therefore a second analysis was performed by using the data on no model, cane trials with white victims only. This time hypothetical data was calculated by combining mean response times from different sized groups. This data is shown in the graph on the right together with the data from the actual groups. It shows that the actual groups did respond faster than would be predicted from hypothetical groups but continues to support the finding that helping increased as a function of group size.

Other results

Help was not just given by one person, but often by several people. On 60% of the 81 no model trials when the victim was given help, the help was given by two or more helpers.

Men were more helpful. Considering the 81 first helpers, 90% were males despite the fact that only 60%, on average, of people in the critical area were males.

Some people displayed the reverse behaviour. On 21 out of the full 103 trials (with and without a model) 34 people left the critical area after the victim collapsed.

Comments from bystanders

More comments were obtained in the drunk condition than in the cane condition. Similarly most of the comments were made on the trials where no help was given within the first 70 seconds. Many women made comments such as *'It's for men to help him'* or *'You feel so bad when you don't know what to do'* (page 295).

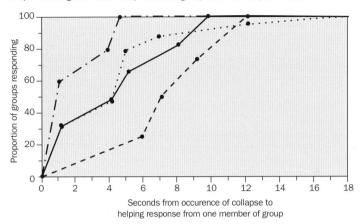

Graph showing the relationship between group size and response time.

Seconds from occurence of collapse to helping response from one member of group

Legend
- – – • Hypothetical 3–person groups
- —— Natural 3–person groups
- · · · · Hypothetical 7–person groups
- — · — Natural 7–person groups

 **Qs 5.12**

1 Why is it important to use percentages rather than the raw data?

2 Do you think it matters that there were more cane than drunk trials? Why or why not?

3 Outline **two** findings related to the drunk/can condition.

4 How do Piliavin *et al.* explain the fact that whites were slightly less willing to help the black victims who were 'drunk' as compared to black victims with canes?

5 Why do you think that the early model elicited more help than the later model?

6 Does this study support the 'diffusion of responsibility' hypothesis? Why or why not?

Try this **5.5**

Try to analyse the data yourself from the table below. What conclusion would you draw about the drunk/cane condition from the spontaneous data alone?

	White victims		Black victims		Total victims	
	Cane	Drunk	Cane	Drunk	Cane	Drunk
Spontaneous (no model)	54/54 100%	11/11 100%	8/8 100%	8/11 73%	62/62 100%	19/22 86%
Trials with a model	3/3 100%	10/13 77%	0/0	2/3 67%	3/3 100%	12/16 75%
Total number of trials	57/57 100%	21/24 88%	8/8 100%	10/14 71%	65/65 100%	31/38 89%

Things you could do ...

Read the original article by Piliavin *et al.* at http://www.garysturt.free-online.co.uk/pil.htm

Read other accounts of bystander research:

'Bystander Phenomenon revisited' for some recent research http://bps-research-digest.blogspot.com/2005/12/bystander-phenomenon-revisited.html

Darley and Latané's book *The Unresponsive Bystander: Why Doesn't He Help?*

Watch a video Excellent discussion of the Bystander effect: http://www.youtube.com/watch?v=z4S1LLrSzVE&feature=related

Discussion

This study explains helping behaviour in situations where escape is not possible and where bystanders are face-to-face with their victims.

The conclusions of this study are summarised in the table on the right.

Piliavin *et al.*'s model for emergency situations

On the basis of the results from this study Piliavin *et al.* proposed a **model** to explain people's response to emergency situations.

This model is summarised below and displayed in the diagram on the right.

- **Emergency situation:** The observation of an emergency situation creates a sense of emotional arousal in the bystander. This 'emotion' will be differently interpreted in different situations. For example, it may be interpreted as fear or sympathy (Schachter, 1964).
- **Heightened arousal:** The arousal is heightened (a) the more one empathises with the victim, (b) the closer one is to the emergency, (c) the longer the emergency continues.
- **Arousal reduction:** The arousal can be reduced by (a) helping directly, (b) getting help, (c) leaving the scene, (d) rejecting the victim as undeserving of help (Lerner and Simmons, 1966).
- **Cost–reward matrix:** The response that is chosen will be a function of the cost–reward matrix outlined on the far right.

Note that this model suggests that helping is motivated by a selfish desire to rid oneself of an unpleasant emotional state rather than being a positive **altruistic** model of helping.

This model can be used to explain the conclusions from the study above right.

Conclusions	Interpretation of each conclusion based on the cost–reward matrix (in coloured diagram below)	
	Costs of helping	**Costs of not helping**
1 A person who is ill is more likely to be given aid than one who appears drunk.	Drunk: high (greater disgust).	Drunk: low (less disapproval because victim to blame for own plight).
2 Men are more likely to help than women.	Women: high (danger).	Women: low (not a woman's role).
3 Some tendency for same-race helping, especially in the drunk condition.	Opposite race: high (more fear if different race).	Same race: higher (disapproval for not helping your own).
4 The amount of help did not decrease as group size increased (as predicted by the **diffusion of responsibility**). If anything the effect was in the opposite direction.	Cane trials: low.	Cane trials: high (more self-blame)
	Diffusion of responsibility increases as costs of helping increase and costs of not helping decrease.	
5 The longer the emergency:		
(a) The less impact the model had on observers.	(a) Arousal already reduced by another means therefore help less likely.	
(b) The more likely it was that individuals left the immediate vicinity.	(b) As arousal increases, there is more need to reduce it and leaving the area is one way to do this.	
(c) The more passengers/participants made spontaneous comments.	(c) Reduces self-blame by discussing reason for not helping.	

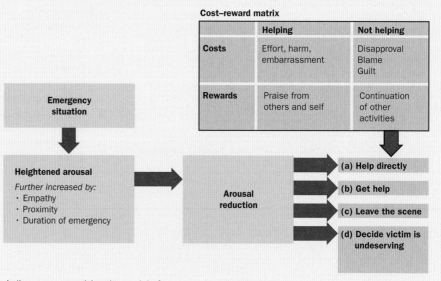

A diagram summarising the model of response to emergency situations proposed by Piliavin et al.

...Links to core studies...

This study was looking for imitative responses of the people on the train so there is a link to the work of **Bandura *et al.*** The study also links to the studies of **Griffiths**, **Milgram** and **Reicher and Haslam** in that it examines human behaviour in real life situations. Because of this the measures are not as precise as you would get in a controlled laboratory study but they capture the richness of human behaviour.

Qs 5.13

1 One interesting finding showed that people were more likely to move from critical area in the drunk condition than the cane condition. Use the cost–reward model to explain why this happened.

2 Use the cost–reward matrix to try to explain the behaviour of one bystander during the Kitty Genovese murder.

3 To what extent are features of this experiment unique and not the same as other helping situations in previous research studies?

4 What overall conclusion would you draw, based on this study, about bystander behaviour. Provide evidence for your conclusion.

5 Piliavin *et al.* suggest that helping is actually a selfish behaviour. Do you agree? Explain your answer.

Evaluating the study by Piliavin *et al.*

The research method
This study was a field experiment.

What are the strengths and limitations of this research method in the context of this study?

One of the research techniques that was used was observation.

What are the strengths and limitations of this research technique in the context of this study?

The self-report technique was also used.

What are the strengths and limitations of this research technique in the context of this study?

The sample
The sample was large and contained a varied mix of participants, but they were all urban.

In what way would the characteristics of the sample affect the results?

Ethics
What ethical issues should have concerned the researchers in this study, and how might they have dealt with these issues?

Reliability
There were two observers involved in this study who observed different things. (This means that inter-rater reliability cannot be assessed.)

How confident can we be about the reliability of their observations? What factors might affect reliability of these measurements.

Validity
Many aspects of the environment were controlled, such as the gender of the victim and the model.

Were there other extraneous variables that might have affected the validity of this study?

Ecological validity
To what extent can we make generalisations about human behaviour on the basis of this study?

Qualitative or quantitative?
Both qualitative and quantitative data was collected in this study.

Give examples of each kind of data from the study.

What are the strengths and limitations of producing this kind of data in the context of this study?

Applications/usefulness
How valuable was this study?

What next?
*Describe **one** change to this study, and say how you think this might affect the outcome.*

> *There are no simple answers.*
> *Evaluating a study requires you to think.*
> *We have provided some pointers here, linked to the **RESEARCH METHODS** and **KEY ISSUES** covered in Chapter 1 (Psychological investigations) and Chapter 7 (Key Issues).*
> *You can read suggested answers on our website www.psypress.com/cw/banyard.*

Producing effective evaluation
When you produce your own answers to the issues on the left there are two things to ensure:
1 Contextualisation
2 Elaboration

The key to **CONTEXTUALISATION** is to ensure that your answer includes some information about this particular study. For example:

> *Question:*
> With reference to the study by Piliavin *et al.*, suggest **one** weakness of a field experiment. **[2]**
>
> *Answer:*
> **STATE:** One strength of a field experiment is that it is conducted in a more natural environment than a laboratory experiment and therefore the results may have greater ecological validity.
> **CONTEXT:** In the Piliavin *et al.* study the research was conducted in a New York subway when people did not know they were being studied so they behaved more naturally than they might in a laboratory experiment.

The key to **ELABORATION** is the three-point rule (see page xii). However, sometimes context is there from the start, so two comments are required. For example:

> *Question:*
> With reference to the study by Piliavin *et al.*, explain why the sample was selected for this study. **[3]**
>
> *Answer:*
> **STATE:** The sample chosen in this study was an opportunity sample of people on the New York subway.
> **COMMENT:** The reason for choosing this sample is that it offered a convenient way to test people's responses to a face-to-face emergency situation.
> **COMMENT:** It also meant that Piliavin *et al.* could study bystander behaviour in a more natural situation because people thought it was really happening.

The social approach
On pages 146–147 and 224–225 we have discussed the **social approach**.

The study by Piliavin *et al.* concerns helping behaviour.
- In what way is this an example of the social approach?
- Discuss the strengths and weaknesses of the social approach using examples from the Piliavin *et al.* study.

Deciding to help

The main message from early studies on bystanders was that people are reluctant to help in emergencies but is this really the case?

James Bulger

The event in the UK that provoked a similar moral panic to the murder of Kitty Genovese (see page 168) was the murder of two-and-a-half-year-old James Bulger in 1993. The boy was abducted from his mother in a shopping centre by two 10-year-old boys. The three boys walked around Liverpool for over two hours before James was tortured and murdered next to a railway line. The haunting image of the time (see picture below) was from CCTV cameras in the shopping centre that captured the moment of abduction.

In a strange coincidence with the Genovese murder, 38 witnesses appeared at the trial of the two 10 year olds. These people had seen or, in some cases, had contact with the boys during their journey across the city. None of them had intervened decisively enough to save the toddler despite the fact that there were signs that something was wrong (for example an injury to the child's head and apparent distress).

Were these witnesses an example of the bystander effect? Such an interpretation is probably neither helpful nor accurate. Another view (for example Levine, 1999) suggests the witnesses' behaviour can be seen in terms of the sense they made of an ambiguous situation and the social categories they used to interpret it. In particular they assumed the boys were brothers and this category of 'family' prohibited any intervention. We don't interfere in 'domestics' and we don't tell other people how to treat their children.

The following witness quotes come from the trial (cited in Levine, 1999): *'I saw a little boy apparently two and a half to three years of age ... He was holding, it looked to be a teenager's hand, which I presumed was his older brother.'*

One witness reported this exchange with one of the boys, *'"I'm fed up of having my little brother." He says, "It's always the same from school" and he said, "I'm going to tell me mum, I'm not going to have him no more."'*

Group membership and bystanders

The studies that followed the Kitty Genovese attack dealt with bystanders as if they were isolated individuals. Recent research has looked at the social identity of bystanders and the groups they have allegiance to. For example, Dovidio *et al.* (1997) found evidence that people were more likely to help members of their own social group (the 'ingroup'). In their study, students were asked to volunteer to help a student distribute **questionnaires** for their research project. They were more likely to offer help if they thought the student was an ingroup member. This work connects to the **Reicher and Haslam** study concerning group behaviour.

Levine *et al.* (2002) reworked one of the early bystander studies (the 'good Samaritan' **experiment** on page 169) and looked at the effect of group identity. They advertised for fans of Premier League football teams to take part in a study. Some Manchester United fans were selected and put together to create a sense of group identity. The fans were directed as a group across the college campus to another room. On the way they witnessed a runner having an accident where he fell over and appeared to hurt himself. In one condition he was wearing neutral clothes and in the other two conditions he wore either a Manchester United shirt (their own team) or a Liverpool (despised rivals) shirt. The injured runner was usually helped when he wore a Manchester United shirt, but he was rarely helped when he wore the other shirts.

Football fans might look like muppets but they'll help their fellow fans.

The London bombs, July 2005

What happens in a real emergency? Do people help or do they look the other way? The London bomb attack produced numerous cases of personal heroism that challenge the view of the uncaring city. If you look, for example, at the pictures of the No. 30 bus that was bombed you can see almost as many people going to help as there are running away. We have remarkable first-hand footage of the events taken by people on their camera phones. In fact the news made the internet blog sites before it was broken on the BBC, which is a new way that people can communicate and help each other.

What follows are some accounts of people involved in the London bombs. Although we selected the quotes we have not tried to put our own explanation on the events. We think they show the remarkable variation of human behaviour and the complexity of human experience.

A woman who was seriously injured in one of the trains commented, *'There was nobody around. There were people talking across from me – people trying to calm each other – but I felt that my experience was quite lonely. It feels like there were lots of lonely individuals in one setting.'*

A man on one of the other trains describes the horror in the carriage, then says, *'Your humanity strikes in, you think is there anyone you can save here or take out with me? A right hand came out and held onto my leg and I tried to see where they were and you couldn't see anything. It was just a mass of bodies and I thought instinctively I've got to get that person out.'*

A former firefighter was widely pictured shepherding a bomb victim to safety as she clutched a surgical mask to her burnt face. He was hailed a hero in the press but he commented, *'I was filled with a certain level of guilt that I was made out to be a hero – the real heroes were the people who lost their lives.'*

A woman on the Piccadilly line train said *'... people so often comment on the arrogance of Londoners and how unfriendly we are – yesterday there was none of that. We all rallied together helping one another get through it – holding hands, sharing water, calming those who were panicked.'*

(BBC, 2005; Yahoo news, 2005)

The evidence seems to show that people will help each other even in extreme situations especially if they feel connected to each other.

Multiple choice questions

1 Which of the following was an IV that was *not* manipulated by the experimenters?
   a Race of victim.   b Drunk or not.
   c Group size.   d Model present.

2 The participants were:
   a Psychology students.
   b General studies students.
   c Passengers on the subway.
   d Both b and c.

3 The victims were:
   a All male and white.
   b All male, black and white.
   c All white, some men and some women.
   d Black and white, men and women.

4 The model intervened:
   a 70 secs after the victim collapsed.
   b 70 secs after the train left the station.
   c 100 secs after the victim collapsed.
   d Both a and c.

5 Which of the following is a DV in this experiment?
   a Willingness to help.
   b Race of helper.
   c Time taken to offer help.
   d All of the above.

6 Passengers were more willing to help:
   a Women.
   b Drunks.
   c Victims with a cane.
   d Black victims.

7 Passengers in the critical area who did not help dealt with their arousal by:
   a Asking someone to help the victim.
   b Turning away from the victim.
   c Making a comment about why they weren't helping.
   d Leaving the critical area.

8 The diffusion of responsibility effect predicts that:
   a Helping increases when group size increases.
   b Helping decreases when group size increases.
   c Helping decreases when group size decreases.
   d Group size has no effect on rates of helping.

9 The results of this study showed that the diffusion of responsibility effect:
   a Occurred.
   b Didn't occur.
   c Could not be measured.
   d The study did not consider this effect.

10 Piliavin *et al.* proposed that the first thing that happens in an emergency situation is:
   a Rewards.
   b Costs.
   c Arousal.
   d Both a and b.

Answers are on page 247.

> *There are three kinds of question that can be asked about the Piliavin* et al. *study, as represented here by sections A, B and C.*
>
> *See page x for further notes on the exam paper and styles of question.*

Exam-style questions

Section A questions

1 Previous psychological research found that people didn't help in emergency situations due to diffusion of responsibility:
   (a) What is meant by the term 'diffusion of responsibility'? [2]
   (b) Explain why this effect was not observed in the study by Piliavin *et al.* [2]

2 Piliavin *et al.* proposed a model of response to emergencies on the basis of the results from their study.
   (a) Identify the **two** factors that influence a person's decision to help or not. [2]
   (b) Use these two factors to explain one of the results from the study. [2]

3 In the study by Piliavin *et al.*, describe what happened on each trial. [4]

4 (a) Describe **one** ethical issue that was a problem in the study by Pilialvin *et al.* [2]
   (b) Describe how Piliavin *et al.* might have dealt with this ethical issue. [2]

5 Piliavin *et al.* designed a study where some of the researchers acted as 'models'.
   (a) Identify **two** of the model conditions. [2]
   (b) Outline **one** conclusion that was drawn from these. [2]

6 Piliavin *et al.* suggested that helping behaviour can be explained using an arousal/cost–reward model. Using this model suggest **two** ways of reducing arousal in the subway emergency. [4]

7 Outline **two** practical problems that occurred in conducting the subway Samaritan study by Piliavin *et al.* [4]

8 In the Piliavin *et al.* study outline **one** quantitative measure recorded by the observers and **one** qualitative measure. [4]

9 Identify the **four** independent variables in study by Piliavin *et al.* [4]

10 In the study by Piliavin *et al.* the victims were dressed identically as a control. Explain how **one** other control was used in this study. [4]

Section B questions

Answer the following questions with reference to the Piliavin *et al.* study:

(a) Briefly outline the previous research or event that was the stimulus for this study. [2]

(b) Describe **two** ethical issues raised by this study. [6]

(c) Give **two** strengths of the field experiment method as used in this study. [6]

(d) Give **two** weaknesses of the field experiment method as used in this study. [6]

(e) Outline the procedures of this study. [8]

(f) Suggest how this study could be improved. Give reasons for your answer. [8]

Section C questions

(a) Outline **one** assumption of the social approach. [2]

(b) Describe how the social approach could explain helping behaviour. [4]

(c) Describe **one** similarity and **one** difference between the Piliavin *et al.* study and any other core studies that take the social approach. [6]

(d) Discuss strengths and weaknesses of the social approach using examples from any core studies that take this approach. [12]

Exam-style questions

The example exam-style questions here are set out like the exam but in Section A of the exam there will be only one question on each of the three social core studies, i.e. three social questions, each worth 4 marks in total.

Section A type questions

1   In Milgram's study the experimenter encouraged participants to continue giving electric shocks using a series of 'prods'.
    (a) Outline **two** of the 'prods' that were used. [2]
    (b) Describe **one** way that the results of Milgram's study can be applied to everyday life. [2]

Stig's answer

(a) He told them 'The experiment demands that you continue'. And also 'You have no other choice'.

(b) You could use this to help training soldiers to obey officers especially in the heat of battle when it is important to obey. This study shows that small steps lead people to obey.

Chardonnay's answer

(a) The participants were encouraged to continue by certain statements given by the experimenter, such as 'Go on'.

(b) You could use the findings to help train policemen in how to effectively tell people what to do for their own safety.

Teacher's comments

Stig, in part (a) you have identified two prods, the second one is not exactly right but is close enough for full marks. Your answer in part (b) identifies a real-life situation and also explains how the insights from this study could be used ('small steps' is the way to get people to obey).

Chardonnay, you have identified one of the prods but not in enough detail to gain any credit – looks like you might have just been guessing. In part (b), you identify an appropriate everyday situation but have not made the all-important link to the study – in what way can Milgram's results be used in this situation?

Stig (2+2 out of 4 marks) Chardonnay (0+1 out of 4 marks)

2   In Milgram's study on obedience 40 participants took part.
    (a) Outline how Milgram obtained this sample. [2]
    (b) Outline **one** strength of using this method to obtain a sample for a study. [2]

Stig's answer

(a) The participants answered an ad that was placed in a newspaper.

(b) One strength of this is you get people who are very willing.

Chardonnay's answer

(a) The participants were recruited by volunteering because they read an advertisement in the newspaper and volunteered to take part.

(b) This is a good way to get participants because you can get access to a wide range of different people so you get a more varied sample than, for example, an opportunity sample.

Teacher's comments

Stig, a bit more detail required for two marks in part (a), for example, you might have included something about the contents of the advert. Again, in part (b) you needed to slightly expand your point, perhaps by saying that volunteers are more likely to engage with the experiment.

Chardonnay, part (a) is fine as you have got advert + volunteering; so 2 marks here. In part (b) you make a nice comparison with a standard opportunity sample. This is always a useful way of adding detail to a question on strengths or weaknesss – make a comparison with an alternative method.

Stig (1+1 out of 4 marks) Chardonnay (2+2 out of 4 marks)

3   In the BBC Prison Study by Reicher and Haslam, participants were given the task of being a prisoner or guard. Describe **two** behaviours that showed the participants were sufficiently engaged with their task. [4]

Stig's answer

One behaviour was that they seemed very involved in what they were doing and got quite upset with the other group (prisoners or guards).
Another behaviour was that they were being filmed so they had to take it seriously.

Chardonnay's answer

The prisoners were clearly unhappy and minded being deprived of things like cigarettes and being locked in their cells. If they weren't really involved they wouldn't have minded so much.
The guards' conversations showed how seriously they took their roles because they discussed it all the time.

Teacher's comments

I think you're guessing here Stig. Your first answer makes some sense but you need to provide evidence to support what you are saying to get the full two marks (what evidence is there that they got upset?). Your second answer isn't really an answer to this question – just because we know they were being filmed that doesn't mean they would have to be engaged with the task.

Chardonnay's answer clearly show she's read the article because she provides answers along the lines as those given in the report, and provides sufficient detail for full marks.

Stig (1+0 out of 4 marks) Chardonnay (2+2 out of 4 marks)

4   Reicher and Haslam sought to explain how inequality in groups may lead to tyranny.

(a) Explain what is meant by 'tyranny'. [2]

(b) Outline the explanation they provided at the end of their study about how tyranny becomes possible. [2]

Stig's answer

(a) Tyranny is when there is an unequal social system and this means one group has power over another group.

(b) Reicher and Haslam suggested that tyranny becomes possible when groups are failing. The members are then willing to abandon their preferred norms and values in preference for establishing a viable social order.

Chardonnay's answer

(a) Tyranny is like having power over some other people.

(b) The explanation given at the end of the article was that groups aren't necessarily anti-social and toxic, nor does group membership mean that people automatically accept roles.

Teacher's comments

This time it is Stig who knows his stuff. He has given an excellent definition of tyranny (taken from the article) and also provides a very clear conclusion about the factors that create tyranny. Well done.

Chardonnay's definition is a bit thin. She deserves one mark for mentioning power but that's about it. Her answer to part (b) shows her familiarity with the study but she hasn't really answered the question. She has described some of the conclusions but not addressed the issue of the factors that lead to tyranny, so no marks even though it shows knowledge of the study.

Stig (2+2 out of 4 marks) Chardonnay (1+0 out of 4 marks)

5   The study by Piliavin *et al.* on subway Samaritans could be described as a field study. Describe **one** strength and **one** weakness of conducting field studies in the context of this study. [4]

Stig's answer

One strength of doing a field study is it is a more natural environment and this was a natural environment.

One weakness is that you can't ask for informed consent.

Chardonnay's answer

Strength of a field study: this study looked at helping behaviour in a natural environment where people might have to help someone.

Weakness: you can't control variables as clearly so it is more difficult to be sure that the DV was changed due to the IV, e.g. in this study that helping was due to crowd size.

Teacher's comments

Both your points are true, Stig, but you have forgotten to relate them to the Piliavin study (contextualisation). Don't forget to read the question carefully to make sure you haven't left anything out.

Chardonnay, you have successfully described both a strength and a weakness and linked them to the Piliavin study. Well done.

Stig (1+1 out of 4 marks) Chardonnay (2+2 out of 4 marks)

6   Piliavin, Rodin and Piliavin conducted a study on subway Samaritans.

(a) Identify **two** of the independent variables in this study. [2]

(b) Describe the effects of **one** of these variables on the behaviour of people in the study. [2]

Stig's answer

(a) Race of the victim and whether he was drunk or had a cane.

(b) They didn't find much effect for race.

Chardonnay's answer

(a) One condition was whether the victim was drunk and the other condition was whether he was ill (holding a cane).

(b) They found that people on the subway were less willing to offer help to a drunk victim than one holding a cane, and if they did offer help they were much slower.

Teacher's comments

Yep, spot on for part (a), Stig. The answer to part (b) needs more information to get the two marks.

Hmmm, Chardonnay. This is a common mistake. Whether the victim was drunk or ill is just one variable, i.e. the 'type of victim' (though two conditions).

Nice detail in part (b) referring to frequency and latency of helping.

Stig (2+1 out of 4 marks) Chardonnay (1+2 out of 4 marks)

Exam-style questions

The example exam-style question here is set out as in Section B of the exam. However, there is no guarantee, in Section B, of a question related to one of the core studies from the social approach.

Section B type questions

7 (a) Describe the aim of the study by Piliavin *et al.* [2]
  (b) Describe how data was collected in the study by Piliavin *et al.* [6]
  (c) Give **one** strength and **one** weakness of the method used to collect data in the study by Piliavin *et al.* [6]
  (d) Explain how the reliability of these measurements could be assessed. [6]
  (e) Outline the findings of the study by Piliavin *et al.* [8]
  (f) Suggest **two** changes to the study by Piliavin *et al.* and outline how these changes might affect the results. [8]

Total [36]

Chardonnay's answer

(a) The aim of the study was to see whether or not people will be helpful.

(b) The data was collected when a group of four students got on a New York subway train. One of them played the 'victim' (collapsed) and another the 'model' (the person who went to help the victim if no-one else did). The other two were females and they were the observers. 70 seconds into the journey, the victim would collapse and lie on the floor until one of the passengers came to help them. If a passenger didn't help them, the model would step in either 70 seconds or 150 seconds after the collapse. The observers noted down things like how long it took before someone helped.

(c) One strength of the method was that it was standardised and the victim always wore the same clothes and always travelled on the same subway line and always collapsed at exactly the same time and so on. This means it was highly controlled and so we can be more certain that the results are valid (i.e. changes in helping behaviour are due to the manipulation of the IV).

One weakness is that there were not enough drunk conditions. The students did not like playing the drunk and so out of all the trials, only about a third of them used the drunk model.

(d) One way to check on the reliability of measurements could be by checking the inter-rater (or inter-observer) reliability. This would involve matching, for each trial, the two observers' records for e.g. time taken to help. For high reliability, they should agree upon the time taken. These two sets of recordings could be correlated with each other and there should be a high positive correlation.

(e) There were lots of findings in this study. First of all, there was a high rate of helping overall. In particular, the white ill person was helped the most. The ill victim was helped very quickly and spontaneously (62/65 conditions). However, the drunk victim was helped less often and less quickly. Males were more likely to be first helpers than females. Also, more comments were made in the drunk condition. Finally, there was no diffusion of responsibility effect.

(f) One change to the study could be to change the setting. For example, instead of doing the study in a subway where everyone can see the victim, it could be in a shopping centre or a park. This might change the results.

Another change could be to have a female victim. Again, this might change the results because women might feel safer to help a female victim even if they wouldn't help a male victim. So more women would help.

Teacher's comments (see mark schemes on pages xii–xiii)

(a) A bit brief/vague Chardonnay – you could have mentioned that their aims included whether type of victim and race of victim had any impact upon helping behaviour, or whether diffusion of responsibility occurs in a real life setting. Really you have only just scraped 1 mark out of 2 here.

(b) This is a fairly standard sort of mistake. It's a question of emphasis on what you decide to include and what you decide to omit. What you have written is perfectly accurate. It's just that you have spent too long describing the procedure and not enough time talking about what data was collected (gender and race of first helper, number of people in the carriage, time taken to help, comments passengers made, any other responses to the emergency such as leaving the carriage). You have also omitted that the data was collected against the different victim conditions (white versus black, and cane versus drunk). What you have written is still creditworthy – but will prohibit you from getting top marks. 4 out of 6 marks.

(c) I particularly like your explanation of validity. Often students say 'that would make it more valid' without giving an example of what it means. So, nice touch, Chardonnay.

For the weakness you give, you need to explain further why this is a weakness and how this might limit the results and conclusions which we can draw, so 3+2 marks here, for a total of 5 out of 6.

(d) This is a fairly good response, Chardonnay. Questions about reliability can be quite tough. However, it is important to point out that in this study the two observers were actually observing different things – one observer noted what people were doing in the critical area and the other noted behaviour in the rest of the carriage. Therefore it would make no sense to calculate inter-rater reliability. At least you have demonstrated an understanding of the importance of inter-rater reliability and used context, so a mid-band mark of 4 out of 6.

(e) This is all accurate stuff, Chardonnay. And you report a range of the results and you have managed to get in a bit of 'fine detail' (62/65 conditions). You should try and remember a few more fine details (difficult, I know) e.g. median speed of helping is 5 seconds for ill but a whopping 109 seconds for drunk. Or you could even include one of the quotes of one of the bystanders ('It's for the men to help'). The reason why remembering these fine details is so good is that they really help you get into that top mark band. Your use of psychological terminology is secure and you obviously understand the results. Therefore, top of the middle band for you with 6 out of 8 marks.

(f) Two valid and potentially interesting suggestions. How would moving the study to a shopping centre change the results? Would there be more or less helping? You need to try and predict what would happen and explain why. You have done this, to some extent, for your second change. Overall, both aspects (description of the changes and how this might affect the results) could do with more description and explanation. So 2+2 here, giving you 4 marks for this question part.

Chardonnay (1+4+5+4+6+4 mark = 24/36 marks)

CHAPTER 6

This chapter looks at three core studies in individual differences:

- *Rosenhan's astonishing demonstration of the unreliability of psychiatric diagnosis.*

- *Thigpen and Cleckley's case study of a woman with three different personalities.*

- *Griffith's investigation into gambling on fruit machines.*

Individual differences

182 Introduction to individual differences

Core study 13
184 Rosenhan (sane in insane places)

184 Starters: madness and schizophrenia
186 The study in a nutshell
187 The study in detail
191 Evaluation
192 Afters: still crazy after all these years
193 Multiple choice questions
193 Exam-style questions

Core study 14
194 Thigpen and Cleckley (multiple personality disorder)

194 Starters: multiple personality disorder
196 The study in a nutshell
197 The study in detail
201 Evaluation
202 Afters: the growing controversy
203 Multiple choice questions
203 Exam-style questions

Core study 15
204 Griffiths (gambling)

204 Starters: addiction
206 The study in a nutshell
207 The study in detail
211 Evaluation
212 Afters: I should be so lucky
213 Multiple choice questions
213 Exam-style questions

214 Exam-style questions

Introduction

What are individual differences?

Much of psychology is concerned with how groups of people behave and their typical or 'average' behaviour. For example, if we were looking at the effectiveness of a new happiness drug we could give the drug to one group of people and a placebo pill to another group, and then consider the average score for each group to see if the drug had any effect on happiness. Most psychologists are interested in these average or **mean** scores. In contrast, the study of *individual differences* focuses on the differences within each group, how individual people differ in their behaviour and personal qualities, and what this tells us about human behaviour.

One strand of work on individual differences tries to measure the differences between individuals in qualities such as personality, intelligence and creativity. These qualities are very difficult to define. We have an everyday understanding of them but when you try to create a precise definition and precise measures the situation becomes a little complicated.

The study of individual differences has always attracted a lot of controversy because it seems to create divisions between people – we are telling people that they have more or less of a human quality than another person. The reason this results in controversy is because of the arguments about why we have individual differences; for example, if one person scores more on an IQ test than another person is that because they are genetically different or because they have been educated differently? The questions become even more controversial when the average scores of groups of people are considered.

Other areas of work that are sometimes included under the general heading of individual differences is the work on people with mental health issues, and also the work on individual identity and group identity.

Is it mad to be happy?

In a gentle parody of psychiatric diagnosis **Richard Bentall** (1992) proposed that happiness should be classed as a mental disorder and referred to under the new name of 'major affective disorder, pleasant type'. He suggested that the relevant literature shows that happiness is statistically abnormal, is made up of a discrete cluster of symptoms, is associated with a range of cognitive abnormalities, and probably reflects the abnormal functioning of the central nervous system. You would think that an article like this would contribute to the sum of human happiness but sadly some people took it seriously and it made them sad. Humour is a serious business.

Personality

A major area of individual differences is the study of personality. Personality is a collection of emotional, **cognitive** and behavioural patterns that are unique to a person. It is an interesting observation that we easily recognise an individual's personality but have great difficulty in describing it. One way that psychologists have attempted to describe personality is to define common traits that we all share and then measure individuals on these dimensions. So, for example, if we say that sociability is a trait then we would devise a sociability test and give everyone a score on that scale. In this way we can build up a picture of an individual (and their individual differences).

According to trait theory, a sociable person is likely to be sociable in any situation because of the traits in their personality. The counter argument is that people behave as the situation demands and it is *where* someone is rather than *who* someone is that best predicts how they will behave.

Psychologists have proposed several models of personality traits and the one most commonly cited at the moment is Costa and McCrae's (1992) *Five Factor Model*, which proposes five key dimensions of personality: extraversion, agreeableness, conscientiousness, neuroticism and openness to new experiences.

Personality types
'Let me have men about me that are fat,
Sleek-headed men and such as sleep o'nights.
Yond Cassius has a lean and hungry look.
He thinks too much, such men are dangerous.'
William Shakespeare, Julius Caesar, Act I, scene ii.

Caesar is making judgements about individual differences in personality from observations of body shape. This approach was also used by **William Sheldon** in his twentieth-century descriptions of three major body types and matching personalities: the endomorph is physically quite round, and is typified as the 'barrel of fun' person. By contrast, the ectomorph is lean and hungry with little body fat. He/she is intense, thoughtful and private. The mesomorph has a more athletic body and tends to be assertive, adventurous and courageous.

Although this typology is intuitively appealing there is very little evidence to support the connection between body shape and personality.

Measuring personality
Most **psychological tests** ask direct questions in similar multi-choice format. These **questionnaires** will usually give you a personal score and you can compare yourself against the scores of others. In this way you can find out whether you are more or less shy, for example, than the average person. These tests are easy to use, easy to answer and require little interpretation.

By contrast, **projective tests** require a lot of interpretation. In such tests a neutral stimulus is used; it is presumed that an individual will project their thoughts and feelings onto this stimulus when describing it. Sometimes

Rorschach-type image

these thoughts and feelings will have been hidden from the individual themselves.

The most famous of these tests is the *Rorschach inkblot test* which is named after Hermann Rorschach (1884–1922) who developed the inkblots, although he did not use them for personality analysis. The individual is shown 10 standard abstract designs, and responses are analysed to give a measure of emotional and intellectual functioning and integration.

The rationale for the test sounds very plausible (and the inkblots are used in the **Thigpen and Cleckley** study) but there is little evidence to support the analyses derived from these tests. One fundamental problem is that analysis has to be carried out by another person whose own inner thoughts and feelings may be projected onto their interpretations.

Differences between people

Self and identity

Who am I? is a question we all face sometimes. One way of exploring this sense of self is to ask people to give 20 answers to this seemingly simple question. We might put down our family associations and the groups we belong to or even the things we own. Some people will put down their religion or their ethnicity or their nationality. They will also put down some personal qualities.

But how do we know who or what we are? One source of evidence is the reaction of other people to us. If people laugh at me then I am funny (or ridiculous) and if people smile at me then I am friendly. These reactions act as a mirror to my personality telling me what other people think of me.

These reactions might also affect how much I value myself. My self-image describes how I see myself and my **self-esteem** refers to how much we approve of or like ourselves. A number of techniques have been used to get information on self concept and self-esteem such as asking people to draw self-portraits. These drawings inevitably disclose something of what we think about ourselves.

Try this   6.1

Try it yourself. Sketch out a self-portrait. It doesn't have to be a great work of art, but think about what you'd put in to show people who you are.

Self-portrait

Benjamin Zephaniah captures a sense of identity through his poetry.

Multiple identities

Nobody can be defined by one quality. We all have a unique mix of personal qualities and social affiliations that help to define who we are.

For many, a key affiliation that contributes to their identity is their football team. The Birmingham poet Benjamin Zephania has been a lifelong supporter of Aston Villa (he has our sympathy – ed.) though his support on the terraces has been well tested in the past.

He says, *'When I was a teenager, I used to come here every other week. It was a lot different then – 25,000 people stood here on the famous Holte End, I was almost the only black face.*

I always remember one game when I came here with my uncle and Villa were winning 2–0 and everybody was happy. And then the other team, I forget who they were, started to come back and beating Villa. The mood changed and suddenly the crowd noticed I was the only black kid and they took it out on me. It was terrible.' (BBC website)

Despite these experiences Zephaniah is now patron of Aston Villa Supporters' Club. In his poem 'Knowing Me', he expresses his passion for the club and shows how it is part of his wider sense of identity.

With my Jamaican hand on my Ethiopian heart
The African heart deep in my Brummie chest,
And I chant, Aston Villa, Aston Villa, Aston Villa,
Believe me I know my stuff.

'Race is an important part of my identity, but I wish it wasn't. I'd like to identify myself as a martial artist, an Aston Villa supporter, or a hip-hop reggae person; but when a policeman stops me on the street it has nothing to do with that.' (The *Guardian*, 21 March 2005)

Online identities

One showcase for our identity can be found on the social networking sites on the internet such as Facebook. Most people who join Facebook post at least one picture of themselves, and commonly many pictures of themselves and their friends. The choice of image is informative of the person's sense of social identity and how they want to project it.

On Facebook you can be whoever you want and you can control your image much more than you can in everyday life. A novel aspect of Facebook is that is allows anyone to broadcast details of their identity and existence to all of the other 950 million users of Facebook worldwide (measured in June 2012). Interestingly it is also estimated that over 80 million of these accounts are fake (BBC 2012). You can be an international star instantaneously with a campaign on Facebook or a video on YouTube. The differences between your identity in real life and your identity in cyberspace is an interesting question for psychology to consider.

One line of research has looked at the identities that people create for themselves in online games. These games, such as *World of Warcraft*, attract thousands of players worldwide who develop friendships and cooperative groups with other gamers. For some people these friendships are more constant than their relationships in real space. One difference between these cyber identities and 'real' life is that the gamer can choose how to present themselves and it is estimated that over half of gamers sometimes use identities with a different gender to their own (Hussain and Griffiths, 2008). Interestingly, it is females who swap gender more than males.

Red hair

Some surprising variables predict differences in individual experience. For example, people with red hair are more sensitive to pain (New Scientist 15 October 2002). A group of red-haired and dark-haired women were given an anaesthetic and then subjected to an electric shock. The process was repeated until the women said they felt no pain. The researchers found that redheads required 20 per cent more anaesthetic to dull the pain.

...Connections...

The psychology of individual differences sparks more heated debate than any other area, because attempts to measure differences between people have been inextricably linked to the idea that psychological characteristics are inherited. Research on individual differences has created an industry of testing that quantifies all imaginable human characteristics. These tests appear in many studies, for example **Thigpen and Cleckley** used psychometric tests to try and establish that Eve had more than one personality. The study by **Reicher and Haslam** used a wide range of techniques to plot the changes in their participants over the course of the study.

Rosenhan: starters

Madness and schizophrenia

The concept of madness has been around for a long time, but the diagnosis of specific mental disorders only dates back around 100 years. The way a society deals with people who are different tells you a lot about that society. Sometimes people are revered for their differentness and sometimes they are persecuted. In the Western world, people who have been categorised as mad have been subjected to an unimaginably wide range of brutal and cruel treatments. They have been feared, ignored, beaten, chained, locked up and tranquilised. In the twenty-first century when we have discovered so much about health, the causes of mental disorders remain largely unknown and the treatments are still very controversial.

Schizophrenia is perhaps one of the most misunderstood and feared conditions. A literal translation of the term is 'shattered mind' which gives rise to the common misconception that it refers to a split personality. The condition was first described by Kraepelin in 1887 and further defined and named by Bleuler in 1911.

Symptoms

The term schizophrenia refers to a collection of serious mental disorders in which the person has persistent problems in perception or reality testing. The symptoms are divided into positive symptoms (those that are additional to normal experience and behaviour) and negative symptoms (reduction in normal experiences or behaviour). The positive symptoms include delusions, hallucinations and thought disorder. The negative symptoms include unusual emotional responses and lack of motivation.

Diagnosis is inevitably based on **self-reports** from the patient and **observations** from expert witnesses such as a psychiatrist. There is no biological test for schizophrenia, so the judgement depends on the expertise of the diagnostician. This makes the condition very different from medical conditions such as measles or meningitis and is one reason why it is difficult to see schizophrenia as a disease.

Louis Wane

Louis Wane (1860–1939) was a popular artist who was most famous for his unusual and sometimes disturbing paintings of cats. The cats had many human features and would be placed in scenes to parody the fads of modern life. He is often referred to in psychology texts because some of the pictures were very vivid and abstract and seemed to indicate a different perception of the everyday world. Wane experienced a number of psychological problems in his life and some commentators suggest that you can see his growing mental distress in the paintings. His behaviour became florid and unpredictable and he is sometimes described as having schizophrenia, though this diagnosis was not made at the time. One of his pictures is shown below.

Categorising people

We find it easy to make judgements of 'oddness' in other people. 'He's never been quite right, you know' we might nudge someone and say, but we find it hard to say what it is that is so odd about the person. Psychological diagnosis is an attempt to classify oddness in people.

Diagnosis

The psychological diagnosis of personality has a long history. The Greeks, for example, recognised diagnoses such as senility, alcoholism, melancholia and paranoia. The first comprehensive system of psychological disorders was created in 1896 by Emil Kraepelin. He believed that mental disorders have the same basis as physical ones, and that the same diagnostic principles should be applied – the careful observation of symptoms. The advantages of introducing a diagnostic system include:

- Diagnosis is a communication shorthand.
- It suggests which treatments are likely to be successful.
- It may point out the cause.
- It aids scientific investigation by collecting together people with similar symptoms.

In 1952, the *Diagnostic and Statistical Manual of Mental Disorders* (DSM) was developed by the American Psychiatric Association. DSM IV is widely used today in the USA. In the UK and the rest of the world it is more common to use the *International Statistical Classification of Diseases and Related Health Problems* (ICD), published by the World Health Organisation.

A diagnosis is arrived at using 'family' (i.e. group) resemblances. If you think of a big family that you know, then you will notice that most of the family members have some similar physical features, yet each member of the family is different from the others. It is a similar recognition process with mental disorders. Each person who has a particular condition has some similar features in their behaviour to other people with the same condition.

MAD

We use the term madness in a number of ways.

- *Feelings of anger: 'she makes me so mad!' we snarl between gritted teeth.*
- *Senseless or laughable behaviours: we might say 'that was a mad idea'.*
- *Showing enthusiasm: 'I'm mad for it'.*
- *Showing irrational behaviour or being mentally unsound.*

All these definitions overlap each other but they are all very distinct as well. The madness we are talking about in this chapter is the fourth definition. Perhaps because we fear this condition we have many different words we use other than mad, for example, crazy, daft, demented, distraught, insane, lunatic, bonkers, cracked, daffy, gag, fruitcake, nuts, wacky. These words have very flexible meanings and can refer to the other definitions mentioned above. This shows how we tend to blur the boundaries between acceptable and unacceptable behaviours.

'The cause of lunacy?' The term lunatic (also loony, lunacy) comes from the Latin word 'luna' meaning moon. It highlights the commonly believed link between madness and the phases of the moon. Modern science has not established a link between the moon and madness but the connection might have arisen from the increased level of light at the full moon. This might have kept people awake and so made them susceptible to sleep deprivation symptoms.

Try this
6.2

Make a list of five people who you think are 'odd' and a list of five people who you think are 'normal'. Now try and make two more lists. First, what are the qualities that the 'odd' people have that the 'normal' people don't? Secondly, what are the behaviours that the 'odd' people do that the 'normal' people don't?

This task should give you some insight into the problems of devising a diagnostic system for mental illness.

Visual and auditory hallucinations

Drugs

People have been aware of hallucinations for centuries. Some have seen them as a gift that provides special visions of life. One way of inducing hallucinations is to take certain drugs, for example LSD or mescaline. These have sometimes been referred to as mind-expanding drugs because of the feeling that the user has of seeing new things that they were not previously aware of. Mescaline is made from South American cacti such as the peyote cactus. It has been used in religious rituals for centuries. Users typically experience visual hallucinations and altered mental states which are often described as pleasurable and illuminating but occasionally there are feelings of anxiety or revulsion.

The dangers with hallucinogens come from the dramatic effect they have on the chemistry of the brain. The unwanted effects can include dizziness, sickness, anxiety, feelings of dying or not being able to return to normal consciousness. None of these are pleasant but the major concern is *hallucinogen persisting perception disorder* (HPPD) which occurs with a number of drugs and leaves the user experiencing hallucinations even when the drug has left their system.

Could it be that people with schizophrenia are having similar altered states?

What is it like to hear voices?

Hearing voices is a relatively common experience. Many people can have internal conversations with their family and friends even when they are alone. People who have recently been bereaved often report hearing the voice of the deceased person. Sometimes, however, the voices appear to be more distanced and often more troubling. The voices might be present all day and have the effect of preventing the voice-hearer from doing things in their daily life. The experience of hearing voices is very varied and difficult to describe.

Joan of Arc was a French heroine of the 100 Years War who inspired the French to many victories over the English. From the age of 12 she heard voices which initially encouraged her in her religious observance, and later told her to do battle with the English. She was eventually captured, tried and burnt by the English who believed her voices came from the Devil. The French, however, believed the voices came from God and after her death she was made a Catholic saint.

Are voices a symptom of illness?

People who hear voices often find it disturbing, and dealing with someone who is hearing voices can also be quite disturbing. In recent times hearing voices has been seen as a symptom of mental disturbance and treated with major tranquillisers. Not everyone responds to this treatment and some people can learn to live with their voices without serious medication. In fact some people regard their voices as positive and there are numerous accounts of people finding their voices inspirational or comforting. Perhaps hearing voices should not always be seen as a symptom of mental disturbance but merely as a variation in human experience.

Mental health in the UK

There is still a lot of stigma attached to mental distress which means that it is often hidden. In its broadest definition, mental distress touches most people during their lives.

- It is estimated that as many as one in six adults in the UK are affected by mental distress at any one time.

- The most common conditions are mixed anxiety and depression which affect about 9% of adults every year.

- Around 700,000 people in the UK have some form of dementia – 5% of people over 65 and 10–20% of people over 80.

- One in four consultations with a GP concern mental health issues. Up to 630,000 people are in contact with specialised mental health services at any one time.

Schizophrenia

The rate of schizophrenia is declining in this country but it is estimated that around 1% of the population will experience episodes during their lifetime and the prevalence of the disorder in any one year is between 2 and 4 in 1000. The prevalence rates are similar for men and women but it tends to show earlier in men with the prevalence in men aged 15–24 twice that of women.

Chemical treatments

The most common treatment for schizophrenia in the UK for the past 50 years has been anti-psychotic medication which is relatively successful in reducing symptoms (WHO, 2001) but has damaging side effects, such as:

- Parkinson-like symptoms characterised by muscle rigidity and tremor.

- *Tardive dyskinesia* (TD) which involves abnormal facial movements, smacking lips, chewing, sucking, and twisting the tongue. TD often persists after the treatment has stopped and cannot be treated.

Sources: ONS 2000, MIND website, Mental Health Foundation website.

ABNORMALITY

Rosenhan and Seligman (1989) suggest that there are seven properties that we can use to help us decide whether a person or a behaviour is abnormal.

1 Suffering *is a common feature of abnormality though it is not always present.*

2 Maladaptiveness *is when a behaviour neither helps the individual nor the groups to which they belong.*

3 Irrationality and incomprehensibility *refers to behaviour that seems to have no rational meaning.*

4 Unpredictability and loss of control: *we expect people to be consistent, predictable and in control of themselves.*

5 Vividness and unconventionality *refers to behaviours that stand out and shock us.*

6 Observer discomfort *refers to behaviour that makes us feel uncomfortable maybe because it breaks some unwritten rules about how we should behave.*

7 Violation of moral and ideal standards: *refers to the rules that we think people should live by.*

...Link to the core study...

What do we mean by the terms 'sane' and 'insane'? Does insanity exist in the individual or the society that judges them? These are the questions that **Rosenhan** is looking at in this study. At the time of the study there was growing unease with the medical approach to mental disorders and growing scepticism at the claims of psychiatrists to be able to diagnose and treat these disorders.

Rosenhan: the core study

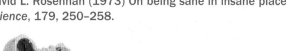

David L. Rosenhan (1973) On being sane in insane places.
Science, 179, 250–258.

See the
CORE STUDY
CHECKLIST
on page xv for
details of what you
need to know for
the exam.

ROSENHAN: THE CORE STUDY

In a nutshell

Context
Experts suggest that it may be more difficult than we think to distinguish between sanity and insanity, normality and abnormality. Judgements about abnormality may actually have less to do with an individual's personality and more to do with the situation in which a person is seen.

Aim
To see if sane individuals would be diagnosed as insane just because they presented themselves to a psychiatric hospital claiming to have psychiatric symptoms.

Study 1

Participants
The participants in this study were the staff and patients in 12 American psychiatric hospitals.

Eight pseudopatients (three women and five men) also took part. A 'pseudopatient' is a sane individual who is pretending to be mentally ill. These pseudopatients were **confederates** and their role was to test the responses of the staff in the mental hospital and observe the behaviour of staff and patients.

Procedure
Rosenhan arranged for the pseudopatients to present themselves to 12 different psychiatric hospitals. The only symptom they reported was hearing voices. In all other ways their behaviour was sane.

Results
All bar one of the pseudopatients was diagnosed as schizophrenic. Once on the psychiatric ward they endeavoured to behave normally and recorded their **observations** in a notebook (**participant observation**). This behaviour was seen as a sign of mental disorder. The average stay was 19 days (range 7–52 days).

Discussion
It may be that psychiatrists are more inclined to call a healthy person sick rather than calling a sick person healthy. It is more dangerous to misdiagnose someone who is ill.

Study 2

Procedure
A further study was conducted to see if this error would persist. Staff at a psychiatric hospital were told the results of the first study and warned that pseudopatients would present themselves over the next three months.

Results
No pseudopatients sought admission yet 41 (out of 193) real patients were suspected by at least one staff member and 23 by at least one psychiatrist.

Discussion
In this study psychiatric staff compensated for the previous results by being more inclined to call a sick person healthy. This suggests that psychiatric diagnosis is highly unreliable.

Study 3

Procedure
Patients approached a staff member and asked questions, such as 'Pardon me, Mr/Mrs/Dr X, could you tell me when I will be eligible for grounds privileges?'

Results
Only 4% of the psychiatrists and 0.5% of the nurses stopped, usually making no eye contact.

As control, a young lady approached staff members on the Stanford University campus, and asked them six questions. All of the staff members stopped and answered all questions, maintaining eye contact.

Discussion
Mental patients are not treated as individuals, they are **depersonalised**.

Conclusion
The label of abnormality changes the way the individual is perceived – 'normal' behaviours in an abnormal setting are seen as abnormal. It is not possible to distinguish the sane from the insane once they are labelled 'abnormal'. Therefore Rosenhan is pointing at a situational rather than dispositional explanation for the diagnosis of mental disorder.

Qs 6.1

1 Explain what is meant by a 'pseudopatient'.

2 Describe what the pseudopatients did to get themselves admitted to a psychiatric hospital.

3 Give **one** example of the qualitative data collected by the pseudopatients.

4 Give **one** example of quantitative data reported in the results of any of the three studies.

5 Describe **one** ethical issue that was raised in this study.

6 Outline **one** conclusion that can be drawn from the first study.

7 Explain why Rosenhan conducted the second study.

8 Explain why the psychiatrists made a different kind of error in the second study.

9 Outline what the third study showed about the treatment of mental patients.

10 In relation to the aims of the study, what conclusions can you draw from the research that was conducted?

The detailed version

Context and aims

Many distinguished researchers have presented the view that the diagnosis of mental illness is *'useless at best and downright harmful, misleading, and pejorative at worst'* (page 251). Rosenhan argues that we may be convinced that we can tell the normal from the abnormal, but the evidence for this ability is not quite as compelling as we think:

- It is common to read about murder trials where the prosecution and defence each call their own psychiatrists who disagree on the defendant's sanity.

- There is much disagreement about the meaning of terms such as 'sanity', 'insanity', 'mental illness' and '**schizophrenia**'.

- Conceptions of normality and abnormality are not universal; what is considered normal in one culture may be seen as quite abnormal in another.

This is not to suggest that there is no such thing as deviant or odd behaviours, nor that 'mental illness' is not associated with personal anguish. Murder and hallucinations are deviant. Depression is linked to psychological suffering.

'If sanity and insanity exist, how shall we know them?' (page 250)

If there is no common ground for defining what is abnormal, then how can we **reliably** identify individuals who are abnormal? Rosenhan's key question is whether a diagnosis of insanity is based on characteristics of the patients themselves or the context in which the patient is seen. This question of personality versus situation can be investigated by getting 'normal' people (that is people who do not have, and have never had, serious psychiatric symptoms) to seek to be admitted to a psychiatric hospital.

- If such 'pseudopatients' are diagnosed as sane this would show that the sane individual can be distinguished from the insane context in which they are found.

- On the other hand, if such pseudopatients are diagnosed as insane then this suggests that it is the context rather than the individual's characteristics that determine the diagnosis. This would mean that the psychiatric diagnosis of 'insanity' has less to do with the patient and more about the (insane) environment in which they are found.

As touch, taste, sight, smell and hearing boarded the charter flight for Havana, Professor Nicholson knew in his heart that he had lost more than just good friends. In fact, he had finally lost his senses.

Cartoon © Nick D. Kim, nearingzero.net. Used by permission.

Aims

Study 1
The initial aim of this study was to see if sane individuals would be diagnosed as insane just because they presented themselves to a psychiatric hospital claiming to have psychiatric symptoms.

Study 2
The first study found that sane individuals (pseudopatients) were diagnosed as insane. This led to a second study which aimed to see if the tendency toward diagnosing the sane as insane could be reversed.

In the first study it is possible that psychiatrists were overcautious because they did not want to miss a diagnosis, i.e. it seemed safer to diagnose a sane person as insane rather than miss a correct diagnosis of insanity.

Therefore the second study sought to see whether, under other conditions, this might be reversed. The aim was to see if psychiatrists and other mental health workers would be undercautious rather than overcautious because they had been told about the mistaken diagnosis in the first study.

Study 3
Rosenhan believed in the power of context. Once an individual is labelled 'insane' others treat that individual differently. To investigate this further a third study was conducted to look at the way staff respond to patients. In particular the focus was on the extent to which staff considered patients as 'individuals'.

Biographical notes

David Rosenhan (1929–2012) was Professor of Law and Psychology at Stanford University, a post he had held since 1970 until his recent death. This classic piece of research on insanity article combines his interest in both law and psychology by looking at the legal definition of abnormality.

Rosenhan recruited his pseudopatients by calling his friends and asking if they were doing anything in the next few weeks. He had no idea that this would mean, for some of them, a stay of several months in a psychiatric hospital. One of the pseudopatients was his friend Martin Seligman with whom he wrote one of the classic textbooks for abnormal psychology.

Rosenhan was well known for his writing, for being a spell-binding lecturer but most of all, for the legacy of this landmark piece of research.

Qs 6.2

1   Outline **one** piece of support for the claim that we cannot tell the sane from the insane.

2   Rosenhan's key question relates to 'personality versus situation'. Explain what this means.

3   How can you use pseudopatients to demonstrate that it is the person rather than the context that matters?

4   Explain the link between studies 1 and 2.

5   Rosenhan tested various hypotheses. Write an alternate hypothesis that relates to Rosenhan's research.

6   Briefly explain the aim of the third study.

Method

Study 1

Participants

This study involves two groups of participants:

1 The staff and patients at 12 different mental hospitals in five states across America. The hospitals represented a range of different kinds of psychiatric institutions – modern and old, well-staffed and poorly staffed. Only one was a private hospital.

2 The 'pseudopatients' who posed as individuals seeking mental health care. There were five men and three women of various ages and occupations (graduate student, psychologist, pediatrician, psychiatrist, painter and housewife). Rosenhan was one of the pseudopatients.

The pseudopatients were **confederates**, briefed by Rosenhan about what to do.

Procedure

Each pseudopatient phoned a hospital and asked for an appointment. On arrival (s)he told the admissions officer that (s)he had been hearing voices which included the words 'empty', 'hollow' and 'thud' spoken in an unknown voice. These symptoms were chosen because they indicated an existential crisis ('Who am I?'), a symptom not previously reported for schizophrenia.

Beyond the description of auditory hallucinations, each pseudopatient stated the facts of their lives as they actually were except for giving their real name, occupation or reason for being at the hospital. None of their life histories were pathological (i.e. abnormal).

Pseudopatients, once they were admitted to the psychiatric ward, ceased to show any symptoms of abnormality. They did display some nervousness because of the shock of being admitted so easily, and also because afraid of being on a psychiatric ward. The reports from the nurses showed that the patients were friendly, cooperative and *'exhibited no abnormal indications'*.

The pseudopatients secretly did not take their medication but otherwise followed the ward routine. They spent their time making notes about their environment – which was seen as a sign of their insanity.

They did not know when they would be discharged; one of the conditions of taking part in the study was that they had to get out by their own devices.

Qs 6.3

1 Study 1 could be described as a naturalistic observation, a controlled observation and a participant observation. Explain why each of these terms might be considered appropriate.

2 Why was it important that a range of hospitals were used in study 1?

3 Identify **two** features of the pseudopatients.

4 In what way were the pseudopatients confederates?

5 Suggest **one** reason why doctors admitted the pseudopatients to hospital.

6 Why do you think Rosenhan chose to use 'existential symptoms' of schizophrenia?

7 In study 1, do you feel that the hospital staff should have judged the pseudopatients as sane or insane? Explain your answer.

8 In study 2, self-report was used as a means of collecting data. Describe how this was done.

9 Give **one** strength and **one** weakness of using this technique in this study.

10 A third investigation took place. What was the independent variable in this study?

11 In studies 1 and 2 independent variables were also tested but there was only one condition for each. Therefore cause-and-effect conclusions can't be drawn. Identify some of the independent variables in studies 1 and 2.

Study 2

The staff in one psychiatric hospital were informed of the results of the first study, which they found hard to believe.

Therefore a follow-up study was organised at this psychiatric hospital. The staff were told that at some time during the next three months, one or more pseudopatients would try to be admitted to the hospital.

Each member of staff was asked to rate all patients who sought admission using a 10-point **rating scale** where 1 and 2 reflected high confidence that the patient was a pseudopatient.

Study 3

Rosenhan decided to test the behaviour of staff members in the psychiatric hospitals. This was a **field experiment** conducted in four of the hospitals or on a college campus. Either a pseudopatient or a young lady (the **independent variable**) approached a staff member and asked questions. The pseudopatients asked one of the following questions:

- 'Pardon me, Mr/Mrs/Dr X, could you tell me when I will be eligible for grounds privileges?'
- 'Pardon me, Mr/Mrs/Dr X, could you tell me when will I be presented at the staff meeting?'
- 'Pardon me, Mr/Mrs/Dr X, could you tell me when am I likely to be discharged?'

The pseudopatient did this as normally as possible and avoided asking any particular person more than once in a day.

Try this   6.3

This is a lengthy and complex report. After you have read through the whole report construct a mobile or some other work of art to illustrate the various strands. This will help you process the various different studies within the report and themes.

Results

Results for study 1

All pseudopatients were admitted and, except one, diagnosed as schizophrenic. Each was eventually discharged with a diagnosis of schizophrenia 'in remission'.

This diagnosis shows the 'stickiness' of the label – once a schizophrenic always a schizophrenic albeit in remission (i.e. symptoms not present at the moment).

The length of hospitalisation varied from 7 to 52 days, with an average of 19 days.

The average daily contact with medical staff ranged from 3.9 to 25.1 minutes, with a **mean** of 6.8 minutes.

Explanation

The failure to detect the pseudopatients' sanity cannot be due to:

* The quality of the hospitals – several were considered to be excellent.
* The time available to observe the pseudopatients – they were in hospital for a reasonable length of time, so there was plenty of opportunity to observe them closely.
* Their behaviour – which was sane (many of the real patients recognised this, saying *'You're not crazy. You're a journalist or a professor'*).

The failure to detect sanity may be because doctors are more inclined to call a healthy person sick than calling a sick person healthy. It is clearly more dangerous to misdiagnose illness than health, and err on the side of caution.

However, what holds for medicine may not hold for psychiatry, especially because psychiatric diagnoses carry personal, legal and social stigmas.

Once you become a patient in a psychiatric hospital, does everything you do provide evidence of your insanity – even if you are sane?

Results for study 2

Over the three months 193 patients were admitted for treatment. None of them were actually pseudopatients but:

* 41 were judged with 'high confidence' to be pseudopatients by at least one staff member.
* 23 were suspected by at least one psychiatrist.
* 19 were suspected by a psychiatrist and one other staff member.

Explanation

The hospital staff were now erring in the opposite direction – they were calling a sick person healthy presumably because they were trying to avoid calling a healthy person sick. Rosenhan commented *'One thing is certain: any diagnostic process that lends itself so readily to massive errors cannot be a very reliable one.'* (page 252)

Results for study 3

The most common response to being questioned by a pseudopatient was a brief reply as the member of staff continued without pausing and making no eye contact. Only 4% of the psychiatrists and 0.5% of the nurses stopped; 2% in each group paused and chatted.

When a young lady approached staff members on the Stanford University campus and asked them six questions, all of the staff members stopped and answered all questions, maintaining eye contact.

Explanation

The avoidance of contact between staff and patients serves to depersonalise the patients, they are not treated as individuals.

Qs 6.4

1. Explain why it took weeks and even months before some patients were discharged.
2. What does the term 'schizophrenia in remission' mean.
3. Describe a situation where the label 'schizophrenia in remission' might be a handicap to an individual.
4. Rosenhan points out that it may be OK to call a healthy person sick when diagnosing physical illness but the same is not true for mental illness. Why?

Things you could do ...

Read the original article by Rosenhan. See if you can find it online, or obtain a copy from your local library (they will order a photocopy if you provide the full reference).

Read other accounts of the research:

Research by Rosenhan is discussed in a chapter of Skinner's Box by Lauren Slater.

Or listen to the BBC's *Mindchangers* programme about this study.

Watch a video

Listen to David Rosenhan on YouTube http://www.youtube.com/watch?v=j6bmZ8cVB4o and http://www.youtube.com/watch?v=qrcuUwTYwwo&feature=related

Watch the Simpson's 'Stark raving Dad'.

Discussion

Stickiness of psychodiagnostic labels

The results show the profound effect of a 'label' on our perceptions of people. Many studies in psychology have demonstrated the same thing. For example, Asch (1946) showed that central personality traits (such as 'warm' and 'cold') have a powerful effect on how we perceive someone's total personality. In the same way, once a person is labelled 'abnormal', this means that all subsequent data about them are interpreted in that light. For example, one pseudopatient who described a warm relationship with his mother but distant one with his father, and good relationships with his wife and children apart from occasional angry exchanges was described by a psychiatrist:

'39-year-old male ... manifests a long history of considerable ambivalence in close relationships, which begins in early childhood ... Affective stability is absent. His attempts to control emotionality with his wife and children are punctuated by angry outbursts ... And while he says he has several good friends, one senses considerable ambivalence ...' (page 253)

In another example a psychiatrist suggested that a group of patients sitting outside the cafeteria before lunch were exhibiting the 'oral-acquisitive nature' of their illness – in reality they didn't have much else to do except turn up for lunch early.

Labels are self-fulfilling for psychiatrists and for the patients themselves. There is a considerable overlap between sane and insane – the sane are not 'sane' all of the time, nor are the insane insane all of the time. It makes no sense to label oneself permanently depressed on the basis of occasional depression. It seems more useful to focus on behaviours.

The experience of psychiatric hospitalisation

The term 'mental illness' is of recent origin. It was coined to promote more humane behaviour towards those who were psychologically disturbed; instead of diagnosing such individuals as witches they were seen to be suffering from a physical illness. However, it is doubtful that people really regard mental illness in the same way as they regard physical illness. You can recover from a broken leg but not from schizophrenia (you remain 'in remission').

The mentally ill are society's lepers. That such attitudes are held by the general population is not surprising; what is surprising is that the professionals (nurses, doctors, psychologists, social workers) hold similar attitudes. Or perhaps it is not surprising given the very limited contact between staff and patients that was observed in this study. For example, the average amount of time that attendants spent 'out of the cage' (the glassed quarters where professional staff had their offices) was 11.3% of their total time at work and much of this was spent on chores rather than mingling with patients. On average the nurses emerged from the cage 11.5 times per shift.

The physicians, especially psychiatrists, were even less available and were rarely seen on the wards. On average the physicians appeared on the ward 6.7 times per day.

Powerlessness and depersonalisation

The staff treated the patients with little respect: punishing them for small incidents, beating them and swearing at them. Such treatment is depersonalising and creates an overwhelming sense of powerlessness. This was further exacerbated by the living conditions: patients cannot initiate contact with staff and personal privacy is minimal (e.g. staff can enter private rooms with no permission, no doors on toilets.

Depersonalisation *can be defined as a sense of being cut off or detached from one's self. This may be experienced as viewing one's own mental processes or behaviour from the outside.*

Sources of depersonalisation

The first source is the attitudes held by all of us towards the mentally ill, attitudes characterised by fear, distrust and also benevolence. Our ambivalence leads to avoidance.

Second, the hierarchical structure of the hospital leads to **depersonalisation**. Those at the top have least to do with patients, and their behaviour inspires the rest of the staff.

There are other sources of depersonalisation, such as lack of money, staff shortages and also the use of psychotropic drugs. Drugs convince staff that treatment is being conducted and therefore further patient contact is not necessary.

Consequences of labelling and depersonalisation

We prefer to invent knowledge (e.g. labelling someone as 'schizophrenic') rather than admit we don't know. This is not merely depressing but frightening. How many people, one wonders, are sane but not recognised as such in our psychiatric institutions? Once hospitalised the patient is socialised by the bizarre setting, a process Goffman (1961) called 'mortification'.

Summary and conclusion

It is clear that we cannot distinguish the sane from the insane. Hospitalisation for the mentally ill results in powerlessness, depersonalisation, segregation, mortification and self-labelling – all counter-therapeutic.

One solution might be to use other approaches to the treatment of mental illness: community mental health facilities to avoid the effects of the institutional setting, or to use **behaviour therapies** which avoid psychiatric labels.

A second solution is to increase the sensitivity of mental health workers and recognise that their behaviour is also controlled by the situation.

...Links to core studies...

This study is one of a select group that had a dramatic effect on public perceptions and continues to have a lasting influence. Other studies in this text to have such an effect include, **Milgram** and **Bandura** *et al.* These studies are all still cited many years after the research was conducted and provide moral stories for the understanding of human behaviour. By looking at unusual (or abnormal) behaviour we gain some clues as to what we mean by normality. Other studies that give us insights about this include **Baron-Cohen** *et al.* and **Freud**.

Qs 6.5

1   In what way is a diagnosis a 'self-fulfilling prophecy'?
2   Why was 'out of the cage' used to assess nurse-patient interaction?
3   Rosenhan suggests that some mental health professionals have negative attitudes towards the mentally ill. Identify **two** pieces of evidence for this view.
4   Explain what the term 'mortification' means.
5   Some people argue that there is nothing to be gained by a diagnosis of schizophrenia. Do you agree?

Evaluating the study by Rosenhan

The research method
A variety of methods were used in this study. The first study is probably best described as a controlled participant observation. Study two involved self-report and observation. Only study 3 was an experiment (a field experiment) – in the other studies various independent variables were tested but there was only one condition for each so cause-and-effect conclusions can't be drawn.

What are the strengths and limitations of these research methods/techniques in the context of this study?

The sample
There were two samples: the hospital staff in study 1 and the hospital staff in study 2. There were a further two samples in study 3: hospital staff and college staff.

In what way are the samples unique? How does this affect the conclusions drawn from the study?

Ethics
All the pseudopatients were volunteers but the hospitals did not agree to take part in the first study and professionals were deceived in all of the studies.

What ethical issues should have concerned the researchers in this study, and how might they have dealt with these issues?

Reliability
Reliability concerns measurement.

What aspects of human behaviour were measured in this study? How could the reliability of these measurements be assessed?

Ecological validity
Observations may lack objectivity which would affect the validity. You might also consider the effect of demand characteristics. The willingness to commit a patient on flimsy evidence may be because the psychiatrist wouldn't suspect for a minute that someone might be pretending and therefore assumes that anyone seeking admission must have a good reason to do so. This may challenge some of the conclusions.

To what extent can we generalise the findings from this study to real life?

Quantitative or qualitative?
Both quantitative and qualitative data were collected in this study.

Give examples of each kind of data.

What are the strengths and limitations of each kind of data in the context of this study?

Applications/usefulness
How valuable was this study? What influence do you think it has had on the treatment of abnormality?

What next?
*Describe **one** change to this study, and say how you think this might affect the outcome.*

There are no simple answers.

Evaluating a study requires you to think.

*We have provided some pointers here, linked to the **RESEARCH METHODS** and **KEY ISSUES** covered in Chapter 1 (Psychological investigations) and Chapter 7 (Key issues).*

You can read suggested answers on our website www.psypress.com/cw/banyard.

Producing effective evaluation
When you produce your own answers to the issues on the left there are two things to ensure:

1   Contextualisation
2   Elaboration

The key to **CONTEXTUALISATION** is to ensure that your answer includes some information about this particular study. For example:

Question:

With reference to Rosenhan's study, describe **one** weakness of using quantitative data. **[2]**

Answer:

STATE: One weakness of using quantitative data is that it can offer no explanation of the behaviour being studied.

CONTEXT: For example, in Rosenhan's study we know the number of times that psychiatrists identified true patients as pseudopatients and Rosenhan guessed why they may have done this (because they were trying to avoid calling a healthy person sick), but he doesn't know this.

The key to **ELABORATION** is the three-point rule (see page vii). For example:

Question:

With reference to Rosenhan's study, describe **one** weakness of the observation method as used in this study. **[3]**

Answer:

STATE: One weakness of observation is the problem of observer bias – that what a person 'sees' is influenced by their expectations.

CONTEXT: In Rosenhan's study the pseudopatients were acting as observers of the behaviour of the hospital staff and might have expected them to show disinterest in the patients.

COMMENT: The effect of this would be that they might have been less likely to notice when the staff were being kind to patients, and this would affect the validity of the data collected.

The individual differences approach

On pages 182–183 and 226–227 we have discussed the **individual differences approach**.

The study by Rosenhan concerns abnormality.

- In what way is this an example of the individual differences approach?
- Discuss the strengths and weaknesses of the individual differences approach using examples from the Rosenhan study.

Still crazy after all these years

Each generation develops its stories to explain the altered states we call madness. We seem to be fascinated and fearful of these states in equal measure and we constantly explore these ideas in fiction.

Reaction to Rosenhan's study

Rosenhan's article created a major storm when it was published. On the one hand there was a barrage of criticism about psychiatrists and their diagnoses; on the other hand the psychiatric profession fought back against Rosenhan, arguing that since psychiatric diagnosis mainly relies on **self-reports** from patients, the study no more demonstrates problems with psychiatric diagnosis than lying about other medical symptoms. Psychiatrist **Robert Spitzer** (1975) claimed:

'If I were to drink a quart of blood and, concealing what I had done, come to the emergency room of any hospital vomiting blood, the behaviour of the staff would be quite predictable. If they labelled and treated me as having a peptic ulcer, I doubt I could argue convincingly that medical science does not know how to diagnose that condition.'

Spitzer had a key role in the development of the DSM (below) and hence increased the number of people defined as mentally disordered.

Making us crazy

One of the biggest controversies about psychiatric diagnosis is whether disorders are real. The current version of the *Diagnostic and Statistical Manual* (DSM) runs to 900 pages, describing more than 300 mental disorders. The DSM defines many sorts of behaviour as mental disorders, some of which do not seem to deserve the label. For example, you or I might call *Oppositional Defiant Disorder* 'being awkward'.

A diagnosis can be worth a lot of money: it may enable a patient to sue an employer for causing illness; it allows the pharmaceutical industry to produce medication for each one. You might not be surprised that some of the main funders of DSM development are pharmaceutical companies. The world thinks it is going mad because the drug companies tell it so, and psychologists collude in this nonsense because it is good for our business as well (Kutchins and Kirk, 1997). An example of the level of psychiatric diagnosis can be seen in the figures for medication prescribed in the UK. In 2010, doctors in England made out over 42 million prescriptions for anti-depressants (more than double the number a decade earlier) at a cost of over £220 million (Ilyas and Moncrieff, 2012). That's an awful lot of pills.

Madness at the movies

For most people their only direct observation of people with serious mental disturbance is at the movies. Sometimes these films can give us a meaningful insight into these altered mental states and films like *The Madness of King George* and *A Beautiful Mind* show the pain in a compassionate way. Other films play on our stereotypes of madness to make great drama. The classic *Psycho* taps into our fears of madness to create one of the most iconic horror films. The risk of violence from people with mental disorders is, however, very low, but many people derive their fears from fictional stories.

One Flew Over the Cuckoo's Nest

Ken Kesey's 1962 cult book of life in a psychiatric hospital in the USA was turned into a film in 1975 starring Jack Nicholson. The film was awarded all five major Oscars and has recently been cited as 'culturally significant' by the US Library of Congress. In the film, Randle P. McMurphy, a serial petty criminal who has been sentenced to a fairly short prison term decides to have himself declared insane so he'll be transferred to a mental institution which he thinks will be more comfortable than prison. In the asylum McMurphy's ward is run by the tyrannical Nurse Ratched, who has crushed the patients into submission.

Jack Nicholson as McMurphy.

As McMurphy takes on Nurse Ratched in a series of power games he becomes a hero to the patients and starts to empower them. All the time the viewer is challenged to question just how sane or insane the inmates are.

McMurphy destabilises the culture of the asylum and he is eventually pacified by a **frontal lobotomy** after he responds violently to one of Nurse Ratched's psychological power games.

The myth of mental illness

What is the difference between a medical and mental disorder? We go to see medical doctors for both conditions and they use similar treatments (e.g. drugs) but is this the best approach? In his critique of the medical model **Thomas Szasz** (1960) raised some general points about the problems of diagnosis. Szasz argued that the medical model is unhelpful to our understanding of psychiatric conditions. The medical model suggests that all psychiatric problems will eventually be understood in terms of simple chemical reactions, and that 'mental illnesses' are basically no different to other diseases. Szasz argued that there are two errors in this view:

1   A disease of the brain is a neurological defect and not a problem of living. For example, a defect in a person's vision may be explained by correlating it with certain lesions in the nervous system. On the other hand, a person's belief, whether this is a belief in Christianity, or Communism, or that their internal organs are rotting, cannot be explained by a defect of the nervous system. Some beliefs are perfectly acceptable and some are thought to be a sign of mental disorder, but they are all beliefs.

2   In medicine when we speak of physical disturbances we mean either signs (for example, fever which is measurable) or symptoms (for example, pain which is reported). When we speak about mental symptoms, however, we refer to how patients describe themselves and the world around them. They might say that they are Napoleon or that they are being persecuted by aliens. These are symptoms only if the observer believes that the patient was not Napoleon, or not being persecuted by aliens. So to see a statement as a mental symptom we have to make a judgement based on our own (and our society's) beliefs.

Szasz suggests that the idea of mental *illness* is used to obscure the difficulties we have in everyday living. Not long ago it was witches and devils that were held responsible for problems in social living. The belief in mental illness is no more sophisticated than a belief in demonology. Mental illness, according to Szasz, is 'real' in exactly the same way as witches were 'real'.

The simple point to draw from Szasz's complex argument is that if you are feeling stressed or down because of things that are happening to you are work or at home then it is unlikely that the problem will be solved by (a) calling it mental illness and (b) dealing with it by taking medication.

Multiple choice questions

1 Which of the following symptoms of schizophrenia did the pseudopatients describe?
   a Having visual hallucinations.
   b Being controlled by outside forces.
   c Hearing voices.
   d Having two minds.

2 How many patients were admitted with a diagnosis of schizophrenia?
   a 8   b 7
   c 6   d 5

3 The average number of days the pseudopatients spent in hospital was:
   a 7   b 12
   c 19   d 26

4 The pseudopatients included:
   a A psychiatrist, a housewife and Rosenhan himself.
   b Only psychologists.
   c Only male participants.
   d The staff at the hospitals in the study.

5 The pseudopatients were discharged with a diagnosis of:
   a Schizophrenia in reverse.
   b Lapsed schizophrenia.
   c Schizophrenia existential.
   d Schizophrenia in remission.

6 In the second study, how many real patients were wrongly identified as pseudopatients by at least one psychiatrist?
   a 19   b 23
   c 41   d 63

7 When the pseudopatients approached a staff member with a question, the psychiatrists stopped and answered the question:
   a 0.5% of the time.   b 1.5% of the time.
   c 2% of the time.   d 4% of the time.

8 Who recognised that the pseudopatients were not real patients?
   a Some nurses.   b Some doctors.
   c Some patients. d All of the above.

9 Which of the following is not true about the label 'schizophrenic'?
   a It creates expectations.
   b It is 'sticky'.
   c It may not be accurate.
   d It is Russian.

10 Behaviour therapies might be preferable to hospitalisation because:
    a They don't involve labels.
    b The patient is not viewed as normal or abnormal.
    c They focus on behaviours.
    d All of the above.

Answers are on page 247.

Exam-style questions

There are three kinds of question that can be asked about the Rosenhan study, as represented here by sections A, B and C.

See page x for further notes on the exam paper and styles of question.

Section A questions

1 In the study by Rosenhan pseudopatients were admitted to mental hospitals.
   (a) Name **two** of the pseudopatients' behaviours which were taken as evidence of abnormality. [2]
   (b) Outline **one** reason why it is difficult to define abnormality and normality. [2]

2 Rosenhan (sane in insane places) suggested mental patients experienced powerlessness and depersonalisation.
   (a) Give **two** examples to support this. [2]
   (b) Outline **one** possible explanation for the behaviour of staff in this study. [2]

3 Rosenhan used the phrase 'stickiness of psychodiagnostic labels'?
   (a) What did he mean by this phrase? [2]
   (b) Give **one** example of how the label 'schizophrenic' affected the way pseudopatient's behaviour was interpreted by staff. [2]

4 In the study by Rosenhan, the pseudopatients were incorrectly diagnosed as schizophrenic. Give **two** possible explanations why the hospital made this mistake. [4]

5 From Rosenhan's study, 'On being sane in insane places':
   (a) Describe what the pseudopatients did to get themselves admitted to a psychiatric hospital. [2]
   (b) Outline **one** reason why doctors admitted the pseudopatients to hospital. [2]

6 Describe **two** ethical issues raised by Rosenhan's study 'On being sane in insane places'. [4]

7 From Rosenhan's study of abnormality:
   (a) Give **one** example of quantitative data that was collected. [2]
   (b) Give **one** example of qualitative data that was collected. [2]

8 In Rosenhan's study 'On being sane in insane places':
   (a) Give **one** example of how the pseudopatients' requests were dealt with by the staff. [2]
   (b) Outline how the staff reactions affected the pseudopatients. [2]

9 In Rosenhan's study pseudopatients sought to be admitted to a hospital. Describe the other participants in this study, aside from the pseudopatients. [4]

10 The pseudopatients in Rosenhan's study were not released from hospital for some time. Explain why it took so long for the hospitals to discharge them. [4]

Section B question

Answer the following questions with reference to the Rosenhan study:

(a) Outline the aim of this study. [2]

(b) Describe the sample used in this study and suggest **one** strength of using this sample. [6]

(c) Give **two** strengths of the observation method as used in this study. [6]

(d) Give **two** weaknesses of the observation method as used in this study. [6]

(e) Outline the results of this study. [8]

(f) Suggest how this study could be improved. Give reasons for your answer. [8]

Section C question

(a) Outline **one** assumption of the individual differences approach. [2]

(b) Describe how the individual differences approach could explain abnormality. [4]

(c) Describe **one** similarity and **one** difference between Rosenhan's study and any other core studies that take the individual differences approach. [6]

(d) Discuss strengths and weaknesses of the individual differences approach using examples from any core studies that take this approach. [12]

THIGPEN AND CLECKLEY: STARTERS

Multiple personality disorder

Multiple personality disorder (MPD) is a psychiatric condition characterised by having at least one 'alter' personality that controls behaviour. The 'alters' are said to occur spontaneously and involuntarily, and function more or less independently of each other. The condition is also referred to as *Dissociative Identity Disorder* (DID).

MPD is defined as the occurrence of two or more personalities within the same individual, each of which is able to take control sometime in the person's life. In the popular imagination it is commonly confused with schizophrenia because of the split personality aspect of it (see page 184). There are very striking differences between the two conditions, most critical of which is the reality testing of the individual (i.e. checking that one's perceptions actually represent reality). People with schizophrenia commonly have problems testing reality and do not see things in the same way as people without the condition. In everyday speech they are experiencing a period of insanity. In the case of multiple personality, none of the personalities have difficulty with reality testing.

The symptoms are:

- The patient has at least two distinct identities or personality states. Each of these has its own, relatively lasting pattern of sensing, thinking about and relating to self and environment.

- At least two of these personalities repeatedly assume control of the patient's behaviour.

- Common forgetfulness cannot explain the patient's extensive inability to remember important personal information.

- This behaviour is not directly caused by substance abuse or by a general medical condition.

What is the cause of MPD?

It is commonly believed that the experiences and symptoms that are labelled as MPD are a response to extremely traumatic situations from which there is no physical means of escape. The traumatic situations might involve physical or emotional pain or anticipation of that pain. If the person 'goes away in their own head' they can remove themselves from the pain and function as if it had not occurred.

MPD: not a new explanation

References to multiple personality go back a long way and appear in the Bible, written 2,000 years ago, for example in the Gospel of St Mark 5: 8–10: 'He ... said to him, "Come out of the man, you unclean spirit!" And Jesus asked him, "What is your name?" He replied, "My name is Legion; for we are many." And he begged him not to send them out ....'

The controversy: does MPD exist?

One view suggests that MPD is real and commonly a response to childhood sexual abuse. The other view suggests that MPD is created in the therapist's office by the use of hypnotism and guided imagery. Look at the information here and come to your own opinion, though it is only fair to say that we (the authors) remain divided about the existence of MPD. It is clear that a small number of people have some powerful experiences where they feel they are not really there and that they are watching what is happening rather than taking part in it. The controversy is about whether the best way to describe this is to call it multiple personality.

What is dissociation?

Your perception of yourself and your experience of the world depend on a number of factors including feelings, thoughts, memories and sensations. You make sense of these inputs to create your view of reality. If some of these information sources become disconnected then it can change your sense of identity or your perceptions of the world. This is what happens in dissociation.

Dissociation is common enough in everyday life. Maybe you are driving somewhere on a familiar route and when you arrive at your destination you realise you can't recall the entire journey. It is almost as if you went into automatic pilot mode. Or maybe you have to give a talk or a performance to a large group of people. You are nervous about it but you keep control of yourself and almost watch yourself doing the performance as if you are in the audience. It almost feels as if someone else is doing it. 'Is that really me?' you ask yourself. In this way we can use dissociation to help us deal with stressful events. Dissociation can be a useful coping strategy to deal with events that are embarrassing, stressful or painful.

Dissociation is also sometimes experienced as a side effect of drugs or alcohol.

Types of dissociation

Amnesia: A loss of memories of specific events or experiences, or sometimes not remembering personal information.

Depersonalisation: This can include out-of-body experiences like seeing yourself as part of a movie, or feeling that your body is not real.

Derealisation: Things around you appear unreal so that objects might appear to change shape or other people seem to be robots.

Identity confusion: A sense of uncertainty about who you are and maybe a struggle inside to define who you are.

Identity alteration: This refers to a dramatic shift in your identity that changes your behaviour in noticeable ways.

The remains of the No. 30 bus blown up in London on 7 July 2005. Some people involved in the incident experienced a sense of not being there – a dissociation for the event.

Dissociation as a response to trauma

The following survivor account of the July 2005 bombs in London shows how one person used dissociation to deal with the initial crisis. She experiences the event as surreal and like a movie.

'It was about three minutes after we left King's Cross when there was a massive bang and there was smoke and glass everywhere. The lights went out, and with the smoke, we couldn't breathe. We sort of cushioned each other during the impact because the compartment was so full. It felt like a dream, it was surreal. The screaming from the front carriage was terrible. It was just horrendous, it was like a disaster movie, you can't imagine being somewhere like that. You just want to get out. I kept closing my eyes and thinking of outside.' (Guardian, 2005)

Readers beware

Whenever you come across symptoms, either medical or psychiatric, there is a tendency to think they describe something about you. This is because they do. In this case we all experience some forms of dissociation in our daily lives. We are all a bit different in different situations. You behave in one way with your friends and another way with your parents; believe me, they are grateful for this.

Altered states and popular delusions

Mesmerism

In the eighteenth century Viennese doctor and showman **Anton Mesmer** developed a technique that eventually took his name – mesmerism. Mesmer discovered that if he could create the right atmosphere he could influence the behaviour of suggestible people. In a theatrical performance he would wear brightly coloured clothes and move around people, waving a magnetised stick and playing the part of a healer. He was able to induce people to dance or fall asleep. The act was similar to the modern day stage hypnotist and circus tent evangelist. Opinion was divided as to whether Mesmer was a conman or whether he had invented something quite remarkable. With royal patronage from the French King, Mesmer set up a Magnetic Institute in Paris but a scientific investigation of his work concluded that the effects experienced by people during mesmerism were due to their imaginations.

Another popular delusion is that we can contact the dead by joining hands and wearing gothic clothes.

Hypnosis

'When using hypnosis, one person (the subject) is guided by another (the hypnotist) to respond to suggestions for changes in subjective experience, alterations in perception, sensation, emotion, thought or behaviour' (APA, 2005).

Hypnosis commonly involves (a) intense concentration, (b) extreme relaxation and (c) high suggestibility. It can be used for entertainment, personal development and therapy. The patients of hypnotherapists are usually people looking for such things as pain relief or a way of giving up smoking. More controversially, some therapists use hypnosis to recover **repressed** memories (false memories) of sexual abuse or memories of past lives. **Freud** started the work into repressed memories (see page 93) and he initially used hypnosis, though wisely moved away from it quite quickly.

Altered states?

Hypnosis is commonly believed to be a trance-like altered state of consciousness. This view sees hypnosis as a route to hidden parts of the mind. An alternative and more plausible view sees hypnosis as a response to social demands where people who are especially suggestible respond to cues from the hypnotist (Wagstaff, 1981). In other words, hypnosis is an extreme example of social conformity where the person behaves as they think they are expected to. Connections are made between hypnotism and mesmerism, and also with a belief in demonic possession and exorcism.

Demonic possession

There are different ways of explaining similar phenomena. The idea of demonic possession sees the victim as having other entities, in this case demons, inside them. The way to remove the demons is through exorcism. This has been carried out in ceremonies such as those caricatured in movies such as *The Exorcist* and more commonly in the USA today at mass religious meetings where the preacher will cast out demons in a dramatic show. Maybe the phenomenon of multiple personality is a different way of explaining a similar experience.

Interpreting unusual experiences

Many unusual experiences have been reported by people. It appears to be a feature of humankind that we try and make the best sense we can of our world. Sometimes this means we have to go beyond the evidence and trust our senses. Not everyone will agree with the way you interpret your world and there are many phenomena that have believers and non-believers.

There is a common belief in near-death experiences where people describe the sensation of going down a tunnel of light, presumably towards the next world. Then there is the issue of alien abduction where people believe they have been abducted and experimented on by beings from other planets (check the internet to see just how common this belief is).

So when we look at the accounts of multiple personality do we judge them as flawed attempts to explain unusual experiences or as the description of a human phenomenon?

Repressed memory therapy

The assumption behind repressed memory therapy (RMT) is that psychological problems such as eating disorders, depression and extreme anxiety are caused by repressed memories. Repressed memories are not in conscious awareness and cannot be recalled without help from a therapist, but is the therapist helping the patient recall something they have forgotten or are they helping them to invent a memory? The repressed memories are often of shocking childhood experiences such as sexual abuse. RMT therapists believe that psychological health can only be restored by recalling and dealing with the repressed memories.

RMT is so controversial that in the UK The Royal College of Psychiatrists has banned members from using therapies designed to recover repressed memories of childhood abuse. In the USA a report for The American Psychological Association in 1996 noted that *'there is a consensus among memory researchers and clinicians that most people who were sexually abused as children remember all or part of what happened to them although they may not fully understand or disclose it. At this point it is impossible, without other corroborative evidence, to distinguish a true memory from a false one.'* (http://www.apa.org/topics/trauma/memories.aspx).

...Link to the core study...

We take it for granted that we have one personality that is relatively consistent and predictable. We ask someone 'How are you today?' and not 'Who are you today?' The revelation of this study was that, for at least one person, this second question was more appropriate. The therapists described an unusual phenomenon and set a pattern for how we would describe this type of experience. They wrote up their case study in medical journals and also presented it to the wider public. Today we are used to seeing personal issues discussed openly (and endlessly) on television but this case was reported at the start of the celebrity psychiatrist circus where psychological problems are given a public airing not only for information but also for entertainment.

The therapists became very famous for the study in contrast to the subject of the case study who was effectively kept hidden for 25 years. Even today there are a lot of unanswered questions about this story. Read the study and decide for yourself whether MPD is real or a creation of therapists.

Thigpen and Cleckley: the core study

Corbett H. Thigpen and Hervey Cleckley (1954) A case of multiple personality.
Journal of Abnormal and Social Psychology, 49, 135–151.

See the CORE STUDY CHECKLIST on page xv for details of what you need to know for the exam.

In a nutshell

Context
The psychiatric disorder 'multiple personality disorder' (MPD) had been reported previously, for example the case of Miss Beachamp (Prince, 1906). However, psychologists generally have been sceptical of the condition.

Aim
To report the case of a patient with MPD.

Participants
Initially 'Eve White' (EW) was referred to a psychiatrist, Dr Thigpen, because she experienced severe headaches and blackouts that had no physical cause.

After several months of treatment the therapist received a letter from EW, with some strange handwriting at the bottom. At her next visit a new 'person' emerged – Eve Black (EB), a very different personality (see 'Thumbnail sketches' above). EB was aware of all EW did but the same was not true in reverse.

Procedure
This was a **case study**, mainly based on the extensive interviews between the two psychiatrists and patient, as well as conversations with the patient's husband and family. Data was collected through **self-report** and interpreted by the psychiatrists.

Quantitative data was also collected using, for example, IQ tests, **projective personality tests** and **EEG** to show a difference between the two Eves.

Thumbnail sketches

Eve White
Demure, retiring, in some respects almost 'saintly', face often looks sad, reads and composes poetry, steadfast, lacking boldness and spontaneity, industrious worker, competent housekeeper, not self-righteous but seldom playful, soft voice, dresses in a simple way, devoted to her daughter.

Eve Black
Party girl, childishly vain, egocentric, enjoys taunting and mocking, does things 'on a whim', immediately amusing and likeable, voice a little 'coarse', uses slang, dresses a little provocatively, posture and gait light-hearted, developed a skin rash when wearing nylon stockings, could never be hypnotised.

Results
When EB was 'out' she often behaved mischievously and would leave EW to be punished. This explained events in EW's past where she could not account for things she did. These past events were substantiated by her husband and parents.

Psychometric and **projective tests** were used to show a difference between the two Eves. EW had a higher IQ and memory function but EB was psychologically healthier – **regressed** rather than **repressed**. In some ways they were one personality at two stages of life. EB's role was to embody all the angry feelings thus enabling EW to maintain a nice, loving persona.

After eight months of therapy a third personality, Jane, emerged. She was superficially a compromise between EW and EB. An EEG showed that EB was different to both EW and Jane.

The solution lay in some integration of the three personalities, but the therapists recognised that it would be morally wrong for them to 'kill off' any one personality.

Discussion
There are a number of explanations for what the therapists observed.

- Eve was a skilful actress, which would require keeping this up over a long period of time.
- Eve was suffering from a hysterical disorder or schizophrenia, though she didn't exhibit the appropriate symptoms.
- The therapists' **observations** were not objective and what they recorded was affected by **observer bias**.
- She was suffering from MPD because there were three distinct personalities.

Qs 6.6

1 Describe the sample in this study and outline **one** weakness with this sample.

2 Why did the psychiatrists refer to the patient as 'Eve White' rather than using her real name?

3 Describe what you think may have caused EW's blackouts.

4 What techniques are used in case studies?

5 Describe **one** strength and **one** weakness of case study in the context of this study.

6 The psychiatrists used projective personality tests (see page 199 for information about such tests). Explain what is involved in such tests.

7 Outline **two** ethical issues raised in this study.

8 Explain what EEG is and what it showed in this study.

9 This study was a longitudinal study. Why was it desirable to conduct this study over a long period of time?

10 How did the therapists confirm some of the evidence provided by Eve?

11 One explanation for the observations that were made was that the therapists' observations were not objective. Explain in what way this is an example of 'observer bias'.

12 How could this observer bias explain the data that were recorded?

13 Outline the evidence that there were three distinct personalities in the one patient.

The detailed version

Context and aim

Multiple personality disorder was reasonably well known in the 1950s, based on a few detailed case studies of patients exhibiting two or more people in one body. However, such cases were rarely encountered by therapists and therefore were viewed with some suspicion. The therapists Thigpen and Cleckley had direct experience of a patient with the disorder forcing them to review the disorder.

Aim
To report the treatment of one patient diagnosed with multiple personality disorder.

Method

Participants
The case study was recorded by Corbett Thigpen and Hervey Cleckley, both very experienced and eminent psychiatrists.

Eve White
The patient was a 25-year-old married woman, 'Eve White' (EW). She was mother to a four-year-old child. EW was referred to the psychiatrist because of 'severe and blinding headaches', and said that 'blackouts' often followed the headaches.

Several months into therapy EW said she was puzzled by a recent trip for which she had no memory. Shortly afterwards Thigpen received a letter (see right). The letter was unsigned but clearly from EW because of the handwriting. The final paragraph was puzzling. Had EW inserted this paragraph as a prank? It was hard to imagine the 'matter-of-fact ... meticulously truthful and consistently sober' EW becoming playful. She denied sending the letter at her next visit, but she remembered starting such a letter. At this time she started to become rather agitated and asked if hearing voices was a sign of insanity. At that moment a strange look came over her face and she put her hands to her head as if seized by a sudden pain. After a tense moment of silence, her hands dropped and with a quick smile and bright voice said 'Hi there, Doc!'

Eve Black appears
EW was transformed from a retiring and conventional figure, lacking attractiveness, into a novel feminine apparition. *'The newcomer [had] a childishly daredevil air, an erotically mischievous glance, a face marvellously free from the habitual signs of care, seriousness and underlying distress, so long familiar in her predecessor. This new and apparently carefree girl spoke casually of Eve White and her problems, always using "she" or "her" in every reference, always respecting the strict bounds of separate identity. When asked her own name she immediately replied, "Oh, I'm Eve Black".'* (page 137)

The procedure

Dr Thigpen, and later Dr Cleckley, spent 14 months (approximately 100 hours) interviewing EW and EB, collecting material about their behaviour and inner lives. The patient's husband and family were also interviewed.

Initially, in order to interview EB, EW had to be hypnotised. Soon it became possible to simply ask to speak to EB and she would come forth.

The largest part of this case study therefore involved interviewing (self-report). Other more objective and quantitative measures were used as well. EW and EB were both tested to assess their personality using psychometric tests (IQ tests and memory tests) and two projective personality tests (drawing human figures and the Rorschach ink blot test). EEG was also used to compare brain activity and a handwriting expert studied their handwriting (not so objective).

Part of the letter received by Dr Thigpen, showing the different handwriting used in the final paragraph.

Biographical notes

Dr Thigpen (1919–1999) and Dr Cleckley (1903–1984)

Corbett Thigpen and **Hervey Cleckley** and their patient were from Augusta, Georgia in the southern USA. Dr Cleckley was chief of psychiatry and neurology at University Hospital of Georgia. His book, The Mask of Sanity, can be read http://www.cassiopaea.com/cassiopaea/psychopath.htm.

Dr Thigpen was a life-long amateur magician. Professionally he was a clinical professor of psychiatry at the Medical College of Georgia. One of his more famous patients was Margaret Mitchell, the author of Gone with the Wind (another Georgian).

Qs 6.7

1 What led EW to seek psychiatric help?
2 Identify **three** differences between EW and EB.
3 What are 'psychometric and projective tests' and how were they used?
4 How did the therapists make 'contact' with EB in order to talk with her?

Thigpen and Cleckley: the core study *continued*

The film The Three Faces of Eve *staring Joanne Woodward (who won an Oscar for her performance of Eve) was based on a book of the same name by Thigpen and Cleckley, both released in 1957.*

Try this 6.4

Try a **role play** with two actors – one the therapist, the other the patient who switches between the different personalities.

Qs 6.8

1 Describe **one** example of something EB did which got EW into trouble.

2 Thigpen and Cleckley reported that they tested EB's claim that she could erase items from EW's memory. How do you think that they may have done this?

3 One problem with self-report data is that it may not be true. How did the therapists obtain confirmation of what EB said?

4 Why were Eve's family members unaware of EB's existence?

5 Give **two** examples of qualitative data collected in this study.

6 Explain the relationship between EW and EB.

7 Why do you think the therapists tried to achieve re-integration of the two personalities?

8 Before the third personality emerged, Eve started to improve. What do you think led to this improvement?

Results

During the first few months of therapy the case seemed fairly ordinary. Several important emotional difficulties were revealed and discussed. These related to marital conflicts and personal frustrations. There was some improvement in the symptoms she experienced but it was clear that EW's major problems had not been settled. Of course everything changed when EB appeared.

Eve Black's life history

Interviews with EB produced the following information. It appeared that EB had enjoyed an independent life since their early childhood. EW had no knowledge of her existence until some time after EB emerged unbidden in the psychiatrists' office. When EB was 'out' EW was completely oblivious of what EB did and was apparently unconscious. By contrast, EB had some awareness of what EW did when EB was not out. She could report what the other did and thought but didn't participate in these thoughts and actions. EB regarded EW's distress about her failing marriage as silly. EB was not cruel but like a *'bright-feathered parakeet who chirps undisturbed while watching a child strangle to death'* (page 138).

EB claimed that during childhood she often emerged to play pranks, though she also lied easily so that it was difficult to take her account as **reliable** evidence.

Confirmation of EB's reports

EW provided indirect support for EB's reports because she could remember punishments and accusations for things she didn't know she had done but which were described by EB.

EW's parents and husband also confirmed EB's stories. For example, EW was punished when, aged six, she wandered off through the woods to play with some other children. Her denials were not believed at the time and she was severely punished. EB had separately reported this incident, saying that she enjoyed the adventure and enjoyed being able to withdraw and leave EW to be punished.

Another incident was reported by EW's husband who lost his temper with EW when he found she'd spent a lot of money on new clothes and hidden them away. EB confessed to being the culprit in this shopping spree.

Eve Black's relationship with Eve White

EB denied any association with EW's child or the husband, whom she despised. She had never made herself known to them nor EW's parents. There would be no reason for them to suspect that EW was really two people and, in any case, EB was able to pass herself off as EW, imitating her tone of voice and gestures. However, EW's parents were aware of unexplained changes in EW, which they described as her 'strange little habits'.

EB reported that she had caused the severe headaches and imaginary voices. She also claimed to be able to wipe EW's memory if she thought very hard about it. One example of this was a report (from a distant relative) that a previous marriage had occurred. EB eventually confessed that when EW was working away from home for a while EB had gone to a dance and ended up marrying a man she scarcely knew. She lived with this man for several months though EW had no recollection of this.

Proceeding with therapy

The aim of therapy was to achieve reintegration of the two personalities. The therapists tried to call out both personalities at once but EW experienced a violent headache and became very distressed; EB tried once and said it gave her *'such a funny, queer, mixed-up feeling that I ain't gonna put up with it no more'* (page 122).

During the course of therapy EW decided to leave her husband and, at that time, her daughter went to live with EW's parents. The headaches, blackouts and voices disappeared and she managed to do well at her job and achieve some stability. EB had been causing less trouble and seldom 'came out', but she did occasionally go on dates with 'bad company'. Fortunately EW was spared the knowledge of this.

A third personality emerges

After eight months the situation changed for the worse again. EW's headaches and blackouts returned. EB was questioned but denied any part in this new development and said she too was experiencing blackouts. During one session of hypnosis EW stopped talking, her eyes shut and her head dropped. After a silence of two minutes, she blinked, looked around the room as if to work out where she was and, in a husky poised voice, said to the therapist *'Who are you?'* It was immediately apparent that this was neither EW nor EB. This new person, Jane, was more mature and bold than EW but not difficult like EB. In a superficial way she could be described as a compromise between the two Eves.

Jane was aware of everything the other two did but could not fully access their memories prior to her emergence. Jane was able to report when EB was lying. She felt free from EW's responsibilities and didn't identify with her role as wife and mother, though she felt compassion towards the child. Jane gradually took over more and more from EW, though she could only emerge through EW and had not found a way to displace EB.

Seeking to solve the problem

The therapists felt that Jane might be able to solve the deepest problems that EW sought treatment for. EB would never provide a solution as she *'would indeed be a travesty of a woman'* (page 146). EW's sense of duty and willingness for self-sacrifice would repeatedly bring her back to a marital situation which she did not have the emotional vigour to deal with. Therefore Jane seemed the only solution. EW admitted, during hypnosis, that the best solution for her child, might be for Jane to take over as mother, a role at which she had not been successful. Jane, however, was reluctant to come between a distressed mother and her child.

EW was not a physically bold person yet a recent event demonstrated another side to her. It was a momentous event which moved Jane deeply. Jane showed her compassion for EW in a letter to the therapists: *'Today [EW] did something that made me know and appreciate her as I had not been able to do before. I wish I could tell her what I feel but I can't reach her. She must not die yet ... She saved the life of a little boy today ... she darted out in front of a car to pick him up ... but instead of putting him down again, the moment his baby arms went round her neck, he became her baby – and she continued to walk down the street carrying him in her arms ... There seemed only one solution to prevent her possible arrest for kidnapping. That was for me to come out and find the child's mother.'* (page 147)

The psychiatrists' responsibility

The therapists recognised their role in 'creating' Jane since her emergence was really due to the process of therapy. They may not have 'caused' her existence but certainly played a part in it.

The therapists were also faced with the decision of how much to encourage her to 'take over' from the others. The therapists did not think themselves wise enough to make such a decision nor did they think the responsibility was theirs: *'Would any physician order euthanasia for the heedlessly merry and amoral but nevertheless unique Eve Black'* (page 146). They believed that they had some choice about which personality to reinforce but ultimately the choice lay with the patient.

Quantitative data

Psychometric tests

	EW	EB
IQ test	110	104
Memory scale	Performance was higher than IQ score	Performance on a par with IQ score

Projective personality tests

	EW	EB
Drawings of human figures and Rorschach ink blot test.	Rigid and not capable of dealing with her hostility. Conflict in role as wife and mother, resulting in anxiety. Result indicates **repression**.	Able to conform to the environment; a healthier profile than EW. Result indicates **regression** – a wish to return to an earlier period of life.

*The projective personality tests suggested that the existence of dual personalities was due to a wish to return to an earlier stage of life (EB in fact used EW's maiden name). EW's hostility towards her roles as wife and mother made her feel guilty which activated the **defence mechanism** of repression, removing the conflict from her conscious awareness. Playing the role of EB permits her to discharge her feelings of hostility towards EW and others. The problem started earlier in life. EW felt rejected by her parents when her twin sisters were born; EW loved them dearly, EB despised them. In a sense EB's role was to embody all the angry feelings thus enabling EW to maintain a nice, loving persona.*

EEG test

*A study was done of the **brain waves** of the three patients using an **electroencephalogram (EEG)**. Tenseness was most pronounced in EB, next EW and then Jane. EW and Jane had a fairly similar alpha rhythm whereas EB's was a little bit faster, on the borderline between normal and abnormally fast. This difference was **significant**. Slightly fast records are sometimes associated with **psychopathic personality** (i.e. a personality disorder characterised by a lack of social conscience). There was also evidence of restlessness and generalised muscle tension in EB's tracings but not in the others.*

Qs 6.9

1   What did the psychometric tests show about the two selves?

2   Much of the data was recalled retrospectively. How do you think this might have affected the reliability of the data?

3   Thigpen and Cleckley wondered about the ethics of deciding which personality could be 'killed'. Do you think this issue was a problem? Explain your answer.

4   Suggest **two** pieces of evidence that support the claim that this patient did have multiple personality disorder and **two** pieces of evidence which suggest that this patient did not have multiple personality disorder.

5   Why did the psychiatrists think that schizophrenia was a possible diagnosis? (Read about schizophrenia on page 96.)

6   Which of Freud's concepts of id, ego and superego goes with each of the three personalities? (See page 96 for details of Freud's concepts.)

7   At one level Eve's problems appear to stem from an unhappy marriage. However, EB had first emerged during her childhood. The results from the projective tests suggest what may have happened. Describe what you think may have caused EW to develop this fragmented personality early in her life.

THIGPEN AND CLECKLEY: THE CORE STUDY

Discussion

Some possible explanations for Eve's behaviour were:

*   She was a skilful actress, although this seems unlikely because it would be hard to see how she could have maintained this act over such a long period of time.
*   It could be that Eve was suffering from a hysterical disorder or schizophrenia, but many of the appropriate symptoms were absent.
*   The therapists' *observations* were not objective.

How does disintegration occur?
Identical twins start as one cell but divide at the very outset. The same could be true of a multiple personality. Can it be re-integrated? Jane appeared to be some sort of fusion of the other personalities, not a mere addition of different traits. Like the fusion of hydrogen and oxygen to make water, Jane was a product genuinely different from both ingredients from which it was formed.

What is personality?
In order to understand multiple personality, we need to understand 'personality'. We hear people say things like 'John Doe has become a new man since he stopped drinking' or 'a friend was not himself the other night' or that 'a woman's absorption in her home resulted in her losing her entire personality'.

In psychiatry the term 'personality' implies a unified total. Dictionaries define it as 'individuality', 'personal existence or identity'. Bearing this in mind Thigpen and Cleckley felt it was appropriate to speak of Eve White, Eve Black and Jane as three 'personalities'.

However, the physical evidence for this was weak. The differences in EEGs and in **psychometric** and **projective tests** were not particularly impressive. A handwriting expert concluded that, even though the handwriting of each personality superficially appeared to be by a different person, they all were clearly written by the same individual.

Final word
Thigpen and Cleckley finished their article with a plea for psychiatry to avoid explanations that offer little real insight. They recognised that they had not been able to propose any new explanation for multiple personalities but found the case very thought-provoking and suggest that further research may yield understanding of this disorder.

 You might look at various websites to collect evidence about the nature of MPD – now called dissociative identity disorder (DID), e.g. www.dissociation.com.

...Links to core studies...

This study has direct links to **Rosenhan's** question about how we can distinguish sanity from insanity. It also links with **Sperry's** account of split-brain surgery. In this work he talks about split consciousness and two people in the same body. There is also a strong link to the work of Elizabeth **Loftus** on memory. She has been prominent in the recovered memory/false memory debate which is central to any evaluation of multiple personality. Finally, there is a link to **Freud** in the use of hypnosis and also the belief in repressed memories of childhood sexual abuse.

Qs 6.10

1   The term 'iatrogenic' is used to describe a disorder that is created by the activity of the doctor. Explain in what way Eve's condition might be described as iatrogenic.
2   There are other explanations for Eve's behaviour apart from a diagnosis of multiple personality disorder. Outline another one of these.
3   Explain why Eve White, Eve Black and Jane might be regarded as three different personalities, rather than one personality.
4   Outline evidence against the view that there were three separate personalities.
5   Was Eve suffering from multiple personality disorder? What is your view? Justify your answer.

Things you could do ...

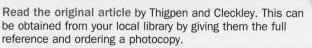

Read the original article by Thigpen and Cleckley. This can be obtained from your local library by giving them the full reference and ordering a photocopy.

Read other accounts of the research:

You can read a much fuller version of this case study in the book *The Three Faces of Eve* by Thigpen and Cleckley.

You can read about other cases of MPD, such as *Sybil*.

Watch a video

Watch the film *The Three Faces of Eve*, available on DVD.

Hear the real Eve (Chris Sizemore) talking as all three personalities http://www.youtube.com/watch?v=BZ3fl18XQ0A

Watch Chris Sizemore being interviewed fairly recently on BBC *Hardtalk* http://www.youtube.com/watch?v=GmNRDvicyOY&feature=related

Evaluating the study by Thigpen and Cleckley

The research method
This was a case study.

What are the strengths and limitations of this research method in the context of this study?

The research techniques
A number of different techniques were used in this study to collect data about the three Eves.

List the different techniques and for each give strengths and weaknesses in the context of this study.

The sample
In what way is the participant in this study unique? How does this affect the conclusions drawn from the study?

Ethics
What ethical issues should have concerned the researchers in this study, and how might they have dealt with these issues?

Reliability
Reliability concerns measurement.

What aspects of human behaviour were measured in this study?

How could the reliability of these measurements be assessed?

Validity
The observations may have been affected by observer bias. The therapists may have 'encouraged' some of Eve's behaviour's.

To what extent can we generalise the findings from this study?

Snapshot or longitudinal?
This case study is **longitudinal** because it takes place over the period of many months.

Consider the strengths and weaknesses of this design in the context of this study.

Qualitative and quantitative
Give examples of both quantitative and qualitative data from this study.

What are the strengths and limitations of each kind of data in the context of this study?

Applications/usefulness
How valuable was this study – for people in general and/or for people dealing with mental illness/multiple personality disorder?

What next?
*Describe **one** change to this study, and say how you think this might affect the outcome.*

There are no simple answers.

Evaluating a study requires you to think.

*We have provided some pointers here, linked to the **RESEARCH METHODS** and **KEY ISSUES** covered in Chapter 1 (Psychological investigations) and Chapter 7 (Key issues).*

You can read suggested answers on our website www.psypress.com/cw/banyard.

Producing effective evaluation
When you produce your own answers to the issues on the left there are two things to ensure:

1 Contextualisation
2 Elaboration

The key to **CONTEXTUALISATION** is to ensure that your answer includes some information about this particular study. For example:

Question:
With reference to the Thigpen and Cleckley study, outline **one** strength of a longitudinal study. **[2]**

Answer:
STATE: One strength of a longitudinal study is that it enables you to observe what happens to someone over a long period of time instead of comparing snapshots of different people.

CONTEXT: In the Thigpen and Cleckley study this was necessary because otherwise you wouldn't understand how the changes in Eve developed over time.

The key to **ELABORATION** is the three-point rule (see page xii). For example:

Question:
Describe **one** difference between the Thigpen and Cleckley study and any other study that could be viewed from the individual difference approach perspective. **[3]**

Answer:
STATE: One difference is in terms of the individual(s) who were focused on.

CONTEXT: In the study by Thigpen and Cleckley the individual was experiencing distress and displaying abnormal behaviour, such as blackouts.

COMMENT: In the study by Rosenhan the individuals studied were sane so this study was looking at abnormality in a different way, specifically to look at the 'stickiness' of psychiatric labels.

The individual differences approach

On pages 182–183 and 226–227 we have discussed the **individual differences approach**.

The study by Thigpen and Cleckley concerns multiple personality disorder.

* In what way is this an example of the individual differences approach?
* Discuss the strengths and weaknesses of the individual differences approach using examples from the Thigpen and Cleckley study.

Thigpen and Cleckley: afters

The growing controversy

Since the account of Eve by Thigpen and Cleckley the story has grown and becomes progressively more controversial. Most striking is Eve's own account of her experience and the differences between this account and that of her therapists.

The real Eve

Christine Sizemore (Eve's real name) always wanted to tell her own story. She was discouraged from doing this by Thigpen because of the possible harm it would do her if she revealed herself to the world. A less charitable interpretation would be that he was also protecting his control over the story. According to Sizemore she agreed to Thigpen and Cleckley preparing academic reports about her for discussion in scientific seminars, but she was not aware they were writing a book for publication to the general public. She was also not aware that Thigpen filmed some of the therapy sessions. The resulting film *Case Study in Multiple Personality* was made available from his university library. When she found out about this, after 20 years, she took legal action to ban its use.

The battle for control of her story was lost before it started as Thigpen and Cleckley published their book and then sold the rights to Hollywood. When *The Three Faces of Eve,* starring Joanne Woodward, was premiered, Thigpen and Cleckley were the stars of the event, but Sizemore was advised to leave town to avoid distress and not to see the film. Joanne Woodward got an Oscar for playing Chris Sizemore, who got nothing, not even any recognition of her existence. The book and the film told of a successful therapy and a happy ending, but this bore little relationship to the truth. Some time later when she tried to write her own account she discovered that Thigpen claimed to have a document signed by her giving him

The real Eve – Chris Sizemore pictured at the 50th Anniversary of the World Premiere of Three Faces of Eve *at the Miller Theatre in Augusta Georgia.*

full rights over her story. In an ironic twist, Christine Sizemore's identity and life story had been taken over by her psychiatrists.

Eventually in 1977 she collaborated with her cousin Elen Pitillo to reveal her identity(ies) to the world with the book *I'm Eve.* This text tells a very different story to that told by Thigpen and Cleckley. It tells a story which starts much earlier in her life, has many more identities and goes on much longer. By the time the book was published she describes herself as being adjusted to her problems and able to live a full and rewarding life.

In 2009, Christine Sizemore came to the UK to speak to two packed houses of A Level students. She also recorded an interview for the BBC's *Hardtalk* series.

Sybil

The public view of MPD has been heavily influenced by films such as *The Three Faces of Eve* and *Sybil.* The story of Sybil (Schreiber, 1973) tells of a woman with 16 personalities, created as a response to childhood sexual abuse. Before the publication of the book and the subsequent movie of the same name there were only 75 reported cases of MPD. Since then the diagnosis rate in the USA has gone through the roof as has the number of personalities believed to exist in the patients.

Sybil was eventually identified as Shirley Mason, who died in 1998 at the age of 75. Her therapist was Cornelia Wilbur, who died in 1992. It is now known that Mason had no symptoms of MPD before she began having therapy with Wilbur. The magazine *Newsweek* (25 January 1999) reported that, according to historian Peter M. Swales (who first identified Mason as Sybil), *'there is strong evidence that [the worst abuse in the book] could not have happened'.*

During her therapy, which included hypnosis and mind-altering drugs, Mason read the literature on MPD including the book *The Three Faces of Eve.* It is commonly believed that the case of Sybil is an example of an *iatrogenic disorder* (that is, one caused by the doctor). A different view is put forward by Philip M. Coons who supports the MPD diagnosis and points out that *'the relationship of multiple personality to child abuse was not generally recognised until the publication of Sybil.'* (http://www.healthyplace.com/communities/personality_disorders/wermany/reading_room/abuse.htm)

A cautionary tale of psychiatric treatment

Bennett Braun was a leading researcher and therapist in MPD in the USA. In 1980 Braun helped establish an MPD facility at the hospital he worked at and by 1984 he was president of the *International Society for the Study of Multiple Personality and Dissociation.* Within 20 years he had been expelled from the *American Psychiatric Association* and can no longer treat anyone for MPD, the condition for which he was considered an expert. How did it get to this?

The best way to answer this is to look at just one of his patients, Patricia Burgus. After a difficult birth of her second child in 1982, Burgus began to experience depression and received conventional therapy. After a while she came in contact with Braun who suggested she and her son should be hospitalised. He suggested that she had MPD and had therefore almost certainly survived some childhood trauma.

In hospital she had a range of therapies including hypnosis and mind-altering drugs, sometimes being woken up in the

middle of the night to have her treatment. During the sessions Braun helped her 'discover' her multiple personalities and in particular her involvement with a satanic cult dating back to the seventeenth century, that she had experienced sexual abuse as a child and that she had given birth to several children who had been sacrificed by the cult. Eventually she described herself as a high priestess who ran the affairs of the cult without her husband or her everyday self knowing anything about it. The lack of any corroborating evidence for these activities or pregnancies did not deter the therapist. Other patients started to incorporate Burgus into their stories and her role of high priestess became established in the collective fantasy of the psychiatric facility.

Burgus' condition got worse and she was transferred to a regular psychiatric ward where she was taken off the medication and started to recover. The multiple personalities quickly disappeared and the satanic cult was shown to be a sham. Several lawsuits were brought against Bennett Braun and his colleagues. Patricia Burgus and her family eventually accepted a settlement of $10.6 million.

Multiple choice questions

1 Which of the following was not one of Eve White's symptoms?
   a Hearing voices.
   b Headaches.
   c Trouble sleeping.
   d Blackouts.

2 Approximately how many hours were spent interviewing the patients?
   a 100   b 120
   c 150   d 200

3 Which of the following is true?
   a EB had access to EW's memories.
   b EW had access to EB's memories.
   c Neither a nor b.
   d Both a and b.

4 Eve Black was described as:
   a Reversed.
   b Repressive.
   c Regressive.
   d Reintegrated.

5 Which of the following is a projective personality test?
   a Wechsler– Bellevue. b Rorschach.
   c Cattell.   d Snoopy Scale.

6 What score did Eve White get on the IQ test?
   a 102   b 104
   c 106   d 110

7 Who was Jane most similar to?
   a EB.
   b EW.
   c Neither EB or EW.
   d Tarzan.

8 The EEG test showed that the alpha rhythms were similar in:
   a EW and Jane.
   b EW and EB.
   c EB and Jane.
   d EW, EB and Jane.

9 Why is it unlikely that the patients were simply acting?
   a They said they couldn't act.
   b The therapy took place over a long period of time.
   c They didn't change their story when hypnotised.
   d All of the above.

10 What other diagnosis, aside from multiple personality disorder, might have been possible?
   a Schizophrenia.
   b Split personality.
   c Depression.
   d Obsessive–compulsive disorder.

Answers are on page 247.

There are three kinds of question that can be asked about the Thigpen and Cleckley study, as represented here by sections A, B and C.

See page x for further notes on the exam paper and styles of question.

Exam-style questions

Section A questions

1 Thigpen and Cleckley were therapists who studied a case of multiple personality disorder.
   (a) Outline **one** problem with the evidence collected in this study. [2]
   (b) Suggest how they might have dealt with this problem. [2]

2 Thigpen and Cleckley diagnosed their patient as suffering from multiple personality disorder. Describe **two** pieces of evidence from the case study that suggest that the patient did have the disorder. [4]

3 In the study by Thigpen and Cleckley the therapist described the first time Eve Black 'appeared'. He noted that Eve White was transformed from a retiring figure into a feminine apparition.
   (a) How did the therapist interpret this observation? [2]
   (b) Give **one** other interpretation of this observation. [2]

4 In the study by Thigpen and Cleckley it might be suggested that the patient had several personalities. Describe **one** piece of evidence that might suggest she did have several personalities and **one** piece of evidence that suggests she didn't have several personalities. [4]

5 Thigpen and Cleckley say that they may have been in part responsible for the appearance of Jane.
   (a) Explain how they might be responsible. [2]
   (b) Outline what they decided to do to resolve the multiple personalities. [2]

6 Outline **one** strength and **one** weakness of the case study method as it was used by Thigpen and Cleckley. [4]

7 (a) Identify **two** psychological tests carried out on Eve White and Eve Black in Thigpen and Cleckley's study. [2]
   (b) Outline **one** weakness with using such tests. [2]

8 With reference to Thigpen and Cleckley's study:
   (a) Describe the qualitative evidence collected. [2]
   (b) Describe **one** strength of using qualitative data in this study. [2]

9 In Thigpen and Cleckley's study:
   (a) Outline the findings from the projective tests. [2]
   (b) Outline **one** conclusion that can be drawn. [2]

10 Thigpen and Cleckley offer various alternative explanations for Eve White's behaviour. Outline **two** of these explanations. [4]

Section B question

Answer the following questions with reference to the Thigpen and Cleckley study:

(a) Briefly outline the research method used in this study. [2]

(b) Explain why this study can be considered a longitudinal study. [4]

(c) With reference to this study, suggest **one** strength and **one** weakness of conducting longitudinal studies. [6]

(d) Describe the procedure followed in this study. [8]

(e) Suggest how the procedure followed in this study could be improved. [8]

(f) Outline the implications of the procedural changes you have suggested for this study. [8]

Section C question

(a) Outline **one** assumption of the individual differences approach. [2]

(b) Describe how the individual differences approach could explain multiple personality disorder. [4]

(c) Describe **one** similarity and **one** difference between the Thigpen and Cleckley study and any other core studies that take the individual differences approach. [6]

(d) Discuss strengths and weaknesses of the individual differences approach using examples from any core studies that take this approach. [12]

Griffiths: starters

Addiction

What are addictive behaviours and how do we explain them? Explanations commonly start with biological (or medical) approaches to addiction that concentrate on the abuse of substances such as alcohol or heroin. These explanations only take us so far because it is clear that people develop a range of addictive behaviours that have nothing to do with chemical substances.

Biological explanations of addiction

Biological explanations of addiction focus on *neurotransmitter* substances in the brain, and on **genetic** differences between people with addictions and people without addictions.

Neurotransmitters

Without going into a full biology lesson, a neurotransmitter is a chemical which moves in the gaps between nerve cells to transmit messages from one nerve cell to another. If you can change the amount of transmitter substance that is available you will have an effect on the transmission of messages in the nervous system. Say, for example, there is a system of nerves that create a feeling of pleasure, and you can increase the available transmitter substance then you might increase the sense pleasure. However, this approach to addiction only takes us so far because it does not take account of the pleasures that are enhanced or restricted by the social situation we are in at the time (Orford, 2001).

Genetics

Studies that analyse the genetic structure of addicted individuals tend to emphasise the role of genetics rather than the environment in addictive behaviours. Some genes have attracted particular attention and have been shown to appear more frequently in people with addictive behaviours than in people without. The problem is that these genes do not occur in all people with the addictive behaviour and they do appear in some people without it. For example, a gene referred to as DRD2 (no, he didn't appear in *Star Wars*) has been found in 42% of people with alcoholism. It has also been found in 45% of people with **Tourette syndrome** and 55% of people with **autism**. It has also been found in 25% of the general population. This means that DRD2 appears more frequently in people with identifiable 'abnormal' behavioural syndromes, but it can not be the sole explanation for the behaviour (Comings, 1998).

Addictive behaviours

One way to think about addiction is to see it in terms of addictive behaviours. This view will include a much wider range of activities than substance addiction. In our everyday speech the term 'addiction' is used as a metaphor for other activities, for example the song 'Addicted to Love' by Robert Palmer. But can we be addicted to love in the same way as we can be addicted to alcohol? Yes we can, says the psychological approach to addictive behaviours put forward by, for example, Orford (2001) who suggests the following definition,

'Addiction: an attachment to an appetitive activity, so strong that a person finds it difficult to moderate the activity despite the fact that it is causing harm.' (Orford, 2001, page 18)

This approach suggests that people can develop addictive behaviours for a wide range of activities including, drug use, alcohol use, gambling, game playing, eating and sex. Although these behaviours appear to be very different, they all involve a number of similar components. Griffiths (1995) suggests that addictive behaviours have six components, which are described on the right. This psychological approach to addictive behaviours highlights the many similarities in a wide range of damaging behaviour patterns, and indicates that the biological (disease) model of addiction is quite limited.

A further similarity between a number of addictive behaviours can be found in the groups that support people who want to change their behaviour, such as Alcoholics Anonymous, or Gamblers Anonymous, and even Weight Watchers. Orford (1985) suggests that when people change their addictive behaviour it often involves them re-inventing themselves, which means they take on a new identity and change their attitudes and values on a wide range of issues. The organisations that support such change often have an almost 'religious approach' to the problem. They frequently require the person to give personal testimony ('I was a sinner', 'I was a drunk', 'I was a gambler') and accept the authority of the group or a 'higher power'. They usually emphasise that the person should change from being self-centred (egocentric) and pleasure seeking (hedonistic), to being humble and ascetic. All this suggests that the person is undertaking a moral (or spiritual) change rather than a medical change.

Do you feel lucky punk?

Components of addictive behaviours (Griffiths, 1995)

1 Salience: this refers to how important the behaviour becomes to the individual. Addictive behaviours become the most important activity for a person so that even when they are not doing it, they are thinking about it.

2 Euphoria: this is the experience people report when carrying out their addictive behaviour. People with addictive behaviour patterns commonly report a 'rush', or a 'buzz' or a 'high' when they are taking their drugs or when they are gambling, for example.

3 Tolerance: this refers to the increasing amount of activity that is required to achieve the same effect. A drug addict might have to increase the intake of drugs and a gambler might have to increase the stakes.

4 Withdrawal symptoms: these are the unpleasant feelings and physical effects which occur when the addictive behaviour is suddenly discontinued or reduced. This can include 'the shakes', moodiness and irritability. These symptoms are commonly believed to be a response to the removal of a chemical that the person has developed a tolerance to. However, they can also be experienced by gamblers (see Orford, 1985), so the effects might be due to withdrawal from the behaviour as well as the substance.

5 Conflict: people with addictive behaviours develop conflicts with the people around them, often causing great social misery, and also develop conflicts within themselves.

6 Relapse: although people sometimes manage to shake off their addictive behaviour, the chances of relapse are very high. Even when the person has been 'dry' for a considerable time, they can quickly develop the same high levels of addictive behaviour.

What is gambling?

Gambling is commonly defined as the activity of wagering money (or something valuable) on an event where you do not know the outcome. The aim of the wager is to win more money (or valuable things). You usually get the result quite quickly.

There are three key components to gambling.

1 The stake: how much is being wagered.

2 The predictability of the event: for some gambling the event is determined mechanically and **randomly**. The lottery is an example of this and some would argue that so are fruit machines (though gamblers would say this is not so). On the other hand some events have some predictability to the outcome and a little bit of skilled knowledge can be used to enhance your chances of winning the bet. For example, if Nottingham Forest were playing Manchester United in a game of football then you could reasonably predict that even if half the United team fell into a hole that suddenly appeared in the middle of the pitch their remaining team mates should still be able to win 6–0. However, this would not prevent many Forest fans betting on their team to win.

Calculating the odds at a race track.

3 The odds: these are agreed between the two people who are gambling prior to the event. They are a ratio of the two possible outcomes and are used to encourage a bet. So, for example, if I am offered odds of 100–1 on Nottingham Forest beating Manchester United then I might well have a flutter because these odds mean that if I bet £1 and by some remarkable turn of events my team wins then I will win 100 times my stake which will be £100.

It's all in the name

Sometimes things can be dressed up with words to appear to be something they are not. Western military refer to civilian deaths caused by their actions as 'collateral damage'. Somehow that doesn't seem so bad as mass murder. In a similar, though less dramatic, way the gambling industry tries to soften our perception of gambling. For example, they refer to the National Lottery as a 'game' and suggest that we 'play the lottery'. But is this really 'playing' and is the lottery a 'game'? Play is often described as an activity where you occupy yourself in amusement, sport, or other recreation. Buying a ticket and scratching out six silver circles (max time 10 seconds) is not much of a game. It's not a game and it's not playing – it's gambling.

Gambling facts and figures

Gambling in the UK is regulated by the Gambling Commission. In 2010–11 the UK betting industry took over £4,700 million of business and employed over 114,000 people. Taxes paid to the UK government from gambling amount to around £1,500 million per year.

On top of this a lot of people gamble online through offshore companies and this does not form part of the figures. This unregulated gambling is estimated to be around a further £2,000 million.

Survey evidence suggests that over 50% of adults in the UK gamble at least once a month and 73% have gambled in the last year but this figure drops to 48% if the National Lottery is excluded.

According to *Guinness World Records*, the highest odds for an accumulator bet were 3,072,887 to 1 by an unnamed woman from Nottingham on 2 May 1995.

There are around 200 licensed bingo operators licensed by the Gambling Commission and they run over 600 clubs employing over 16,000 people. Punters spend over £650 million each year in bingo clubs and a further £600 million on other bingo games.

Since its launch in 1994, the National Lottery has given over £34 billion in prizes and created over 2,000 millionaires. Total National Lottery ticket sales for the year to 31 March 2012 were over £6,500 million,

In gambling space, no one can hear you lose

One of the features that gambling companies use to encourage you to stake money is to make you more aware of winning than losing. When you lose on a fruit machine (which is most of the time) you don't hear anything. But when you win the machine makes enough noise to wake the dead. The machine clatters – the sound that signifies WINNER and everyone knows it.

Fruit machines are designed to magnify wins and minimise the sense of losing.

an increase of over £650 million on the previous year. That is an average of £100 stake for every person in the country. Over £100 million of prizes went unclaimed.

Problem gambling

The gambling industry committed to donate a minimum of £5 million per year between 2009 and 2012 to help fund problem gambling related research, education and treatment.

Depending on how it is measured the rate for problem gambling in the UK is estimated between 0.7% or 0.9%. These rates are similar to those in other European countries (such as Germany and Norway) and are lower than countries such as the USA and Australia.

Sources: Gambling Commission website, National Lottery Commission website and Gambling Aware website.

...Link to the core study...

Traditional views of addiction saw it as a medical condition but is this so? **Griffiths** is exploring the idea that we develop addictive behaviours for a whole range of activities of which addiction to chemical substances is just one example. The strength of the addiction therefore lies not in the substance but in the habits that develop around it. In truth we can become addicted to almost anything: eating, drinking, gambling, sex, exercise, internet gaming and many more. One of the many difficulties in exploring these behaviours is to distinguish between people who are enthusiastic about something and so do it a lot, and those who are addicted. It's a fine line and not everyone agrees where that line should be drawn.

Griffiths: the core study

Mark D. Griffiths (1994) The role of cognitive bias and skill in fruit machine gambling. *British Journal of Psychology, 85*, 351–369.

See the CORE STUDY CHECKLIST on page xv for details of what you need to know for the exam.

GRIFFITHS: THE CORE STUDY

In a nutshell

Context
Psychologists have sought to understand gambling by looking at what people are thinking when they gamble. Thought processes can be described in terms of **heuristics** which can present a distorted picture of the world. For example, the 'illusion of control' distorts reality because we erroneously believe we have control over events.

Aim
The aim of this study was to record the **cognitive** processes of regular fruit machine gamblers (RGs) to see if they were more irrational than non-regular fruit machine gamblers (NRGs).

There were three specific **hypotheses**:

1. There are no differences between RGs and NRGs in terms of skill.
2. RGs produce more irrational verbalisations when gambling than NRGs.
3. RGs regard themselves as more skilled at fruit-machine gambling than NRGs.

Additionally it was suggested that participants in the thinking aloud condition would take longer.

Participants
Sixty participants (30 RGs and 30 NRGs) were recruited through advertisements and, for some of the RGs, by personal contact. There was a gender imbalance in the RG group (29 males and 1 female). The **mean** age was 23.4 years.

Procedure
Each participant played a fruit machine in a local arcade starting with a £3 stake (=30 free plays). They were asked to try to stay on for 60 gambles. After that (when they would have won back their original stake plus £3) they could take the money or continue playing.

There were three forms of assessment:

- *Behavioural* – skill of RGs and NRGs was observed on seven **dependent variables** such as total plays, total time, play rate and end stake.
- *Thinking aloud* – half the RGs and half the NRGs were asked to think aloud while playing to gain insight into their cognitive processes. These verbalisations were tape-recorded.
- *Post-experiment interview* – participants were asked their views on what skills were involved and to assess their own skill level.

Key term: heuristics and cognitive biases

*A **heuristic** is a strategy used to work something out or solve a problem – it may be a set of rules (such as a recipe for a cake), an educated guess or just common sense. It is a guideline of what to do in specific situations.*

You may have some general heuristics for solving problems, such as 'if it doesn't work try reading the instructions' or 'if I want to know what's on TV tonight I check the listing in the newspaper' or 'when my teacher asks a question I just say the first thing that pops into my head'. It's a plan of action.

*Heuristics don't guarantee a solution (whereas algorithms do) and they may lead to **cognitive biases** that skew the way a person perceives the world.*

Results
Behavioural data – there was no indication that RGs were actually more skilful then NRGs. There were only two **significant** differences, e.g. RGs played faster than NRGs and the RGs in the thinking aloud group had the longest intervals between wins. Another difference emerged in terms of behaviour after breaking even; 71% of the RGs who broke even continued playing whereas only 29% of the NRGs did.

Thinking aloud – **content analysis** was used to identify the differences in the statements made by RGs and NRGs. RGs produced significantly more irrational verbalisations (14%) than the NRGs (2.5%).

Post-experimental interview – most RGs reported that fruit machine playing involved equal chance and skill and rated themselves as skilled, whereas the same was not true of NRGs.

Discussion
All four hypotheses were supported, suggesting that cognitive distortions may underlie gambling behaviour.

This suggests that pathological gambling might be treated using a cognitive approach such as audio playback therapy.

Qs 6.11

1. What are the two conditions of the independent variable?
2. Sometimes this study is mistakenly called a field experiment. What makes it a quasi-experiment rather than a field experiment?
3. Identify (a) a one-tailed hypothesis and (b) a null hypothesis from this study.
4. Describe the sampling technique(s) that were used.
5. Outline **one** weakness of the sample that was used.
6. What ethical issues are important in this study and how could the researchers deal with each of them?
7. Identify the experimental design used in this study.
8. Identify **at least one** control used in this study.
9. Describe **one** similarity and **one** difference between the results about RGs and NRGs.
10. State **two** conclusions you would draw from the results of this study.
11. Explain why a cognitive approach to the treatment of gambling might be appropriate, based on the results of this study.

The detailed version

Context and aim

A number of psychologists have been interested in the cognitive psychology of gambling, in other words what is going on in the minds of gamblers. Two approaches have been used: 'normative decision theory' and 'heuristics and biases'.

Normative decision theory
Normative decision theory is concerned with rational decision making. The theory claims it can predict the decisions a gambler will make. However, research has not found support as it appears that choices are often irrational. In fact the theory would not predict that people would gamble in the first place because the odds are against them!

Heuristics and biases
Wagenaar (1988) proposed that heuristics are the best way to understand the cognitive processes involved in gambling, i.e. the thought processes that go on when a person is gambling. The problem for gamblers is that the heuristics they choose produce distortions because they are selected on the wrong occasions. Wagenaar identified 16 such distortions, the six most important ones being:

1   *Illusion of control* – i.e. behaviours which give you the illusion you are in control, such as choosing your own lottery ticket or having a favourite fruit machine. Such control makes the player think there is skill involved.

2   *Flexible attributions* – gamblers' **self-esteem** is bolstered by attributing success to their own skill and attributing failure to some external influence. Similarly they put a spin on events so that a loss becomes described as a 'near win' or as something that could have been predicted in advance (called **hindsight bias**).

3   *Representativeness* – a belief that **random** events have a pattern, e.g. if you toss a coin nine times and keep getting heads it must be increasingly likely that tails will come up next time. Observed events do not represent true odds exactly (try one of the activities below).

4   *Availability bias* – people's judgements reflect the frequency of relevant instances. For example, you hear about lots of people who have won the pools (increased 'availability' of information), which makes you think it is more common than it is.

5   *Illusory correlations* – people (mistakenly) believe that some events are **correlated** with success, for example rolling dice softly to get low numbers.

6   *Fixation on absolute frequency* – measuring success in terms of absolute rather than relative frequency. Gamblers may win a lot but relative to the number of times they gamble their successes are small.

All of these heuristics lead to biases in cognitive processing, i.e. distortions in a person's thinking.

The cognitive psychology of fruit machine players
In previous research Griffiths (1990 a, b, c) found that regular fruit machine gamblers used a variety of heuristics during gambling, especially to explain big losses or for bad gambling. Gamblers believed their actions to be, at least in part, skilful and also gained a sense of control through the familiarity with a particular machine.

Do you wonder what to do when you walk into a supermarket? Does your mind go blank when everyone looks at you? The world is a confusing place and we are faced with all sorts of choices all the time. Therefore it helps to have a variety of guiding principles that direct our behaviour in commonly encountered situations. These are heuristics.

Aim and hypotheses

The aim of this study was to compare the behaviour of regular and non-regular fruit machine gamblers – RGs and NRGs. There were three hypotheses:

1   There are no differences between RGs and NRGs on objective measures of skill (seven behavioural dependent variables, listed on the next page).

2   RGs produce more irrational verbalisations than NRGs (assessed using the 'thinking aloud method').

3   RGs are more skill oriented (i.e. focused on skills involved in gambling) than NRGs on subjective measures of skill (assessed by **self-reports** in post-experimental **semi-structured interviews**).

A fourth hypothesis was mentioned: participants in the thinking aloud condition would take longer than those not in this condition.

For the purposes of this experiment:

*   Fruit machine skill was defined as *'the ability of the individual to affect the outcome of gambling positively (e.g. more gambles with initial money staked and/or more winnings with initial money staked)'*.

*   Irrational verbalisations were those that were *'contrary to reason (e.g. personification of the machine or use of heuristics)'*.

Qs 6.12

1   Describe your own example of a heuristic (look on the internet).
2   Select **two** distortions described by Wagenaar and explain how they could explain the behaviour of fruit machine gamblers.
3   How are heuristics used when gambling?
4   How was 'fruit machine skill' operationalised?
5   Give an example of an irrational verbalisation.

Try this   6.5

Representative heuristic

You can investigate the representative heuristic by placing 50 pieces of red paper and 50 pieces of blue paper in a hat. Draw out 10 slips of paper – did you get five of each colour?

Randomness

You can also try asking people to 'mimic' the rolling of a dice. They should write down (or say) 100 digits between 1 and 6. Were there any consecutive digits that were the same? People avoid this because it doesn't 'feel' random. Try rolling a dice 100 times and see what happens.

Griffiths: the core study *continued*

Method

Participants

Sixty participants took part (**mean** age 23.4 years), half were RGs (29 males and 1 female) and half were NRGs (15 males and 15 females). RGs gambled at least once a week, NRGs gambled once a month or less (but had used fruit machines at least once in their lives).

The participants were recruited through poster advertisements around local university and college campuses. A number of the RGs were recruited via a gambler known to the author.

The gender imbalance was unfortunate but fruit machine gambling is dominated by males.

Procedure

Each participant was given £3 to gamble on a fruit machine in a local arcade (this amount of money was equivalent to 30 free plays). Participants were asked to play FRUITSKILL unless they objected – so some players choose a different game. They were asked to try to stay on their machine for at least 60 gambles (i.e. break even and win back £3). At that point they were allowed to either keep the £3 or carry on gambling.

When designing the study there were two considerations which relate to the **ecological validity** of the study:

- *The setting*: the **experiment** took place outside the **laboratory** because some researchers have questioned whether participants in a laboratory study of fruit machine gambling behave as they would in other more natural settings.
- *Money*: using someone else's money may reduce the excitement and risk taking involved in gambling. However, allowing participants to keep their winnings may compensate for this.

Behavioural data: assessing skill levels

Each player was tested individually. Griffiths was nearby and observed their behaviour, recording the seven **dependent variables**:

Behavioural dependent variables used to assess skill of RGs and NRGs.

Dependent variable	Operational definition
Total plays	Total number of plays during play session
Total time	Total time in minutes of play during one play session
Play rate	Total number of plays per minute during a play session
End stake	Total winnings in number of 10p pieces after a play session was over
Wins	Total number of wins during a play session
Win rate (time)	Total number of minutes between each win during a play session
Win rate (plays)	Total number of plays between each win during a play session

Thinking aloud: assessing verbalisations

Half the participants in each group were **randomly allocated** to the thinking aloud condition. The reason that only half the participants did this was in case it had some effect on their behaviour. Previous research has found no effect except a slight slowing down of performance. This led to the fourth **hypothesis** to be tested that 'thinking aloud participants would take longer to complete the task than non-thinking aloud participants'.

The following instructions were given to the 'thinking aloud' participants:

'The thinking aloud method consists of verbalising every thought that passes through your mind while you are playing. It is important to remember the following points:

1   *Say everything that goes through your mind. Do not censor any of your thoughts even if they seem irrelevant to you.*
2   *Keep talking as continuously as possible, even if your ideas are not clearly structured.*
3   *Speak clearly.*
4   *Do not hesitate to use fragmented sentences if necessary. Do not worry about speaking in complete sentence.*
5   *Do not try to justify your thoughts.'*

The verbalisations were tape recorded using a lapel microphone and later transcribed.

Interview: assessing subjective judgement of skill

After playing the machines participants were interviewed using a **semi-structured interview**. They were asked their opinion about the level of skill involved in fruit machine playing and asked to judge their own skill level.

Try this
6.6

Try the thinking aloud method yourself. You can do it while engaged in any activity, such as noughts and crosses or you too can play a fruit machine (there are a number of free online sites for playing fruit machines!).

You might tape record yourself or a partner and try to analyse your thoughts using the coding system produced by Griffiths. The full system can be found on our website at www.psypress.com/cw/banyard

You could then try to perform a content analysis on your data as described on the facing page.

Biographical notes

Professor Mark Griffiths *is Europe's only Professor of Gambling Studies (Nottingham Trent University). He is Director of the International Gaming Research Unit and has won numerous awards for his research (e.g. John Rosecrance Research Prize, CELEJ Prize, Joseph Lister Prize, etc.). He has published over 1,500 articles in refereed journals, books, book chapters and has also appeared on over 2,000 radio/television programmes. He is also a very active blogger (see http://drmarkgriffiths.wordpress.com).*

Jamie Davies interviewed Mark, asking him about his own gambling 'Yes I do [gamble], roulette is the game that I play – but when I'm playing roulette I'm actually buying entertainment rather than trying to win money. When I am playing on slot machines though I call it 'research!' (see www.psychblog.co.uk/ interview-the-gambling-man-prof-mark-griffiths-119.html).

Results

Analysis of behavioural data

A number of differences between the RGs and NRGs were noted but only two **significant** differences were found on the dependent variables:

- RGs had a significantly higher playing rate (eight gambles per minute as compared to six per minute for NRGs).
- RGs who thought aloud had a significantly lower win rate in number of gambles (i.e. the number of gambles between each win was significantly lower than for NRGs).

An additional observation was made about how RGs and NRGs behaved once they broke even. Ten of the 14 (71%) RGs who broke even after 60 gambles carried on gambling until they had lost everything. Whereas only two out of seven (29%) NRGs did – a highly significant difference.

Analysis of interview

The post-experimental semi-structured interviews yielded answers to the following questions:

- *Is there any skill involved in playing the fruit machine?* Most NRGs said 'mostly chance' whereas most RGs said 'equal chance and skill'.
- *How skilful do you think you are compared to the average person?* NRGs viewed themselves as below average whereas RGs said 'above average' or 'totally skilled'.
- *What skill (if any) is involved in playing fruit machines?* RGs identified the following skills: knowledge of 'feature skills', knowledge of when the machine will pay out and knowledge of not playing when it has just paid out.

There were also some indirect skill factors. For example, RGs objected to gambling on a particular machine because they weren't familiar with it.

Analysis of thinking aloud

The verbalisations were analysed by performing a **content analysis** of the transcriptions. In order to do this Griffiths first of all produced a list of **behavioural categories** (**coding system**) by looking through the transcriptions and identifying 30 *utterance categorisations*. Some examples of the categories can be seen in the table below. Griffiths then categorised the statements made by each participant. The number of utterances in each category for each participant was adjusted as a percentage of the total for that participant. Finally, totals were calculated for RGs versus NRGs.

Attempts were made to establish the **reliability** of the categorisations. This was done using two other raters. **Inter-rater reliability** was low because one rater knew very little about fruit machine gambling and therefore couldn't understand the terminology; the second rater had not been present during the recording of the utterances and therefore had no context and could not make as much sense of the utterances as the author.

Some of the significant findings from the table below include:

- RGs made significantly more percentage verbalisations in categories 1 and 21.
- NRGs made significantly more percentage verbalisations in categories 14, 15 and 31.
- RGs also referred to their mind going blank and feeling frustrated, topics rarely mentioned by NRGs.
- RGs produced significantly more irrational verbalisations (14%) than the NRGs (2.5%).
- Overall both groups used more rational than irrational verbalisations.

RGs used a variety of **heuristics**, for example gamblers used **hindsight bias** to explain their loses: *'I had a feeling it wasn't going to pay very much after it had just given me a "feature" and there were many flexible attributions, such as "…two nudges, gotta be … oh, you son of a bitch, you (the machine) changed them". Some gamblers had completely erroneous perceptions: "I'm only going to put one quid in to start with because psychologically I think it's very important … it bluffs the machine".'* Note that many of the comments above contain personification, for example stating that the machine *'is in a bad mood'* or *'doesn't like me'*.

*Utterance categorisations used in the **content analysis** with mean scores for NRGs and RGs, and **significance** values.*

		NRGs	RGs	Sig*
Irrational verbalisations				
1	Personification of the fruit machine, e.g. *The machine likes me.*	1.14	7.54	0.0004
2	Explaining away loses, e.g. *I lost because I wasn't concentrating.*	0.41	3.12	0.026
4	Swearing at the machine, e.g. *You bastard.*	0.08	0.60	0.042
Rational verbalisations				
7	Reference to winning, e.g. *I won 40 pence I think.*	6.77	9.79	0.042
14	Questions relating to confusion/non-understanding, e.g. *What's going on here?*	13.24	1.56	0.000
15	Statements relating to confusion/non-understanding, e.g. *I don't understand this.*	4.81	1.72	0.008
16	Reference to skill, e.g. *I only won because I was so quick.*	1.47	5.34	0.024
17	Humour, e.g. Two melons – *I like it when I get my hands on two melons.*	0.89	0.41	0.40
21	Reference to the 'number system', e.g. *I got a '2' there.*	1.45	9.49	0.003
25	Hoping/needing a certain feature to appear in the win line, e.g. *I need an orange to win.*	0.77	3.28	0.014
28	Reference to luck, e.g. *My luck's in today.*	0.69	0.52	0.76
31	Miscellaneous utterances, e.g. *I think I'll get a bag of chips after playing this.*	25.53	11.73	0.000

Sig* = significance, the lower the number the more significant the difference. The acceptable level for significance was the 1% level or .01

Qs 6.13

1. How was the independent variable operationalised?
2. Why do you think participants might have behaved differently if the study had been conducted in a laboratory rather than a natural setting?
3. Identify **three** key aspects of the 'thinking aloud method'.
4. Explain what is involved in content analysis.
5. How was reliability assessed in this study?
6. Inter-rater reliability was low. Outline **one** reason put forward for this.
7. In what way does this low reliability challenge the validity of the findings from the think aloud data?
8. Give **one** example of quantitative data collected in this study, and **one** example of qualitative data.
9. Describe **one** strength of both kinds of data in the context of this study.

Discussion

Hypothesis 1
The behavioural data show that, on the whole, there were no differences between RGs and NRGs, supporting **hypothesis** 1. It was found that RGs gambled more times than NRGs using the same amount of money which might imply RGs have greater skill. However, it may be that the skill of RGs is little more than being able to 'gamble up' small wins into larger ones using 'nudge' and 'hold' buttons.

It is possible that gamblers spend time on fruit machines not to win but because it is intrinsically rewarding in itself and choose machines to maximise their playing time.

Hypothesis 2
The analysis of verbalisations shows that RGs did make more irrational verbalisations than NRGs, supporting hypothesis 2. However, RGs made far fewer irrational verbalisations than the 80% previously reported by Ladouceur *et al.* (1988). Nevertheless the rate of irrational verbalisations supports the general notion of **cognitive bias** in RGs.

NRGs produced more statements of confusion/non-understanding than RGs but this was not surprising as many aspects of the game were new to them. Another key difference was that NRGs rarely reported 'my mind has gone blank' whereas a number of RGs stopped speaking for up to 30 seconds. This was probably because they were on 'automatic pilot', a characteristic of experienced players in any game (e.g. chess) where thought processes are not controlled by conscious cognitive processes.

Hypothesis 3
Skill orientation differed between RGs and NRGs, supporting hypothesis 3. RGs were more skill oriented in their self-comparison ratings and in questions related to skill factors. Fisher (1993) identified three major skills:

1 *Choosing which machine to play*, including knowing how much has been put in to a machine and how much it has paid out. These skills were listed in this study.
2 *Knowing the reels*, i.e. knowing the order of the symbols (unique to each machine) which enables the 'nudge' feature to be used effectively. Knowledge of reels and of nudges were reported as separate skills in this study.
3 *Gambling,* i.e. using the gamble button. Players believe this increases winnings but machine manufacturers report it is entirely **random**, therefore it is a 'pseudo-skill'.

Other genuine skills were reported in this study including light oscillation (pressing a button when particular symbols are lit up) and knowing the number system.

Hypothesis 4
Those participants in the thinking aloud condition did take longer to gamble than those who were not 'thinking aloud' but this difference was not **significant**.

Conclusion
The real difference between RGs and NRGs is probably cognitive; RGs think more skill is involved than there actually is. There are also cognitive differences in the way RGs react towards the machine itself, such as **personification** – although this may be a general tendency to personify something which one is in regular contact with.

Recommendations
The 'thinking aloud method' produced descriptions of behaviour rather than explanations. In order to explain behaviour (i.e. predict when a particular **heuristic** will be used) rigged fruit machines might be used where sequences of wins and losses are manipulated to reveal the heuristics in the thoughts reported.

The results of this study may be used to rehabilitate gamblers. If cognitive biases stimulate gambling then cognitive therapies may be appropriate. 'Audio playback therapy' might involve taping a player's thoughts (as captured by 'thinking aloud') and playing this back to highlight the irrational verbalisations. This was tried with four of the RGs in this study who said they were surprised by what they said and thought.

www.CartoonStock.com

Qs 6.14

1 For each of the **four** original hypotheses, state a conclusion that can be drawn in relation to this hypothesis and provide **one** piece of evidence to support each conclusion.
2 Do you feel that any of the results/ conclusions are surprising? Explain why or why not.
3 Griffiths felt that the think aloud method could be improved. Explain why.

Things you could do ...

Read the original article by Griffiths This can be obtained from your local library by giving them the full reference and ordering a photocopy.

Read other accounts of research on gambling: see Dr Griffiths' blog http:// drmarkgriffiths.wordpress.com

Watch a video
On YouTube *Meet the Gambling Professor: An Interview to Mark Griffiths*.

Also on YouTube is a programme on gambling made by BBC for Discovery, *Against all odds*.

...Links to core studies...

This study is difficult to categorise. It is placed in the chapter on individual differences but it just as easily could be placed in cognitive psychology (because of the faulty thinking of gamblers) or social psychology (because social psychology embraces explanations of behaviour in the real world). This study tells us something about the rewards of gambling and we can explain some of these using a **behaviourist** analysis (like **Bandura et al.**).

Evaluating the study by Griffiths

There are no simple answers.

Evaluating a study requires you to think.

*We have provided some pointers here, linked to the **RESEARCH METHODS** and **KEY ISSUES** covered in Chapter 1 (Psychological investigations) and Chapter 7 (Key issues).*

You can read suggested answers on our website www.psypress.com/cw/banyard

The research method
This was a quasi-experiment but also conducted in a natural environment.

What are the strengths and limitations of these research methods in the context of this study?

Research techniques
Other research techniques were used in this study: observation, self-report ('think aloud' and semi-structured interview) and a content analysis.

What are the strengths and limitations of these research techniques in the context of this study?

The experimental design was Independent measures.

What are the strengths and limitations of this design in the context of this study?

The sample
There were various significant characteristics of the sample: some were volunteers, they were college students and almost all of the RGs were male.

In what way do such characteristics affect the representativeness of this sample?

In what way might college students differ in their gambling behaviour to others? How does this affect the conclusions drawn from the study?

Ethics
Gambling is not generally approved of and it has the potential to become addictive.

What ethical issues should have concerned the researchers in this study, and how might they have dealt with these issues?

Reliability
Content analysis was conducted using a coding system developed and applied by Griffiths. There was low agreement with other raters.

How does this affect the conclusions drawn from this study?

Ecological validity
Griffiths considered issues relating to ecological validity – the setting where gambling took place was natural but the fact that participants were not using their own money reduced the naturalness.

To what extent can we generalise the findings from this study to real life?

Quantitative or qualitative?
Both quantitative and qualitative data were collected in this study.

Select one kind of behaviour and give an example of how it was measured quantitatively and qualitatively.

What are the strengths and limitations of each kind of data in the context of this study?

Applications/usefulness
How valuable was this study? What influence do you think it has had on the treatment of abnormality?

What next?
*Describe **one** change to this study, and say how you think this might affect the outcome.*

Producing effective evaluation
When you produce your own answers to the issues on the left there are two things to ensure:
1   Contextualisation
2   Elaboration

The key to **CONTEXTUALISATION** is to ensure that your answer includes some information about this particular study. When there are three marks you need to add further material. For example:

> *Question:*
> Discuss the reliability of the findings of Griffiths' study. **[3]**
>
> *Answer:*
> **STATE:** Reliability refers to the consistency of data.
> **CONTEXT:** In Griffiths' study he considered the reliability of the content analysis by having three people code the 'think aloud' verbalisations.
> **COMMENT:** In fact the three coders did not produce consistent results which would lead us to doubt the reliability of Griffiths' results. However, he suggested that the reasons the reliability was low was because one rater was inexperienced and the other didn't understand the context.

The key to **ELABORATION** is the three-point rule (see page xii). This rule generally applies to 3 mark questions. However, sometimes elaboration is required in a 2 mark question. For example:

> *Question:*
> With reference to Griffith's study of gambling, discuss the ecological validity of the findings. **[2]**
>
> *Answer:*
> **STATE:** Griffiths' study is high in ecological validity because it was conducted in the gambler's natural environment.
> **COMMENT:** This means that the gamblers would have been behaving in the way they usually do and their behaviour would represent their usual gambling behaviour. This means it can be generalised to gambling behaviour in the real world.

The individual differences approach

On pages 182–183 and 226–227 we have discussed the **individual differences approach**.

The study by Griffiths concerns gambling addiction.

*   In what way is this an example of the individual differences approach?
*   Discuss the strengths and weaknesses of the individual differences approach using examples from the Griffiths study.

I should be so lucky

Gambling is a growing industry in this country and people are being given more opportunities to make bets all the time. Will gambling become the new crack?

Things that increase addictive behaviours

Availability

There are a number of environmental factors that affect the incidence of addictive behaviours in a society. One factor that affects the level of alcoholism is the availability of alcohol and the average consumption of alcohol by the general population. Comparison studies have found near perfect **correlations** between the number of deaths through liver cirrhosis (generally attributed to alcohol abuse) and the average consumption of alcohol in different countries (Orford, 1985). The availability factor also affects the consumption of cigarettes as shown in the study below.

If we examine the pattern of cigarette consumption compared with the retail price of cigarettes in this country we can observe a remarkable relationship. The chart below shows how the curve for consumption is the mirror image of the curve for retail price (Townsend *et al.*, 1994). Since 1970 any increase in price has brought about a decrease in smoking. At the time of the study there was a slight decrease in the price of cigarettes (figures adjusted to take account of inflation) and a corresponding rise in smoking. This rise in smoking was particularly noticeable in young people, and according to Townsend *et al.* regular smoking by 15-year-old boys increased from 20% to 25% and by 16–19-year-old girls from 28% to 32%. This connection between price and consumption suggests an obvious policy for governments who want to reduce smoking.

Social cues: tobacco advertising

In their response to the Health of the Nation strategy (published by DoH, 1992), the British Psychological Society (1993) called for a ban on the advertising of all tobacco products. This call was backed up by the government's own research (DoH, 1993) which suggested a relationship between advertising and sales. Also, in four countries that have banned tobacco advertising (New Zealand, Canada, Finland and Norway) there has been a **significant** drop in consumption.

Tobacco advertising has now been banned in the UK and in Europe and smoking has been banned in all public buildings in the UK. This is still quite a recent event so the effect on levels of smoking is not yet known. One clear effect though is that more smokers are experiencing hypothermia after huddling in alleys outside bars and restaurants as they try and find somewhere to have a cigarette.

Gambling

If social cues and availability are two key features that encourage addictive behaviours then it is likely that the UK will see an explosion in problem gambling in the next few years. Gambling companies are very visible with their sponsorship of sporting events and on prime time television (Lotto). People are also shown positive images of gambling through sports shows and game shows. On top of this the internet offers more and easier opportunities to burn your money.

Just-world effect

The *just-world effect* (Lerner, 1980), refers to the tendency of some people to believe the world is 'just' and so therefore people 'get what they deserve'. They believe that good things do (or should) happen to good people and bad things should happen to bad people. The National Lottery in the UK is a good example of this in that who gets to win is a complete lottery (the clue is in the name) but the press seem to think that the prizes should go to the 'deserving poor'. There are a lot of negative comments when someone with a criminal record wins the big prize, for example Michael Carroll from Norfolk was relentlessly vilified in the press after his big win in 2002.

Psychological studies have found that people who believe in a just world are more likely to believe that rape victims contributed to the assault by their behaviour, that sick people caused their illness and the poor deserve to have no money. The big problem with this type of thinking is the world is not just and the bad guys sometimes win and sometimes bad things happen to good people.

Rather surprisingly it has been shown that belief in a just world has some benefits for the believers. They are likely to have less depression, less stress and greater life satisfaction (Bègue, 2005). I guess it just goes to show that self-delusion is good for you.

Michael Carroll, self-styled 'King of the Chavs', still standing despite being vilified by the press.

The relationship between the price of cigarettes and consumption 1971–1990.

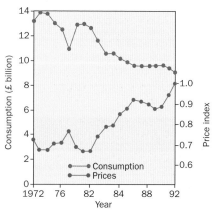

The gambler's fallacy

'I'm going to win today. I can feel it in my bones.' Gamblers (and casual punters) often develop irrational beliefs about their ability to control or predict events.

Among the many irrational beliefs is the idea that a **random** event can be affected or predicted by other random events. This is known as the *gambler's fallacy*. So when watching a roulette wheel, if the little ball hasn't fallen in the number 18 hole for a long while you might believe that 'law of averages' will mean that it must turn up soon. The trouble is that there is no such thing as the 'law of averages' and the chances of the ball dropping into number 18 on the next turn of the wheel are exactly the same as they were on the last one and the one before that.

This faulty thinking can take a number of forms as gamblers might risk their money in the belief that they are having a 'run of luck' or that their 'run of bad luck' will end soon.

An interesting version of this can be seen in people's choices of numbers for the National Lottery. A sequence of related numbers is just as likely to turn up as a series of not related numbers. So the chances of winning on 1, 2, 3, 4, 5, 6 are the same as 8, 12, 17, 34, 36, 42, but who would pick the first sequence? It just seems impossible that such a combination could win.

Multiple choice questions

1 Normative decision theory suggests that gambling is:
   a Rational.
   b Irrational.
   c Both rational and irrational.
   d Neither rational or irrational.

2 Wagenaar suggested that certain heuristics may explain gambling. Which of the following was NOT one of them?
   a Illusion of control.
   b Temperamental bias.
   c Availability bias.
   d Representativeness.

3 Griffiths predicted that regular gamblers would be:
   a Better than NRGs on objective measures of skill.
   b The same as NRGs on objective measure of skill.
   c Less skilful than NRGs on objective measures of skill.
   d This was not one of his predictions.

4 In the study there were:
   a More males.   b More females.
   c Equal numbers.   d They were all males.

5 The method used to assess what participants were thinking was called:
   a Thinking aloud.
   b Private thinking.
   c Audio thinking.
   d Thinking bias.

6 RGs were found to be:
   a More irrational than NRGs.
   b Less irrational than NRGs.
   c There was no significant difference between the two groups in terms of irrationality.
   d They were mad, bad and dangerous to know.

7 How many hypotheses were supported by the results?
   a 1   b 2
   c 3   d 4

8 When asked to speak their thoughts, some of the RGs stopped speaking for short spells. The explanation given was:
   a They were losing money.
   b They were on automatic pilot.
   c They went into escape mode.
   d Both b and c.

9 In the discussion Griffiths suggests that fruit machine gamblers play because:
   a They want to win money.
   b They are stupid.
   c The game is intrinsically rewarding.
   d All of the above.

10 A possible therapy that could be developed is called:
   a Thinking aloud therapy.
   b Audio thinking therapy.
   c Audio playback therapy.
   d Auditory therapy.

Answers are on page 247.

There are three kinds of question that can be asked about the Griffiths study, as represented here by sections A, B and C.

See page x for further notes on the exam paper and styles of question.

Exam-style questions

Section A questions

1 In the study on gambling by Griffiths there are four hypotheses.
   (a) State **one** of these hypotheses. [2]
   (b) Explain how evidence was collected to support this hypothesis. [2]

2 Griffiths refers to heuristics in his study on gambling.
   (a) Explain what a heuristic is. [2]
   (b) Describe **one** of the heuristics that might explain gambling behaviour. [2]

3 In Griffiths' study of gambling describe **one** similarity and **one** difference that was found between regular and non-regular gamblers. [4]

4 Griffiths used a method called 'thinking aloud' to gain insight into gamblers' behaviour.
   (a) Briefly outline what this method involved. [2]
   (b) Give **one** weakness of using this method to assess gambling. [2]

5 From the study by Griffiths,
   (a) Give **one** example of a rational verbalisation. [2]
   (b) Give **one** example of an irrational verbalisation. [2]

6 In the study by Griffiths on gambling,
   (a) Identify **two** dependent variables used to objectively measure skill. [2]
   (b) For one of these variables state the associated finding. [2]

7 In the study by Griffiths,
   (a) Identify **two** pieces of quantitative data gathered in this study. [2]
   (b) Outline **one** strength of quantitative data used in this study. [2]

8 In the study by Griffths outline **two** ethical issues that were raised. [4]

9 In Griffiths' study into gambling,
   (a) Outline **one** way that the sample was representative. [2]
   (b) Outline **one** way that the sample was not representative. [2]

10 In the Griffiths' study describe **two** ways that the procedure was standardised. [4]

Section B question

Answer the following questions with reference to the Griffiths study:

(a) State **one** of the hypotheses investigated in this study. [2]

(b) Describe the sample used in this study and give **one** weakness of using this sample. [6]

(c) Outline the procedure of this study. [6]

(d) Outline the findings of this study. [6]

(e) Discuss the reliability of the findings of this study. [6]

(f) Describe and evaluate changes that could be made to the way this study was conducted. [10]

Section C question

(a) Outline **one** assumption of the individual differences approach. [2]

(b) Describe how the individual differences approach could explain gambling. [4]

(c) Describe **one** similarity and **one** difference between the Griffith study and any other core studies that take the individual differences approach. [6]

(d) Discuss strengths and weaknesses of the individual differences approach using examples from any core studies that take this approach. [12]

Exam-style questions

The example exam-style questions here are set out like the exam but in Section A of the exam there will be only one question on each of the three individual differences core studies, i.e. three individual differences questions, each worth 4 marks in total.

Section A type questions

1   Rosenhan conducted a study where pseudopatients sought treatment in mental hospitals.

    (a)   Outline **one** way in which the hospital staff were treated unethically. [2]

    (b)   Suggest what might have been done to deal with this unethical treatment, and what effect this might have had on the results. [2]

Stig's answer

(a) The staff didn't know they were part of a study.

(b) If the staff knew the truth the study would have been pointless.

Chardonnay's answer

(a) The staff were deceived: not aware that pseudopatients would be presenting themselves and, in the second study, didn't know that really there weren't any pseudopatients.

(b) One way would be to debrief all staff afterwards and offer them the opportunity to withdraw their data. However, then the results would be biased because of attrition.

Teacher's comments

Stig, you're right in part (a) but it would be a good idea to identify the ethical guideline. Similarly in part (b) you are probably right in speculating that the study would have been pointless – but why? More specifically, to answer the question you need to refer to the actual results of the study!

Chardonnay, you have given a very clear answer in part (a), over and above the requirements of the question. Your part (b) is an excellent answer showing quite a sophisticated understanding of ethical issues.

Stig (1+0 out of 4 marks) Chardonnay (2+2 out of 4 marks)

2   In the study by Rosenhan (sane in insane places):

    (a)   Describe **one** example of how the hospital staff dealt with requests for information from the pseudopatients. [2]

    (b)   Outline **two** effects this had on the pseudopatients. [2]

Stig's answer

(a) Most of them gave a brief answer without eye contact and just walked on.

(b) It depersonalised them.

Chardonnay's answer

(a) The staff largely ignored the patients.

(b) The effects were that the patients didn't feel they counted and were not real people. They were depersonalised and it lowered their self-esteem.

Teacher's comments

Stig, to the point and spot on in part (a). This is a good example of getting full credit without waffling. In part (b) the question asks for two effects, so only 1 mark awarded – a mark carelessly thrown away.

Chardonnay, your answer is a bit too brief in part (a), it just doesn't display a sufficiently detailed knowledge of the study. You might have added 'and walked away when spoken to'. In part (b), you have given two effects – depersonalisation and reduction in self-esteem so fine for 2 marks.

Stig (2+1 out of 4 marks) Chardonnay (1+2 out of 4 marks)

3   In the study on multiple personality disorder Thigpen and Cleckley used psychometric tests:

    (a)   Identify **two** tests completed by Eve. [2]

    (b)   Explain why it was necessary for an independent tester to analyse the results of the tests carried out on Eve. [2]

Stig's answer

(a) Eve did an IQ test and a personality test.

(b) It was better to have an independent tester so that he wouldn't affect how she performed.

Chardonnay's answer

(a) Eve did an IQ test and a projective personality test (the Rorschach test).

(b) They employed an independent tester so that the tester was not biased in how they interpreted Eve's responses or that she didn't act up to him how she might have done with Thigpen and Cleckley who she knew quite well.

Teacher's comments

Stig, 1 mark for IQ test, but your second answer ('personality test') is a bit too vague to gain credit. For part (b) your answer is again lacking in detail; you need a bit more by way of explanation – so just 1 mark again.

Chardonnay shows you how it's done. Both of her answers are spot on. She has described the personality test in more detail in part (a). In part (b) she provides plenty of detail giving a full explanation – over and above what is required for 2 marks.

Stig (1+1 out of 4 marks) Chardonnay (2+2 out of 4 marks)

4   Thigpen and Cleckley's study of multiple personality disorder focused on one individual, Eve. This is a case study. Give **one** strength and **one** weakness of the case study method in the context of this study. [4]

Stig's answer

One strength of the case study method is that it allows you to study one individual case of multiple personality or other abnormal disorder. Such cases are very rare so it is really the main way to study the disorder while giving sufficient detail.

A weakness is that any individual is unique, there were special things about Eve's case which are unique and therefore the conclusions drawn from this may not apply to other cases.

Chardonnay's answer

Strength: Case studies allow us to gain rich detail about one individual case.

Weakness: The problem is that the individual is likely to be unique in some way and we can't generalise from this case.

Teacher's comments

This time Stig you are the one who provided bucket loads of detail and gets full marks – but not just because of the detail. You have carefully read the question and realised that you also had to include the context, i.e. effectively relate your answer to Thigpen and Cleckley's study.

Chardonnay, you are right about the strength and weakness of a case study but you haven't connected each of these to the Thigpen and Cleckley study.

Stig (2+2 out of 4 marks) Chardonnay (1+1 out of 4 marks)

5   Griffiths suggested that regular fruit machine gamblers would be more irrational than non-regular gamblers.

(a) Explain why he expected to find this difference. [2]
(b) Identify **one** piece of evidence from the study that shows that regular gamblers are more irrational than non-regular gamblers. [2]

Stig's answer

(a) Griffiths expected to find that regular gamblers would be more irrational than non-regular gamblers because they can't be thinking rationally or they wouldn't be gambling.
(b) The regular gamblers said more irrational statements than the non-regulars (14% versus 2.5%).

Chardonnay's answer

(a) Griffiths expected this difference because another psychologist proposed that gamblers use heuristics which distort cognitive processes and this leads to irrational behaviour.
(b) The regular gamblers made more percentage verbalisations which were irrational whereas the non-regular gamblers made more percentage verbalisations which were rational.

Teacher's comments

Stig, there is no need to repeat the question in your answer; your somewhat lengthy answer doesn't actually say very much. However there is a glimmer of knowledge here – one argument against normative decision theory is that it predicts people would not gamble at all, as you say. In part (b) you have given a briefer answer and the inclusion of the percentages gives you full marks.

Chardonnay as usual you have given a careful and well-informed answer for part (a) but in part (b) it's your turn to write a lot of words but say very little – really all you have said is that there was a difference. You did say 'percentage verbalisations' which is the key point about where the evidence comes from, but not sufficient for 2 marks.

Stig (1+2 out of 4 marks) Chardonnay (2+1 out of 4 marks)

6   In his study on gambling Griffiths endeavoured to ensure that the design was ecologically valid.

(a) Describe **one** aspect of the design that aimed to achieve this. [2]
(b) Explain how this would have made the study more ecologically valid. [2]

Stig's answer

(a) Using real fruit machines was one way to do this.
(b) This would mean the participants played the machines like they would normally in everyday life.

Chardonnay's answer

(a) The study was conducted in a fruit machine arcade.
(b) If the study was in a lab then they might have been less relaxed but in an everyday natural setting people are likely to behave more like they do in real life.

Teacher's comments

You need to read what you have written Stig; of course they are real fruit machines but Griffiths could have used real fruit machines in a lab. It's more natural than playing a fruit machine on the internet though, so 1 mark. Chardonnay's got the key factor – real machines in a *natural* setting.

In part (b) Stig you've thrown away another mark by not spelling out the detail – why would they behave differently in the real arcade than in the lab? Chardonnay has included this detail for the full 2 marks.

Stig (1+1 out of 4 marks) Chardonnay (2+2 out of 4 marks)

Exam-style questions

The example exam-style question here is set out as in Section B of the exam. However, there is no guarantee, in Section B, of a question that includes one of the individual differences core studies.

Section B type questions

7 (a) What was the aim of the Rosenhan study? [2]
   (b) Describe the sample used in the Rosenhan study and give **one** limitation of it. [6]
   (c) Describe how data was gathered in the Rosenhan study. [6]
   (d) Give **one** strength and **one** weakness of observational studies. [6]
   (e) Suggest **two** changes to the Rosenhan study and outline any methodological implications these changes may have. [8]
   (f) Outline the results of the Rosenhan study. [8]

Total [36]

EXAM-STYLE QUESTIONS

Chardonnay's answer

(a) The aim of the Rosenhan study was to see whether diagnosis of abnormality (schizophrenia) is really valid and reliable. In particular, is abnormality just a feature of the situation that people are in, rather than a characteristic of the person?

(b) The main sample was the hospitals that were visited by the pseudopatients and the staff (nurses, doctors, orderlies) who were in these hospitals. Altogether, there were 12 hospitals and Rosenhan says that they were varied in terms of whether they were state run or private run, and whether they were old or modern. One limitation of this sample is that it is still quite a small proportion of the mental hospitals in America – probably there were several hundred of them at the time.

(c) A lot of data was gathered in this study – both qualitative and quantitative. In the main study, the pseudopatients were hospitalised (mostly diagnosed with schizophrenia) and they observed mainly the staff while they were there. The data was also how long they had to stay in hospital before they were discharged. In the second study, the data was gathered from doctors and nurses according to whether they thought there were pseudopatients when in fact there were none.

(d) One strength of an observational study is that it is looking at behaviour which really happens (rather than what people say happened). This should mean that the study has some validity.

One weakness of observational studies is that even though you can see what is going on, you do not necessarily know why people behaved in that way – why they did things. It might be that observational studies actually give a limited understanding of behaviour because we don't know the reasons why.

(e) One change (if the study were done today) could be to use CCTV on the wards as well as the pseudopatients to collect data. This would mean that the pseudopatients would not have to take notes so much (and might not be thought of as so obsessive); and that more data could be collected, from places even when the pseudopatient wasn't present, e.g. things that might be said about him or her in the cage. This change would give more data and could be quite revealing. Also, it might actually be more objective as the data doesn't just rely upon the collection of a participant observer who might be over-involved and over-emotional about what is going on.

A second change would be to interview the doctors and nurses afterwards so that you could get a better idea about why they made the mistake.

(f) The results of the Rosenhan study were that all the pseudopatients were admitted and that they remained in hospital for an average of 19 days (range of 7 to 52 days). While they were in the hospital, in general, there was a lot of powerlessness and depersonalisation. Patients were generally ignored by staff who spent most of their time in 'the cage' (their office). There was a tendency to interpret their behaviour as abnormal, e.g. when waiting for the canteen, it was said patients had 'oral acquisitive nature' rather than they were just waiting there because they were bored. The diagnosis was 'sticky' as even when they were discharged, they were signed off with 'schizophrenia in remission' rather than absolutely fine. This study showed that psychiatrists tend to call a sick person healthy; but the second study showed that doctors also could make the reverse error (calling a healthy person sick) as doctors and nurses thought that real patients were pseudopatients.

Teacher's comments (see mark schemes on pages xii–xiii)

Overall, Chardonnay, your answer is about the right length and you have devoted proportionate time to each of the six question parts.

(a) This is spot on Chardonnay. Lots of people overlook the situation versus disposition aspect of Rosenhan's aim, so well done.

(b) Again, candidates often trip up here and say that the sample were the pseudopatients; you're right, the main sample was the hospitals and staff. There is some detail here (the variety, etc.) though you didn't remember that the hospitals represented five different states; still it is good enough for the full 3 marks. The limitation part is marked separately and you have made a valid point here, but could have developed your point by talking about the possible lack of representativeness of US mental hospitals, for instance. 4 out of 6 marks.

(c) In a way this is quite a tricky question to answer because there could be a huge amount to say – but only 6 marks available. Therefore, you do have to be quite shrewd. This is a mid-band answer. For the top band you needed just a few more details, such as the sort of behaviours recorded by the pseudopatients in the main study.

(d) Valid points here, Chardonnay. However, you haven't elaborated the strength as much as would be appropriate for full marks and so this only just qualifies for 2 out of 3 marks. Although the question does not ask for reference to the Rosenhan study it may be to your strength to use an example to clarify your point. Your weakness is described more fully and so attracts 3 out of 3 marks.

(e) Two good ideas, however not so good on the execution. For the first change, you haven't given much description of the change itself, for example, would there be multiple cameras per ward, who would analyse the footage? You need to give just a bit of extra detail here. Good discussion of impact upon results.

The second change is altogether too brief. You have identified the change and have given some hint about the likely impact upon results. For full marks both parts (change and its effect) should be much more detailed. For example: *They could be asked about why they admitted the pseudopatient in the first place and why they said or did certain things, e.g. why they ignored patients, spent so much time in 'the cage', etc. This would have no impact upon original results – but it would help us understand why they did some of the things they did, e.g. why the doctors admitted them – did they 100% believe they were schizophrenic, or were they just being cautious?*

(f) It is always more than handy to have some useful details up your sleeve such as some exact numbers for the main results. You also have some of the key themes (depersonalisation, stickiness) of the results and display both range and detail of understanding.

Chardonnay (2 + 4 + 4 + 5 + 5 + 7 marks = 27/36 marks)

CHAPTER 7

This chapter looks at the overarching themes in your study of psychology.

Exam questions on G542 relate core studies to these themes, which means that the content of this chapter needs to be used in conjunction with the core studies in Chapters 2–6.

Approaches, perspectives, issues and methods

218 Approaches
218 The cognitive approach
220 The developmental approach
222 The physiological approach
224 The social approach
226 The individual differences approach

228 Perspectives
228 The behaviourist perspective
230 The psychodynamic perspective

232 Issues
232 Ethics
234 Ecological validity
236 Longitudinal and snapshot studies
238 Qualitative and quantitative data

240 Methods
240 Case studies
242 Reliability and validity

Other methods are covered in Chapter 1 of this book
24 Experiment (laboratory and field)
16 Self-report
4 Observations

244 Exam-style questions

The cognitive approach

The **cognitive approach** is the dominant way of looking at people in modern psychology. The approach became the most popular approach in psychology departments once the problems with the **behaviourist perspective** (see page 228) could not be ignored any longer. The behaviourists viewed people as a 'black box', and they studied what impinged on the black box (stimuli) and what came out of the black box (responses) but they did not pay much attention to what went on inside the black box. I know this will come as no surprise to most readers, but quite a lot goes on inside our heads and a lot of our behaviour can be affected by mental events as well as physical events.

The cognitive approach in the core studies
Studies in this text that fit directly into the cognitive approach:
- The eyewitness studies of **Loftus and Palmer**.
- The autism study by **Baron-Cohen et al.**
- The conservation study by **Samuel and Bryant**.
- **Savage-Rumbaugh et al.'s** study of language acquisition in chimpanzees.

Other studies in the text that use some of the techniques or ideas:
- The split-brain study by **Sperry**.
- **Maguire et al.'s** study of London taxi drivers.
- The gambling study by **Griffiths**.

Key ideas in the cognitive approach

1 The computer metaphor

Cognitive psychology came to the forefront of psychology in the 1950s. **George Miller** hosted a seminar in the USA in 1956 where Newell and Simon presented a paper on computer logic, Noam Chomsky (see the study on Kanzi by **Savage-Rumbaugh et al.**, page 61) presented a paper on language, and Miller presented his famous paper on 'The magic number seven plus or minus two'. Each of these presentations defined their field and modern cognitive psychology is often dated to this event.

At the heart of the cognitive approach is the idea that we can study the human mind by comparing it to the processes of machines. In the UK **Donald Broadbent** was a strong supporter of the information-processing models of cognition. These models were based on the communication technology of the time and were commonly represented as telephone exchanges to represent the way messages were sorted and distributed.

As technology developed so did the science of how people behave intelligently in the world. The models were now based on computer processes. This brings up a question about whether cognitive psychology is studying the cognitive processes of people or the cognitive processes of computers. It also brings up a much deeper question about what it means to be human and be alive. Can a computer think? Can it be aware of itself? Can it have a **Theory of Mind**? (For this last question see the study on **autism** on page 50.)

The cognitive model of the mind is often influenced by the technology of the time. In the 1950's the most sophisticated information processing machine was a telephone exchange, and this was used as a template for describing how we process cognitive information.

2 Matching with the findings of neuroscience

The cognitive approach is based on models of how we think and perceive the world. These models are commonly shown as diagrams of boxes in the head. The big question that arises is whether these boxes can be matched to structures in the brain. If so, then all well and good and we can build up our car-engine model of the brain. If not, then what do the boxes mean? The big example is memory, which is commonly represented as a collection of boxes, but extensive work on the brain has failed to find an area that we can call 'memory' (see pages 110–111 and 222–223 on the physiological approach).

3 Experimentation

The first psychology **laboratory** was set up by **Wilhelm Wundt** (1823–1920) in Leipzig, Germany in 1879. According to Wundt, psychology was the study of immediate experience – which did not include any issues of culture or social interaction. About half the work in the lab was on the topics of sensory processes and perception, though they also looked at reaction time, learning, attention and emotion. The main method that was used in the laboratory was *introspection*, which is a form of self-**observation**.

Modern cognitive psychology mainly uses **experimental methods** to collect its evidence. In fact it is rare to see any other method in the top scientific journals. The advantages of this method are that you can make clear statements about the impact of a single variable on the way we think and we can test findings through replication. Among the downsides are the simple (and very boring) nature of the tasks that participants are asked to do and the sad fact that **replications** are rarely carried out.

4 Relevance to everyday life

Many experiments in cognitive psychology are carried out in psychology **laboratories** where participants are asked to respond to small changes on a computer screen. The question that arises is whether this relates to the ways we make sense of the world in everyday life. For example, if you want to test my memory then asking me to remember a list is perhaps not the best way because I never bother to do this in everyday life as I have a pencil and paper and write down those things. And I use my memory for capturing not just lists but emotions and connections and everything else that makes being alive such a rich experience. The studies in this text are not really representative of cognitive psychology in that they all have everyday relevance, but if you look at the cognitive approach you will see that it mainly deals with abstract tasks in unreal situations.

APPROACHES

Who am I?

When we think about who I am and how I came to be like this the *cognitive approach* focuses on thought processes (or cognitions). It makes comparisons to technology like computers.

Powerful computers are able to memorise, recall, calculate and make sense of complex data. The cognitive approach builds up models of human cognition as if it were like a computer. So, am I really a biological computer? And are my thoughts, feelings and memories just the stirrings of my hard drive? This is an uncomfortable idea and most of us like to think that we are more than a computer, but if so what are we?

If we go down this route then we might say that sometimes there is a problem with the computer programme (**Baron-Cohen et al.**'s study on autism), or maybe it makes faulty judgements due to context (**Loftus and Palmer** on memory) or maybe the hardware just does not allow certain cognitions to develop (**Savage-Rumbaugh et al.**'s work on chimpanzee language).

Try this   **7.1**

The computer challenge

(a) Make a list of the things that computers and humans can do. To get you started there is: (i) storing information, (ii) calculating, (iii) recalling.

(b) When you've completed that list try to identify the differences between the ways that humans and computers do these tasks.

(c) Now try to make a list of the things that people can do that computers can't.

AI: artificial intelligence

One of the key strands of cognitive psychology is artificial intelligence (AI). It is the science and engineering of making intelligent machines, especially intelligent computer programs. The origins of AI can be seen in the work of British scientist **Alan Turing** in the 1950s on intelligent machines. Turing is particularly famous for his work on code breaking during the Second World War (1939–45) using the Enigma machines he helped to create.

Turing's claim

Turing held that, in time, computers would be programmed to acquire abilities that rivalled human intelligence.

As part of his argument Turing put forward the idea of an 'imitation game', in which a human being and a computer would be questioned under conditions where the questioner would not know which was which. This would be possible if the communication was entirely by written messages.

Turing argued that if the questioner could not distinguish them, then we should see the computer as being intelligent. Turing's 'imitation game' is now usually called 'the Turing test'.

When is a robot not a robot?

The blurred lines between people and machines have been a recurring theme in fiction for years. Films such as *Blade Runner*, *AI*, *Short Circuit* and *Star Trek* explore the idea and challenge us to tell the difference between a living person and an intelligent machine. The robots behave like people and we feel the same way towards them as we do to human beings. Will we eventually build a machine that is so like a human being that we can not tell the difference? And if so will it matter? Can we still switch them off or reboot them when we feel like it? Horror films of the past such as Frankenstein looked at attempts to create biological life, but perhaps we are much closer to creating cognitive life? Don't forget to switch off the computer tonight.

Will the study of artificial intelligence eventually create a robot that is indistinguishable from a human being?

Wonders of cognition

Cognitive psychology often seems quite mechanical and abstract but some researchers explore the more remarkable qualities of our cognition.

Synaesthesia

What is the colour of the letter M, or the number 6, or a prelude in E-minor? How do red circles taste? What do they sound like? If you know the answer to one of these questions you probably enjoy (or suffer from) synesthesia. Most of us, however, do not and the questions therefore look very strange. Surely this is the road to madness if you can taste images or see colours in sounds. This is not the case, however, and we probably all have some small experiences like this.

Synesthesia (from the Greek syn = together, and aisthesis = perception) is the experience of a *cross-modal association*. In other words the stimulation of one of your senses causes a perception in one or more different senses. According to Baron-Cohen et al. (1996) at least 1 in 2000 of the population experiences synesthesia although many suspect it is more common. It is hard to obtain an estimate because many synesthetes are unaware that what they perceive is unusual.

The study of synesthesia helps us to learn more about how the brain processes sensory information and how it makes abstract connections between inputs that seem to be unrelated.

Inattentional blindness

Sometimes we don't seem able to see things that are right under our noses. Simons and Chabris have carried out a number of studies to investigate this, the most famous of which creates a task where people are unable to spot a gorilla walking in full view across a scene. They ask people to concentrate on one feature of the scene and because people focus on it so much they don't notice the man in the monkey suit (see http://www.theinvisiblegorilla.com/gorilla_experiment.html).

Variations of this task find similar results. For example, when people were asked to listen out for key words in some recorded conversation they didn't notice that one of the other voices was saying 'I am a gorilla' over and over again. Also when radiographers were asked to look at scans of a lung to find signs of tumours they totally missed the image of a gorilla that was added to the scans.

When people are shown the thing that they missed they are utterly amazed that they could have missed it, and when you see how large the gorilla is you'll be amazed as well.

The developmental approach

The **developmental approach** looks at the changes that individuals go though during their lives. Developmental psychologists are interested in how we develop from the 'cradle to the grave'. In fact, modern scientific techniques mean that we can track development even before the cradle and so we should really say from 'conception to the grave'.

Some psychologists see the changes as developing steadily and progressively, and some describe the changes as going through a series of stages. The interest for all developmental psychologists is in the things that bring about these changes. The main focus of developmental psychology is on children because it is in the first few years of life that we can observe the most dramatic changes.

The developmental approach in the core studies
Studies in this text that fit directly into the developmental approach:
- The Bobo study of **Bandura et al.**
- The conservation study by **Samuel and Bryant**.
- The Little Hans case study by **Freud**.
- **Savage-Rumbaugh et al.'s** study of language acquisition in chimpanzees.

Other studies in the text that use some of the techniques or ideas:
- **Thigpen and Cleckley's** study of multiple personality.
- The autism study by **Baron-Cohen et al.**

Key ideas in the developmental approach

1 Similarities and differences

Psychologists can look for the features that all children share and are important to the development of any child, or they can look at the features that are different between one child and another. This issue appears in most areas of psychology as we try to understand what makes us tick.

There are some things about you that are like nearly all other individuals (for example, nearly all people develop language and nearly all people smile and laugh), there are some things about you that are like a lot of other people (for example, the religious beliefs that your have) and there are some things about you that are unique to you (your personality and, in fact, your genetic make-up is unique even if you are a twin). We are different to everyone else yet we share a lot with everyone else.

Psychologists tend to focus in their studies either on the uniqueness or the similarities. This is because we can't study everything at once but it is worth looking at the other viewpoint when thinking about each of the studies in this text. At the two ends of the spectrum, the **Bobo study** looks at how all children can develop aggressive behaviours and at the other end **Freud** looks at the unique case of Little Hans.

On the facing page we look at issues of diversity. There is a danger in thinking that all children have the same experiences of life. This is not the case and information here and also on page 75 highlights the diverse experiences of children.

2 Stages

If children develop bit by bit then we do not need to talk about stages, but if development involves re-organisation and the emergence of new strategies and skills then it is more useful to talk about stages. For example, in everyday speech we commonly refer to informal stages such as the 'terrible twos'.

Baby showing the diving reflex, an innate (inherited) behaviour.

Stages are favoured by a lot of psychologists and in this text we have Piaget's stages of **cognitive development** in the study by **Samuel and Bryant** and also **Freud**'s stages of psychosexual development. The study by Bandura et al. does not suggest stages but merely that we change our behaviour in response to new experiences and observations.

The stage approach helps us to see the sequence of development that occurs in many children, but among the concerns about the use of stages are: (a) do they occur in *all* children rather than just most? (b) do all children go through them in the same order? (c) do children always move up the stages or can they sometimes go back to earlier stages? and (d) are there any cultural differences and if so why?

3 Nature and nurture

The **nature–nurture** debate looks at the relative importance of genetics (nature) over experience (nurture) in the development of behaviour. Clearly some aspects of behaviour have a strong genetic component. For example, children can develop crawling and walking on their own even they usually have a lot of support and encouragement. Also, they develop language without tuition suggesting a readiness to learn this skill. The fact that we can't teach language to other animals shows that language is a unique human skill.

Do the effects of nature go as far as personality and everyday behaviour? It is a topic that crops up in everyday conversations as people try and judge why people behave in the way that they do. When we hear someone say something like, 'He's very musical, just like his uncle' we can see that the speaker thinks there is a genetic link for musical ability. We clearly share some characteristics with our parents but how much is that due to being brought up by them or how much to sharing their genetic structure?

4 Timing and plasticity

Are there key times for certain behaviours to develop and what happens if that development is disrupted? For example, babies up to the age of about six months display a diving reflex which means that if they go under water they automatically hold their breath and make swimming like movements. This reflex fades by the age of one. The work of **Sigmund Freud** and **John Bowlby** suggest that early attachments with family members have an effect on later life and if those attachments are not formed by a certain age the effects will be long lasting. Plasticity refers to the amount that a behaviour can change and adapt or how rigid it will be once it has developed.

Who am I?

When we think about who I am and how I came to be like this the *developmental approach* focuses on our early life experiences. Maybe I am prone to anxiety and insecurity because of an unhappy event when I was three (**Freud**). Maybe I make the moral judgements that I do because I haven't fully developed my thought processes (**Samuel and Bryant**) and maybe I hit my cousin because I watch a lot of TV and I copy the behaviour of action heroes (**Bandura et al.**).

The developmental explanation of who we are is the one we most commonly used. It is our autobiography. We tell people stories about the events in our lives and the listeners draw some conclusions about who we are and why we behave in the way that we do.

The strength of this autobiographical approach is that we can find common features between our stories and the stories of other people. This helps us to understand other people because we can compare them to ourselves. 'Oh that happened to you as well? That is why we are so alike.'

The weakness of this approach is that it is too easy to find explanations for things after the event. Coupled with this is our very bad memory for our childhood and our tendency to embellish stories of past events.

'If you want your children to be intelligent, read them fairy tales. If you want them to be more intelligent, read them more fairy tales.'
Albert Einstein

Try this   **7.2**

What is a child?

This is not such a silly question as you might think. We use terms like child, toddler, teenage and adult but what are we referring to other than age?

What does a child know when it is born? What can it do? Can it make sense of the world when it opens its eyes? Does it have a range of instincts that develop as it grows? Alternatively, is it born with a 'blank slate' onto which experience will write the knowledge that gives the child its personality and cognitive skills?

Use your skill and judgement and observations of relatives to note the differences between children and adults. Make as long a list as you can. When you've done that try and put most of them under the headings, emotion, behaviour and thought. This might help you get inside the head of the child you were a few years ago and get an idea of how different the world was to you back then.

'All children are artists. The problem is how to remain an artist once he grows up.' Pablo Picasso

Different stories of parenting

Cinderella: is it all true?
One of the strongest themes in fairy tales is of the wicked stepmother. The story of Cinderella has been around in many cultures for centuries. It is estimated that over 350 versions of it exist starting with one recorded in the ninth century in China. In this version Cinderella doesn't have a fairy godmother but is helped by a magical fish (a glass kipper perhaps?). The story has developed over the centuries but the role of the wicked stepmother remains constant.

Is the story so powerful because it relates to a truth we know but dare not speak about? There is an uncomfortable line of research developing that points to the negative effects of being in a stepfamily. We'll put in the usual caveats and say that many children in stepfamilies have a perfectly acceptable life, although Bowlby is recorded as saying *The myth (of the wicked step-parent) has some validity to it. A step-parent is a very unsatisfactory parent for a child to have. It is nobody's fault. It's a fact.'* (Maddox, 1998).

Evolutionary psychologists go a step further and suggest that we are going against thousands of years of evolution when we try to nourish and support our partner's children as if they were our own. On the front cover of their book *The Truth about Cinderella*, Daly and Wilson (1998) state *'having a step-parent is the most powerful risk factor for severe child maltreatment yet discovered'*. You can see why this work is controversial.

Black, White or Mixed Race?
Racially mixed couples are no longer a rare phenomenon. It is estimated that a third of British people of Afro-Caribbean origin under the age of thirty who are currently married or co-habiting have white partners. Tizard and Phoenix (1993) explored the issue of mixed-race identity by interviewing young people from a range of social backgrounds, all of whom had one white and one African or Afro-Caribbean parent. The interviews looked at adolescents' perception of their racial identity, its role in their lives, their feelings about having one black and one white parent, their attitude to black and white people, allegiance to black and white cultures, their experience of, and ways of coping with racism. They found that many young people have very positive dual identities, as both black and white, and resist demands from others about the kinds of identities they should have.

New families

The pattern of family life is changing in this country. At least one in three children will experience parental separation before the age of 16. Most of these children go through a period of unhappiness; many experience low **self-esteem**, behaviour problems, and loss of contact with part of the extended family.

Children are usually helped by good communication with both parents, and most settle back into a normal pattern of development (Dunn and Deater-Deckard, 2001). Many children have experience of being in a stepfamily. Becoming part of a stepfamily seems to be helpful for younger children but to be harder for older children to adapt to (Hawthorne et al., 2003). Older children seem to appreciate step-parents more when they act in a supportive and friendly way rather than being involved in discipline or control.

There are also issues around the role of fathers in successful parenting and some fathers argue for greater access to their children. The group called 'Fathers 4 Justice' campaigns for a child's right to see both their parents and all their grandparents. One of the consequences of Bowlby's work was that in divorce cases the courts started to give custody to mothers rather than the traditional placement with fathers. The result of this has been that fathers (and grandparents) have sometimes been cut out of the child's life and been allowed only limited access.

The physiological approach

The **physiological approach** has an underlying assumption that people are biological machines. These biological machines are made up of chemicals and cells which control our thoughts, feelings and behaviour.

This approach also sees us developing through the processes of evolution and therefore most if not all of parts of our brain and body have developed because they are adaptive (in other words they have made us more likely to survive and reproduce).

The physiological approach in the core studies
Studies in this text that fit directly into the physiological approach:
- The study of taxi driver brains by **Maguire *et al*.**
- **Dement and Kleitman's** study of sleep.
- **Sperry's** spilt-brain studies.

Other studies in the text that use some of the techniques or ideas:
- **Reicher and Haslam's** prison study.
- **Griffiths'** study of gambling behaviours.

Key ideas in the physiological approach

1 Biological machines

The idea of a physiological approach in psychology starts with the French scientist and philosopher **René Descartes** (1596–1650). At the time he was writing, a number of scientists were studying the human body as if it were a machine. Descartes suggested that we are made up of two principal components, a body and a soul. He argued that a body without a soul would be an automaton that was completely controlled by external stimuli and its internal chemistry. According to Descartes we are a ghost in a machine, and he set about trying to understand how the machine works.

Looking at the body we can see that the eye has the properties of a glass lens and we can describe our movement with the science of levers. The machine metaphor seems to work quite well and so it is an obvious next step to apply this idea to the brain. Perhaps we don't have a ghost operating the machine at all, maybe we are nothing but a machine. And that is the physiological approach.

The past hundred years have seen an explosion in brain research and we now know a lot more about how the brain is wired and how it influences our behaviour. Despite all this research the big questions still remain unanswered. In particular what makes the collection of chemicals and cells in the brain become the reflective, thinking, feeling organism that is aware of itself and able to act and make choices. If there isn't a ghost in the machine then how is this biological machine managing to work itself?

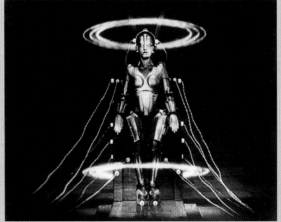

In the classic silent movie Metropolis a robot is created that takes the place of a real person without anyone knowing. If we are biological machines will this be possible one day?

2 Interpreting data

It is estimated that the adult human brain has 10^{11} (one hundred billion) neurons (or nerve cells) and each of these cells has on average 7,000 connections (synapses) to other neurons. The number of messages that can be sent is beyond our imagination.

Within this spectacular array of activity we try to impose some meaning. We do that by drawing lines on the diagrams and labelling areas but if you looked at a brain you would be hard pressed to actually see the structures that are drawn on the diagram. We are only beginning to get a picture of what goes on in the brain and so interpreting the data is a difficult process. One thing we can be sure of is that whatever is in the textbooks today will have been rewritten in 10 years time.

3 Localisation of function

Our understanding of machines is that they are made up of components. This model has been applied to the brain and so we have maps of the brain that identify components that are responsible for particular tasks.

Researchers have been able to identify all manner of brain sites that have a specific impact on behaviour, for example on page 110 we describe the work of **Paul Broca** who found one of the areas in the brain that affects the production of language. Although this work has told us a lot, not all of the searches for brain components have been successful. For example, the attempt by **Karl Lashley** (1890–1959) to look for the part of the brain responsible for memory. Despite decades of work with rats in which he systematically removed parts of their brains to observe the effects on their memory, he was unable to find a specific site.

A big question that arises from this **localisation** approach is that if we are made up of lots of bits then where and what is the 'me' that operates all these bits. Are we just a collection of bits?

4 Implications

If we think of people as biological machines then it suggests certain solutions to everyday problems. Look at the following quote from physiological psychologist Peter Milner:

'I am interested in organisms as pieces of machinery, and I would like to know much the same about them as I once wanted to know about the gadgets I saw around me: first, what happens when the controls or inputs are manipulated and, a little later, how it happens.' (Milner, 1970, page 1)

This quote has a strange irony to it. If I went to my doctor and said *'I feel like a machine. I am a gadget. One of my bits is going wrong, could you fix it please'*, the doctor might regard this statement as a sign of my mental instability and immediately send for the straight jacket. If, on the other hand, I make this statement to a conference of psychologists, and make it not about myself but about 'people', then I can be hailed as a scientific genius.

The idea that we can regard people as objects in science means that people might be treated as objects in everyday life. When objects breakdown we fix them by the use of spare parts (brain surgery) or by throwing them away (murder). It is difficult not to be shocked at such a brutal approach to people and to such a pessimistic vision of human behaviour and experience.

Who am I?

When we think about who I am and how I came to be like this the *physiological approach* focuses on our brains and nervous system. Am I my brain? If not, what else am I? And if I am just my brain, then what is studying me at the moment? It must be my brain. Yes, my brain studying my brain? Don't think about this too much as it will hurt. Check it out. Look in the mirror and try to see the physiological machine.

One strength of the physiological approach is that there is a lot of evidence concerning the influence of the brain on behaviour. The fact that we can't explain all behaviour in this way is seen by physiological psychologists as being because we have yet to discover all the mechanisms of the brain but that one day we will be able to map out the physiology of behaviour in the way that we have mapped out the human **genome**.

The main problem with this approach is that it does not correspond to our experience of being alive. We experience our lives as if we have choices. If our lives are just the product of chemical reactions then there can be no choice. And if there is no choice then there can be no good or bad, no right from wrong.

Brains are not just for thinking

There is an online museum of Scientifically Accurate Fabric Brain Art (http://harbaugh. uoregon.edu/Brain). This is the world's largest collection of anatomically correct fabric brain art, including the brain below knitted by Karen Norberg. The museum's curator says: 'While our artists make every effort to insure accuracy, we cannot accept responsibility for the consequences of using fabric brain art as a guide for functional magnetic resonance imaging, trans-cranial magnetic stimulation, neurosurgery, or single-neuron recording.'

There is also a sister site, the Gallery of Wooden Brain Art. And you might take a look at the Brain Handbag (see http://www.mindhacks.com/ blog/2007/ 11/a_handbag_shaped_li.html). It is clear that the idea that we only use 10% of our handbag is a myth.

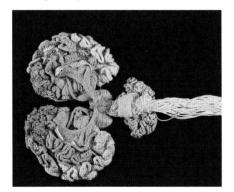

Applications of the physiological approach

Serotonin and Prozac

There is currently a widely held theory that depression is caused by lowered levels of the neurotransmitter serotonin. The basic idea here is that depression is mainly a physiological condition and can be alleviated by chemicals that boost the levels of serotonin. The most common class of drugs to do this is *SSRIs* (selective serotonin reuptake inhibitors); the most commonly known is *Prozac*.

In the UK in 2010 there were over 42 million prescriptions for anti-depressants and over 17 million for anti-anxiety medication (Ilyas and Moncrieff, 2012). The number of anti-depressants taken in the UK has quadrupled in fifteen years. There is little difference in the effectiveness of the many different anti-depressant drugs although there is a difference in price and the SSRIs are much more expensive and cost the NHS over £220 million each year.

Between 60% and 80% of people report improvement in their mood or behaviour when taking anti-depressants.

Among the problems with SSRIs are the side effects of which the most worrying is the evidence linking the drug to suicidal thoughts. The UK government recommends that SSRIs are not given to under 18s for this reason.

The biggest issue is the idea that a single chemical in a complex structure like the brain will bring about changes in complex emotions like depression. If someone has a problem in living, perhaps they are not getting on with people at school or work or maybe they have recently lost someone close to them, then it is difficult to see how a pill will change anything.

Psychosurgery

Psychosurgery can be dated to a research report given at a talk in London by Jacobsen and Fulton in 1935. They had been training two chimpanzees to carry out a memory task. One of them, called Becky, was particularly temperamental and became very distressed when she failed the task. She would fly into a tantrum and refuse to try again. Fulton and Jacobsen surgically removed part of the **frontal lobes** of her cerebral **hemispheres** which have a lot of connections with the *limbic system*. They reported that Becky no longer became distressed during the memory task.

Egas Moniz was at the talk and speculated whether it would be possible to reduce anxiety states in people by a similar operation. Within a year, Moniz had started to carry out **frontal lobotomies** on distressed patients. By 1950 over 20,000 people around the world had been treated in this way, including prisoners and children.

Was the operation effective? As with many forms of treatment, the effectiveness was assessed by the people carrying out the operations. Surprisingly enough, they thought that the operations were very successful. However, it eventually became clear that the benefits of this sort of gross destruction of brain tissue were often very small, and sometimes the consequences were disastrous. Moniz himself, who won the Nobel prize in 1949, was shot in the spine by one of his own lobotomised patients. This operation is relatively rarely used today, but it is worth reflecting on how the report of one chimpanzee's behaviour could lead to so many people having their brains mashed.

Try this 7.3

One way of exploring how common the physiological approach is to our everyday explanations is to look at the way we describe daily activities. Make a list of the things that we do or explanations that we make which have some physiological assumptions behind them. This list can include things you eat or drink, and changes you think happen inside you, such as hormones.

Just to get you started, what about having a cup of coffee in the morning to help us get up? We assume (largely correctly) that the chemicals in coffee will give us a lift.

The social approach

The **social approach** is concerned with the interactions between people. It therefore looks for explanations of behaviour in terms of social communication, social judgements and social relationships. In many ways this approach does not lend itself to tightly controlled **experiments** because human interactions are affected by so many variables at the same time. The puzzle for social psychologists is to find an appropriate methodology that allows us to make inferences about human behaviour while at the same time allowing that behaviour to occur in as natural a setting as possible. The key areas in the social approach are:

- **Social perception and judgement** is about how we make sense of and judge people and groups.
- **Social interaction** is about how we relate to others and so includes areas like conflict and cooperation and relationships.
- **Social influence** is concerned with the ways in which our interactions with other people affect the way we think, feel and behave and covers issues such as persuasion, attitude change, obedience and conformity.
- **Self-perception and identity** is concerned with how we make sense of ourselves and how we judge ourselves.

The social approach in the core studies
Studies in this text that fit directly into the social approach:

- **Milgram's** study on obedience.
- **Reicher and Haslam's** study on resistance to **tyranny**.
- **Piliavin *et al.*'s** study on helping behaviour.
- The Bobo study by **Bandura *et al.***

Other studies in the text that use some of the techniques or ideas:

- **Loftus and Palmer's** study on eyewitness judgements.
- **Rosenhan's** study about behaviour and judgements in psychiatric hospitals.
- **Griffiths'** study on gambling behaviour.

Former Prime Minister Tony Blair. Did groupthink play a part in the decision to attack Iraq in 2003?

Groupthink

An example of social influence is the work of **Irving Janis** on *groupthink*. Janis first used the term to describe a situation where each member of a group tries to match their opinion to those that they believe are held by the rest of the group. Although this is usually not a problem, in some situations the group might end up agreeing to a decision that each individual thinks is unwise. Sometimes a group of people can talk themselves into a bad decision.

Groupthink tends to occur on committees and in large organisations and Janis originally studied a number of military decisions made by US governments.

In the UK, the Butler Report looked at how the government arrived at the decision to attack Iraq in 2003. The report commented on the informal meetings that took place between a select group of advisers to Prime Minister Tony Blair. This was referred to as a 'kitchen cabinet' to describe where the discussions and decisions took place. The suggestion is that a small group of largely unelected advisers held meetings without formal rules and were led by the charisma of Tony Blair (*The Times*, 2004). Maybe they developed a groupthink, convincing each other that going to war was the best decision.

Key ideas in the social approach

1 Social Influence

Social influence has been one of the big concerns in social psychology. But when we use the social approach to explain behaviour how can we collect our evidence? If you ask people whether they are influenced by adverts they will usually say no. If this was the case then advertisers in the UK are wasting £16 billion each year. The influence of advertising is one of the easier things to study because you can measure sales before the advertising campaign and again after the campaign.

More than most other areas in psychology, the social approach has to wrestle with ethics. If we want to investigate social influence then we either need to carry out a study where we actually attempt to influence people or we look on as someone else attempts to influence people. The problems here are obvious in that we are trying to change someone's behaviour or judgement without them knowing.

The knee-jerk reaction is to say that this is unethical and should not be allowed but there is another side. Think of all the attempts to influence you every day. Teachers, religious leaders, health professionals and family members are all trying to influence you. They would probably argue that it is for a good cause. If they manage to influence you to stop a risky behaviour then is that unethical?

If we just observe interactions like the example of groupthink on the left, then it is difficult to be sure that our explanation is the best one available.

2 Self-perception

If we want to look at how we perceive ourselves then we have to rely on **self-report** measures. These vary from simple-answer **questionnaires** to **unstructured interviews**, but there is one issue with all of them – we are collecting data on how the participant wants to be seen by others and not direct information on how they see themselves.

How do we know ourselves? A theory put forward by **C.H. Cooley** (1902) suggested that self-concept is influenced by an individual's beliefs about what other people think of him/her. We see ourselves reflected in the behaviour of others. If people laugh at my joke then I am funny, if they scowl at me, I am bad, and so on. People are a mirror to show me what I am like.

The mirror is not always accurate because I can misinterpret what people really think of me.

Sometimes we perceive ourselves as others do and sometimes we get it very wrong. For example, Kruger and Dunning (1999) explored the breadth and depth of human incompetence and, in particular, self-delusion. They suggested that incompetent people overestimate their own ability. They asked people to rate how funny some jokes were and also to rate how good they were at judging humour. The people who were worst at judging humour (in the jokes) believed they were actually good at it. They got similar results with logic test and law entrance exams. For this work Dunning and Kuger received the 2000 IgNobel Prize for Psychology.

Who am I?

When we think about who I am and how I came to be like this the *social approach* focuses on our interactions and relationships with other people. Maybe I am compliant because of the people I am with or what I think people expect of me (**Milgram**). Maybe I choose to help people because they seem to be like me (**Piliavin *et al.***).

Maybe one way to describe me is to look at the groups I belong to (**Reicher and Haslam**). *Las Madres de La Plaza de Mayo* (see right) defined themselves by their campaign for justice. Spend a few moments thinking about the groups you belong to that define your identity. These might be relationships (such as families) or social categorisations (such as ethnicity) or social groups (such as the local trainspotting club).

The Mothers of Plaza de Mayo

This is a story that illustrates the best and the worst of humanity. It shows how people can behave in terrible ways towards other human beings and also how groups of people can come together under a common cause to resist tyranny and, in this case, to prevail.

On April 30, 1977, during the military dictatorship in Argentina (1976–83), 14 women gathered in front of Government House in Buenos Aires to demand information about their missing children. In protest they wore white head scarves with their children's names embroidered on to symbolise the blankets of the lost children. The women did not have access to the media which was controlled by the Junta, but by using word of mouth they managed to expand their protest. From the beginning they had to face threats and fear but they still continued their search for the truth. At the end of 1977, 12 of the women were detained by a paramilitary squad and never heard from again. Despite this brutality the protests continued and undermined the government. The problem for the government was that it professed to be committed to the values of the Catholic church while at the same time dishing out some violent treatment to a group of peaceful and unarmed women.

It is estimated that 30,000 people were 'disappeared' by the military death squads and that around 500 children were born to women in the concentration camps and then given to high-ranking officials. These children were deprived of their natural parents and their identity. On 8 December 2005, 28 years after they 'disappeared' themselves, the remains of the founding Mothers Azucena Villaflor, Maria Ponce de Bianco and Esther Ballestrino de Careaga were cremated and their ashes buried in honour at Buenos Aires, Plaza de Mayo. The people who carried out these atrocities have still not been brought to trial.

3 Social perception

If you ask two people to describe the same event then most likely they will come up with different accounts, especially of why things happened the way they did. You can look on this as a problem for the social approach or an opportunity. It is an opportunity because it gives us a chance to investigate the things that affect our judgements of people and events.

An example of work on social perception is *attribution theory* – the theoretical models of **Fritz Heider**, **Harold Kelley** and **Edward E. Jones**. It is concerned with the ways in which people explain (or attribute) the behaviour of others. For example, it distinguishes between *situational* (what's happening outside of you) and *dispositional* explanations (what's happening inside). Imagine you arrange to meet someone outside a club and they arrive late. You might well blame them because they didn't leave enough time to get there (dispositional explanation) whereas they might explain it as due to the bus not turning up (situational explanation).

We commonly explain our own behaviour in terms of situations while believing that other people are personally in control of theirs. This bias is called the *fundamental attribution error* and is the cause of numerous domestic arguments. We always feel sure that we know *why* a friend behaved like they did, but if you think about it you can't even be sure why you did some of your own behaviour.

4 Social interaction

The social approach looks to understand people in the context of their interactions with others. A brief think about this will tell you that this is a difficult ask because of all the different interactions that are going on between people in any interaction. How can you identify the most important factors?

It is possible to run studies that look at limited variables and they can give us some insights but can't capture the whole story. An early example of this approach is the experimental work of **Norman Triplett** in 1897 into the effects of competition on performance. Triplett observed that racing cyclists achieved better times on a circuit when they had someone pacing them. In a ride of 25 miles the average times per mile were:

- alone: 2 min 29.9 secs
- with a pacer: 1 min 55.5 secs
- in competition: 1 min 50.4 secs

He went on to observe this improved performance in other tasks and found, for example, that children wound fishing reels faster when there were other children also winding fishing reels in the same room.

The individual differences approach

The **individual differences approach** commonly looks to measure and rank people and categorise us by the small differences that distinguish one person from another. In some ways the remarkable thing about people is how much they share. People are able to communicate, they seek out other people and they have warm attachments to other people that endure over time. There are remarkable similarities in the ways that people make sense of the world but at this point in our history we seem most concerned by what distinguishes one person from another rather than what unites us. Hence the rise in importance of individual differences in psychology.

The most influential development in individual differences has been **psychometric tests**, which aim to provide simple and reliable ways to measure attitudes, cognitions, abilities and aptitudes of people.

The individual differences approach in the core studies
Studies in this text that fit directly into the individual differences approach:

- **Rosenhan's** study about behaviour and judgements in psychiatric hospitals.
- The multiple personality study by **Thigpen and Cleckley**.
- **Griffiths'** study on gambling behaviour.

Other studies in the text that use some of the techniques or ideas:

- **Reicher and Haslam's** study on resistance to **tyranny**.
- The autism study by **Baron-Cohen** *et al.*
- **Freud's** case study of Little Hans.

The history of individual differences

The study of individual differences can be traced back to the work of **Francis Galton**. He invented and defined the field. In 1884 Galton created a mental testing **laboratory** – the **anthropometric** lab for testing data about people, such as visual acuity, strength of grip, colour vision, hearing acuity, hand preference, etc. He hoped to use these measures to estimate people's hereditary intelligence.

Before Galton, psychology had been looking for general principles of experience. By contrast, Galton's anthropometric laboratory looked for individual differences and operated within his cousin Darwin's ideas of individual variability and selection. Although we would not recognise Galton's tests as measures of mental abilities today they do mark the beginning of mental testing.

Galton is also credited with developing a staggering range of techniques and concepts that define the field even today (see Fancher, 1996) such as **self-report questionnaires**, twin studies, **scattergraphs** and **correlations**. He also invented the term **nature–nurture** to describe the difference between environmental and inherited influences.

The above is a phenomenal list but it is only a selection of his output and you can add word association to it. Galton devised a word association technique; his paper on this was read by Freud and contributed to the development of one of the major techniques of **psychoanalysis**.

And if you're still not impressed then he also invented the weather map, and hence weather forecasting.

Although there were many other psychologists who helped develop the field of individual differences we thought we'd showcase Galton because of the originality and breadth of his contribution.

Key ideas in the individual differences approach

1 Evolution

If you had to pick one scientific idea that had the greatest effect on modern thought then you might well pick the theory of evolution. This theory has transformed the way we look at ourselves and continues to exert an influence on psychology particularly with the growing interest in genetic explanations of behaviour. **Charles Darwin** argued that human beings were descended from animal ancestors and demonstrated the similarities in the physical structures of people and animals, even down to the structure of the brain.

Natural selection
The two key ideas of Darwin's theory are:

- *Genetic variation* – all individuals are genetically unique (an example of individual differences – if all members of a species were entirely uniform there would be no evolution), and
- *Selection* – the individuals who successfully breed are the ones who are better adapted to the environment they are living in.

The genetic features that make some individuals survive and reproduce are likely to be passed on to the next generation. This is a process of selective breeding where the selection is done by the environment (i.e. *natural* selection). The issue this raises for humans is that we are able to tamper with natural selection by the development of medicine that keeps people alive, and by the development of laws that prevent murderous disputes, or regulate fertility through the conventions of marriage. Maybe this will have an effect on how the species develops. If so then what should we do about it?

Hope for us all: *Charles Darwin (1809–1882) did not do very well at school, and in his autobiography he said of his education that 'Nothing could have been worse for the development of my mind ...' (Darwin, 1969, page 27)*

2 Eugenics

Eugenics refers to the attempt to improve the quality of human beings through selective breeding. So, for example, if we wanted to improve the general level of intelligence in the country we would encourage intelligent people to have lots of children and unintelligent people to have none. Of course this only works if the factors that lead to differences in intellectual performance can be inherited.

There are many problems with the eugenics approach to intelligence including the controversial assumptions that:

- There is a single human quality that we can call intelligence rather than many different types of intelligent behaviour.
- Intelligence can be reliably and validly measured.
- Intelligence is a fixed quantity and cannot be improved.
- The differences in intelligence between people are mainly due to genetic factors.

Who am I?

When we think about who I am and how I came to be like this the *individual differences approach* focuses on how you can be categorised and measured. This allows us to compare you to other people and so when you think about yourself it is in terms of how much alike or unalike you are to the other people around you. As a result you see yourself as a set of characteristics such as sociable or intelligent or extravert.

It is worth thinking about whether you can be defined and described with these labels and categories.

Not so intelligent?

'It is an important and popular fact that things are not always what they seem. For instance, on the planet Earth, man had always assumed that he was more intelligent than dolphins because he had achieved so much – the wheel, New York, wars and so on – whilst all the dolphins had ever done was muck about in the water having a good time. But conversely, the dolphins had always believed that they were far more intelligent than man – for precisely the same reasons.'

Douglas Adams, The Hitchhiker's Guide to the Galaxy

3 Psychometrics

There's more to creating a psychometric scale than just coming up with a series of questions. Over a hundred years of testing has developed a series of sophisticated techniques for measuring people using **questionnaires**.

In the first place techniques have been developed to measure the **reliability** of the test. These techniques examine individual questions and tell you how much they contribute to the final score and how consistent they are.

Second, there is the issue of **validity** and the tests need to be checked against other measures to see if you are measuring what you claim to be measuring.

Third, the tests are **standardised** which means that they are given to a large number of people and their scores are used to give information on what a certain group of people will score on that test and you can compare your results with that.

It is important to note, however, that not all things that are measurable are important and not all things that are important are measurable.

The problem for the individual differences approach is that it focuses on measurement and ignores some important psychological qualities that are hard to measure. For example, what can be more important than a person's compassion or maybe their sense of humour or the breadth of their imagination, and yet these are very difficult to measure and so do not form part of psychological discussions about individual differences.

Psychometric tests give us data that is easy to use but does it capture the real quality of a person?

4 Differences and commonalities

When we study people we can focus on their unique qualities or we can focus on the qualities they share with other people.

If we focus on the uniqueness then we are likely to use the **qualitative approach** and build up a picture of the subjective experience of that person (this is called an *idiographic approach*). **Case studies** often use this approach and in this text you will find accounts of Little Hans (**Freud**) and Eve (**Thigpen and Cleckley**) that draw on this approach.

There are clear advantages to this approach because we are all unique individuals who have our own experiences of the world. The reason it is not favoured in research, however, it that it does not allow us to make generalisations and comparisons.

If we focus on the characteristics that people share (called the *nomothetic approach*) then we are likely to use the **quantitative approach**, and most likely use psychometric tests. We get data that is easy to present and easy to generalise from but we lose something of the individual's special qualities.

Testing intelligence

The first tests that we can recognise as IQ tests were developed in France by **Alfred Binet** who was commissioned by the minister of public education to develop a technique to identify children in need of special education, and from this the intelligence test was born. The test was used to give an estimate of a child's mental age by comparing the child's performance on various tasks with the performance of children of various ages. It was later suggested that the mental age of the child should be divided by the chronological age to give an index of intelligence and so the notion of IQ was developed (the formula is given below). This is an example of norm referencing.

Intelligence Quotient (IQ) = Mental Age / Chronological Age x 100

Binet believed that children who were in need of extra help could be identified by these tests, but he vigorously argued against the idea that intelligence is a fixed quantity that can not be improved by further help. This approach got sadly lost in the translation of tests into English and in their transportation to America. In contrast to the approach of Binet, the fiercest supporters of intelligence testing in the English speaking world were scientists who believed that individual differences are mainly due to genetic factors, and who proposed eugenic solutions to the perceived problems of society. For example, **Lewis Terman** who introduced the IQ test to America, wrote:

'If we would preserve our state for a class of people worthy to possess it, we must prevent, as far as possible, the propagation of mental degenerates.' (Lewis Terman, 1921, cited in Kamin, 1977)

To paraphrase Terman, he is saying we must stop poor and uneducated people from having children. All this would seem unpleasant but unimportant were it not for that fact that over half of the states in the USA brought in sterilisation laws for the 'feeble minded' and carried out tens of thousands of operations (Kamin, 1977).

The **behaviourist perspective** looks to understand people in terms of the rewards and punishments they receive (their reinforcement history). When behaviourists observe behaviour they are looking at what precedes a behaviour (the stimulus) and what follows it (the **reinforcement**). They believe they can use these observations to understand and predict behaviour and can then change the stimuli and rewards in order to change the behaviour.

The history of behaviourism

The term 'behaviourism' was first used by **John B. Watson** (1878–1958) in a paper written in 1913 in which he outlined a plan for behaviourism – an approach that was to dominate psychology for the next 50 years.

Watson suggested we should ignore concepts of intangible things like 'the mind' and concentrate on what we can observe and measure. The things people do (in other words, their behaviour) can be observed and measured and so Watson proposed that psychology should study this behaviour and record and analyse it using the techniques of science.

Before Watson put forward his theory of behaviourism psychology was mainly looking at the internal workings of the mind. This work was making limited progress because it was difficult to get evidence on how the mind works because first there was no agreement on what the mind is and secondly there was no way to measure it or record what it did.

Watson revolutionised psychology by his support for **experimental methods** and his assumption that humans are like other animals therefore suggesting that we can study animals to find out about human behaviour.

Watson also argued that we are born with a *tabula rasa* (blank slate), and we develop our personality, intelligence, etc. through our experiences in life. In other words we are born equal and the differences between us come from experience and not from breeding. This idea captured the public imagination because it taps into the USA *Declaration of Independence* which states: *'We hold these truths to be self-evident, that all men are created equal …'*. It is part of the American Dream that people can achieve because of their efforts and abilities rather than because of their class, and behaviourism gave scientific life to that dream.

Watson also suggested that psychology should aim to develop techniques that can control and alter human behaviour.

Watson's behaviourism was a truly revolutionary approach.

The behaviourist perspective in the core studies

Behaviourism is concerned with explaining why we do things (our behaviour) and how that behaviour can be changed if necessary. It is therefore relevant to all of the core studies in this text, and is used explicitly in a number of them, for example:

- In the Kanzi study (**Savage-Rumbaugh *et al.***), our furry friend learned to make his first signs through rewards. Pressing a lexigram for food became associated with getting that food.
- The Bobo doll study (**Bandura *et al.***) is an extension of behaviourism and looks at how behaviour is changed through observing other people.

Behaviourism also links to some of the other issues, for example:

- **Ethics:** if behaviourism can be used to control people and change their behaviour then who decides which behaviours should be changed and who controls the controllers?

Key ideas in the behaviourist perspective

1 Classical conditioning

In Russia **Ivan Pavlov** (1849–1936) investigated reflex behaviour and discovered that dogs can learn to produce a reflex response to new stimuli. Most famously, he is reported to have trained dogs to salivate when they heard the sound of a bell because this was associated with food. This type of learning is called **classical conditioning**.

Pavlov discovered one of the ways in which animals learn. In this case they learn to perform reflex behaviours (one they were born with) in response to new stimuli. In the famous example, the dogs were already able to salivate and Pavlov trained them to show this behaviour to a new stimulus. This is a very common experience as attested by one of the authors who regularly went to a local Asian restaurant where he would choose 'Hot Meat' off the menu. After a few visits to the restaurant he only had to read the words 'Hot Meat' on the menu in order to start salivating, and, in fact, just typing it now has brought about the same response.

Of course there is more to classical conditioning than salivating to food and it can explain how we develop a number of emotional and sexual responses. The principle of this type of learning is still used in **behaviour therapies**.

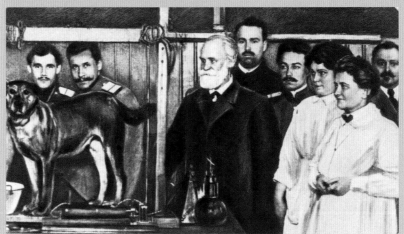

Pavlov and his associates at the laboratory.

2 Learning by trial and success

At the same time that Pavlov was getting his dogs to salivate, American psychologist **Edward Lee Thorndike** (1874–1949) was investigating how animals learn. In contrast to Pavlov, Thorndike was interested in how they learned new behaviours. In one series of observations he placed a cat in a 'puzzle box' and measured the time it took to escape. Over a number of trials the time taken to escape decreased yet the animal showed no sign of insight into the problem. It got out but it did not understand how it did it. From his observations he developed the Law of Effect which states that *the consequence of a successful behaviour is that it is more likely to recur in similar circumstances*. This provides a description of learning that does not require ideas such as 'the mind'.

PERSPECTIVES

Who am I?

When we think about who I am and how I came to be like this the *behaviourist perspective* focuses on our personal history or reinforcements. The behaviourists believed that we can understand an animal or a person by thinking of it as a *machine*, and looking at what goes into the machine (stimulus or inputs) and measuring what comes out (responses or outputs). This view sees the animal or person as a passive puppet who responds to stimuli with no more control than we have to a reflex action like a knee jerk. Put in this way it sounds harsh and simplistic though it has led to a number of effective applications.

Try this   7.4

Try to mould the behaviour of a friend or family member by smiling at them every time they say a particular word, for example smiling whenever they say 'whatever' or 'banana'. Smiles are a very powerful reinforcer and people will try and get smiles from others much of the time. See if you can increase the number of times that they say your chosen word through this simple reinforcement programme.

3 Operant conditioning and B.F. Skinner

Behaviourists such as **B.F. Skinner** (1904–1990) explored the principles of learning using behaviour as the main focus of their study. A key concept is the role of reinforcement. This is commonly defined in terms of the effect on behaviour, so, for example, a stimulus is said to be reinforcing if the behaviour it is associated with appears more frequently, and a stimulus is said to be punishing if a behaviour appears less frequently. This is an important point because some things that might appear as punishment, for example shouting at a child who is behaving in an irritating way might in fact lead to the behaviour appearing more frequently and so the shouting has to be seen as reinforcing rather than punishing.

Skinner used the above procedures to explain an array of complex behaviours in humans believing that it was unnecessary to look for underlying causes of behaviour, but only the reinforcement contingencies that could be used to change that behaviour. This approach to the study of behaviour led to a certain view about people and the ways they make sense of the world. Perhaps one of the most startling demonstrations of the power of **operant conditioning** was the work by Skinner (1960) during the Second World War (1939–45) in developing a missile guidance system using live pigeons. He was able to train them to recognise landmarks on maps and to peck a screen so that a missile could be directed to its target. Sadly,

Mrs Skinner views her daughter Debbie in an air crib which is often misreported as being a human Skinner Box.

although the system worked, the military decided against sending the heavily armed pigeons out on active service. Can't think why.

4 Black-box psychology

The behaviourist approach is based on a black-box model of people. In other words the approach looks at stimuli (what goes into the box) and responses (what comes out of the box) but it doesn't look at what goes in inside the box. All the things that we experience every day such as our thoughts and feelings do not figure in this approach. To say that this gives a limited view of human behaviour and experience would be a massive understatement of the issue.

The **cognitive** revolution of the 1950s moved psychology on from this behaviourist approach by looking inside the box to try and see how all the gubbins worked. Looked at like this we can say that the cognitive approach is still a behaviourist approach and uses a similar machine metaphor to describe people but it goes beyond looking at stimuli and responses.

Behaviourism: Psychology's big idea

It is possible to argue that behaviourism is psychology's 'big idea' because it has stood the test of time and, if anything, is growing in popularity today. Behaviourism offers a straightforward way to change behaviour and there is little doubt that it can be successful.

Therapies

Behaviourism has produced a wide range of therapies. For example, personal change is attempted through the use of classical conditioning techniques such as *aversion therapy* (where an unpleasant stimulus is paired with an unwanted behaviour), or *systematic desensitisation* (where a pleasant feeling is paired with a feared situation). Rewards are used to try and change health behaviours and time-outs are used to reduce disruptive behaviours. Modern therapies such as *cognitive behaviour therapy* (CBT) use a modified version of behavioural techniques to help people change the ways they think and behave.

Advertising

Classical conditioning is used to link up emotions with product. The UK's favourite advert (directed by film director Ridley Scott and available on YouTube) creates a feeling of warmth and nostalgia and pairs this feeling with a make of bread (Hovis). Many adverts use a similar technique to create emotional associations with the product.

Gambling

A lot of people like a flutter. There is something exciting about putting a stake on an event and it is a good feeling to win. The people who make gambling machines know this and try to create an experience of gambling that is rewarding even when you don't win, so that you will try again. One of these techniques is to give you the idea that your nearly won. If you get two numbers the same on a scratch card you feel as if you nearly won but really you just lost.

The psychodynamic perspective

The **psychodynamic** perspective views all human behaviour and experience in terms of the inner conflicts of the mind. The approach concentrates on the structure of the mind which has parts we are aware of (the conscious) and parts we are unaware of (the unconscious). The approach comes initially from the work of Freud but also includes ideas from the many people who developed Freud's ideas.

The psychodynamic approach sees the individual as being in continual conflict with the various drives inside them and that good mental health is achieved by resolving these conflicts as best you can. The approach goes further than looking at individuals to explain how societies develop and function, and comments on governments, religion, families and just about everything. To the believers it can explain everything, and to the non-believers it can explain next to nothing.

The approach (a way of explaining events and experiences) is often mixed up with Freud's theories and there is a good reason for this because there is considerable overlap. It is not possible to understand the approach without having some basic idea of the theories (see also page 96).

The psychodynamic perspective in the core studies

Some would argue that all psychology and in fact all human life can be explained from a psychodynamic perspective. The common view, however, in UK university psychology departments is that Freud is only of historical interest. You are more likely to study him if you take English at university than if you take psychology.

That being said, it is possible to see his influence in many of the core studies and in many of our public services. For example:

*   The study of Eve (**Thigpen and Cleckley**) highlights her inner conflicts and her early life experiences as an explanation for her adult behaviour.
*   It is possible to explain some people's obedience (see **Milgram**) as their responses to the relationship they had with their father.
*   **Freud**'s study of Little Hans illustrates psychoanalysis
*   Freud's focus on the first five years had a massive impact on our attitudes to children in the 20th century. On page 74 you can read about attachment and the work of **John Bowlby** who did a lot to improve the way that we deal with young children.

Anatomy is destiny

Freud claimed that *anatomy is destiny*, that is, your sex determines your main personality traits. Men are men and women are women. This idea has created a lot of debate with, for example, one of Freud's colleagues, **Karen Horney** who took the opposite view. She said that culture is more important than biology as the main influence on personality. **Psychoanalysis** does not seem to understand women as well as it does men. For example Freud wrote, *'Nor will you have escaped worrying about this problem – those of you who are men; to those of you who are women this will not apply – you are yourself the problem'* (1933).

Karen Horney suggested that psychoanalysis appears to understand men better than women is because the psychodynamic approach has been dominated almost exclusively by male thinking and has therefore evolved into a masculine enterprise.

Dreaming

'You should bear in mind that the dreams which we produce at night have, on the one hand, the greatest external similarity and kinship with the creations of insanity, and are, on the other hand, compatible with complete health in waking life' (Freud, 1910).

Freud's idea that dreams are essential for good mental health has received a lot of support over the years. If you were not allowed to dream then it is likely that you would soon start experiencing different mental states that might well include paranoia and anxiety.

Key ideas in the psychodynamic perspective

1 The unconscious mind

According to **Sigmund Freud** the unconscious mind is that part of our mind which we are not aware of. Freud believed that the unconscious contains all manner of unresolved conflicts and has a powerful effect on our behaviour and experience. One of the ways to access the unconscious according to Freud was to examine the mental processes that we have less control of such as our dreams.

'Freud considered laughter the conservation of psychic energy. Then again, Freud never played Friday night, second house, at the Glasgow Empire.' British comedian Ken Dodd

Many of us remember our dreams and sometimes puzzle on what they mean. Freud believed that all dreams are meaningful and, in fact, the meaning is the cause of the dream. The issue is figuring out, by looking at the symbols in the dream, what it means. Freud also suggested that all dreams are the fulfilment of wishes, that is something that we want to happen, but those wishes are sometimes so shocking to us that we disguise them in many ways.

In his analysis of dreams and symbols Freud suggests that many of the things we dream of are symbols for sex. In particular anything long and thin, or capable of getting bigger is seen as a phallic (penis) symbol. A cigar can be a classic phallic symbol but Freud recognised that sometimes you might just want to smoke some tobacco and so wrote *'Sometimes a cigar is just a cigar'*.

2 Psychosomatic: mind and body

The term *psychosomatic* is commonly used but little understood. The two parts of the term refer to the mind (psycho) and the body (somatic) and suggest a connection between the two. This was a revolutionary idea at the end of the nineteenth century and Freud was one of the people who developed it.

In 1885 Freud went to Paris to visit the French neurologist **Jean-Martin Charcot** who specialised in treating patients suffering from a variety of unexplained physical symptoms such as paralysis that had no obvious medical cause. Charcot believed that his patients were suffering from a form of hysteria which had developed from their emotional response to a painful (traumatic) event in their past. They suffered, in his view, not from the physical effects of the event, but from the idea they had formed of it. Under hypnosis, Charcot was able to relieve the symptoms. Freud returned to Vienna and started to use hypnosis with people who were showing symptoms of hysteria to see if he could get to the mental causes of the disorder.

It is hard to convey quite how dramatic this idea was at the time, but it is part of Freud's legacy that we take it for granted today that there is a connection between our state of mind and the general health of our body.

Who am I?

When we think about who I am and how I came to be like this the *psychodynamic perspective* focuses on early life experiences. According to Freud I am the product of the emotional relationships I had in the first five years of life. My worries and hang-ups can be traced back to events at that time.

As an adult I am constantly trying to balance the demands of the different sides of my personality. My superego and id battle for control (see page 96), and my **defence mechanisms** (see page 96) protect me from emotional distress.

I am not fully aware of many of the things that affect me but if I observe my dreams and behavioural mistakes I can get some insight into my unconscious.

Little Red Riding Hood, the most analysed fairy tale character ever.

3 The importance of early childhood experiences

Freud believed that our personalities are formed during the first five years of life. The poet **William Wordsworth** (he of the daffodils) used the phrase *'the child is the father of the man'* to capture the influence that our early experiences have on our adult personality.

Freud believed that disturbances in adult life have their roots in early experiences and therefore the way to resolve these disturbances is to use the talking cure (psychoanalysis) to go back to the source of the problem. The aim of the talking cure was to find the hidden emotion from the past that was bottled up and was having a bad effect on the person. This is another legacy from Freud that we take for granted today, that blocked up emotions will bring all sort of problems, Whether this is true or not is still fiercely debated but what is undeniable is the popular belief that it is true.

Over the course of many interviews with many patients Freud discovered a recurrent and disturbing theme. When the talking cure unravelled the various troubling events it ended up at a childhood sexual experience. Freud initially suggested that many instances of adult mental disturbance were caused by sexual experience (abuse) as a child. The word controversial does not do justice to the response that this idea provoked. Freud later retracted the theory and suggested instead that the children had imagined the sexual contact but never actually experienced it. This second idea is even more controversial today because we are much more ready to accept that children experience unwanted sexual advances from adults.

4 Instincts

In his early writings Freud argued that a child is born with a drive (or instinct) to seek bodily pleasure. This is called the **libido** which today we associate with adult sexuality and so using the term to refer to babies seems odd. Freud's view was that the driving force of the libido is there from birth and it becomes focused on different things during our development. The libido ends up as the drive for reproduction (the sex drive) but starts off in babies as a drive to get pleasure from sucking things like dummies.

In his later writing Freud developed the idea of two competing instincts inside us, one struggling for life (*Eros*) and one struggling for death (*Thanatos*). He summarised his view by writing *'The goal of all life is death'*. It sounds very strange to us that we should have an internal urge to die but if we look at it in a broader way then it makes more sense. The drive for life is a drive for activity, action and unpredictability (chaos). Although we might have a lust for life and seek out exciting events and people we don't want this all of the time. Sometimes we want to chill ('young people' talk) or take it easy and have a cup of tea ('old people' talk). When we chill we are looking for less stimulation, we want the world to be slower, quieter, more predictable and less demanding. If you take this to its obvious conclusion then we are most at peace and least troubled when we are dead. The drive for peace and quiet is ultimately the drive for ultimate peace and quiet, i.e. death.

'Time spent with cats is never wasted'. This is perhaps the most controversial thing Freud ever wrote, especially to the many cat haters in this country.

Fairy tales

Why do some stories have a big effect on us? Freud would suggest that they tap into some deep fears or wishes. Take for example the story of *Little Red Riding Hood* (Hoodie for short). This is a fairy story of a little girl who goes into the wood to see Granny. Sadly Granny has been eaten by a Wolf who takes her place in Granny's bed. When Hoodie arrives she does not realise that her Granny has been replaced by a Wolf. How can this be? Is she blind? How can there be a problem telling the difference between a wolf and your granny? The story is quite ridiculous but as children we suspend our disbelief and go along with the story. To see how ridiculous it is change the part of the Wolf to a talking Banana, and when you get to the bit that Hoodie can't tell the difference between Granny and Banana, the story falls apart.

A Freudian answer to this puzzle is that to the child the wolf and Granny are in fact one and the same person. To a child, adults are very unpredictable. Sometimes they are kind and caring and give you treats and sometimes they get angry and shout at you. The reasons for these changes are not obvious to the child who sees the adult as having two sides – Granny and the Wolf.

This fairy tale has been the subject of numerous other Freudian interpretations and if you're interested, see what you can find online.

Ethics

Ethics are the values and customs of a person or a group. They deal with issues such as right and wrong, good and bad, and what it means to be responsible for our actions. Every group has a code of behaviour that gives some guidance on how to behave. Sometimes this code is written down and our laws are an example of this. If you break the law and get caught you will be given a punishment. Not all parts of the good behaviour code are written down and we have to pick them up from the people we mix with. You often only find out about the code when you accidentally break it, so for example if you turn up to a party in a gorilla costume then people will laugh but if you turn up to a funeral in the same costume there will be less laughter.

What are ethics?

The ethics of a behaviour can be judged using four categories (Daeg de Mott, 2001): consequences, actions, character and motive. When we look at *consequences*, we judge whether a behaviour is right or wrong by looking at the result of the behaviour. If it leads to a result that brings about an improvement for someone's life, we might think it is a good thing. When we look at the *actions*, however, we look at the act itself, and consider what it is that the person is doing. The category of *character* is concerned with whether the person is a good (or virtuous) person who is generally ethical. When we look at *motives*, we are concerned with the intentions of the person carrying out the behaviour, and we consider whether they were trying to do something good.

Nothing is clear cut in the study of ethics and these categories sometimes give us different assessments. The puzzle is to decide whether you think the behaviour is ethical or not. Look at the following two examples and see what you think.

Example one: therapy
Rapoff *et al.* (1980) used an ammonia spray to punish a deaf-blind five-year-old boy who was engaging in serious self-injurious behaviour (self-mutilation), and in so doing reduced the amount of his self-harming behaviour.

This sounds a shocking thing to do and many of you will immediately decide that this treatment is unethical but we are going to argue the opposite. The *consequence* of this action, if it is successful, is that the boy will have a better quality of life. The *act* does not look to be a good thing, but we might well judge the *motives* of the therapist to be sound because he or she wants to help the child. Depending on what we believe about therapists in general or what we know about Rapoff in particular we can make an assessment of *character* and decide whether we trust them to do the right thing. Considering that there are no easy solutions when dealing with very challenging children and that this solution at least avoids the use of medication, you might be inclined to judge this as an ethical treatment. Feel free to disagree.

Example two: the Milgram study
Milgram's study (see page 150) is commonly cited in psychology texts as an example of research that broke ethical guidelines. However, the *consequences* of the study were that we have a much sharper insight into human behaviour. The *act*, again, does not look good but Milgram's *motives* were to find out about human behaviour and, in particular, why people are able to commit atrocities. We would also argue that Milgram's *character* was sound as shown by the way that he tried to deal with **ethical issues** before and after the study.

Try this 7.5

The ethical question is: if you believe someone has information that you want, how far can you go to get that information? Think about this for:

a A kidnapper telling you where the victim is.

b Your brother telling you where he has hidden the TV remote.

Ethics in the core studies
The study of ethics is concerned with judgements about right and wrong. All psychological research can be judged against an ethical code. It is important to realise, however, that ethical codes change over time and so it is not helpful to judge behaviour from 100 or even 50 years ago against the ethics of the twenty-first century.

If you select any of the core studies it is possible to find at least one of the ethical guidelines that has been infringed. For example, **Milgram's** participants experienced a stressful situation that stayed with some of them for the rest of their lives (see Blass, 2004). In the Bobo doll study (**Bandura *et al.***) some of the children were left in a room with a violent adult and most of them ended up in tears. The issue to consider along with the guidelines is the value of the research, or in other words, was it worth breaking the ethical guidelines?

Ethics are also a concern in **case studies** (see page 240), such as **Thigpen and Cleckley's** study of Eve. The subject of the case study may be harmed by their involvement with the psychologists, or at least not benefit as much as they might.

In Eve's case the therapists took control of her story and misrepresented what happened. They also tried to prevent her from publishing her own story.

Ethics and psychology

In psychology we are interested in the moral and ethical codes that people develop and live by, but that is not the concern on this page. What we are interested in here is the ethical code that psychologists develop for their own behaviour. Psychologists deal with people in a number of ways including doing research with them and offering them therapy or advice. In order to ensure the safety of the people who come into contact with psychologists, psychologists have developed some guidelines of good practice which are commonly referred to as ethics.

Many studies are criticised for their lack of ethics. It is not acceptable for participants to be harmed during the course of any study. However, what constitutes 'harm'? Is it harmful for a person to experience mild discomfort or mild stress? Is it acceptable to lie to participants about what an **experiment** is about? Such **deception** may be necessary so that participants' behaviour is not affected by knowing what the aim of the experiment is.

Ethics is a topic that has no straightforward answers. Psychologists have to weigh up various factors when deciding whether a study is ethically acceptable. Professional organisations such as the *British Psychological Society* (BPS) produce ethical guidelines or 'codes of conduct' to help do this.

Ethical guidelines for psychologists and psychological research

We have listed below the guidelines from the *The British Psychological Society Code of Ethics and Conduct* (BPS, 2009) which are based on four ethical principles: *respect, competence, responsibility* and *integrity*. Of course, nothing is ever simple and judgements about ethics depend on more than just a set of guidelines, including how useful the research will be. For example, if a study might create a life-saving drug then a certain amount of risk might be acceptable but if the study is for a beauty product then the risk is not necessary or acceptable.

Respect

General respect: Psychologists should respect people's individuality and not show any prejudice on the basis of age, gender, disability, ethnicity, religion, etc.

Privacy* and *confidentiality: It is important to keep records but any disclosure needs to be agreed with the person who gave the information or data.

Informed consent: Are the participants aware of the procedures they are letting themselves in for and make an informed choice to proceed? Informed consent means that clients should not be deceived about what is going on.

Self-determination: The participant should be in control of the situation and aware that they can withdraw whenever they like.

Competence

Awareness of professional ethics: Ethics are an important part of professional life and it is expected that psychologists make themselves aware of ethical principles and codes.

Decision making: Making ethical decisions is more difficult than it seems and it is important to be careful and thoughtful when making those decisions.

Recognising limits of competence: It is important to recognise what you know and also what you don't know.

Recognising impairment: It is important to be able to reflect on your own competence and make the decision to seek help and stop working. This is a tough call to make.

Responsibility

General responsibility: It is important to ensure that people are not harmed by a psychologist's action or even inaction. Not as easy as it sounds, for example to protect a psychiatric patient from harm a therapist might recommend that they do not take the medication but that might result in an increase in their symptoms and put other people at risk from their disturbed behaviour.

Continuity of care: Therapy could go on forever and psychologists should put limits on their interactions with people.

Protection of research participants: It stands to reason that research should not harm people and all potential risks to well-being and dignity are removed. It's easier said than done.

Debriefing: The investigator should discuss with the participants their experience of the research in order to monitor any unforeseen negative effects or misconceptions.

Integrity

Honesty and accuracy: There are many people who misrepresent their training and expertise – the internet is awash with them as are the sofas of daytime television studios. Also, some research findings are misrepresented and 'sexed-up' to make them media friendly.

Avoiding exploitation and conflicts of interest: It is obviously good practice to keep personal and professional lives separate but that is not always possible and at these times the psychologist needs to seek ethical support and approval.

Maintaining personal boundaries: The code of practice is very strong in stating that psychologists should 'refrain from engaging in any form of sexual or romantic relationship with persons to whom they are providing professional services, or to whom they owe a continuing duty of care, or with whom they have a relationship of trust'.

Addressing ethical misconduct: If confronted about ethical behaviour it is expected that psychologists will cooperate with any enquiry in a positive way. Also it is expected that, regardless of friendship or other constraints, a psychologist will report behaviour of colleagues that they believe to be in conflict with the ethical code. This again is a tough one because it is one of the basic rules of human interaction not to snitch, but it is not acceptable to just turn a blind eye to situations you know are wrong.

An ineffective ethics committee.

Missing guidelines

The principles in the list on the left offer a framework for the conduct of research. It is debateable whether they are a full list of the things that psychologists ought to be concerned about. There are some omissions from the list that we might like to add as extra guidelines of good practice. For example, what about:

The use of the research: We can ask psychologists to try to ensure that their findings are used to help people rather than to harm them. So if, for example, psychologists found out what features of a casino encourage people to gamble more than they want, they could tell the casino or they could tell the punters. If they tell the casino then that organisation will most probably use that information to persuade punters into losing more money at the gaming tables.

You might think of some other issues of right/wrong, good/bad that psychologists should consider. The discussion isn't closed.

Some decisions are easier than others

Sometimes ethics can create difficult dilemmas. Imagine that you are a mental health worker and you are dealing with someone who is temporarily mentally disturbed. They describe hearing voices that are telling them to do violent things to people. You believe that forcing them into a psychiatric facility will have a bad effect on them and might prolong this psychotic episode. You also believe that this person is unlikely to actually harm anyone.

The problem is that you have to make a call about the welfare of the ill person and also the safety of the general public.

*Which is more important, the needs of the individual or the needs of the community? As a mental health worker you have to make that ethical call. In this text we criticise the therapists (**Thigpen and Cleckley**) who worked with Eve (see page 202) but there is a case that they were making an ethical judgement to protect Eve from further harm.*

Ecological validity

There's **validity** and there's **ecological validity** – both terms were introduced in Chapter 1. Validity concerns whether a researcher is testing what they intended to test. This is discussed again at the end of this chapter.

Ecological validity is a wider concept – it concerns whether the results of a study can be related to people's *everyday behaviour*, to 'real' and natural social settings as opposed to the research setting where the results were produced. 'Ecological' is a word meaning 'environments'. So ecological validity is about taking a result from one setting and applying it to other settings, but we have to think about more than the setting when we try to think about realness.

Ecological validity in the core studies
Ecological validity relates to every one of the core studies. On this spread we look at studies by **Loftus and Palmer** and **Piliavin et al.** and **Milgram**.

The issues apply to studies conducted in a **laboratory** such as **Bandura et al.**, studies conducted in the field such as **Savage-Rumbaugh et al.**, **case studies** such as **Freud's** study of Little Hans, **observations** such as **Rosenhan** and so on.

To what extent can we make generalisations about everyday life from these studies?

What creates high ecological validity?

One of the main concerns for any researcher is that the findings of the study can be used to explain behaviour. This may seem obvious but consider this:

> A researcher conducts a study in a laboratory to see how people react to **leading questions**. Participants are shown a film clip of a car accident and asked questions about the speed the cars were travelling. The study shows that people think the car was travelling faster if they are asked 'How fast were the cars going when they smashed into each other?' rather than being asked 'How fast were the cars going when they hit each other?'

What we really want to know is not about how people behave in a laboratory when watching a film clip (**Loftus and Palmer**) – but about how real-life eyewitnesses behave when they see a real car accident.

When thinking about ecological validity there are three key factors to consider:

1. Think about the task
How much is the film clip and the questions like the 'real' experience an eyewitness would have? If you have seen a car accident you will know that it is very frightening – the noise of the cars hitting each other, the smell of broken metal, the distress of the people. … The task in Loftus and Palmer's study was not very much like 'real' life (everyday life). It wasn't very ordinary (i.e. it was artificial).

2. Think about the setting
A laboratory is one setting. A street near where you live is another setting. The same street 50 years ago is yet another setting. When we conduct research we generalise the results of the setting to other settings. That's where the word 'ecological' comes in because it refers to the setting.

3. You are being watched
In a laboratory participants know they are being studied because they have come to the laboratory and been briefed about what is going to happen. This is likely to mean they don't behave 'normally' (naturally). In the subway Samaritan study by **Piliavin et al.** the participants didn't know their behaviour was being studied. In **Milgram's** study the participants knew they were being studied but they didn't know that their obedience levels were being studied.

If we want to be really picky …
Ecological validity can be further divided into:

Population validity – *generalising from the participants in a study to other groups of people.*

Historical validity – *generalising from the time period in which a study was done to more recent times.*

Four studies for you to consider

Study 1: a laboratory study
Milgram (1963) arranged for participants to deliver painful electric shocks to a 'learner' in a laboratory. He found that 65% of the participants were fully obedient.

Milgram repeated this study in many different situations:

- The location was moved to a run-down office. Levels of obedience dropped from 65% to 48% in this more realistic setting. One of the features of the setting was that it lacked the prestige of the Yale laboratory.

- When the teacher was in the same room as the learner, obedience levels dropped to 40%. This shows that when features of the situation change, willingness to obey legitimate authority changes. In this version there was face-to-face contact.

- When the teacher held the learner's hand on a shock plate, obedience levels dropped to 30%.

In a sense these results show that we cannot generalise from one setting to another because obedience levels changed from one setting to another.

However, taken together the results point to the same conclusion – situational factors affect obedience to unjust authority. This supports the validity of Milgram's initial conclusions.

Study 2: a field study
When research is conducted in the 'field' it is generally regarded as more 'natural' because the environment is more natural.

Hofling et al. (1966) conducted a study of obedience in a US hospital. Nurses were telephoned by a 'Dr Smith' who asked the nurses to give 20 mg of a drug called *Astroten* to a patient. This order contravened hospital regulations in a number of ways:

- nurses were told not to accept instructions on the phone;
- nor from an unknown doctor;
- nor for a dose in excess of the safe amount (the dosage was twice that advised on the bottle);
- especially for an unknown drug.

Nevertheless, 21 out of 22 (95%) nurses did as requested.

This study supports the validity of Milgram's study because the results are the same – both studies found high levels of obedience to unjust authority.

When the nurses involved in the study were interviewed afterwards they said, in their defence, that they had obeyed because that's what doctors expect nurses to do – they behaved as nurses do in real life, or did they? Consider study 3.

ISSUES

Are experiments artificial?

*No. **Experiments** are neither artificial or not artificial – a laboratory study might be more artificial than a **field experiment** because the task is artificial, the setting differs to other settings and participants are aware they are being studied – but the key is the laboratory not the fact that it is an experiment.*

Testing a hypothesis on the moon

Galileo predicted that objects all fall at the same rate no matter what their mass. So, if you simultaneously drop a feather and hammer from the same height they should land at the same time.

However, you can't demonstrate this on earth because air resistance would slow the feather. The Apollo 15 space mission used the artificial setting of the Moon to test Galileo's prediction.

*We need artificial conditions to test **hypotheses** to eliminate **extraneous variables**. The results from such artificial studies can then be confirmed by field studies with less control.*

A moon astronaut testing Gallileo's hypothesis about gravity, 'In my left hand, I have a feather; in my right hand, a hammer.'

Study 3: another field study

Rank and Jacobsen (1975) conducted another study with nurses, this time in Australia. But there were other important differences:

*   The drug was familiar (*Valium*).
*   The nurses could consult with peers.

The result this time was a complete reversal to the study by Hofling *et al.* This time 16 out of 18 (89%) *refused* to obey the legitimate authority.

Rank and Jacobsen's study used *more real-life tasks* – in this study the nurses dealt with a familiar drug and were allowed to consult with each other. So this study was more like everyday life than Hofling's study.

Study 4: a real-life event

The historian **Christopher Browning** (1992) described an incident in the Second World War – more of a case history than a 'study', but we can use the evidence to consider obedience.

Police Battalion 101 was commanded by Major Wilheim Trapp. In one encounter between German troops and civilians the Major Trapp had orders to shoot all the Jews in the small Polish town of Józefów. Trapp told his battalion of 500 men that such a mission was not to his liking but orders are orders. However, he told his battalion that if they did not feel up to the mission they should step forward. One man stepped forward and after a time another 10 joined him.

According to Milgram's findings far more should have stepped forward and disobeyed – the task involved many of the factors that Milgram had found led to reduced obedience (the face-to-face contact, there were some disobedient peers, and there was absence of pressure from the authority figure).

On the other hand, Milgram also suggested that one reason for high levels of obedience is that people don't have time to think. The suddenness of Trapp's offer may explain the high levels of 'just obeying orders'.

Police Battalion 101, just obeying orders.

What can we conclude?

You might think that Milgram's study was very artificial. Yes, it was in an invented setting and it was an unusual setting for the participants but, on the other hand, the 'lab setting' was just used as a convenient way to test authority (the 'experimenter' was the authority figure).

Hofling *et al.*'s study was conducted in a more natural setting than Milgram's but there were aspects of this study that were unusual (not like everyday experience) – it would have been very unusual for a nurse to be asked to administer an unknown drug let alone in twice the safe dosage. When the tasks were made more everyday (in the study by Rank and Jacobsen), obedience levels changed quite dramatically.

Another issue with Hofling's study is that it concerned one particular kind of authority relationship – doctors and nurses. When the nurses in Hofling's study were interviewed afterwards they said that the reason they obeyed was because they saw it as part of their job to obey the orders of doctors. Does this mean that research using nurses doesn't tell us that much about everyday obedience?

Browning's study challenges some of Milgram's conclusions. The results of this case history are based on what people really did and therefore should be high in ecological validity. On the other hand, they were German officers and we might feel that we cannot generalise to all people from this **sample**.

There are no simple answers, but there are lots of interesting discussions about what psychological research really tells us!

No study really lacks ecological validity ...

It's a question about how high or low a study is in ecological validity. Most studies have bits of both.

All research conducted in the real-world is not automatically ecologically valid and all lab studies are not automatically ecologically invalid.

Longitudinal and snapshot studies

How does behaviour develop and change during our lives? This is an interesting question for psychologists but it is difficult to get the evidence. One way to collect evidence is to study a group of people as they change and develop. This is called a **longitudinal study** and it involves repeated observations over long periods of time. The first obvious problem with this type of study is that it takes a long time to get any results because you have to wait for the people to age in real time.

The alternative is to have a cross-sectional or **snapshot study** where *different* groups of people are studied at different stages of their development at one point in time. The clear advantage of this is that the data can be collected within a relatively short space of time but we can't know whether our results are due to the development of the behaviour or to differences in the experiences of the different groups.

Imagine a study into the skills of using computers. A study carried out today would probably find that people aged 15 would on average be brilliant at using computers, that people who are 35 would be pretty good at most aspect of computer use and that people who are 65 would on average be only fair to middling at computer use. Does this mean that computer skills decline with age? Probably not because there is a much better explanation – that people who are now 65 never used computers when they were 15 (personal computers were unheard of then) and so did not learn the skills, which would explain their low performance in their 60s.

Movies and snapshots

The difference between longitudinal and snapshot studies is like the difference between Flickr and YouTube.

Research studies that just take one set of data are sometimes referred to as snapshot studies. These studies have captured some aspect of behaviour or experience at one moment in time, like a snapshot. This is the most common way to collect data in psychology and the picture we get of behaviour is fine because we know every picture paints a thousand words (Telly Savalas). But if we explore the metaphor we can see some of the drawbacks to these psychological snapshots.

People pose for snapshots. Look through your photos. How many of your snaps have people smiling (usually cheesy and with their arms out)? Now look at how often people are smiling in their daily life. We smile when people look at us and when we think we are being observed. The rest of the time we rest our smile muscles. The snapshots you see on Facebook or Myspace would suggest that people are forever smiling to the point that their faces have got stuck in some hideous rictus like *The Joker*. If you just use snapshots as evidence then you would think the whole world is riotously happy every minute of the day.

The moving image tells a different story. It is harder to keep up the happy image when the cameras roll continuously as numerous people have found out on *I'm a Celebrity ...*

Self-portraits

A picture of Noah everyday turned into a film.

Movies can give a unique insight into people but a good portrait can still catch the depth of a person. What about if you combined the two? On YouTube and elsewhere on the internet there are projects by individuals where they have taken a picture of themselves everyday and then combined them into a movie to capture how they have changed.

For example look at Noah who took a picture of himself every day for 12½ years.

www *http://www.youtube.com/watch?v=iPPzXlMdi7o&feature=plcp or search for Homer Simpson's version.*

The simplicity of modern technologies allows you to try something like this yourself. Take a picture of yourself or a friend or a pet everyday for a couple of months.

Longitudinal and snapshot methods in the core studies

Among the core studies that take measures over time are the **case studies** of Little Hans (**Freud**) and Eve (**Thickpen and Cleckley**). In the case of Eve, the report by Thigpen and Cleckley reads as a summary of several months of therapy. The story is much longer even than that and is told in Eve's own account of her life. It is an interesting postscript to Freud's study that Hans came to see Freud when he was a young man and appeared to have no recollection of the issues that form the basis for the powerful description in the case study.

There are also links to other issues covered in this text. The key ones concern the quality of the data that we get from these types of study. Are the data **reliable** and **valid**? How can we ensure the quality of our data over time because it is difficult to maintain our control of all the variables in the study.

Social research

Longitudinal studies are used in social research to track such issues as poverty and health. This type of study can dig deeper into the issues. For example, say the proportion of people in poverty in the UK is 10% in 1990 and also 10% in the year 2000, we might want to know whether this 10% is mainly the same group of people or different people.

Longitudinal studies vary enormously in their size and complexity. At one extreme a large group of people may be studied over decades. For example, the longitudinal study of the *Office of Population Censuses and Surveys* collects data on a 1% **sample** of the British population that was initially identified at the 1971 census.

This data is used to see what factors such as housing or employment can be shown to correlate with illness or early death. At the other extreme, some longitudinal studies follow up a single case over a period of time.

Try this 7.6

Think about how your own psychological variables have changed over time. For example, think back five years and then 10 years and make a list of (a) the differences in the way you think, (b) the differences in the way you behave and (c) the differences in the way you feel. If that seems too tricky then try mapping out your tastes in (a) food, (b) music and (c) television.

ISSUES

Longitudinal studies

Pictures of the same person as she (gracefully) ages.

Snapshot studies

Picture of three generations of the same family.

	Longitudinal studies	Snapshot studies
Time	Longitudinal studies take a long time, which makes them more expensive and also requires patience because you have to wait a long time for the results.	Snapshot studies can be done much more quickly (in a few moments or a few months instead of many years).
Attrition	**Attrition** is a problem for longitudinal studies because some of the participants inevitably dropout. The problem is that it may be certain kinds of participants (the ones who are less motivated or more unhappy or who have done less well) which leaves a biased sample.	This is much less of a problem for studies that take place over a short space of time.
Participant variables	In longitudinal studies participant variables are controlled. **Participant variables** are characteristics such as IQ, sociability, interests and so on.	The groups of participants may be quite different. The participant variables in a snapshot design are not controlled in the same way that they are controlled in an **independent measures design**. This means that differences between groups may be due to participant variables rather than the **independent variable**.
Cohort effects	**Cohort effects** occur when a group of people are all the same age. They share certain experiences, such as children born just before the war had poor diets in infancy due to rationing.	
	We may not be able to generalise the findings from a study that looks at only one cohort because of the unique characteristics of that cohort.	Cohort effects may produce spurious results. For example, one snapshot study compared IQs of 20-somethings with 80-somethings and found the **mean** IQ of the latter group was much lower, concluding that ageing led to a decreased IQ. The reason, however, might well be because the 80-somethings had lower IQs when they were 20-somethings (e.g. due to poorer diet).

Cohorts

People who grew up in the 1960s (like Phil and Cara) have many shared experiences and attitudes which makes them different to, say, people who are teenagers in the twenty-first century. They remember Sergeant Pepper as if it was yesterday. They were brought up in a world without computers, sat nav, cheap foreign travel or even Pot Noodles. This means that a study of adolescents in the 1960s might have different findings to a study conducted today because of the very different experiences of these people. This is called a cohort effect.

The Beatles (as if you didn't know), a 1960s phenomenon.

The significant difference is not simply the time taken for longitudinal versus snapshot studies but the fact that, in a longitudinal study, what is being observed is changes in behaviour over time. In a snapshot study a behaviour is recorded at one moment in time.

Examples of longitudinal studies

Snapshot studies are much the default in psychology and social science due to issues of cost and convenience. There are, however, some examples of longitudinal studies that you can access and provide a fascinating picture of the UK and its people.

The Centre for Longitudinal Studies (http://www.cls.ioe.ac.uk) is home to three UK studies that are studying a group of people born around the same time. You might be able to guess when the children were born from the title of the three projects: *The 1958 National Child Development Study* which follows the lives of 17,000 people born in the same week; *The 1970 British Cohort Study* which is following a further 17,000 people also born in the same week; and *The Millennium Cohort Study* is following 19,000 people born during 2000–01 and has already collected five sets of data.

These projects are building up a rich picture of development in UK people and should be able to give us insights into a range of issues on health and well-being. We are personally hoping for conclusive evidence that the 3Cs diet (cake, chips and cider) is the best way to ensure a long life.

The most visible of the birth cohort studies is the *Up Series*. This set of television documentaries by Michael Apted has followed the lives of 14 UK children since 1964. Every seven years the programme makers revisit the same 14 people to see what has happened to them. The series started with a clear agenda about class differences in the UK and the differences in opportunity for children depending on the family they are born into. The series confirms all our expectations about the way that many people have restricted opportunities in this country, and to be fair, not much has changed in the last 50 years.

Qualitative and quantitative data

Qualitative data are about 'qualities' of things. They are descriptions, words, meanings, pictures, texts and so forth. They are about what something is like, or how something is experienced. Good examples of studies included in this book which are based on the collection of qualitative data are **Freud's** case study of Little Hans and **Reicher and Haslam's** prison simulation, though quantitative data was also collected in this study. Studies which mainly deal with qualitative data are in the minority in this book and this reflects the dominance of quantitative data in psychological research.

Quantitative data are about 'quantities' of things. They are numbers, raw scores, percentages, means, standard deviations, etc. They are measurements of things, telling us how much of something there is. Most of the studies in this book deal with quantitative data. For example, the memory study by **Loftus and Palmer** records estimates of speed and **Samuel and Bryant's** study of children's judgements records the number of children who make a particular judgement.

How do I love thee?

In one of the most famous love poems of all time Elizabeth Barrett Browning starts by asking:

'How do I love thee? Let me count the ways.'

If she had been looking for quantitative answers she might well have continued:

'Well I can think of 3 maybe 4 on a good day.'

Although this would probably have been an accurate answer it would not have done much for the romance in the relationship. In fact she goes on to describe her experience in rich terms:

'I love thee to the depth and breadth and height My soul can reach, when feeling out of sight For the ends of Being and ideal Grace.'

*Our complex emotional and **cognitive** worlds can only be partly described with numbers but fortunately we have the richness of language to capture our experience.*

Try this　　　　　　　7.7

To Quant or to Qual? That is the question. Look at the terms below and figure out which applies best to qualitative or quantitative data.

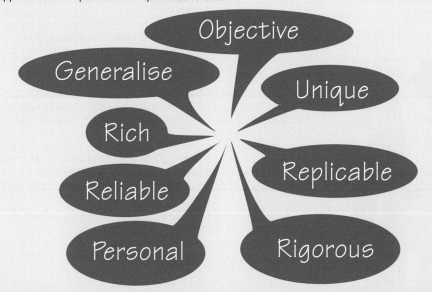

The answers are not as straightforward as you might think and in some cases they are a matter of opinion. The debate between advocates of the two types is very fierce and often insulting. Maybe people use qualitative measures to cover up for not being able to use statistics; or do people use quantitative measures to avoid difficult questions and personal experience?

Qualitative and quantitative data in the core studies

Measurement is a key part of any psychological study. You might well argue that it is the main puzzle for any researcher. How do I measure this behaviour or cognition or emotion so that I can best understand what is happening with it? If you want to measure aggressive behaviour, as in the Bobo doll study (**Bandura *et al.***), then you might count the number of physical acts or the number of shouts. This gives you one measure of aggression but sometimes people can create a very aggressive atmosphere without doing anything or saying anything. To capture this you would have to add first hand accounts of the situation to put alongside your quantitative measures.

One of the other issues that this one ties into very closely is that of **reliability** and **validity**. The argument for quantitative measures is that they can appear to be very reliable and very reassuring. If we are being prescribed a medication we might be interested to hear some recommendations of it by previous users but we want to know (a) how many people got better using it, and (b) how much better they got. The bottom line for most of the core studies is that they use a mixture of data in order to describe and analyse human behaviour and experience.

Using the terms correctly

People sometimes refer to research methods as being either qualitative or quantitative. This is misleading, however, because it implies that certain methods always produce certain kinds of data.

For example, **experiments** are usually referred to as 'quantitative' and **textual analysis** is usually described as 'qualitative'. Experiments, however, can sometimes produce both kinds. **Milgram** described the behaviour of his participants in some detail (qualitative), as well as measuring the extent to which they were prepared to comply with the demands of the experimenter (quantitative).

On the other hand, **textual analysis** can be 'quantitative'. For example, the **Savage-Rumbaugh** study reports detailed **observational** data (qualitative) but the final analysis looks at how many words the chimpanzees learned (quantitative). For this reason it is more accurate to use the terms qualitative and quantitative to refer to 'data', rather than 'research method'.

(The **qualitative approach** to research is discussed on page 243.)

ISSUES

7.8

Try to produce qualitative AND quantitative measures for the same material. Use the source on the right as the material to work with.

1   Produce a *qualitative* analysis: one way that qualitative data can be summarised is by identifying repeated themes. These should be based on the participants' own meanings, that is they should be groupings as seen from the participant's perspective rather than ones imposed by the researcher. This enables the researcher to reduce the total material (hours of videotapes or pages of **interview** transcripts) to manageable proportions. The themes or patterns may be illustrated by using quotes from the participant(s).

2   Produce a *quantitative* analysis of the data: to do this you have to convert the data to numbers, for example count up how many times a particular theme is mentioned. You can then represent this data in a bar chart (see **descriptive statistics** on page 13).

Less than 36 hours into the experiment, Prisoner #8612 began suffering from acute emotional disturbance, disorganised thinking, uncontrollable crying, and rage. In spite of all of this, we had already come to think so much like prison authorities that we thought he was trying to 'con' us – to fool us into releasing him.

Prisoner #8612 told other prisoners, 'You can't leave. You can't quit.' That sent a chilling message and heightened their sense of really being imprisoned. #8612 then began to act 'crazy,' to scream, to curse, to go into a rage that seemed out of control. It took quite a while before we became convinced that he was really suffering and that we had to release him.

The only prisoner who did not want to speak to the priest was Prisoner #819, who was feeling sick, had refused to eat, and wanted to see a doctor rather than a priest. While talking to us, he broke down and began to cry hysterically, just as had the other two boys we released earlier. I took the chain off his foot, the cap off his head, and told him to go and rest.

While I was doing this, one of the guards lined up the other prisoners and had them chant aloud: 'Prisoner #819 is a bad prisoner. Because of what Prisoner #819 did, my cell is a mess, Mr. Correctional Officer.' They shouted this statement in unison a dozen times.

(Zimbardo, http://www.prisonexp.org)

Visual methods

What does a tattoo tell us about the person?

In our daily lives we are surrounded by images, and we make sense of the world using our sense of sight. With the explosion in the use of digital technologies we commonly present ourselves through images, and explore information in pictorial form. Traditional psychology deals with data that is either verbal or numerical and has developed a range of sophisticated methods to analyse this data such as *structural equation modeling* for numerical data (quantitative), and *discourse analysis* for verbal data (qualitative). There are also methods for exploring visual data but these are less used in research or teaching.

Think about this – why did you choose those particular pictures to upload to Facebook? Looking at other people's chosen images tells you something about how they want to be seen. The same applies to the visual image we create for our appearance. If we wanted to study tattoos for example we need to investigate the images as well as asking people about them. This is where visual methods come in.

Idiographic and Nomothetic

The debate over the relative merits of qualitative and quantitative data has a long history in psychology. There has been a tension between those who put most value on studying individuals and those that look for common features in groups of people. The study of the individual is called the **idiographic** approach whereas **nomothetic** is more the study of a cohort of individuals.

- *Nomothetic* is a tendency to generalise, and is expressed in the natural sciences. It describes the effort to develop laws that explain objective phenomena, for example, in physics we have laws of motion. An example in psychology is the attempt to identify and measure underlying features in personality and cognition.

- *Idiographic* is a tendency to specify, and is expressed in the humanities. It describes the effort to understand the meaning of accidental and often subjective phenomena. In psychology, first-hand accounts of personal experience are a good example of this approach.

The magic of the Ronettes

How can we capture the richness of human experience? We want to record our experiences and compare them in some way. If we say one song is better than another then we have applied a simple form of measurement. If we want to create a top 10 of music then we have to develop some measurement criteria to do that. We might want to use a combination of qualitative and quantitative measures. You might want to know who the best-selling artist (quantitative) was but you also need to know what someone feels when they listen to the music. You can investigate this with measures of **brain waves** (quantitative) or changes in skin conductance (also quantitative) but will these measures be enough to provide an explanation of what the music makes us feel? The experience of music is very personal and rich and it is hard to see how numbers would be able to capture the full response to the greatest song ever performed which is *Be My Baby* by the Ronettes *(what do you mean you've never heard of it?).*

You can't explain the magic of the Ronettes only in numbers.

Mixed methods

As you look through the core studies you'll often see a mix of data in the report. For example, the core study on multiple personality by **Thigpen and Cleckley** has a wide range of data as shown in the table below.

Quantitative measures
Scores on personality tests
IQ scores
Memory test scores
EEG measures of brain activity

Qualitative measures
Clinical interviews with patient(s)
Interviews with family members
Observations by therapists
Letter sent to therapists
Responses to Rorschach test

Case studies

Case studies provide some of psychology's best stories. In this text we have looked at a number including the story of Little Hans by **Freud** who used detailed case studies as the main evidence for his theories, the multiple personalities of Eve described by **Thigpen and Cleckley**, and the development of language in Washoe recorded by Gardner and Gardner and Kanzi by **Savage-Rumbaugh** *et al.*

These case studies give us detailed information on Hans, Eve and Kanzi and they provide some unique insights into behaviour and experience. Freud uses the story of Hans to support the existence of the **Oedipus complex** in boys, and Thigpen and Cleckley used Eve's story to support their view of **multiple personality disorder**. The study of the use of lexigrams by pygmy chimps provides evidence that animals can use abstract signs to communicate.

All the stories are engaging and have stood the test of time. There is still considerable interest in all of them and they commonly appear in introductory psychology textbooks. Their appeal goes beyond the boundaries of psychology and several case studies have become well known to the general public. There is no doubt that they have contributed to our understanding of ourselves and others but it is also important to look at the scientific value and personal consequences of these.

'There is no psychology; there is only biography and autobiography.'
American Psychiatrist Thomas Szasz

Biography and autobiography

Case studies are scientific biographies. They try to tell the story of someone and use key details to illustrate psychological theories. Some of the problems that authors have when they attempt to write a biography also come up with case studies.

For example, the entertainer Cilla Black wrote her own autobiography and said *'I had to do the book because there was an unauthorised biography which didn't tell it like it was.'* How could someone else tell the story of your life? Only you have seen it from the inside. But, if we left the story of your life just to you, then we would also have some problems. The story I would tell about myself is bound to be different to the stories that other people would tell about me. Autobiographies are very different to biographies; this is not to say that we tell lies about ourselves or others but just that seeing a story from the inside is very different to seeing it from afar. Case studies are most commonly biography rather than autobiography and so have that outsider view of the events.

The British author Rebecca West identified the problem for biographers and case study authors when she wrote, *'Just how difficult it is to write biography can be reckoned by anybody who sits down and considers just how many people know the real truth about his or her love affairs. Nobody can know the real truth, perhaps not even yourself.'*

The US author Mark Twain highlights the weakness of biographies when he wrote, *'Biographies are but the clothes and buttons of the man. The biography of the man himself cannot be written.'* The words on the page can only capture the performances that we give everyday and not the internal world of our thoughts and feelings.

Biographies and case studies commonly seem to be about exceptional people doing exceptional things. It is perhaps not surprising that we are drawn towards people who have different experiences to ourselves. This concentration on differentness can give a false impression about ordinary people living regular lives. As Mark Twain wrote, *'There was never yet an uninteresting life. Such a thing is an impossibility. Inside of the dullest exterior there is a drama, a comedy, and a tragedy.'*

Your mother was right – you are very special. In fact, you are unique, and your experience of life and your life story is all your own.

Case studies in the core studies

Case studies provide the starting point for a lot of work in psychology. An unusual experience or behaviour is observed and studied and it can give some general insight into human experience and some personal insight into one special life. The study of multiple personality has developed from records of case studies like that of Eve (**Thigpen and Cleckley**). Sigmund **Freud** developed his theories from detailed analysis of a small number of case studies of which Little Hans is one example. You might well argue that the chimp research of **Savage-Rumbaugh** *et al.* is also based on case studies as is the work of **Sperry** on split brains.

There are links to other issues in that a lot, but by no means all, of case study evidence is collected as **qualitative data** rather than as **quantitative data**. Much of it has a **longitudinal** element as well, as the authors try and give a rich picture of the subject of their study. It is also worth underlining the need to retain a sceptical eye of this evidence because our access to the evidence is often fiercely controlled by the authors of the studies.

A number of studies are based on the experiences of chimpanzees (see page 62). Such subjects are never given the opportunity to tell their side of the story. Such animals are often wild before being trained to speak. We think they aren't just wild, they are furious.

Whose story is it anyway?

One of the issues concerns authorship. If my life story was going be told in a book or a scientific paper then I would like to have some say in it. Apart from anything else it is my story and I ought to be able to tell it. This is the position Eve (Christine Sizemore) was in, but her attempts to tell her own story were impeded and discouraged by her therapists who had authored papers and a book about her (see page 202). And if you were Hans wouldn't you like to contribute to the story? The therapists took control of their patients' life stories and in some cases made money out of it. On the facing page we write about David Reimer. He was unaware until he was an adult that his story appeared in many textbooks of psychology and sociology across the world. Genie (see facing page) and HM (see page 113) also have their stories widely told without their **informed consent**.

The underlying theme here concerns vulnerable people. Children, people with mental ill-health and the poor are all groups that have vulnerabilities and whose stories are less credible and less likely to be heard if it comes from their own mouth. It is still their story though and they know more about it than anybody else. It is an important **ethical issue** for psychologists to consider.

METHODS

Examples of case studies in psychology

Phantom limbs

The neurologist **V.S. Ramachrandran** uses case studies to explore ideas about how the brain works. In his Reith Lectures for the BBC in 2003, Ramachandran described one patient with a phantom left arm (which means they feel the presence of the arm even though it had been amputated). He blindfolded the patient and then touched him around his body using a cotton bud and asked him what he felt. Everything was as you'd expect until he touched the left side of the patient's face. Ramachandran reports that *'when I touched his cheek he said oh my god doctor, you're touching my left thumb, my missing phantom thumb and he seemed as surprised as I was. Then I touched him on the upper lip and he said oh my god you're touching my phantom index finger.'*

Only by exploring a person's first hand unique account do we get this level of insight into the problem. And if you want to know why the patient had those sensations then go check out http://www.bbc.co.uk/radio4/reith2003/lectures.shtml.

Nelson's phantom

If you look up in Trafalgar Square in London you will see this statue. It shows Nelson with one arm and an empty sleeve. His arm was amputated after it had been shattered by a musket bullet. Nelson developed a strong sensation of a phantom arm and even felt his (non-existent) fingers squeezing into his (non-existent) palm. These sensations led Nelson to say that his phantom was a direct proof of the existence of the soul. If an arm can survive being completely destroyed then why not the whole person?

Genie

Genie was brought up in terrible conditions for the first 13 years of her life, during which she was continually restrained by her father, often strapped to a chair, and never spoken to. When she was discovered she was unable to speak. She seemed to be an ideal case to use to answer a number of scientific questions about the development of language.

Her subsequent care and exploitation by psychologists is a matter of some dispute (Rymer, 1993). For years she lived with the family of one of the psychologists who was studying her and she was well cared for. But when the research money ran out, Genie was abandoned back into abusive environments. Genie's mother successfully sued some of the psychologists involved for 'extreme, unreasonable, and outrageously intensive testing, **experimentation**, and **observation**'. It is argued that concern for psychological research was placed before compassion for the child.

Try this   7.9

Try to write **two** case studies/biographies.

For the first one choose a family member and get them to tell you something about themselves, maybe an interesting event or the way they feel about something. Write it down and show it to them to see if they agree with what you have written.

For the second one, write a story of something you have done. It could be something exciting like your backward pogo stick journey down Everest or something everyday like babysitting for an evening.

For both case study stories look at what was left out and how difficult it is to create a full and accurate record.

The boy brought up as a girl

The heading for this case study sounds like the subject of a daytime TV show. It is much more than that, however, it is the story of a personal and scientific tragedy.

David Reimer was born in rural USA in 1965 along with his twin brother Brian. When they were eight months they each had a minor operation on their penis for medical reasons. The doctor made a mistake and burnt off David's penis. The parents were referred to **Dr John Money**, who believed that it was possible to bring a child up as a girl even if he had been born a boy. This was his own view, and a rather controversial one, so the case of David Reimer provided him with an opportunity to get evidence to support his theory.

In brief, John Money advised the parents to bring David up as a girl and to keep his true identity from him. The parents accepted Money's advice and David became Brenda. As far as the world knew the change was a success and Money published reports saying that the child was well adjusted in her new identity. Nothing could have been further from the truth, however, and although Brenda was strongly encouraged to be feminine she never adjusted to life as girl and at the age of 14, when she/he discovered the truth, decided to live as a male.

Some years later biologist **Milton Diamond** (1997) made contact with David who was shocked to hear that his story had been presented as a successful example of gender reassignment. He spoke extensively to Diamond and later to journalist Jon Colapinto (2000) who published David's story. He also appeared in television documentaries.

In 2002 Reimer's twin brother Brian took his own life with an overdose of anti-depressants and David's life became more troubled after this. During the next two years he was made redundant and his explosive anger and periods of depression created tensions in his marriage. On 4 May 2004 he took his own life.

Evaluating case studies in psychology

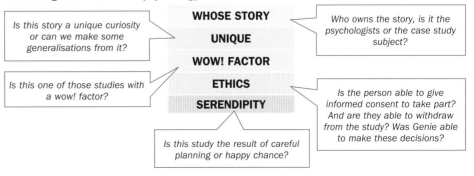

Is this story a unique curiosity or can we make some generalisations from it?

WHOSE STORY

UNIQUE

WOW! FACTOR

ETHICS

SERENDIPITY

Who owns the story, is it the psychologists or the case study subject?

Is this one of those studies with a wow! factor?

Is the person able to give informed consent to take part? And are they able to withdraw from the study? Was Genie able to make these decisions?

Is this study the result of careful planning or happy chance?

Reliability and validity

The issues of **reliability** and **validity** are fundamental when considering the value of research. These topics were discussed extensively in Chapter 1 and that may be enough for you, but we thought we'd give you a few more things to think about …

> reliability = consistency
> validity = testing what you intended to test

Reliable but not valid

If a measurement is not reliable then it can't be valid. In Chapter 1 we used the example of the 'psychomeasure' IQ test as something that would be reliable but not valid.

Here's another example. We often worry about our weight and would prefer to be about 10 kilo lighter. Phil comes up with a good idea. He just resets my bathroom scale so it looks as if I am 10 kilo lighter. Every day I get on my bathroom scales and feel good because I have lost weight. It's a reliable measurement – but not valid – because it's not my 'real' weight.

Valid but not reliable

In general it is difficult to imagine any test or assessment being valid if it isn't reliable. However, we've come up with one possibility: in a **questionnaire** a researcher has a choice between using **open** or **closed questions**. For example:

- Open question – *Explain what you feel about the stress of taking exams.*
- Closed question – *Which of the following represents how you feel about taking exams: Scared I might fail, don't feel I have revised enough, not really worried.*

One strength of using open questions is that you are more likely to find out what people really do think and feel, i.e. the data collected represents everyday life better (increased validity).

One of the weaknesses of using open questions is people might give different answers from one day to the next for various reasons (for example, differences in their mood). This reduces reliability.

So open questions may tend to have greater validity but tend to have less reliability.

Reliability in the core studies

Reliability mainly concerns measurement and you can find this in every core study.

- In **experiments** the **dependent variable** is measured, for example in the study by **Baron-Cohen *et al***. The *Eyes Task* (a **psychological test**) was used to assess **Theory of Mind**.
- Or in the study by **Maguire *et al*.** brain size was measured by counting pixels.
- In the study by **Bandura *et al*.** the children's aggressive behaviour at the end of the study was measured using **observational techniques** (**behavioural categories**). And in this study aggression was also assessed beforehand using **rating scales**.

Reliability

Reliability means we assume that if the same measurement was repeated we would get the same or similar result.

- Reliable data is consistent. So the question you must ask is 'Is this data consistent with data collected elsewhere?'
- Reliable data is evidence you can trust. So the question you must ask is 'Can we trust it?'

Think about this …

A researcher interviews school students about their homework practices. How can the researcher check reliability?

Answer: The researcher might ask the student's parents and teachers about their homework.

WRONG! This would be a check on the *truthfulness* of the answers. To check *reliability* the SAME interviewer would ask the SAME participants the SAME questions and the responses would be compared to see if they are consistent.

If anything is changed that would explain why the end result is not consistent – but we just want to know if the measuring tool is inconsistent.

Replication – reliability or validity?

One of the cornerstones of good science is **replication** – repeating a study several times to see if the same results are found. Getting the same results suggests that the result must be 'real' rather than just a fluke. For example, if you repeated **Loftus and Palmer's** study and found that your participants gave the highest speed estimates for the verb 'hit' what does this tell us about the original results? Does it show the results lack reliability or validity?

It's reliability

Bailey (2012) considered the following example. In Piaget's **conservation task** children of six usually say the longer line of counters has more, even though there is the same number of counters in each line. From this we can conclude that children of this age can not conserve number. The result is reliable. We can trust it. However, **Samuel and Bryant** showed that it was not a valid measure of conservation because, if you ask only one question instead of two, children of six can conserve. So a repetition of Piaget's study only demonstrates reliability.

It's validity

Milgram replicated his original research in a number of different studies (see page 234). These replications confirmed his original finding – that situational factors determine obedience levels. In this case replication demonstrates validity.

What's the answer?

If a researcher repeats the same study EXACTLY then they are demonstrating reliability. They may use different participants but it is essentially the same study. However, replication usually involves making other changes. For example, the study by Rank and Jacobsen (see page 235) was not an EXACT repeat of Hofling *et al*.'s study. In general this is how psychologists use replication – to demonstrate or challenge the validity of an explanation rather than demonstrate the reliability of the method.

Validity in the core studies
Validity involves a balance between control and generalisability.
Both are important.

- In the **laboratory experiment** by **Loftus and Palmer** both the
task and the environment were not very realistic. However,
a high level of control was possible so we could claim
that changes in the **dependent variable** were due to the
independent variable.

- In the **field experiment** by **Piliavin et al.** the task and the
environment were more 'real', however **extraneous variables**
could not be controlled.

Validity

Validity concerns the issue of whether any observed effect is a genuine one – psychologists
want to discover what is really true about human behaviour. In order to believe in their
results we need to be assured that no extraneous variables have intervened (low control).
We want to feel that the **sample** of people studied does represent a group of people in
the 'real world' (the population of people we claim to be representing). We want to know
that the task that was studied was similar to what people actually do as part of everyday
behaviour. We want to be convinced that the participants were acting naturally and not
trying to behave like they think they should behave.

One little warning ...
Sometimes students get confused about the 'right result'. Validity is about being right
but not in the way you might think. Consider this – a researcher produces the hypothesis:
'Boys are more aggressive than girls'. A study is conducted and the results support the
hypothesis. The researcher was 'right' in the sense that the results confirm the hypothesis
but that doesn't mean he was 'right' in the sense that boys are actually more aggressive
than girls. The researcher might have used a **questionnaire** with **leading questions** to
measure aggressiveness. So even though he was 'right' the result is meaningless.

Just because the prediction turns out as expected doesn't mean that it represents
something 'real'.

Reliable, yes, but are they valid – i.e. are they real
watermelon?

*As a matter of fact they are. You grow them by
placing the young fruit in a square box that shapes
the growth. It's a wonder they haven't caught on.*

Is it reliability or validity?
Sometimes it is easy to get confused
between the two. We all do!

Consider this example:

*An observational study is conducted of
children playing in a park. The observers
record their observations using a set of
behavioural categories. Their observations
are quite different to each others.*

Is this a matter of reliability or validity?

It may represent low reliability because
the observations are not consistent.

It may represent low validity because the
differences occurred because the categories
were ambiguous so each observer
interpreted them differently.

Both answers are acceptable. In the end
what matters is how you explain it. So don't
worry too much – just explain yourself as
clearly as possible!

Qualitative data and the qualitative approach

Reliability and validity are usually discussed using examples of **quantitative data**.
Qualitative data cannot be treated in the same way.

First of all reliability concerns measurement and qualitative data are not measured.
Examples are selected and may be summarised. Themes or categories may be identified
and the number of instances in each category can be counted. Thereby you end up with
something quantitative but otherwise reliability doesn't really make sense in the context
of qualitative data.

However, to be fair, the **qualitative approach** is less concerned with the ideas of
reliability and validity, preferring instead to talk about the richness, diversity and
changeability of human behaviour and experience. The idea of the 'qualitative approach'
is different to just thinking about 'qualitative data' (which is collected in many studies).

The *quantitative* approach to research assumes there is one reality and, when conducting
research, this is what we are trying to discover. By contrast, the qualitative approach
disputes this idea of one single reality. The approach argues that 'reality' changes
depending on whose perspective you are considering.

For example, when trying to understand aggressive behaviour, the meaning of such
behaviour is different depending on whether you are the aggressor or the person
being aggressed against. Both realities are relevant to understand the meaning of the
behaviour. Qualitative researchers wish to understand human behaviour through these
differing perspectives and therefore they embrace the concept of no one single reality.

Validity is still an important concept because the researcher is seeking to achieve an
accurate representation of the participants or phenomenon's reality. One solution is
triangulation, whereby pieces of evidence from several different sources are compared
(they may be from both quantitative and qualitative approaches). If they all point in the
same direction that confirms the meaningfulness of the findings.

A word from Piaget

In the core study by **Samuel and Bryant** *you
looked at a part of Piaget's theory of* **cognitive
development***. In this theory Piaget proposed that
our mental abilities grow as we get older. It is not
just a question of getting more knowledge – it's a
question of thinking in a different way.*

*How does this happen? According to Piaget it
happens because new information challenges
your existing categories. You may feel, after
reading this spread, that it is all confusing – but
this is all part of your cognitive development. Out
of confusion comes understanding!*

Exam-style questions

The example exam-style question here is set out as in Section B of the exam.

Section B type question

1 Choose **one** of the core studies below. And answer parts **(a)–(f)** on your chosen study:

- Freud: Little Hans
- Thigpen and Cleckley: multiple personality disorder
- Savage-Rumbaugh: symbol acquisition by pygmy chimpanzees

(a) What was the aim of your chosen study? [2]
(b) Give **two** examples of qualitative data that were collected in your chosen study. [4]
(c) Describe the sample in your chosen study and suggest **one** strength of this sample. [6]
(d) Give **one** strength and **one** weakness of the case study method as used in your chosen study. [6]
(e) Outline the procedure of your chosen study. [8]
(f) Suggest improvements to your chosen study and outline implications for these improvements. [10]

Total [36]

Chardonnay's answer

(a) The aim of the Savage-Rumabaugh study was to look at the language acquisition of chimps.

(b) One example of qualitative data was that Kanzi tossed a hard nut at a person to open it. If they didn't understand then he would slap the nut with his hand. A second example of qualitative data was when Kanzi took advantage of the naïve experimenter when he took him to the back of the enclosure where he would not usually get to travel. In all other cases he took the most direct route to the forest locations.

(c) The sample in the Savage-Rumbaugh study was two pygmy chimps and two common chimps. The pygmy chimps were brother and sister Kanzi and Mulika. One strength of this sample is that they were quite easy to obtain because they were born in captivity at the language centre and so the researchers had easy access to them.

(d) One strength of the case study method is that it allows us to gather a great deal of detailed data. For example, we know a great deal about Kanzi's language development over time and that some of his first symbols he acquired without formal training included apple, chase and Austin. This detail increases the validity of the study. One weakness of the case study method is that it lacks generalisability. This means the sample isn't representative.

(e) Kanzi was born to a language chimp and was brought up in a language centre. The study took place over 17 months. When Kanzi's mother was removed for mating, researchers noticed that he was using lexigrams spontaneously to communicate. The researchers started to classify his symbols as correct/incorrect, spontaneous and imitative. Kanzi also undertook formal tests of matching symbols to spoken English, symbols to photos, and symbols to synthesised speech. This was compared with other apes like common chimpanzees and his sister Mulika. Kanzi was also tested taking a blind researcher round the 55 acre forest to find specific locations for food, e.g. mushrooms in the look-out. When he was outside the symbols were recorded using a pointing board. Inside the lexigrams were connected to a computer to record which symbols were used.

(f) To improve the study the researchers could have used more pygmy chimps that were from different mothers. Although this would have been difficult because pygmy chimps are rare it would have shown if Kanzi and Mulika were similar to others of their species or, on the other hand, particularly clever (because they have the same mother). This would have increased the validity of the study. Another change would have been to have raised Austin and Sherman in exactly the same way as Kanzi and Mulika. They were older at the beginning of the study so it may be that they did not acquire language so well because they did not have the same opportunities. This would have increased the validity. A third improvement would have been to have continued the study for longer than 17 months to give more detail.

Teacher's comments (see mark schemes on pages xii–xiii)

(a) Chardonnay, this aim is not sufficient for full marks. You need to be more explicit e.g. to compare the language acquisition of pygmy chimpanzees with common chimpanzees.

(b) These are two excellent examples of qualitative data that have come directly from the study. Full marks.

(c) There really is not enough detail here to describe the sample, so barely obtains 2 marks. You could say something about their ages and name the common chimpanzees. In the strength you have given a good example but again it needs to be contextualised a little more for full marks, so 2 + 2 marks out of a total 6.

(d) Chardonnay, your strength is very good – lots of detail here and the use of examples. However, the weakness is not contextualised and really lacks explanation. For example, what are we trying to represent? 3 + 1 marks out of a total of 6 marks.

(e) This is a good answer, although you have included some details that are not part of the procedure (e.g. where Kanzi was born). You could also describe how there was a test of language acquisition that was videotaped and then compared to real-time coding to check for reliability. However, there is enough detail here for a top band response. Well done.

(f) Chardonnay, you have given two excellent improvements and explained well how they would have affected the study and also given some other implications (e.g. it would be difficult because pygmy chimps are rare). Your third improvement is weaker because you haven't explained any implications for that change. Overall a good response though.

Marks 1 + 4 + 4 + 4 + 7 + 7 = 27/36

Section C type question

2   (a) Outline **one** assumption of the behaviourist perspective. [2]
    (b) Outline how the behaviourist perspective could explain the acquisition of language. [4]
    (c) Describe **one** similarity and **one** difference between any studies that could be viewed from the behaviourist perspective. [6]
    (d) Discuss strengths and weaknesses of the behaviourist perspective using examples from any studies that could be viewed from this perspective. [12]

Total [24]

Stig's answer

(a) The behaviourist perspective says that everything about us is to do with our learning.

(b) In the Savage-Rumbaugh study the chimpanzees did acquire language. Kanzi was better than Austin and Sherman and managed to produce over 2000 combinations. He did much better on the formal tests than the others. He used a lexigram for this.

(c) One similarity between the Savage-Rumbaugh study and the Bandura study was the location in which the research took place. Savage-Rumbaugh was in an ape language centre in USA. Bandura's study took place at a university campus nursery school in California, USA.

One difference between Savage-Rumbaugh and Bandura was the size of the sample. Savage-Rumbaugh used one ape (Kanzi) and compared to 3 others. Bandura had 252 children.

(d) A strength of the behaviourist perspective is that it is highly scientific and controlled. In the Bandura study the children were all given exactly the same toys to play with in the same 3 rooms. This means that the results are likely to be very valid because other variables that could affect behaviour are removed, making the findings both valid and reliable.

A weakness is that behaviourism makes people seem as if they are machines and reduces their behaviour down to simple factors when we are complex. For example, Bandura says that we are aggressive only because we imitate when it could be because we are born that way.

A second strength of the perspective is that it is easy to understand. If our behaviour is down to learning then people can understand that really well.

A further weakness in the Savage-Rumbaugh study is that it is unethical to take apes out of their natural environment and do experiments on them.

Teacher's comments (see mark schemes on pages xii–xiii)

(a) Stig, you have missed the crucial word 'behaviour' in your assumption. Reference to 'learning' is just enough for one mark.

(b) This is a common mistake in (b). You haven't made it clear how the perspective (which you said is about our learning) links to the acquisition of language. Repeating facts about this study is not sufficient to gain any marks.

(c) You have given a clear similarity between these two studies.

In the differences you have again stated what the difference is and used the Savage-Rumbaugh example well. However, there were 72 children in the Bandura study. 3 + 2 marks.

(d) Stig, you have started your answer to (d) very well with a clearly described and illustrated strength and weakness (demonstrating sound understanding). Things go downhill after that! You haven't explained what 'easy to understand' means. Your final weakness is study-specific and not about the approach as a whole – a common weakness in responses to section C type questions on strengths/weaknesses of the **approach**. This means you achieve just 6 marks.

Marks 1 + 0 + 5 + 6 = 12/24

Exam-style questions

Section C type question

3 (a) Outline **one** assumption of the psychodynamic perspective. [2]
   (b) Describe how the psychodynamic perspective could explain the development of phobias. [4]
   (c) Describe **one** similarity and **one** difference between any studies that could be viewed from the psychodynamic perspective. [6]
   (d) Discuss strengths and weaknesses of the psychodynamic perspective using examples from any studies that could be viewed from this perspective. [12]

Total [24]

Chardonnay's answer

(a) One assumption of the psychodynamic perspective is the way we have a conscious, subconscious and unconscious mind. All of these can influence our behaviour.

(b) Phobias can develop as a result of ego forming defence mechanisms. This is because of the conflict in the unconscious. For example, Little Hans was going through the Oedipus complex so he wanted to have a sexual relationship with his mother. As he knew (unconsciously) that his father would hate him and punish him with castration, his ego developed a defence mechanism to protect him from this conflict. So instead of him being afraid of his father he became afraid of horses.

(c) One similarity between Freud and Thigpen and Cleckley is that they are both case studies which gathered a lot of detail about one person.

One difference between Freud and Thigpen and Cleckley is the way the data was gathered. Thigpen and Cleckley interviewed Eve directly in their 100 hours of interviews about her multiple personality disorder. Freud analysed Little Hans by using Little Hans' father as they wrote to each other. Freud did not speak to Little Hans directly.

(d) One strength of the psychodynamic perspective is that it enables researchers to build up a comprehensive understanding of the individual through lots of rich detailed data. Thigpen and Cleckley undertook 100 hours of interviews with Eve to discover her multiple personality disorder. This increases the validity of the data because they were asking open questions and she was able to respond in a detailed way.

Another strength of the psychodynamic perspective is that it does not oversimplify our understanding of behaviour. It uses psychological and physiological explanations to help us understand the individual. For example, it was Little Hans' id (the innate part of his psyche) that demanded attention from his mother and wanted his desires to be satisfied. This was shown in his dream about wanting to take a crumpled giraffe away from a big giraffe.

One weakness of the perspective is that it can be unethical. For example, in the Thigpen and Cleckley study the researchers made a decision about which part of Eve's personality should dominate. This meant that Eve could not give her consent properly.

A second weakness is that the perspective is very subjective. For example, it was Freud's own theory that Little Hans' dreams and fantasies were demonstrating the phallic stage. It could be that Little Hans wished his sister dead simply because he wanted to be an only child rather than a fear of castration. There is no way to verify this interpretation scientifically as it is based on one person's opinion.

Teacher's comments (see mark schemes on pages xii–xiii)

(a) Chardonnay this is an excellent response, showing a good understanding of the perspective. Well done.

(b) The psychodynamic perspective is obviously your forte Chardonnay. You have explained this development of phobia really clearly and related it to the Freud study. Another full mark answer.

(c) You have provided an excellent difference between your two chosen studies but in your similarity you haven't explicitly used examples from the studies. You need to provide some examples of the 'rich detailed data' gathered in the two studies to support your claim. In the second paragraph you have stated the difference and then provided examples to support this for the full 3 marks. The similarity only scores 1 out 3 marks.

(d) Wow Chardonnay, you are really showing off now! Here are two strengths, very well described and illustrated. Students often say (incorrectly) that the psychodynamic perspective oversimplifies behaviour so it is good that you see oversimplification given as a strength here. Your first weakness is not of the same calibre of your other one. The issue of ethics does count as a weakness of the psychodynamic perspective – the problem with your answer is that the justification is not totally correct. Thigpen and Cleckley did not decide which part of Eve's personality should dominate – in fact they decided the opposite, that it would not be ethical to do this and left the decision to Eve. However, it is true that Eve could not give her consent properly.

Overall this is an excellent response to the part (d) question so almost full marks.

Marks 2 + 4 + 4 + 11 = 21/24

ANSWERS
to multiple choice questions

Chapter 2 MCQ answers

Loftus and Palmer (MCQs on page 49)	1c 2a 3c 4b 5c 6a 7b 8b 9b 10c
Baron-Cohen *et al.* (MCQs on page 59)	1a 2d 3d 4d 5a 6d 7b 8a 9c 10c
Savage-Rumbaugh *et al.* (MCQs on page 69)	1b 2c 3d 4b 5c 6a 7b 8a 9a 10d

Chapter 3 MCQ answers

Samuel and Bryant (MCQs on page 85)	1d 2d 3d 4b 5d 6c 7d 8b 9a 10d
Bandura *et al.* (MCQs on page 95)	1a 2c 3d 4d 5d 6b 7d 8a 9b 10d
Freud (MCQs on page 105)	1b 2b 3c 4d 5b 6b 7d 8c 9a 10d

Chapter 4 MCQ answers

Maguire *et al.* (MCQs on page 121)	1c 2d 3b 4c 5a 6c 7a 8d 9a 10b
Dement and Kleitman (MCQs on page 131)	1d 2b 3c 4a 5d 6d 7a 8c 9b 10b
Sperry (MCQs on page 141)	1c 2b 3d 4a 5a 6c 7d 8c 9b 10c

Chapter 5 MCQ answers

Milgram (MCQs on page 157)	1a 2a 3c 4b 5d 6b 7a 8d 9d 10c
Reicher and Haslam (MCQs on page 167)	1d 2d 3d 4c 5b 6a 7b 8d 9a 10d
Piliavin *et al.* (MCQs on page 177)	1c 2c 3b 4a 5d 6c 7d 8b 9b 10c

Chapter 6 MCQ answers

Rosenhan (MCQs on page 193)	1c 2a 3c 4a 5d 6b 7d 8c 9d 10d
Thigpen and Cleckley (MCQs on page 203)	1c 2a 3a 4c 5b 6d 7c 8a 9b 10a
Griffiths (MCQs on page 213)	1a 2b 3b 4a 5a 6a 7c 8d 9c 10c

REFERENCES

Aitchison, J. (1983) *The articulate mammal: An introduction to psycholinguistics* (2nd edn). New York: Universe Books. ▸**page 60**

Akelaitis, A.J. (1944) A study of gnosis, praxis and language following section of the corpus callosum and anterior commissure. *Journal of Neurosurgery*, 1, 94–102. ▸**page 135**

Allport, G.W. (1968) The historical background of modern psychology. In G. Lindzey and E. Aronson (eds) *Handbook of Social Psychology* (2nd edn, vol. 1. pp. 1–80). Reading, MA: Addison-Wesley. ▸**page 146**

Anderson, C.A., Shibuya, A., Ihori, N., Swing, E.L., Bushman, B.J., Sakamoto, A., Rothstein, H.R., Saleem, M. and Barlett, C.P. (2010) Violent video game effects on aggression, empathy, and pro-social behavior in Eastern and Western countries: A meta-analytic review. *Psychological Bulletin*, 136 (2), 151–173. ▸**page 92**

APA (2005) http://www.apa.org/divisions/div30/define_hypnosis.html (accessed Jan 2006). ▸**page 191**

Arendt, H. (1963) *Eichmann in Jerusalem*. London: Penguin. ▸**page 156**

Asch, S.E. (1946) Forming impressions of personality. *Journal of Abnormal and Social Psychology*, 41, 258–290. ▸**pages 29, 190**

Asch, S.E. (1955) Opinions and social pressure. *Scientific American*, 193, 31–5. ▸**page 148**

Aserinsky, E. and Kleitman, N. (1955) Two types of ocular motility occurring in sleep. *Journal of Applied Physiology*, 8 (1), 1–10. ▸**page 125**

Bailey, B. (2012) Replication: The difference between reliability and validity. *The Psychologist*, 25 (7), 484. ▸**page 242**

Bandura, A. (1986) *Social Foundations of Thought and Action*. Englewood Cliffs, NJ: Prentice-Hall. ▸**page 87**

Bandura, A. (2004) Swimming against the mainstream: the early years from chilly tributary to transformative mainstream. *Behaviour Research and Therapy*, 42, 613–630. ▸**page 87**

Bandura, A., Ross, D. and Ross, S.A. (1961) Transmission of aggression through imitation of aggressive models. *Journal of Abnormal and Social Psychology*, 63(3), 575–582. ▸**page 88**

Baron-Cohen, S., Burt, L., Smith-Laittan, F., Harrison, J. and Bolton, P. (1996) Synaesthesia: Prevalence and familiality. *Perception*, 25(9), 1073–1079. ▸**page 219**

Baron-Cohen, S., Leslie, A.M. and Frith, U. (1986) Mechanical, behavioural and intentional understanding of picture stories in autistic children. *British Journal of Developmental Psychology*, 4, 113–125. ▸**page 58**

Bartlett, F.C. (1932) *Remembering*. Cambridge: Cambridge University Press. ▸**page 40**

Bassett, K., Green, G. and Kazanjian, A. (2000) Autism and Lovaas Treatment: A systematic review of effectiveness evidence. Vancouver, BC: BC Office Of Health Technology Assessment. ▸**page 58**

Baumrind, D. (1964) Some thoughts on ethics of research: After reading Milgram's behavioural study of obedience. *American Psychologist*, 19, 421–423. ▸**page 156**

BBC (2000) Cherie Blair 'bad role model'. http://news.bbc.co.uk/1/hi/uk/660867.stm. ▸**page 86**

BBC (2003) Sesame Street breaks Iraqi POWs. http://news.bbc.co.uk/1/hi/world/middle_east/3042907.stm. ▸**page 130**

BBC (2005) Reliving the London bombing horror. http://news.bbc.co.uk/1/hi/uk/4346812.stm; London explosions: Your accounts http://news.bbc.co.uk/1/hi/talking_point/ 4659237.stm (accessed December 2005). ▸**page 176**

BBC (2012) Facebook has more than 83 million illegitimate accounts. BBC News website. Available at http://www.bbc.co.uk/news/technology-19093078 (accessed September 2012). ▸**page 183**

Bègue, L. (2005) Self-esteem regulation in threatening social comparison: The role of belief in a just world and self-efficacy. *Social Behaviour and Personality*. See http://www.findarticles.com/p/articles/mi_qa3852/is_200501/ai_n9520808/pg_3 (accessed December 2005). ▸**page 212**

Bennett-Levy, J. and Marteau, T. (1984) Fear of animals: What is prepared? *British Journal of Psychology*, 75, 37–42. ▸**page 20**

Bentall, R.P. (1992) A proposal to classify happiness as a psychiatric disorder. *Journal of Medical Ethics*, 18, 94–98. ▸**page 182**

BEO (2004) Behavioural observation, University of Bern, http://www.psy.unibe.ch/beob/proj_ex.htm and http://www.psy.unibe.ch/beob/home_e.htm (accessed September 2004). ▸**page 8**

Bishop, K.M. and Wahlsten, D. (1997) Sex differences in the human corpus callosum: myth or reality? *Neuroscience and Biobehavioural Reviews*, 21 (5), 581–601. ▸**page 132**

Blass, T. (2004) *The Man who Shocked the World: The Life and Legacy of Stanley Milgram*. New York: Basic Books. ▸**page 148**

Boden, M.A. (1977) *Artificial Intelligence and Natural Man*. New York: Basic Books. ▸**page 60**

Bowlby, J. (1965). *Child Care and the Growth of Love* (2nd edn). London: Penguin Books. ▸**page 72**

Bowler, D.M. (1992) 'Theory of Mind' in Asperger Syndrome. *Journal of Child Psychology and Psychiatry*, 33, 877–895. ▸**page 54**

Brazelton, T.B. (1973) *Neonatal Behavioral Assessment Scale*. Philadelphia, PA: J.B. Lippincott. ▸**page 73**

Brazelton, T.B., Koslowski, B. and Tronick, E. (1976) Neonatal behavior among urban Zambians and Americans. *Journal Academy of Child Psychiatry*, 15, 97–108. ▸**page 73**

British Psychological Society (1993) *Code of conduct, ethical principles and guidelines*. Leicester: The British Psychological Society. ▸**page 212**

Broadcasting Standards Commission (BSC) (2002) Briefing Update: Depiction of Violence on Terrestrial Television. ▸**page 92**

Browning, C. (1992) *Ordinary Men: Reserve Police Battalion 101 and the Final Solution in Poland*. New York: HarperCollins. ▸**page 235**

Bryan, J.H. and Test, M.A. (1967) Models and helping: naturalistic studies in helping behaviour, *Journal of Personality and Social Psychology*, 6, 400–407. ▸**page 171**

Burger, J.M. (2009) Replicating Milgram: Would people still obey today? *American Psychologist*, 64 (1), 1–11. ▸**page 156**

Bushman, B.J. and Anderson, C.A. (2001) Is it time to pull the plug on the hostile versus instrumental aggression dichotomy? *Psychological Review*, 108, 273–279. ▸**page 87**

Carmichael, L., Hogan, P. and Walter, A. (1932) An experimental study of the effect of language on the reproduction of visually perceived forms, *Journal of Experimental Psychology*, 15, 73–86. ▸**page 46**

Carson, B.S. (2002) Gifted hands that heal (interview by Academy of Achievement). http://www.achievement.org/auto doc/page/car1int-1 (accessed October 2005). ▸**page 136**

Clark, M. (2001) in O'Connell, A.N. and Russo, N.F. (ed.) (2001) *Models of Achievement: Reflections of Eminent Women in Psychology*. New York: Columbia University Press. ▸**page 147**

Colapinto, J. (2000) *As Nature Made Him: The Boy Who was Raised as a Girl*. New York: HarperCollins. ▸page 241

Comings, D.E. (1998) Why different rules are required for polygenic inheritance: lessons from studies of the DRD2 gene. *Alcohol*, 16, 61–70. ▸page 204

Cooley, C.H. (1902) *Human Nature and the Social Order*. New York: Scribner. ▸page 224

Coolican, H. (1996) *Introduction to Research Methods and Statistics in Psychology*. London: Hodder and Stoughton. ▸page 19

Corballis, M.C. (1999) Are we in our right minds? In S. Della Salla (ed.) *Mind Myths: Exploring Popular Assumptions about the Mind and Brain*. Chichester: John Wiley and Sons. ▸page 136

Coren, S. (1996) *Sleep Thieves*. New York: Free Press. ▸page 130

Corkin, S. (1984) Lasting consequences of bilateral medial temporal lobectomy: Clinical course and experimental findings in H.M. *Seminars in Neurology*, 4, 249–259. ▸page 113

Costa, P.T., Jr. and McCrae, R.R. (1992) Normal personality assessment in clinical practice: The NEO Personality Inventory. *Psychological Assessment*, 4, 5–13. ▸page 182

Crabb, P.B. and Bielawski, D. (1994) The social representation of material culture and gender in children's books. *Sex Roles*, 30 (1/2), 69–79. ▸page 9

Daeg de Mott, D. K. (2001) Ethics. *Gale Encyclopedia of Psychology*. Available: www.findarticles.com. ▸page 232

Daly, M. and Wilson, M. (1998) *The Truth About Cinderella*. London: Weidenfeld & Nicolson. ▸page 221

Daniel, T.C. (1972) Nature of the effect of verbal labels on recognition memory for form. *Journal of Experimental Psychology*, 96, 152–157. ▸page 46

Darley, J.M. and Batson, C.D. (1973) 'From Jersualem to Jericho': A study of situational and dispositional variables in helping behavior. *Journal of Personality and Social Psychology*, 27, 100–108. ▸page 169

Darley, J.M. and Latané, B. (1968) Bystander intervention in emergencies: Diffusion of responsibility. *Journal of Personality and Social Psychology*, 8, 377–383. ▸page 169, 171

Darwin, C. (1969) *The Autobiography of Charles Darwin: with original omissions restored*, edited with appendix and notes by his grand-daughter, Nora Barlow. New York: W.W. Norton. ▸page 226

Darwin, C.A. (1871) *The Descent of Man and Selection in Relation to Sex*. London: John Murray. ▸page 68

Dement, W.C. (2001) *The Promise of Sleep*. London: Pan. ▸page 130

Dement, W. and Kleitman, N. (1957) The relation of eye movements during sleep to dream activity: An objective method for the study of dreaming. *Journal of Experimental Psychology*, 53 (5), 339–346. ▸page 124

DeVries, R. (1969) Constancy of generic identity in the years three to six. *Monographs of the Society for Research in Child Development*, 34 (3, Serial No. 127). ▸page 75

Diamond, M. (1997) Sexual identity and sexual orientation in children with traumatized or ambiguous genitalia. *Journal of Sex Research*, 34(2), 199–211. ▸page 241

Dodds, P., Muhamad, R. and Watts, D. (2003) An experimental study of search in global social networks. *Science*, 301, 827–829. ▸page 149

Donaldson, M. (1982) Conservation: What is the question? *British Journal of Psychology*, 73, 199–207. ▸page 77

DoH (Department of Health) (1992) The Health of the Nation: a strategy for health in England. London: HMSO. ▸page 212

DoH (Department of Health) (1993) One year on: a report on the progress of the health of the nation. London: HMSO. ▸page 212

Dollard, J., Doob, L.W., Miller, N.E., Mowrer, O.H. and Sears, R.R. (1939) *Frustration and Aggression*. New Haven, CT: Yale University Press. ▸page 87

Dovidio, J.F., Gaertner, S.L., Validzic, A., Matoka, A., Johnson, B. and Frazier, S. (1997) Extending the benefits of recategorization: Evaluations, self-disclosure, and helping. *Journal of Experimental Social Psychology*, 33, 401–420. ▸page 176

Draper, P. (1978) The Learning Environment for Aggression and Anti-Social Behavior among the !Kung. In Montagu, A. (ed.) *Learning Non-Aggression: The Experience of Non-Literate Societies*, pages 31–53. New York: Oxford University Press. ▸page 87

Dunn, J. and Deater-Deckard, K. (2001) *Children's Views of their Changing Families*. York: York Publishing Services/Joseph Rowntree Foundation. ▸page 221

Eagly, A.H. (1978) Sex differences in influenceability. *Psychological Bulletin*, 85, 86–116. ▸page 28

Eberhardt, J.L. (2005) Imaging race. *American Psychologist*, February–March, 181–190 (available online at http://www.apa.org/journals/features/amp602181.pdf). ▸page 120

Ekman, P. (1992) An argument for basic emotions. *Cognition and Emotion*, 6, 169–200. ▸page 54

English, M. (2011) Young Bonobo shows signs of autism. Discovery News. http://news.discovery.com/animals/young-bonobo-autism-110922.html (accessed August 2012). ▸page 63

Fancher, R.E. (1996) *Pioneers of Psychology* (3rd edn). New York: W.W. Norton. ▸page 226

Festinger, L., Riecken, H.W. and Schachter, S. (1956) *When Prophecy Fails*. Minneapolis: University of Minnesota Press. ▸page 6

Fick, K. (1993) The influence of an animal on social interactions of nursing home residents in a group setting. *American Journal of Occupational Therapy*, 47, 529–534. ▸page 7

Fisher, S. (1993) The pull of the fruit machine: A sociological typology of young players. *Sociological Review*, 41, 446–474. ▸page 210

Freud, A. (1946) *The Ego and the Mechanisms of Defense*. New York: International University Press. ▸page 92

Freud, S. (1905) *Three essays on the theory of sexuality*. Republished 1977. Harmondsworth, Middlesex: Penguin. ▸page 97

Freud, S. (1909) Analysis of a phobia in a five-year-old boy. In J. Strachey (ed. and trans.) *The Standard Edition of the Complete Psychological Works: Two Case Histories* (vol. X), pages 5–147. London: The Hogarth Press. ▸page 98

Freud, S. (1910) The origin and development of psychoanalysis. *American Journal of Psychology*, 21, 181–218. ▸page 230

Freud, S. (1933) *New Introductory Lectures on Psycho-Analysis*. London: Hogarth. ▸page 230

Frith, U. (1989) Autism: *Explaining the Enigma*. Oxford: Basil Blackwell. ▸page 56

Frith, U. and Happé, F. (1999) Theory of mind and self consciousness. What is it like to be autistic? *Mind and Language*, 14, 1–22 ▸page 51

Gado, M. (2005) A cry in the night: the Kitty Genovese murder. http://www.crimelibrary.com/serial_killers/predators/kitty_ genovese/11.html (accessed December 2005). ▸page 168

Ganis, G., Rosenfeld, J.P., Meixner, J., Kievit, R.A. and Schendan, H.E. (2011) Lying in the scanner: Covert countermeasures disrupt deception detection by functional magnetic resonance imaging. *NeuroImage*, 55 (1), 312–19, PMID: 21111834. ▸page 120

Gardner, B.T and Gardner, R.A. (1969) Teaching sign language to a chimpanzee. *Science*, 165, 664–72. ▸page 60

Garth, T.R. (1925) A review of racial psychology. *Psychological Bulletin*, 22 (June), 343–364. ▸page 147

Goffman, E. (1961) *Asylums*. Garden City, NY: Doubleday. ▸page 190

Golby, A.J., Gabrieli, J.D.E., Chiao, J.Y. and Eberhardt, J.L. (2001) Differential responses in the fusiform region to same-race and other-race faces. *Nature Neuroscience*, 4, 845–850. ▸page 120

Griffiths, M.D. (1990a) The cognitive psychology of gambling. *Journal of Gambling Studies*, 6, 31–42. ▸**page 205**

Griffiths, M.D. (1990b) Addiction to fruit machines: A preliminary study among males. *Journal of Gambling Studies*, 6, 113–126. ▸**page 205**

Griffiths, M.D. (1990c) The acquisition, development and maintenance of fruit machine gambling in adolescents. *Journal of Gambling Studies*, 6, 193–204. ▸**page 205**

Griffiths, M.D. (1995) *Adolescent Gambling*. London: Routledge. ▸**page 204**

Grossman, D. (1995) *On Killing: The Psychological Cost of Learning to Kill in War and Society*. Boston, MA: Little, Brown and Co. ▸**page 92**

Guardian (2005) http://www.guardian.co.uk/attackonlondon/story/0,,1525460,00.html (accessed September 2007). ▸**pages 183, 190**

Hall, P. and Smith, K. (2011) Analysis of the 2010/11 British Crime Survey intimate personal violence split-sample experiment. Home Office. Available at http://www.homeoffice.gov.uk/publications/science-research-statistics/research-statistics/crime-research/analysis-bcs-ipv-2011?view=Binary (accessed September 2012). ▸**page 92**

Happé, F. (1994) An advanced test of Theory of Mind: Understanding of story characters' thoughts and feelings by able autistic, mentally handicapped, and normal children and adults. *Journal of Autism and Developmental Disorders*, 24, 129–154. ▸**page 54**

Harlow, J.M. (1868) Recovery from the passage of an iron bar through the head. *Publications of the Massachusetts Medical Society*, 2, 327–347. ▸**page 110**

Haslam, S.A. and Reicher, S. (2008) Questioning the banality of evil. *The Psychologist*, 21(1), 16–19. ▸**page 156**

Haslam, A. and Reicher, S. (2012) This is not about obedience: Reappraising Milgram's Yale studies. *Psychology Review*, 18 (2), 2–4. ▸**page 156**

Hawthorne, J., Jessop, J., Pryor, J. and Richards, M. (2003) *Supporting Children through Family Change: A Review of Interventions and Services for Children of Divorcing and Separating Parents*. York: York Publishing Services/Joseph Rowntree Foundation. ▸**page 221**

Hayes, K.J. and Hayes, C. (1952) Imitation in a home-raised chimpanzee. *Journal of Comparative Physiological Psychology*, 4, 450–9. ▸**page 60**

Hayes, K.J. and Nissen, C.H. (1971) Higher mental functions of a home-raised chimpanzee. In Schrier, A.M. and Stollnitz, F. (eds). *Behaviour of Non-human Primates*, 4, 50–115. New York, Academic Press. ▸**page 60**

Hobson, R.P. (1984) Early childhood autism and the question of egocentrism. *Journal of Autism and Developmental Disorders*, 14, 85–104. ▸**page 53**

Hofling, K.C., Brontzman, E., Dalrymple, S., Graves, N. and Pierce, C.M. (1966) An experimental study in the nurse-physician relationship. *Journal of Mental and Nervous Disorders*, 43, 171–178. ▸**page 235**

Home Office (2003) World Prison Population List, http://homeoffice.gov.uk/rds/pdfs2/r188.pdf (accessed December 2005). ▸**page 158**

Horne, J.A. and Reyner, L.A. (1995) Sleep-related vehicle accidents. *British Medical Journal*, 310, 565–567. ▸**page 130**

Hughes, H. (1992) Impact of spouse abuse on children of battered women. *Violence Update*, August 1, 9–11. ▸**page 92**

Humphreys, L. (1970) *The Tearoom Trade*. Chicago: Aldine. ▸**page 4**

Hussain, Z. and Griffiths, M. (2008) Gender swapping and socialising in cyberspace: An exploratory study. *Cyberpsychology and Behaviour*, 11 (1), 47–53. ▸**page 183**

Ilyas, S. and Moncrieff, J. (2012) Trends in prescriptions and costs of drugs for mental disorders in England, 1998–2010. *British Journal of Psychiatry*, DOI: 10.1192/bjp.bp.111.104257. ▸**page 190, 223**

International Centre for Prison Studies (2008) http://www.kcl.ac.uk/depsta/rel/icps/worldbrief/highest_to_lowest_rates.php (accessed January 2008). ▸**page 158**

James, W. (1890) *Principles of Psychology*. New York: Holt. ▸**page 39**

Joliffe, T. (1997) Central f in adults with high-functioning autism or Asperger Syndrome. Unpublished PhD Thesis, University of Cambridge. ▸**page 55**

Jordan, R.H. and Burghardt, G. (1986) Employing an ethogram to detect reactivity of black bears (*Ursus americanus*) to the presence of humans. *Ethology*, 73, 89–155. ▸**page 5**

Kamin, L.J. (1977) *The Science and Politics of IQ*. Harmondsworth, Middlesex: Penguin. ▸**page 227**

Keller, K.L. (1987) Memory factors in advertising: The effect of advertising retrieval cues on brand evaluations. *Journal of Consumer Research*, 14, 316–333. ▸**page 40**

Kellogg, W.N. and Kellogg, I.A. (1933) *The ape and the child*. New York: McGraw-Hill. ▸**page 60**

Kosslyn, S. (1975) Information representation in visual images. *Cognitive Psychology*, 7, 341–370. ▸**page 3**

Kruger, J. and Dunning, D. (1999) Unskilled and unaware of it: How difficulties in recognizing one's own incompetence lead to inflated self-assessments. *Journal of Personality and Social Psychology*, 77, 1121–1134. ▸**page 224**

Kunzig, R. (2004) Autism: what's sex got to do with it? *Psychology Today*, Jan/Feb [full text at http://cms.psychologytoday.com/articles/pto-3207.html]. ▸**pages 55, 58**

Kutchins, H. and S.A. Kirk. (1997) *Making us Crazy: DSM – the Psychiatric Bible and the Creation of Mental Disorder*. New York: Free Press. ▸**page 190**

Ladouceur, R., Gaboury, A., Dumount, M. and Rochette, P. (1988) Gambling: Relationship between the frequency of wins and irrational thinking. *Journal of Psychology*, 122, 409–414. ▸**page 210**

Laird, J.D. (1974) Self-attribution of emotion: The effects of facial expression on the quality of emotional experience. *Journal of Personality and Social Psychology*, 29, 475–86. ▸**page 29**

Lamb, M.E. and Roopnarine, J.L. (1979). Peer influences on sex-role development in preschoolers. *Child Development*, 50, 1219–1222. ▸**page 6**

Latané, B. and Darley, J.M. (1968) Group inhibition of bystander intervention in emergencies. *Journal of Personality and Social Psychology*, 10, 215–221. ▸**page 169**

Latané, B. and Rodin, J. (1969) A lady in distress: inhibiting effects of friends and strangers on bystander intervention. *Journal of Experimental Social Psychology*, 5, 189–202. ▸**page 173**

Lerner, M.J. (1980) *The Belief in a Just World: A Fundamental Delusion*. New York: Plenum. ▸**page 212**

Lerner, M.J. and Simmons, C.H. (1966) Observer's reaction to the 'innocent victim': Compassion or rejection? *Journal of Personality and Social Psychology*, 4, 203–210. ▸**page 174**

Levant, R. (2007) Visit to the U.S. Joint Task Force Station at Guantanamo Bay: A first-person account. *Military Psychology*, 19(1), 1–7. ▸**page 166**

Levine, M., Cassidy, C., Brazier, G. and Reicher, S. (2002) Self-categorisation and bystander non-intervention: two experimental studies. *Journal of Applied Social Psychology*, 7, 1452–1463. ▸**page 176**

Levine, R.M. (1999) Rethinking bystander non-intervention: social categorisation and the evidence of witnesses at the James Bulger murder trial. *Human Relations*, 52, 1133–1155. ▸**page 176**

Lewin, R. (1980) Is your brain really necessary? *Science*, 210, 1232–1234. ▸**page 111**

Loftus, E. (1979) *Eyewitness Testimony*. Cambridge, MA.: Harvard University Press. ▸**page 48**

Loftus, E. (1997) Creating false memories. *Scientific American*, 277(3), 70–75. [full text at http://faculty.washington.edu/eloftus/Articles/sciam.htm]. ▸page 48

Loftus, E. and Palmer, J.C. (1974) Reconstruction of automobile destruction. *Journal of Verbal Learning and Verbal Behavior*, 13, 585–589. ▸page 43

Loftus, E. and Pickrell, J. (1995) The formation of false memories. *Psychiatric Annals*, 25, 720–725. ▸page 48

Lorenz, K.Z. (1966) *On Aggression*. New York: Harcourt, Brace & World. ▸page 86

Luchins, A.S. (1957) Primacy-recency in impression formation. In C. Hovland (Ed.) *The Order of Presentation in Persuasion*. New Haven, CT: Yale University Press. ▸page 29

Maddox, B. (1998) The Grimms got it right – renowned Grimm's Fairy Tales authors, Jakob and Wilhelm Grimm; stepfamily horror stories and step parents, *New Statesman*, October 16. ▸page 221

Maguire, E.A., Gadian, D.G., Johnsrude, I.S., Good, C.D., Ashburner, J., Frackowiak, R.S.J. and Frith, C.D. (2000) Navigation-related structural changes in the hippocampi of taxi drivers. *Proceedings of the National Academy of Science, USA*, 97, 4398–4403. ▸page 114

Manchester Evening News (2005), www.manchesteronline.co.uk, 3 May 2005. ▸page 86

Marshall, J. (1969). *Law and Psychology in Conflict*. New York: Anchor Books. ▸page 43

Matsumoto, D. (1994). *People: Psychology from a cultural perspective*. Pacific Grove, CA: Brooks/Cole. ▸page 84

McCabe, D., Castel, A. and Rhodes, M. (2011). The influence of fMRI lie detection evidence on juror decision-making. *Behavioral Sciences and the Law*. DOI: 10.1002/bsl.993. ▸page 120

McGarrigle, J. and Donaldson, M. (1974) Conservation accidents. *Cognition*, 3, 341–50. ▸page 82

McGlade, H.B. (1942). The relationship between gastric motility, muscular twitching during sleep and dreaming. *American Journal of Digestive Diseases*, 9, 137–140. ▸page 128

Mental Health Foundation (no date) Mental Health Statistics. Available at http://www.mentalhealth.org.uk/help-information/mental-health-statistics (accessed September 2012). ▸page 185

Merrin, W. (2005) *Baudrillard and the Media: a Critical Introduction*. Cambridge: Polity. ▸page 158

Milgram, S. (1960) Conformity in Norway and France: an experimental study of national characteristics. Dissertation: Harvard University. ▸page 148

Milgram, S. (1963) Behavioural study of obedience. *Journal of Abnormal and Social Psychology*, 67, 371–378. ▸pages 156, 234

Milgram, S. (1970) The experience of living in cities: a psychological analysis. *Science*, 167, 1461–1468. ▸page 169

Milgram, S. (1974) *Obedience to Authority: An Experimental View*. New York: Harper & Row. ▸page 156

Milgram, S. (1977) The familiar stranger: An aspect of urban anonymity. In S. Milgram, *The Individual in a Social World* (pp. 51–53). Reading, MA: Addison-Wesley. ▸page 149

Miller, N.E. and Dollard, J. (1941) *Social learning and Imitation*. New Haven, CT: Yale University Press. ▸page 84

Miller, S.A. (1982). On the generalisability of conservation: A comparison of different kinds of transformation. *British Journal of Psychology*, 73, 221–230. ▸page 84

Milner, P. (1970) *Physiological Psychology*. New York: Holt, Rinehart and Winston. ▸page 222

Moore, C. and Frye, D. (1986) The effect of the experimenter's intention on the child's understanding of conservation. *Cognition*, 22, 283–298. ▸page 84

Mowrer, O.H. (1947) On the dual nature of learning – A reinterpretation of 'conditioning' and 'problem-solving'. *Harvard Educational Review*, 17, 102–148. ▸page 102

Muir, H. (2003) www.newscientist.com/article.ns?id=dn367. ▸page 51

Myers, R.E. (1961) Corpus callosum and visual gnosis. In J.R. Delafresnaye (ed.), *Brain Mechanisms and Learning*. Oxford: Blackwell. ▸page 135

Neimark, J. (1996) The diva of disclosure, memory researcher Elizabeth Loftus. *Psychology Today*, 29 (1), 48. ▸page 44

Neisser, U. (1982) *Memory Observed*. New York: Freeman. ▸page 40

Neisser, U. and Harsch, N. (1992) Phantom flashbulbs: False recollections of hearing the news about the Challenger. In E. Winograd and U. Neisser (eds) *Affect and Accuracy in Recall: Studies of 'flashbulb' memories* (vol. 4, pp. 9–31). New York: Cambridge University Press. ▸page 41

Nelson, L.D. and Norton, M.I. (2005) From student to superhero: situational primes shape future helping. *Journal of Experimental Social Psychology*, 41, 423–430. ▸page 87

NOMS (2008) http://www.hmprisonservice.gov.uk/assets/documents/1000334D20080104SPSWEBREPORT.doc (accessed January 2008). ▸page 158

Ogden, J.A. and Corkin, S. (1991) Memories of H.M. In W.C. Abraham, M.C. Corballis and K.G. White (eds) *Memory Mechanisms: A Tribute to G.V. Goddard*. Hillsdale, NJ: Erlbaum. ▸page 113

Orford, J. (1985) *Excessive Appetites: A Psychological View of Addictions*. Chichester: John Wiley. ▸page 212

Orford, J. (2001) *Excessive Appetites: A Psychological View of Addictions* (2nd edn). Chichester: John Wiley. ▸page 204

Orne, M.T. (1962) On the social psychology of the psychological experiment: with particular reference to demand characteristics and their implications. *American Psychologist*, 17, 776–783. ▸page 29

Orne, M.T. and Holland, C.C. (1968) On the ecological validity of laboratory deceptions. *International Journal of Psychiatry*, 6 (4), 282–293. ▸page 153

Orne, M.T. and Scheibe, K.E. (1964) The contribution of nondeprivation factors in the production of sensory deprivation effects: The psychology of the 'panic button'. *Journal of Abnormal and Social Psychology*, 68, 3–12. ▸page 29

Ornstein, R.E. (1972) *The Psychology of Consciousness*. San Franciso: Freeman. ▸page 140

Palinkas, L.A., Suedfeld, P. and Steel, G.D. (1995) Psychological functioning among members of a small polar expedition. *Aviation, Space and Environmental Medicine*, 66, 943–950. ▸page 130

Papert, S.A. (1999) *Mindstorms: Children, Computers and Powerful Ideas* (2nd edn). New York: Basic Books. ▸page 77

Papez, J.W. (1937) A proposed mechanism of emotion. *Journal of Neuropsychiatry and Clinical Neuroscience*, 7(1), 103–112. ▸page 111

Parkin, A. J. (1996) H.M.: The medial temporal lobes and memory. In C. Code, C.W. Wallesch, Y. Joanette, and A. B. Lecours (eds), *Classic Cases in Neuropsychology*. London: Psychology Press. ▸page 113

Piaget, J. (1954) *The Construction of Reality in the Child*. New York: Basic Books. ▸page 74

Piliavin, I.M., Rodin, J. and Piliavin, J.A. (1969) Good Samaritanism: an underground phenomenon? *Journal of Personality and Social Psychology*, 13 (4), 289–299. ▸page 170

Pinker, S. (2002) *The Blank Slate: The Modern Denial of Human Nature*. New York: Penguin. ▸page 73

Premack, D. and Premack, A.J. (1983) *The mind of an ape* (1st edn). New York: Norton. ▸page 60

Premack, D. and Woodruff, G. (1978) Does the chimpanzee have a Theory of Mind? *The Behavioral and Brain Sciences*, 4, 515–526. ▸page 50

Prince, M. (1906) *The Dissociation of Personality*. New York: Longmans, Green. ▸page 196

Raffaele, P. (2006). The smart and swinging Bonobo. *Smithsonian*, 37 (8), 66. ▸page 63

Raine, A. (2004) Unlocking Crime: The Biological Key, BBC News, December http://news.bbc.co.uk/1/hi/programmes/if/4102371.stm (accessed October 2005). ▸page 120

Ramsay, G. (1953). Studies of dreaming. *Psychological Bulletin*, 30, 432–455. ▸page 128

Rank, S.G. and Jacobsen, C.K. (1977) Hospital nurses' compliance with medication overdose orders: A failure to replicate. *Journal of Health and Social Behaviour*, 18, 188–193. ▸page 235

Rapoff, M.A., Altman, K. and Christophersen, E.R. (1980) Suppression of self-injurious behaviour: determining the least restrictive alternative. *Journal of Mental Deficiency Research*, 24(1), 37–46. ▸page 232

Reicher, S. and Haslam, S.A. (2006) Rethinking the psychology of tyranny: The BBC prison study. *British Journal of Social Psychology*, 45, 1–40. ▸page 160

Richeson, J.A., Baird, A.A., Gordon, H.L., Heatherton, T.F., Wyland, C.L., Trawalter, S. and Shelton, J.N. (2003) An fMRI investigation of the impact of interracial contact on executive function. *Nature Neuro-science*, 6, 1323–1328. ▸page 120

Ronson, J. (2004) The road to Abu Ghraib – part two. *The Guardian*, October 30. page 18. ▸page 166

Rose, S.A. and Blank, M. (1974) The potency of context in childrens' cognition: An illustration through conservation. *Child Development*, 45, 499–502. ▸pages 76, 77

Rosen, J. (2007) The Brain on the Stand. *New York Times*, 11 March 2007. Available at http://www.nytimes.com/2007/03/11/magazine/11Neurolaw.t.html?pagewanted=all (accessed September 2012). ▸page 120

Rosenblith, J.J. (1959) Learning by imitation in kindergarten children. *Child Development*, 30, 69–80. ▸page 90

Rosenhan, D.L. (1973) On being sane in insane places. *Science*, 179, 250–258. ▸page 186

Rosenhan, D.L., and Seligman, M.E.P. (1989) *Abnormal psychology* (2nd edn). New York: Norton. ▸page 185

Rosenthal, A.M. (1964) *Thirty-Eight Witnesses: The Kitty Genovese Case*. Berkeley: University of California Press. ▸page 168

Rosenthal, R. (1966) *Experimenter Effects in Behaviour Research*. New York: Appleton. ▸page 28

Ross, J.M. (1999) Once more onto the couch. *Journal of the American Psychoanalytic Association*, 47, 91–111. ▸page 94

Rutter, M. (2005) The adoption of children from Romania/The social and intellectual development of children adopted into England from Romania. The Research Findings Register, summary number 55. http://www.ReFeR.nhs.uk/ViewRecord.asp?ID=5 (accessed 18 April 2006). ▸page 73

Ryan, J. (2004) Army's war game recruits kids. *San Francisco Chronicle*, 23 September. ▸page 92

Rymer, R. (1993) *Genie: Escape from a Silent Childhood*. London: Michael Joseph. ▸page 241

Sacher, W. (1993) Jugendgefährdung durch Video- und Computerspiele? [Is there a danger to youth from video and computer games?] *Zeitschrift für Pädagogik*, 39, 313–333. ▸page 92

Samuel, J. and Bryant, P. (1983) Asking only one question in the conservation experiment. *Journal of Child Psychology*, 22 (2), 315–318. ▸page 78

Savage-Rumbaugh, S., McDonald, K., Sevcik, R.A., Hopkins, W.D. and Rupert, E. (1986) Spontaneous symbol acquisition and communicative use by Pygmy Chimpanzees (Pan paniscus). *Journal of Experimental Psychology*, 115(3), 211–235. ▸page 62

Schachter, S. (1964) The interaction of cognitive and physiological determinants of emotional state. In L. Berkowitz (ed.) *Advances in Experimental Social Psychology*, Vol. 1. New York: Academic Press. ▸page 174

Schopler, J. and Matthews, M.W. (1965) The influence of the perceived causal locus of partner's dependence on the use of interpersonal power. *Journal of Personality and Social Psychology*, 2 (4), 609–612. ▸page 171

Schreiber, F.R. (1973) *Sybil*. New York: Warner Books. ▸page 202

Shayer, M., Demetriou, A. and Perez, M. (1988) The structure and scaling of concrete operational thought: Three studies in four countries and only one story. *Genetic Psychology Monographs*, 114, 307–376. ▸page 84

Sidoli, M. (1996) Farting as a defence against unspeakable dread. *Journal of Analytical Psychology*, 41(2), 165–178. ▸page 102

Skinner, B.F. (1960) Pigeons in a pelican. *American Psychologist*, 15, 28–37. ▸page 229

Slater, M., Antley, A., Davison, A., Swapp, D., Guger, C. Barker, C., Pistrang, N. and Sanchez-Vives, M.V. (2006) A virtual reprise of the Stanley Milgram Obedience Experiments. PLoS ONE,1(1), e39 doi:10.1371/journal.pone.0000039 [http://www.plosone.org/article/fetchArticle.action?articleURI=info%3Adoi%2F10.1371%2Fjournal.pone.0000039]. ▸page 156

Smith, P. and Bond, M.H. (1993) *Social Psychology across Cultures: Analysis and Perspectives*. New York: Harvester Wheatsheaf. ▸page 200

Sperry, R.W. (1964) from 'James Arthur Lecture on the Evolution of the Human Brain'. Quoted on http://faculty.washington.edu/chudler/quotes.html (accessed October 2005). ▸page 132

Sperry, R.W. (1968) Hemispheric disconnection and unity in conscious awareness. *American Psychologist*, 23, 723–733. ▸page 132

Spitzer, R.L. (1975) On pseudoscience in science, logic in remission, and psychiatric diagnosis: a critique of Rosenhan's 'On being sane in insane places'. *Journal of Abnormal Psychology*, 84, 442–452. ▸page 190

Szasz, T.S. (1960) *The Myth of Mental Illness*. London: Paladin. ▸page 198

Tajfel, H. and Turner J.C. (1979) An integrative theory of intergroup conflict. In S. Worchel and W.G. Austin (eds) *The Social Psychology of Intergroup Relations* (S. 33–47). Monterey, CA: Brooks/Cole Publishers. ▸page 158

Terman, L. M. (1921) Intelligence and its measurement: A symposium (II.). *Journal of Educational Psychology*, 12, 127–133. ▸page 227

Terrace, H.S. (1979) *Nim*. New York: Alfred A. Knopf. ▸pages 61, 68

Terrace, H.S., Petitto, L.A., Sanders, R.J. and Bever, T.G. (1979) Can an ape create a sentence? *Science*, 206, 891–902. ▸page 68

The Times (2004) Blair promises to end 'kitchen cabinet' government, www.timesonline.co.uk/article/0,,15629-1185343,00.html. ▸page 224

Thigpen, C.H. and Cleckley, H. (1954) A case of multiple personality. *Journal of Abnormal and Social Psychology*, 49, 135–151. ▸page 196

THINK (2004) www.thinkroadsafety.gov.uk. Tiredness kills – how to avoid driver tiredness. June 2004. ▸page 130

Tizard, B. (1986) *The Care of Young Children: Implications of Recent Research*. London: Thomas Coram Research Unit Working Paper No. 1. ▸page 72

Tizard, B. and Phoenix, A. (1993). *Black, White or Mixed Race?* London: Routledge. ▸page 221

Tizard, B. and Phoenix, A. (2001). *Black, White or Mixed Race? Race and Racism in the Lives of Young People of Mixed Parentage*. London: Routledge. ▸page 221

Townsend, J, Roderick, P. and Cooper, J. (1994) Cigarette smoking by socioeconomic, sex, and age: effects of price, income, and health publicity. *BMJ*, 309, 923–927. ▸page 212

Uttal, W.R. (2003). *The New Phrenology: The Limits of Localising Cognitive Processes in the Brain*. Cambridge, MA: MIT Press. ▸page 112

Van Horn, J., Irimia, A., Torgerson, C., Chambers, M., Kikinis, R., and Toga, A. (2012). Mapping Connectivity Damage in the Case of Phineas Gage. *PLoS ONE*, 7 (5) DOI: 10.1371/journal.pone.0037454. ▸page 110

Wada, T. (1922). An experimental study of hunger and its relation to activity. *Archives of Psychology*, 8 (57). ▸page 128

Wagenaar, W. (1988) *Paradoxes of gambling behaviour*. London: Erlbaum. ▸page 205

Wagstaff, G.F. (1981) *Hypnosis, Compliance and Belief*. New York: St Martins Press. ▸page 191

Watson, J.B. (1924) *Behaviorism*. New York: Peoples Institute Publishing Company. ▸page 228

Webb, W.B. and Agnew, H.W. (1975) Are we chronically sleep deprived? *Bulletin of the Psychonomic Society*, 6, 47–48. ▸page 130

Wells, G.L. and Bradfield, A.L. (1998) 'Good, you identified the suspect': Feedback to eyewitnesses distorts their reports of the witnessing experience. *Journal of Applied Psychology*, 83, 360–376. ▸page 48

Wells, G.L. and Olson, E.A. (2003) Eyewitness testimony, *Annual Review of Psychology*, 54, 277–295. ▸page 48

WHO (2001) *Mental Health: New Understanding, New Hope*. ▸page 185

Women's Aid (2012) Children. Available at http://www.womensaid.org.uk/domestic_violence_topic.asp?section=0001000100220002anditemTitle=Children [accessed September 2012]. ▸page 94

Yahoo news, 2005) http://news.yahoo.com/fc/World/London_Bombings (accessed January 2005). ▸page 176

Zimbardo, P.G. (1969) The human choice: individuation, reason and order versus deindividuation, impulse and chaos. Nebraska Symposium on Motivation, 17, 237–307. ▸page 161

GLOSSARY with INDEX

A

abnormality 52, 54, 56, 102, 120, 147, 182, 185, 186–192, 194–202, 204

Abu Ghraib 166

abuse 44, 48, 58, 75, 94, 96, 166, 168, 194, 195, 200, 202, 204, 212, 231, 241

addiction (gambling) ix, 204–205, 212

advertise 18, 40, 41, 70, 151, 159, 178, 206, 208, 212, 224, 229

aggression (core study) 3, 6, 11, 27, 31, 66, 74, 82, 88–95, 102, 147, 174, 190, 210, 220, 221, 224, 228, 232, 234, 238, 242

aggression see also violence 3, 6, 9, 27, 33, 86–87, 88–94, 97, 99, 111, 113, 120, 159, 220, 238, 242, 243

agraphia The inability to write, resulting from brain damage. 136

Ainsworth, Mary 74

alcoholism 184, 204, 212

algorithms 206

alien ix, 6, 76, 168, 192, 195

alien hand syndrome 138

Allport, Gordon W. 146

alpha wave 122, 199

alternate hypothesis A testable statement about the relationship between two variables. Alternative to the null hypothesis. 25, 33

altruistic Behaviour that benefits another, possibly at a cost to the donor. 174

Alzheimer's disease 112, 113

American Psychiatric Association (APA) 184, 202

American Psychological Association (APA) 147, 156, 159, 166, 195

American Sign Language (ASL) 60, 63

American Society for the Advancement of Science 156

American see also USA 43, 45, 51, 61, 75, 89, 120, 125, 135, 147, 148, 149, 151, 159, 171, 186, 227, 228, 240

amnesia 113, 194

Amnesty International 130

amygdala 111, 115

anal stage In psychoanalytic theory, the second stage of psychosexual development when the organ focus of the id is on the anus. 97

anarchic hand 138

Ang San Suu Kyi 146

animal language see also language acquisition (core study) 60–68, 219, 220

animals in research see also chimpanzees 7, 16, 20, 56, 60–61, 62–68, 77, 86, 111, 114, 115, 118, 133, 135, 220, 228, 240

animism 68, 76

anonymity 15, 17, 159

anthropometric The science of measuring the human body. 226

anthropomorphism 61, 68

anti-anxiety drug 223

anti-depressant 192, 223, 241

anti-psychotic 185

anti-semitism 97

anxiety 5, 92, 96, 98–102, 123, 126, 150, 164, 185, 195, 199, 221, 223, 230

apes 61, 62–68

aphasia A condition characterised by difficulties in the production and/or understanding of language. 136

Apollo 15 space mission 235

appearance-reality distinction 77

Arendt, Hannah 156

Argentina 225

army 94, 111, 148, 158

artificial intelligence 219

AS examination x–xiii

Asch, Solomon 29, 148, 190

Ashburner, John see Maguire et al. (core study)

Asperger syndrome An autistic spectrum disorder where individuals are deficient in social skills but, unlike other autistics, have a normal IQ. Some individuals (although not all) exhibit exceptional skill or talent in a specific area. 50, 52–58

Asperger, Hans 50

atrocity 156

attachment 74, 204, 220, 226, 230

attribution 61, 207, 209, 225

attribution theory 225

attrition The loss of participants from a study over time, which is likely to leave a biased sample or a sample that is too small for reliable analysis. 237

auditory 132, 133, 185, 188

Auschwitz 148

Austin (common chimpanzee) 62–66

Australia 84, 163, 205, 235

Austria 97, 99

authoritarianism Favouring absolute obedience to authority, either by submitting to authority or wielding authority. 160–164

autism A mental disorder which usually appears in early childhood and typically involves avoidance of social contact, abnormal language, and so-called 'stereotypic' or bizarre behaviours. 2, 50–51, 74, 204

autism (core study) 2, 3, 31, 52–59, 61, 63, 66, 74, 82, 111, 118, 218, 219, 220

autistic savant 51

autistic spectrum disorder (ASD) A classification that unities a range of different disorders that share similar characteristics, such as difficulty in social relationships and difficulty in understanding what is in other people's minds. 'Low' functioning autism is at one end of the spectrum and 'high' functioning Asperger syndrome at the other end. 50, 52, 58

availability bias 207

aversion therapy 229

B

Bandura et al. (core study) 3, 6, 11, 27, 31, 66, 74, 82, 86–87, 88–95, 102, 147, 174, 190, 210, 220, 221, 224, 228, 232, 234, 238, 242

Bandura, Albert 86–87

bar chart A graph used to represent the frequency of data. The categories on the x-axis have no fixed order, and there is no true zero. 5, 13, 20, 27, 65

Barney the singing dinosaur 130

Baron-Cohen et al. (core study) 2, 3, 31, 50–51, 52–59, 66, 74, 75, 82, 111, 118, 190, 218, 220, 226, 242

Baron-Cohen, Sacha 55

Baron-Cohen, Simon 51, 55, 58, 220

Basic Emotion Recognition Task 52–55

Baumrind, Diana 156

BBC Prison study (core study) 3, 23, 160–167, 222, 238

behaviour checklist An operationalised list of the behaviours to be recorded during an observational study. 5, 7, 8, 9, 10, 27

behaviour therapy (see also cognitive behaviour therapy) Methods of treating psychological disorders through conditioning (classical and operant conditioning). Undesirable behaviours are unlearned. 58, 190, 228

behavioural categories Operationalising a target behaviour, i.e. dividing it into a set of constituent behaviours. These can be used in the form of a behaviour checklist or a coding system. 5, 6, 9, 24, 209, 242, 243

behaviourist perspective (behaviourism/ behaviourist) An approach to explaining behaviour which holds the view that all behaviour can be explained as a result of classical or operant conditioning (i.e. nurture, environment). The approach is only concerned with the behaviours themselves rather than any internal mechanisms in order to explain behaviour – thus 'behaviourism'. 58, 66, 68, 74, 86, 92, 104, 190, 210, 218, 228–229

Bentall, Richard 182

benzene ring 123

beta wave 122

Bible *see also* Good Samaritan 194

Big Brother house 123

big mark questions 7, 8

bilateral Having two sides. In terms of the brain this refers to functions that are present in both sides (hemispheres) of the brain, such as hearing. Some bilateral functions are controlled by the same side of the brain (= ipsilateral) and some are controlled by the opposite side (= contralateral). 138

Binet, Alfred 76, 227

Black, Cilla 240

Blade Runner 122, 133, 219

Blair, Cherie 86

Blair, Tony 60, 224

blank slate 221, 228

blind test A study where some of the people involved are prevented from knowing certain information that might lead to conscious or subconscious bias on their part, which would invalidate the results. 65, 116

Bobo doll 3, 27, 31, 74, 87, 88–95, 220, 224, 228, 232, 238

bomb 74, 148, 166, 176, 194

Bonobos *see* chimpanzees

boredom effect An order effect. In a repeated measures design participants may do less well on a later condition because they have lost interest. 26, 28

Bowlby, John 74, 220, 221, 230

Bowlingual 68

BPS code of ethics *see* British Psychological Society

BPS Research Digest blog 120, 173

brain *see also* split-brain ix, 2, 9, 29, 38, 39, 40, 52, 54, 56, 58, 110–140, 185, 192, 197, 204, 218, 219, 222–223, 226, 239, 241, 242

brain damage 58, 114, 117, 118, 140

brain scan 110–111, 112–113, 114–121, 140

brain scans (core study) 31,111, 114–121, 128, 218, 222, 242

brain stem 132

brain waves The brain produces electrical signals that vary in voltage. A brain wave is the rapid alternation between high and low voltage. This voltage change

is translated by an EEG machine into a series of wavy lines. 122, 124–128, 199, 239

brain, diagram of 115, 123, 132

Brazelton, T. Berry 75

British Psychological Society (BPS) code of Human Research Ethics 14, 15, 24, 232, 233

Broadbent, Donald 218

Broca, Paul 110, 222

Browning, Christopher 235

Browning, Elizabeth Barrett 238

Bryant, Peter 81

Bulger, James 168, 176

Burma 146

burnout 164

bystander effect/behaviour/apathy 168, 169, 170–176

C

Canada 87, 212

Carson, Benjamin 140

case study A research method that involves a detailed study of a single individual, institution or event. Case studies provide a rich record of human experience but are hard to generalise from. 15, 46, 62, 98–102, 111, 160, 162, 195, 196–202, 220, 226, 232, 236, 238, 240–241

castration 97, 98

castration anxiety Anxiety created by the fear of losing the genitals or injury to them. Freud proposed that this is experienced by boys during the Oedipal stage of development. 99, 100

CAT scans Computerised Axial Tomography, a picture of the brain is constructed by taking a series of x-rays 180° around the head. 111, 114

ceiling effect An effect that occurs when test items are too easy for a group of individuals. Therefore too many people do very well, i.e. 'hit the ceiling'. 54, 55, 56

cerebral commissures The fibres that connect the two hemispheres of the brain, including the corpus callosum. 135

cerebral cortex 123, 132

Challenger space shuttle 41, 130

Charcot, Jean-Martin 96, 97, 230

checklist *see* behaviour checklist

Chernobyl 130

child psychology see developmental psychology 74

children in research 2, 3, 6, 8, 9, 15, 21, 27, 39, 50, 51, 53, 54, 56, 58, 62–68, 74–105, 123, 128, 140, 147, 220–221, 225, 227, 230, 231, 232, 237, 240, 242

children's drawings 84

chimpanzees (aka chimps) IX, 23, 50, 60–69, 218, 219, 220, 223, 238, 240

Chomsky, Noam 61, 68, 218

Cinderella 221

Civil rights movement 147

Clark, Mamie and Kenneth 147

classical conditioning Learning that occurs through association. A neutral stimulus is paired with an unconditioned stimulus, resulting in a new stimulus-response (S-R) link. 228, 229

Cleckley, Hervey 197

Clever Hans 61, 68

clinical Medical practice. 97, 161, 162, 163, 164

clinical interview A form of semi-structured or unstructured interview similar to the kind of interview used by a GP when determining a medical diagnosis. 16, 23, 239

clinical psychologist A psychologist who treats patients with mental disorders. 160, 162

closed question A question that has a range of answers from which respondents select one; produces quantitative data. Answers are easier to analyse than those for open questions. 17, 20, 23, 242

co-variable The measured variables in a correlational analysis. The variables must be continuous. 32–33

coding system A systematic method for recording observations in which individual behaviours are given a code for ease of recording. 5, 8, 209

cognitive/cognitive processes (cognition) Related to the process of thought; knowing, perceiving or believing. 3, 28, 37–69, 76, 82, 86, 120, 140, 182, 206–210, 218–219, 229, 238

cognitive alternatives 160–164

cognitive approach An approach to understanding behaviour which suggests that the key influence on how an individual feels and acts is how the individual thinks about a situation. 218–219, 229

cognitive behaviour therapy 229

cognitive bias A distortion of judgement or thinking that occurs in particular situations. 206, 207, 210

cognitive development The changes in a person's mental structures, abilities and processes that occur over their lifespan. 74, 79, 84, 220, 243

cognitive psychology 37–69

cohort effect An effect caused because one group of participants has unique characteristics because of time-specific experiences during their development. 237

Columbia University 87, 147

common chimpanzees 62–66

computer ix, 24, 38, 60, 61, 62, 64, 112, 122, 218–219, 236, 237

concentration camp 148, 225

concrete operational stage 76, 78, 79

concurrent validity A means of establishing validity by comparing an existing test or questionnaire with the one you are developing. If the two tests show a significant positive correlation this establishes the concurrent validity of the new test/questionnaire. 22, 54, 56

confederates An individual in an experiment who is not a real participant and has been instructed how to behave by the investigator. 88, 148, 151, 170, 186, 188

confidentiality An ethical issue concerned with a participant's right to have personal information protected. 15, 17, 23, 233

conjoined twins 140

consciousness 76, 96, 110, 111, 133, 135, 138, 185, 195

consent see informed consent 154, 162

conservation 76–77, 78–85, 218, 220, 242

conservation (core study) 31, 46, 56, 74, 78–85, 218, 220, 221, 238, 242, 243

conservation task A method for testing the ability to distinguish between reality and appearance, for example to understand that quantity is not changed even when a display is transformed. 76, 78, 80, 242

content analysis A kind of observational study in which behaviour is observed indirectly in written or verbal material. May involve an initial qualitative analysis to produce categories, which then can be represented with qualitative data (examples from each category) or quantitative data (the frequency of particular behaviours in each categories). 206, 209

control condition In an experiment with a repeated measures design, the condition that provides a baseline measure of behaviour without the experimental treatment, so that the effect of the experimental treatment may be assessed. 54, 78, 80, 90

control group In an experiment with an independent groups design, a group of participants who receive no treatment. Their behaviour acts as a baseline against which the effect of the independent variable may be measured. 42, 45, 82, 88, 114, 115, 116, 117, 118

control in research 2, 6, 10, 24, 26, 27, 28, 30, 31, 40, 52, 55, 56, 62, 64, 80, 81, 88, 90, 91, 114, 116, 117, 118, 153, 186, 224, 235, 236, 237, 243

controlled observation A form of investigation in which behaviour is observed but under conditions where certain variables have been organised by the researcher. 6–7, 153

Cooley, C.H. 224

corpus callosum 132, 133, 134, 135

correlation Determining the extent of the relationship between two variables. Usually a linear correlation is predicted, but the relationship can be curvilinear. 2, 8, 13, 22, 32–33, 41, 114, 117, 118, 124, 125, 127, 207, 212, 226

correlation coefficient A number between −1 and +1 that tells us how closely the co-variables in a correlational analysis are related. 8, 32

cortisol A hormone produced by the adrenal gland during periods of prolonged stress. 162

counterbalancing An experimental technique designed to overcome order effects. Counterbalancing ensures that each condition is tested first or second in equal amounts. 26

covert observation see also undisclosed observation 6

cross-cultural study 84, 148

cross-modal association 219

cyber identity 183

cyranos 149

D

Da Vinci, Leonardo 130

Dandy, Walter E. 140

Darley, John 168, 169, 171, 172, 173

Darwin, Charles 68, 97, 226

daytime TV viii, 233, 241

debrief A post-research interview designed to inform the participants of the true nature of the study and to restore them to the state they were in at the start of the study. xiv, 4, 14, 15, 16, 150, 152, 153, 156, 163, 233

deception An ethical issue, most usually where a participant is not told the true aims of a study (e.g. what participation will involve) and thus cannot give truly informed consent. Very occasionally deception may involve the provision of false information. 10, 14, 16, 24, 82, 232, 233

defence mechanism In psychoanalytic theory, the strategies used by the ego to defend itself against anxiety, such as repression, denial and projection. viii, 96, 98, 104, 199, 231

deindividuation A psychological state in which individuals have lowered levels of self-evaluation (e.g. when in a crowd or under the influence of alcohol) and decreased concerns about evaluation by others. 160, 161

Delgardo, Jose 111

demand characteristics A cue that makes participants unconsciously aware of the aims of a study or helps participants work out what the researcher expects to find. This is likely to affect the participants' behaviour. 20, 22, 28, 29, 30, 31, 82, 91

Dement and Kleitman (core study) 31, 33, 122–123, 124–131, 222

Dement, William 128, 130

dependent variable A measurable outcome of the action of the independent variable in an experiment. 24, 26, 27, 28, 30, 32, 80, 153, 160, 162, 164, 170, 206, 207, 208, 242, 243

depersonalisation A change in the experience of self where people have a feeling of watching themselves act, while having no control over a situation. viii, 186, 190, 194

depression 39, 160, 162, 163, 164, 185, 187, 190, 195, 202, 212, 223, 241

Deprivation (motional) 51, 74

Descartes, Rene 222

descriptive statistics Methods of summarising a data set such as measures of central tendency (mean, median, mode) and the use of graphs. xiv, 12, 13, 16, 17, 27, 239

developmental approach This approach seeks to understand behaviour in terms of the changes which occur as we age, in particular the complementary effects of nature and nurture. 220–221

developmental disorder 52, 54

developmental psychology 39, 63, 74–108

Diamond, Milton 241

Dick, Philip K. 122, 133, 138, 140

diffusion of responsibility An explanation for bystander behaviour; when in a group in an emergency situation, each individual feels less responsibility because responsibility is shared and therefore spread out. 169, 170, 171, 174

disclosed observation 6, 10

discourse analysis 239

discrimination 75, 133, 146, 147, 161

dispositional factors/explanation 151, 186, 225

dissociation 194, 202

dissociative identity disorder see also multiple personality disorder 194, 200

diving reflex 220

Dodd, Ken 230

Dr Strangeglove 138

dreams 16, 18, 20, 33, 96, 97, 100, 101, 111, 122–123, 124–131, 133, 194, 228, 230, 231

dropped letter technique 149

DSM 184, 192

DV see dependent variable

E

Ebbinghaus, Hermann 40

ecological validity Concerning the ability to generalise a research effect beyond the particular setting in which it is demonstrated to other settings. xiv, 9, 10, 30, 31, 40, 56, 208, 234–235

EEG A method of detecting activity in the living brain. Electrodes are attached to a person's scalp to record general levels of electrical activity. 112, 122, 123, 124–128, 196–200, 239

ego 96

ego defence mechanisms *see also* defence mechanisms 96, 98

Eichmann, Adolf 156

Einstein, Albert ix, 51, 76, 221

electroencephalogram *see* EEG

EMG 122

emotion ix, 2, 3, 12, 29, 41, 50, 52, 54, 56, 58, 68, 74, 86, 94, 96, 97, 110, 111, 118, 120, 122, 132, 133, 134, 137, 138, 174, 182, 184, 190, 194, 195, 198, 199, 218, 221, 223, 228, 229, 230, 231, 238, 239

empathising 58, 174

EOG Electro-oculogram, measures the electrical difference that exists between the front and the back of the eye. This enables eye movements to be recorded. 122, 124–126

epilepsy 113, 133, 134, 135, 140

episodic memory Memory for events. 118

eros 231

Estonia 149

ethical guidelines 156, 232–233

ethical issue The conflict which arises in research between research goals and participant's rights. 2, 4, 10, 14–15, 16–17, 24, 82, 156, 161, 166, 232–233, 240

ethics xiv, 4, 14–15, 16–17, 24, 31, 33, 48, 96, 113, 134, 156, 160, 161, 162, 163, 164, 166, 224, 228, 232–233, 241

ethics committee 15, 162, 233

eugenics 226, 227

Eve White and Eve Black 138, 183, 196–203, 227, 230, 232, 233, 236, 240

event sampling An observational technique in which a count is kept of the number of times a particular behaviour (event) occurs. 5, 6, 7, 8, 10, 18

evolution 111, 118, 130, 221, 222, 226, 228, 229

experiment (experimental method) A research method that involves the direct manipulation of an independent variable in order to test its possible causal relationship with a dependent variable. xiv, xv, 2, 11, 19, 24–31, 32, 33, 40, 42–47, 48, 52–57, 77, 78–83, 84, 88–93, 111, 113, 114–119, 124–129,133, 134–139, 159, 160–165, 169, 170–175, 176, 188, 191, 206–211, 218, 224, 225, 228, 232, 235, 238, 241, 242, 243

experimental design A set of procedures used to control the influence of participant variables in an experiment. 24, 26, 27

experimental group In an experiment with an independent groups design, a group of participants who receive the experimental treatment (the independent variable). 43, 88, 89, 114, 115

experimenter bias The effect that the experimenter's expectations have on the participants and thus on the results of the experiment. 28, 31

extraneous variable In an experiment, any variable other than the independent variable that might potentially affect the dependent variable and thereby confound the results. 24, 26, 28, 30, 31, 80, 88, 89, 164, 235, 243

extreme male brain 58

Exxon Valdex 130

Eyes Task 2, 52–56

eyetracking 3

eyewitness testimony (core study) The evidence provided in court by a person who witnessed a crime, with a view to identifying the perpetrator of the crime. ix, 16, 31, 42–48, 128, 218, 224

F

Facebook 11, 183, 236, 239

facilitated communication 58

fairy tales 221, 231

false memory 46, 48, 102, 195

familiar strangers 149

fatigue effect An order effect. In a repeated measures design, participants may do less well on one condition rather than another because they have become tired or bored. 26, 28

field experiment A controlled experiment that is conducted outside a lab. The key features are that the independent variable is still manipulated by the experimenter, and therefore causal relationships can be demonstrated. The environment is more familiar and therefore participant behaviour may be more 'natural'. 31, 170, 188, 235, 243

field study Any study that takes place away from the laboratory and within the context in which the behaviour normally occurs. 31, 164, 234, 235

Finland 212

flashbulb memory 41

fMRI scan A method used to scan brain activity while a person is performing a task. It enables researchers to detect which regions of the brain are rich in oxygen and thus are active. 112, 114, 118, 120

football 18, 40, 58, 86, 176, 183, 205

Frackowiak, Richard *see* Maguire *et al.* (core study)

France 51, 133, 158, 227

Frankenstein 123, 219

free will The view that our behaviour is determined by our own will rather than by other forces. 111

Freud (case study) 2, 23, 46, 74, 82, 96–97, 98–105, 111, 128, 147, 190, 200, 220, 226, 227, 230, 234, 236, 238, 240

Freud family 104

Freud, Anna 104

Freud, Sigmund 86, 92, 97, 195, 221, 226, 230–231

Freudian 3

Freudian slip 97

Frith, Christopher *see* Maguire *et al.* (core study)

frontal lobotomy A form of psychosurgery in which fibres running from the frontal lobes to other parts of the brain are cut. 129, 135, 192, 223

frontal region of the brain (frontal lobe) The region of the brain (cortex) above and behind the eyes, involved in fine motor movement and thinking. 52, 54, 56, 113, 120, 132, 134, 223

fruit machines 205–210

frustration 68, 87, 110, 147, 198

fundamental attribution error 225

G

Gabriel, Peter 68

Gadian, David *see* Maguire *et al.* (core study)

Gage, Phineas 110, 112

Gall, Franz Joseph 112

Gallileo 235

Galton, Francis 226

galvanic skin response (GSR) 3

gambler's fallacy 212

gambling ix, 204–205, 229

gambling (core study) 3, 206–213, 218, 222, 224, 226

Gardner, Randy 130

Gazzaniga, Michael 140

gender reassignment 241

Gender Recognition of the Eyes 52, 54

Gender *see also* sex 9, 28, 52, 54, 56, 58, 88–91, 114, 183, 206, 208, 233,

generalisability 18, 30, 161, 243

generalised anxiety disorder An anxiety disorder that involves excessive worry about anything and everything. 100

genetic 50, 52, 54, 56, 92, 120, 182, 204, 220, 226, 227

Genie 241

GLOSSARY with INDEX

genome 222

Genovese, Kitty 168, 170, 176

Georgia State University 63

Germany 97, 123, 133, 148, 150, 151, 158, 205, 218, 235

Gernika 148

Golgi stains 110

Good, Catriona *see* Maguire *et al.* (core study)

gorilla 6, 232

Great Ape Trust 68

Greece 84

Greek 50, 97, 184

Gregory, Richard 39

grey matter The term used to describe certain parts of the brain. It is found on the surface of the brain and also deep inside, within structures such as the hypothalamus and hippocampus. It is the part of the brain that is most dense in neural connections (which makes it look grey) and associated with higher order thinking. 114, 116, 117, 120

Griffiths (core study) 3, 154, 174, 204–205, 206–213, 218, 222, 224, 226

Griffiths, Mark 183, 204, 208

Grossman, David 94

groupthink 224

Guantanamo Bay 166

H

hallucinations 130, 184, 185, 187, 188

Hans *see* Little Hans or Clever Hans

Happé 51, 54

Harvard University 149

Haslam, Alex (*see also* Reicher and Haslam, core study) 156, 163

Heider, Fritz 225

helping behaviour 30, 146, 149, 168–174, 224

hemisphere (brain) The forebrain is divided into two halves, or hemispheres. Each half is largely the same, containing the same specialised regions with the exception of those functions that are lateralised, such as language. 29, 114, 117, 132–140, 223

hemispherectomy 140

hemispheric deconnection *see* split-brain

hereditary 123, 226

heuristic A strategy used to solve a problem or work something out. It can be a set of rules, an educated guess or just common sense. 206–210

Hezbollah 94

hindsight bias The tendency to see past events as being more predictable than they were before they took place. 207, 209

hippocampus A structure in the subcortical area of each hemisphere of the forebrain (i.e. 'under' the cortex, deep inside the brain). It is associated with memory. It is part of the limbic system, therefore involved in motivation, emotion and learning. viii, 113, 114–118, 134

historical validity 234

Hitchhiker's Guide to the Galaxy 169, 227

HM 113, 118, 240

Holocaust 148, 149

Hopkins, William *see* Savage-Rumbaugh *et al.* (core study)

Horney, Karen 230

horses 61, 96, 98–102, 104, 115

hypnosis 48, 96, 159, 194, 195, 196, 197, 199, 200, 202, 230

hypothalamus 111, 116, 123, 132

hypothesis A precise and testable statement about the world, specifically of the relationship between data to be measured. It is a statement about populations and not samples. xiv, 2, 25, 26, 33, 113, 123, 149, 151, 206, 208, 210, 235

I

iatrogenic 202

ICD 184, 192

id 96, 231

idiographic approach 227, 239

IgNoble Prize 68, 104, 117, 224

line graph 13

illusion of control 206, 207

Illusion *see* visual illusion

imitative learning s*ee also* nonimitative learning 88–90, 92

impression formation 29

inattentional blindness 219

independent measures An experimental design in which participants are allocated to two (or more) groups representing different research conditions. Allocation is achieved using random or systematic techniques. 24, 26, 27, 28, 42, 78, 237

independent variable In an experiment, an event that is directly manipulated by an experimenter in order to test its effect on another variable (the dependent variable). 24, 26, 27, 28, 30, 32, 52, 80, 88, 153, 160, 162, 170, 188, 237, 243

India 149

individual differences 5, 19, 39, 111, 126, 138, 160, 182–213

individual differences approach An approach to understanding behaviour that focuses on the ways that people differ and understanding those differences, for measuring variations in individual scores on tests of intelligence or personality. 23, 226–227

individualist culture A culture that values independence rather than reliance on others, in contrast to many non-Western cultures that could be described as collectivist. 47

inferential statistics Procedures for drawing logical conclusions (inferences) about the population from which samples are drawn. xiv, 13

informed consent An ethical issue and an ethical guideline in psychological research whereby participants are given comprehensive information concerning the nature and purpose of the research and their role in it, in order that they can make an informed decision about whether or not to participate. 4, 10, 14, 15, 16, 24, 82, 113, 233, 240, 241

inherited 54, 92, 183, 220, 226

insanity *see* abnormality

instinct 86, 176, 221, 231

institutional review board 15

intelligence 3, 9, 14, 28, 29, 32, 39, 50, 52, 54, 56, 58, 61, 68, 76, 84, 111, 132, 147, 182, 218, 219, 226, 227, 228

inter-rater reliability The extent to which there is agreement between two or more observers (raters). 8, 10, 30, 90, 209

intervening variable A variable that comes between two other variables and can be used to explain the relationship between the two variables. 33

interview A research method that involves a face-to-face, 'real-time' interaction with another individual and results in the collection of data. 16–17, 18, 20–23, 146, 239

interviewer bias The effect of an interviewer's expectations, communicated unconsciously, on a respondent's behaviour. 22

introspection 218

invasion of privacy *see* privacy

investigator bias The effect that the investigator's expectations have on participants in a research study and thus on the results of the study. 28, 82

ipsilateral A description for behavioural functions that are controlled by the same side of the cerebral hemisphere. 138

IQ 50, 55, 56, 237

IQ test 23, 32, 76, 137, 182, 196, 197, 199, 227, 239, 242

Iraq 130, 158, 166, 224

Itard, Jean-Marc Gaspard 51

IV *see* independent variable

J

James Bulger see Bulger, James
James, William viii, 39, 44
Janis, Irving 224
Joan of Arc 185
Johnsrude, Ingrid see Maguire et al. (core study)
Joliffe, Therese see Baron-Cohen et al. (core study)
Jones, Edward E. 225
Jung, Carl 82
just-world effect 212

K

Kanner, Leo 50
Kanzi 56, 60–69, 218, 228, 240
Kitty Genovese see Genovese, Kitty
Kleitman, Nathaniel see Dement and Kleitman (core study) 125, 128

L

L'Enfant Sauvage 51
laboratory Any setting (a room or other environment) specially fitted out for conducting research. 6, 25, 31, 45, 76, 124, 125, 150, 152, 153, 154, 156, 168, 170, 171, 208, 218, 226, 228, 234, 235
laboratory experiment An experiment carried out in the controlled setting of a laboratory. 31, 42, 43, 78, 88, 161, 169, 170, 172, 243
language xiii, ix, 39, 50, 51, 52, 58, 60–61, 62–68, 75, 76, 77, 97, 110, 134–140, 218, 219, 220, 222, 238, 240, 241
language acquisition (core study) 11, 23, 56, 60–61, 62–69, 75, 218, 219, 220, 228, 234, 238, 240
LaPiere, Richard 147
Las Madres de la Plaza de Mayo 225
Lashley, Karl 222
Latané, Bibb 168, 169, 172, 173
Latané, Bibb 168, 169, 171, 172, 173
latency period 97, 104
lateralisation 133,137
leading question A question that is phrased in a way (e.g. 'Don't you agree that...?') that it makes one response more likely than another. 16, 22, 23, 41, 42–46, 82, 98, 100, 234, 243
learning 39, 51, 58, 60, 61, 62–68, 76, 82, 86, 87, 88–92, 102, 104, 113, 115, 118, 133, 140, 150–154, 185, 218, 219, 220, 228–229, 238
Learning difficulties 50, 52, 58, 233
left brained thinking 140
legitimacy The extent to which something is fair or right. 160–164

lexigram A symbol used to represent a word but is not necessarily indicative of the object referenced by the word. 62–65, 228, 240
libido In psychoanalytic theory, the libido is the id's sexual (biological) drive. At each stage of psychosexual development, the libido becomes focused on a part of the body. 100, 231
lie detector test 3, 120
lie scale 16
limbic system 111, 223
Little Hans (core study) 2, 20, 46, 98–105, 128, 220, 226, 227, 230, 234, 236, 238, 240
Little Red Riding Hood 231
lobotomy see frontal and unilateral lobotomy
localisation Certain areas of the brain are associated with specific behavioural functions. 111, 222
Loftus and Palmer (core study) xiv, 16, 24, 31, 40–41, 42–49, 100, 118, 128, 147, 164, 218, 219, 224, 234, 238, 242, 243
Loftus, Elizabeth 44, 48, 102, 200
London bombs 176, 194
London Olympics 146, 166
longitudinal study A study conducted over a long period of time. It is often a form of repeated measures design in which participants are assessed on two or more occasions as they get older. 62, 63, 236–237
Lorber, John 111
Lorenz, Konrad 86
Lovaas method 58
Lovaas, Ivar 58

M

madness see mental disorder
magic 77, 84, 197, 218, 221, 239
Maguire et al. (core study) 31, 111, 112–113, 114–121, 128, 218, 222, 242
Maguire, Eleanor 117
Matata 60, 63–66
matched Making two or more groups of participants similar with respect to key characteristics such as age, essentially a matched participants design. 52, 54, 80, 89, 114
matched participants design An experimental design in which pairs of participants are matched in terms of variables relevant to the study, such as age, IQ, perceptual ability and so on. One member of each pair receives one level of the IV and the second pair member receives the other level of the IV. This means that participant variables are better controlled than is usually the case in an independent groups design experiment. 88, 54, 114, 160, 162

McCartney, Paul 68, 123
McDonald, Kelly see Savage-Rumbaugh et al. (core study)
mean A measure of central tendency. The arithmetic average of a group of scores, calculated by dividing the sum of the scores by the number of scores. 8, 13, 18, 20, 27, 31, 42, 43, 52, 55, 79, 80, 81, 89, 91, 114, 115, 117, 126, 173, 182, 189, 206, 208, 209, 237
mechanistic approach 38
median A measure of central tendency. The middle value in a set of scores when they are placed in rank order. 13, 172
memory 14, 19, 24–25, 26–27, 30, 32, 40–41, 42–49, 50, 51, 86, 97, 104, 113, 114–121, 128, 130, 132, 137, 151, 195, 196–200, 218, 219, 222, 223, 238, 239
mental disorder (mental illness) see also phobias, multiple personality disorder, depression 56, 63, 76, 96, 98, 99, 111, 128, 182, 184, 185, 186--193, 192, 194–200, 222, 231, 240
mental health 74, 104, 118, 120, 182, 230
mental hospital see psychiatric hospital
mental illness see mental disorder
mental map 3, 113, 114, 118, 149
mental processes see cognitive 38, 40, 76, 97, 110, 117, 138, 218, 230, 243
mental retardation 58
mental state 50, 53, 54, 56, 58, 96, 164
mesmerism 195
Metropolis 222
microsleep 130
Milgram (core study) ix, 2, 11, 31, 111, 148–149, 150–157, 158, 164, 169, 174, 190, 224, 225, 230, 232, 234–235, 242
Milgram, Stanley 148–149, 159, 168, 169, 238
Miller, George 218
Mixed race 221
MMR vaccine 50
modal group The group that has the most common scores/items. 13, 16, 20, 153
mode A measure of central tendency. The most frequently occurring score in a set of data. 13
model A person who is imitated. 86–95, 146, 170–174
modelling 64, 86–92, 170–172
Molaison, Henry see HM
Money, John 241
Moniz, Egas 222
moral 102, 133, 148, 169, 176, 185, 190, 196, 199, 204, 221, 232
mortification 190
Mortimore, Catherine see Baron-Cohen et al. (core study)
Mowrer, Hobart 104
Mr Men 84

MRI scan Magnetic resonance imaging, produces a three-dimensional image of the static, living brain which is very precise and provides information about the function of different regions. 112, 114–119, 140

Mulika 62–69

multiple personality disorder A type of mental disorder where two or more relatively independent personalities are believed to exist in one person. The separate personalities have become 'dissociated' (separated) from each other, hence the name 'dissociative personality disorder' is also used. Dissociation may occur as a consequence of stress. 194–195

multiple personality disorder (core study) 46, 138, 194–195, 196–203, 220, 226, 239, 240

murder 86, 94, 111, 112, 120, 148, 156, 168, 170, 176, 187, 205, 222, 226

My Lai 148

N

National Lottery 205, 212

natural experiment *see* quasi-experiment

natural selection 226

naturalistic observation A research method carried out in a naturalistic setting, in which the investigator does not interfere in any way but merely observes the behaviour(s) in question. 6–7, 10

nature Those aspects of behaviour that are innate and inherited. 'Nature' does not simply refer to abilities present at birth but to any ability determined by genes, including those that appear throughout the lifespan through maturation. 118, 220

nature–nurture The discussion about whether behaviour is due to innate or environmental factors. 115, 220, 226

Naughty Teddy 84

Nazi 97, 148, 151, 156, 158

near-death experience 195

Necker cube 39

negative correlation A relationship between two co-variables such that as the value of one co-variable increases, that of the other decreases. 32–33, 114, 117, 118

Neisser, Ulrich 40, 41

neuroimaging *see* brain scan

neuroscience 39, 112, 218

neuroses A mental disturbance characterised by distress but where the patient has not lost touch with reality, as distinct from psychosis. 102

neurotransmitter 204, 223

New Zealand 212

Newton, Isaac 51

Nicholson, Jack 192

night terrors 123

Nim Chimpsky 66, 68

Nobel prize 68, 135, 223

nomothetic approach 227, 239

non-participant observation Observations made by someone who is not participating in the activity being observed. 6

nonimitative learning 62, 64, 65, 91

normative decision theory 207

Norway 148, 149, 205, 212

Nottingham Forest football vi, viii, 205

NREM 122, 124–131

null hypothesis An assumption that there is no relationship (difference, association, etc.) in the population from which a sample is taken with respect to the variables being studied. 25, 33

nurse 186–190, 192, 234–235

nurture Those aspects of behaviour that are acquired through experience, i.e. learned from interactions with the physical and social environment. 118, 220

O

obedience 148, 149, 234–235

obedience (core study) 2, 14, 31, 111, 150–157, 224, 230, 234, 235, 242

observation (in social learning theory) 92

observation/observational study A research technique where a researcher watches or listens to participants engaging in whatever behaviour is being studied. 2, 3, 4–11, 15, 16, 18, 19, 23, 24, 30, 31, 32, 62–65, 75, 90, 99, 128, 150, 160, 162, 184, 186, 196, 200, 218, 234, 238, 239, 241, 243

observational methods An overall plan for conducting an observation, such as deciding to control certain elements of the environment (a controlled observation). 6–7, 10–11

observational techniques The application of systematic strategies to record observation data, such as the use of time sampling or behavioural categories. 4–7, 10–11, 27, 92, 242

observer bias In observational studies there is a danger that observers' expectations affect what they see or hear. 9, 10, 196

occipital lobe 132

Oedipus complex Freud's explanation of how a boy resolves his love for his mother and feelings of rivalry towards his father by identifying with his father. Occurs during the phallic stage of psychosexual development. 97, 98–105, 240

One Flew Over the Cuckoo's Nest 192

one-tailed hypothesis States the direction of difference (e.g. more or less) between two groups of participants or between different conditions, or the relationship (positive or negative) between co-variables. 25, 33

one-way mirror A mirror that is reflective on one side but transparent on the other. This allows observers to watch participants without them being aware of the observers' presence (covert observation). 6, 8, 90, 152, 154

open question In an interview or questionnaire, a question that invites respondents to provide their own answers rather than select one of those provided. Tends to produce qualitative data. 17, 20, 152, 242

operant conditioning Learning that occurs when we are reinforced for doing something, which increases the probability that the behaviour in question will be repeated in the future. Conversely, if we are punished for behaving in a certain way, there is a decrease in the probability that the behaviour will recur. 68, 92, 229

operationalise Providing variables in a form that can be easily tested. 24–25, 26, 27, 90, 208

opportunity sample A sample of participants produced by selecting people who are most easily available at the time of the study. 18–19, 21

oral stage 97

order effect In a repeated measures design, an extraneous variable arising from the order in which conditions are presented. 26, 28

P

Pakistan 84

Palestinian 110, 158

Palmer, John *see* Loftus and Palmer (core study)

Pan paniscus *see* chimpanzees

Pan troglodytes *see* chimpanzees

Paralympics 146

paralysis 97, 122, 123, 124, 230

parietal lobe 132

participant observation Observations made by someone who is also participating in the activity being observed, which may affect their objectivity. 6, 10, 186

participant variable Characteristics of individual participants (such as age, intelligence, etc.) that might influence the outcome of a study. 27, 28, 237

Pavlov, Ivan 81, 228

Penfield, Wilder 112, 132, 133

Pepys, Samuel 61

perception 38–39, 44, 46, 52, 54, 118, 122, 132, 138, 148, 168, 184, 185, 190, 194, 195, 209, 218, 219, 221, 224–225

permeability Refers to the ability to move from one place to another. A membrane that is permeable allows substances to pass through it. 160–167

personality test 23, 196–199, 239

personality, personality development 2, 20, 54, 98–102, 110, 111, 112, 132, 134, 137, 138, 151, 161, 162, 164, 182, 183, 184, 186, 187, 190, 194–203, 220, 221, 226, 228, 230, 231, 239

personification Attributing human characteristics to animals, inanimate objects or abstract notions. 207, 209, 210

pet 7, 68, 236

PET scan 112

phallic stage 97

phantom limb 241

phobia A group of mental disorders characterised by high levels of anxiety that, when experienced, interfere with normal living. 20, 96, 98–104

phrenology A pseudoscience that links bumps on a person's head to certain aspects of the individual's personality and character. 2, 112

physiological approach 222–223

physiological psychology 39, 75, 110–143, 162

Piaget, Jean 53, 56, 74, 76–77, 78, 79, 82, 84, 111, 220, 242, 243

Picasso, Pablo 221

Piliavin *et al.* (core study) 31, 92, 154, 164, 168–169, 170–177, 224, 225, 234, 243

Piliavin, Irving M. and Jayne 172

pilot study A trial run of a research study, involving only a few participants who are representative of the target population. It is conducted to test any aspects of the research design, with a view to making improvements before conducting the full research study. 5, 9, 15, 20, 21, 151, 152

pluralistic ignorance 168

pons 123

population validity Concerning the extent to which the findings of a study can be generalised to other groups of people besides those who took part in the study. 234

positive correlation A relationship between two co-variables such that as the value of one co-variable increases, this is accompanied by a corresponding increase in the other co-variable. 32–33, 114, 117, 118, 124, 125, 127

practice effect An order effect. In a repeated measures design, participants may do better on one condition rather

than another because they have completed it first and are therefore may have improved their ability to perform the task. 26, 28

pre-operational stage 76, 77, 78, 79

prejudice 4, 97, 120, 146–147, 149, 161, 233

presumptive consent A method of dealing with lack of informed consent or deception, by asking a group of people who are similar to the participants whether they would agree to take part in a study. If this group of people consent to the procedures in the proposed study, it is presumed that the real participants would agree as well. 14

primacy effect 29

primate see chimpanzee 50, 60, 63

Princess Diana 41

Prison see BBC prison study 48, 130, 158, 159, 169, 192, 223, 239

privacy An ethical issue that refers to a zone of inaccessibility of mind or body and the trust that this will not be 'invaded'. Contrasts with confidentiality. 4, 10, 15, 17, 159, 233

procedural memory 118

projective test Psychological tests that assess attitudes and personality by asking respondents to give their interpretation of a picture. The respondent 'projects' their own attitudes onto the picture and reveals them in the descriptions provided. 23, 182, 196–200

protection from harm An ethical issue. During a research study, participants should not experience negative physical (e.g. pain or injury) or psychological effects (e.g. lowered self-esteem or embarrassment). 14, 233

Prozac 223

pseudopatient 186–193

pseudoscience A claim, belief or practice which is presented as scientific, but does not adhere to a valid scientific method, lacks supporting evidence or plausibility, cannot be reliably tested, or otherwise lacks scientific status. 112

psychiatric hospital 186–187, 188–192, 224, 226

psychiatrist 48, 50, 150, 166, 184, 185, 186–192, 195, 196–202, 240

psychoanalysis A form of psychotherapy, originally developed by Sigmund Freud, that is intended to help patients become aware of long-repressed feelings and issues by using techniques such as free association and dream analysis. 82, 96–97, 98–104, 226, 230, 231

psychodynamic perspective 102, 230–231

psychological harm 14, 17, 24, 82

psychological test A method used to assess psychological abilities, such as

personality or intelligence or emotional type. This could be qualitative or quantitative. 20, 23, 152, 182, 242

psychometric test The quantitative measurement of any psychological ability. 'Metric' means measurement. 20, 162, 183, 196–200, 226, 227

psychopathic personality A mental disorder where an individual is incapable of feeling remorse for their actions or empathy for others. 120, 199

psychosexual development 220

psychosurgery 120, 223

psychsomatic 230

PsyOps 130, 166

pygmy chimpanzees 62–69, 240

Q

qualitative 61, 77

qualitative approach An approach to research that emphasises individual experience rather than seeking to form general rules about behaviour. 146, 227, 238, 239, 243

qualitative data Information in words or images that cannot be counted or quantified. Qualitative data can be turned into quantitative data by placing them in categories and counting frequency. 12, 17, 32, 150, 153, 238–239, 240, 243

quantitative approach 227, 239

quantitative data Information that represents how much or how long or how many, etc. A behaviour is measured in numbers or quantities. 12, 17, 32, 196, 197, 199, 238–239, 240, 243

quasi-experiment A research design that is 'almost' an experiment but lacks one or more features of a true experiment. For example the independent variable may not have been directly manipulated and/or participants may not have been randomly allocated to conditions. 31, 52

questionnaire A research method in which data is collected through the use of written questions, which may be open or closed questions. 2, 16–17, 18, 19, 20–23, 26, 32, 43, 44, 58, 87, 128, 149, 154, 159, 168, 176, 182, 224, 226, 227, 242, 243

quota sampling Similar to a stratified sample except participants are selected from strata using opportunity sampling rather than a random sampling technique. 21

R

R.E.M. 122

race 120, 147, 169, 170–174, 183, 221

racism 120, 160, 162, 221

Rainman 56

Ramachandran, V.S. 241

random Happening without any pattern, all events have an equal chance of being selected. 13, 18, 21, 55, 64, 122, 125, 160, 162, 205, 207, 210, 212

random allocation Allocating participants to experimental groups or conditions using random techniques. 27, 28, 31, 89, 150, 159, 160, 208

random number tables 18

random sample A sample of participants produced by using a random technique such that every member of the target population being tested has an equal chance of being selected. 18–19

rapid eye movement sleep (REM sleep) Rapid eye movement sleep, during which the body is paralysed except for the eyes which are active and the brain is very active. REM sleep is often equated with dreaming, but dreams can also occur in NREM sleep. 122, 123, 124, 125

rating scale A means of assessing attitudes or experiences by asking a respondent to rate statements on a scale of 1 to 3 or 1 to 5, etc. 17, 20, 160, 162, 163, 188, 242

realism The aim of portraying things as they really are. 30

recency effect 29

recovered memory see false memory

reductionist 135

regression In psychoanalytic theory, a defense mechanism where an individual deals with anxiety by returning to an earlier ego state rather than coping with unacceptable impulses in an adult way. 96, 196, 199

Reicher and Haslam (core study) 3, 23, 92, 158–159, 160, 167, 174, 176, 183, 222, 224, 225, 226, 238

Reicher, Steve 156, 163

Reimer, David 240, 241

reinforcement If a behaviour results in a pleasant state of affairs, the behaviour is 'stamped in' or reinforced. It then becomes more probable that the behaviour will be repeated in the future. There is both positive and negative reinforcement – both lead to an increased likelihood that the behaviour will be repeated. 86, 104, 228–229

relapse 204

reliability A measure of consistency which means that it is possible to obtain the same results on subsequent occasions when the measure is used. 8–10, 22, 23, 30, 33, 60, 62, 64, 90, 120, 128, 187, 198, 209, 227, 236, 238, 242–243

REM rebound 128

REM sleep see also rapid eye movement sleep 31, 33, 122–131

repeated measures A type of experimental design in which each participant takes part in every condition under test. 24, 26, 28, 78

replication The opportunity to repeat an investigation under exactly the same conditions in order to test the method used (reliability) or findings (validity). xiv, 7, 21, 26, 31, 68, 156, 161, 218, 242

representative heuristic 207

representative sample A sample selected so that it accurately stands for or represents the population being studied. 18, 19, 21

repressed memory therapy 195

repression In psychoanalytic theory, a defence mechanism whereby anxiety-provoking material is kept out of conscious awareness as a means of reducing anxiety levels and coping. 44, 96, 97, 98–102, 195, 196, 199

right brained thinking 140

right to withdraw An ethical issue; participants should have the right to withdraw from participating in an experiment if they are uncomfortable with any of the procedures. 14, 16

Robertson, Mary see Baron-Cohen et al. (core study)

Rodin, Judith see Piliavin et al. (core study)

role model 86, 87, 88, 146

role play A controlled observation in which participants are asked to imagine how they would behave in certain situations and act out the part. This method has the advantage of permitting the study of certain behaviours that might be unethical to study or difficult to find in the real world. 126, 136, 152, 159, 164, 172, 198

Ronettes 239

Rooney, Wayne 86

Rorschach inkblot test 182, 197, 199, 239

Rosenhan (core study) 11, 92, 111, 118, 128, 147, 184–185, 186–193, 200, 224, 226, 234

Rosenhan, David 187

Ross, Dorothea see Bandura et al. (core study)

Ross, Sheila see Bandura et al. (core study)

Rubin, Edgar 38

Rupert, Elizabeth see Savage-Rumbaugh et al. (core study)

Russia 61, 128, 156, 158, 228

Rutter, Michael 75

S

Sally Anne test 53

sample A selection of participants taken from the target population being studied and intended to be representative of that population. xiv, 15, 18–19, 21, 23, 26, 89, 150, 235, 236, 237, 243

sampling (in an observation) In an observational study, a system to determine when observations are recorded. The alternative is to simply record everything that happens. 5, 6, 7, 10, 11

sampling/sampling technique The process of taking a sample. 18–19, 21, 24, 26, 128

Samuel and Bryant (core study) 31, 46, 56, 74, 76–77, 78–85, 218, 220, 221, 238, 242, 243

Samuel, Judith 81

sane in insane places (core study) 11, 92, 111, 118, 128, 147, 186–193, 200, 224, 226, 234

sanity see abnormality

Savage-Rumbaugh et al. (core study) 11, 23, 56, 60–61, 62–69, 75, 218, 219, 220, 228, 234, 238, 240

Savage-Rumbaugh, Sue 63

scanning see brain scan 112, 113, 114, 115, 118, 136

scattergraph A graphical representation of the relationship (i.e. the correlation) between two sets of scores. 13, 20, 32–33, 226

scepticism ix, 58, 68, 77, 111, 185, 196, 240

schizophrenia 184, 185, 186–193, 194, 196, 200

science viii, ix, 2, 63, 111, 112, 113, 120, 122, 123, 130, 132, 133, 135, 141, 146, 156,184, 218, 219, 222, 228, 239, 242

Second World War ix, 74, 148, 150, 151, 158, 161, 219, 229, 235

seizures see epilepsy

self-concept (and self) 50, 158, 174, 183, 190, 194, 224

self-efficacy Our belief in our own competence in any given situation, i.e. how much you believe you can do something. 86, 162, 163

self-esteem The feelings that a person has about their self-concept. 17, 20, 24, 147, 158, 162, 183, 207, 221

self-fulfilling 190

self-perception 224

self-report Any research method where participants are asked to report their own attitudes, abilities and/or feelings, such as a questionnaire, interview or some psychological tests (if a test measures an ability then it is not a self-report method). 2, 16–17, 18, 20–23, 30, 32, 184, 192, 196, 197, 207, 226

self-selected sample A sample of participants produced by participants themselves determining whether they will take part in a study. This is generally taken to be equivalent to a volunteer sample but strictly speaking it can include situations where, for example, a participant crosses the road and their behaviour is recorded as part of an observational study. 18–19

Seligman, Martin 185, 187

semi-structured interview An interview that combines some pre-determined questions (as in a structured interview) and some questions developed in response to answers given (as in an unstructured interview). 16, 23, 207, 208, 209

serotonin 223

Sevcik, Rose *see* Savage-Rumbaugh *et al.* (core study)

sex 4, 6, 47, 54, 58, 68, 88, 89, 91, 96, 132, 171, 204, 205, 228, 230, 231

Shakespeake, William 68, 90, 122, 123, 182

Sheldon, William 182

Sherif, Muzafer 147

Sherman 62–69

Sidoli, Mara 104

significant A statistical term indicating that the research findings are sufficiently strong to enable a researcher to reject the null hypothesis under test and accept the alternate hypothesis. xiv, 12, 13, 25, 45, 54, 55, 79, 91, 117, 118, 124, 127, 128, 162, 163, 171, 172, 199, 206, 209, 210, 212

single blind A type of research design in which the participant is not aware of the research aims and/or of which condition of the experiment they are receiving. If the researcher is also 'blind' about the aims/conditions the design is called 'double blind'. 26, 28

situational factors/explanations 151, 159, 160, 186, 225, 234, 242

situational variable A factor in the environment that could act as an extraneous variable, such as noise, time of day or the behaviour of an investigator. 28

six degrees of separation 149

Sizemore, Chris 200, 202, 240

Skinner, B.F. 229

sleep 182, 122–123, 195

sleep and dreaming (core study) 31, 33, 124–131, 222

sleep deprivation 128, 130, 184

sleep stages 122

sleep-spindles Waves of brain activity that occur in bursts lasting for roughly a second during slow wave sleep. 122, 126

sleeptalking 122, 123

sleepwalking 122, 123

slow wave sleep One of the phases of sleep. Brain waves have low frequency and high amplitude. This stage of deep sleep is associated with bodily growth and repair, such as the production of growth hormones. Most common during the early hours of sleep. 123, 126

snapshot study A study carried out over a very short period of time such as hours and days, in comparison to a longitudinal study. May be used to specifically refer to studies looking at the effects of age. 236–237

social approach The approach to understanding behaviour that focuses on how conspecifics (members of one's own species) influence what we do and think. 224–225

social cognitive theory 87

social desirability bias A tendency for respondents to answer questions in such a way that presents themselves in a better light. 16, 22, 23

Social identity 164, 176, 183

social identity theory 156, 158, 160, 161

social influence see obedience 146, 159, 224

social learning theory The basic assumption of this theory is that people learn through observing the behaviour of models, mentally rehearsing the behaviours they display, then later imitating them in similar situations. 86–87, 88–92, 102

social perception 54, 224, 225

social psychology 39, 146–180, 210, 236

somebody else's problem (SEP) field 169

spatial memory 114–118, 137, 140

SPE see Stanford Prison Experiment

Sperry (core study) 23, 31, 111, 132–133, 134–141, 200, 218, 222, 240

Sperry, Roger 132, 133, 135

spinal cord 112, 123, 132

Spitzer, Robert 192

split-brain (core study) 31, 133, 134–141, 200, 218, 222

SSRIs 223

St Valentine 133

standardise To compare a measure against criterion or normally distributed scores. 53, 90, 227

standardised instructions A set of instructions that are the same for all participants so as to avoid investigator effects caused by different instructions. 22, 28

Stanford Prison Experiment (SPE) 159, 160, 161, 166, 169

Stanford University 44, 87, 89, 128, 159, 186, 187, 189

Star Trek 219

stepfamilies 221

stereotypes 9, 192

Strange Stories task 52–55

stratified sample A sampling technique in which groups of participants are selected in proportion to their frequency in the population in order to obtain a representative sample. The aim is to identify sections of the population (strata) that need to be represented in the study. Individuals from those strata are then selected for the study using a random technique. 21

structural equation modelling 239

structured interview Any interview in which the questions are decided in advance 16, 23

structured observations The researcher uses various 'systems' to organise observations, such as a sampling technique and behavioural categories. 5, 6–7, 10, 18, 75

subway Samaritan (core study) 31, 170–177, 234

subway train 149

superego 96, 231

Superman 87

suprachiasmatic nucleus 123

Sybil 200, 202

synaesthesia 219

systematic allocation In an independent measures design, deciding which participants to place in which groups by using a rule, such as the first five go in group 1 and the next five in group 2, etc. 27, 28

systematic desensitisation 229

systematic sample A method of obtaining a representative sample by selecting, for example, every 5th, 7th or 10th person. 18

systemitising 58

Szasz, Thomas 192, 240

T

Tajfel, Henri 147, 158

Tammet, Daniel 51

target population The group of people that the researcher is interested in. The group of people from whom a sample is drawn. The group of people about whom generalisations can be made. 18–19, 21, 26, 243

tattoo 239

taxi drivers 113–118

television viii, 40, 41, 74, 94, 160, 164, 168, 195, 212, 233, 237, 241

temporal lobe 115, 132, 133

Terman, Lewis 227

terrorism 158, 159, 161

terrorist 94, 158, 166

test–retest A method used to check reliability. The same questionnaire, interview or psychological test is given to the same participants on two occasions to see if the same results are obtained. 22, 30

textual analysis A qualitative method used to study the meaning of communications. 238

thalamus 123, 132

Thanatos 231

The Knowledge 113, 115

Theory of Mind An individual's understanding that other people have separate mental states and that the other people see the world from a different point of view from their own. 50, 52–57, 61, 66, 218, 242

therapy viii, 48, 58, 60, 86, 98, 104, 195, 196–199, 202, 206, 210, 228, 229, 232, 233, 236

theta wave 122

Thigpen and Cleckley (core study) 23, 46, 75, 102, 138, 147, 182, 183, 194–195, 196–203, 220, 226, 227, 230, 232, 233, 236, 239, 240

Thigpen, Corbett 197

thinking aloud method 206–210

Thorndike, Edward Lee 228

Three Faces of Eve 198, 202

Three Mile Island 130

three-point rule A rule used to describe how to elaborate exam answers – state the point, provide context and give an example or further explanation/comment. xi

time sampling An observational technique in which the observer records behaviours in a given time frame, e.g. noting what a target individual is doing every 15 second or 20 seconds or 1 minute. At this time point the observer may select one or more categories from a behaviour checklist. 5, 10, 11, 18

ToM *see* Theory of Mind

torture 130, 148, 186, 176

Tourette syndrome 52–55, 204

triangulation 243

Triplett, Norman 225

Turing test 219

Turing, Alan 219

Twain, Mark 240

two-tailed hypothesis A form of hypothesis that states a difference, correlation or association between two variables but does not specify the direction (e.g. more or less, positive or negative) of such a relationship. 25, 33

tyranny The arbitrary or unrestrained use of power by one group over another. 146, 158–159, 160–167, 224, 225, 226

U

unconscious 28, 42, 96–97, 98–105, 137, 198, 230–231

undisclosed observation Observing people without their knowledge, e.g. using one-way mirrors. 6–7, 10

unilateral lobotomy A lobotomy is a form of psychosurgery in which fibres running from the frontal lobes to other parts of the brain are cut. Unilateral means it is performed on only one side of the brain. 135

University of Wisconsin 172

unstructured interview The interviewer starts out with some general aims and possibly some questions, and lets the interviewee's answers guide subsequent questions. 16, 23, 224

unstructured observation Every instance of a behaviour is recorded in as much detail as possible. This is useful if the behaviours you are interested in do not occur very often. 5, 6–7, 10

Up series 237

USA *see also* American IX, 48, 50, 75, 94, 120, 130,140, 147, 148, 149, 151, 158, 184, 192, 195, 202, 205, 218, 227, 228, 241

V

validity Refers to whether an observed effect is a genuine one. This includes the extent to which a researcher has measured what he/she intended to measure and the extent to which the findings can be applied beyond the research setting. viii, 9, 10, 16, 22–23, 30–31, 33, 52, 54, 221, 227, 234–235, 238, 242–243

Victor, the wild boy of Aveyron 51

Vietnam 148, 159

violence *see also* aggression ix, 75, 86, 88, 93, 94, 192

visual illusions 39

volunteer bias In a self-selected sample, the participants may have special characteristics, such being more highly motivated and therefore do not represent the target population. 19

W

Washoe 60, 63, 68, 240

Watson, John B. 86, 228

weapon focus effect 48

West, Rebecca 240

white matter Regions of the brain occupied by the axons of neurons and glial cells. White matter coordinates communication between different brain regions. 116

Whitman Charles 111

Wordsworth, William 231

World Health Organisation 74, 184

World Trade Centre, New York 41, 158

Wundt, Wilhelm 218

Yale University 149, 150, 151, 156, 234

Z

Zambia 75

Zephania, Benjamin 183

zero correlation In a correlation, the lack of a significant relationship between co-variables. 32–33

Zimbardo, Philip 149, 159, 160, 161, 166, 239